EUROPEAN MIGRATION

Centre for Economic Policy Research (CEPR)

The Centre for Economic Policy Research (CEPR) was founded in 1983 to enhance the quality of economic policy-making within Europe and beyond, by creating excellent, policy-relevant economic research, and disseminating it widely to policy influencers in the public and private sectors and civil society. A second goal was to unify and integrate the European economics research community.

CEPR is based on a new model of organization called a 'thinknet': a distributed network of economists who are affiliated with, but not employed by, the Centre, collaborating through CEPR on a wide range of policy-relevant research projects and dissemination activities. CEPR's network of Research Fellows and Affiliates comprises around 600 economists, based primarily in Europe in universities, research institutes, central bank research departments, and international organizations. No research is performed at CEPR's London headquarters, which serve a purely administrative function, defining research initiatives with the network, seeking funding, organizing research-related activities, such as meetings and publications, and working to disseminate the findings of project teams.

This distinguishes CEPR from traditional think-tanks, which employ researchers directly, and typically take an institutional position. In contrast, CEPR has a pluralist and non-partisan stance: the Centre takes no institutional policy positions, and its publications carry a wide range of policy conclusions and recommendations. The opinions expressed in this book are those of the authors and not necessarily those of CEPR or its supporting funders.

Chairman	Guillermo de la Dehesa
President	Richard Portes
Chief Executive Officer	Stephen Yeo
Research Director	Mathias Dewatripont

Centre for Economic Policy Research
90–98 Goswell Road
London EC1V 7RR
UK

Tel: +44 (0)20 7878 2900   Fax: +44 (0)20 7878 2999
Email: cepr@cepr.org   Web site: www.cepr.org

European Migration

What Do We Know?

Edited by
KLAUS F. ZIMMERMANN

OXFORD
UNIVERSITY PRESS

OXFORD

UNIVERSITY PRESS

Great Clarendon Street, Oxford OX2 6DP

Oxford University Press is a department of the University of Oxford.
It furthers the University's objective of excellence in research, scholarship,
and education by publishing worldwide in

Oxford New York

Auckland Cape Town Dar es Salaam Hong Kong Karachi
Kuala Lumpur Madrid Melbourne Mexico City Nairobi
New Delhi Shanghai Taipei Toronto

With offices in

Argentina Austria Brazil Chile Czech Republic France Greece
Guatemala Hungary Italy Japan Poland Portugal Singapore
South Korea Switzerland Thailand Turkey Ukraine Vietnam

Oxford is a registered trade mark of Oxford University Press
in the UK and in certain other countries

Published in the United States
by Oxford University Press Inc., New York

© CEPR 2005, excepting the contribution by Chiswick and Sullivan

British Library Cataloguing in Publication Data

Data available

Library of Congress Cataloging in Publication Data

Data available

Typeset by Newgen Imaging Systems (P) Ltd., Chennai, India
Printed in Great Britain
on acid-free paper by
Biddles Ltd., King's Lynn, Norfolk

ISBN 0-19-925735-3   978-0-19-925735-5

3 5 7 9 10 8 6 4 2

Acknowledgements

Preliminary versions of many of these papers were presented at the CEPR conference 'European migration: what do we know?' held in Munich on November 14–15th 1997, and organized as past of CEPR's Human Resources research programme (succeeded by the Labour Economics and Public Policy programmes in 1998). We gratefully acknowledge financial support for this meeting from the European Commission through the Human Capital and Mobility programme (Networks)–contract number CHRX-CT94-0515.

Contents

List of figures ix

List of tables xii

List of contributors xvii

1. Introduction: What We Know About European Migration 1
   Klaus F. Zimmermann

2. From Boom to Bust: The Economic Integration of Immigrants in Postwar Sweden 15
   Tommy Bengtsson, Christer Lundh, and Kirk Scott

3. Migration in a Scandinavian Welfare State: The Recent Danish Experience 59
   Peder J. Pedersen

4. Irish Migration: Characteristics, Causes, and Consequences 89
   Alan Barrett

5. Migration, Migrants, and Policy in the United Kingdom 113
   Timothy J. Hatton and Stephen Wheatley Price

6. The Netherlands: Old Emigrants–Young Immigrant Country 173
   Jan C. van Ours and Justus Veenman

7. German Migration: Development, Assimilation, and Labour Market Effects 197
   Thomas Bauer, Barbara Dietz, Klaus F. Zimmermann, and Eric Zwintz

8. Immigrant Adjustment in France and Impacts on the Natives 263
   Amelie Constant

9. Italian Migration 303
   Daniela Del Boca and Alessandra Venturini

10. Greek Migration: The Two Faces of Janus 337
    Nicholas P. Glytsos and Louka T. Katseli

11. Migrations in Spain: Historical Background and
    Current Trends   389
    Olympia Bover and Pilar Velilla

12. International Migration from and to Portugal:
    What Do We Know and Where Are We Going?   415
    Maria I. B. Baganha, Pedro Góis, and Pedro T. Pereira

13. Aliyah to Israel: Immigration
    under Conditions of Adversity   459
    Shoshana Neuman

14. The New Immigrants: Immigration and the USA   507
    Barry R. Chiswick and Teresa A. Sullivan

15. Canadian Immigration Experience: Any Lessons for Europe?   573
    Don J. DeVoretz and Samuel A. Laryea

16. Europeans in the Antipodes: New Zealand's
    Mixed Migration Experience   601
    Rainer Winkelmann

Index   633

Figures

2.1. Sweden's migration exchange, 1946–2000 (no. of migrants) 17
2.2. Distribution of immigration to Sweden by
     sender regions, 1946–2000 (per cent) 18
2.3. Sweden's migration exchange with different regions,
     1946–2000 (no. of migrants) 19
2.4. Cohort return migration by years in Sweden,
     1968–2000 (per cent) 21
2.5. Numbers of asylum-seekers and residence permits granted
     due to refugee or humanitarian reasons, 1984–97 26
2.6. Proportion of employed foreign citizens, people born abroad,
     and people born in Sweden, age-standardized
     1970–90 (per cent) 29
2.7. The proportion of unemployed. Foreign citizens and
     total population, 1977–2000 (per cent) 30
2.8. Highest educational level of people (1) born in Sweden,
     (2) born outside of Sweden, and (3) immigrated in
     1991–4, aged 25–64 42
3.1. Relative distribution of the stock of immigrants and
     descendants by global region in 1980 and 2004 62
3.2. Relative distribution of the stock of immigrants and
     descendants from European countries in 1980 and 2004 62
3.3. Relative distribution of the stock of immigrants and
     descendants from Asian countries in 1980 and 2004 63
3.4. Migration flows. Denmark, 1946–2002 63
3.5. Net emigration to other Nordic countries, EU countries,
     African and Asian countries, 1985–2002 64
3.6. Percentage skill composition of emigrants from
     Denmark by destination, 1989 68
3.7a. Unemployment rates by country of origin. Danes
     and immigrants, 2002 71
3.7b. Participation rate by country of origin. Danes and
     immigrants, 2002 71
3.7c. Employment rates by country of origin. Danes and
     immigrants, 2002 72

3.8. Unemployment rates by citizenship and gender, 1980–2002   73
3.9. Labour force participation rates. Foreign citizens and
      all in Denmark, 2000   74
5.1. Total immigration and emigration, 1964–98   116
5.2. British and foreign net immigration, 1964–98   117
6.1. Birth-surplus in the Netherlands,
      1900–2000 (1,000 persons)   175
6.2. Immigration surplus in the Netherlands,
      1900–2000 (1,000 persons)   176
6.3. Immigration from former Dutch colonies,
      1945–2000 (1,000 persons)   177
6.4. Immigration from Morocco and Turkey,
      1945–2000 (1,000 persons)   178
7.1. Immigration and emigration, 1950–2000 (in 1,000)   200
7.2. Immigration, labour force, nonlabour force (in 1,000),
      1954–2000   204
7.3. Guest workers by country of origin, 1955–2000 (in 1,000)   208
7.4. GNP growth and growth of foreign employment,
      1955–2000   209
7.5. Inflow of ethnic Germans by country of origin,
      1950–2001 (in 1,000)   210
7.6. Asylum seekers by continent of origin,
      1979–2000 (in 1,000)   215
7.7. Internal migration and unemployment, 1960–2000   223
7.8. Internal migration and vacancies, 1960–2000   224
7.9. GNP growth and growth of internal migration   224
7.10. Migration streams beween East and
      West Germany, 1957–1998   225
8.1. Stock of foreign population by nationality (in thousands)   268
8.2. Inflow of foreign population by nationality as a
      per cent of total inflows   268
9.1. Italian migration abroad (thousands), 1876–1981   305
9.2. Emigrants by main destination, 1870–1940 (percentages)   306
9.3. Remittances of Italian emigrants, 1876–1980
      (5-year mean values) (in 1938 liras)   314
10.1. Greek total net migration, 1960–99   340
10.2. Emigration and repatriation of Greeks to and
      from Germany, 1955–97   341
10.3. Greek emigration areas, 1955–77   344

10.4. Regional shares of emigrants (1955–77) and
       returnees (1970–85) (Greece = 100)   345
10.5. Total emigrants' remittances (in million dollars), 1965–97   349
10.6. Emigrants' remittances as a percentage of import
       payments and export receipts   350
11.1. Spanish emigration, 1822–2000   393
11.2. Spanish emigration by origin region
       (in per capita terms), 1962–2000   395
11.3. Net inter-regional migrations (in per capita terms),
       1962–99   397
11.4. Inter-regional migrations (in per capita terms), 1962–99   399
11.5. Inter-regional migrations: emigrants
       (in per capita terms), 1962–99   405
11.6. Inter-regional migrations: immigrants
       (in per capita terms), 1962–99   406
11.7. Intra-regional migrations (in per capita terms), 1962–99   407
11.8. Intra-regional migrations (in per capita terms), 1962–99   408
11.9. Foreign immigration, 1983–99   411
11.10. Foreign residents in Spain: total and by origin,
       1942–2000   411
11.11. Foreign immigrants, by origin, as a percentage
       of the total, 1983–99   412
14.1. Percentage of foreign-born, by country: 1990   524
14.2. English language proficiency of the foreign-born, 1990   534
14.3. Proportion of foreign-born in selected occupations
       ages 25–64, by sex, 1990   547
14.4. Marital status of the foreign-born and native-born
       populations ages 18 and over, 1990   552
15.1. Canada's historical immigration flows   574
15.2. Distribution across source countries   575
15.3. Immigration by class: summation, 1968–76   577
15.4. Labour market displacement model   584
16.1. New Zealand net permanent and long-term migration,
       1946–2001   603
16.2. Age-employment profiles, men and women, 1981
       and 1996   620
16.3. Age-log income profiles of immigrants and
       New Zealand-born residents, by English background
       and sex   626

Tables

2.1. Number of immigrants living in Sweden in 2000   17
2.2. Employment and unemployment rates in 1997
     (per cent)   30
2.3. Employment rates and unemployment rates in 1999 of
     people born abroad by immigration year, age-standardized
     (per cent)   31
2.4. Early retirements 1990-7. Number of retirees in
     per cent of each group according to birth country and
     sex. Age-standardized values (per cent)   38
3.1. Share of immigrants and refugees in employment
     by length of residence   81
3.2. Impact on public sector revenue and expenditures.
     Average per person. DKK, 1995   82
4.1. Components of population change in intercensal
     periods, 1871-1996   91
4.2. Net migration by sex, 1871-1986   92
4.3. Net migration classified by age for intercensal periods
     between 1946 and 1986   93
4.4. Percentage emigrating of second and third-level
     education leavers   95
4.5. Accounting for the variation in Irish emigration   99
5.1. UK net immigration by country of origin or destination
     (thousands per decade)   118
5.2. Ethnic minorities in the 1991 census (GB)   132
5.3. Fluency in English and education qualifications   134
5.4. Labour force status of working age males   136
5.5. Predicted percentage rates of employment in
     England, 1993-4: white and non-white males
     aged 25-64 with mean characteristics   142
5.6. Predicted percentage rates of unemployment
     (ILO definition) in England, 1993-4: white and non-white
     aged 25-64 with mean characteristics   146
5.7. Average characteristics of white and non-white
     male employees aged 25-64 in England, 1993-4   150

5.8. Predicted hourly wage rates for white and non-white
     male employees in England, 1993–4 with
     mean characteristics   156
5.9. Population change and net migration, 1961–96   162
6.1. Population growth and migration in the Netherlands,
     1900–2000 (1,000 persons/year)   175
6.2. Unemployment rates (unemployment as per cent of
     labour force) and non-employment rates (employment
     as per cent of working age population)   180
6.3. Average educational attainment by immigrant
     status, 1998   181
6.4. Labour market participation (as a percentage of
     population) and unemployment rate (as a percentage of
     total labour force) by immigrant status (15–65 years)   185
6.5. Job levels of employed workers by immigrant
     status, 1998   186
7.1. Immigration and emigration, 1950–2001 (in 1,000)   201
7.2. Foreign population and foreign labour force, 1955–73   207
7.3. Foreign population and foreign labour force, 1974–88   212
7.4. Unemployment rates, Germans and foreigners,
     1970–2002   213
7.5. Foreign population and foreign labour force, 1989–2001   216
7.6. Earnings assimilation of German immigrants   229
7.7. Private households receiving social security benefits,
     West Germany, 1995   238
7.8. Elasticities of native wages with respect to a 1% increase
     in foreign employment   245
8.1. Population by nationality and place of birth   267
9.1. Emigration and migration rate (per 1,000), 1876–1985   304
9.2. Regional contribution and direction (per cent national
     migration)   305
9.3. Return migration   307
9.4. Time series regression for Italian emigration, 1878–1913   311
9.5. Stock of foreign resident population in absolute value,
     as share of domestic population and by area of origin
     and most important nationality of origin   317
9.6. Determinants of immigration   321
9.7. Wage competition between natives and foreigners   324

9.8.   The results of the probit regression of the probability of
          moving from unemployment to employment for those
          looking for their first job   325
9.9.   Legalizations by countries of origin (millions)   329
10.1.   Number of emigrants (1955–77) and returnees (1970–85)
          by region   345
10.2.   Occupational composition of the Greek–German
          migration   347
10.3.   Determinants of emigration to Germany (selected studies)   364
10.4.   Determinants of remittances   367
10.5.   Surpluses and shortages of agricultural labour and
          proportion of emigrating population, 1976   370
10.A.1.   Greek total net migration   381
10.A.2.   Emigration and repatriation of Greeks, 1955–97,
          selected regions   382
10.A.3.   Total emigrants' remittances, 1965–97
          (in million dollars)   383
11.1.   Regional unemployment rates   398
11.2.   Final estimated migration equation using pooled
          cross-sections for 1987–91   402
11.3.   Predicted probabilities (%)   403
11.4.   Intra-regional migration, by size of town of origin
          and destination (as a percentage of the population
          in the corresponding size of town of residence)
          Men aged 20 to 24   409
11.5.   Equations for intra-regional migration using pooled
          data for the 17 Spanish regions, over the 1979–95 period   409
12.1.   Portuguese emigration for selected countries, 1950–88   421
12.2.   Origin of Portuguese immigrants' spouses and the
          children of Portuguese origin (%) spouses   424
12.3.   Socioprofessional category of immigrants of the
          male sex according to age and dates of entrance and
          of the male individuals born in France of
          Portuguese origin   424
12.4.   Legal foreign residents, 1980–97   436
12.5.   Requests for residency permits, by nationality
          (Special Legalization Program, 1992/3 and 1996)   438
13.1.   Waves of Jewish immigration, 1882–1998   463
13.2.   Sources of population growth: Jewish and non-Jewish
          population, 15/5/1948–96 (thousands)   464

13.3.	Jewish immigration waves, 1882–May 1948	466
13.4.	Years of schooling: Soviet immigrants and the Israeli Jewish population, 1978	476
13.5.	Occupational distribution: Soviet immigrants and the local Jewish population	477
13.6.	Occupational and schooling of Israeli workers (1990) and immigrants (per cent)	477
13.7.	Growth-rates of product and population	488
13.8.	Growth-rates—various countries, 1950–68	489
14.1.	Immigration and proportion foreign-born in the United States, 1871–1998	510
14.2.	Region of origin of immigrants, by period of immigration, 1921–1998 (per cent)	511
14.3.	Foreign-born population of the United States, by region of birth and period of immigration, 1990	512
14.4.	Foreign-born population aged 25–64, by region of birth and period of immigration, 1990	513
14.5.	Top twenty countries of birth among the foreign-born, and selected demographic characteristics, 1990	518
14.6.	Schooling attainment among the foreign-born aged 25–64, by sex, region of birth, and period of immigration, 1990	531
14.7.	English-language fluency of the foreign-born aged 25–64, by sex, region of birth, and period of immigration, 1990	535
14.8.	Labor force participation rates of the foreign-born aged 25–64, by sex, region, of birth, and period of immigration, 1990	539
14.9.	Occupational attainment and self-employment status of men aged 25–64, by region of birth, 1990	544
14.10.	Occupational attainment and self-employment status of women aged 25–64, by region of birth, 1990	545
14.11.	Household type of persons aged 18 and over, by nativity and immigrant status, 1990	550
14.12.	Recent immigrants residing with relatives, by relationship, age, and hemisphere of birth of the immigrant, 1960–90	551
14.13.	Fertility of foreign-born women, by region of birth and period of immigration, 1990	554
14.14.	Earnings of foreign-born men aged 25–64, by region of birth and period of immigration, 1990	557

14.15. Household income of the foreign-born, by region
       of birth and period of immigration, 1990   561
14.16. Poverty rates of the foreign-born, by region of birth
       and period of immigration, 1990   562
15.1. Social and economic attributes by place of birth, 1996 580
15.2. Social and economic attributes by place of birth, 1981 581
15.3. Social and economic attributes by place of birth, 1971 582
15.4. Elasticities of factor complementarities, 1980
       (125 Canadian industries)   586
15.5. Ratio of foreign-born to total labour force from
       selected largest Canadian industries, 1980   588
15.6. Elasticities of factor complementrary: above average
       in foreign-born intensive industries, 1980   589
15.7. Elasticities of factor complementaries, 1990
       (in 107 industries)   590
15.8. The impact of a 20% increase in the stock of recent
       immigrants on wages   593
15.9. Occupation by ethnic origin for females in
       Vancouver, 1991   595
15.10. Occupation by ethnic origin for males in
       Vancouver, 1991   596
15.11. Oaxaca type comparisons by ethnicity in Canada, 1991   597
16.1. New Zealand's changing population structure, 1945–66   604
16.2. New Zealand's working age immigrant composition
       by region of origin, 1981 and 1986   606
16.3. Summary of points scored in general skills category   612
16.4. Educational attainment, New Zealanders, all immigrants
       and recent immigrants, 1981 and 1996 (%)   616
16.5. 1996 Age distribution of working age of immigrants and
       New Zealand-born persons   617
16.6. Parental and (de facto) marital status of immigrants
       and New Zealand-born residents, 1996 (%)   617
16.7. Proportion of immigrants speaking English proficiently,
       by region-of-origin, 1996   618
16.8. Relative income and welfare benefits, immigrants and
       New Zealanders, 1981 and 1996   621
16.9. Adjusted income differentials and population shares
       of recent immigrants by region-of-origin, 1981 and 1996 623

Notes on contributors

Maria I. B. Baganha is Associate Professor of Sociology at the University of Coimbra, Portugal, and Senior Research Fellow at the University's Centre for Social Studies (CES). She is also a member of the International Steering Committee of Metropolis, and a member of several international academic journals.

Alan Barrett is a Senior Research Officer with the Economic and Social Research Institute, Dublin and a Research Fellow of the Institute for the Study of Labor (IZA), Bonn. Between 2001 and 2004, he spent two years with the Irish Finance Ministry and one year in economic consulting, before returning to the ESRI. He has published articles in journals such as the *Journal of Population Economics, Labour Economics* and the *Industrial and Labour Relations Review.*

Thomas Bauer is Professor of Economics at the Ruhr-Universität Bochum and member of the executive board of the RWI-Essen. He is also Research Fellow of the Institute for the Study of Labour (IZA), Bonn, Research Affiliate of the Centre for Economic Policy Research (CEPR), London and the Centre for Comparative Immigration Studies (CCIS) at the University of California-San Diego, USA. His research interests include migration, population economics, economics of education, and applied microeconometrics.

Tommy Bengtsson is Professor of Demography and Economic History at Lund University. He is also a Research Associate with the Labour Economics Programme of the Centre for Economic Policy Research (CEPR), London and a Research Fellow of the Institute for the Study of Labour (IZA), Bonn.

Olympia Bover is a Staff Economist at the Research Department of the Bank of Spain, International Research Associate at the IFS, a Research Fellow of the Centre for Economic Policy Research (CEPR), London and the Institute for the Study of Labour (IZA), Bonn. Her published papers have appeared in the *Journal of Labour Economics, Economic Journal, Journal of Econometrics, Economic Policy, Oxford Bulletin of Economics and Statistics, Investigaciones Económicas,* and contributed volumes.

Barry R. Chiswick is Distinguished Professor and Head of the Department of Economics at the University of Illinois at Chicago. He is also Program

Director for Migration Studies at the Institute for the Study of Labour (IZA), Bonn. He has done extensive research on a variety of aspects of international migration on four continents and across historical periods.

Amelie Constant is a Senior Research Associate and the Deputy Programme Director of Migration at the Institute for the Study of Labour (IZA), Bonn. Before she joined the IZA, Bonn, she was at the University of Pennsylvania, and the Population Studies Centre. At the IZA, she is also heading the German research activities in a bi-national project, studying the social and labour market integration of migrants in Denmark and Germany. She has published in the *Journal of Population Economics, International Migration,* and *Applied Economics Quarterly.*

Daniela Del Boca is Professor of Economics at the University of Turin, Director of the Centre for Household Income, Labour, and Demographics (CHILD), and Fellow of the Institute for the Study of Labour (IZA), Bonn and of the Italian Academy at Columbia University. Her articles have appeared in several books and journals such as the *American Economic Review, Journal of Human Resources, Journal of Population Economics, Labour Economics, Review of Income and Wealth,* and *Review of Household Economics.* She is Co-editor of *Labour* and Associate Editor of *Review of Economics of the Household.*

Don J. DeVoretz, Professor of Economics, is currently investigating the phenomenon of brain circulation. He is the Director of the Centre of Excellence of Immigration and Integration, Vancouver and there also of the RIIM Program 'Immigration and Integration in the Metropolis'. He is a Research Fellow of the Institute for the Study of Labour (IZA), Bonn. 2004 he has become the Willy Brandt Guest Professor at the Malmö University's 'International Migration and Ethnic Relations' programme (IMER), Sweden.

Barbara Dietz is a Senior Researcher at the East European Institute in Munich and a Research Fellow at the Institute for the Study of Labour (IZA), Bonn. She has conducted qualitative and quantitative studies on East–West migration and the integration of immigrants from Eastern Europe and the former Soviet Union into the German economy and society.

Nicholas P. Glytsos is Principal Researcher at the Centre of Planning and Economic Research (KEPE), Athens.

Pedro Góis is a sociologist, Lecturer in the Faculty of Fine Arts University of Porto and Permanent Researcher at the Center for Social Studies in the University of Coimbra, Portugal.

Timothy J. Hatton is Professor of Economics at the Australian National University and the University of Essex, he is a Fellow of the Centre for Economic Policy Research (CEPR), London and of the Institute for the Study of Labour (IZA), Bonn. His publications on international migration include a book on the international labour market in the late nineteenth century. More recently he has focused on analyzing trends in migration and asylum since the 1960s.

Louka T. Katseli Professor of Economics, is presently Director of the OECD's Development Centre in Paris. She is on leave from the Department of Economics at the University of Athens. She has been actively engaged in public-policy making from a number of posts: Director of the Centre of Planning and Economic Research in Athens, Special Economic Adviser to the Prime Minister of Greece, Member of the European Monetary Policy Committee, Member of the EU's Comité des Sages for the Restructuring of the Social Charter, and Member of the United Nations Development Policy Committee. She is also a Research Fellow of the Institute for the Study of Labour (IZA), Bonn.

Samuel A. Laryea is a Senior Economist with the Labour Market Policy Research Unit, Human Resources and Skills Development Canada, Government of Canada. His publications and research interests cover a wide range of issues including the labour market impacts of immigration, Canada's brain drain to the United States, and developmental issues pertaining to Sub-Saharan African countries.

Christer Lundh is Professor of Economic History at the Lund University, Sweden. He was the head of the Welfare Policy Council of the Centre for Business and Policy Studies (SNS). He has published several books on immigration and integration of immigrants in Sweden.

Shoshana Neuman is an Associate Professor and head of the Department of Economics at Bar-Ilan University. She is currently a Research Fellow of the Centre for Economic Research Policy (CEPR), London, of the Institute for the Study of Labour (IZA), Bonn, leader of the Israeli team in an EU project on Work and Gender and active on several national committees. She has published numerous articles on labour economics and economics of education. She received research grants and awards, recently from the European Union, the Israeli Central Bureau of Statistics, the Pinhas Sapir Centre for Development, and Arc en Ciel.

Peder J. Pedersen is Professor of Economics, University of Aarhus, and the Danish National Institute of Social Research in Copenhagen and a Research Fellow of the Institute for the Study of Labor (IZA), Bonn. Current research interests are labour economics, income distribution and the economics of the welfare state.

Pedro T. Pereira is Full Professor at the Universidade da Madeira, Portugal, Research Associate of the Centre for Economic Policy Research (CEPR), London and Research Fellow of the Institute for the Study of Labour (IZA), Bonn. He previously held a position as Associate Professor at the Universidade Nova de Lisboa, Portugal. He is a fellow of the TSER Project 'Labour Demand, Education and the Dynamics of Social Exclusion'. He has published several articles in collected volumes and in international journals and has edited several books.

Kirk Scott is an Assistant Professor at the Department of Economic History at Lund University, Sweden.

Teresa A. Sullivan, Professor of Sociology, is currently Executive Vice Chancellor for Academic Affairs at the University of Texas, Austin. She has won three major teaching awards for her undergraduate teaching.

Jan C. van Ours is Professor of Economics at the Department of Economics, Tilburg University. He is fellow of the Centre for Economic Policy Research (CEPR), London, the William Davidson Institute (Ann Arbor) and the Institute for the Study of Labor (IZA), Bonn. He has published in such journals as *Journal of Political Economy, Journal of Labor Economics, Economic Journal, European Economic Review, Oxford Economic Paper, Oxford Bulletin of Economics and Statistics.* He was awarded with the Hicks-Tinbergen medal of the European Economic Association.

Justus Veenman is Professor of Economic Sociology at the Erasmus University Rotterdam, and Director of the Institute for Sociological and Economic Research (ISEO) at the Erasmus University. He has published numerous articles and books on integration issues.

Pilar Velilla is a Staff Economist at the Research Department of the Bank of Spain.

Alessandra Venturini is currently Professor of Economics at the University of Turin, Italy, and a Research Fellow of the Institute for the Study of Labour (IZA), Bonn. She was Visiting Professor at Brown University, Providence, Visiting Researcher at the Institute of Development Studies of Sussex University, Visiting Researcher at the International Institute of Labour Studies at the ILO in Geneva. She has published many articles in *European Economic Review*, *Journal of Population Economics* and a book which summarizes her interests, *Postwar Migration in South Europe* (Cambridge University Press, 2004).

Stephen Wheatley Price is Senior Lecturer in Economics at the University of Leicester, UK and a Research Fellow of the Institute for the Study of Labour (IZA), Bonn, Germany. His main research interests are in labour and population economics, especially the labour market performance of the UK.

Rainer Winkelmann is Professor of Statistics and Empirical Economic Research at the University of Zurich. He was Senior Research Associate at the Institute for the Study of Labour (IZA), Bonn, where he also served as Programme Director for the Institute for the Study of Labour (IZA), Bonn, Research Program 'The Future of Labor'. He has published a book *Econometric Analysis of Count Data*, and numerous papers in edited books and national and international journals such as *Economica*, *Econometric Reviews*, *Empirical Economics*, *Industrial and Labour Relations Review*, *Journal of Business and Economics Statistics*, *Journal of Econometrics*, *Journal of Economic Surveys*, *Journal of International Economics*, *Journal of Population Economics*, and *Weltwirtschaftliches Archiv*.

Klaus F. Zimmermann is Professor of Economics at the University of Bonn, Director of the Institute for the Study of Labour (IZA), Bonn, President of the German Institute for Economic Research (DIW Berlin), Honorary Professor of Economics at the Free University of Berlin. He is also a Fellow at the Centre for Economic Policy Research (CEPR), London, an Associate Research Fellow of the Centre for European Policy Studies (CEPS), Brussels, a Research Associate of the Centre for Comparative Immigration Studies (CCIS) at the University of California-San Diego and a Member of the Advisory Group of Economic Analysis (GEA) to the President of the EU Commission. Moreover, he holds the post of Editor-in-Chief of the *Journal of Population Economics* and is author of numerous books and papers in refereed journals and collected volumes. He was awarded the John G. Diefenbaker Award of the Canada Council for the Arts.

Eric Zwintz is Consultant for Research and Technology at the Bayerischen Staatsministerium für Wirtschaft, Munich. He studied economics at the University of Munich and was a Research Associate of the SELAPO Centre for Human Resources in Munich.

1. Introduction: What We Know About European Migration

Klaus F. Zimmermann

1.1. Introduction

Globalization has brought a new challenge to Europe: migration. It comes through various channels. First, there is unskilled migration. The poor of the world are knocking at the door of the rich. Fortress Europe still stands, but at its borders from the east and the south there is illegal immigration of unknown size. These innocent aliens team up with the rising excess supply of native unskilled workers who seek permanent gainful employment, more and more often with limited success. If the current trends continue, the resulting unemployment will further increase in the future, causing more social and economic disruptions.

A second channel is migration of the most skilled among the labour force. Human capital is the ultimate resource of the twenty-first century, and all developed societies face a large and growing excess demand for skilled labour, which is not satisfied by the local labour force and educational system. The lack of qualified workers decreases the incentive to hire low-skilled workers. Developed countries are increasingly competing to attract international skilled labour to fill the gaps. However, Europe, contrary to North America, Australia and, New Zealand, has no position in the international labour market for highly skilled people. Migration, return migration, onward migration, and circular migration are new challenging phenomena in a phase of internationalization of the labour market.

Trade is the third source of labour imports. If people do not move or are not allowed to move, trade may take the place of labour imports. For instance, cheap labour is embodied in imports of goods, and this threatens home production and low-skilled workers in particular. Virtual migration is the ultimate threat: many jobs can be done through the Internet. Jobs in the industrialized world may disappear without any real move of foreign workers.

Fourth, the expansion of the European Union will trigger further immigration into major European countries and create new market opportunities in Central and Eastern Europe. This is, certainly, a transition issue, whereas the inflow of low-skilled people has already largely taken place through illegal immigration. The European Union countries now need to ensure that the mobile highly skilled Eastern Europeans are not attracted only to the traditional immigration countries.

There are pros and cons to this unavoidable development. The challenge is to use migration as an instrument for the better. In a steady state, with migrants to be assimilated, and with similar human capital and physical capital, there is no real advantage, but also no disadvantage for the host nation. In a simple constant-returns production function world, the production possibilities shift outwards with no effects on income distribution and welfare levels. However, when migrants are different, when they bring variety and willingness to adjust the host economy speedily to its long-run needs, they are of invaluable help.

The migration literature has dealt with these challenges in a limited way. The growing interest in this field and the challenges for Europe are documented in the contributions by Bauer and Zimmermann (1997), Brücker et al. (2002), and Zimmermann (1994, 1995*a*, 1995*b*). Research has clustered around four major themes: (1) the determinants of migration; (2) the assimilation of the migrants; (3) the effects of immigrants on the natives; and (4) migration policy. A number of recent books deal with these issues: the series of articles contained in the four volumes on *The Economics of Migration*, selected by Zimmermann and Bauer (2002) from a rich literature on mobility, focus particularly on work within this framework relevant to the European situation. The book *Migration*, edited by Faini et al. (1999), investigates the interactions between migration, trade, and development. *Immigration Policy and the Welfare System*, edited by Boeri et al. (2002), provides a recent update and an overview of migration data and policy issues for Europe and the United States. A newer book, *How Labor Migrants Fare*, edited by Zimmermann and Constant (2004), contains fresh research from the *Journal of Population Economics* on the particular issue of how migrants adjust to the labour market of the host country and how they perform in society.

There is still a substantial lack of empirical evidence for European countries. This volume complements the literature by filling this gap, and hence, will provide a major source of reference. It collects original country chapters for all major European countries and contrasts the European evidence with experiences from most of the traditional immigration countries. The research agenda is as follows. First, the migration flows since the Second World War are studied and evaluated, and a review of major migration policy regimes is provided. Secondly, the available empirical evidence measuring the adjustments of migrants in the host country in terms of wages, unemployment, and occupational choices is summarized. This draws, where possible, from hard evidence contained in econometric estimates. Thirdly, we investigate how migrants affect the labour market of the host country, and evidence is provided from econometric studies evaluating the wage and employment consequences of immigration.

Surprisingly, we reach the valid conclusion that immigration is largely beneficial for the receiving countries. There might be phases of adjustment, but there is no convincing evidence that natives' wages are depressed or that unemployment is increasing as a consequence of migrant inflows. However, there is a growing impression that migration serves the needs of the labour market less and less well. This suggests to policy-makers that there is a need for a stronger focus on the economic channels of immigration. This book provides a conceptual basis for such a policy, and contains the required empirical facts and the institutional background.

Section 1.2 of this chapter contains an overview of the relevant research questions and instruments as well as some empirical findings and policy issues. Section 1.3 summarizes the major findings about assimilation and labour market impacts in the countries studied in this book. Section 1.4 concludes.

1.2. The Political Economy of Immigration

The measurement of migration in Europe reflects rather different concepts of nationality. Germany and the Southern European countries define citizenship by the *jus sanguinis* principle, which grants citizenship to all people who are descendants of the same ethnicity. France and Great Britain define citizenship by the *jus soli* principle, which grants citizenship to all people born in the country. As a consequence, second generation migrants will disappear in the population in one country, while they are still counted as foreigners in the other country. Hence, the European Union statistics provide data only on the basis of measures of nationality, and not of the status of the foreign-born as, for instance, is the case in the United States. This has to be kept in mind when comparing empirical findings across regions.

After the Second World War, Europe became one of the main regions receiving migrants of the world. Following a distinction made by Zimmermann (1995a), there are four relevant phases of postwar migration into Europe: (a) periods of postwar adjustment and decolonization; (b) labour migration; (c) restrained migration; and (d) dissolution of socialism and afterwards.

The first period covers the years between 1945 and the early 1960s. During this period, Germany experienced an inflow of about twenty million people displaced by the war. Great Britain, France, Belgium, and the Netherlands were affected by return migration from European colonies and the inflow of workers from the former overseas territories. In the United Kingdom, there was increased immigration from the newly independent Commonwealth countries, starting with the Caribbean countries and continuing with people from the Indian subcontinent. More than one million Algerians of French origin have been repatriated to France after the independence of Algeria. The Netherlands experienced an inflow of about 70,000 immigrants from Indonesia in 1946, followed by a second wave of additional 60,000 immigrants in 1950 when Indonesia became independent.

The second phase of labour migration lasts until the first oil-price crisis in 1973/4. The strong economic growth and the resulting labour shortages in the second half of the 1950s and the 1960s induced a number of Western European countries to open up for immigration. Some of the countries even established an active recruitment policy, or guest-worker regime. Germany, Austria, the Netherlands, Switzerland, Denmark, and Sweden actively recruited unskilled workers from the Southern European countries. Net immigration to the north from the Mediterranean countries in the 1955–73 period amounted to about five million migrants. Labour migration in this period was mainly motivated by wage differences between the south and the north. Germany and Switzerland opted for temporary migration as a response to labour shortages. However, Switzerland with its rotation principle was more successful with this policy than Germany was with the guest-worker system. German work contracts and residence permits were temporary, but since these temporary arrangements were not enforced, the guest-worker programmes resulted in permanent migration. Return migrants to Belgium, the Netherlands, the United Kingdom, and France were also permanent as a consequence of decolonization.

Restraint migration is the third phase of postwar migration into Europe. In the face of increased social tensions and fears about recession after the first oil-price shock, the governments all over Europe stopped active recruitment from 1973. Immigration policies became more restrictive affecting labour migrants exclusively. Although the guest-worker system was designed for temporary workers, return migration started only slowly. As a consequence, the main channels of immigration became family reunification and humanitarian immigration.

The fourth phase of European migration can be identified at the end of the 1980s, when migration flows to Western Europe have been dominated by East–West migration and the inflow of asylum seekers and refugees. Ethnic Germans migrating to Germany played a substantial role in this process. Whereas in the 1970s and 1980s, asylum seekers originated mainly from Asia and Africa, the inflow of asylum seekers and refugees from European countries increased significantly in the 1990s. This was a direct consequence of the dissolution of the political regimes in the former socialist states in Eastern Europe, but also of the clashes between Turks and Kurds in the southeast of Turkey. Around 1992 some European countries, especially Germany, became more restrictive towards the immigration of asylum seekers and refugees. But most European countries did not further restrict their refugee and asylum policies. Sweden, Denmark, the Netherlands, and Switzerland continued to accept larger numbers of refugees.

How do the migrants fare? This is a question of assimilation and integration into the labour market of the host country. Bauer et al. (2000) deal with this issue and incorporate a study of natives' sentiments towards immigrants. According to the standard economic models in this field, the degree of assimilation is influenced by the individual determinants, the characteristics of the home country, the migration motive, and the expected migration duration. The greater the similarity between the sending and the receiving countries in relation to their economic development, the more rapid is the assimilation. Individuals who migrate for economic reasons and permanent migrants are expected to assimilate faster than noneconomic and temporary migrants. A key issue is the international transferability of human capital. Human capital acquired at home may not be fully transferable to the host country. Hence, there is an expected negative relationship between the transferability of human capital and the initial immigrant–native earnings gap. The lower the international transferability of human capital, the higher is the earnings disadvantage of the immigrants at the time of migration. With increasing time of residence in the host country, migrants invest in country-specific human capital of the receiving country and adapt their stock of human capital acquired in the home country. As a consequence, the human capital of the migrants grows relatively to the human capital of the natives, and the earnings of the immigrants approach but may not reach those of the natives.

How do the natives fare in the face of immigration? Borjas (1994) and Bauer and Zimmermann (1997) investigate this question. A key issue here is the situation of the labour markets in the host country; they might be either competitive or in disequilibrium. A further point of departure is that labour is heterogeneous and of diverse quality, while it depends on whether immigrants are unskilled or skilled. Another issue is whether skilled and unskilled workers are complements or substitutes to natives. A reasonable (and standard) assumption is that skilled and unskilled workers are complements. Then one scenario is that immigrants are substitutes to unskilled natives and complements to skilled natives. Increased immigration may depress wages and increase unemployment of the unskilled workers, and may induce the opposite effects for skilled natives. The scenario is reversed for skilled immigration. Hence, in a situation of unskilled unemployment and excess demand for skilled work, it makes sense to import highly skilled labour migrants. This will foster growth, and increase demand for unskilled native workers. Their wages will increase and the unemployment will decrease, respectively. This explains how migrants can be friends or enemies to natives in the labour market. It remains an empirical matter. Therefore, it is important to examine the evidence across countries.

1.3. Migrants: Friends or Foes?

The concept of the book is to compare the empirical findings on migration in major European countries after the Second World War in a unified framework. Are migrants taking jobs away and depressing the wages of the natives? Do they adjust to the host country, in the sense that they perform well, as well as or even better than natives in the labour market? Or are they just a burden for the welfare state?

1.3.1. Northern Europe: Welfare Magnets and Historical Inheritance

In the first part, the book contains four chapters about Northern Europe. Two chapters are from the Nordic welfare states, Sweden and Denmark, that do not seem to receive many typical labour migrants. The two others are about Ireland and Great Britain that share a common migration experience through the large Irish emigration to the British island. Ireland has traditionally been an emigration country, while the United Kingdom has largely restricted immigration to people from its former colonies.

The chapter on Sweden reports that over the longer recent period, the official Swedish goal to integrate the immigrants to provide them with the same opportunities and the same standard of living as that of native Swedes has failed. Social and economic exclusion among migrants is much higher than among natives. This is highly problematic, since one-fifth of the Swedish population is of foreign origin: about 10 per cent are foreign-born and another 10 per cent have at least one foreign parent born outside Sweden. However, the exclusion is a more recent experience. It seems to have been caused as much by a changing composition of the migrants as by changes in labour demand for quantity or skills. The number of non-European migrants has increased due to the immigration of relatives and refugees, although the relatively high levels of education persisted. The demand-pressure for high-level skills and the tight labour market regulations have pushed migrants into self-employment and the informal sector.

As in Sweden, the labour market integration of immigrants from less-developed countries and refugees in Denmark has not been very successful. First generation migrants are not faring well in comparison to the natives, but second generation migrants are becoming more similar to the native Danes. The relative success of second generation migrants can be traced to the relevance of parental capital and to neighbourhood effects, especially that of improving educational levels. Immigrants and refugees tend to concentrate in a few neighbourhoods in the bigger cities, resulting in subsequent political tensions.

Contrary to these welfare states, for most of its recent history, Ireland has been a country of emigration. Hence, most of the experiences found in the economic literature deal with this part of the story. It is clear that out-migration reacted substantially to the poor economic perform-ance of the country, and reducing the labour market problems through out-migration has been positive for the country. Many of the Irish migrated to Britain, whereas the educational levels of the movers had increased. More recently, and associated with the rising success of the Irish economy, the country has experienced net-inflows. In the mid-1990s Ireland seemed to have benefited from the inflow of skilled people who have contributed well to the economy and assisted in reducing earnings inequality. There is also some evidence that return-migration brought back people with increased skills that made the original outflow even more beneficial.

While Ireland is losing its tradition as an emigration country, Britain is struggling with its inherited state of being a colonial power. While migration is largely driven by economic incentives, the free flow of labour has been distorted by growing policy intervention. As a consequence, migration policy has become inextricably linked with domestic race-relations policy. This chapter observes that the ethnic minority population exhibits rising educational levels, especially in the second and subsequent generations. Labour market disadvantages seem not to reflect discrimination, but the assimilation process, whereby immigrants improve their labour market status with length of residence. The immigration effects on the native labour market have hardly been studied in Britain so far, but the impacts have been evaluated at most as being modest. It is concluded that the social and political impacts vastly outweigh any conceivable economic effects.

1.3.2. Western Europe: Attractive Labour Markets

Western Europe encompasses the traditionally attractive labour markets of Germany, Switzerland, Austria, the Benelux countries, and to a certain extent, France. This volume contains chapters on the Netherlands, Germany, and France. The literature on Germany especially provides substantial evidence concerning assimilation and the impact on the natives.

In the Netherlands, ethnic minorities are in a disadvantaged socio-economic position. As in other parts of Western Europe, immigration in the past was largely related to decolonization and the labour hiring process of the 1960s, where migrants obtained jobs in low-paid industries. Many migrants from the labour hiring period faced difficulties because their situation was particularly hit by the economic recession of the 1980s. In addition, cultural aspects, less functional social networks and human capital factors are probably culprits of the immigrants' plight of marginalization. The more recent improvements in the Dutch labour market gave rise to an interesting question: would the situation of the migrants improve in proportion to economic recovery? While labour market participation rates are rising and unemployment rates declining, the economic improvement of immigrants is not as strong as that of natives.

The most important European immigration country is Germany which, in the same way as the Netherlands, has been traditionally the port for many labour migrants. Germany, however, has also attracted substantial inflows of noneconomic migrants such as relatives, refugees, and ethnic Germans from Eastern Europe. Since migrants from the hiring period were largely chosen because they were similar to blue-collar workers and they were paid by law as natives, there hardly can be much of an economic assimilation process. Ethnic Germans were generally found to assimilate, although at a slow rate, which has become more problematic with the recent waves of ethnic German immigrants. Foreigners today are under more labour market pressures than natives, largely as a consequence of occupational status, and not of behaviour. Self-employment is a channel to integrate into the economy. There is no real indication that migrants depress native wages or increase their unemployment risk. Immigration effects are either small or insignificant, or they are positively improving the economic situation of the natives.

France has gone through the similar phases of decolonization and labour hiring as the Netherlands. French immigration policy had focused on people willing to accept the French language and culture. Given this emphasis in society, it is not surprising that few economic studies have examined assimilation and the impact on the natives. The majority of the immigrant population in France are manual workers and suffer from poor labour market conditions. Also, second generation migrants are not fully integrated, although they carry the French passport. Again, the impact of foreigners on the natives is not considered to be harmful, but their contribution to economic growth is rather modest.

1.3.3. Out-migration and the New Waves to the South

For large periods after the Second World War, the Southern European countries experienced net out-migration. They are now in the process of becoming traditional immigration countries, expecting people from Northern Africa and other less developed parts of the world. The volume investigates Italy, Greece, Spain, and Portugal.

Italy has largely lost its status as an emigration country, which became evident during the period from 1970 to 1980. Nowadays, only a few highly skilled and specialized workers leave the country in search of better job opportunities. Italy has turned into a host country, receiving immigrants from Eastern Europe and developing countries, in part as illegal migrants. The available studies on the native impacts of foreign work hardly provide any support for the position that the labour markets between the groups are highly competitive. This chapter even surveys some evidence of complementarity between migrants and natives, suggesting that immigration may actually improve the labour market conditions of the natives. If the relationship is negative, as in the illegal sector, the estimated effect is small and indicate a negligible economic importance, with the exception of the illegal part in the agricultural sector where natives and migrants are strongly competitive.

The chapter on Greece confirms the regime shift found in Italy. The turnaround here occurred around 1974, when return migration began to exceed emigration. After the collapse of the socialist regimes in Eastern Europe, the outflow to Greece became strong, dominated by illegals. By the mid-1990s, the stock of illegal migrants in Greece (mostly Albanians) was estimated to be around 500,000 people. They are mostly in agriculture, but also in the construction and service industries. Studies show that foreign workers in agriculture largely took available vacancies and even generated their own jobs. Immigration did not raise the overall unemployment of natives, although in some selected industries such as construction and services there were some negative effects.

Emigration to Europe also stopped in Spain around 1973. Since then, migration has become more internal, with a strong rise in intraregional migration from the early 1980s. Research reported in this chapter supports the hypothesis that this increase in migration is a response to the increased employment opportunities in the service sector in all regions since the late 1970s. Although foreign immigration is still a small proportion, its size is growing strongly and it is rapidly gaining attention. There is not much evidence for the impact on the native labour market. However, a lift on some restrictions on immigration policy in 1991 is used to study the effects. The chapter reports a small positive elasticity for wages and total employment to the migration change. At the same time, the effect was negative for unskilled labour.

The chapter on Portugal also deals with emigration and immigration separately. While traditionally the country was mostly characterized by emigration, immigration has played a predominant role since the 1980s. The stock of foreign population grew steadily, and the complexity of the issue increased with a rising heterogeneity of the migrants. More and more migrants came from countries with which Portugal had never had any trade or historical links. Low-skilled workers were largely settling into the densely populated Lisbon area. While those low-skilled people came from Zaire, Senegal, Pakistan, Romania, and Moldavia, the highly skilled migrants in Portugal are from European countries and Brazil.

1.3.4. Lessons from the Traditional Immigration Countries

The final part of this section deals with the experiences of some traditional immigration countries: Israel, the United States, Canada, and New Zealand.

Israel has always encouraged and supported the immigration and absorption process as part of a pro-immigration ideology and immigration policy. This country's experiences are of high scientific interest, since they exhibit a large, rich, and diverse pool of migrants. Israeli migrants come from a wide range of countries and have diverse educational and professional backgrounds. The Israeli experience is therefore well suited for deriving lessons on the questions of assimilation and impact on the host economy. The assimilation evidence is that immigrants start with very low earnings. While their earnings adjust rapidly, it nevertheless takes a long time for them to approach the standards of the natives. Initially, the immigrants receive an insignificant return to imported human capital, either schooling or experience. With increased duration of residence, the returns increase, but a gap between them and comparable natives remains. Occupational convergence is also slow. Explained by aggregate demand effects, the overall evaluation of the impact on the natives seems to be positive. However, the effect of immigration differs for different native occupational groups due to the occupational convergence of highly skilled immigrants, who first compete with low-skilled natives and then work their way up to highly skilled occupations.

The United States of America is often seen as the model immigration country. Its migration history provides a rich source of knowledge, which is impossible to examine in full in this volume. The chapter on the United States hence concentrates on the new migrants of the 1990s. Three dominant findings emerge: immigration has increased absolutely and relatively; the diversity of immigrants has increased in terms of nearly every measured characteristic; and immigrants converge impressively with the native-born in their demographic and economic characteristics. The new immigrants are predominantly from Asia and Latin America and show more diversity in skills than the recent immigrants from the traditional source countries (Europe and Canada). While there is convergence over time, the limited skills of some groups cause rising problems, nonetheless. The low skills result in very low earnings, and often also in low employment, and hence in a high incidence of poverty. Since the economy now offers far fewer opportunities for low-skilled workers, this calls for a careful observation in the future.

While there seems to be a universal need in all immigration countries to screen migrants more carefully from the perspective of the local labour market needs, the potential model country for this type of policy seems to be Canada. Hence, the Canadian experience is of particular value for Europe. It seems that Canada's balanced immigrant programme of

50 per cent economic immigrants and 50 per cent other leads to low short-run displacement or wage compression in the native segment of the labour market. The policy of admitting people with substantial amounts of human capital strengthens the positive outcomes of the labour market integration and reduces the need to provide additional training and physical capital to the migrants. An initial occupational segmentation in the Canadian labour market supports the positive impact of immigration on the natives. Hence, the key lesson of the Canadian experience is to screen economic migrants according to their human capital.

The experiences of New Zealand with a selective immigration policy following the needs of the local labour markets are somewhat different. Although geographically located far away from Europe, New Zealand is a country that has preserved its European, e.g. British, heritage more strongly than Australia, Canada, or the United States have done. It is, therefore, of particular interest for European immigration policy. This chapter shows that while the Canadian type point system applied in the last decades worked quite well and was efficient administratively, it has failed to generate the economically successful migrants who could foster New Zealand's economic growth. While the formal level of qualifications of people selected by the system were indeed very high, compared with the native-born or with previous generations of immigrants, their unemployment rates were also high and they had to face low income levels. Hence, a selection according to qualification levels is not a guarantee for a successful integration in the host country.

1.4. Conclusions

In recent years, migration has become a major challenge for researchers and policy-makers. The focus has been to investigate the demographics of the movements, the assimilation and integration patterns this process causes, and the effects migrants have on the welfare of the native population. The design of coherent migration policy is crucial, where Europe lags behind the traditional immigration countries in North America and Australasia. This book summarizes for the first time the existing evidence in Europe and contrasts it with the experiences of those traditional countries. It provides a complete picture of migration policies across countries and draws policy conclusions.

This introductory chapter has indicated that there is indeed a huge and rich experience of the causes and consequences of migration for the host countries and the migrants themselves. The lessons one can draw so far are that in the past, the labour market integration of migrants has been slow, but steady, and their impact on the natives has not been very strong, but mostly beneficial. However, with globalization and the particular pressure on low-skilled workers and the increased demands on highly skilled people, the rules of the game have changed. The economic position of the new immigrants has become weaker. From this perspective, a selective immigration policy seems to be even more important than before. The successful Canadian experience seems to be quite supportive of such a position. The limits of the Canadian model, however, are shown by the failure of New Zealand to implement it successfully. Hence, policy-makers have to understand better what the deficits of this case were, and how to avoid them in a European framework.

References

Bauer, T. and Zimmermann, K. F. (1997). 'Integrating the East: the labour market effects of immigration', in Black, S. W. (ed.) *Europe's Economy Looks East— Implications for Germany and the European Union* (Cambridge: Cambridge University Press), 269–306.

——, Lofstrom, M., and Zimmermann, K. F. (2000). 'Immigration policy, assimilation of immigrants and natives' sentiments towards immigrants: evidence from 12 OECD Countries', *Swedish Economic Policy Review*, 7: 11–53.

Boeri, T., Hanson, G., and McCormick, B. (2002). *Immigration Policy and the Welfare System* (Oxford: Oxford University Press).

Borjas, G. J. (1994). 'The economics of immigration', *Journal of Economic Literature*, 32: 1667–717.

Brücker, H., Epstein, G., McCormick, B., Saint-Paul, G., Venturini, A., and Zimmermann, K. F. (2002). 'Managing migration in the European welfare state', in Boeri, T., Hanson, G., and McCormick, B. (eds.), *Immigration Policy and the Welfare System* (Oxford: Oxford University Press), part I, 1–167.

Faini, R., de Melo, J., and Zimmermann, K. F. (1999). *Migration. The Controversies and the Evidence* (Cambridge: Cambridge University Press).

Zimmermann, K. F. (1994). 'Some general lessons for Europe's migration problem', in Giersch, H. (ed.) *Economic Aspects of International Migration* (Berlin et al.: Springer-Verlag), 249–73.

—— (1995a). 'European migration: push and pull', *Proceedings of the World Bank Annual Conference on Development Economics 1994, World Bank Economic Review*, and *World Bank Research Observer*, 313–42.

Zimmermann, K. F. (1995*b*). 'Tackling the European migration problem', *Journal of Economic Perspectives*, 9: 45–62.

— and Bauer, T. (2002). *The Economics of Migration*, vols. I–IV, (Cheltenham/ Northampton: Edward Elgar Publishing Ltd).

— and Constant, A. (2004). *How Labour Migrants Fare* (Berlin et al.: Springer-Verlag).

2. From Boom to Bust: The Economic Integration of Immigrants in Postwar Sweden

Tommy Bengtsson, Christer Lundh, and Kirk Scott

2.1. Introduction

Today about one-fifth of the Swedish population is born, or has at least one parent born, outside the country. This puts Sweden about three times above the European average when it comes to the size of the immigrant population. Among its neighbours, Denmark has the highest proportion of immigrants, about the European average, while the figures for Norway and Finland are much less. The official Swedish aim is to integrate the immigrants in order to give them the same opportunities and the same standard of living as native Swedes. Has this goal been achieved? The answer is no. Today the exclusion from the regular labour market and unemployment among immigrants is much higher and the standard of living is much lower than among natives. However, this was not the case in the past. In the 1960s, the immigrant population had a higher employment rate than the native population and therefore had higher average earnings. The question is whether this development is a result of the changes in the composition of immigrants from labour to refugee and from European to non-European, or whether it is due to changes in the demand for labour in terms of volume and skills.

Sweden became a net immigration country during the great depression in the 1930s. During the previous one hundred-year period, Swedes migrated in large numbers—in the beginning to neighbouring countries, Denmark and Germany, then further away, to North America in particular. In all, about 1.2 million Swedes migrated. This figure should be compared with the Swedish population, which in 1900 was about five million. The inflow of refugees from the other Nordic and Baltic countries was quite substantial during and immediately after the Second World War. The demand for labour was great, and a change in policy made it possible for these immigrants to get jobs. In 1954 the labour market opened up when the Nordic countries became a common labour market. Despite large-scale immigration of labour migrants and refugees, from Finland and Eastern Europe respectively, and an increase in the female labour force participation rate, the demand for labour was still unmet. Sweden therefore opened up for large-scale non-Nordic labour immigration in the 1950s and 1960s. Workers from Southern and south-eastern Europe came to Sweden either on tourist visas or actively recruited in their homelands. And they did well.

As a result of trade unions' protest against the liberal immigration policy at the end of the 1960s, the policy changed and labour immigration became restricted. The new regulations made it possible for the trade unions to decide whether labour immigration should take place or not. At the beginning of the 1970s the Swedish Confederation of Trade Unions instructed the trade unions to reject applications for labour permits from non-Nordic citizens who wanted to immigrate into Sweden. In practice, this almost stopped the non-Nordic labour immigration to Sweden. The immigration of relatives and refugees continued however, which actually led to an increase in the number of non-European immigrants. These new immigrants faced problems in the labour market that were not experienced by the earlier immigrants. Not only the composition of immigrants changed, but also the demand for labour. Few unskilled jobs were produced in the declining industrial sector and there was a general shift towards demand for higher and more complex skills. Since the regulations of the Swedish labour market make it practically impossible for outsiders to compete with lower wages, the new immigrants have to a considerable extent turned to self-employment and work in the informal labour market. Still, they have higher unemployment, lower employment rates, lower earnings and a higher degree of dependence on the social welfare system than natives. In addition, in the beginning of the 1990s Sweden went from almost full employment to a high level of unemployment, a situation that also faces most other countries in Europe. Thus, Sweden was facing labour market and social problems not met since the great depression, if at all. Against this background we will, in Section 2.2, give an overview of migration to Sweden and its migration policy after the Second World War. We will then turn to the income development of immigrants in Section 2.3, and to effects of immigration on the labour market and the economy in general in Section 2.4, before we turn to the conclusions in Section 2.5.

2.2. Migration and Migration Policy[1]

2.2.1. Migration—An Overview

All through the postwar period, large-scale immigration to Sweden has been taking place. In total, 2.2 million people immigrated during the period 1946 to 2000 (see Figure 2.1.) Even though return migration was considerable, this immigration has resulted in 1.8 million people of foreign origin (including the second generation) living in Sweden in 2000, constituting about one-fifth of the total population (see Table 2.1).

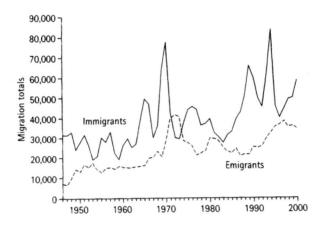

Figure 2.1. Sweden's migration exchange, 1946–2000 (no. of migrants)
Source: SOS, Befolkningrörelsen; SOS Folkmängdens förändringar; SOS Befolkningsförändringar; SOS Befolkningsstatistik

Table 2.1. Number of immigrants living in Sweden in 2000

	Foreign citizens	Swedish citizens	Total
Born outside Sweden (First generation)	394,609	609,189	1,003,798
Born in Sweden* (Second generation)	82,703	734,645	817,348
Total	477,312	1,343,834	1,821,146

*At least one of the parents was born outside Sweden.
Source: SOS, Befolkningsstatistik.

[1] Section 2.2 is based on Lundh and Ohlsson 1994*a*, 1994*b*, and 1999; Lundh 1994, and official statistics where other references are not made.

During the postwar period the pattern of immigration has undergone radical change, however, as has the economic role which immigrants have played and migration policy itself. Therefore, immigration since the Second World War can be divided into two phases.

The first phase covers the years from the end of the Second World War up until the early 1970s. During this phase, labour immigration predominated even though there was some refugee immigration. Most labour migrants came from the Nordic countries, but as immigration for those who wanted to work in Sweden became free in practice in the 1950s (see below), migration from the rest of Western Europe increased (see Figures 2.2. and 2.3). Additional labour was recruited or came as work-seeking tourists from Germany, Austria, and Italy in the 1950s and from Yugoslavia, Greece, and Turkey in the early 1960s. During the entire period, about 60 per cent of the immigrants came from the Nordic countries. The importance of Finnish immigration increased, and by the 1960s the Finns were by far the largest immigrant group. In 1965–7, on average

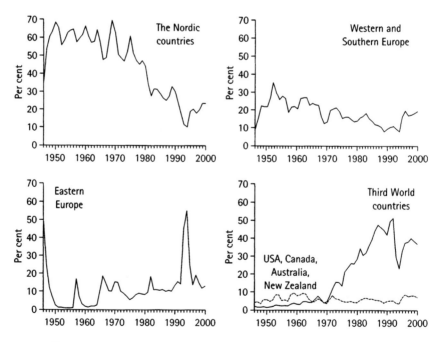

Figure 2.2. Distribution of immigration to Sweden by sender regions, 1946–2000 (per cent)

Sources: SOS Befolkningsrörelsen; SOS Folkmängdens förändringar; SOS Befolkningsförändringar; SOS Befolkningsstatistik

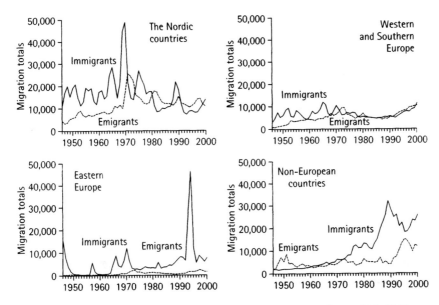

Figure 2.3. Sweden's migration exchange with different regions, 1946–2000
(no. of migrants)

Sources: SOS Befolkningsrörelsen; SOS Folkmängdens förändringar; SOS Befolkningsförändringar;
SOS Befolkningsstatistik

16,000 persons per year moved from Finland to Sweden. The migration
was so large that about one-third of the Finnish population lived or had
once lived in Sweden. At that time, the second largest immigrant group
was the Yugoslavs, with about 5,000 persons per year.

During the second phase, from the early 1970s onwards, the importance
of labour migration gradually decreased. New regulations in 1968 made it
much more difficult for non-Nordic citizens to apply for work permits
in Sweden, and from the early 1970s labour immigration from non-Nordic
countries gradually diminished to no more than about 200 per year. As the
standard of living rose in the other Nordic countries and as the differences
in unemployment first levelled off and then reversed, Nordic labour
immigration also declined, beginning in the middle of the 1970s. In the
1980s and 1990s, the migration exchange between Sweden and most
Western and Nordic countries has levelled out, and net migration from
these countries has been close to zero.

Instead, the elements of refugee and family reunion immigration have
come to play an ever-increasing role during the second phase. During and
immediately after the war, there had been extensive refugee immigration,

especially from the Baltic and Nordic countries, but as the refugee situation in Europe stabilized in the 1950s the number of refugee immigrants to Sweden decreased. Between 1950 and 1968, an average of no more than 1,300 refugees per year immigrated, coming from refugee camps in Europe. Since 1968, the number of refugee immigrants multiplied. In the 1970s, refugees from Latin America predominated; during the 1980s refugees from the Middle East and in the 1990s refugees from the former Yugoslavia were of great importance, which we will look into in more detail shortly.

Thus, the change in the migration flows from labour migration to refugee and family reunion migration also involves a change in the composition of the countries of origin. During the first phase, most immigrants came from the Nordic or other Western European countries, while immigrants from Third World countries and Eastern Europe have predominated during the second phase. In 1990-7, no more than 13 per cent of the total immigration was classified as labour migration, while 35 per cent of the immigrants were refugees and 44 per cent were related to Swedes or immigrants already living in Sweden.

The difference between labour migrants and refugee and family reunion migrants should not, however, be exaggerated. To some extent, the decline in non-Nordic labour migration and the increase in refugee and family reunion migration is due to the change in the Swedish migration policy, so that part of the latter migration under other circumstances would have been classified as labour migration. Furthermore, after entering Sweden, most refugees and family reunion immigrants form part of the labour supply. This is also the historical experience for Sweden. The refugees who immigrated to Sweden from Eastern Europe, from the Baltic States, Hungary, Czechoslovakia, and Poland from the Second World War up to the 1960s, have had a labour market performance similar to labour immigrants from other parts of Europe.

Even though there has been considerable immigration to Sweden, emigration should not be neglected. Thus, while on average about 39,000 persons immigrated per year in the period 1946-97, about 23,000 people emigrated per year. Even though some Swedes emigrated, the majority of the emigrants were former immigrants moving home. Return migration can be studied on a cohort basis from 1968 and onwards. As can be seen in Figure 2.4, about 40 per cent of the 1968 immigrant cohort had left after seven years and 50 per cent after twenty years.

It is also obvious from Figure 2.4 that the frequency of return migration is less for immigration cohorts of more recent times. This is a reflection of the fact that labour migration has gradually been replaced by refugee

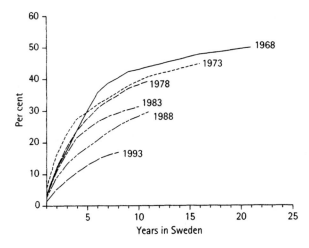

Figure 2.4. Cohort return migration by years in Sweden, 1968–2000 (per cent)
Sources: SOS Befolkningsstatistik

immigration and that family reunion migration has come to affect relatives of refugees rather than relatives of labour migrants. Among labour migrants, the desire to go home after some years of work in Sweden seems to be strong. Of the 1970 and 1980 immigration cohorts, as many as 50–60 per cent of the Danes, Norwegians, and Finns, who are typically labour migrants, had left Sweden after less than five years. The corresponding return migration for typical refugee immigrants like Poles and Iranians was much less. Of the 1980 immigration cohort, no more than 6–8 per cent had left Sweden five years after the entry. Even if the desire to return to the home country might be as strong for refugees as for labour migrants, it is the political situation in their home country that determines whether it is possible to return. In many cases refugees have to wait a long time for the possibility of returning.

The phenomenon of re-immigration to Sweden among those immigrants who leave Sweden to go back to their home country is quite common. Since 1968, about one-third of the emigrants (including Swedish citizens) returned within five years. Among the Finns the migration traditions have been extra strong, and from the middle of the 1980s the frequency of re-immigration has been about 40 per cent. Of those Chilean citizens who took the opportunity to move back to Chile in 1985 when this became possible, about 50 per cent had returned to Sweden within four years. Regarding re-immigration, it can be mentioned that some people seem to make migration a part of their lifestyle and everyday life, as in the Finnish case. Others, like the Chileans, develop social networks during their time as refugees, which prove difficult to break up, especially for the second generation immigrants.

Several studies show that there has been a strong influence on immigration to Sweden of business cycles in both the sender countries and in Sweden. There is a positive effect of Swedish business cycle movements on changes in immigration for the period from the end of the Second World War to the early 1970s. Immigration was high in times of boom and vice versa, often with a delay of a year between the peak (and trough) of the boom and the immigration maximum (minimum).[2] It has also been shown that in this period labour market conditions in Sweden had a considerable influence on emigration and return migration from Sweden.[3] During the period after the early 1970s, the influence of Swedish business cycles on immigration seems to have been weaker, probably because the element of labour migration has decreased in importance, but there is still a general positive effect. For some immigrant groups, not only labour migrants but in some cases also family reunion migrants (for instance Chileans), this effect was quite strong.[4]

Sweden has, with the exception of two years, experienced net immigration through all the postwar period, even though the sender countries have varied over time. The existence of structural net immigration has been explained in terms of differences in the standard of living, the liberal Swedish immigration policy and established migration traditions. It has been shown that through the entire postwar period between two-thirds and three-quarters of the total immigration to Sweden came from countries where the GNP per capita was less than 80 per cent of Sweden's. As soon as the difference in the standards of living between the sender country and Sweden began to level out, immigration dropped. Some of the refugee and family migration might also be explained in terms of established migration traditions. The Greek and Turk immigration in the 1960s and 1970s, the Chilean immigration in the 1980s, and the Bosnian immigration in the 1990s were to a large extent dependent on the fact that there were already immigrated populations from these countries in Sweden who provided information and facilitated immigration and assimilation in Sweden.

---

[2] Wadensjö 1972; Ohlsson 1975; Ohlsson 1978; Lundh and Ohlsson 1999.
[3] Geschwind 1958; Widstam 1962.
[4] Gustafsson et al. 1990; Lundh and Ohlsson 1999.

2.2.2. The Liberalization of Migration Policy, 1946–68

The economic basis for the vast labour immigration between 1946 and the 1970s was shortage of labour. The period was characterized by rapid economic and industrial growth. GNP increased by about 4 per cent per year and the manufacturing industry by even more, especially in the early 1960s when the yearly growth rate was about 7 per cent. From the 1940s to the early 1960s, central authorities recommended a yearly net immigration of about 10,000 persons to compensate for the lack of labour. In these decades this number was equivalent to 8–12 per cent of an average cohort of 16-year-old men and women ready to enter the labour market. In order to make labour immigration possible, three measures were taken to open up the Swedish labour market for foreign labourers.

First, all Nordic citizens were given free entry to the Swedish labour market. In 1942, many of refugees from the Nordic countries fled to Sweden and lived there until the war was over. In 1943 it was decided that Danish and Norwegian citizens should be allowed to work in Sweden without having to apply for special work permits. When the war was over, these rules were not changed, which made it possible for Danes and Norwegians to immigrate and work in Sweden. In 1954 an agreement on a Common Nordic Labour Market was signed, which extended the Swedish rules to all Nordic countries. Any Nordic citizen could move to another Nordic country, settle there and work there, without having to apply for visa, work permit, or residence permit.

Secondly, steps were taken to organize the recruitment of foreign workers in their home countries and in different ways to facilitate their immigration to Sweden. In the 1940s, recruitment campaigns were organized by the companies themselves, which were sometimes criticized by the authorities in the countries in which the campaigns were held. In the 1950s, another form of recruitment was organized. Swedish companies who wanted to employ foreign workers applied to the Swedish National Labour Market Board, which organized the recruitment in co-operation with the corresponding authority in the sender country in question. This kind of organized import of labour was not very large, but comprised mostly skilled workers in industry and restaurants. In the 1960s, unskilled workers were also recruited in this way.

Thirdly, a general liberalization was undertaken of the legislation and the practice through which foreigners should be allowed to enter, settle down, and work in Sweden. Gradually the demand for visas for non-Nordic citizens was abandoned, and the 1954 alien legislation was in principal positive to labour immigration under the condition that no domestic labour was available. The practice during the 1950s and 1960s was that non-Nordic citizens were allowed to come to Sweden as tourists for three months, during which time they were free to seek employment. If they succeeded in getting an employment offer, they could apply for work and residence permits, which were hardly ever rejected. Between 1961 and 1965, over 90,000 foreigners applied for work permits for the first time and another 140,000 applied for prolonged or altered work permits. Of the first-time applications, less than 5 per cent were rejected, and of the applications for prolonged or altered permits, as few as two per thousand were rejected.

2.2.3. The Restrictive Migration Policy and its Exceptions, 1968–96

In 1968, a radical change in migration policy was undertaken. The aim was to regulate labour immigration from the non-Nordic countries. The new regulations meant that it was no longer possible to enter Sweden as a tourist, seek employment and apply for a work permit when an employment offer was at hand. Instead, non-Nordic citizens had to apply for work permits in their home countries, which in practice made it difficult to present an employment offer. The applications were given special examination by the labour market authorities and the trade unions, which could approve or not depending on whether domestic labour was available. Especially after 1972, when the Swedish Trade Union Confederation recommended the trade unions to reject all applications for work permit by non-Nordic workers, it became practically impossible for non-Nordic citizens to immigrate in order to work in Sweden.

The background of the change towards a more restrictive migration policy was among other things the rapid increase in labour immigration from Finland, Yugoslavia, and Greece in the early 1960s. These were immigrant groups who did not speak Swedish, were mostly agricultural workers without industrial and trade union traditions, and, as far as the Yugoslavs and the Greeks were concerned, were culturally and religiously distant. In some factories and small towns the foreign presence became suddenly large and provoked the domestic workers and unions. Even the situation in the housing market became tense. In the recession of 1966 some trade unions tried to influence the government to regulate the free labour immigration into Sweden. The Swedish National Labour Market Board was also in favour of more regulations in the field of migration.

The attempt to restrict the non-Nordic labour immigration was not only an attempt on the part of the trade unions to reduce wage competition induced by the influx of foreign labour. It was also an effort to integrate the foreign workers in the Swedish Model; for example, the system of co-operation and negotiation in the labour market and in working life. Starting in 1968, when the new restrictive immigration policy was introduced, a special integration policy was developed in order to adapt immigrants to Swedish society. This contained such institutions as state support to immigrant magazines and organizations, immigrant language teaching in public schools, and compulsory education in Swedish during working hours without payroll deductions.

When changing the migration policy in 1968, the politicians did not aim for, or even predict, a shift from labour migration to refugee and family reunion migration and from Nordic and Western European migrants to Third World and Eastern European migrants. Factors other than the change in the migration policy contributed to this. First, there was a general decline in the demand for labour reflecting the fact that the increase in GNP after the oil crisis in 1974 was much less than in the 1950s and 1960s. Furthermore, as a result of rationalizations, the number of employees in the industrial sector declined from the early 1960s. In the 1970s and 1980s, new jobs generally arose in the service and public sectors. The new economic policy in the early 1990s aimed at improving the state finances and reducing inflation contributed to the severe economic crisis that reduced the demand for labour still more. In short, the decline in demand for labour, especially in low-skilled jobs, is the main reason why the change in migration policy in 1968 was soon followed by the almost total disappearance of non-Nordic labour immigration. Labour migration from the Nordic countries also declined, but mainly as a result of an equalization in the standard of living.

Secondly, in the 1970s, 1980s, and 1990s, refugee migration on a worldwide scale has developed in a way that was not predicted in 1968. The new migration policy contained a few exceptions from the rule that non-Nordic immigration should be restricted. Refugees should be allowed to enter Sweden and family reunion should be supported. Looking back, in 1968 about 1,300 refugees immigrated to Sweden per year, of which less than 400 per year came actively seeking asylum. In the period 1968–96, the picture became totally different. The vast majority of the refugee immigrants were given residence permits after seeking asylum upon arrival in Sweden. On average, 8,600 asylum seekers per year were given a residence permit between 1968 and 1997. For single years, as for instance

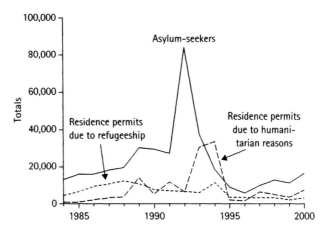

Figure 2.5. Numbers of asylum-seekers and residence permits granted due to refugee or humanitarian reasons, 1984–97

Source: Asylsökande och beviljade uppehållstillstånd 2000, Statistiska meddelanden BE65SM0101

in 1992 when the war in Bosnia led to the mass migration of refugees, the number of asylum-seekers increased to over 84,000 in Sweden (see Figure 2.5). In the 1990s the Immigration Board approved less than half of the applications for asylum in the first place. Still, many of those who were refused asylum as refugees later on were given residence permits on other grounds. Between 1990 and 1997, the average number of residence permits due to refugeeship or for humanitarian reasons corresponded to two-thirds of the number of asylum-seekers in the same period. Besides the political situation in many developing countries, the rapid development of transportation and communication have contributed to the increase in the number of asylum-seekers in the recent decades.

When family reunion was made an exception from the restrictive immigration policy in 1968, it was the reunion of Swedish families and families of labour immigrants that the legislators had in mind. As the number of labour migrants decreased and the number of refugees increased, a gradually larger proportion of family reunion immigration concerned refugees. In 1992–5, about 45 per cent of the residence permits based on family reunion were granted to relatives of refugees.

2.2.4. The Common Nordic Labour Market and the Common European Labour Market

Immigration from the other Nordic countries to Sweden has in practice been free ever since the end of the Second World War. The constitution of the Common Nordic Labour Market in 1954 gave Swedes the same opportunities to work in the other Nordic countries as had previously been offered to Danes and Norwegians in Sweden. There is no doubt that the common Nordic labour market facilitated movements in the Nordic area, but the directions of the migration flows indicate their dependence on underlying economic conditions.[5]

Structural net immigration from other Nordic countries has been based on two conditions. First, the existence of a demand for foreign labour in Sweden, and secondly, a considerably higher standard of living in Sweden than in the other countries. Thus, net immigration from Denmark occurred up to the 1950s, from Norway up to the 1960s, and from Finland up to the 1970s (with the exception of 1971-2). In the 1990s, however, there has been net emigration of about 2,000 persons per year from Sweden to the other Nordic countries, which reflects both the difficult situation in the Swedish labour market in general and wage differentials between Sweden and its neighbours for certain occupational groups.

Between 1954 and the early 1970s, the Swedish labour market was, in practice, open for European citizens who wanted to work in Sweden. During this period there was a net immigration from Western and Southern Europe that levelled out in the 1970s and 1980s. Just as in the Nordic case, this can be explained by the decreasing demand for labour in Sweden from the middle of the 1970s and the convergence out of the standard of living.

In 1994, Sweden joined the Common European Labour Market. It has been stated that migration within the European Union is low and has diminished over time.[6] There is little evidence that the Swedish entrance affected immigration to Sweden to any particular extent. Between 1994 and 2000, the average non-Nordic immigration from the EES/EU countries was 9,000 persons, while about 10,000 emigrated. Thus, cultural barriers and other moving costs have not been counter-balanced by a higher living standard in Sweden attracting labour migrants once the institutional barriers were torn down. On the contrary, in a Western European context the standard of living in Sweden has fallen in the 1990s. Given this, and given the international orientation of many large Swedish companies, the Swedish entrance into the European common labour market has facilitated emigration and thereby contributed the net emigration of about 3,000 Swedish citizens per year to EES/EU countries since 1994.

---

[5] Fischer and Straubhaar 1996.
[6] Lundborg 1993.

2.3. Immigrants' Labour Market Integration

2.3.1. Employment and Unemployment

There exists a relative abundance of information on first generation immigrants' employment at a certain point in time, either produced by Sweden statistics (e.g. censuses and labour force surveys) or from academic studies.[7] Sections 2.3.1 through 2.3.3 discuss the labour market attachment of the first generation of immigrants, while Section 2.3.4 examines the conditions of the second generation.

From a labour market integration standpoint, the process of obtaining employment is likely to be of greater interest in Sweden than the process of income assimilation. The reason for this is the relatively high level of unionization in the country (over 80 per cent of the workforce including white-collar workers) and the prevalence of collective bargaining. This implies that the labour market dynamics in Sweden are largely found in the employment process and labour market matching, rather than in income disparity.

The general picture derived from cross-sectional data is that the employment rates of immigrants relative to natives have declined during the postwar period. The employment rate of foreign citizens in 1950 was 20 per cent higher than the rate of the total population after standardizing for sex and age. By the middle of the 1970s the employment rate of foreign citizens was equal to the rate of the total population, and thereafter there has been a sharp decrease in the employment rate of immigrants relative to natives. The employment rate of foreign citizens in the middle of the 1990s was 30 per cent below the rate of the total population.[8]

It is clear that the development of employment rates of people born abroad was similar to those of foreign citizens, even though the level was somewhat higher, implying some positive selection of naturalization (see Figure 2.6).[9] In 1970, immigrant men had an employment rate that exceeded natives, but ever since there has been a decline in the employment rate of the immigrants. Immigrant women, also, had a higher employment rate than Swedes in 1970, but even if the rate rose somewhat after 1970, they were caught and passed by Swedish women who gradually increased their employment rate.

---

[7] Wadensjö 1972; Ohlsson 1975; Jonung 1982; Reinans 1982; Ekberg 1983; 1990a, 1993b; Harkman 1994; Bevelander 1995, 2000; Scott 1999; Rosholm et al. 2001; Ekberg and Andersson 1995.   [8] Ekberg and Rooth 2000.   [9] Bevelander 2000.

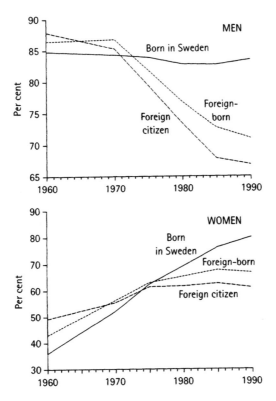

Figure 2.6. Proportion of employed foreign citizens, people born abroad, and people born in Sweden, age-standardized 1970–90 (per cent)
Source: Bevelander 1995

One would expect the unemployment pattern of immigrants to be in line with the development of employment rates, and, even if there are no annual statistics before 1977, there is some evidence that this was the case. Scattered data from the 1960s and early 1970s indicate that immigrants experienced about the same rate of unemployment as natives. On the other hand, unemployment among immigrants was more sensitive to business fluctuations than unemployment among natives. Since the end of the 1970s, the unemployment rate of foreign citizens has been considerably higher than the rate of the natives. As can be seen in Figure 2.7, from 1977 till the early 1990s it was twice as high as the unemployment rate of the total labour force. In the 1990s, the unemployment rate of foreign citizens has been even higher, about three times as high as for natives.

Thus, it is obvious that the labour market situation for immigrants has undergone profound changes in the last two decades. More recent cohorts

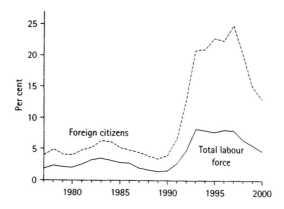

Figure 2.7. The proportion of unemployed. Foreign citizens and total population, 1977–2000 (per cent)
Source: AKU råtabeller, AKU grundtabeller

have lower employment rates and higher unemployment rates than their countrymen who had been in Sweden longer time.

The present situation, with low employment rates and high unemployment among immigrants, is not only a result of the extreme trough in the business cycle after 1991–the deterioration started earlier on. This is shown, for example, by the fact that many immigrants also faced problems of finding jobs in the years of economic boom in the 1980s. The recession in the early 1990s multiplied the newcomers' problems of finding jobs, however, and contributed to the exclusion of 'old' immigrants from the labour market. As can be seen in Table 2.2, in 1997 as much as 16–26 per cent of the immigrants were unemployed, depending on sex and the definition of the term 'immigrant'. Furthermore, as little as 41–55 per cent of the immigrant population aged 16–64 was employed. As a consequence, immigrant households were over-represented among social assistance recipients. Immigrant households have, to a larger extent than natives,

Table 2.2. Employment and unemployment rates in 1997 (per cent)

	Employment rate		Unemployment rate	
	Men	Women	Men	Women
Foreign citizens	47.3	41.1	26.4	23.2
Foreign-born population	55.0	50.1	18.7	16.3
Total population	72.4	68.9	8.5	7.5

Source: SCB unpublished statistics; AKU Grundtabeller 1997.

Table 2.3. Employment rates and unemployment rates in 1999 of people born abroad by immigration year, age-standardized (per cent)

Year of immigration	Employment rate		Unemployment rate	
	Men	Women	Men	Women
1970–1979	65	63	8	6
1980–1987	61	53	15	14
1988–1992	53	46	20	16
1993–1998	38	29	26	22
The foreign-born population	58	52	15	12
The total population	75	71	6	5

Source: Ekberg and Rooth 2000.

become recipients of social transfers to the extent that almost half of all social welfare payments in the mid-1990s went to immigrant households.[10]

There are large differences in employment rates between immigrants from different regions, with Nordic and Western European immigrants having the highest rates, followed by Southern Europeans and those from developing countries. Formal education and time in Sweden can only partially explain differences in employment probabilities between immigrants from different regions. Even after controlling for individual characteristics, micro studies of immigrant employment in Sweden show the same graduated picture.[11]

The increasing difficulty in obtaining employment has led to declining employment rates evident in cross-sectional studies. Some nationalities exhibit extremely low employment rates, such as Iranians (42 per cent for men and 36 per cent for women according to the labour force survey of 1997). A look at the longer picture isn't quite as grim, however. The cross-sectional figures are often a reflection of labour market entry difficulties. During the period 1984 to 1994, 70 per cent of Iranian men did succeed in obtaining some sort of employment within five years of obtaining their permanent residence permit. In addition, those with higher levels of education from their home country tend to do better than their uneducated peers in the longer run. The employment level of Iranians with academic degrees after five years is 85 per cent, which can be compared with the

[10] Broomé et al. 1996; Franzén 1997.
[11] Bevelander 2000; Åslund 2001; Roslund et al. 2001.

corresponding level for Iranians with primary education of 69 per cent, and those Iranians who lack educational information come in at 56 per cent. Differences between Iranian men by education are thus very large, much larger than differences across nationalities.[12]

It has also been found that the returns to education and labour market training in Sweden are not substantial in terms of employment prospects for refugees.[13] Rather it is more important to acquire a foothold in the labour market than to acquire formal human capital. This is also consistent with the need for culture-specific human capital, since employment would naturally expose the refugee to the workings of the Swedish labour market.

In an attempt to alleviate the economic problems caused by the creation of high immigrant concentrations in certain municipalities, the Swedish government began a programme in 1985 of spreading refugee immigrants throughout the country upon arrival. The effects of this 'all of Sweden' policy were recently evaluated and the results were striking.[14] Rather than reducing unemployment, it was found that the probability of idleness eight years after arrival was actually *increased* by 6 percentage points due to the new programme. This then led to a study of the effects of ethnic enclaves. Despite the negative association that enclaves have in the Swedish debate, the results show that they actually reduce idleness.

One area in which immigrants tend to be over-represented is self-employment.[15] Recent studies show that immigrants from almost all nationalities have a higher likelihood of becoming self-employed than natives, and that it is especially those non-Nordic immigrants who arrived before 1980 who are likely to set up shop for themselves.[16] One possible explanation of this over-representation is that self-employment may offer an entrance to a labour market that otherwise excludes outsiders. The self-employed can, through longer work days and help from family members, reduce wage costs and thus compete in a manner impossible in the tightly regulated regular labour market, where work hours and minimum wages are fixed collectively.[17]

2.3.2. Earnings and Wages

Due to poor wage statistics for Sweden, little is known about immigrants' wages. Early studies indicate that there were little or no differences

[12] Bengtsson and Scott 1998.   [13] Rooth 1999.
[14] Edin, Fredriksson, and Åslund 2001.   [15] Scott 1999.   [16] Hammarstedt 2001.
[17] Broomé et al. 1996.

in wages between immigrants and natives with the same jobs in the 1960s and early 1970s.[18] However, since the 1980s a tendency to wage discrimination has emerged.[19] Because of the poor wage statistics, most Swedish studies refer to immigrant *earnings* rather than immigrant wages.[20]

The average earnings of immigrants are to a large extent a function of the immigrants' employment rates, job structure, and number of working hours per year. In the middle of the 1960s, foreign citizens on average earned 20 per cent more than Swedish citizens, mainly because of the high employment in full-time jobs of immigrant women.[21] In the 1960s and early 1970s, immigrants' earnings were concentrated in the middle income bracket while the proportions of immigrants with high or low income bracket were less.[22] Again, the reason that few had low relative earnings was probably due to a greater number of hours worked, especially of immigrant women, and the reason that there were few with high incomes was the fact that most immigrants worked in industrial jobs. It is difficult, however, to say (because of the lack of wage statistics) that immigrants earned more on average than natives due to higher hourly wages, or more likely, more hours worked per week.

Since the 1970s, the earnings of immigrants have gone down, with studies of the 1970s and early 1980s showing a growing proportion of immigrants with low earnings.[23] In the 1980s, immigrant earnings relative to native earnings deteriorated, and recent studies reveal low yearly average earnings and large proportions of low-income earners.[24] In 1992, the average earnings of foreign citizens were 60 per cent of the earnings of Swedish citizens.[25]

Common in the immigration literature is the concept of 'catch-up'.[26] The idea here is that immigrants enter the country with lower wages, but as their true productivity is revealed or they acquire location-specific human capital their earnings increase at a faster rate than natives. This process was evident in Sweden until the 1970s, but an examination of the 1990 census shows that there may now exist little earnings catch-up.[27] Several studies

---

[18] Wadensjö 1975.   [19] Wadensjö 1994*b*.

[20] There have been sensitivity studies carried out which show that the yearly earnings commonly used in Swedish studies are highly correlated with wages, so this is not deemed too problematic.   [21] Ekberg and Andersson 1995.

[22] SCB 1977; Wadensjö 1972.   [23] Arbetsmarknadsdepartementet 1981; Ekberg 1983.

[24] Aguilar and Gustavsson 1991; Ekberg 1994*b*; Scott 1999.

[25] Ekberg and Andersson 1995.   [26] Chiswick 1978; Borjas 1981, 1985.

[27] Scott 1999.

show these changes in immigrant labour market position over the past thirty years, and that there exist large differences between the adaptation of older and newer immigrants, as well as differences between nationalities.

One study observed immigrants (foreign-born) who arrived prior to 1970 and were still living in Sweden in 1970, that is, mostly labour immigrants.[28] For each of these immigrants, a Swedish 'twin' was created, with the same age, sex, occupation, and residential place in 1970. The immigrants were followed in the following censuses through 1990, and were in each point in time compared with their Swedish 'twins'. This approach means that some of the included immigrants successively are lost because of return migration or death, but it also means that new immigrants after 1969 are not included in the study. Thus, Ekberg's twin studies are mainly studies of the careers of labour immigrants who came in the 1950s and 1960s.

Among the old immigrants, small differences were found compared to Swedes as far as social mobility and the development of earnings were concerned. Of those foreign-born who were still employed in 1990, men earned only 2 per cent less than natives and women 3 per cent more. Still, the upward social movement of immigrants tended to be somewhat slower than for natives. The immigrants also tended to leave the labour market earlier than natives, and that the average earnings of immigrants were therefore smaller than that of the natives.

Although the difference between the total immigrant population and the natives was small, the difference between various immigrant groups was considerable. Some nationalities such as Poles and Czechs experienced high upward occupational mobility, while, on the other hand, immigrants from Yugoslavia and Greece were less fortunate in their labour market careers.

A longitudinal study found that earnings of men and women born in Sweden are greater than earnings of immigrants born outside Sweden, and that this gap cannot be fully explained by differences in observed human capital.[29] As with the employment picture presented in the previous section, the immigrant–native earnings gap is different for different nationalities. The earnings in this study tend to increase with time in the country (as opposed to the cross-sectional evidence from the 1990 census), and when the sample is limited to those with Swedish upper secondary education the gap is reduced. Taking account of variations in occupation also only accounts for part of the gap.

[28] Ekberg 1990*a*, 1990*b*, 1991, 1994*a*, 1995.   [29] LeGrand and Szulkin 1999, 2000.

The same picture is seen in another longitudinal study examining 1968-93.[30] In this study there exists a fairly clear demarcation in periods, with the time up until the mid-1980s being more favourable for immigrant incomes than the time afterwards. Here we also see differences in earnings gaps between nationalities, when controlling for human capital, demographic, and occupational differences. Those immigrants from countries closer to Sweden, such as Norway or Germany tend to do much better than those from more distant nationalities such as Somalia.

It is also clear that the old and the new immigrants experienced very different labour market careers in the 1980s and 1990s. It is clear that the lower employment rates and earnings of the latecomers remained even after controlling for the number of years in Sweden.[31] Thus, the difference in career seems not only to be a matter of how long immigrants had been in Sweden, but also when they arrived. In terms of the negative effects of the 1990s recession, it seems as if the refugees who arrived during the previous fifteen years were the hardest hit, experiencing great difficulties in even gaining a foothold in the labour market.[32]

As with employment, the effects of the all of Sweden policy on earnings were examined.[33] Here it was found that, eight years after arrival in Sweden, this integration policy had effectively reduced earnings by 25 per cent compared to what would have existed given the previous immigrant policy. Again the effects of ethnic enclaves on income is positive, as was the case for employment.

That these differences in wages persist after controlling for observed characteristics also leads one to the conclusion found in Section 2.3.1: the Swedish economy may have reorganized itself in a manner which favours those with country-specific human capital. The will give natives an obvious comparative advantage over their immigrant counterparts. The fact that living in enclaves increases income and employment possibilities also lends support to this idea, since here one cannot reasonably assert the importance of Sweden-specific human capital.

2.3.3. Social Benefits Dependency, Sickness and Early Exits

This section deals with immigrant's dependency on social benefits, sickness insurance benefits, and early retirement benefits–relative to natives'.

---

[30] Scott 1999.   [31] Bevelander 1995; Scott 1995; Bevelander and Scott 1996.
[32] Edin and Åslund 2001.   [33] Edin et al. 2001.

The literature in this area can be divided into two groups: the social and economic and the epidemiological and medical. Health, likewise, has two components, one medical and one social. This is the case with regard to both somatic and psychological diseases. Information about sickness and economic compensation for sickness can therefore provide us with insights on how well immigrants are socially and economically integrated, just like details on job prevalence and income development.

2.3.3.1. Health

Epidemiologists in the USA, Australia, Canada, and Great Britain show that in the 1950s and 1960s the health conditions among immigrants differed from those who stayed behind.[34] The children grew taller compared to those who still lived in the sending countries, and the disease pattern differed. Many of the early studies of the influence of changes in lifestyle factors on cancer and coronary heart diseases use data on immigrants, since they provide a 'natural experiment'. Typical of those studies is the comparison between those who migrated and those who stayed. Later research has instead focused on the difference between immigrants and natives.

Knowledge about the health of immigrants is, however, still limited in Sweden.[35] Few studies have been done with a 'natural experiment' approach. The studies of coronary heart diseases among immigrants from Finland to Sweden are exceptions.[36] The focus has instead been on how the health of immigrants compares with that of natives. Still, few studies have been done and a more general study of mortality and causes of death have not been done for immigrants. Only a smaller study of Stockholm County, which shows a higher mortality below sixty-five years of ages for immigrants, has been made.[37] Studies of perinatal and infant mortality show small differences between immigrants and natives.[38]

Some differences in health of immigrants relative to Swedes are documented. Screening of asylum seekers show that they have higher prevalence of infections and parasitical diseases. Tuberculosis is more frequent among immigrants than natives. Genetic disposition for age-diabetes exists in some of the home countries of the immigrants. Differences are

---

[34] Hjern 1995.   [35] Riksförsäkringsverket 1996.

[36] The study showed that the incidence of arteriosclerosis is diminishing the longer the Finnish immigrants have stayed in Sweden, but that it still has higher prevalence than in Swedes. Alfredsson et al. 1982.   [37] Diderichsen 1989.

[38] Aurelius and Ryde-Blomqvist 1978; Mjönes and Koctürk 1986.

also found in cancer of the gastrointestinal system.[39] Asylum seekers also show a higher prevalence of psychological diseases than natives (due to torture and traumatic events) and immigrants from Eastern Europe, former Yugoslavia, and the Mediterranean countries have a higher incidence of suicide than Swedes. Somatic damages from the home country (war, torture) are likely to be important, but the diagnoses for those arriving in 1988–90 do not show any proof.[40] Thus, the difference in health among immigrants as a group relative to Swedes is rather small. Later research shows, however, that the differences within the group of immigrants are rather large.

2.3.3.2. Early retirement

The proportion of the population which retired early between the ages of 16 and 64 years varies strongly with birth country and over time. While about 6 per cent of Swedish-born males took early pensions during the 1990s, the figures for immigrants from the other Nordic countries were 11–12 per cent after standardizing for age-composition. The group with the highest degree of early retirement are labour immigrants from the former Yugoslavia, especially females. As shown in Table 2.4, this figure fell throughout the 1990s. This is, however, a statistical fallacy, since the reason is that a large group of refugees from Bosnia and other parts of former Yugoslavia have entered the group. Several other groups, including immigrants from Greece, Turkey, and Finland, have similar levels of longterm sickness spells and early retirements.

It is unlikely that well-defined somatic diseases are of major importance for differences between various immigrant groups and natives in sickness leave and early retirement. The health differences in somatic and psychological diseases aren't that large, as shown in the previous section. Early retirements are instead often due to somatic disorders of the locomotive system caused by monotonic jobs.[41] It is also likely that general labour market conditions–unemployment, closing of factories, investment in new machinery, etc.–are of great influence on early retirement.[42] Thus, the proportion of early retirements shown in Table 2.4 is not only a result of differences in health but also in employment conditions and the labour market in general. The dependency on sickness benefits and early

---

[39] Hjern 1995.   [40] Riksförsäkringsverket 1996.   [41] Riksförsäkringsverket 1996.
[42] The exception is the immigrants who retired after a short stay in Sweden (less than five years). They often have a specific disease panorama (psychological diseases or retardation), see Riksförsäkringsverket 1996.

Table 2.4. Early retirements 1990–7. Number of retirees in per cent of each group according to birth country and sex. Age-standardized values (per cent)

	1990	1991	1992	1993	1994	1995	1996	1997
Men								
Sweden	6.1	6.1	6.3	6.5	6.5	6.3	6.2	6.0
Other Nordic countries	11.0	10.9	11.8	12.2	12.3	11.8	12.0	12.1
Other EU countries	9.2	9.7	9.9	8.1	7.9	7.3	9.0	8.1
Former Eastern Europe	7.6	8.3	8.7	8.1	7.9	7.3	7.5	7.4
Former Yugoslavia	18.6	18.6	19.9	17.6	14.4	13.8	12.9	12.9
Africa	7.0	9.7	7.1	7.6	7.0	8.9	11.8	11.4
Asia	7.0	9.7	7.1	8.5	8.7	8.2	9.4	9.8
North America	3.6	2.4	2.6	2.8	3.1	2.2	2.6	2.2
Latin America	2.9	3.4	5.4	6.7	6.6	9.5	7.6	7.9
Women								
Sweden	7.2	7.4	7.8	8.2	8.2	8.2	8.2	8.2
Other Nordic countries	13.3	13.9	14.3	15.0	14.9	14.5	14.4	14.3
Other EU countries	11.3	11.6	12.4	13.2	14.8	15.0	14.1	14.3
Former Eastern Europe	11.8	12.2	12.8	12.5	12.0	10.7	11.1	11.0
Former Yugoslavia	27.1	29.4	31.4	28.1	20.9	19.1	18.1	17.8
Africa	3.1	0.3	0.3	3.3	5.6	9.4	10.2	8.4
Asia	7.4	7.4	7.5	9.2	10.0	11.1	11.5	11.5
North America	15.1	9.0	9.2	6.7	6.6	7.0	6.8	7.2
Latin America	11.6	11.5	11.5	14.3	13.9	14.7	14.5	15.0

Source: Riksförsäkringsverket 2001.

retirement pensions among immigrants is therefore a net indicator of health and integration at the workplace.

2.3.3.3. Sickness benefits

We find large differences in sickness compensation by immigrant group and sex.[43] There are also large differences between educational levels.[44] Education interacts with home country. The level of sickness benefit claimed by immigrants from Western Europe corresponds to that paid to Swedes with the same education but immigrants from Southern Europe

---

[43] Riksförsäkringsverket 1996.
[44] Bengtsson and Scott (forthcoming); Riksförsäkringsverket 1966.

show very different figures, particularly low-educated women.[45] The issue is the same as for early retirement; sickness leave is not only due to sickness but also to workplace dissatisfaction. Immigrants had, however, more long-term absences also after controlling for all sectors of employment.[46] A problem here is that it is difficult to control for specific workplace conditions and fuel conditions which might explain as much as half of the variation in sickness absence between immigrants and Swedes.[47] The figure is likely to be higher if more information about workplace and work history were known. The share of sickness leaves related to workplace accident is, however, low. Jobs typically held by foreign-born women have on average only 5 per cent absences due to work injuries. The figure is about the same for men.[48] There is consequently no relation between workplace accidents and total sickness compensation. Thus a large share, perhaps as high as 50 per cent, of the difference between immigrants and natives in sickness benefits cannot be attributed to the specific workplace.

2.3.4. Second Generation of Immigrants

Unlike established immigration countries such as the USA and Canada, Sweden is only recently seeing second generation immigrants—the Swedish-born children of immigrants—entering the labour force. Given this fact, there have to date been very few studies of the intergenerational integration of immigrants into the Swedish economy.

The previous sections have discussed the importance of country-specific human capital for the labour market success of newly arrived immigrants. If this is the case, then one would expect the second generation to do comparatively better than their parents. This would be due to the fact that they were raised in Sweden, and should thus have no problems with the language and a school transcript which is easily understood by prospective employers.

There are also reasons to believe that they will not do as well as children of natives, however. The first is that they are likely to be raised in a home environment, which is considerably different from that of their schoolmates. This exposure to different values and traditions could be seen

---

[45] Immigrants had fewer absences, both short and longterm, before 1992 according to Andrén 2001. The result is different from that found, for example, by Bengtsson and Scott (forthcoming), which may be a result of sampling or the fact that Andrén does not control for number of years in Sweden.   [46] Bengtsson and Scott (forthcoming).
[47] Riksförsäkringsverket 1996.   [48] Wadensjö 1997.

as non-assimilation and may have some negative effect. The most likely source of problems, however, is found in the names and appearances of the second generation. Given the fact that they have similar sounding names and are similar in appearance to their parents, they may well be the target of statistical discrimination. If employers know that their employees need certain location-specific skills, and that immigrants are less likely to possess these skills, then they may discriminate against those of the second generation, based solely on the name on an application.

Several studies have examined the extent to which the second generation has become more 'Swedish' than their parents. Three studies of educational investment arrive at similar conclusions. One study examined transitions into upper secondary and university studies, and found that the children of immigrants are just as likely to enter higher levels of education as their 'Swedish' counterparts (i.e. native persons with native parents), when controlling for social category.[49] The second study examined completed years of education, and found that the stock of second generation in 1994 had approximately the same number of years of schooling as did the 'Swedish' population in the same age categories.[50] The third study examines completed educational level, and finds in most cases no effects of ethnic origin on educational attainment when controlling for parental economic status. For those groups showing effects, the effect is positive, rather than negative.[51]

When it comes to the second generation's attachment to the labour market, the assumed outlook is bleak. This is partially because of the situation mentioned above, but also because social and labour market status tends to be transmitted through generations, and the first generation has had difficulties establishing itself. One would imagine that they will be better off than their parents, but not as well off as 'Swedes'. A study of the situation in 1994 shows that the second generation immigrants born before 1970 had approximately the same employment rates as 'Swedes', while those born after 1970 have a different situation.[52] For these younger individuals, there is a noticeable difference between their employment rates and those of first generation immigrants with the same national background. Compared with their 'Swedish' contemporaries, however, there also exist considerable differences, with the 'Swedes' being better off.

The earnings of second generation immigrants have also been studied, and it was found that there did exist differences between these individuals

[49] Eriksson and Jonsson 1993.   [50] Ekberg 1997a, 1997b.   [51] Österberg 2000.
[52] Ekberg 1997a, 1997b.   [53] Österberg 2000.

and 'Swedes'.[53] On average the effect of ethnicity was found to be negative, but this 'ethnic penalty' was most pronounced in the earnings category under SEK 100,000. In an examination of individuals earning more than SEK 100,000, very few ethnicities displayed these negative effects, leading to the conclusion that the impact is mainly seen at the point of entry into the labour market. This finding was echoed in another study, which found the negative effects of the second generation to be most pronounced in the employment process.[54]

Generally it can be said that the second generation is better off than their immigrant forebears, but that they have yet to assimilate fully into the Swedish economy. In terms of occupational segregation there seems to be a lessening of the segregation noticed in the first generation, but the second generation still displays some deviation from the total population's occupational distribution.[55]

2.3.5. Sweden-Specific Human Capital and Discrimination

Most international and Swedish economic studies of immigrant labour market integration have been carried out within the human capital tradition. Within this kind of approach, it is assumed that the individual's labour market career is influenced by individual characteristics. Models usually control for some demographic variables and put emphasis on explaining variables such as education, vocational training, labour market experience, and sometimes motivation.

As was previously stated, there are clear differences between immigrants and natives as far as employment and earnings are concerned. Immigrants are less likely than natives to be employed and therefore are more likely to be on unemployment benefit or social assistance. Partly as a consequence, immigrants usually earn less than natives. Clear differences can also be observed within the immigrant population itself. Migrants of the 1950s or 1960s do a lot better than those who immigrated in the 1980s and 1990s, and in the latter period labour migrants usually do better than refugees and immigrants from industrialized countries in Europe and America do better than immigrants from the Third World. Second generation immigrants generally do better than immigrants of the first generation.[56]

To what extent then is it possible to explain such differences in labour market performance through individual differences in human capital? As

[54] Månsson and Ekberg 2000.   [55] Ekberg 1997a, 1997b.
[56] Ekberg and Rooth 2000.

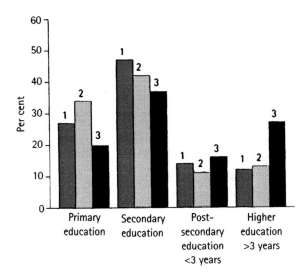

Figure 2.8. Highest educational entry of people (1) born in Sweden, (2) born outside of Sweden, and (3) immigrated in 1991–4, aged 25–64
Source: SCB, Utbildningsnivå för utrikes födda. Rapport från enkätundersökning våren 1995. Bakgrundsfakta till Arbetsmarknads- och Utbildningsstatistiken 1995: 4

far as theoretical education is concerned, there is little difference between immigrants and Swedes (see Figure 2.8). The total immigrant population (foreign-born) is somewhat over-represented among the low and highly educated, but the deviation from the Swedish average is slight. On the other hand, the newly arrived immigrants are generally more highly educated than Swedes, which partly is due to the fact that they are younger than the average Swedish population. But even after age standardization it is clear that the immigrants of the 1990s have larger proportions of people with post-secondary and higher education.[57]

Most research in recent years points in the direction that merely individual investments in human capital, measured as level of education and experience, cannot explain differences between immigrants and natives, and between national and cohort groups within the immigrant population. This approach needs to be complemented with a demand side approach including a broader concept of human capital.[58] Supplementary explanations have therefore been put forward, emphasizing increasing demands for nation-specific human capital and discrimination.

[57] Broomé et al. 1996.
[58] Arai et al. 1999; Scott 1999; Bevelander 2000; Österberg 2000, Vilhelmsson 2000.

Some studies accentuate the increasing importance of 'Sweden-specific' skills in the 1980s and 1990s.[59] This increase was a result of the process of economic structural transformation, which can be described at both the aggregate and micro level. At the aggregate level, the industrial sector has been decreasing since the middle of the 1960s, meaning that new jobs were generally created in the service sector. At the firm level, technology and work organization was changing with the introduction of information technology and the replacement of the Fordist concept by lean production. The economic structural change meant a transformation of working life and changing demands for skills. There was a drop in the demand for unskilled foreign workers for low qualified jobs in industry and an increase in the demand for language skills and 'social competence' that to a high degree is culture-specific, which is unfavourable to newly arrived immigrants.

This explanation was presented in some studies in the middle of the 1990s and has been frequent ever since. In some studies the hypothesis that economic structural change and shifts in technology and organization increased the importance of language skills and other Sweden-specific knowledge, plays the major role in explaining the worsening of immigrant performance in the Swedish labour market in the 1980s and 1990s.[60] In other studies the importance of Swedish-specific human capital is seen as a residual or a supplementary explanation.

It may seem logical that economic transformation and technological and organizational changes have induced a demand for labour with higher qualifications and Sweden-specific knowledge. It is a fact that immigrants in the 1980s and 1990s did a lot worse that those who arrived earlier and it is also without doubt that immigrants from less developed countries in the Third World experience a much worse labour market than immigrants from Europe and America. In spite of its logic, it is difficult in empirical studies, to verify fully this hypothesis. It is not easy to isolate the effect of a change in the demand for unqualified labour with little Sweden-specific skills from other possible changes over time, for instance in discrimination practices. It could be hypothesized that an increase in the demand for Sweden-specific skills would increase the statistical discrimination as well.[61] There is also some evidence of the existence and even increase in preferential discrimination.[62] However, discrimination does not explain all the differences between nationalities in labour market performance—some

---

[59] Lundh and Ohlsson 1994a–b; Broome et al. 1996; Bevelander and Scott 1996; Bengtsson and Scott 1998; Scott 1999; Bevelander 2000.   [60] Scott 1999; Bevelander 2000.

[61] Broomé et al. 1996.   [62] Rooth 2001.

studies give support to the hypothesis that technological and organizational changes in the firms have led to an increase in the demand for Sweden-specific skills.

One micro-level study shows that the deterioration in immigrant employment prospects during the 1980s and 1990s were similar for immigrants in both Denmark and Sweden, despite differing macroeconomic climates.[63] This may be interpreted as the effects of organizational change being a large determinant in the current labour market dilemma of immigrants in Scandinavia, and perhaps also elsewhere.

Second generation immigrants generally do better than the first generation of the same national origin.[64] Immigrants that were so young when arriving in Sweden that they completed education within the Swedish educational system are more likely to have a good labour market career than immigrants with a foreign education.[65] Such results indicate that Swedish language and Sweden-specific human capital are important for the performance in the labour market.

According to one study, the risk of being unemployed is greater for individuals of the second generation of immigrants if they are from developing countries and if both parents were born abroad.[66] For Western Europeans (and Scandinavians in particular) it is little or no disadvantage to have two foreign-born parents, since their native human capital is easily transformed into a Swedish setting. For children of immigrants from developing countries the fact that both parents are born abroad means about 15 percentage points higher risk of being unemployed than second generation immigrants with one native parent. This difference is interpreted in terms of access or lack of Sweden-specific knowledge. Since second generation immigrants from developing countries should experience about the same level of appearance-forced discrimination whether one or two parents were born abroad, the results support the idea that Sweden-specific knowledge is important for individuals' labour market careers.

Some studies find discrimination to be of great importance in explaining the differences between natives and immigrants and among immigrant nationalities in the labour market performance.[67] Statistical discrimination, in particular, has been found to be one explanation for the lesser employment opportunities of immigrants and the wage gap between

---

[63] Rosholm et al. 2001.   [64] Ekberg 1997a, 1997b.
[65] Schröder and Vilhelmsson 1998.   [66] Rooth 2001.
[67] Arai, Regner and Schröder 1999.

natives and immigrants.[68] In most studies, discrimination is treated like a residual: that is; those differences that are left when all possible human capital factors are controlled for, which makes the results somewhat imprecise. However, one study of adopted children gives substantial support to the idea that preferential discrimination does exist in the Swedish labour market.[69] In this study foreign-born men adopted as children by native married couples were compared to Swedes with regard to the probability of their being unemployed in the age groups twenty to thirty-five. It was found that there was no difference in the likelihood of being unemployed between adopted persons with Swedish looks (whites) and Swedes, whereas adopted persons with non-Swedish looks (nonwhites) were much more likely to be unemployed. Since all adopted persons, regardless of looks, could be assumed to have acquired Sweden-specific human capital (Swedish education, Swedish language skills, Swedish networks), such remaining differences could be related to the colour of the skin; this is interpreted as discrimination.

2.4. The Economic and Labour Market Effects of Immigration

2.4.1. Economic Growth

The main economic argument in favour of a liberal immigration policy in the 1950s and 1960s was that immigration would mitigate the shortage of labour in boom periods and in expanding branches of industry. It would thereby stabilize business conditions, neutralize bottlenecks in production, counteract too sharp wage increases and contribute to economic growth on the whole. This was the spirit of the age when Sweden in the early 1950s accepted the OEEC's labour statute, pledging to facilitate European labour mobility, and the agreement on a common Nordic labour market.

It is not easy to calculate the importance of immigration to economic growth, especially not in the long run. It has been held that immigration played a somewhat different role in the Swedish economy in the 1960s compared with the 1950s. In the 1950s, which was a period of transformation and structural change, immigration was supplementary to Swedish labour. A large fraction of the immigrants were skilled workers such as engineers and technicians who were employed in key jobs in expanding companies. These immigrant workers were crucial in the transformation

---

[68] Bevelander 2000; Le Grand and Szulkin 1999.   [69] Rooth 2001.

process, where new techniques of production, new machinery and new products were introduced. Thus, through the human skills of the immigrants, labour immigration contributed not only to an increase in production, but also to an increase in productivity.

In the 1960s, which were characterized by industrial expansion, the role of immigration changed and immigrant labour now became complementary to native labour. The increase in productivity was now led by the new technique and economies of scale, and given this it was mainly unskilled labour that was demanded. The shortage in labour was more general than previously and unskilled workers from Finland, Yugoslavia, and Greece dominated immigration in the 1960s.

While international economic empirical research points in different directions when it comes to the question of the effects of immigration on economic growth, there is only one Swedish study in this field. Ekberg studied the effects on GNP per capita and consumption per capita in Sweden by using a combined demographic–economic model with endogenous technical progress.[70] He compared two alternatives, one without immigration and one with the level of net immigration that was typical in the 1950s and 1970s. His result showed that the positive effect of immigration was insignificant.

Ekberg's conclusion is that the effect of immigration on economic growth is to a large extent dependent on the geographical and occupational mobility of the immigrants.[71] His own studies of immigrants (foreign-born) who entered Sweden prior to 1970, through recent decades presented a contradictory picture in this regard.[72] On the one hand, the immigrants have had a larger geographic mobility than natives, especially directed towards large cities such as Stockholm, Gothenburg, and Malmoe. These labour migrants were once recruited to economically expansive industrial regions and moved later on to other expanding parts of the country. Therefore, they probably had a positive influence on economic growth. On the other hand, the immigrant groups with the highest geographic mobility have at the same time had the lowest social mobility. To a large extent they have remained in the same sort of unqualified jobs as they were once recruited to when they arrived in Sweden. Altogether, Ekberg claims that it is hard to draw any specific conclusions on the effect of immigrants' geographical and occupational mobility on economic growth.[73]

---

[70] Ekberg 1977, 1983.   [71] Ekberg and Andersson 1995.
[72] Ekberg 1993a, 1995a.   [73] Ekberg and Andersson 1995.

2.4.2. Employment and Wages/Earnings

Theoretically, one would expect that the increase in the labour supply resulting from immigration would give rise to lower wages for the native labour force and an increasing competition for available jobs. However, international empirical studies indicate that the effects of immigration on both employment and wages have been quite small. The Swedish case fits well into this picture.

Fischer and Straubhaar argue it is probable that, due to the low migration intensities involved, it is impossible to reveal any *general effects* of migration on wages. This would be the case only in branches using foreign labour intensively.[74] Ekberg finds that the total effect of immigration on employment and wages was rather small in the 1960s and 1970s as a result of contradictory effects in different sectors of the economy and for different groups of native labour.[75] For low-skilled native labour, immigration exerted downward pressure on wages, while the effect of immigration on well-educated labour was the opposite, that is, positive. Sectors employing large numbers of low-skilled Finnish workers, say construction and the manufacturing industry, saw slightly lower wage increases, which Ekberg interprets as downward pressure on wage increases causing the immigration of large number of Finnish workers.[76] Another possible explanation is that, generally speaking, immigrant workers replaced natives in the goods producing sector, often in the branches that showed lower growth-rates, while the natives went to the service sector.[77]

Thus, it seems unlikely that immigration in the period of labour migration had any negative effect on the native employment and wages in general and particularly not in the expansive industries and branches. This raises the question of whether this was also true for the 1980s and 1990s when immigration was dominated by refugees and not by labour.

There are two facts that speak in favour of this. First, the general level of unemployment was very low until 1992, so low that economists in the 1980s claimed that it was even below the NAIRU.[78] Even though the rate of unemployment of immigrants (foreign citizens) was twice as high as the

[74] Fischer and Straubhaar 1996.   [75] Ekberg 1977, 1983.
[76] Ekberg 1993a.   [77] Ohlsson 1975; Lundh and Ohlsson 1994b.
[78] The nonaccelerating inflation rate of unemployment (NAIRU) is the rate of unemployment that is consistent with a stable rate of inflation. The concept is used by neoclassical economists and is interchangeable with the concept 'natural' rate of unemployment.

Swedes' in the 1980s, their contribution to the job competition and wage pressure could hardly be more than marginal.

Secondly, the growing numbers of immigrants without employment in the 1980s and 1990s must not all necessarily be regarded as an immigrant labour supply surplus. It is well known that it is difficult to calculate empirically the labour supply. The economic structural change and the transformation of working life make it even more difficult to judge to what extent newly arrived immigrants should be regarded as an unemployed part of the labour force who compete with natives for jobs and whose existence exerts pressure on the wage level. To the extent that the skills of these immigrants don't match the demand for labour, for example, language skills or social competence, they don't compete with natives for jobs and they don't exert any pressure on wages. It is generally agreed that there has been a change in the demand for labour skills which has been unfavourable to new immigrants, especially those who come from countries with languages and traditions very unlike the Swedish. In the 1990s, newly arrived immigrants competed with natives for unqualified jobs in sectors which were no longer growing, while their competitiveness was much less in highly-skilled jobs where language skills and communication-related competence are required.

Thus, the effect of immigration on native employment and wages was generally small and limited to immigrant-intensive branches. However, the question still remains whether this depended only on the fact that the numbers of immigrants have been too few to have any larger impact and to influence the entire labour market or if it was due to the Swedish wage formation system.

It is well known that the Swedish labour market model was characterized by wage formation through negotiations and collective agreements between quite centralized trade unions and employers' associations. Practically the entire labour market was covered by the collective agreement system, which was a prerequisite for the compressed wage structure that has characterized the Swedish labour market since the 1960s. The Swedish model was the institutional framework which made it possible for trade unions to exclude undesirable non-Nordic labour from the market by applying their veto to applications for work permits and to prevent wage competition from immigrant workers through the minimum wage level in the collective agreements.

Given the difficulties imposed by this insider/outsider phenomenon, immigrants in the 1990s showed a new employment pattern, working less as full-time, regularly hired employees and more often as part-time and temporary workers, as self-employed or in the grey or black market. In some branches where the proportion of self-employment is high, generally taxi, restaurant, domestic service, and small food shops, it is obvious that immigration has had a strong wage effect. Since immigrants are prevented from using wages to compete with natives in the highly regulated wage market, they often turn to self-employment. Working many hours per day and using family-members as labour in family firms, they are able to lower their hourly wage/income to the level that is competitive in the market, thereby exerting a downward wage pressure and competing for jobs.

2.4.3. Net Contributions to the Welfare State

It is well known that immigrants usually have a larger share of their population in economically active ages than do natives. Therefore, one would expect immigrants' contributions to the public sector in terms of taxes to exceed the public costs for immigrants' in terms of education, health, pensions, etc. Thus, labour immigration would lead to an income transfer from immigrants to natives via the public sector.

However, the results of international studies in the field point in different directions, which is probably due to the fact that the studies were carried out in different countries with different labour market regimes and welfare systems and at different points in time with different labour market situations.

To what extent immigrants in practice are net contributors to the public sector depends on the labour market situation. If many immigrants suffer from high unemployment, are kept out of employment in the regular market or are marginalized in the black market, the balance between public incomes and costs for the immigrant group will surely be affected.

The distribution effects of immigration via the public sector have been calculated in four Swedish cross-sectional studies and one cohort study. The first cross-sectional study referred to the situation in 1969 and was intended for a situation of marginal immigration.[79] The study concluded that there was a positive income effect for natives.

The second study concerned the distribution of incomes via the public sector between the entire immigration population and the native population in 1970 and 1976.[80] The result was in accordance with the previously mentioned study. The immigrants paid, in general, more taxes than they

---

[79] Wadensjö 1972.   [80] Ekberg 1983.

cost in terms of transfers and public consumption. In 1970 this meant a transfer to the average native household of 1,000–2,000 SEK in 1995 purchasing power. The net transfer in 1976 was somewhat smaller.

The third cross-sectional study referred to the average situation in 1980–5 and included only foreign citizens and parts of the public sector.[81] The study showed that the income effect of immigration was neutral.

The fourth cross-sectional study referred to 1991 and comprised the total immigrant population.[82] The study also included an estimation of the net costs of immigration in 1995, based on some assumptions, for example on the employment rates of the newly arrived groups (1991–3), which were not known at the time of the study. The study exposed that there was a negative income effect of immigration to the natives in 1991 and 1995, e.g. there was a transfer of income from natives to immigrants. In 1991, the public net cost related to immigration was 5–10 billions or 470–940 Kroners (SEK) per immigrant. In 1995, the net cost of the public sector was calculated to 20 billions, or 1,700 Kroners (SEK) per immigrant.

These cross-sectional studies indicate a chronology in the distribution effect of immigration, which is confirmed by a study of different immigration cohorts' net effects on the public sector.[83] During the period of labour immigration, incomes were transferred from immigrants to natives. As long as the public sector was rather small, the proportion of this distribution was also small but, along with the growth of the welfare state, the distribution effect grew. Around 1970, the transfer of incomes from immigrants to natives corresponded to about one per cent of the GNP.

During the course of the 1970s, the proportion of the distribution decreased and in the early 1980s there was a balance between immigrant-induced public costs and revenues. In the middle of the 1980s a shift occurred, and since then there has been a transfer of incomes in the opposite direction, from natives to immigrants, which increased in the 1990s. In 1991, the distribution of incomes from natives to immigrants via the public sector, corresponded to one per cent of the GNP, and in 1995 to two per cent of the GNP. To a large extent, this development was due to the massive refugee immigration and the weak labour market attachment of the new immigrants.

From Ekberg's and Andersson's study it is clear that it is the immigration of the 1980s and 1990s that has provoked the negative income effects of immigration.[84] If one takes into consideration the population contribution

[81] Gustafsson et al. 1990.   [82] Ekberg and Andersson 1995.
[83] Gustafsson and Larsson 1997.   [84] Ekberg and Andersson 1995.

of immigrants arriving prior to 1980, the income effect of the early immigration is neutral. The employment rates for these early cohorts are satisfactorily high, over 70 per cent on average. In fact, it is the large number of new immigrants in the 1980s and early 1990s with much lower employment rates that has led to a shift in the direction of income transfers in the 1980s. In 1992, only 63 per cent of those who immigrated in 1980–7 were employed, and no more than 47 per cent of those who came in 1988–90.

The importance of the immigrant's employment rate is clear from Ekberg's and Andersson's calculation of the income effect of immigration in 1991, under the assumption that new immigrants reach the same employment rate as the natives fairly quickly. The calculation showed that the public costs for immigrant-related allowances and public consumption decreased by three billions SEK, while the tax incomes went up eight billions SEK. Together this meant that a better labour market attachment of the new immigrants would mean a net contribution to the public sector of about two billions SEK instead of a net cost of 5–10 billions SEK, which was the actual situation.

2.5. Concluding Remarks

Sweden is among the countries in Europe with the highest number of immigrants relative to its population. One-fifth of the Swedish population is of foreign origin, with the majority from non-Nordic countries. About 10 per cent of the population are foreign-born and another 10 per cent have at least one parent born outside Sweden. The main bulk of the early immigrants, i.e. those who came from the end of the Second World War up to the middle of the 1970s, was from the neighbouring Nordic countries, from Finland in particular, and from Western and Southern Europe. Whether entering Sweden as labour immigrants or refugees (primarily dissidents from Eastern Europe), they earned well and became fully integrated into the society.

As a result of a change towards a more restricted immigrant policy, non-Nordic labour immigration practically stopped in the 1970s, while the immigration of refugees and tied movers increased. The refugee immigrants mainly came from countries outside Europe, first from Latin America, later from Asia, including the Middle East, and from Africa. Despite a booming Swedish economy in the 1980s, many of the newly arrived immigrants faced severe problems getting jobs. This was particularly true for those with low education. This was the situation, *nota bene*, at a time when the demand for labour was high. Thus one could say that there was a mismatch between the supply and the demand for immigrant labour during the 1980s, well before the business recession and increasing unemployment of the early 1990s.

The collapse of the labour market in the beginning of the 1990s as a result of a demand shock induced by the economic recession, the change in economic policy towards price stability and the public budget restrictions, made the labour market situation for immigrants worse. Non-European refugee immigrants who arrived in the 1980s or 1990s were to a large extent excluded from the labour market. Their employment opportunities were worse than those of natives and European immigrants, their unemployment rates were higher and their earnings lower. As a consequence, immigrant households were over-represented among social assistance recipients. Immigrants of the second generation have done better than the parental generation. However, the labour market situation was obviously worse for second generation immigrants of non-European origin compared with children of natives. Even the previously successful labour immigrants experienced worsening conditions in the labour market in the 1990s. Partly as a result of monotonic jobs in the manufacturing industry, problems with the locomotive system often led to longterm sickness and early retirement. Thus, while the newcomers and their children to a large extent were excluded from the Swedish labour market, the early immigrants were also being forced out of working life.

From the bulk of studies on immigrant integration into the Swedish labour market, it is obvious that individual characteristics alone cannot explain why immigrants have done worse than natives or the large differences between nationalities. The difference in the educational level is small between the Swedish born and foreign-born populations. There are large variations between nationalities and between immigrant cohorts, however. Labour immigrants from the Nordic countries and Southeastern Europe were generally less educated than Swedes, while immigrants from Eastern and Western Europe as well as North Americans, were on average better educated than Swedes. Even though there are exceptions, non-European immigrants of the early 1990s were better educated than Swedes, even after age standardization. Several micro studies show that education has a general positive effect on the probability of getting employment and on earnings, but it does not explain the differences in these respects between non-Europeans and natives (and Europeans). On the contrary, if educational level is controlled for, the disadvantage of newcomers of non-European origin increases. In terms of health, there are no major differences between foreign-born and natives in well-defined somatic or mental diseases.

Thus, there is no major shift over time in formal education or health that can explain why immigrants during the last decades have done worse in the labour market than previous ones. The only shifts in immigration that could be observed are the change in nationality composition and the shift from labour immigration to refugee immigration (including tied movers). The change in migration flows has made immigration to Sweden more heterogeneous than before. Many immigrants originate from countries that are not only geographically, but also economically, socially, and culturally more distant than earlier immigrants were. However, before the 1970s or 1980s, refugees were as integrated into the Swedish labour market as labour migrants. As far as we know from the small numbers of immigrants from outside Europe before the 1970s, their labour market situation was not substantially different from other immigrants.

Several studies therefore underlined the need to look also at changes in the demand for labour when analysing the mismatch during the 1980s and onwards. A structural change in the demand for labour, towards an increasing demand for labour with Sweden-specific skills, derived from changes in technology and working life organization, has been pointed out as a possible explanation. As a consequence, the increase in the demand for Sweden-specific human capital led to discriminatory behaviour of firms that was unfavourable to immigrants. The structural transformation of the economy had also reduced the number of low-skilled jobs in the industrial sector. Thus, in a period when the demand for Swedish language skills and other Sweden-specific competence was increasing, Sweden received extensive immigration of refugees from regions more distant from Sweden than ever before. These immigrants were refugees, and were not selected on their labour market qualifications.

The difficult labour market situation for immigrants to Sweden during recent decades has clear parallels with other Western European countries, including the Nordic ones. New immigrants came from countries further away than before and faced problems of getting jobs, in particular if they were poorly educated. Meanwhile, due to a general technological and organizational change in working life, a shift in the demand for labour occurred in the firms towards workers with greater country-specific skills. Thus, the problems seem to be similar in many mature industrial economies. However, the way they were solved was different and dependent on institutions and political traditions.

The Swedish institutional set-up made it extremely difficult for immigrants, like other outsiders (youth, long-term unemployed), to enter the labour market in a situation of economic transformation with high unemployment due to the recession, since the opportunity to compete with low wages was in practice no longer possible. The Swedish labour market is highly regulated and wages are determined by negotiations between trade unions and employers. Unlike the US and many European countries where trade union influence have declined in the 1980s and 1990s, trade unions in Sweden are still in a very strong position. Over 80 per cent of the employees (including white-collar workers) are unionized, and collective agreements cover the entire regular labour market. In practice, it is impossible to underbid or offer someone work for wages below the standard of the collective agreements.[85] Some immigrants (and natives) turn to self-employment in order to escape the labour market regulations on minimum wages.

Non-European immigrants of the 1980s and 1990s, and to a somewhat lesser degree their Swedish-born children, have experienced a much longer period of labour market entrance than did the previous immigrant cohorts. This is partly due to the institutional pattern in combination with the labour market situation, and partly to the increase in the demand for Sweden-specific human capital. As for all outsiders, they run the risk of this difficult entry into the labour market turning into a definite barrier against all future labour market participation. In this respect, the situation for non-European immigrants of the 1980s and 1990s constitutes the first failure of the Swedish unemployment and immigrant integration policy.

References

Aguilar, R. and Gustavsson, B. (1991). 'The earnings assimilation of immigrants', *Labour*, 5.

Alfredsson, L., Ahlbom, A., and Theorell, T. (1982). 'Incidence of myocardial infarction among Finnish immigrants in relation to their stay in Sweden', *International Journal of Epidemiology*, 11: 225–8.

Andrén, D. (2001). *Work, Sickness, Earnings, and Early Exits from the Labour Market: An Empirical Analysis Using Swedish Longitudinal Data* (Göteborg: Nationalekonomiska Institutionen).

---

[85] Lundh 2002.

Arai, M., Regner, H., and Schröder, L. (1999). *Är arbetsmarknaden öppen för alla?*, Bilaga 6 till Långtidsutredningen 1999. Finansdepartementet.

Arbetsmarknadsdepartementet (1981). *Invandrarkvinnor och jämställdhet*. DSA 1981:1 (Stockholm).

Aurelius, G. and Ryde-Blomqvist, E. (1978). 'Pregnancy and delivery among immigrants', *Scandinavian Journal of Medicine*, 6: 43–8.

Bengtsson, T. and Scott, K. (1998). Labour Market Entrance and Income Assimilation. An Analysis of Longitudinal Data from Sweden, 1970–1994. Paper presented at the ESF Conference 'Migration, Development and Policy' in Espinho, Portugal, 21–6 April 1998.

— (forthcoming). 'Immigrant consumption of sickness benefits in Sweden, 1982–1991', *Journal of Socio-Economics*.

Bevelander, P. (1995). *Immigrant Labour Force Participation in Sweden 1960–1990* (Department of Economic History, Lund University).

— (2000). 'Immigrant employment integration and structural change in Sweden, 1970–95' (Lund and Södertälje: Almqvist and Wiksell International).

Bevelander, P. and Scott, K. (1996). 'The employment and income performance of immigrants in Sweden, 1970–90', in *Yearbook of Population Research in Finland 1996, 33*.

Borjas, G. (1994). 'The economics of immigration', *Journal of Economic Literature*, 32.

Broomé, P., Bäcklund, A.-K., Lundh, C., and Ohlsson, R. (1996). *Varför sitter 'brassen' på bänken? Eller Varför har invandrarna så svårt att få jobb?* (Stockholm: SNS Förlag).

Brune, Y. (1993). *Invandrare i svenskt arbetsliv*. Tranås.

Diderichsen, F. (1989). *Storstadsutredningen*. SOU 1989:111.

Edin, P.-A. and Åslund, Olof (2001). Invandrare på 1990-talets arbetsmarknad. (Stockholm: FIEF).

—, Fredriksson, P., and Åslund, O. (2001). 'Ethnic enclaves and the economic success of immigrants–evidence from a natural experiment', in Åslund, O., *Health, Immigration and Settlement Policies* (Uppsala).

Ekberg, J. (1977). 'Longterm effects of immigration', *Economy and History*, 20.

— (1983). *Inkomstomsteffekter av invandring*. Lund Economic Studies, 27. (Lund).

— (1990a). *Invandrarna på arbetsmarknaden*. D. S. 1990:35 (Stockholm: Allmänna förlaget).

— (1990b). 'Immigrants–their economic and social mobility', in Persson, I. (ed.), *Generating Equality*. (Oslo: Oslo University Press).

— (1991). *Vad hände Sedan? En studie av utrikes födda på arbetsmarknaden*. (Växjö).

— (1993a). *Geografisk och socioekonomisk rörlighet bland invandrare* (Stockholm: ERU/Fritzes).

— (1993b). *Sysselsättning och arbetsmarknadskarriär bland invandrare, Rapport till Invandrar och flyktingkommittén*. (Kulturdepartementet Stockholm).

Ekberg, J. (1994a). 'Economic progress among Immigrants in Sweden', Scandinavian Journal of Social Welfare, 3.
— (1994b). 'Är invandrarna fattiga?', Ekonomisk Debatt. 22.
— (1995). 'Internal migration among immigrants', in Lundh, C. (ed.), Demography, Economy and Welfare. Scandinavian Population Studies, Vol. 10 (Lund).
— (1997a). 'Hur är arbetsmarknaden för den andra generationens invandrare?', Arbetsmarknad & Arbetsliv, vol. 3, no. 1.
— (1997b). Andra generationens invandrare. Demografi och arbetsmarknad. (Växjö: Högskolan i Växjö).
— and Andersson, L. (1995). Invandring, sysselsättning och ekonomiska effekter. Ds 1995:68. (Stockholm).
— and Rooth, D-O. (2000). Arbetsmarknadspolitik för invandrare. Bilaga till Språk och arbete–svenskundervisning för invandrare och invandrarnas arbetsmarknad. Riksdagens revisorer. Rapport (2000/01:3).
Eriksson, R. and Jonsson, J. O. (1993). Ursprung och utbildning. SOU 1993:85.
Fischer, P. A. and Straubhaar, T. (1996). Migration and Economic Integration in the Nordic Common Labour Market. Nord 1996:2. (Århus).
Franzén, E. (1997). 'Invandrare och socialbidrag', Socialvetenskaplig tidskrift, 4, no. 4.
Geschwind, H. (1958). 'Invandrares vistelsetid i Sverige', Statistisk tidskrift, no. 3, 1958.
Gustavsson, B. and Larsson, T. (1997). 'Invandrare och offentliga sektorns budgetrestriktion–En redovisningsövning', Ekonomisk Debatt, no. 3.
Gustavssons, B., Zamanian M., and Aguilars, R. (1990). Invandring och försörjning. (Göteborg: Daidalos).
Hammarstedt, M. (2001). Self-Employment Among Immigrants in Sweden. An Analysis of Intragroup Differences. (Växjö University, School of Management and Economics).
Harkman, A. (1984). Sysselsättning och arbetslöshet. (Stockholm: Stockholms Läns Landsting. Regionplanekontoret).
Hjern, A. (1995). Migrationsmedicinsk forskning. En översikt. MFR-rapport 1 (Stockholm:Medicinska Forskningsrådet).
Jonung, C. (1982). Migrant Women in the Swedish Labour Market, Report no. 3. (DEIFO, Stockholm).
Le Grand, C. and Szulkin, R. (1999). 'Invandrarnas löner i Sverige: Betydelsen av vistelsetid, invandrarland och svensk skolgång', i Arbetsmarknad & Arbetsliv, 5, no. 2.
— (2000). Permanent Disadvantage or Gradual Integration: Explaining the Immigrant-native Earnings Gap in Sweden. (Stockholm University, Swedish Institute for Social Research).
Lundborg, P. (1993). 'Arbetskraftens fria rörlighet i Europa', in Bernitz et al. (eds.), Vad betyder EG?, (Stockholm: SNS Förlag).
Lundh, C. (1994). 'Invandrarna i den svenska modellen–hot eller reserv?'. Arbetarhistoria, no. 2.

— (2002). *Spelets regler. Institutioner och lönebildning på den svenska arbetsmarknaden 1850-2000* (Stockholm: SNS Förlag).

Lundh, C. and Ohlsson, R. (1994a). *Från arbetskraftimport till flyktinginvandring,* (Stockholm: SNS Förlag).

— (1994b).'Immigration and economic change', in Bengtsson, T. (ed.), *Population, Economy and Welfare in Sweden,* (Berlin: Springer-Verlag).

— (1999). *Från arbetskraftimport till flyktinginvandring,* (Stockholm: SNS Förlag).

Mjönes, S. and Koctürk, T. (1986). 'Growth, nutritional status and infant mortality of Turkish immigrant preschool children', *Scandinavian Journal of Primary Care,* 4: 183-90.

Månsson, J. and Ekberg, J. (2000). *Second generation Immigrants in the Swedish Labour Market.* (Växjö University, School of Management and Economics).

Ohlsson, R. (1970). 'Economic Fluctuations and Immigration to Sweden, 1945-67', *Economy and History,* 13.

— (1975). *Invandrarna på arbetsmarknaden* (Lund).

— (1978). *Ekonomisk strukturförändring och invandring,* (Lund: CWK Gleerup).

Paulson, S., Schierup, C.-U., and Ålund, A. (1994). 'Den interna arbetsmarknaden– etniska skiktningar och dekvalificering', in Schierup, C.-U. and Paulson, S. (Eds.), *Arbetets etniska delning.* (Stockholm: Carlsson).

Reinans, S. (1982). *Utlänningar på arbetsmarknaden.* DEIFO. Rapport nr 19. (Stockholm).

Riksförsäkringsverket (1996). *Invandrarna i socialförsäkringen. Sjukskrivning, rehabilitering och förtidspensionering under 1990-talet.* (Stockholm: RVF Redovisar 1996:11).

— (2001). *Invandrares förtidspensioner under 1990-talet* (Stockholm: Riksförsäkringsverket. RFV redovisar 2001:7).

Rooth, D.-O. (1999). *Refugee Immigrants in Sweden. Educational Investments and Labour Market Integration.* (Lund University, Department of Economics).

Rosholm, M., Scott, K., and Husted, L. (2001). 'The Times they are a-changin'. Organizational change and immigrant employment opportunities in Scandinavia', IZA Discussion paper 258.

SCB (1977). *Invandrarnas levnadsförhållanden 1975.* Levnadsförhållanden, no. 9 (Stockholm).

Schröder, L. and Vilhelmsson, R. (1998). 'Sverigespecifikt humankapital och ungdomars etablering på arbetsmarknaden', *Ekonomisk Debatt,* 28, no. 8.

Scott, K. (1999). *The Immigrant Experience. Changing Employment and Income Patterns in Sweden, 1970-1993.* (Lund: Lund University Press).

— (1995). *Migrants in the Labour Market. Employment Patterns and Income (Development of Immigrants to Sweden, 1970-90.* Department of Economic History, Lund University).

Wadensjö, E. (1972). *Immigration och Samhällsekonomi.* Lund.

— (1975). 'Renumeration of Migrant Workers in Sweden', *International Labour Review.*

Wadensjö, E. (1994*a*), 'Sverige och invandringen från öst', in Layard, R., Blanchard, O., Dornbusch, R., and Krugman, P. *Invandringen från öst.*

—— (1994*b*). *The Earnings of Immigrants in Sweden.* Paper for the Sixth Annual Conference of the European Association of Labour Economics. (Warsaw, September 22–5, 1994).

—— (1997). 'Invandrarkvinnornas arbetsmarknad', i *Glastak och glasväggar. Den könssegregerade arbetsmarknaden.* SOU 1997:137.

Widstam, T. (1962). 'Invandringen till Sverige och återutvandringen under 1950-talet', *Statistisk tidskrift*, no. 5.

Vilhelmsson, R. (2000). *Ethnic Differences in the Swedish Youth Labour Market*, (Stockholm University, Institutet för social forskning, licentiatserien nr 15, 2000).

Åslund, O. (2001). 'Health, immigration, and settlement policies' (Uppsala University, Department of Economics).

Österberg, T. (2000). *Economic Perspectives on Immigrant and Intergenerational Transmissions.* (Göteborg University, Department of Economics).

3. Migration in a Scandinavian Welfare State: The Recent Danish Experience

Peder J. Pedersen

3.1. Introduction[1]

The share of people in Denmark who are immigrants or descendants of immigrants is close to the average European level. By 2004 the share of immigrants and refugees and descendants of immigrants and refugees, including people who have become Danish citizens, was 8.2 per cent of the total population.

The postwar history of migration in Denmark falls into a number of phases each with specific characteristics. The early postwar period was characterized by net migration of Danish citizens, mainly to Australia and Canada. The background was a fairly high level of unemployment until the late 1950s compared with the full employment experience of most other Western European countries, cf. Pedersen (1996*a*). From the late 1950s to the first round of oil price shocks in 1974, the Danish labour market was characterized by full employment, close to a situation of excess demand for labour. The net migration of Danish citizens was at a low level. At the same time, guest workers came in mainly from Yugoslavia and Turkey. The end of full employment in 1974 was accompanied by a stop to guest-worker immigration; however, workers who had entered the country in the preceding period were allowed to stay. Many guest workers remained in Denmark and had after 1974 the option of family reunion as a new source of immigration.

Since 1954, Danish citizens have had access to free labour mobility between the Nordic countries and have since 1972, by entry to

A very preliminary version of the paper was presented at the CEPR/SELAPO Conference 'European Migration: What Do We Know'. Comments from participants at the conference and from Nina Smith and Klaus Zimmermann are gratefully acknowledged. Peter Bason, Deniz Arikan, Eva Rytter, and Anette K. Jensen have been very helpful in digging up data.

[1] This paper presents a selective review of the trends in international migration and related research in Denmark. The selection has been of mainly quantitative indicators and research with the exclusion of more qualitative studies of the problems and prospects connected with the process of moving to a new country.

the European Economic Community, had access also to the labour markets in the other member countries of the European Union. In that sense, Danish citizens had—until the entry by Finland and Sweden to the European Union—the broadest access to the labour markets in the rest of Europe. However (as surveyed below) actual mobility was fairly low. At this low level, net mobility of Danish citizens responded to cyclical differences between Denmark and respectively the other Nordic countries and the other member countries of the European Union.

From the mid-1970s to the mid-1980s immigration was at a low level, dominated by family reunions among guest workers, of mainly Turkish origin. In the second half of the 1980s immigration increased again. Family reunions were still part of the picture, but at the same time the number of refugees increased strongly, mainly coming from Poland, Iran, Iraq, Lebanon, and Sri Lanka. The final phase in the 1990s has also been dominated by an inflow of refugees, this time mainly coming from the former Yugoslavia and from Somalia.

In the following, Section 3.2 contains a more detailed survey of the aggregate migration to and from Denmark. Part of these flows are related to the labour market. The statistical sources have no indication of which part of the migration flows are directly motivated by entry to a job, abroad or in Denmark. A major part of the mobility relative to other Nordic and EU countries is, however, most probably labour market related or related to education. We therefore consider research concerning those flows in more detail in Section 3.2. Section 3.3 contains a brief survey of the major trends in Danish immigration policy while Section 3.4 reviews a number of indicators of the labour market integration of immigrants and refugees. The same indicators are reviewed in relation to second-generation immigrants, i.e. descendants of immigrants and refugees. Subsequently, Section 3.4 contains a brief survey of the available research regarding labour market integration.

In Section 3.5 we summarize a number of welfare related issues concerning immigration, including results regarding the impact from immigration on public sector expenditures and tax revenue. Furthermore, this section reviews some results regarding the internal mobility in Denmark among immigrants and refugees. This is of special relevance concerning refugees who are initially dispersed fairly evenly throughout the country, but subsequently tend to move to urban neighbourhoods dominated by immigrants and refugees. Finally, a number of concluding comments are found in Section 3.6.

3.2. Aggregate Stocks and Flows of Migration

In 2004 the total number of immigrants and descendants was about 442,000 persons.[2] Their relative distribution by region of origin is shown in Figure 3.1. In 2004 about 230,000 persons came from or descend from people coming from different European countries, including Turkey, while close to 150,000 are from Asian countries. Figure 3.1 illustrates the big shift in composition taking place between 1980 and 2004. It is evident that immigration from Asia and Africa is a post-1980 phenomenon.

Figure 3.2 shows in the same way the relative distribution for a number of European regions and countries in 1980 and in 2004. It is evident that the increase in the stock of immigrants and descendants from ex-Yugoslavia and from Turkey is dominated by the development since 1980. For immigrants and descendants from Turkey the main factor behind the post-1980 development is family reunions, while the main factor in the case of ex-Yugoslavia is the war in the country, especially in Bosnia. Regarding the Nordic and the EU countries the stocks are nearly stationary in the post-1980 period.

Finally, Figure 3.3 shows the relative distribution of the stock of immigrants and descendants from a number of Asian countries. For people with Iraq, Iran, and Lebanon as countries of origin, immigration is fully a post-1980 phenomenon. For people from Vietnam and from the rest of Asia the stock increase is predominantly a post-1980 development. Immigrants and descendants from Pakistan is the only group with a more significant presence prior to 1980.

After this brief survey of the changes in the stocks of immigrants and descendants we proceed to an equally brief survey of the migration flows between Denmark and the rest of the world. Figure 3.4 shows the long-run trends in the migration flows during the last nearly sixty years. The figure includes all movements independent of the citizenship of the migrants. A number of episodes in recent migration history are evident from Figure 3.4. In the postwar years up to the end of the 1950s the situation was one of net emigration mostly to North America, New Zealand, and Australia. The

---

[2] The statistical terminology used by Statistics Denmark is to classify a person as an immigrant if she or he is born abroad by parents who both are non-Danish, or if one parent is non Danish and the other is unknown. If both parents are unknown and the person is born abroad, she or he is also classified as an immigrant. Descendants are defined as persons born in Denmark by parents who both are of non-Danish origin. The country of origin is defined as the country where the persons's mother was born. Immigrants from a number of typical refugee countries are classified as refugees by their country of origin as there is no administrative classification in the statistical registers.

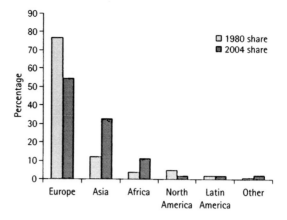

Figure 3.1. Relative distribution of the stock of immigrants and descendants by global region in 1980 and 2004
Source: Statistics Denmark

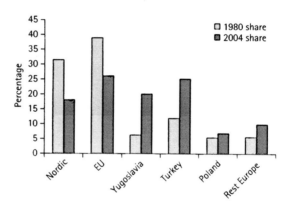

Figure 3.2. Relative distribution of the stock of immigrants and descendants from European countries in 1980 and 2004
Source: Statistics Denmark

migration flow was mostly made up of Danish citizens with emigration motivated by a fairly high unemployment rate in Denmark up to the end of the 1950s in contrast to most other Western European countries.

This was followed by years of full employment or excess demand for labour up to 1973. In the first phase of those full employment years net migration was negligible. In the latter part, there was net immigration reflecting an inflow of guest workers. This came to an end in 1973 when

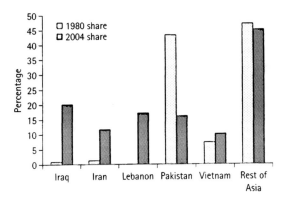

Figure 3.3. Relative distribution of the stock of immigrants and descendants from Asian countries in 1980 and 2004
Source: Statistics Denmark

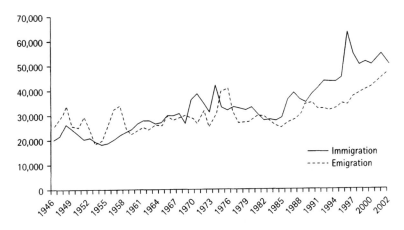

Figure 3.4. Migration flows. Denmark, 1946–2002
Source: Statistics Denmark

the oil price shock implied an end to full employment which was accompanied by a stop to guest-worker immigration.

Since 1973, there is only one episode of net emigration, i.e. in 1974–5, when Danish migration to Sweden occurred as a reaction to the steep increase in unemployment at home at the same time as labour demand in Sweden was unaffected by the international recession. In the remaining part of the period since the mid-1970s, the flows are dominated by family reunions from the guest-worker countries and especially after 1980 by an inflow of refugees, cf. below.

The net flows to four groups of countries during the most recent seventeen years are shown in Figure 3.5. Net migration flows to the other Nordic and EU countries are approximately at the same level and follow the same pattern. During the deep recession in the late 1980s in the Danish economy, net emigration was positive both to the other Nordic and EU countries. From 1993 a strong cyclical upswing in the Danish economy was accompanied by a switch to net immigration from these country groups. Migration relative to the typical refugee nations follow quite a different pattern, with net immigration from Asian countries following a declining trend until the mid-1990s, followed by a new increase. Net immigration from Africa, especially from Somalia, follows an increasing trend until the mid-1990s, followed by a decrease in the second half of the 1990s.

To summarize, we find a number of broad trends in the postwar Danish migration history. Overall, the stock of people in the population being immigrants or descendants of immigrants has risen from a very low level to around 7–8 per cent. The postwar years fall into a number of distinct episodes. Up to the late 1950s, with fairly high unemployment, there was a net emigration of Danish citizens. In the subsequent full employment years, guest workers were coming mainly from ex-Yugoslavia and Turkey. The oil price shock of 1974 was accompanied by a stop to guest worker immigration and a temporary migration of Danish citizens to Sweden. The main trends in the following quarter of a century has been immigration

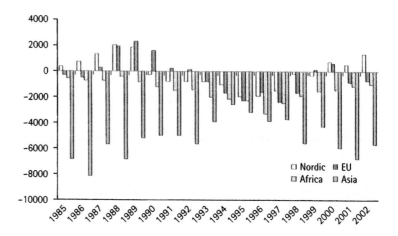

Figure 3.5. Net emigration to other Nordic countries, EU countries, African and Asian countries, 1985–2002
Source: Statistics Denmark

due to family reunions and an inflow of a number of waves of refugees, especially in the years after 1980.

3.2.1. Worker Flows

Available data do not make it possible to distinguish between flows followed immediately by entry to a job and other migration flows. Evidence in this area is consequently circumstantial and indirect. On the immigration side, people who arrived back in the 1960s and early 1970s entered jobs immediately. Refugees, on the other hand, by the nature of their motivation to migrate, did not represent a flow of workers like the first wave of immigrants from ex-Yugoslavia, Pakistan and Turkey.

The present section summarizes evidence on the flows between Denmark and the other Nordic countries and between Denmark and the other EU countries. As mentioned, there is no direct evidence in the data concerning which part of these flows are at the same time flows to and from jobs. Econometric analyses in this area have implicitly assumed that differences in job opportunities and in unemployment rates have been the dominant motivating factors behind these flows.

As mentioned in the introduction, Danish citizens have had access to both the labour markets of the other Nordic countries, since 1954, and of the other EU countries since 1972. However, the actual migration flows have been fairly low all along. The broad aspects of mobility between the Nordic countries are surveyed in Fischer and Straubhaar (1996), which is a study celebrating the forty-year anniversary of the free Nordic labour market. One of the general conclusions in Fischer and Straubhaar (1996) is the low level of intra-Nordic mobility, with the big migration from Finland to Sweden in the 1960s and 1970s as the only exception. In the Danish context, the only exception is the increase in migration to Sweden in 1974–5 which however neutralized only a small part of the big cyclical decline in employment. Fischer and Straubhaar (1996) conjecture that something like 70 per cent of the intra-Nordic mobility has been directly job-related. Until the late 1970s migration flows were dominated by unskilled workers. We return to this aspect below in discussing a study with specific reference to skill migration after 1980. In their general discussion of migration determinants Fischer and Straubhaar (1996) conclude that unemployment and vacancy rate differentials have been the main determinants of intra-Nordic worker flows, while wage differences are found to be unimportant, cf. however the results from a disaggregate analysis below, Røed (1996).

A final general conclusion is that return migration is very high in a Nordic context, indicating the temporary nature of a major part of the intra-Nordic migration flows.

In the Danish case, Fischer and Straubhaar (1996) stress the general low level of migration to other Nordic countries throughout the fifteen years from the mid-1970s to 1990 where Denmark had a high and mostly increasing level of unemployment in contrast to the other Nordic countries. Lundborg (1991) concludes in a study of the intra-Nordic mobility flows that the 'missing' Danish migration, with the 1974–5 episode as an exception, is due to the unemployment insurance system, where benefits in the early 1980s were generous to unskilled workers and, practically, of indefinite duration.

A simple econometric analysis of the flow of migrants from Denmark to Norway and Sweden is found in Pedersen (1996b) covering the years 1970–90.[3] The dependent variable is the annual net mobility. While Norwegian and Finnish migration to another Nordic country predominantly has been to Sweden, Danish residents have had a choice between going to Norway or to Sweden, conditional on a decision to migrate to another Nordic country.[4] A number of specifications were tried. The explanatory variables in the preferred specification of Danish net mobility to Sweden are the relative change in Danish unemployment with a positive sign, the absolute change in vacancies in Sweden, also with a positive sign, and the difference between the absolute changes in employment in Norway and Sweden. This last variable has a significantly negative coefficient indicating the option for choice between two destinations depending on labour market trends in the two countries. Pedersen (1996b) also reports return migration rates for different cohorts of emigrants by year of migration and finds an extremely stable pattern. This indicates that return migration is independent of the cyclical state of the home country at the time of return. The labour market variables are thus of primary importance only for the gross out-migration flows.

Some results concerning mobility between Denmark and the other EU countries are reported in Pedersen (1993). The period under study is the years from the early 1970s when Denmark joined the EU until 1990. The dependent variable is the net mobility of either residents or citizens

---

[3] The flows in this analysis consist of residents in the country of origin without distinguishing between Danish and non-Danish citizens.

[4] In principle, Finland is also a potential destination. Mostly due to the language barrier, flows to Finland have been very small.

of Denmark in relation to six other EU countries.[5] Net mobility is significantly related to the change in unemployment rates in Denmark and in the other EU countries along with the lagged level of net mobility. Alternative regressions use the growth-rate differential between Denmark and the other EU countries as explanatory variable with slightly more significant results.

While the analyses reported above refer to aggregate migration flows, Pedersen (1993) and Schröder (1996) report results from studies of migration by skill for the years 1980–9. The results regarding Denmark are part of a broader analysis including the three Scandinavian countries, cf. Pedersen (1996c). For all three countries, data were made available on the skill level of all migrants in the period.[6] It was possible using these data, to construct intra-Scandinavian 'skill mobility balances'. The results from this part of the analysis are reported in Schröder (1996) and Røed (1996). The possibility of disaggregating the mobility flows by skill levels leads to some interesting results. The impact on mobility from unemployment rate differentials is declining with increasing educational levels. On the other hand, income or wage differentials have an increasing impact on mobility with increasing educational levels, which contrasts the general conclusion regarding intra-Nordic migration flows in Fischer and Straubhaar (1996). For Denmark it was found in Røed (1996) that the EU membership had a negative impact on Danish mobility to the other Scandinavian countries for those with basic or college level education. For people with a university level education no such effect was found.

By level of education, the main difference regarding Danish emigration in the 1980s was found between people with a long university education and all other educational groups, who had lower migration rates which were fairly close to each other. For the group of highly educated people, the annual migration rate varied between 0.6 and 1.0 per cent. Some characteristic differences are found concerning the choice of destination for migrants with different educational background. Figure 3.6 shows the composition on four different educational levels for the whole group of emigrants and for emigrants to the Scandinavian and the EU countries respectively.

---

[5] Belgium, France, Germany, Italy, the Netherlands, and the UK. Unemployment and growth rates are aggregated in the analysis to an EU average by use of Danish export weights.

[6] These data refer to citizens of the three countries only. For non-Scandinavian citizens, comparable skill data were not available.

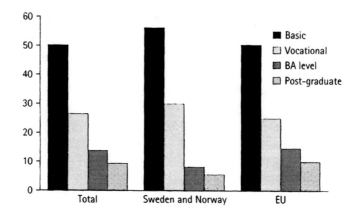

Figure 3.6. Percentage skill composition of emigrants from Denmark by destination, 1989
Source: Pedersen (1993)

The main differences are the higher shares with basic and vocational training going to the Scandinavian countries, while a greater share of the migrants to the EU countries have medium or long university educations. Skill emigration is also the topic in Pedersen et al. (2003). For Denmark, Norway, and Sweden, micro datasets on all emigrants in 1981, 1989 and 1998 were made available in combination with 5 per cent samples of the whole population in the three years prior to the selected emigration years. The emigration propensity was increasing with the level of education in all three countries. In Denmark, there was no trend towards increasing emigration propensities in the 1990s. For highly educated people emigration propensities peaked in 1989, probably reflecting the cyclical situation. The higher outflow thus reflects greater stocks of more educated people, and not jumps in the propensity to leave a welfare state with high and progressive taxation. The return migration pattern by skill groups is at the same level comparing the late 1990s and the late 1980s.

Finally, concerning worker flows it was mentioned above that no precise statistical evidence is available regarding which part of migration flows, represents direct entry into jobs. In relation to mobility between Denmark and other OECD countries, the conjecture mentioned above was, about 70 per cent represented mobility into jobs. For the first wave of guest workers from Yugoslavia, Turkey, and Pakistan in the late 1960s and early 1970s, entry to unskilled jobs was close to 100 per cent. For the post-1974 immigration, the share of those coming from non-OECD countries who entered a job immediately after arrival was much lower, but the precise level is not known. Some aspects of the labour market integration for those groups is treated below in Section 3.4.

3.3. Immigration Policy

Until now, there has not been a consistent long-run immigration policy in Denmark. As in many other countries, immigration from non-OECD countries has been politically controversial. This is not the case for migration to and from the other Nordic and EU countries, which is dominated by mobility to jobs or education.

The entry of guest workers back in the 1960s and early 1970s was economically motivated. There immigrants took up unskilled jobs in the low end of the wage distribution. As mentioned above, this immigration came to an end with a legal change in 1973, the so-called guest worker stop. Since then, family reunions and descendants have also migrated to Denmark. In the years after the guest worker stop, immigration from outside the OECD area was formally regulated by a mix of national legislation and obligations due to ratification of international refugee conventions. Refugees and asylum seekers, who were granted a residence permit, were in principle expected to enter the labour market and to provide for themselves and their family. To this end, a number of programmes were introduced consisting of language classes and labour market entry courses.

As evident from the survey in Section 3.4 the aim of labour market integration has not been fulfilled. Part of the explanation is that the major wave of refugee immigration occurred in a period of high unemployment. Furthermore, the highly organised Danish labour market is characterised by a low variance in the wage distribution and a relatively high level of the adult minimum wages. Immigrants and refugees during this period were consequently met by many barriers, i.e. a high unemployment level, also for native-born, insufficient knowledge of the language, and for many a lack of the necessary educational qualifications to pass the threshold created by the minimum wage. Beside these barriers, there is also evidence of discrimination by employers or potential colleagues.

The consequence of this has been that many immigrants and refugees have been provided for by cash income transfers for long periods of time. This is part of another problem regarding integration policy, that of the division of the financial responsibility regarding immigrants and refugees between the state and municipal authorities. Social welfare benefits including rent subsidies is a municipal expenditure. Thus, municipalities have an incentive to transfer immigrants and refugees to programmes financed by the state. Battles between different administrative levels is however hardly an efficient way to realize a consistent long-run labour market policy. Another area of political tension was related to the geographical distribution of immigrants and refugees over the country. The distribution soon became very uneven with the consequence that some municipalities had low or no expenditures in this area, whereas others came under financial pressure. Questions regarding the geographical distribution of immigrants and refugees are discussed further in Section 3.5.

In 1998, the Parliament enacted a new legal base concerning immigrants and refugees. In this new law, labour market integration is the main explicit objective. This is to be achieved by a combined effort concerning language courses, education, labour market programmes, and by creating a higher priority regarding the problem in the local communities through a change in administrative responsibility towards the municipalities, away from the state and county administrations. The background in a cyclical upswing beginning in 1994 creates a better environment than back in the 1987–93 period when large numbers of immigrants and refugees arrived during a deep recession of long duration. A more comprehensive survey of Danish immigration policy can be found in Pedersen and Smith (2001). Most recently, policy reforms have been introduced to reduce the number of new entrants from less developed countries, by tightening both the rules regarding residence permits to refugees and regarding tied movers.

3.4. Labour Market Integration of Immigrants

We begin this section with a brief survey of the current labour market state of immigrants and refugees. Next, we proceed to an equally brief survey of the development in aggregate unemployment during the years since 1980 for Danish citizens and for immigrants and refugees. Finally, we summarize results from the relatively few econometric studies of unemployment dynamics and wages among immigrants and refugees, and among the relatively few second-generation descendants of people in this group. Asylum seekers are not included in the statistical registers from which data are drawn before they receive a residence permit.

Figures 3.7a–c summarize the labour market situation in 2002 for the major groups of immigrants and refugees by their country or region of origin. For comparison the figures include Danish citizens consisting also of foreign-born people who have obtained citizenship.

Figure 3.7a shows the rates of unemployment calculated as the number of unemployed relative to the whole population in the labour force in the relevant group. The unemployment rates are extremely high at 10–14 per cent, compared with 5 per cent for Danes, for immigrants from less developed countries. For immigrants from more developed countries, unemployment rates are at the same level as for Danish citizens.

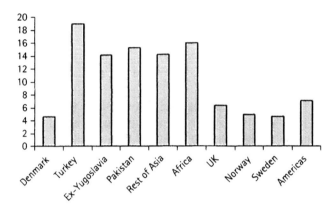

Figure 3.7a. Unemployment rates by country of origin. Danes and immigrants, 2002
Source: Statistics Denmark

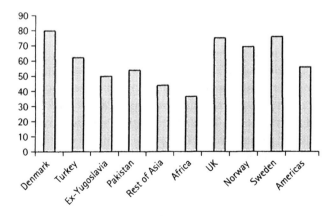

Figure 3.7b. Participation rate by country of origin. Danes and immigrants, 2002
Source: Statistics Denmark

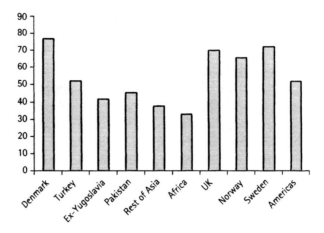

Figure 3.7c. Employment rates by country of origin. Danes and immigrants, 2002
Source: Statistics Denmark

Figure 3.7b shows participation rates for the same groups. The variation in participation rates is very big, indicating that it could be highly misleading to judge labour market integration by looking only at unemployment rates. People from former-Yugoslavia is a case in point. The unemployment rate is lower than the rate for people from Turkey, while the participation rate until recently was significantly lower. This reflected that the group from former-Yugoslavia is a composite of people who arrived at the time of the guest worker immigration and more recently arrived as refugees from Bosnia. The latter group was–initially–not given a permanent residence permit, and consequently many of them had not even the opportunity to attempt an entry to the labour market.

We find the same low participation rates for people coming from Asia and Africa. The refugee status is here also part of the explanation for the low participation rates. The employment rates shown in Figure 3.7c are thus more reliable indicators concerning entry to the labour market.

The two oldest immigrant groups from Turkey and Pakistan have employment rates of about 40–50 per cent, i.e. significantly lower than the level found among Danes, while the groups dominated by recently arrived refugees have employment rates of 30–40 per cent. The econometric studies discussed below have concentrated on analyses of the incidence and duration of unemployment among immigrants and refugees. Based on the evidence contained in especially Figure 3.7b, it might be equally important to study the participation decision and the potential and real restrictions on participation.

Over time there are big and persistent differences in the unemployment rates between Danish citizens and foreign citizens as a group, cf. Figure 3.8, showing the development from 1980 to 2002.

During the whole recession from 1986–7 to 1994, foreign citizens have unemployment rates above 20 per cent. On top of the effects from the recession, the figure also reflect the impact from the increasing net immigration during these years, cf. Figure 3.4. During the cyclical upswing since 1994, unemployment rates among foreigners have gone down steeply, but still they remain, significantly above the level among natives.

As mentioned above, participation rates are equally or more important than unemployment rates as indicators of labour market integration. Figure 3.9 shows participation rates by age in 2000 for foreigners as a group and for the whole population. A difference of 20–30 percentage points for the core age groups signals that integration by this measure is still a distant goal. The rather few econometric studies of the integration process in the labour market have concentrated on unemployment, employment and wages. The topics in Hummelgaard et al. (1995) are unemployment and residential mobility among immigrants and refugees from less developed countries. The question of geographical distribution and concentration among these groups are discussed below. Here we concentrate on the results concerning unemployment. The data base used in this and a number of subsequent studies is unique in the sense that it consists of register based information on all immigrants and refugees aged between fifteen and sixty-six years. This 100 per cent sample is combined with a 10 per cent representative sample of the whole population, making

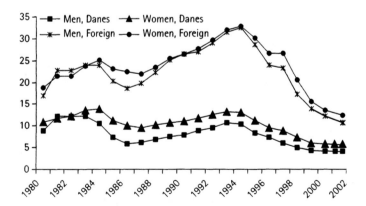

Figure 3.8. Unemployment rates by citizenship and gender, 1980–2002
Source: Statistics Denmark

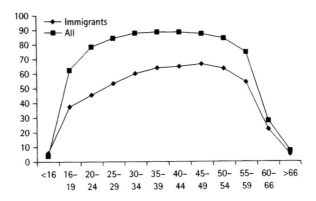

Figure 3.9. Labour force participation rates. Foreign citizens and all in Denmark, 2000
Source: Statistics Denmark

a panel dataset covering the period 1984 and currently until 1998. Data are also available on descendants of immigrants and refugees. Among the drawbacks of the data are a lack of knowledge about the educational background of immigrants and refugees at the time of their arrival to Denmark and about their language ability regarding Danish. Further, the data lack a clear distinction between immigrants and refugees. This is solved by classifying everybody coming from the typical refugee nations as refugees, and classifying people coming from all other countries as immigrants.

Based on monthly observations of individual labour market states, the data are used to construct spells of unemployment which are used in duration analyses estimating a Weibull hazard model. People in the sample are included in the analysis if they have at least one year of labour market experience in Denmark. The unemployment experience is decomposed into the risk of unemployment and the duration in case of unemployment. The risk of unemployment was twice as high for first generation refugees as for the population as a whole. It was even higher for immigrants. This should be seen, however, along with the major differences in participation rates, which are much higher for immigrants than for refugees, cf. Figure 3.7b. For descendants of immigrants and refugees, the second generation, the unemployment risk is on level with the one for the population as a whole. For both refugees and immigrants the risk of unemployment is a decreasing function of residence in Denmark. The decline is much stronger among refugees than among immigrants and differs considerably depending on the country of origin. Once again it should be emphasized that we are comparing conditional risks and not the risks for the two respective groups in their totality.

The average duration of unemployment spells is also much longer among immigrants and refugees than among the whole population. Integration by this measure is much closer for the second-generation immigrants who—very much dependent on education—on average only have slightly longer average duration of unemployment than the whole population. The panel structure of the data makes it possible to follow the employment share as a function of the duration of residence. For men aged 30–39 years the employment share reaches 50 per cent after ten years in the country. The initial levels differ greatly, 30 versus 5 per cent after one year, for immigrants respectively refugees, while the levels for the two groups are about the same ten years later. For women, there is a takeover point after five years and the ten years employment share for refugee women is at the same level as for men, and significantly higher than for immigrant women.

In the duration analysis a main result is a negative duration dependence in the hazard rate out of unemployment. There is a high risk of spell recurrence and consequently a rather low probability of an exit to a long-term job. There are significant differences depending on gender and country of origin regarding the chances of obtaining a regular long-term job. Especially immigrant women are a vulnerable group with respect to labour market integration.

Finally, Hummelgaard et al. (1995) discuss how the barriers in the labour market increase the risk and duration of unemployment for those immigrants and refugees who have entered the labour market. Many of the barriers taken up in the discussion are related to discrimination. Education has been emphasized as one of the important factors regarding success or not in the labour market. But in the case of second-generation immigrants who have received their education in Denmark, the Social Commission (1992) found a systematic higher risk of unemployment for second-generation immigrants compared with young Danes with the same education. This is especially important concerning vocational training, which is partly composed of a practical apprenticeship in a firm. Second-generation immigrants have greater problems finding an opportunity for practical apprenticeship than their Danish counterparts, Ottosen (1993), Pilegaard Jensen et al. (1992). This part reflects without doubt discrimination. Another part reflects that a broad social network in the local community is important for finding a practical apprenticeship job, and this network is for obvious reasons fragmented for immigrants and refugees.

Another piece of evidence regarding discrimination as a barrier is found in Melchior (1990). She had information for a group of immigrants about their vocational or university education in their country of origin. Melchior found that this was without significance for the success or not in the Danish labour market.

Insufficient language skills are an important barrier for first-generation immigrants, which is reduced but not overcome by courses in Danish for immigrants and refugees, Ottosen (1993). Insufficient knowledge of Danish is not a problem for second-generation immigrants. The barriers for this group seem to a large extent to vary with their country of origin. This could be related to big differences regarding the socioeconomic status of their parents back in their home countries, and different attitudes regarding the importance of giving their children an education in Denmark.

A more specific study of education and unemployment among young first or second-generation immigrants is found in Hummelgaard et al. (1998). People in the sample with a foreign background are divided into two groups, descendants who were born in Denmark and immigrants arriving before the age of fourteen years. Regarding the educational background, there are significant differences between the two groups with a foreign background and between them and the native population. Among descendants, the share with a university education is the same as for the native population. The main difference is a lower share with a vocational education and a higher share without any formal education after school. The young immigrants have lower shares, both with a theor-etical and a vocational education. Two-thirds of the young people aged 20–29 years in this group has no formal education after school. Regarding the ambition of labour market integration this is obviously a severe handicap. Among the young immigrants, the share with a formal post-school education is lower, on average, the older the person was at the time of arrival to Denmark. The variation with regard to national background is very big, from 80 per cent without any post-school education among young immigrants from Turkey, to 30–40 per cent among people from the former Soviet Union and Eastern Europe. This might, as mentioned before, reflect equally large differences in the socioeconomic background of parents coming from different countries.

Formal education is important for entry to a labour market with a high average wage, a low variance in the wage distribution and a relatively high minimum wage. The labour market experience of the group of young descendants and immigrants is the second topic in the study. Regarding participation, descendants and immigrants arriving before the age of thirteen have the same participation rate as the population as a whole and also by gender. Young immigrants and refugees arriving after the age of twelve, i.e. having had most of their eventual school years outside Denmark, have much lower participation rates.

For descendants, a standard calculation shows that one-third of the unemployment difference relative to the whole population can be ascribed to educational differences. Part of the remaining two-thirds reflects discrimination as documented by Hjarnø and Jensen (1997). By country of origin, the unemployment rate is highest for young people from Turkey and lowest for people from the former Soviet Union and Eastern Europe. The average duration of unemployment compared with the native population is 20 per cent higher for descendants and 50 per cent higher among young immigrants.

The transition out of unemployment is modelled by estimation of a Weibull hazard function. Dummy variables for being a descendant or an immigrant arriving in the age interval 0–12 years are significant and negative, indicating a lower transition rate out of unemployment. Education is important, and especially a university education is found to be very important for descendants and immigrants. In spite of this, and considering the big differences in educational levels and composition summarized above, dummies for national background are not significant in the Weibull estimation. Finally, a significant negative duration dependence is found which is numerically bigger for descendants and young immigrants.

The Ministry of Economic Affairs (1997) presents a wage estimation on cross-section data for 1995, including the time in Denmark among the explanatory variables. The data set is a 10 per cent sample of wage and salary earners in private firms with 10 or more employees and is restricted to people 18–59 years old. There is a significant wage assimilation effect for immigrants. There seems, however, to be a break in the relationship implying wage assimilation for people arriving before the mid-1980s. For people arriving during the next decade there is no clear relationship between the wage and the length of residence in Denmark. This period was characterized by the entry of refugees in fairly great numbers, cf. Section 3.2. The regression analysis does not correct for selectivity or for changes in the composition of immigrants on countries of origin.

Updated versions of the database used in Hummelgaard et al. (1995, 1998) are used in a number of more recent analyses of different aspects of labour market integration, Husted et al. (2000, 2001), Nielsen et al. (2001) and Rosholm et al. (2000). Husted et al. (2001) analyses employment and wages for first-generation male immigrants in the core age group with data for the period 1984-95. A panel data model is estimated. The model takes account of the selection bias from missing wage observations, and from missing observations on education from the home country and abilities in Danish. The extent of employment assimilation differs much between immigrants and refugees, by national origin and according to whether a person has acquired an education since arrival in Denmark. Length of residence is equally important and a 'reference person' comes fairly close to the employment probability of a native after 5-10 years of residence. The wage assimilation is found to depend very much on experience in the Danish labour market. Fast employment integration is followed by a nearly complete closing of a wage gap between immigrants and natives. Considering the highly organized nature of the Danish labour market, this is hardly surprising.

The problem analysed in Husted et al. (2000) is whether immigrant women are exposed to double discrimination in the labour market, i.e. gender discrimination like native female workers and ethnic discrimination on top of that. The data base is the same as in Husted et al. (2000a). The main result is that double discrimination is not found in the Danish labour market. The only exception is women from Pakistan for whom ethnic wage discrimination is found on top of gender discrimination. A somewhat worrying result in Husted et al. (2001) is the lack of a significant positive return to education acquired by immigrants while in Denmark.

The topic in Nielsen et al. (2003) is the eventual impact from the parents' generation of immigrants on education and on labour market entry among their descendants, the second-generation immigrants. The main purpose is to study the impact from 'parental capital', 'ethnic capital' and neighbourhood characteristics—concepts taken from the US literature—on four different areas, i.e. whether second-generation immigrants acquire a vocational education or not, the waiting period from completion of an education until entry to a job, the duration of the first spell of employment and finally the wage rate earned in the first job.

Data are from registers and cover the years 1985-97 for 18-35-year-old descendants matched with a sample of natives in the same age group. One unique fact regarding these data is that information is also available on the parents and on the neighbourhood where the childhood was spent. Different econometric methods are used to study the impact from parental and ethnic capital. Among the main results are a significant impact from parental capital on achieving an education or not and strong neighbourhood effects on the probability of getting an education and on the waiting period to the first job. The neighbourhood effects result in a lower probability of getting an education and in longer duration until entry to the first job.

Rosholm et al. (2001) suggest an explanation of the increasing difficulties integrating immigrants from ever more distant cultures into modern service-oriented societies. The analyses build on comparable microdata for Sweden and Denmark covering the period 1985-95 where the two countries went through very different cyclical circumstances with excess demand for labour in Sweden until around 1990 at the same time as unemployment was high and increasing in Denmark throughout the late 1980s and early 1990s. In spite of this, the two countries experienced the same increasing problems integrating new immigrants into the labour market. Rosholm et al. (2001) point to the structural changes in the organization of jobs and work, demanding much more language and sociocultural skills, along with the disappearance of traditional, monotonous and isolated industrial jobs as the common underlying factor.

The studies discussed until now are all based on register data. Mogensen and Mathiessen (2000) contains numerous results on the problems in the integration of immigrants and descendants from less developed countries into the Danish welfare state and the labour market. A new element in Mogensen and Mathiessen (2000) is the construction and use of survey data in combination with information from administrative registers. A representative survey is carried out with immigrants and descendants from eight less developed countries and with a control group of Danes. The survey data are combined with a number of register based datasets, resulting in a comprehensive description of how the immigrants in this group meet different aspects of a modern welfare state.

These data make it possible to analyse the purely financial incentives for immigrants regarding the choice between having or getting a job compared to living on income transfers from the public sector, cf. Schultz-Nielsen (2000a, 2001). It turns out that major incentive problems exist in this area. For immigrants and descendants in employment, the detailed data make it possible to calculate and compare the economic situation in the job to a counterfactual where the individual instead collected unemployment insurance benefits. It turns out that some 20 per cent of employed immigrants and descendants would be better off, regarding their disposable income, collecting benefits instead of working. For unemployed persons for obvious reasons wages are not observed, so the same calculation can not be made. Instead, unemployed immigrants were asked in the survey regarding their own expectation as to how getting a job would influence their disposable income. About 20 per cent reported they expected less or the same disposable amount of money in case they got a job. It seems beyond doubt that the combined impact from the tax and benefit structures in the Danish welfare state creates non-trivial incentive problems, which are higher for immigrants and descendants from less developed countries as their actual or potential wages are relatively low.

Schultz-Nielsen (2000*b*, 2001) presents results from logit analyses of the probability of being employed for immigrants from less developed countries. A number of attitude related variables coming from the survey are included among the explanatory variables. The results are interesting as the data makes it possible to explore areas outside the register based spheres, but they are on the other hand to some extent influenced by an unclear causal structure. Some of these variables, which are found to have a significant impact on the probability of being employed are at the same time themselves more or less influenced by whether the person has a job or not.

3.5. Welfare Related Issues

Immigration can, broadly speaking, influence welfare by two routes. The first is the impact in real economic terms on production, employment, real wages, and the wage distribution. The other is the impact from immigration on public sector finances in the receiving country. The first of these routes is until now of little importance in the Danish context, cf. Ministry of Economic Affairs (1997). This is due primarily to the fairly low level of immigration in combination with the hitherto low employment rates for immigrants and refugees. The total employment for this group is 1–1.5 per cent of the economy-wide level of employment. The Ministry of Economic Affairs simulates the impact from immigration on a number of real economic magnitudes using parameter values found in different studies in the literature. Overall, the conclusion is that the impact on the real economy until now has been negligible, but that the impact is expected to increase with the share of employment among immigrants.

The employment share is increasing with the duration of residence in Denmark, see Table 3.1, but the level is still low for the group that has spent more than ten years in Denmark. For comparison Table 3.1 includes corresponding numbers from a Norwegian study going somewhat longer back in time. The numbers are not directly comparable; e.g. the composition of

Table 3.1. Share of immigrants and refugees in employment by
length of residence

Denmark, 1995		Norway, 1993	
1–5 years	8.4	<4 years	8.2
5–10 years	14.7	4–8 years	36.9
>10 years	27.7	9–13 years	50.4
		14–23 years	53.7
		>23	65.1

Source: Ministry of Economic Affairs, 1997.

countries off origin differs between Denmark and Norway. Even with these modifications it is interesting to note that integration by this measure seems to have gone much faster in Norway.[7]

Part of the slow employment integration might relate to the high and mostly increasing level of unemployment until 1994. The Ministry of Economic Affairs points to another area, that of the weak or non-existent economic incentives to supply labour for part of the immigrant population due to very high composite marginal tax rates, cf. Schultz-Nielsen (2000a, 2001) referred to above. Due to means tested transfers an immigrant family with children could confront a composite marginal tax rate of 0.90 or more if they change from being provided for by income transfers to unskilled jobs.

The other route by which immigration influences welfare is through the eventual impact on revenue and expenditures for the public sector, both in a static and in a dynamic perspective. The Ministry of Economic Affairs (1997, ch. 6) presents the results from a static exercise for the year 1995 using register based data for a representative sample of the total population. Public expenditures and taxes are individualized as far as possible. The sample is divided into three groups: group 1 consisting of immigrants from OECD countries; group 2 are immigrants and refugees from other countries; and group 3 is the rest of the population. The main results are shown in Table 3.2.

The total net contribution in 1995 was −11.3 billions DKK for group 2, immigrants and refugees from non-OECD countries, while immigrants from OECD countries had a net contribution of 1 billion DKK. The difference reflects the low employment share for group 2 leading to a high level of income transfers in the form of social welfare benefits, unemployment

[7] Note however that aggregate unemployment profiles have been very different in the two countries with much lower unemployment throughout the period in Norway.

Table 3.2. Impact on public sector revenue and expenditures. Average per person. DKK, 1995

	Group 1	Group 2	Group 3
Income transfers	45,700	70,100	49,400
Individual consumption of public services	43,900	82,100	44,700
Direct taxes	62,300	38,700	68,400
Indirect taxes	38,000	31,600	40,700
Net contribution	10,600	−82,000	15,000
Average income from work	111,700	54,600	131,900
No. of persons	91,560	137,310	3,917,940

Source: Ministry of Economic Affairs (1997)

insurance benefits for those who are eligible, means-tested and non-means-tested child benefits and rent support, which is also means tested. The high average individual consumption of public sector services is related among other things to expenditures for asylum centres for refugees applying for a residence permit, integration programmes, and school expenditures for children of immigrants and refugees. The fairly low average tax payments once again reflects the low employment share, which is also evident when comparing average incomes from work between the three groups in the analysis.

Wadensjö (2000, 2001) and Wadensjö and Orrje (2002) building on more recent data present detailed results regarding the impact on public sector finances from immigration. The main emphasis is put on the importance of the extent and the speed of labour market integration. The results indicate clearly that the low labour market attachment among immigrants from less developed countries is the main factor behind the net transfer from the public sector to people in this group. This is also the case, cf. Wadensjö (2001: 68), for immigrants from less developed countries with ten or more years of residence in Denmark. Compared with Ministry of Economic Affairs (1997), Wadensjö (2001) and Wadensjö and Orrje (2002) find a small reduction of the average net transfers to immigrants from less developed countries, presumably reflecting the improved employment situation from 1995 to 1997.

The responsibility regarding expenditures related to the entry of immigrants and refugees are divided between the state, counties, and municipalities. The rules governing this administrative division are not necessarily optimal in relation to the goal of fast integration. A short study of these aspects based on survey data from a sample of municipalities is found in Christoffersen and Andersen (1997).

This division of the financial responsibility for the different programmes directed to immigrants and refugees is one reason why the geographical dispersion of immigrants and refugees is of interest. Another aspect follows from the observation that an initial administratively organized dispersion of refugees over the country after the granting of a residence permit, is followed by mobility towards urban centres with a high concentration of ethnic minorities. This behaviour can be interpreted in at least two different ways. First, it has always been normal behaviour in immigration countries that recently arrived immigrants stick together with fellow countrymen who have arrived earlier. In this way a social network is established faster than if residence occurs among people with a different language and a different culture. The opposite interpretation is that this behaviour tends to create ghettos that will slow down the integration in the new society, that is, the need to learn the new language quickly and to create a network in the new country becomes less imperative. The eventual negative effect from this could be a more difficult situation regarding labour market entry, cf. Nielsen et al. (2000) discussed above.

Residential mobility models for immigrants and refugees have been estimated by Hummelgaard et al. (1995) and Graversen et al. (1997). The data set used by Hummelgaard et al. is described above. Mobility is studied by estimation of a logistic model. Residential mobility by immigrants and refugees is dominated by moves to areas with a high concentration of ethnic minorities. A number of background variables result in a significantly lower mobility. This is found for an indicator for having stable employment, for the duration of residence in Denmark, for living in a couple, for being provided for to a large extent by public income transfers and for living in a neighbourhood with a large proportion of ethnic minorities. In relation to integration, these findings seem to point in different directions. A significant higher propensity to be mobile is found for people with weak or no attachment to the labour market.

Graversen et al. (1997) analyse mobility for people, both immigrants and natives, living in 'problem housing estates', defined as estates receiving support from a special programme run by the Ministry of Social Affairs. A non-trivial share of the inhabitants in those housing estates are immigrants and refugees. The mobility pattern is analysed by estimation of a logit model. Among the findings are that people from ethnic minorities to a much larger extent than Danes remain in those estates. The study tried to determine—in relation to the ghetto aspect raised above—whether there was a critical share of people from ethnical groups, making for much higher out-mobility among Danes living in the estates, if this critical level was crossed. No such critical level was found.

3.6. Concluding Comments

The present share of immigrants and descendants in Denmark is close to the average Western European level. International migration in recent decades was surveyed above separately for Danish citizens and foreigners. Danish citizens have free access to the labour markets in the other Nordic countries (since 1954) and in the other EU countries (since 1972). Net migration flows have however been small, but responsive to economic indicators in Denmark and abroad.

Immigration to Denmark falls in a number of phases in the postwar years. Guest workers arrived in the decade up to the first oil price shock mainly from Yugoslavia and Turkey. After the enactment of a legal stop to guest-worker immigration in 1974, there have been three different kinds of immigration flows: family reunions related to those who arrived prior to 1974: immigration from other OECD countries; mainly Nordic and other EU countries; and an inflow of refugees during the 1980s and 1990s.

The labour market integration of immigrants from less developed-countries and refugees has not been very successful. Participation rates are low, especially for refugees, and unemployment has been high among those who have successfully entered the labour market. First-generation immigrants from less developed countries have a much higher risk of unemployment and a much higher duration in case of unemployment compared with the native population. Second generation immigrants have the same risk of unemployment as the native population and only a slightly higher average duration. The main problems regarding labour market integration are related to high aggregate unemployment at the time of arrival, to a high minimum wage, to discrimination and to barriers in the form of lacking language skill and lack of relevant educational qualifi-cations. The risk of unemployment is discussing and the share of people in stable employment is increasing with the duration of residence in Denmark. The share with stable employment is about 50 per cent after ten years for men in the age group 30–39 years. For first-generation immigrants from less developed countries, wage assimilation is found to be dependent on experience in the Danish labour market and on duration of residence.

The economic incentives for having or getting a job compared with being provided for by income transfers from the public sector are weak for a non-trivial share of immigrants from less-developed countries, reflecting the combined impact of a fairly low actual or potential wage, high taxes and means-tested benefits. For second-generation immigrants, an impact is also found for parental capital and neighbourhood effects, particularly on the probability of getting an education. This is of major importance regarding both entry to the labour market and for keeping a stable employment situation.

The welfare issues of immigration are related to the impact on real economic magnitudes and on public sector revenue and expenditures. No dynamic analysis is available for Denmark for these issues. Static analyses regarding the situation in the mid-1990s indicate a negligible real impact due to the fairly small stock of immigrants in combination with a low degree of labour market integration for immigrants from outside the group of high income countries. The static impact on public sector revenue and expenditures was estimated to be on the level of −82,000 DKK as an average amount per immigrant or refugee from less developed countries. The total net contribution from this group of immigrants was estimated to be −11.3 billions DKK corresponding to 1.2 per cent of GNP in 1995. The average net contribution is increasing with the duration of residence in Denmark, but is still negative for those with more than ten years of residence. In more recent studies the improved cyclical situation since 1995 is found to have reduced the average net transfer to immigrants from less developed countries.

Immigrants and refugees have tended to concentrate in a number of neighbourhoods in the bigger cities. A few quantitative studies have analysed this residential pattern, which has consequences for the allocation of public expenditures between municipalities—with subsequent political tensions—, and which also has eventual negative consequences for labour market integration.

References

Christoffersen, H. and Andersen, L. M. (1997). *Kommunaløkonomi, flygtninge og indvandrere. (Municipal Finances, Refugees and Immigrants)* (AKF, Copenhagen).

Fischer, P. A. and Straubhaar, T. (1996). *Migration and Economic Integration in the Nordic Common Labour Market* (Nord 1996:2. Copenhagen).

Graversen, B. K., Hummelgaard, H., Lemmich, D., and Nielsen, J. B. (1997). *Residential Mobility in Danish Problem Housing Estates* (AKF, Copenhagen).

Hjarnø, J. and Jensen, T. (1997). *Diskrimination af unge med indvandrerbaggrund ved jobsøgning. (Discrimination against youth with an immigration background in situations of job search).* Danish Centre for Migration and Ethnical Studies. Working Paper no. 21.

Hummelgaard, H., Husted, L., Holm, A., Baadsgaard M., and Olrik, B. (1995). *Etniske minoriteter, integration og mobilitet. (Ethnical minorities, integration and mobility)* (AKF, Copenhagen).

—, Graversen, B. K., Husted, L., and Nielsen, J. B. (1998). *Uddannelse og arbejdsløshed blandt unge indvandrere. (Education and unemployment among young immigrants)* (AKF rapport, Copenhagen).

Husted, L., Nielsen, H. S., Rosholm, M., and Smith, N. (2000). *Hit Twice? Danish Evidence on the Double- Negative Effect on the Wages of Immigrant Women.* CLS Working Paper 00–06.

—, —, —, and — (2001). Employment and Wage Assimilation of Male First Generation Immigrants in Denmark. *International Journal of Manpower,* 22: 39–68.

Jensen, T. P., Gammeltoft, P. and Larsen, A. H. (1992). *Hvem får praktikplads–og hvordan fungerer PKU-ordningen? (Who gets an apprenticeship job–and how is the functioning of the PKU programme?)* (AKF, Copenhagen).

Lalonde, R. J. and Topel, R. H. (1997). 'The economic impact of international migration and the economic performance of migrants', ch. 14 in M. R. Rosenzweig and O. Stark (eds.) *Handbook of Population and Family Economics* (North-Holland, Amsterdam).

Lundborg, P. (1991). 'Determinants of Nordic migration to Sweden', *Scandinavian Journal of Economics:* 363–75.

Melchior, M. (1990). *Flygtninge i Danmark. (Refugees in Denmark)* (SFI Rapport 90:1. Copenhagen).

Ministry of economic affairs. (1997). *Økonomiske konsekvenser af indvandring.* (Economic Consequences of Immigration), ch. 5 in *Økonomisk oversigt, December 1997.* (Economic Survey, December 1997, Copenhagen).

Mogensen, G. V. and Mathiessen, P. C. (eds.) (2000). *Integration i Danmark omkring årtusindskiftet. Indvandrernes møde med arbejdsmarkedet og velfærdssamfundet. (Integration in Denmark around the turn of the milennium. The meeting of immigrants with the labour market and the welfare* state). The Rockwool Foundation Research Unit. Aarhus University Press.

Nielsen, H. S., Rosholm, M., Smith, N., and Husted, L. (2003). 'Intergenerational transmissions and the school-to-work transition of 2nd generation immigrants.' *Journal of Population Economics,* 16:755–86.

Ottosen, M. H. (1993). *Os og dem–gensidig tilpasning? (Us and Them– Reciprocal Adaptation?)* Foreigners in Denmark 2, SFI, Pjece 37 (Copenhagen).

Pedersen, P. J. (1993). 'Intra-nordic and Nordic-EC Labour Mobility', ch. 11 in J. Fagerberg and L. Lundberg (eds.) *European Economic Integration: A Nordic Perspective* (Avebury. Aldershot).

— (1996a). 'Postwar growth of the Danish economy', ch. 17 in N. Crafts and G. Toniolo (eds.) *Economic Growth in Europe Since 1945*. CEPR (Cambridge University Press).

— (1996b). 'Aggregate intra-Nordic and Nordic-EC mobility', ch. 3 in Pedersen (ed.) (1996).

— (ed.) (1996c). 'Scandinavians without borders–skill migration and the European integration process'. Separate book in E. Wadensjö (ed.) *The Nordic Labour Markets in the 1990s*, vol. II (North-Holland, Amsterdam).

—, Røed, M., and Schröder, L. (2003). Emigration from the Scandinavian Welfare States. Chapter 4 in T. M. Andersen and P. Molander (eds). *Alternatives for Welfare Policy: Coping with Internationalization and Demographic Change* (Cambridge University Press).

— and Smith, N. (2002). International Migration and Migration Policy in Denmark, pp. 219–36 in R. Rotte and P. Stein (eds.) *Migration Policy and the Economy: International Experiences* (Ars et Unitas. Hans Seidel Stiftung. Munich).

Røed, M. (1996). 'Educational background and migratory behaviour in the Scandinavian labour market', ch. 6 in Pedersen (ed.) (1996c).

Rosholm, M., Scott, K., and Husted, L. (2001). The Times They Are A'Changin. Organizational Change and Immigrant Employment Opportunities in Scandinavia. *IZA Discussion Paper* No. 258.

Schröder, L. (1996). 'Scandinavian skill migration in the 1980', ch. 5 in Pedersen (ed.) (1996c).

Schultz-Nielsen, M. L. (2000a). *Integrationen på arbejdsmarkedet–og de samfundsøkonomiske forholds betydning*. (Integration in the labour market–and the importance of factors in the aggregate economy), ch. 3 in Mogensen, G. V. and P. C. Mathiessen (eds.) (2000).

— (2000b). *Hvilke individuelle faktorer har betydning for integrationen på arbejdsmarkedet? (Which individual factors are important for labour market integration?)*, ch. 4 in Mogensen, G. V. and P. C. Mathiessen (eds.) (2000).

— (2001). *The Integration of Non-Western Immigrants in a Scandinavian Labour Market: The Danish Experience*. The Rockwool Foundation Research Unit. Study no. 7 (Copenhagen).

Social Commission. (1992). *Sortering for livet*. (Sorting for life) (Copenhagen).

Wadensjö, E. (2000). *Omfördelning via offentlig sektor: en fördjupad analys. (Redistribution via the public sector: an in-depth analysis)*, ch. 9 in Mogensen, G. V. and P. C. Mathiessen (eds.) (2000).

— (2001). 'Immigration, the labour market, and public finances in Denmark'. *Swedish Economic Policy Review*, vol. 7, no. 2:59–84.

— and Orrje, H. (2002). *Immigration and the Public Sector in Denmark*. The Rockwood Foundation Research Unit (Aarhous University Press).

4. Irish Migration: Characteristics, Causes, and Consequences

Alan Barrett

4.1. Introduction

The topic of migration, or more specifically emigration, has been of enormous importance for Ireland since the early part of the last century. Although the Irish Famine of the late 1840s was the catalyst that prompted the large-scale exodus of the second half of the nineteenth century, O'Rourke (1995) has pointed out that 1.5 million people emigrated from Ireland between Waterloo and the Famine; this was equivalent to a rate of 7 per 1000. However, it was the Famine which generated the outflow which in turn contributed to the population of what is now the Republic of Ireland declining from 6,529,000 in 1841 to 3,222,000 at the turn of the century.[1]

For much of the twentieth century, emigration remained high and the population decline continued until 1961. But even in the 1960s when the population grew, emigration continued. The 1970s saw unprecedented inflows but net outflows resumed in the 1980s, thereby leaving emigration as a defining feature of Ireland's demographic and economic experience. The exceptional economic growth that Ireland experienced in the mid and late-1990s brought with it renewed inflows, made up of returning Irish migrants and non-Irish immigrants.

In this chapter, we will discuss what has been learnt about the Irish migration experience through the research of economists. The chapter is organized as follows. In Section 4.2, we present the most important features of the migration flow from (and to) Ireland. In Section 4.3, we consider the work that has been undertaken in order to identify the factors that have given rise to the migratory pattern. Section 4.4 contains a discussion of the work which has sought to look at Irish emigrants in their

---

[1] As discussed in O'Rourke (1995), some have argued that the outflow from Ireland would have been as high as it was, even in the absence of the Famine; however, the argument is made strongly by O'Rourke that the Famine did indeed create a discontinuity in the Irish migration experience.

destinations. Section 4.5 is taken up with the studies that have asked how the large-scale emigration has affected the economy. Nearly all of the material presented in Sections 4.2 to 4.5 relates to the large outflows that occurred up until the 1990s. However, in Section 4.6, we look at some papers that have studied the inflow of the 1990s. In Section 4.7 we summarize what we know about Irish migration.

4.2. The Migration Flow

In order to begin this examination of research into Irish migration, it is useful to take an overview of population and migration figures going back over the last 130 years. The direction that the research has followed has been motivated by the particular realities of Irish migratory history and so some familiarity with that history will enhance our understanding of the research. In Table 4.1, we present statistics on population change, the natural increase and net migration for the intercensal periods from 1871 to 2001.

It can be seen from the table that between 1871 and 1961, Ireland experienced almost continuous population decline. This pattern of decline predates 1871, however; the population of Ireland was 6,529,000 in 1841 and declined continuously to a low point of 2,818,000 in 1961. What is clear from Table 4.1 is that this pattern of population decline arose because net migration from the area exceeded the natural increase, apart from a period in the late 1950s, up until the 1960s. And even in the 1960s, while population growth had resumed, net emigration was still occurring.

Taking the figures up until the 1970s, it is clear that the research efforts would be directed at different elements of emigration. Given the turn-around in the 1970s and the emergence of net inflows, it might have been the case that efforts would have focused on elements of immigration or return migration. However, with the re-emergence of large-scale outflows in the 1980s, the experience of the 1970s began to look like a temporary phenomenon and so emigration maintained its position as the focus of researchers' efforts. The re-emergence of net inflows in the 1990s has now altered this and immigration is now beginning to be studied.

The numbers in Table 4.1 disguise shifts that have occurred in some dimensions of Irish migration so we will briefly outline a number of these. Much of the discussion has been taken from NESC (1991), O'Gràda and Walsh (1994) and Sexton (1996) and relates to the outflows before the 1990s.

Table 4.1. Components of population change in intercensal periods, 1871–1996

Intercensal period	Population change	Natural increase (i.e. births less deaths) Annual averages	Net migration
1871–1881	−18,317	+31,855	−50,172
1881–1891	−40,133	+19,600	−59,733
1891–1901	−24,688	+14,954	−39,642
1901–1911	−8,214	+17,940	−26,154
1911–1926	−11,180	+15,822	−27,002
1926–1936	−357	+16,318	−16,675
1936–1946	−1,331	+17,380	−18,711
1946–1951	+1,119	+25,503	−24,384
1951–1961	−14,226	+26,652	−40,877
1961–1971	+15,991	+29,442	−13,451
1971–1981	+46,516	+36,127	+10,389
1981–1991	+8,231	+28,837	−20,606
1991–1996	+20,074	+18,426	+1,648
1996–2001	+42,600	+22,100	+20,500
		Rates per 1,000 average population	
1871–1881	−4.6	+8.0	−12.7
1881–1891	−10.9	+5.3	−16.3
1891–1901	−7.4	+4.5	−11.9
1901–1911	−2.6	+5.6	−8.2
1911–1926	−3.7	+5.2	−8.8
1926–1936	−0.1	+5.5	−5.6
1936–1946	−0.4	+5.9	−6.3
1946–1951	+0.4	+8.6	−8.2
1951–1961	−4.9	+9.2	−14.1
1961–1971	+5.5	+10.2	−4.6
1971–1981	+14.5	+11.3	+3.2
1981–1991	+2.4	+8.3	−5.9
1991–1996	+5.6	+5.2	+0.5
1996–2001	+11.4	+5.9	+5.5

Sources: Sexton (2001).

Destination

With regard to the destinations of Ireland's emigrants, a major shift occurred at the beginning of the 1930s. For much of the last century, the majority of Irish emigrants went to the United States; between 1880 and 1921, 87 per cent of emigrants went to the United States whereas only 10 per cent went to Britain. The Great Depression reduced the employment

Table 4.2. Net migration by sex, 1871–1986

Intercensal period	Annual average ('000)			No. of females per 1,000 males
	Males	Females	Persons	
1871–1881	−24,958	−25,314	−50,172	1,010
1881–1891	−29,257	−30,476	−59,733	1,042
1891–1901	−20,315	−19,327	−39,642	951
1901–1911	−11,764	−14,390	−26,154	1,223
1911–1926	−13,934	−13,068	−27,002	938
1926–1936	−7,255	−9,420	−16,675	1,298
1939–1946	−11,258	−7,453	−18,711	662
1946–1951	−10,309	−14,075	−24,384	1,365
1951–1961	−21,786	−19,091	−40,877	876
1961–1971	−6,236	−7,215	−13,451	1,157
1971–1981	+5,806	+4,583	+10,389	789
1981–1986	−8,283	−6,094	−14,377	736
1986–1991	−14,820	−11,920	−26,740	804

Source: 1871-1986 taken from NESC (1991); 1986-91 from Sexton (1996).

opportunities available to emigrants and so the Irish began to go to Britain in greater numbers. It is estimated that by the late 1940s over 80 per cent of the outflow went to Britain and this continued into the 1970s. The proportion going to Britain has dropped since but it was still the main destination for most Irish emigrants in the 1980s. Figures for the mid-1990s, however, show the British share to have fallen to 44 per cent; the shares to other destinations are as follows: rest of the EU, 14 per cent; USA, 14 per cent; rest of the world, 27 per cent (Central Statistics Office 1997).[2] The dominance of Britain as the destination of Irish emigrants in recent decades is reflected in the research which will be discussed below.

Sex

If one takes a long-term look at Irish migration, there appears to be a balance across the sexes in terms of numbers emigrating. However, during certain sub-periods, there were notable imbalances between the sexes, as can be seen from Table 4.2.

---

[2] The resumption of sizeable emigration to the United States was partly related to an increase in illegal immigration, especially in the 1980s, and also to the visa lotteries which the United States government have run since the late 1980s. A large number of visas were specifically reserved for Irish nationals in the lotteries. Barrett (1996) presents evidence on the skill levels of the lottery immigrants relative to other immigrants for Ireland and eight other countries.

In the late nineteenth century, the numbers of males and females in the net outward flow was about equal. But in the twentieth century there were some interesting imbalances. In the period 1936–46, the net outflow was mainly male and this can probably be explained by the nature of the opportunities which arose during the war. Immediately after this period, females were the dominant group in the net outflow; this was probably related to the fact that many women may have delayed their migration. In the 1950s, the dominance of men in the outflow returned. It has been argued that this was probably related to the contraction in male employment over the period. In a similar way, the 1960s saw a greater expansion in male employment and a rise in the female outflow again, relative to the male outflow. The 1960s was also a period during which restrictions on women's entry and continued presence in the labour force continued and this may have contributed to the greater female outflow. The net inflow of the 1970s contained a relatively higher number of males. The 1980s male outflow was again employment related in that, like the 1950s, the numbers of male job losses was greater than the number of female job losses.

Age

In order to see the age distribution of the net migration, consider Table 4.3.

For most of the periods of net outflows, it can be seen that the outflow is concentrated in the 15–24-year age category and so emigration is a young person's pursuit. In the 1950s, however, during a period of very depressed economic activity, the numbers emigrating in the 25–34 age category were almost equal to those in the 15–24 age band. Another noteworthy point

Table 4.3. Net migration classified by age for intercensal periods between 1946 and 1986

Persons (at end of period)	('000)					
	1946/51	1951/61	1961/71	1971/81	1981/6	1986/91
0–14	−4.4	−22.9	+23.1	+47.4	−6.3	−9.3
15–24	−66.3	−146.9	−90.8	−10.2	−48.5	−105.3
25–34	−43.6	−140.0	−64.7	−1.1	−19.1	−35.1
35–44	−8.1	−44.5	+8.1	+39.6	−1.6	+24.6
45–64	−3.7	54.3	−15.8	+9.8	−2.9	−1.2
65+	+9.6	+11.5	+7.3	−18.2	+6.5	−7.4
Total	−116.6	−397.1	−132.8	+103.7	−71.9	−133.7

Source: Taken from NESC (1991).

arises in the 1960s. Even though there is a net outflow, it can be seen that there was an inflow of those in the 35–44 and in the 0–14 age bands. What this points to is older emigrants returning with families. This is seen more strongly in the 1970s; the net inflow is made up of the very young (0–14) and those over thirty-five. We also see in the 1970s that even in a period of net inflow, emigration was an option still being exercised by those in the 15–34 age group.

Education/Occupation

In spite of its obvious relevance from a national economic viewpoint, for many years there was practically no systematic information on the occupational and social structure of the net outflow. However, O'Gráda and Walsh (1994) make the point that the scale of emigration in the 1940s and 1950s was large enough to make it broadly representative of society at large. As such, many of the emigrants in this period would have been rural and unskilled. This is borne out by figures from the 1940s which show that 73 per cent of the male emigrants were in either agricultural or unskilled occupations, while 57 per cent of the female emigrants were in domestic service (Commission on Emigration 1956).

O'Gráda and Walsh (1994) also argue that the change in the structure of occupations between 1946 and 1971 point to a continued outflow that was largely unskilled. Most of the contraction in employment over this period occurred in low-income occupations. As the level of unemployment did not increase in this period, it appears highly likely that those who would have occupied low-skilled jobs in Ireland, had they been available, emigrated.

With rising levels of educational attainment in Ireland in the late 1960s and 1970s, an emigrant stream that was representative of society would have shown increasing skill levels. An analysis of the social-group make-up of the gross outflow in 1987–8 provided evidence that the outflow was indeed representative of Irish society (NESC, 1991, based on data from the Labour Force Survey of 1988). This analysis was based on the social group of the emigrant's head of household and so did not address directly the skill level of the emigrants themselves. In order to find some evidence on this point, we can look at Table 4.4 which is taken from O'Gráda and Walsh (1994).

From this table we can see that in the 1980s the proportion emigrating of those who have acquired a third-level qualification is higher than the proportion emigrating who leave school after second level. As such, there is evidence that the outflow consisted of the more highly skilled in the 1980s, thus altering the character of Irish emigration. Two qualifying

Table 4.4. Percentage emigrating of second and third-level education leavers

Year of leaving	Second-level	Third-level	
		Primary degree	Higher degree
1980	1.7	8.0	17.0
1981	1.1	7.6	21.9
1982	1.8	8.1	18.8
1983	3.5	9.4	15.3
1984	4.1	14.3	19.4
1985	5.7	16.2	27.1
1986	6.1	19.5	24.4
1987	10.5	25.6	28.9
1988	14.7	26.1	27.6
1989	9.9	24.9	30.8
1990	8.1	19.0	24.1

Source: Taken from O'Gráda and Walsh (1994).

points should be made. First, it could be that the second-level school leavers may emigrate after a period of time has elapsed, whereby they may not have been captured in the numbers shown in Table 4.4. Second, although a high proportion of graduates may have emigrated in the 1980s, there is a belief that many of them ultimately returned thus reducing concerns about the extent to which Ireland was experiencing a 'brain drain'.

To summarize, in the earlier part of the century Irish emigrants were most likely to go to the United States; however, from 1930 onwards, Britain became the primary destination. Over time, there has been a balance between the proportions of males and females emigrating, although in certain subperiods, there have been imbalances. Emigrants have typically been in the 15–24 year age bracket, although at times of particular economic depression older individuals have left also. Finally, whereas before the 1970s emigrants would have been largely unskilled, reflecting the population in general, emigration in more recent years has been more skilled in nature. This is partly because of improved educational levels in Ireland, but it may also be because emigration became more selective of the better educated.[3]

---

[3] The higher education levels of more recent Irish emigrants will be seen again in Section 4.4 when the characteristics of Irish people in their destinations are considered. The 'education selection' effect will also be seen again, in Section 4.3, part B, when studies looking at the determinants of emigration are explored.

4.3. The Factors Behind the Migration Flow

From the previous section it is clear that Ireland has experienced significant population outflows for many decades. In this section, we will look at the factors which have generated this outflow. Taking a broad overview, NESC (1991) identified a number of factors which combined to produce the outcome. For much of the twentieth century, Ireland's economic development lagged behind that of other countries. Ireland also had a relatively high birth rate which put pressure on labour supply. Irish people had ready access to the United States in the earlier part of the century and continue to have ready access to Britain. They have also had a network of previous emigrants who could ease the transition to life in the destination country. Given the combination of these circumstances, it is not surprising that the outflow occurred.

NESC (1991) and others have taken a more rigorous look at the factors which have generated the migration stream and it is to these studies that we now turn. The studies in this area can be broken into two types, those which have viewed the issue from a macro perspective and those which have pursued a micro perspective. We will consider each group, and the lessons derived from them, in turn.

A. Macro studies

To be precise, the studies in this sub-section are generally concerned with the determinants of year-to-year fluctuations in net migration and not with migration determinants *per se*. They all show that the Irish and British labour markets are closely linked because of the migration mechanism and focus on how migration responds to differences in labour market conditions between Ireland and Britain. Clearly, it is also the case that labour market conditions in Ireland would have responded to migration so in a sense the focus of the studies is incomplete. In Section 4.5 below, the issue of how migration affected Ireland will be considered.

An early study of the determinants of year-to-year fluctuations in Irish migration is that of Walsh (1974). The general approach adopted by Walsh in this paper has been followed by others so it is useful to outline the approach in some detail. His starting point is a model of the following form:

$$M_{ijt} = \alpha + \beta_1 Y^*_{it} + \beta_2 Y^*_{jt} \tag{1}$$

$$M_{jit} = \alpha' + \beta'_1 Y^*_{it} + \beta'_2 Y^*_{jt} \tag{2}$$

$$N_{ijt} = (\alpha - \alpha') + (\beta_1 - \beta'_1)Y^*_{it} + (\beta_2 - \beta'_2)Y^*_{jt} \tag{3}$$

where M_{ijt} is the gross migration flow from country i to country j in period t, N_{ijt} is the net flow between the two countries and $Y^{\bullet}_{it}$ is a measure of the expected lifetime income that would accrue to an individual in location i. Equation (3) can therefore be interpreted as saying that the net migration flow will depend on relative labour market conditions in the two countries.

Walsh's purpose was to establish how best to estimate a reduced-form model of the type described by Equation 3. In particular, he was interested in establishing if the expected income terms should be entered as ratios, levels or differentials and how the expected income term should be specified. For current purposes, however, our interest arises from what his results say about Irish migration.

Walsh estimated various forms of Equation (3) using data on the net migration flow from Ireland and wage and unemployment data from Ireland and Britain for the period 1951 to 1971. While some of the net migration flow may not have been to or from Britain, it will be remembered from Section 4.2 that the vast bulk of emigration during this period was to that destination. His results show that Irish net migration was responsive to relative labour market conditions in Ireland and Britain, with both wage differentials and unemployment differentials appearing to be significant in the estimated equations.

The empirical approach in Walsh (1974) suffered from a particular weakness. The net migration equations were estimated using ordinary least squares; however, as mentioned in the paragraph introducing this sub-section, it is most improbable that variables such as Irish wages and Irish unemployment were exogenous. In order to overcome this problem, it would be necessary to estimate the net migration as part of a simultaneous system. Geary and McCarthy (1976) present an early attempt to do this. In this paper, Geary and McCarthy are attempting to develop an econometric model of price and wage inflation in a small open economy. They include a migration equation in their system and estimate it using Irish data from the period 1951 to 1971. The results of their estimation are similar to Walsh's in that net migration responds to differences in the unemployment rate between Ireland and Britain and to differences in wage rates.

While the papers of Walsh (1976) and Geary and McCarthy (1976) demonstrated that Irish net migration was responsive to relative labour market conditions in Ireland and Britain, it was subsequently shown that the migration equations which they had estimated suffered from instability and were not very useful in predicting migration flows. Keenan (1981) re-estimated the migration equations from these earlier papers, along with some specifications from other papers of this type, and uncovered this instability. Hence, although the link between the Irish and British labour markets had been established empirically, the task remained of refining the modelling of Irish migration.

One contribution to this migration equation specification issue is contained in the paper of Geary and O'Gráda (1989). The innovation introduced by them was to incorporate tax and welfare considerations into the expected income term. They define a variable, labelled the 'retention ratio', as follows:

$$RET_i = UR_i RR_i + (1 - UR_i)(1 - t_{2i})(1 - t_{1i}) \qquad (4)$$

UR_i is the unemployment rate, for country i, RR_i is the replacement rate, t_{2i} is the employee social insurance contribution rate and t_{1i} is the income tax rate. RET is therefore the expected proportion of a pound of gross income retained by the individual in country i. Expected income is then defined as RET multiplied by average earnings. The ratio of UK to Irish expected income (labelled RELY) is then entered into the migration equation, as follows:

$$M_{it} = b_0 + b_1 RELY_{it} + b_2 M_{i,t-1} \qquad (5)$$

where $M_{i,t-1}$ is the lagged dependent variable.

Geary and O'Gráda concluded that the estimation of an equation specified in the manner just described generated a 'strong, well-behaved and stable relationship'. While this element of their work was later called into doubt (see below), they nonetheless uncovered a dimension to the Irish migration story which was of considerable importance in the 1980s, that is, the tax and welfare dimension (again, see below).

The most recent attempt at estimating migration equations is in O'Gráda and Walsh (1994) which is presented in Table 4.5. The dependent variable used is once again aggregate net migration. WDIFF and UEDIFF are the gaps between Irish and UK wages and unemployment rates. In specification (4), an alternative wage-gap term is used, HTWDIFF, which is defined as follows: [WIR (1 − URIRL) − WUK (1 − URUK)]. A dummy variable is also included to capture the years in which there was net inward migration (DUM70S); T is a time trend. All but one of the equations is estimated over the period 1953 to 1990. The results show again how Irish migration is determined by relative labour market conditions. They also show that the unemployment term is more precisely estimated and that the elasticity associated with the unemployment coefficient is greater than that of the wage coefficient. Finally, they re-estimated equations of the Geary and O'Gráda (1989) type; from their results it appears that the more traditional specifications perform better.

Table 4.5. Accounting for the variation in Irish emigration

Equation Number							
	(1)	(2)	(3)	(4)	(5)	(6)	(7)
Constant	6.382	6.091	7.987	14.041	6.192	4.597	3.749
	(2.00)	(1.75)	(2.10)	(8.87)	(1.05)	(2.79)	(1.41)
WDIFF	− 0.081	− 0.062	− 0.202	−	− 0.005	−	− 1.45
	(− 0.70)	(− 0.49)	(− 1.22)	(− 0.02)	(− 1.36)	−	−
HTWDIFF	−	−	−	− 0.0029	−	−	−
				(1.65)			
UEDIFF	1.814	1.851	1.467	− (1.65)	1.775	2.156	0.987
	(2.67)	(2.53)	(1.85)		(5.87)	(1.95)	(− 4.64)
DUM70s	− 9.503	− 9.292	− 7.800	− 8.634	−	− 9.472	− 7.951
	(− 7.93)	(− 6.84)	(− 4.40)	(− 6.01)	(− 7.34)	(− 7.92)	−
T	− 0.422	− 0.417	− 0.533	− 0.592	− 0.499	0.363	− 0.244
	(− 3.94)	(− 3.27)	(− 3.42)	(− 5.36)	(− 1.86)	(− 5.49)	(− 2.21)
R^2	0.865	0.888	0.885	0.858	0.751	0.880	0.916
Method	OLS	AR(1)	AR(1)	AR(1)	AR(1)	AR(1)	OLS
Period	53–90	53–90	53–88	53–90	53–90	53–90	62–86
D-W	1.31	2.28	2.27	1.96	2.03	2.34	1.79

Source: Taken from O'Gráda and Walsh (1994).

The problem identified by Keenan (1981) remains in that estimated migration equations continue to perform poorly in predicting the migration flow. Nevertheless, it is still argued that including a migration equation is crucially important when building marco-models (Barry and Bradley 1991). The migration mechanism is a core element of the functioning of the Irish economy and so any attempt to provide an overview of the working of the economy must include migratory considerations. As mentioned above, in Section 4.5 the wage/unemployment/migration link will be returned to when the effect of emigration on Irish wages and unemployment rates are assessed.

B. Micro studies

A regularly recurring theme in the literature on Irish migration is the lack of data on those who left. Hence, in trying to gain insights into the mass exodus from the perspectives of the emigrants, the sources are extremely thin. A handful of studies do, however, exist and so we will distill the lessons from them.

The most comprehensive study of the migratory decisions in the 1960s is that of Hannan (1970). In 1965, Hannan set about interviewing over 500 young people in a rural part of Ireland. The area selected was typical of many rural areas at the time in that it had experienced significant outflows over a long period. The young people were selected in such a way that they were at a stage where they had begun to think about their futures and whether they would remain in the area or not. They were asked a range of questions which sought to ascertain such things as their attitudes to their community, their ambitions and aspirations, along with background characteristics such as social class, parents' education levels and so on.

Hannan's first task was to establish links between a range of variables and an intention to migrate. He found that one of the strongest generators of an intention to migrate was a belief that occupation and income aspirations could not be satisfied in the community in question. He also found that alienation from the local community lead to an intention to migrate but that family obligations reduced the likelihood of planned migration.

In 1968, Hannan conducted a follow-up survey. His primary motivation was to assess the extent to which the intentions which people had expressed in 1965 had been translated into action. The dataset which was generated was subsequently analysed by O'Gráda (1986) who estimated logit regressions with a dependent variable indicating whether the individual had emigrated or not. The analysis produced a number of results which include the following. Education had a positive effect on the likelihood of emigration. Similarly, the existence elsewhere of family members who could assist in the transition to a new environment also increased the likelihood of emigration. The father's occupation appeared to work as a proxy for family wealth and tended to be negatively related to the likelihood of emigration. Finally, a variable which captured the mother's attitude to migration was also found to increase the probability of emigration. While there may be an element of ex-post rationalization being captured by this effect, O'Gráda concludes from this result and other pieces of evidence that there was an important element of joint decision-making in regard to emigration. While much migration modelling focuses on the costs and benefits to the individual, such a framework does not appear to be adequate for the emigration being analysed here.

A more recent analysis of individual migration decisions is contained in NESC (1991). The sample used in this study was drawn from the group who left secondary school in 1982. The group were first interviewed in May 1983; they were then re-interviewed in November 1984 and yet again between November 1987 and February 1988. For some of the analysis an extra group from the 1981 cohort of school leavers who had entered third level were added; the full sample amounted to 1990. As mentioned in Section 4.2, the 1980s were a period of heavy emigration and so this sample was able to tell much about the nature of migration in this important period.

One of the clear findings was that emigration was strongly linked to education. Again, this is something that arose in Section 4.2; the out-migration from Ireland in the 1980s appears to have been selective of the better educated. The likelihood of emigration was also found to be positively associated with socioeconomic status, where this was measured using an index which accounted for variables such as father's occupation and level of education. Those who came from more remote areas were also more likely to emigrate. In contrast, the group that was least likely to emigrate were the less educated, working-class, urban youth.

Another interesting issue uncovered in NESC (1991) is that much of this emigration was not a function of joblessness; rather it was related to under-achievement in the labour market in the sense that those with various levels of education were not able to find positions in which their skills were fully used. The picture that emerged was of a type of emigration whereby better educated individuals were using this option as part of a general career strategy. It has been shown that in Ireland in the 1980s a significant degree of 'trading down' occurred. The job market was sufficiently weak that employers were able to fill positions with individuals of ever increasing qualifications (Breen 1984). They may also have been responding to tax related incentives, as the Irish tax system became increasingly punitive in the 1980s (Callan and Sutherland 1997). Hence, these individuals simply moved to Britain where they could use their skills more profitably. At the same time that this was occurring, however, there was still a group of very low-skilled individuals emigrating.

The data used in NESC (1991) were also used by Reilly (1993) but he extended the analysis to look at the issue of return migration. In jointly modelling the decision to migrate and subsequently to return, he finds weak evidence that the less educated are more likely to return while the more educated are more likely to stay away. However, he finds that the country to which the individuals emigrated has a stronger effect on the likelihood of return. In particular, those who emigrated to Britain were more likely to stay away than those who emigrated to the United States or to mainland Europe. While the absence of large Irish communities in mainland Europe relative to Britain, plus language difficulties, may explain the higher rate of return migration from there, the rate of return migration from the United States is less readily explained. One possible explanation is that much of the Irish emigration to the United States in the 1980s was illegal in nature; hence, the emigrants may not have viewed their migration as a long-term choice.

Before leaving the area of studies into the decisions of individuals to migrate, we will draw on a sociological qualitative study of the group of 1980s Irish emigrants just mentioned, those who worked illegally in the United States. Corcoran (1993) observed this group and sought to discover, amongst other things, why they had left Ireland. In so doing she provides an interesting insight into the migration motives of this group. She develops a three-way classification of motivations and we mention it here by way of highlighting the issues which were driving the large-scale emigration of the 1980s. One of her groups is labelled the 'bread and butter' emigrants. These are people who were unemployed in Ireland before leaving or could only find small amounts of work. A second group is labelled the 'disaffected adventurers'. These were people who were employed in Ireland but who saw their career advancement as being severely limited in the Ireland of the 1980s and who viewed the tax system as being overly harsh. These appear to be the group that NESC (1991) uncovered and which were discussed above. The final group is labelled the 'holiday-takers'; these are people from relatively wealthy backgrounds who were treating the stay in the United States as merely a working holiday.

The most important summary point to be taken from this sub-section is that in the 1980s it appears that the more educated were leaving. This was possibly due to taxation and to the 'trading down' which was occuring whereby higher qualifications were required for lower positions due to the very poor state of the labour market. Given the finding of Reilly (1993) that the less educated were more likely to return, the possibility of a 'brain drain' seemed quite real.

4.4. The Irish Away

Many studies in the economics of migration explore the issue of how well immigrants assimilate into their new environment. In the Irish context, what is of greater interest is how Irish emigrants fared in their destinations. Unfortunately, there are very few studies to our knowledge that consider this issue in a manner that satisfactorily explores the idea of assimilation. Generally what has been done is simply to take a snap-shot of the Irish in Britain and to compare them to the British population. While this tells us something about the standing of the Irish immigrant community in Britain, it tells us nothing about the assimilation of Irish individuals over time. Nevertheless, we will discuss these studies and distil the information that does exist.

Hughes and Walsh (1976) drew on information in the UK Census of 1971 and on special tabulations compiled by the UK Office of Population Censuses and Surveys in 1971 to document the occupational, industrial and socioeconomic structure of Irish emigrants in Britain. Their work focused on those who had arrived in Britain in the previous year and in the previous five years; as such, the group they were looking at were relatively recent arrivals and so while the data presented tell us something about entry level positions, they tell us less about assimilation.

For male emigrants, the picture to emerge is that of concentration in a number of occupations, industries, and socioeconomic groups. A third of them were 'construction workers' or 'labourers n.e.c.', a finding which confirms the stereotype of the Irish construction worker in Britain. Nearly 60 per cent were in the skilled, semiskilled and unskilled manual socioeconomic groups. This impression of the Irish males in Britain corresponds with the impression of those who were leaving at the time, as discussed in Section 4.2. For females, the occupational distribution reveals a higher occupational status for Irish women in Britain than for Irish men. In addition, while it was shown using chi-square tests that both Irish men and Irish women in Britain had different occupational distributions than the British labour force, the female distributions were more similar than the males. It was also shown that the occupational distribution of those who had been there longer was closer to that of the British, so this amounts to some evidence of assimilation.

A more recent study of the Irish in Britain is that of Hornsby-Smith and Dale (1988). The angle of the assimilation issue which they consider is how well the second generation do relative to the first generation. They take their data from General Household Survey's of 1979 and 1980 and look at those who were born in the Republic of Ireland (the first generation), those born in Britain but with at least one Irish parent (the second generation) and those born in Britain of British parents (the native population).

Like the other work which has been discussed already, they observe first generation Irish men to be more heavily represented in the semi-skilled and unskilled socioeconomic categories than their British counterparts. Irish women, however, appear to have higher education levels and a higher occupational status. It is also observed that the Irish experience a good degree of social mobility between the first and second generations; in terms of educational attainment, the second generation Irish have levels of attainment that are at least as high as their British counterparts. What is perhaps of greater interest in this paper, however, is the contrasting experiences of second generation Irish people from the Republic and from Northern Ireland. While those from the Republic experience upward mobility across the generations, those from Northern Ireland experience downward mobility.

A more recent study of this type is contained in NESC (1991). A number of sources is drawn upon to generate information on the Irish in Britain. The British Labour Force Surveys from 1985 to 1987 are used to establish the occupational distribution of the Irish relative to the British and a number of interesting findings emerge. Like earlier studies, the Irish are seen to be more heavily concentrated in the lower ends of the socio-economic distribution. But based on remarks made already in this chapter on the changing nature of the emigrant outflow, it is not that surprising that a different picture emerges if the Irish are looked at by age group. It is shown that the occupation attainment level of the Irish aged 16–24 had improved relative to the older generation of Irish immigrants. (This is also found in Halpin (1997) where he uses British Labour Force Surveys from 1994, second quarter, to examine the characteristics of the Irish in Britain.) However, there is also evidence that some Irish people are not doing as well as they might expect given their educational levels. The conclusions drawn are as follows: Irish third-level graduates are getting into occupations appropriate to their levels of education; however, those with second level education are not achieving occupation levels that might be expected of them. NESC (1991) also report the type of second generation assimilation found by Hornsby-Smith and Dale (1988).

Again distilling an important summary point, the view of the Irish abroad corresponds with what would be expected, given what we have already described when discussing who left. In particular, the nature of Irish emigration appears to have changed in that modern day Irish emigrants are more educated than was previously the case. Before leaving the issue of the Irish abroad, it is interesting to briefly consider how the Irish in the United States have fared. Perhaps because the United States has declined in importance for Irish emigrants, there appears to be little recent work devoted specifically to the Irish there. However, Reilly (1993) offers some discussion based on Borjas (1987). Borjas finds that the Irish do considerably less well than immigrants from the UK. Given the lower skill levels of earlier cohorts of Irish emigrants, this is perhaps not surprising. However, Borjas also finds that there is little difference between Irish emigrants from the 1950s and the 1970s, relative to US natives, which is surprising.

4.5. The Effects of Large-Scale Emigration

Many writers on the Irish economy took the view that the large-scale emigration of most of the last century was not only a symptom of economic failure but also a cause. A number of arguments has been put forward to support this view. Among them are the following: emigration reduced the size of the domestic market and thus reduced opportunities to avail of economies of scale; emigration robbed the country of the brightest and the best; the outward flow reduced the urgency of achieving higher growth-rates.

An alternative and more positive view of emigration would see emigration as contributing to a convergence between Irish living standards and those elsewhere, as a shifting labour supply curve moved along a labour demand curve. It has been pointed out that had net migration been zero in the postwar years, the population of the Republic of Ireland would have been between a quarter or a third larger than it now is. It is hard to imagine that the additions to the labour force implied by such population estimates would not have had a depressing effect on wages and/or would not have increased unemployment. A number of studies have attempted to uncover empirical evidence on the issue of how emigration effected variables such as wages and unemployment and so we now consider these.

There appears to have been convergence between Irish and British wages in the latter part of the nineteenth century and early twentieth century (O'Rourke 1995; Boyer, Hatton, and O'Rourke 1994). Given the relative failure of Ireland to industrialize at that time, the authors on this topic attribute the relative Irish wage growth to emigration. There is some disagreement, however, over where Irish wages stood relative to British wages between the 1930s and the 1960s. O'Rourke (1994) shows, using data from the International Labour Organization, that in three industries (building and construction, engineering, and printing and publishing) Irish wages were actually higher than British wages in the years 1926 to the mid-1980s, except for a period between 1952 and 1964 during which relative Irish wages collapsed. This prompts him to ask if 'labour flowed uphill' and the chapter contains some possible explanations of the apparent paradox.

A more recent paper by Curtis and Fitzgerald (1996) presents a somewhat different view of relative wages in Ireland and Britain, at least as far as relative levels are concerned. Using data on industrial wages from the Central Statistics Office which are more broadly based than the data used by O'Rourke, they show that the ratio of Irish industrial wages relative to those in Britain was only around 75 per cent in 1930s. The ratio then fell to around 60 per cent at the beginning of the war and then rose again after the war. These movements in the ratio are consistent with those presented in O'Rourke (1994), as is the fall in relative Irish wages in the 1950s. However, according to Curtis and Fitzgerald, a convergence in wages between Ireland and Britain began in the early 1960s, with the Irish/British wage ratio rising from around 60 per cent in 1960 to 95 per cent in the late 1970s. The ratio then hovered around the 95 per cent mark until 1990.

Given the broader nature of the data in Curtis and Fitzgerald paper relative to those used by O'Rourke, it is possible that while wages were higher in the industries O'Rourke considered, this was not generally true. Hence, labour may not have 'flowed uphill'. O'Gràda and Walsh (1994) have suggested that there may have been entry barriers to the high-wage occupations identified by O'Rourke; hence the relevant wages facing Irish emigrants were indeed lower in Ireland than in the UK. However, a question that remains from the Curtis and Fitzgerald paper is why the convergence occured after 1960 and not between 1930 and 1960. Curtis and Fitzgerald suggest that the opening of the Irish economy in the 1960s contributed to the convergence in wages, but the mechanism remains unclear. They conclude with the point that UK wages play an important role in determining Irish wages.

With respect to unemployment, two papers have suggested that net migration may have had the effect of creating a stable differential between Irish and British unemployment rates. In the first of these papers, Honohan (1984) makes the point that most studies that have looked at the links between the Irish and British labour markets have done so through the types of migration equations discussed in Section 4.3. As these suffer from serious data problems, he sees an advantage in simply looking at Irish and UK unemployment rates. He maintains that closely related movements in the two rates are at least consistent with a story which says that in times of high UK unemployment, Irish emigrants return home or chose not to move, thus increasing Irish unemployment. Similarly, as UK unemployment falls, emigration resumes and the Irish unemployment problem eases. His empirical work indicates that Irish unemployment did indeed react to movements in British unemployment and that over time, Irish unemployment would converge to an equilibrium relationship with UK unemployment whereby it stood at 5 per cent above the UK level.

This issue was re-visited by Honohan (1992) using data up to the last quarter of 1991. While arguing that UK unemployment still has a strong influence on Irish unemployment, he believed that the equilibrium gap was no longer constant and had risen. He suggests that the reduced strength of the link may be a result of a growing group of long-term unemployed in Ireland who do not form part of a once mobile labour force and who instead remain in Ireland even if unemployed.

In discussing the effect of emigration on wages and unemployment separately, the impression is incorrectly given that the effects are determined separately. This is of course untrue; as mentioned in Section 4.3 above, migration, unemployment, and wages are all jointly determined. The fact that the studies have been presented here in this disjoint way reflects the way in which our understanding in the area has been advanced and also that a need for a more comprehensive understanding remains.

Before leaving this area, we will consider two additional studies. In spite of the importance of emigration in the Irish macroeconomic experience and the questions it gives rise to in terms of effects, there are only a limited number of studies which have tested with any degree of rigour what the effects might have been. Walsh (1989) attempts to assess the degree to which there may have been a causal relationship between high net out migration and low growth in GNP. He employs the Sims' (1972) time series tests for causality, using data on Irish net migration and real GNP per capita from the period 1948 to 1987. While he finds there to be evidence that GNP affected net migration, no evidence is found for the reverse affect. Hence, the argument that net migration retarded GNP growth is not supported. On a much more informal level, it has been pointed out that the huge outflow of the 1950s did not appear to impede growth in the 1960s; likewise, the population inflows of the 1970s preceded the economic stagnation of the 1980s. Thus, there is further doubt surrounding the negative view of emigration.

Some additional insights into the impact of migration on the economy can be gained from an exercise reported in NESC (1991). Using the HERMES-Ireland model of the macroeconomy (details of which are reported in Bradley et al. 1989), a simulation was conducted that estimates the impact of a rise in UK unemployment of 4 per cent. Such a rise would reduce Irish emigration and this effect is captured by the migration equation in the model. The impacts on a range of macroeconomic variables five years after the event are estimated. It is estimated that net emigration would fall by 35,000 and the unemployment rate would rise by 2.6 percentage points. While real GDP would rise by 0.9 per cent, GDP per capita would fall by 2.8 per cent. Hence, the migration fall would reduce living standards in Ireland.

4.6. Studies of the Inflow of the 1990s

From 1994 to 2000, Ireland experienced exceptionally high rates of economic growth. Given the discussion above on the link between poor economic conditions and the historic outflow from Ireland, it is unsurprising that the improved conditions led to a population inflow. For the year ended April 2001, the net inflow was 26,300. This is in striking contrast to the annual average net inflow of just 1,648 in the early 1990s and the annual average net outflow of over 20,000 in the 1980s (see Table 4.1). The inflow over the 'Celtic Tiger' period was evenly split between returning emigrants and non-Irish immigrants—for example, in 1999, 54 per cent of the inflow were Irish while in 2000 the Irish percentage in the total inflow was forty-three.

With Ireland's migration experience beginning to take on the character of the core Europe countries, the research agenda has moved in a similar manner. Just as economists elsewhere have looked at immigrant characteristics and the effects of immigration on the domestic labour market, Irish papers on these topics are now emerging.

Barrett and Trace (1998) used the Labour Force Surveys of 1994 through 1997 to examine the educational qualifications of the population inflow over that period. As noted above, the emigrants of the 1980s were more highly educated than the population in general and so it would be expected that the returning migrants would be similarly educated. This was what Barrett and Trace found, but their findings with respect to non-Irish immigrants were perhaps more surprising. The immigrants were also more highly educated than the domestic population but their qualifications were also higher than the returning migrants. This suggested that Ireland in the mid-1990s was an attractive destination for highly skilled people.

Barrett et al. (2002) examine the effects of this highly-skilled inflow of the mid-1990s. Their starting point is an observation that earnings inequality increased in Ireland between 1987 and 1994 but that the distribution of earnings was relatively stable between 1994 and 1997. They hypothesize that the pattern may be partly explained by the inflow from 1994 onwards. While the demand for highly skilled labour was likely to have been increasing over the entire period, Barrett et al. suggest that the supply of skilled labour which the inflow brought about would have dampened wage pressures from 1994 on. They estimate a structural model of the Irish labour market and simulate the impact of the migratory inflow. They find evidence to suggest that the skilled inflow did indeed act to reduce wage increases at the top of the earnings distribution, thereby acting to reduce earnings inequality.

The issue of the labour market outcomes of returning migrants has been explored in Barrett and O'Connell (2000). They use survey data from 1998 on a sample of people who graduated from Irish universities and colleges in 1992 to see if there is a wage premium for having left Ireland and returned. The possibility of such a premium is based on the notion that migration can form part of the human capital accumulation process. Skills acquired away from Ireland may make former emigrants more productive than their colleagues who remained in Ireland, thereby allowing them to earn a wage premium. The results suggest that a premium does exist for men although not for women. The premium is largest for men who stated that they left for labour market reasons as opposed to tourism-oriented reasons – they are observed to earn 15 per cent more than similar graduates who never left Ireland.

The summary lesson from these three papers is that immigration into Ireland in the 1990s was positive for the country. The inflow was skilled and appeared to produce a 'win-win' situation of increased GNP and reduced earnings inequality. However, the volume of research on immigration is still small. It will be necessary to see a larger body of research before a more comprehensive picture will emerge of Ireland's experience of immigration.

4.7. Summary and Conclusion

The purpose of this chapter has been to establish what we know about Irish migration. We can summarize our knowledge as follows. For most of its recent history, Ireland has experienced net outward migration. A number of factors have generated the conditions whereby such outward flows could be expected; these include the lower level of development of the Irish economy relative to elsewhere, the ready access which Irish people have had to other countries and the existence of networks of Irish emigrants which facilitated emigration. The year-to-year fluctuations have been affected by relative labour market conditions in Ireland and Britain so it appears that Irish people were reacting to economic stimuli when migrating. This is borne out by studies of the decision to migrate in which it has been shown that lack of a job, or of a satisfactory job, lead to emigration.

Up until the 1960s, the emigration flow seemed to be broadly representative of Irish society; the result of this was that many emigrants were relatively unskilled. With improving educational standards in Ireland since the late 1960s, an outflow that was broadly representative of society would have shown an increased level of education. However, there is evidence to show that this effect was added to by emigration that was somewhat selective of the more educated in the 1980s.

The nature of the outflow from Ireland is reflected in the characteristics of the Irish when viewed abroad. It had previously been the case that the Irish in Britain were in lower occupational categories. However, more recent emigrants are located further up the occupational ladder. In addition, an amount of upward social mobility between first and second generation Irish appears to occur.

One of the main impacts of emigration on the Irish labour market has been to reduce unemployment. While there is evidence that wage convergence between Ireland and Britain occurred in the nineteenth century and early part of the twentieth century, such convergence is not evident between the 1930 and 1960. After 1960, convergence seems to have re-emerged and there is now a close link between movements in Irish and British wages.

Clearly, the Irish research on migration has been dominated by matters related to emigration. With the recent surge in economic growth, the net inward migration that was experienced in the 1970s has returned and some papers are emerging on Ireland's experience of immigration. In the mid-1990s Ireland appears to have benefited from an inflow of skilled people who have contributed to economic growth and who have also assisted in reducing earnings inequality. There is also evidence to suggest that previous outflows may have been beneficial in the sense that when emigrants return they bring with them skills that are valued in the Irish labour market.

On the assumption that the economic gains made by Ireland are maintained, it is likely that immigration rather than emigration will be the focus of research for economists and sociologists interested in this area. Among the issues that will be important are the degree to which non-Irish immigrants assimilate into the Irish labour market and the degree to which second generation immigrants experience social mobility. While the inflow to date appears to have been relatively skilled, this may change and so the implications of a less skilled inflow may also be a topic for research.

References

Barrett, A. (1996). 'The greencard lottery winners: are they more or less skilled than other immigrants?, *Economics Letters*, 52: 331–5.

—, FitzGerald, J., and Nolan, B. (2002). 'Earnings inequality, returns to education and immigration into Ireland', *Labour Economics* 9 (5).

— and O'Connell, P. J. (2000). 'Is there a wage premium for returning Irish migrants?', *Economic and Social Review*, 32, no. 1.

— and Trace, F. (1998). 'Who is coming back? The educational profile of returning migrants in the 1990s', *Irish Banking Review*, Summer.

Barry, F. and Bradley, J. (1991). 'On the causes of Ireland's unemployment', *Economic and Social Review*, 22: 253–86.

Bradley, J., Fitzgerald, J., Hurley, D., O'Sullivan, L., and Storey, A. (1989). *HERMES-Ireland, A Model of the Irish Economy: Structure and Performance*, Dublin: Economic and Social Research Institute.

Borjas, G. J. (1987). 'Self-selection and the earnings of immigrants', *American Economic Review*, 77: 531–53.

Boyer, G. R., Hatton, T. J., and O'Rourke, K. (1994). 'The impact of emigration on real wages in Ireland, 1850–1914', in T. J. Hatton and J. G. Williamson (eds.), *Migration and the International Labour Market 1850–1939*, (London: Routledge).

Breen, R. (1984). *Education and the Labour Market: Work and Unemployment among Recent Cohorts of Irish School Leavers* (Dublin: Economic and Social Research Institute, General Research Series Paper No. 119).

Callan, T. and Sutherland, H. (1997). 'Income supports in Ireland and the UK', in T. Callan (ed.), *Income Support and Work Incentives: Ireland and the UK* (Dublin: Economic and Social Research Institute, Policy Research Series Paper No. 30).

Central Statistics Office (1997). *Population and Migration Estimates April 1997* (Dublin: Central Statistics Office).

Commission on Emigration and Other Population Problems (1956). *Report*, Dublin: Government Publications Office.

Corcoran, M. P. (1993). *Irish Illegals: Transients between Two Societies* (Westport, Connecticut: Greenwood Press).

Curtis, J. and Fitzgerald, J. D. (1996). 'Real wage convergence in an open labour market', *Economic and Social Review*, 27: 321–40.

Geary, P. T. and McCarthy, C. (1976). 'Wage and price determination in a labour exporting economy: the case of Ireland', *European Economic Review*, 8: 219–33.

— and O'Gráda, C. (1989). 'Post-war migration between Ireland and the United Kingdom: models and estimates', in Gordon, I. and A. P. Thirlwall (eds.), *European Factor Mobility: Trends and Consequences* (London, MacMillan).

Halpin, B. (1997). 'Who are the Irish in Britain? Evidence from large-scale surveys', Working Papers of the ESRC Research Centre on Micro-Social Change, Paper 97-15, (Colchester: University of Essex).

Honohan, Patrick (1984). 'The evolution of unemployment in Ireland 1962–83', in Baker, T., Callan, T., Scott, S., and Madden, D. (eds.), *Quarterly Economic Commentary* (May) (Dublin: Economic and Social Research Institute).

— (1992). 'The link between Irish and UK unemployment', in Baker, T., Scott, S. and Cantillon, S. (eds.), *Quarterly Economic Commentary* (Spring), (Dublin: Economic and Social Research Institute).

Hornsby-Smith, M. P. and Dale, A. (1988). 'The assimilation of Irish immigrants in Britain', *British Journal of Sociology*, 39: 519–44.

Hughes, J. G. and Walsh, B. M. (1976). 'Migration flows between Ireland, the United Kingdom and the rest of the world, 1966–71', *European Demographic Information Bulletin*, 7: 125–49.

Keenan, J. G. (1981). 'Irish migration: all or nothing resolved?', *Economic and Social Review*, 12: 169–86.

NESC (National Economic and Social Council) (1991). *The Economic and Social Implications of Emigration*, prepared for the Council by Sexton, J. J., Walsh, B. M., Hannan, D. F., and McMahon, D. (Dublin: National Economic and Social Council).

O'Gráda, C. (1986). 'Determinants of Irish emigration: a note', *International Migration Review*, 20: 650–6.

— and Walsh, B. M. (1994). 'The economics effects of emigration: Ireland' in Asch, B. J. (ed.), *Emigration and Its Effects on the Sending Country* (Santa Monica, California: Rand).

O'Rourke, K. (1995). 'Emigration and living standards in Ireland since the famine', *Journal of Population Economics*, 8: 407–21.

— (1994). 'Did labour flow uphill? International migration and wage rates in twentieth-century Ireland', in Grantham, G. and McKinnon, M. (eds.), *The Evolution of Labour Markets*, London: Routledge.

Reilly, B. (1993). 'What determines migration and return? An individual level analysis using data for Ireland' (University of Sussex, mimeo).

Sexton, J. J. (1997). 'Ireland', in *Third Report for the OECD Continuous Reporting System on Migration (SOPEMI)*' (Paris: OECD).

— (2001). 'Ireland', in *Trends in International Migration–SOPEMI 2001*' (Paris: OECD).

Sims, C. A. (1972). 'Money, Income and Causality', *American Economic Review*, 42, 540–552.

Walsh, B. M. (1974). 'Expectations, information, and human migration: specifying an econometric model of Irish migration to Britain', *Journal of Regional Science*, 14: 107–20.

— (1989). 'Tests for macroeconomic feedback from large-scale migration based on the Irish experience: a note', *Economic and Social Review*, 20: 257–66.

5. Migration, Migrants, and Policy in the United Kingdom

Timothy J. Hatton and Stephen Wheatley Price

International migration has been an important phenomenon in Britain. During the last fifty years migration in general, and immigration in particular, has become a key policy issue. Economic considerations have always been a part of the debate, but they have been subordinated to the more overtly social and political questions. For this and other reasons, the economic analysis of international migration, the experience of migrants and their impact on the wider economy is less advanced than is the case for some other countries in Europe and North America. The purpose of this paper is to draw together a number of somewhat disparate threads embracing the history of migratory movements, public policy towards immigration and race, the economic experience of immigrants and the overall impact on the economy. The first section charts the changing historical pattern of migration to and from Britain. This is followed by a sketch of the development of immigration policy linking it with developments in domestic race relations. This highlights the important distinction between migrants and ethnic minorities. We then examine the numbers, composition, educational qualifications, and labour market status of ethnic minorities in Britain in the 1990s. In the light of recent research analysing the labour market experience of immigrants, we review this literature in depth and present some of the new findings on employment, unemployment, and earnings of migrants, distinguishing between different ethnic groups and between immigrants and the native-born. In the final section we offer some speculations about the possible overall effects of migration on the British economy.

The authors are grateful to the conference organizers and to the participants at the conference for their comments. We are also grateful for comments on a subsequent draft from Richard Berthoud, David Blackaby, Sajal Lahiri, and John Muellbauer. The Quarterly Labour Force Survey of the United Kingdom is used with the permission of the Office for National Statistics, United Kingdom, and the Data Archive at the University of Essex.

5.1. Migration to and from the UK: The Changing Balance

The historical pattern

Like most countries of Western Europe, Britain has traditionally been a country of emigration. In the late nineteenth century (1870–1913) net emigration of British citizens amounted to 131,000 or 3.4 per thousand per annum of the UK population. The total net loss was 5.6 million and it is estimated that in the absence of this net movement the population would have been 16 per cent higher than it actually was in 1911. It therefore had important effects on the demographic structure of the population and on conditions in the labour market. But migration was then, and it remains now, a two-way process. In the late nineteenth century the inward movement of British citizens averaged about half of the outward movement. These figures are taken from (third-class) passenger movements between UK ports and destinations outside Europe. While some of them would have been short-term visitors, the vast bulk of them were emigrants, travelling in the steerage compartments of emigrant ships.

The overwhelming majority of British emigrants went to English-speaking destinations in the New World. Of total gross emigration 1870–1913, 53.8 per cent went to the United States, 25.4 per cent to Canada, and 16.5 per cent went to Australia and New Zealand combined. Of the remainder, the majority went to Cape Colony and Natal in present-day South Africa. Besides being English speaking, these countries had strong imperial or historic ties with Britain. Most emigrants were young and about three-fifths were male. Most travelled as individuals rather than in family groups but they typically were joining friends or relatives in the destination country. They were largely induced by high wages (relative to Britain) and by essentially free entry—indeed for much of the period there were subsidized passages to the southern hemisphere.[1] Very few emigrants went to other parts of the empire and to non-empire countries (other than the United States), and those who did so usually returned.

About half of the gross emigration, and an even larger share of net emigration, was from Ireland, then part of the UK. The Irish migration which became a flood following the great famine of the late 1840s, flowed to the same destinations as those from mainland Britain, although a rather greater share went to the United States. For Ireland alone, rates of emigration were the highest anywhere in Europe and, largely as a result of the

---

[1] For a detailed analysis of the structure and determinants of UK emigration 1870–1913, see Hatton (1995). On emigraton from Europe in general, its causes and effects, see Hatton and Williamson (1998).

exodus, the Irish population fell by a third between 1913 and 1951. A significant minority of the Irish migrants went to Britain, although formally this was internal migration.[2] Within Great Britain, the Irish were by far the largest group of immigrants as revealed by census enumerations. But there was also a small net inflow of non-British citizens that grew with the arrival of significant numbers of Eastern European Jews from the 1880s. There were very few immigrants from countries outside Europe.[3]

The era of mass migration ended shortly after the First World War. The American Immigration Acts of 1921 and 1924 are often seen as a watershed for international migration. British emigration to the United States fell to a fraction of its former levels and it never even reached the quota level. Emigration to other destinations also declined in the 1920s as compared with before 1914. In the 1930s, for the first time, there was net immigration to Britain, and from overseas as well as continued immigration from the (now independent) Irish Free State. Nevertheless, the pattern and composition of international migration remained essentially that of the prewar era. It was only after the Second World War that it began to change.

The postwar period
International migration revived after the Second World War. As the costs of travel declined and air travel became more common, the total number of seaborne travellers is no longer an adequate measure of migration. The most useful source for postwar statistics is the *International Passenger Survey* (IPS), a survey of arrivals and departures by sea and by air taken since 1964. Migrants are identified in these statistics as those who have been abroad for at least a year and intend to stay for at least a year after arriving or who are departing for an intended stay of at least one year abroad. The survey samples only about 0.2 per cent of all passengers, and only a small minority (about one per cent) of these are migrants. Although the survey collects data on age, sex, nationality, and reasons for migration as well as the country of origin or destination, the sample size is too small to draw reliable inferences about small subgroups.[4] Until 1963 the

---

[2] Irish emigration declined over time, largely because of the improvement in Irish wages and living standards relative to those in destination countries (Hatton and Williamson 1993).

[3] The statistics suggest substantial inward and outward movements of foreign citizens but many of these were European migrants transiting through British ports. Because the statistics only count journeys to and from extra-European ports they cannot be used to calculate net migration of foreign nationals to Britain.

[4] The standard error for the whole survey for 1990 is 12,000 on a base of 267,000, or 4.5 per cent. For a subset of the sample, for instance migrants to and from Europe, it is proportionately larger: 8,000 on a base of 66,000 (Bailey 1992, Appendix).

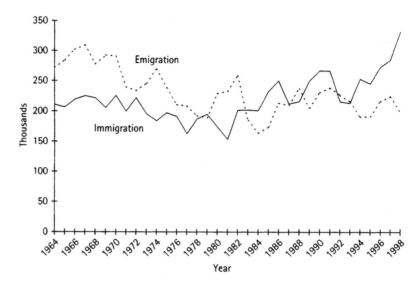

Figure 5.1. Total immigration and emigration, 1964–98
Source: OPCS, International Migration, (various issues).

passenger statistics exclude those travelling to and from European countries. From 1964 these were included, although Irish migrants are still
excluded from the statistics.

Other sources, though more useful for some purposes, are less comprehensive in coverage. The Labour Force Survey (LFS), an annual survey analysed more extensively below, identifies foreign migrants who are potential
members of the labour force and includes a question on length of stay. Work
permit data from the Department of Employment and National Insurance
registrations from the Department of Social Security provide a complete
count but they embody different criteria related to employment. The Home
Office data on immigration control, settlement and asylum reflects the process
of naturalisation rather than covering all immigrants. All these sources, like
the decennial census and other population surveys mentioned below, are
sources of information on immigrants but contain nothing on emigrants.[5]

Between 1946 and 1998 total emigration was 10.5 million while immigration was 9.0 million. The net emigration balance of 1.5 million represents only 28,000 per year, or about 0.5 per thousand of the population.
Net emigration was highest in the early years up to the mid-1960s but the
outward balance diminished in the 1970s. As Figure 5.1 shows, from 1983

[5] For a more detailed discussion of these sources of statistics and a comparison of flow data
derived from them, see Ford (1994).

there was net immigration in most years. And as Figure 5.2 shows, this change in the balance was largely due to a decline in the net outflow of British citizens rather than to a rise in the net inflow of foreign nationals. British citizens include those born abroad and naturalized immigrants. But the pattern is roughly the same for the British-born (the dotted line) and it is driven largely by a decline in the outflow rather than by a rise in the inflow.

The long-run trend in the net balance would look somewhat different if the Irish were included. Migrants from the Irish Republic remain the largest single group of foreign nationals enumerated in Britain. Net immigration of Irish was about 20,000 per annum in the 1950s but it declined sharply and turned into an outflow of about 13,000 per annum in the 1970s before reviving again in the 1980s (Garvey 1985:30). Thus if the Irish were included in the statistics, the net emigration balance of the early postwar decades would be somewhat reduced. A source of measurement error in the more recent decades arises because of arrivals (not initially counted as immigrants) who subsequently claimed asylum, or switched to longer-term visas, or simply overstayed. Adjustments for these categories (also including the Irish) produce an average inward balance of 73,000 per annum from 1983 to 1998 as compared with 37,000 on the unadjusted figures (see Dobson et al. 2001:39).

The destinations of British emigrants followed its historical pattern until the early 1970s. Although net emigration to the United States remained

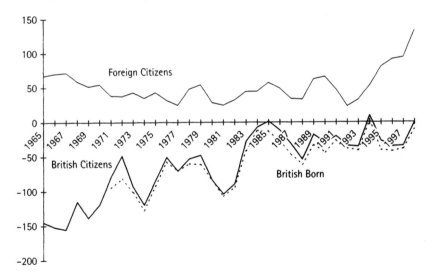

Figure 5.2. British and foreign net immigration, 1964–98
Source: OPCS, International migration, (various issues).

Table 5.1. UK net immigration by country of origin or destination (thousands per decade)

	1969–78	1979–88	1989–98
Commonwealth			
Australia	−286.3	−187.1	−52.3
Canada	−112.2	−71.4	−15.3
New Zealand	−63.3	−3.4	+24.6
South Africa	−99.3	−8.6	+45.2
Other African Commonwealth	+76.1	+48.4	+56.6
Bangladesh, India, Sri Lanka	+124.0	+111.8	+93.1
Pakistan	+46.1[1]	+87.5	+59.2
Caribbean Commonwealth	−4.5[3]	+5.0	+5.4
Other Commonwealth	+56.6	+17.5	+34.9
Foreign			
European Union	−56.9[4]	+29.5[5]	+133.7[6]
Rest of Europe	−18.1	−7.2	+19.1
United States	−21.7	−75.5	−19.8
Rest of America	+5.6	−2.0	−6.8
Middle East	+54.3[2] {	−55.1	+0.6
Other Foreign		+39.1	+77.9

Source: OPCS *International Migration*, 1978, 1988, 1998.
Notes: (1) From 1973 only; (2) Includes Pakistan 1968–72; (3) West Indies only; (4) Coverage reflects enlargement in 1973; (5) Reflects enlargement in 1981 and 1986; (6) As constituted in 1995.

modest, there were high rates of net emigration to Australia, Canada, New Zealand, and South Africa until the mid-1970s. The bulk of the decline in the net emigration balance can be accounted for by the falling net emigration to these traditional destinations (Table 5.1). The counter-balance to the net emigration of British citizens was the net immigration of non-British citizens. As Table 5.1 indicates, the bulk of these were from former colonies and from Commonwealth countries. From the mid-1980s, net immigration from these countries declined somewhat and there was growing net immigration from Europe, both within and outside the European Union.

Although immigration from the countries of the New Commonwealth, including Pakistan (henceforth NCW), has been the focus of debate and policy, it accounts for only a quarter of total gross immigration. As we shall see, the focus of attention has been almost exclusively on the immigration of ethnic Asians and Afro-Caribbeans.[6] The arrival of large

[6] The figures for gross immigration from the New Commonwealth and Pakistan include a significant minority of white immigrants and they therefore overstate the numbers of ethnic Blacks and Asians. However this is offset to an unknown extent by the arrival of Afro-Caribbeans and Asians from other countries.

numbers of nonwhite immigrants in Britain is the major new feature of the postwar period. The beginning of this new era is often marked by the arrival in 1948 of an immigrant ship, the *Empire Windrush*, carrying 492 immigrants from Jamaica.[7] In the first postwar decade the numbers arriving were small but growing, and mostly from the Caribbean. From the late 1950s these were joined by growing numbers from India, which rose to a peak in the 1960s. There followed a surge from Pakistan, which peaked in the 1970s, and one from Bangladesh, which reached its height in the 1980s. Since the mid-1980s these waves have subsided and the sources of net immigration have become more diverse.

Economic incentives and policy

Migration movements are sometimes characterized as systems or regimes. One typology divides these migration systems into settlement systems, labour systems, refugee systems, and illegal immigration systems (Coleman 1994: 46-7). Such typologies do not have strong analytical roots and they relate more to the legal and political framework under which migration takes place rather than to the fundamentals driving immigration. Furthermore, because of persistence in migration patterns, migration streams often continue long after the original basis for them has disappeared. Nevertheless they are useful as a preliminary guide and for drawing comparisons between countries.

As we have seen, Historic, imperial, and linguistic ties have been an important feature underlying the pattern of British emigration. In the case of the United States it lasted for two centuries after the end of empire. The quota system of the 1920s effectively continued the preferential treatment of British immigrants until 1965. Preferential treatment of British immigrants to Canada and Australia lasted well into the postwar period. Free access for British immigrants to Canada was ended in 1948 but preferential treatment lasted much longer. In Australia, until the 1970s, policy was aimed almost exclusively at attracting British and Irish immigrants, and the positive inducement of assisted passages lasted until 1973.[8] While these permissive conditions were reinforced by chain migration effects, the chief driving force in the long run was the substantial economic incentives as reflected in the gaps in real wages and per capita income.

---

[7] The *Empire Windrush* is important only because of the public comment and parliamentary debate it aroused. Other ships which arrived shortly before or after attracted less attention.

[8] For an outline of these policies, see Paul (1997: 30-9).

The major new element in British migration history, the arrival of immigrants from the New Commonwealth fits uneasily with the concept of a settlement system although colonial ties are important. Neither can it easily be characterized as a guest-worker-type labour system. As we shall see, very few of these immigrants were recruited either through government programmes or directly by employers. Only about 10 per cent came with a specific offer of a job (Coleman 1994: 38–9). These immigration flows took place despite a policy stance to keep them out rather than because of positive encouragement. British Government policy has evolved through taking progressively tougher measures against a perceived incipient flood of immigration from the NCW countries. In the face of such policies, the size of the potential flows is hard to judge. But it has been argued that emigration from less developed countries increases as economic development takes place (Massey 1988). If so then this would help to explain why there was less pressure in the earlier years and why the policy of exclusion was progressively escalated.[9]

For the period since 1975 a recent study used the net immigration balance for the source or destination areas in Table 5.1 to assess the economic forces that have determined the net migration flows (Hatton 2001). One important determinant is the stock of previous immigrants. Every thousand of the foreign-born living in Britain generates a further 120 immigrants a year. This reflects the 'friends and relatives effect', no doubt enhanced by the family reunification element of immigration policy. Interestingly, the immigrant stock effect is almost exactly the same magnitude for the emigration of UK citizens as it is for the immigration of foreign citizens. Economic incentives as reflected in unemployment rates and levels of per capita income at home and abroad were also important determinants of net immigration.[10] But in the long run these effects were relatively modest, accounting for a rise in total net immigration of about 12,000 per annum between 1975–9 and 1994–8.

A more intriguing finding is that rising inequality in Britain relative to that in source/destination countries is associated with declining emigration of British citizens. For those towards the top of the income

[9] This is also consistent with the progressive weakening since the 1950s of the link between domestic economic conditions and the immigration rate from New Commonwealth countries (Peach 1978).

[10] An earlier study of aggregate time series by Muellbauer and Murphy (1988) indicated that housing costs were an important component of the incentive to migrate to Britain. Their estimates suggest that rising house prices, especially in the Southeast of England, inhibited immigration to Britain in the late 1980s.

distribution the incentive to move to the traditional destination countries has gradually diminished. For those further down the income distribution, increasingly skill selective policies in those countries have made it harder to emigrate. Net immigration of non-British citizens also reflects the selectivity associated with rising inequality but the effects differ across source areas, and the overall positive effect on net immigration is more modest than for British citizens. British immigration policy seems to have been mildly selective—an effect that is reflected in the positive effects on immigration of source country schooling levels.

Although economic incentives are important, a minority of immigrants enter Britain on work permits. Before 1973 work permits were not required for immigrant workers from the Commonwealth and from that time they ceased to be required for immigrants from EU countries. The number of work permits issued fell from over 50,000 per annum in the early 1970s to less than 16,000 in the early 1980s and then gradually increased, surpassing the 50,000 mark again in the late 1990s. Forty-four per cent of these were long-term permits and another 44 per cent were short-term, and the remainder were trainees entering under the Trainee and Work Experience Scheme. More than four-fifths of these were classed as managerial or professional and a quarter of them were moving as transfers within the same firm. These highly skilled workers tend not to settle permanently and are sometimes called 'executive gypsies' (Coleman and Salt 1992: 436). Labour migrants from EU countries, not requiring work permits, tend to be less skilled, particularly those from Southern Europe.

Among immigrants from outside the EU, acceptances for settlement by the Home Office declined from about 70,000 per annum in the early 1970s to 50,000 per annum in the early 1990s. The proportion from NCW countries declined from about 60 per cent in the 1970s to less than 50 percent in the 1980s. By the late 1980s more than two-thirds were entering as husbands, wives, or dependants (mainly children). Among immigrants from the Indian subcontinent, there was a sharp decline in the number of children admitted but some increase in the number of fiancées, wives, and husbands (Coleman and Salt 1992: 453; Coleman 1994: 57). These flows largely are the persistent effects of earlier labour migration, and the shift from children to spouses reflects the decline in young first-generation immigrants and the maturing of the second generation. During the 1990s this process was gradually reversed: the total number of acceptances for settlement increased, while the family reunification share declined.

A relatively small proportion of those accepted for settlement have been refugees although those granted asylum or 'exceptional leave to remain' is the fastest growing category since the early 1980s. Prior to this, few asylum seekers applied or were accepted although there were certain exceptions such as the 29,000 Ugandan Asian refugees who were admitted in 1972–3. In 1979 there were only 1,563 applications and this total increased gradually during the 1980s; it then rose sharply to an average of nearly 50,000 in the 1990s. As a result the number of applications to the UK have rapidly caught up with those to other European countries such as France and Germany. Although applications from specific countries can be related to particular wars and disturbances, others are not so directly linked. Changes in laws governing asylum in the early 1990s raised rejection rates even among groups such as Sri Lankans, Turkish Kurds, and refugees from the Balkan states (Skellington 1996: 76). During the 1990s nearly two-thirds of asylum applications were rejected but nevertheless a total of nearly 120,000 were granted refugee status or given exceptional leave to remain (Dobson et al. 2001: 257). Thus, despite the British Government's hard line on 'economic refugees', asylum seekers have formed a growing proportion of foreign-born immigrants to Britain.

5.2. British Government Policy on Immigration and Race

The evolution of immigration policy
The British Government's immigration policy has developed through a number of stages. It has been driven essentially by concerns about race rather than by concerns about immigrants *per se*. The total number of immigrants or the gross immigrant flow has rarely been a matter for concern. Much more important has been the preoccupation with the colour, creed, and ethnic background of immigrants. As a result, immigration policy has not been directly influenced by prevailing conditions in the labour market. Thus, immigration policy cannot be seen, even in the early postwar period, as anything resembling the guest-worker systems of France and Germany. Policy has been conditioned largely by relations with Commonwealth countries and in particular with the New Commonwealth. Policy developments can be seen largely as a retreat from obligations created under the British Empire, and only gradually given up under the Commonwealth.

Until 1905 there was an open immigration policy. The Aliens Act of 1905, which gave the Home Secretary the power to refuse entry to those who were infirm, criminal, or who could not support themselves, was strengthened by the Acts and Orders of 1914, 1919, and 1920. Although these gave wide-ranging powers over immigration, they applied only to non-British subjects. All subjects of the Crown were entitled to free entry to Britain and this covered all Britain's colonies and dominions. The Nationality Act of 1948 essentially reaffirmed that right and extended it to the newly independent former colonies. This commitment, a symbol of Commonwealth solidarity, quickly proved to be an enduring stumbling block to the development of an immigration policy which would keep out some (mainly non-white) immigrants and allow relatively free entry to other (mainly white) immigrants. From 1945 it created a tension which remained unresolved until the Commonwealth Immigrants Act of 1962.

Even before 1948 there was no free entry for immigrants from the British Empire in Asia and Africa. Immigration was restricted by the actions of British officials in Empire countries. The 'problem' of Black and Asian immigrants was largely one of seamen who failed to return to their country of origin and stowaways. But with the growing movement to independence, beginning with India and Pakistan in 1947, British officials lost the power to control immigration from these countries at source. Instead, the British government urged the governments of India, Pakistan, countries of the Caribbean, and West Africa to impose their own restrictions, often under the implicit threat that failure to do so would hasten the enactment of legislative controls. As Spencer (1997) shows, the success or failure of such diplomatic methods is reflected in the pattern of early postwar immigration. In the early 1950s the government of Jamaica did not cooperate with these policies, while the governments of India and Pakistan did. As a consequence, in the early years, non-white immigration came largely from the Caribbean and not from the Indian subcontinent.[11] This fragile balance could not last long and 'when the system broke down in 1959–60, the recourse to legislation was swift' (Spencer 1997: 38).

The growing numbers arriving from the New Commonwealth occurred despite, rather than because of, British Government policy. Very little positive encouragement was given to immigration despite the very tight labour market, as reflected in an unemployment rate of less than 2 per cent in the two decades after 1945. The settlement of some 100,000 Polish immigrants (many of whom were ex-servicemen) under the Polish Resettlement Act of 1947 and the recruitment of some 86,000 workers from the Baltic States, Yugoslavia, and the Ukraine under the European Voluntary

---

[11] Other factors were important as well in the early Jamaican immigration: high unemployment in Jamaica and the restriction of West Indian immigration into the United States under the McCarran-Walter Immigration Act of 1952 (Layton-Henry 1992: 31).

Workers programme were short-term consequences of war and recon-struction.[12] It is notable that, at the very same time, ex-servicemen and wartime immigrants from Jamaica in the West Indies were being repat-riated from Britain, or discouraged from returning to Britain. But boom conditions continued to draw immigrants, and this led to mounting con-cern in the 1950s about the growing non-white communities. Nevertheless, restrictive legislation was delayed. The essential problem for the govern-ment was how to restrict immigration from some parts of the Common-wealth and not from others, and how to limit entry from Commonwealth countries while maintaining free entry from the Irish Republic (outside the Commonwealth), without rupturing Commonwealth relations.[13]

The Commonwealth Immigration Act of 1962 represents the first break with the past only in the sense that a longstanding desire to restrict New Commonwealth immigration was embodied in legislation. The timing of the legislation reflected the declining importance of the Commonwealth and the rising tide of African, Caribbean and Asian immigration; it owed very little to domestic labour market conditions.[14] From 1 July 1962, new conditions were laid down for entry. In order to enter Britain an immigrant needed to be issued with a voucher which would be issued to those either with a pre-arranged job (Category A), special skills (Category B), or where there were specific domestic needs for labour (Category C). The 1962 Act also allowed the admission, in addition to the primary migrants, of wives, fiancées, and children up to age sixteen. In practice a somewhat wider variety of dependants was admitted. In 1965 and 1969 these conditions we tightened, admission under category C was abolished, and the numbers admitted under A and B were restricted. This tightening of the rules during the 1960s reflects the continuing immigration from the New

---

[12] The Poles were mainly army personnel exiled to Britain during the War. Those entering under the EVW scheme were displaced persons from camps in Germany and Austria. Considerable help was given to the Poles to resettle but those recruited under the European Voluntary Workers' scheme received less favourable treatment and many of them returned home (Rees 1993: 92–5). For a detailed history of the EVW scheme, see Kay and Miles (1992).

[13] These tortuous negotiations are described by Paul (1997: 93–106).

[14] Confidence in the usefulness of Commonwealth links was seriously undermined by the Suez crisis of 1957 and by the growing view that Britain's future economic security lay with Europe not the Commonwealth, a view which found expression in Britain's first application to join the European Economic Community in 1961. According to Spencer: 'The government concern since 1949, through a period of full employment had been to find ways to control immigration from the Caribbean, Africa and the Indian sub-continent, not immigration in general. The timing of its discussions of the question had everything to do with variations in the number of Asian and Black immigrants arriving and nothing to do with population flows in general or the number of job vacancies in British industry (1997: 127).

Commonwealth, running at between 30,000 and 50,000 per annum—numbers far in excess of those in the 1950s.

Free right of entry was maintained for those with passports issued by the British government and those who were born in the UK until the Commonwealth Immigrants Act of 1968, when UK passport holders were made subject to immigration controls unless they, a parent or a grandparent had been born, adopted or naturalized in Britain. The Act was provoked by the arrival of growing numbers of Asians formerly settled in the East African countries of Kenya, Uganda and Tanganyika. Many of these settlers had exercised their right to British passports when the host countries became independent.[15] The 1971 Immigration Act can be seen as a step to redefine British citizenship in line with this immigration policy. It distinguished 'patrials' and 'non-patrials'. Patrials were defined as British or Commonwealth citizens who had themselves, or whose parent or grandparent, had been born, adopted, registered, or naturalized in Britain; non-patrials had no more rights than aliens. The 1971 Act was symbolic in two ways: it ended the unrestricted entry of British subjects (honoured more in the breach than in the observance) and it became effective on the same day (1 January 1973) that Britain joined the European Community—opening new rights of entry to EC nationals.

The decade 1962–71 marked a defining shift in the legal framework for British immigration policy—a shift away from Commonwealth obligations and towards redefining British citizenship. It kept the door open to the descendants of (relatively recent) British settlers, mostly in the United States, Canada, and Australia, while closing it to the chiefly non-white immigrants from the New Commonwealth. But despite increasingly restrictive legislation immigrants from the New Commonwealth continued to flow in. During the early 1960s an increasing proportion gained entry on the basis of family reunification rather than as primary immigrants. It was estimated that under the voucher system, each voucher taken up admitted on average 3.7 immigrants (Spencer 1997: 139).

Controlling the numbers admitted under various forms of family reunification became a major concern from the late 1960s. In 1969 entry was refused to foreign husbands and fiancés of settled migrant women but, because of the unequal treatment of the sexes that this implied, the rule was removed in 1974. A new test of the genuineness of the relationship was imposed in 1977 and in 1980 the test was strengthened and the right

---

[15] The Ugandan Asians who arrived in 1972–3 were admitted by special dispensation outside the Act.

was restricted to the husbands or fiancés of women who were either born in Britain or who were British citizens.[16] These rules were challenged on the grounds of discrimination under the European Convention for Human Rights and the British Government response in 1985 was to 'level down' by extending the existing restrictions on husbands (and fiancés) to wives (and fiancées) (Howard 1993: 110–13). These rules were further tightened in the Immigration Act of 1988 which extended the 'independent of public fund' test to the dependants of pre-1973 immigrants.

The debate of the late-1970s raised once more the issue of unequal treatment of different groups of British citizens. Until then British nationality was still defined by the 1948 British Nationality Act under which there were still some 950 million British subjects throughout the world (Coleman and Salt 1992: 440). This was changed under the British Nationality Act of 1981 which was an attempt to bring British nationality more in line with immigration policy. The Act superseded the traditional status of British subject and created three types of British citizenship: British citizens, British Dependent Territories citizens, and British Overseas citizens. Only the first of these gave automatic right of entry, and it extended only to those born, adopted or naturalised, registered as citizens, or those permanently settled, and it descended only to the first generation born abroad to British citizens born in the UK (see Layton-Henry 1992: 191–5). In the early 1990s the perceived threat was the growing number of asylum seekers, most of whom were regarded as poor unskilled 'economic migrants', rather than as genuine asylum seekers. There was also growing concern about the number of immigrants entering Britain on tourist visas who subsequently claimed asylum. The Asylum and Immigration Act of 1993 removed a visitor's right of appeal if refused entry. The Act evidently halved the number granted asylum between 1993 and 1994. It also increased dramatically the number held in detention pending decisions at the same time as raising the number who were repatriated. The Asylum and Immigration Act of 1996 removed the right to all state and local authority benefits (including housing) from those claiming asylum after arrival and those whose applications had been rejected but who still remained. The Immigration and Asylum Act of 1999 further modified the asylum and appeals system, strengthened enforcement powers, and increased sanctions against the carriers of illegal entrants.

---

[16] The 1980 regulations permitted elderly dependants to enter only if they were wholly maintained by their children or grandchildren living in Britain.

Thus immigration policy in the 1990s once more represents a tightening of restrictions in response to perceived threats of undesirable immigration.[17]

Race Relations Policy

Black and Asian populations have been seen as separate and distinct both ethnically and culturally and this has been reflected both in immigration policy and in the treatment of these groups within the UK. In the early postwar period Black and Asian immigrants were viewed with suspicion and they were considered less likely to assimilate. Thus, the Royal Commission on Population concluded in 1949 that additional immigrants could only be welcomed without reserve if 'the migrants were of good human stock and were not prevented by their religion or race from intermarrying with the host population and becoming merged in it' (quoted in Holmes 1988: 210). So assimilation was viewed as the key objective with regard to immigrants and at that time this meant complete absorption. The contrast between the official view of Blacks and Asians and of Europeans as immigrants could not have been sharper. The fact that women from the Baltic were recruited precisely in order that they 'would intermarry and add to our native stock' makes the point (Kay and Miles 1992: 124). The fact that miscegenation was regarded with abhorrence effectively meant that, for non-white immigrants, a lack of assimilation on the one hand, and full integration on the other, were both undesirable.

The basis of deep-rooted prejudice against Blacks and Asians has been attributed to Britain's imperial past. Nations who had, until very recently, been subject peoples, and had often been cast in the role of servants or slaves, were widely depicted as culturally and socially inferior (Layton-Henry 1984: 1–7). This seems to have been the view held by senior government officials, at least until the 1960s. Prejudice against Black and Asian immigrants was often justified by the notion that they brought with them disease, crime, and low morals and that they were not suitable for employment and likely to be a burden on the welfare state. But despite its best efforts, the Interdepartmental Working Party of 1959–61 found very little evidence to sustain a case against these communities (Spencer 1997: 109–15).

---

[17] According to one observer 'asylum policy seems to be in a cycle of unending restrictionism' (Hansen 2000: 235). Another recent example of restrictions in response to perceived threats of an immigration surge is the curtailing of immigration opportunities to the citizens of Hong Kong when the colony was handed over to China in 1997.

Much clearer was the fact that non-white immigrants were a focus of racial tension in working-class communities and this was reflected in spates of race riots in inner city areas where Blacks and Asians were concentrated. Such unrest occurred in Liverpool in 1948 and in Deptford and Birmingham in 1949, and broke out again much more seriously in 1958 with prominent disturbances in Nottingham and Notting Hill in London. Race became a key issue in the 1964 election when an overtly racist Conservative candidate ousted the shadow Foreign Secretary, winning the constituency of Smethwick against the national trend. Political tension flared again in 1968 when the anti-immigrant National Front came to prominence and the senior Conservative politician Enoch Powell made his infamous speech warning of 'rivers of blood' unless the immigrant tide was stemmed.[18] The fact that this antagonism was based on race rather than class or culture is reflected by the negative reaction to the Kenyan Asians (Layton-Henry 1992: 53).

The 1960s saw immigration and race moving to the top of the political agenda. It was driven by the growing visibility of immigrant communities, fear of violence and unrest, increasing polarization of political opinion, and growing evidence that there was serious racial discrimination against non-whites, particularly in the spheres of housing and employment. This escalation in the importance of race as a political issue was paralleled by progressive moves in race relations policy. In 1962 the (non-statutory) Commonwealth Immigrants Advisory Council was established to advise the government the promotion of racial harmony. The Race Relations Act of 1965 made it unlawful to practise discrimination but provided no effective tools to counter it. This was followed by the Race Relations Act of 1968 which strengthened the Race Relations Board formed under the 1965 Act and specifically outlawed racial discrimination in employment, housing, and a number of other spheres. Both these acts also set up bodies to promote racial harmony positively.

It is notable that in the 1960s initiatives on race relations marched almost in lockstep with increasing restrictions on immigration. These two arms of policy have sometimes been seen as contradictory; pro-immigrant on the one hand and anti-immigrant on the other (Spencer 1994). They have sometimes been explained as a response to growing politicization and

[18] Powell specifically attacked the bill that was to become the Race Relations Act, 1968, arguing that the numbers and concentration of Black and Asian immigrants would pose serious barriers to assimilation and proposing not only a stop to immigration but also a policy of repatriation of non-white immigrants and their children. This anti-immigrant stance was widely supported in the opinion polls (Layton-Henry 1992: 80).

polarization of the race issue: appeasing the anti-immigrant lobby with tougher immigration controls and appealing to pro-immigrant sentiment with positive efforts to promote racial harmony and to outlaw discrimination (Jones 1977: 160–2). While these measures were undoubtedly a response to social and political pressure, both strands of policy can be seen as reflecting the growing assimilationist view of New Commonwealth immigration.[19] Promoting equal opportunity and fostering improved race relations would, it was hoped, diffuse social tensions, while restricting immigration would reduce further tensions arising from the arrival of new cohorts of (yet to be assimilated) immigrants.

Despite these measures, racial disharmony continued into the 1970s. Evidence accumulated of discrimination towards non-whites, even after anti-discrimination legislation,[20] and a further Race Relations Act was introduced in 1976. This Act outlawed indirect discrimination–any unjustifiable requirement which would disadvantage a particular racial group–and it set up a new Commission for Racial Equality. The restrictionist tendency also remained strong. In 1978 Margaret Thatcher acknowledged that some Conservative supporters had switched to the National Front and she promised that a new Conservative government would allay the fears of the white majority that they 'might be swamped by people of a different culture'. While the incoming government drew support away from the National Front and introduced the 1981 Nationality Act, it did nothing to quell social tension which, in most peoples minds, worsened between 1975 and 1981 (Anwar 1986: 27). The riots which broke out in the inner city areas of Toxteth (Liverpool) and Brixton (London) in 1981 were widely believed to have had a strong racial element[21] and the number of individual racial attacks also increased (Layton-Henry 1984: 116).

During the 1980s racial tensions were never far from the surface and evidence of deep-seated racial prejudice continued to accumulate. Despite the Race Relations Act, a number of studies showed continuing discrimination in housing, employment, and education. More troubling still was the evidence of violence against ethnic minorities. Police statistics

---

[19] That view, and the difficulties associated with presenting it, can be identified in the debate about the 1996 Asylum and Immigration Act (Spencer 1998).

[20] The most compelling evidence was from 'situation tests' by Political and Economic Planning in which similarly qualified white and non white actors applied for jobs and for rental housing. These indicated that Blacks and Asians had a much higher probability of being refused–even when compared with other non-whites. On the influence of these studies, see Layton-Henry (1992: 56–7).

[21] This was also suggested in the Report by Lord Scarman on these incidents.

indicated a doubling of the number of racial attacks between 1988 and 1993–4. Although statistics from the British Crime Survey show no sharp increase over this period, they reveal a much higher level of racial incidents than do the police statistics (Virdee 1995: 24). Indeed it seems likely that the police statistics reflect increased reporting and growing awarness of racial incidents rather than rapidly growing incidence. The focus of race relations policy in the 1990s was on the criminal justice system but efforts to introduce new legislation with stiffer penalties for racially motivated crimes failed to gain Parliamentary support.[22]

Thus while the essential framework of race relations policy remained unchanged in the 1980s and early 1990s, there was a growing focus on the way that public policies towards law and order, education and health, as well as employment, impinged on non-whites. At the same time the focus shifted away from immigrants and towards ethnic minorities. While the government stuck firmly to the assimilationist approach there was a growing weight of opinion that attempts to anglicize ethnic minorities, particularly in education, were not only failing to counter disadvantage but reinforcing separateness.[23] The alternative, multicultural approach argued for the integration of ethnic minority cultures into the mainstream. Thus the burden of adjustment would shift away from ethnic minorities and towards the white population. But, in practical terms, this approach has yet to gain much ground in public policy.

5.3. Immigrants and Ethnic Minority Groups in Britain

Numbers and distribution
The sources of data concerning immigrants and ethnic minority groups living in Britain have been limited until comparatively recently. Prior to 1971 the decennial census recorded only place of birth. Census statistics show that, in 1951, 4.4 per cent of the population of England and Wales was foreign-born, rising to 6.5 per cent in 1971 and increasing more slowly thereafter. In 1991 the foreign-born were 7.4 per cent of the population of

---

[22] Biases in the attitude of the metropolitan police towards ethnic minorities was brought into sharp relief by the enquiry following the failure to bring to justice the murderers of a black youth, Stephen Lawrence. There has also been a vigorous debate about whether Blacks and Asians are more likely to be arrested and imprisoned than whites (Ftizgerald 1988).

[23] As one observer puts it, educational policies 'were formulated as much out of concern for the effects of the growing immigrant school population on the opportunities for white pupils as in response to the needs of the minority ethnic groups themselves' (Mason 1995: 69).

Great Britain and 45 per cent of these were born in the NCW countries. Some of the foreign-born would have been of British extraction and many more would have become British citizens. Only about 3 per cent of the resident population enumerated in 1991 were citizens of foreign countries.

Over time, place of birth became an increasingly poor indicator of the size of the ethnic minority population because of the growing numbers of second-generation immigrants. In the 1971 census a question was asked about parental birthplace (and also date of migration) and from this, and an analysis of surnames (in order to eliminate those of British origin born in NCW countries), an estimate was derived for the population of NCW origin. It indicated that ethnic minorities were 2.7 per cent of the population of Great Britain but this estimate was considered to have a wide margin of error. This estimate was updated to 1981, suggesting a population of over two million or 4.0 per cent.[24] The proposal to include a question on ethnic group in the 1981 census was abandoned (itself a reflection of the sensitivity of the race issue). Not until 1991 was a question on ethnicity included in the census and this indicated an ethnic minority population of just over 3 million, or 5.5 per cent of the total.

The most important alternative source on the population stock is the Labour Force Survey (LFS). This was undertaken biennially from 1973, annually from 1983, and quarterly from 1992. Estimates from the LFS indicate numbers for the ethnic minority population which are broadly consistent with census based estimates for 1971, 1981, and 1991. In the following section we use the data from the LFS to analyse employment status and wage outcomes for immigrants and ethnic minorities as compared with the native white population. Alternative sources are the influential surveys undertaken by the Policy Studies Institute in 1966–7, 1974–5, 1982, and 1994. These oversample the ethnic minority population and have been an important source of evidence on the characteristics of different ethnic minority groups and for comparison with the white population.[25]

There are a number of different ways of defining the ethnic minority population, principally according to colour or race, religion, language or culture, or country of extraction. The 1991 census divided ethnic minority populations into seven groups (plus other), based on a combination of race and region of extraction. Of the 5.5 per cent who categorized themselves as

---

[24] For a comparison of alternative estimates for 1981, see Jones (1996: 11).

[25] One crucial difference between the LFS and the PSI studies is that the former surveys are undertaken only in English whilst the latter offer the option of an interview in the respondent's first language. The LFS therefore may not capture those immigrants with poor English language ability.

Table 5.2. Ethnic minorities in the 1991 census (GB)

Ethnicity	Population share	Born overseas	Female	Age under 16	Age 60+
White	94.5	4.2	51.7	19.3	22.1
Black Caribbean	0.9	46.3	52.1	21.9	10.9
Black African	0.4	63.6	49.7	29.3	2.7
Black Other	0.3	15.6	50.9	50.6	20.7
Indian	1.5	58.1	49.7	29.5	6.8
Pakistani	0.9	49.5	48.5	42.6	3.7
Bangladeshi	0.3	63.4	47.8	47.2	3.3
Chinese	0.3	71.6	50.5	23.3	5.7
Other Asian	0.4	78.1	52.6	24.4	4.1
Other	0.5	40.2	48.3	41.7	5.0

Source: 1991 Census, Ethnic Group and Country of Birth, vol. 2, London: HMSO, 1993.

ethnic minorities, Indians, Pakistanis, and Bangladeshis make up about a half, while those describing themselves as Black Caribbean, Black African, or Black Other make up a further 30 per cent. As Table 5.2 shows, nearly half of the total ethnic minority population was born in Britain although only about a third of the Black Africans, Bangladeshis, Chinese, and Other Asians were second generation. The proportion is particularly high for Black Other, many of whom described themselves as 'Black British'.

The proportions of men and women is fairly equal, a notable convergence as compared with a decade earlier, partly reflecting the influence of family reunification.[26] But the age structure is rather less similar to that of the white population. As Table 5.2 shows, except for Black Caribbeans and Black Other, the share aged sixty or over is less than 10 per cent. This reflects the fact that most immigrants were young on arrival (typically in their twenties or younger) so that only those remaining from the earliest cohorts of immigrants have reached retirement age.[27] The counterpart is the large proportion of those under sixteen, the vast majority of whom were born in Britain. This feature is also heightened by relatively high birthrates and large family sizes for some of the ethnic minority groups, particularly the Pakistanis and Bangladeshis. LFS data reveal that a third of Pakistani and Bangladeshi families had three or more dependent children under 16 (Jones 1993: 19).

[26] LFS data for 1982 indicates that females were 43 per cent of African Asians, 42 per cent of Pakistanis and 41 per cent of Bangladeshis (Jones 1993: 21).

[27] It may also be the case that some of these immigrants have return migrated upon retirement.

Census and other data also reveal a very marked concentration of ethnic minority populations in certain parts of Britain. These concentrations were established early on in the settlement patterns of successive waves of immigration. Ethnic minority populations remain heavily concentrated in urban centres, with 45 per cent located in the Greater London area alone as compared with 10 per cent of the white population. Other major areas of settlement are the Midlands and the industrial/urban parts of Lancashire and Yorkshire. Even within urban areas, minority populations are concentrated in certain localities, often the more depressed inner city areas. Thus in the London area, in the boroughs of Brent, Newham, Tower Hamlets, Hackney, Ealing, and Lambeth, ethnic minorities exceeded 30 per cent of the population in 1991. Many of these areas have ethnic communities dominated by one particular ethnic minority group. For example Bangladeshis made up 23 per cent of the population of Tower Hamlets, Black Caribbeans made up 15 per cent of the population of Lambeth while Indians predominated elsewhere in London (e.g. Brent, Newham, and Ealing) and in the Midlands.[28]

The overall numbers of ethnic minority groups, their demographic structure and their concentration in certain urban areas has a number of implications. First, their exposure to the predominantly white British culture may be less than it would appear at first sight. Second and more important, as the literature from the 1970s onwards has increasingly emphasized, these ethnic minorities must be considered as communities and not just as individuals or families. Third, the maintenance of distinctive cultures is both a cause and a consequence of geographical concentration.

Language fluency, education, and skills

Education, vocational qualifications, and language fluency are important for adaptation to the host country environment and for success in the labour market. Lack of these skills can be a key source of disadvantage. Many of the early postwar immigrants had little education and poor language skills. But these deficits relative to the white population have eroded over time because of rising education levels in source countries, because of

---

[28] As Peach (1998) shows, geographic concentration is much more marked among Bangladeshis and Pakistanis than among Indians or Caribbeans. Even greater concentration can be discerned when these broad categories are divided into localities of origin—often reflecting chain migration effects. Thus the concentration of those with Jamaican origins in the Clapham area is often traced back to the arrivals on the *Empire Windrush* who were initially accommodated there.

Table 5.3. Fluency in English and education qualifications

Ethnicity	English spoken fairly well		Highest qualification below 'O' level		Highest qualification degree	
	men	women	men	women	men	women
White	–	–	31	38	11	8
Caribbean	–	–	44	34	6	3
Indian	81	70	35	40	24	19
African-Asian	91	86	32	32	20	15
Pakistani	78	54	48	60	11	7
Bangladeshi	75	40	60	73	10	3
Chinese	76	76	31	25	26	17

Source: Modood and Berthoud 1997, pp. 60, 65–6.

the changing selectivity in migration, and because an increasing proportion of ethnic minorities have been educated in Britain. The 1991 census contains information on higher educational qualifications but the best source of information is the most recent PSI study of ethnic minorities. This is because interviews were conducted by a member of the same ethnic minority group as the respondent, in the interviewees' first language and language fluency was assessed by the interviewer rather than self-reported (see Modood and Berthoud 1997: 11).

Table 5.3, extracted from the PSI study, shows that fluency among ethnic minorities ranged from 91 per cent for African Asian men to only 40 per cent for Bangladeshi women. Although rates of language fluency were significantly lower for those not born in Britain, they rise sharply with length of time since migration, particularly for those groups with initially low levels of language fluency. This finding is consistent with the results from studies of other countries such as the United States and Australia[29] where increases in fluency have been seen as leading to improvements in wages and labour market success. However, those who were over the age of 25 at migration appear to have improved their fluency less markedly—a finding also consistent with other evidence. The PSI data also suggests that language acquisition is less marked when the individual concerned lives in an area in which there is a high density of members of the same ethnic minority group, particularly where they comprise more than 10 per cent of the population (Modood and Berthoud

[29] See for example, Chiswick and Miller (1995).

1997: 62). Of course this may also reflect a tendency for those with poor language proficiency to gravitate to high ethnic minority density areas. Shields and Wheatley Price (2001, 2002) have demonstrated that these results are robust to multivariate analysis.

While studies of earlier periods showed significantly lower educational attainment among ethnic minorities as compared with whites, the most recent evidence suggests a significant catching up. The earlier studies noted a tendency for polarization in the educational attainment of ethnic minorities—with large proportions both of highly qualified individuals and of individuals with no qualifications. This too has become less marked as a larger share of the ethnic minority population has been educated in Britain. As Table 5.3 indicates, among men, slightly larger proportions of Caribbeans and Pakistanis and a much larger proportion of Bangladeshis have no qualifications or qualifications below 'O' level, as compared with whites. Among women, Pakistanis and Bangladeshis stand out. It is notable also that Indians, African-Asians, and Chinese have much larger proportions with degree-level qualifications than whites.

These comparisons tend to conceal some important compositional differences. Since early migrants tended to be less qualified than later migrants and since first-generation immigrants as a whole tend to be less qualified than the second generation, the younger members of most of the ethnic minorities compare even more favourably with whites. Although among young males aged 16–24, ethnic minorities as a whole had 32 per cent with no or sub-'O' level qualifications compared with 22 per cent for whites, the proportions are equal for females.

More notable are the high participation rates in post-16 education among ethnic minorities, particularly among Indians and African Asians and to a lesser extent among Pakistanis and Bangladeshis. According to Modood and Berthoud, 'No ethnic group had a lower participation rate in post-16 education than white people and some had a much higher rate' (1997: 76). In Table 5.4 the percentage of 16–24 year old males in full-time education, calculated from the Quarterly Labour Force Survey, is reported both by ethnic and immigrant status. These figures confirm the PSI study but also highlight interesting differences between the native-born and foreign-born. Among Whites, Blacks and Mixed/Other ethnic groups immigrants have participation rates 15–20 per cent higher than their native-born counterparts, while Pakistani and especially Indian native-born males are more likely to engage in full-time education. Interestingly, Irish immigrants have a lower participation rate in full-time education than any other group.

Table 5.4. Labour force status of working age males

Ethnicity	16–24 years old		25–34 years old		35+ years old	
	native-born	foreign-born	native-born	foreign-born	native-born	foreign-born
Active in the labour market						
White	79.9	61.5	95.6	90.2	85.7	88.0
Irish	–	88.1	–	94.5	–	76.2
Black	65.9	51.4	91.3	78.0	93.8	81.5
Indian	55.9	64.2	91.8	91.6	74.5	86.6
Pakistani	54.9	59.3	95.7	94.4	·	77.3
Mixed/Other	59.2	40.6	88.3	73.2	81.3	85.2
Full-time education			*Self-employed*			
White	16.6	31.6	12.9	9.3	18.8	21.7
Irish	–	11.1	–	21.5	–	22.5
Black	26.5	41.0	6.5	9.1	–	8.8
Indian	42.1	30.2	13.9	20.1	–	25.6
Pakistani	40.0	37.0	18.2	17.3	–	28.4
Mixed/Other	35.8	55.3	9.6	12.1	–	20.4
ILO unemployed						
White	19.5	23.3	10.8	9.6	8.8	9.8
Irish	–	15	–	17.8	–	18.9
Black	48.3	66.6	32.2	34.3	26.6	27.0
Indian	26.7	23.5	13.7	11.2	–	13.2
Pakistani	43.9	43.0	30.0	22.0	–	24.9
Mixed/Other	33.0	27.5	17.6	21.1	–	14.2

Source: Authors' calculations based on data from the Quarterly Labour Force Surveys of the United Kingdom.
Notes: Percentage rates of the whole working age (16-64 years olds) population are reported, except for the "self-employment" and ILO unemployment rates which are a percentage of the Labour force (or economically active population). They are derived using the whole sample of each Quarterly Labour Force Survey from 1992q4 to 1994q3. The 1991 Census weights were used to provide population estimates provided each reported cell contained a statistically reliable sample size (over 10,000 equivalent persons), otherwise the cell is left blank. Full-time education rates are only reported for 16–24 year olds and self-employment rates are only provided for 25+ year old men as the other categories contained too few cases.

Thus although among ethnic minority adults there remain significant numbers with low language proficiency and little education, the evidence indicates a very strong educational drive, as reflected by the behaviour of the younger (mostly second or third) generation, among Indian and, to a lesser extent, Pakistani men (see also Leslie and Drinkwater 1999). While

Black native-born young men are less likely to engage in full-time education than their foreign-born counterparts, they still have a much higher
participation rate than whites. It has been suggested that this is a reflection
of lack of job opportunities for young ethnic minority workers. But survey
evidence indicates that ethnic minority respondents are no more likely to
cite poor job prospects as a reason for continuing in education than whites
(Jones 1993: 35; Modood and Berthoud 1997: 77).

Labour market status
Table 5.4 also provides information on the labour market status of working
age men. The different percentages of 16–24 year old men, active in the
labour market, largely reflect their participation in education. Amongst
25–34 year olds, 90 to 95 per cent of men are active in most categories. The
slightly lower rates for foreign-born Blacks and Mixed/Other reflects the
higher proportion of these groups still engaged in full-time education and
the relative attractiveness of university level education in the United
Kingdom for mature and postgraduate studies. The lower activity rates
reported for Indian native-born, Irish, and Pakistani foreign-born 35+
year-olds may indicate that these groups have increased probabilities of
being long-term sick or unable to work, since they are no more likely to
have retired early than other groups.

The self-employment rates given in Table 5.4 show that there is a greater
propensity to work for oneself amongst Indians and Pakistanis compared
with the native-born white population. Qualitative evidence indicates that
this is a positive choice among Indians while, for Pakistanis, it is more
likely to be associated with poor employment prospects (Metcalf, Modood,
and Virdee 1996).[30] It may also reflect the fact that some of these men were
engaged in entrepreneurial activity in East Africa prior to immigration or
the provision of culturally specific goods and services in their own communities. For Pakistanis this inclination has carried across the generations
to the native born, whereas for native born Indians their self-employment
rate is much closer to the white natives' rate. Interestingly white foreign-
born 35+ men and Irish immigrants are more likely, while all Blacks are
less likely, to be self-employed than native whites. Evidently, self-
employment is not envisaged as an escape route from discrimination
among Blacks.

Finally, in Table 5.4 the International Labour Office definition of
unemployment rates are given, again by broad age group. The youth

---

[30] More recent quantitative evidence can be found in Clark and Drinkwater (1998, 2000).

unemployment problem is clearly evident, with the rate among young males being up to twice as large as that for over 25-year-olds. There are also marked differences between ethnic groups that dominate the native-born/foreign-born comparisons (of which only the 16–24 year old Black and 25–34 year old Pakistani differences are noteworthy). Irish-born males are less likely than other foreign-born whites to be unemployed when young, but are more likely when over the age of 25. All ethnic minority groups in all categories are more likely to be unemployed than whites. Black and Pakistani males have the greatest difficulty in obtaining employment while Indian labour force participants seem to be able to access jobs almost as easily as native-born whites. It is unlikely that the hypothesis of discrimination can account for these differences between culturally similar groups. However, these are only average differences and take no account of differences in characteristic endowments. We now turn to a review of more rigorous econometric evidence concerning the labour market performance of native and foreign-born men.

5.4. Immigrants, Ethnic Minority Groups, and Jobs

The literature
There have been few econometric investigations into the employment and unemployment experience of immigrants in the United Kingdom.[31] However, the labour market experience of the ethnic minority population has recently received considerable attention.[32] Blackaby, Clark et al. (1994), using pooled General Household Survey data, and Blackaby, Leslie et al. (1998), using information from the Quarterly Labour Force Survey of the United Kingdom, provide some evidence that the employment prospects

---

[31] Indeed, there is little descriptive evidence either. Salt (1995), using the Spring 1992 and 1993 Quarterly Labour Force Surveys, investigates whether the foreign (defined according to nationality) working population in the UK differs from that of the UK labour force, with regard to occupation and region of residence. He does not consider employment or unemployment rates. However, Woolford (1994) presents some descriptive statistics concerning the Irish (nationality) population in the UK, based on the Spring 1993 Quarterly Labour Force Survey. He shows that they are more likely to be unemployed, or working in the construction sector, than other economically active persons in the UK.

[32] Descriptive investigations include Daniel (1968), Smith (1977), Brown (1984), and Modood and Berthoud (1997) based on surveys of the West Indian and South Asian population, Jones (1993) who uses the 1988–90 annual Labour Force surveys to provide a national picture, as does Sly (1994, 1995) using the Quarterly Labour Force Survey. Sly (1996) and Sly et al. (1997) use both the annual and Quarterly Labour Force surveys to examine trends in the labour market participation of ethnic groups over the last ten years.

for ethnic minorities have worsened over time, and that difficulties accessing employment appear to be more serious than differences in earnings, once employed.[33]

Recently, Blackaby, Leslie, and Murphy (1999) and Blackaby, Drinkwater et al. (1997) have used the annual Labour Force Survey (pooled over 1988–91) and the 1991 Census, respectively, to investigate unemployment rates among Britain's ethnic minorities. They find, using an Oaxaca-type (1973) decomposition methodology, that for some groups (Black Africans and the Irish) characteristic differences explain the majority of the unemployment rate gap, while for other groups (Bangladeshis, Indians, and Pakistanis), the differential rewards to these characteristics are to blame. The variations in the size of the latter component are attributed to a number of factors including different amounts of discrimination, the differential response of ethnic minority groups to discrimination (Blackaby, Leslie, and Murphy 1999), and greater amounts of non-assimilation[34] by some groups and different endowments of unobserved ability, particularly in the English language (Blackaby, Drinkwater et al. 1997).

As Blackaby, Drinkwater et al. (1997) acknowledge, the use of such a decomposition methodology is problematic and provides results which are very difficult to interpret precisely. The variation in unemployment attributable to differential returns to characteristics also captures reporting errors in the data source, measurement errors endemic in the definitions of the characteristics used, and systematic variations in unobserved ability such as may be the case for immigrants (Chiswick 1978; Borjas 1985, 1987). Furthermore, since the majority of ethnic minorities in the UK were born abroad, that part of their human capital which was acquired in a foreign country may not be perfectly transferable to the UK labour market (Chiswick 1978). Recent immigrants may also lack the location-specific human capital necessary for labour market success in the UK (Chiswick 1982), especially English language fluency.

In the study by Blackaby, Leslie, and Murphy (1999), only a dummy variable is included for those born abroad, whereas, in Blackaby, Drinkwater et al. (1997), separate logistic regressions are performed for all ethnic minority natives as well as Irish and other white immigrants. However, there are no controls for country of origin nor an examination of

[33] See also Leslie et al. (1998).
[34] It is unclear what Blackaby et al. (1997) mean by this term.

the adjustment process over time spent in the United Kingdom.[35] Furthermore, the definition of unemployment, used in the 1991 Census leads to higher reported rates of unemployment (see Blackaby et al. 1997) and makes comparisons with other government surveys, and across countries, difficult.

Other studies that have examined these issues include Mayhew and Rosewell (1978) who used the 1971 census to investigate occupational crowding among immigrants. They found that Irish, Pakistani, and West Indian workers were disproportionately working in low-paid (undesirable) jobs whereas Indians and Commonwealth Africans had accessed better types of employment with white immigrants crowded into the higher paying jobs. Stewart (1983), using the National Training Survey, also finds a significant gap in occupational attainment for non-white immigrants, with respect to native-born whites. In addition, Gazioglu (1994) provides some evidence that Bangladeshi and Turkish men, living in London, experience considerable job disamenities and Shields and Wheatley Price (1999a, 1999b) document the disadvantage experienced by ethnic minotriy men in accessing employer-funded job-related training.

Wheatley Price (2001a, 2001b) conducted the first UK studies to examine the employment and unemployment experience of male immigrants. Using the model of immigrant adjustment, proposed by Chiswick (1982) and Chiswick and Hurst (1998), hypotheses concerning the impact of education, potential labour market experience, familial characteristics and region of residence on the employment rate[36] and on the likelihood of being unemployed (according to the International Labour Office definition)[37] are examined for white and non-white, native and foreign-born, males. The data on males aged 25–64 and residing in England were obtained from the Quarterly Labour Force Survey (QLFS) of the United Kingdom, pooled over two years (1993–4).

---

[35] Indeed the 1991 Census does not record the year of immigration, thus making this analysis impossible.

[36] The employment rate is defined as the total number of men who report being paid employees, self-employed, voluntary workers or engaged in government training schemes as a proportion of the total male sample.

[37] The economically inactive are excluded from this sample. Therefore this is not the opposite of the employment rate. The proportion of the population claiming unemployment benefit–the official measure of unemployment in the UK–is also examined by Wheatley Price (2001b). Since these results broadly follow the pattern of the ILO unemployment findings, and because they are not useful for inter-country comparisons, we do not report them here.

New results on employment adjustment

According to Wheatley Price (1998*a*), immigrant white men are less likely on average to be employed (76.1 per cent) than their native-born counterparts (80.1 per cent). Among non-whites there is little difference in the employment rate (68.8 per cent for native-born males, 66.9 per cent for immigrant men). In his sample, over half of all foreign-born whites arrived in the UK before 1965, with the proportion arriving over the next two decades continuously falling from 12.6 per cent between 1965 and 1969 to 5.0 per cent in the early 1980s. 16.5 per cent of immigrant whites arrived in the last decade. Ireland is by far the largest source country, accounting for 30 per cent of the sample. Many of the non-Irish white immigrants have British nationality and immigrated to the UK while they were still children (Shields and Wheatley Price 1998). Immigrants without British or Irish nationality are most likely to originate in the USA, Canada, New Zealand, and Australia, or in the rest of Europe.

By contrast, only 7.8 per cent of non-white immigrants were present in the UK before 1960. During the 1960s about 40 per cent of this sample entered the country, with a further 17 per cent arriving in the early 1970s. The proportion of non-white immigrants who arrived during the next ten years is dramatically smaller until 1985–94, when about 16.5 per cent of the sample arrived. Not surprisingly, less than one per cent of non-white immigrants were born in the major western industrialised countries. However, the Indian subcontinent accounts for nearly 50 per cent of the non-white foreign born sample (India–24 per cent; Pakistan–15 per cent) with a further 11.3 per cent having been born in Kenya and Uganda, many of whom are of South Asian origin. The Caribbean, Africa, and the Middle East are also major source regions.

The results of the logistic regression analysis of employment, undertaken by Wheatley Price (1998*a*), and based on Chiswick's (1982) model, are presented in Table 5.5 as predicted percentage probabilities of employment. The separate employment effect of each characteristic, on an otherwise average person, is shown for both the continuous and dummy variables.[38] A native-born white male with average characteristics has a predicted employment rate of 83.3 per cent. This compares with 80.2 per cent for the average foreign-born white male, 71.7 per cent for a native-born non-white and 69.4 per cent for an average non-white immigrant.

---

[38] For the continuous variables, the predicted employment is calculated for an average male with two less (or two more) years of education and five less (or five more) years of potential labour market experience. For the dummy variables we evaluate the predicted probability of an otherwise average person when each characteristic holds.

Table 5.5. Predicted percentage rates of employment in England, 1993–4: white and non-white males aged 25–64 with mean characteristics

Variable	Native-born		Foreign-born	
	White	Non-white	White	Non-white
Person with average characteristics	83.34	71.71	80.22	69.42
2 less years of education	80.22	68.15	77.43	69.31
2 more years of education	86.05	73.01	82.74	69.54
5 less years of experience	85.39	66.37	82.14	72.79
5 more years of experience	78.95	73.48	76.38	63.01
Not married or living together	66.27	50.63	63.32	54.07
Married or living together	86.51	84.52	83.86	71.90
No dependent children aged <16	84.73	77.75	81.03	71.74
One dependent child aged <16	83.83	64.41	81.99	68.73
Two dependent children aged <16	81.93	63.09	78.30	73.20
Three dependent children aged <16	67.28	38.06	72.58	59.66
Living in the Midlands	83.87	76.52	77.44	68.72
Living in the North	79.36	73.12	78.81	67.11
Living in the South	86.16	78.70	82.72	78.03
Living in Greater London	82.08	66.12	79.08	67.22
Immigrated Pre-1955	–	–	80.15	72.20
Immigrated 1955–1959	–	–	84.64	77.36
Immigrated 1960–1964	–	–	84.42	73.84
Immigrated 1965–1969	–	–	83.32	73.91
Immigrated 1970–1974	–	–	79.33	74.81
Immigrated 1975–1979	–	–	79.47	72.29
Immigrated 1980–1984	–	–	64.53	65.98
Immigrated 1985–1989	–	–	80.07	59.17
Immigrated 1990–1994	–	–	63.14	35.52
Born in Ireland	–	–	75.97	–
Born in the USA	–	–	91.09	–
Born in Canada, NZ or Australia	–	–	87.19	–
Born in SW Europe	–	–	85.81	–
Born in Italy	–	–	82.81	–
Born in Germany	–	–	80.44	–
Born in NW Europe	–	–	85.64	–
Born in SE Europe	–	–	75.13	–
Born in Eastern Europe	–	–	71.94	–
Born in USA/CAN/NZ/AUS/EUR	–	–	–	73.51
Born in the Middle East or N Africa	–	–	72.30	61.49
Born in Kenya	–	–	–	81.37

Table 5.5. (*Continued*)

Variable	Native-born		Foreign-born	
	White	Non-white	White	Non-white
Born in Uganda	–	–	–	73.73
Born in Central & E Africa	–	–	–	54.66
Born in W Africa	–	–	–	58.42
Born in W, Central & E Africa	–	–	91.12	–
Born in S Africa	–	–	83.35	68.76
Born in Jamaica	–	–	–	72.00
Born in the rest of the Caribbean	–	–	–	68.58
Born in the Caribbean	–	–	59.39	–
Born in Bangladesh	–	–	–	53.72
Born in Sri Lanka	–	–	–	76.01
Born in Pakistan	–	–	–	62.46
Born in Bangladesh, SL or Pakistan	–	–	73.56	–
Born in India	–	–	78.18	73.15
Born in HK, Malaysia or Singapore	–	–	72.92	77.25
Born in the rest of the world	–	–	80.54	73.75
Sample size	67,679	593	3,206	3,560

Source: Wheatley Price (1998*a*).

Decreasing the number of years of education by two, from its mean value, reduces the employment rate of white natives by an average of 3.1 per cent, by 3.56 per cent for non-white natives, 2.79 per cent for an average white immigrant and by only 0.11 per cent for a non-white immigrant. This provides strong evidence to suggest that the education obtained by this latter group is either of such poor quality that it counts for nothing in terms of employment in England, or it is hardly transferable to the UK, perhaps due to language difficulties.

For native-born whites, five years less in the labour market increases the probability of employment by 2 per cent, while non-white natives lose 5.34 per cent. In comparison, white immigrants gain only a 1.92 per cent advantage, for five less labour market years abroad, while non-white immigrants increase their probability of employment by 3.37 per cent. Therefore white immigrant men receive lesser penalties, for potential work experience gained abroad than non-white men, reflecting the increased relevance of their acquired labour market skills to the UK environment or the fact that employers find such attributes easier to assess.

For immigrants, the extent of the initial employment disadvantage is evident from the predicted employment rates for those who immigrated between 1990 and 1994. Only 63.1 per cent of white immigrants, with average characteristics who arrived in that period, are likely to be employed, whilst the employment rate for non-white immigrants is predicted to be just 35.5 per cent. Evidently, the white immigrants come with more pre-arranged jobs, are better informed about the opportunities available in the English labour market before they arrive, or are more effective in their initial job search. For white immigrants, the employment rate rises to 80 per cent and stays there after just a few years in the English labour market, closely following the pattern of assimilation found by Chiswick (1982) and Chiswick and Hurst (1998) in the United States.[39] There is also some evidence of cyclical factors influencing employment rates (e.g. 1980–4 and 1985–9) which may be caused by return migration, especially of Irish immigrants.

For the average non-white immigrant the initial assimilation in employment is rapid. Over the first five years, employment rates jump by nearly 24 per cent. This pattern is in line with the predictions of Chiswick's (1982) model. The continued adjustment of non-white immigrants, over the first 20–5 years in the UK (to an employment rate of nearly 75 per cent), indicates that these men must have been less well prepared for the English labour market, than whites. They take much longer to adapt, suggesting that this process may be hindered by their foreign qualifications, lack of English language fluency, adverse unobserved characteristics or by discriminatory attitudes. Some of this disadvantage persists as their employment rates remain below those of white natives, though immigrants are more likely to be employed than non-white natives after about fifteen years in England.

It is evident from the predicted probabilities associated with the country group dummy variables that place of birth is important in determining the employment prospects of immigrants. For white immigrants, having been born in the United States or West, Central and East Africa raises the employment rate by over 10 per cent above the average for that group. Those coming from Canada, New Zealand, Australia, South West and North West Europe also experience at least a 5 per cent employment advantage. White immigrants from Eastern Europe, the Middle East, and North Africa, Hong Kong, Malaysia and Singapore have a lower predicted employment rate (by 7–8 per cent).

---

[39] An alternative explanation of such findings is that they result from a decline in immigrant quality over time (Borjas 1985, 1987).

Among non-white immigrants, those born in Kenya perform the best (12 per cent better than the mean person), with Sri Lankans (6.6 per cent) and those from Hong Kong, Malaysia and Singapore (7.8 per cent) also performing well above average. However, immigrants from Pakistan, the Middle East and North Africa have a 7–8 per cent employment rate disadvantage, with those born in West Africa (11 per cent), Central and East Africa (15 per cent) and Bangladesh (16 per cent) being least likely to find employment in the English labour market.

New results on unemployment incidence
The results of a similar analysis of ILO unemployment are presented in Table 5.6 (taken from Wheatley Price 1998*b*). According to this study, a native-born white male, with average characteristics, has a predicted ILO unemployment rate of 7.87 per cent. This compares with 8.79 per cent for the average foreign-born white male, 20.8 per cent for a native born non-white with mean characteristics and 16.5 per cent for an average non-white immigrant.

Increasing the number of years of education by two, from its mean value, decreases the ILO unemployment rate of white natives by 2.57 per cent percentage points and that of non-white natives by 1.33 per cent. For the average white immigrant two more years of education lowers the predicted ILO unemployment rate by 2.26 per cent and that of non-white immigrants by 1.27 per cent. Evidently, non-whites face difficulties translating their education into jobs that whites do not.

Changing the years of potential labour market experience makes little difference to the predicted ILO unemployment rates of the white groups. The non-white native-born, who are much younger on average, are more likely to be unemployed (by 1.74 per cent) if they have been in the labour market for five years less. The corresponding figure for the average non-white immigrant, reflecting the reward to potential labour market experience gained abroad, is 2.22 per cent. There is an enormous increase in the probability of being unemployed for single, over cohabiting, men and for fathers of several dependent children. ILO unemployment rates vary systematically across the English regions, unlike employment rates. For all groups, living in the South is associated with the lowest unemployment rates, while living in London substantially increases the likelihood of unemployment for each group.

Focusing now on the foreign-born groups we see that white immigrant men face a severe initial ILO unemployment rate of 19.8 per cent.

Table 5.6. Predicted percentage rates of unemployment (ILO definition) in England, 1993–4: white and non-white males aged 25–64 with mean characteristics

Variable	Native-born		Foreign-born	
	White	Non-white	White	Non-white
Person with average characteristics	7.87	20.75	8.79	16.52
2 less years of education	11.53	22.15	11.73	17.88
2 more years of education	5.30	19.42	6.53	15.25
5 less years of experience	8.09	22.49	8.58	14.88
5 more years of experience	7.94	20.60	9.10	18.74
Not married or living together	18.00	40.71	20.17	28.87
Married or living together	6.35	10.60	6.99	14.93
No dependent children aged <16	6.87	16.88	7.64	14.83
One dependent child aged <16	8.00	26.85	9.27	18.18
Two dependent children aged <16	8.98	26.19	10.42	14.37
Three dependent children aged <16	17.67	45.44	14.92	21.92
Living in the Midlands	7.31	18.70	10.05	16.11
Living in the North	8.77	21.20	8.02	17.01
Living in the South	7.09	17.13	7.36	11.01
Living in Greater London	9.94	29.24	10.42	19.07
Immigrated Pre-1955	–	–	6.70	18.52
Immigrated 1955–1959	–	–	8.24	12.55
Immigrated 1960–1964	–	–	7.31	13.69
Immigrated 1965–1969	–	–	7.90	13.83
Immigrated 1970–1974	–	–	7.52	13.62
Immigrated 1975–1979	–	–	11.84	14.77
Immigrated 1980–1984	–	–	19.32	20.88
Immigrated 1985–1989	–	–	7.49	25.68
Immigrated 1990–1994	–	–	19.82	41.00
Born in Ireland	–	–	12.19	–
Born in the USA	–	–	3.44	–
Born in Canada, NZ or Australia	–	–	4.02	–
Born in SW Europe	–	–	7.83	–
Born in Italy	–	–	6.42	–
Born in Germany	–	–	10.75	–
Born in NW Europe	–	–	7.03	–
Born in SE Europe	–	–	11.02	–
Born in Eastern Europe	–	–	11.92	–
Born in USA/CAN/NZ/AUS/EUR	–	–	–	14.90
Born in the Middle East or N Africa	–	–	13.59	24.76
Born in Kenya	–	–	–	10.17

(continued)

Table 5.6 (*Continued*)

Variable	Native-born		Foreign-born	
	White	Non-white	White	Non-white
Born in Uganda	–	–	–	10.50
Born in Central & E Africa	–	–	–	32.20
Born in W Africa	–	–	–	25.26
Born in W, Central & E Africa	–	–	2.23	–
Born in S Africa	–	–	8.64	13.48
Born in Jamaica	–	–	–	18.74
Born in the rest of the Caribbean	–	–	–	17.89
Born in the Caribbean	–	–	30.20	–
Born in Bangladesh	–	–	–	26.87
Born in Sri Lanka	–	–	–	12.65
Born in Pakistan	–	–	–	23.65
Born in Bangladesh, SL or Pakistan	–	–	12.36	–
Born in India	–	–	11.17	13.64
Born in HK, Malaysia or Singapore	–	–	11.49	9.11
Born in the rest of the world	–	–	6.32	10.47
Sample size	59,763	539	2,774	2,954

Source: Wheatley Price (1998*b*).

This disadvantage, in comparison with the average white native-born worker, is eliminated after about 15–20 years, and thereafter white immigrants experience marginally lower rates. The 1985–9 and the 1970–4 cohorts, however, have much lower rates of ILO unemployment than a smooth adjustment process would predict. The surviving members of the first two of these cohorts of white immigrants may be positively selected, in terms of unobserved ability, or they are positively scarred by the economic climate prevailing at the time of immigration (see Chiswick et al. 1997).

As far as non-white immigrants are concerned, the evidence in support of Chiswick's (1982) model is much stronger. In terms of ILO unemployment, the initial unemployment rate faced by recent non-white immigrants is very large at 41 per cent. However, this rate is halved over the first five to ten years as local labour market knowledge and skills are acquired, but it never converges to that of white natives.

Even after controlling for all of the above variables, the country of birth of immigrants plays an important role in determining the unemployment rates of these men. For white immigrants, as was the case for employment, having been born in West, Central, and East Africa, the USA or Canada, New Zealand, and Australia results in the lowest unemployment rates (under 5 per cent). Whites born in the rest of the world, Italy, North West and South West Europe are also less likely to be unemployed than the average white immigrant male. Those born in Germany, South East Europe, India, Hong Kong, Malaysia, and Singapore, and in the Eastern Bloc experience ILO unemployment rates below the Irish (at 12.2 per cent).

Among non-white immigrants, even those born in Hong Kong, Malaysia, and Singapore, who have the lowest ILO unemployment rates, are more likely to be out of work than an average white immigrant. Those from Kenya have the next lowest rates, with immigrants from the Western industrialized countries of North America, Europe, and Australasia, Uganda, South Africa, Sri Lanka, India, and the rest of the world also having below average predicted probabilities of unemployment. However, immigrants from Jamaica and the Caribbean are 2–3 per cent percentage points more likely to be unemployed than an average non-white foreign-born male, while those from Pakistan, the Middle East, and North Africa and West Africa have ILO unemployment rates of about 24–25 per cent. Non-whites from Bangladesh (26.9 per cent) and Central and East Africa (32.2 per cent) have the highest predicted percentage ILO unemployment rates of all male immigrants. These males must have either much poorer quality of schooling and labour market skills, face great difficulties transferring the human capital acquired before migration, be negatively selected in terms of unobserved characteristics or have little knowledge of the English language.

In summary, the results presented above show that there are large differences in the employment and unemployment experience of 25–64 year old males in the English labour market, according to ethnic and immigrant status. For both groups of immigrant workers, there is evidence that the adjustment process, outlined by Chiswick (1982) and Chiswick and Hurst (1998), is valid in the English labour market. For whites, convergence with the experience of comparable white natives occurs rapidly over the first five years in the English labour market and is completed within fifteen years of immigration. However, non-white immigrants never attain the levels of labour market status enjoyed by whites. Their initial adjustment is also most rapid in the first five years in the UK and continues for a further twenty years.

5.5 Wage Outcomes

Employee characteristics
Using data from the Quarterly Labour Force Survey, Table 5.7 provides a summary of the average characteristics for 25-64-year-olds, white and non-white, male employees in England in 1993-4. Among the white immigrant groups, those with British nationality entered the country at a relatively young age, whereas those with other nationalities entered relatively late in life compared to Irish and non-white immigrants (Shields and Wheatley Price 1998). Most of the white British immigrants are children of temporary emigrants from the UK, who may have gone abroad in the Armed Services or in public service jobs. A large number would have returned to undertake education in the UK either alone, in boarding schools, or with their parents. This is reflected in the fact that they, uniquely amongst the immigrant groups, receive the majority of their education in the UK and have on average very little foreign potential experience.

Concerning acquired skills, white immigrants of British and other nationalities have undergone more, but Irish men have received less, years of education than white native-born workers. Non-white native and foreign-born men also have acquired substantially more years of education than native-born whites. With regard to potential experience the picture is reversed. All immigrants have less total years of potential labour market experience than white natives, again with the exception of the Irish who have substantially more. Most of this potential experience was undertaken in the UK, with white (other) immigrants having received substantially more potential experience in their country of origin than Irish or non-white immigrants. Native-born non-white male employees have considerably less potential experience than all other groups, since they are much younger.

The ethnic composition of native- and foreign-born non-white employees is very different. Blacks account for nearly 50 per cent of the native-born employees, but only 22 per cent of the foreign born sample, whilst Indians are the largest immigrant group (40 per cent) but contribute only 22 per cent of native-born employees. The relatively recent migrations of the Pakistani and Bangladeshi communities is reflected in their proportion of the foreign-born being nearly three times that of the native-born sample. Even these figures may mask important differences in the country of origin. The Black group consists of those originating in Africa, the Caribbean, and elsewhere and the Indian group is comprised of those actually born in India and those

Table 5.7. Average characteristics of white and non-white male employees aged 25–64 in England, 1993–4

Variable	Native-Born		Foreign-Born			
	White	Non-white	White-British	White-Irish	White-other	Non-white
Acquired skills						
Years of education received abroad	–	–	3.77	8.68	12.29	10.65
Years of education received in the UK	11.9	13.0	9.84	3.02	2.48	3.05
Years of experience obtained abroad	–	–	1.16	3.88	6.44	4.08
Years of experience obtained in the UK	24.4	12.8	20.75	26.41	14.34	18.38
Ethnic composition (%)						
Black	–	47.8	–	–	–	22.1
Indian	–	21.6	–	–	–	40.1
Pakistani/Bangladeshi	–	6.0	–	–	–	7.0
Mixed/other	–	24.6	–	–	–	20.8
Industrial sector (%)						
Construction/transport	25.2	25.4	21.1	33.9	20.5	19.7
Financial Services	11.9	17.9	14.2	9.5	17.9	10.4
Manufacturing	32.4	23.9	24.5	25.9	29.9	34.1
Non-financial services	12.6	18.7	13.4	13.2	17.0	17.4
Public	18.0	14.2	26.8	17.5	14.7	18.5

Occupational level (%)						
Managerial	21.2	20.1	34.2	19.0	25.0	12.9
Professional	13.2	10.4	19.9	11.1	17.9	12.9
Associate professional	9.8	11.9	7.4	8.5	13.8	8.0
Clerical/secretarial	7.1	11.9	9.4	7.4	2.7	8.7
Craft and related	17.5	14.9	8.5	15.9	10.7	17.7
Personal/protective	6.3	3.7	7.1	6.9	13.8	8.2
Sales	4.2	4.5	2.8	1.6	0.4	3.5
Plant and machinery	15.2	15.7	8.3	19.6	10.3	19.4
Other	6.3	6.0	2.0	9.0	4.5	8.5
Employment conditions						
Weekly earnings (£)	354.5	302.1	420.2	335.6	455.6	300.6
Usual hours worked	44.8	42.3	44.9	46.3	47.2	41.9
Sample size	20,181	135	351	189	224	634

Source: Authors calculations based on data from the Quarterly Labour Force Surveys of the United Kingdom.

born in East Africa. With larger sample sizes the differing labour market characteristics of these groups could be investigated.

Irish immigrants are more likely to be employed in the construction and transport sector, and be under-represented in the financial sector, than other groups. Non-white native and white (other) foreign-born males are the most likely to be employed in the financial services, while non-white immigrants and white native-born workers are mainly to be found in the manufacturing jobs. Non-whites are the most likely to be engaged in the nonfinancial service sector. White (British) foreign-born male employees are substantially over-represented in the public sector and in managerial and professional occupations.

White (other) immigrants also are disproportionately employed in the higher occupational levels while non-white immigrant employees are the least likely to attain a managerial position. Non-white native-born males do not appear to face the same difficulties as their occupational distribution is very similar to that of native-born whites. Among white immigrants the Irish appear to have the least favourable occupational distribution and receive by far the lowest weekly wage. White (other) and white (British) foreign-born males earn substantially more than other employees with the former group also having the longest working week. Non-white men appear to earn significantly less, on average, than white natives and work shorter hours.

Econometric investigations of immigrant and ethnic minority earnings
There have been two main problems with empirical studies of immigrant earnings in the United Kingdom, namely the absence of suitable data and the (almost exclusive) focus on discrimination. With regard to data, economic researchers have until recently relied largely on single annual General Household Surveys (GHS)[40] (Chiswick 1980; McNabb and Psacharopoulos 1981; Blackaby 1986), pooled annual General Household Surveys (Blackaby–Clark et al. 1994, 1995; Blackaby–Leslie et al. 1997; Bell 1997), and small-scale localized surveys (e.g. Dex 1986; McCormick 1986; Gazioglu 1996).[41] The first data source suffers from very small

[40] Stewart (1983) uses occupational data from the National Training Survey but associates an average earnings figure, obtained from the General Household Survey, with it.
[41] The series of Policy Studies Insititute (PSI) surveys, undertaken with mainly sociological questions in mind (Daniel 1968; Smith 1977; Brown 1984; Modood and Berthoud 1997), contain only about 2,000 members of the ethnic minorities which, when a suitable sample has been isolated (e.g. immigrant men of working age), leaves relatively small sample sizes. In addition, only the data used in Smith (1977) and the most recent survey results (summarised in Modood and Berthoud 1997) are still available. Although the fourth PSI survey provides only grouped wage data and contains no information on hours of work its main advantage lies in the quality of the samples of ethnic minorities and the inclusion of questions on English language speaking fluency.

sample sizes.[42] Larger datasets can be obtained by pooling over a large number of years (leading to the second type of data) but this requires assumptions about the invariance of labour market conditions over time. The third source of data has been narrowly focused on particular groups in specific locations.[43]

There has been a need for a national picture and thus a nation-wide dataset.[44] The Quarterly Labour Force Survey (QLFS) of the United Kingdom, undertaken since 1992, is the only source which includes information on country of birth and the timing of immigration, a reliable ethnicity question, and information on earnings. By pooling a small number of quarters, statistically reliable sample sizes can be obtained to enable separate earnings functions to be estimated for white and non-white native-born and foreign-born groups (see Blackaby, Leslie et al. 1998; Shields and Wheatley Price 1998).

The second main failure of previous studies has been the focus on discrimination.[45] With the exception of Chiswick (1980) and Dex (1986) none of the earlier studies, cited above, took account of the fact that most of ethnic minority population in the United Kingdom, had been born abroad, received some or all of their schooling there and may lack speaking and writing fluency in the English language.[46] The use of Oaxaca-type decomposition techniques to measure discrimination also ignores the fact that these immigrants may have different distributions of unobserved characteristics due to the self-selection processes associated with migration (Chiswick 1978; Borjas 1985, 1987). Furthermore, there has been little disaggregation into individual ethnic or immigrant groups, despite there being substantial differences in other aspects of their labour market performance (Jones 1993) which cannot be explained by discrimination alone

[42] The study, by Mackay (1996), using data from the British Household Panel Study, also suffers from a small sample.

[43] Second generation West Indian school leavers in Birmingham and London in the case of Dex (1986), West Indian and Asian heads of households in Birmingham in McCormick (1986) and Turkish and Bangladeshi fathers and sons in a London borough in the case of Gazioglu (1996).

[44] The 1991 Census of the United Kingdom and the annual Labour Force Survey (1973–91) have been found lacking in this regard since they did not ask information about income.

[45] McNabb and Psacharoulos (1981), Dex (1986), Blackaby (1986), Blackaby, Clark et al. (1994, 1995), Blackaby, Leslie et al. (1996, 1997). Discrimination is also the main focus of the PSI studies.

[46] Indeed the only one of these studies that has information on English language ability is Gazioglu (1996). Recently, however, Shields and Wheatley Price (2002) have combined average hourly occupational wage information from the QLFS with the fourth PSI survey data in order to investigate the influence of language fluency on wages. Dustmann and Fabbri (2003) have investigated similar issues using the wage information in the PSI and Family and Working Lives Survey, as have Leslie and Lindley (2001) and Blackaby et al. (2001) using the PSI data. All the studies find that language fluency significantly increases earnings by 10–20 per cent.

(Blackaby, Leslie and Murphy 1999). In addition the earnings performance of white immigrants has been mainly ignored.

Chiswick (1980) was the first study to examine the earnings experience of immigrants to Great Britain. He found that there was little difference in the earnings of white native-born and white foreign-workers, but that non-white immigrants earn substantially less. Interestingly, he shows that the non–white immigrants receive a lower return to schooling,[47] than that received by white immigrants or white natives. He also finds for all immigrants that years of experience in the UK are no more productive than those attained before migration.[48] More recently, Bell (1997) found initial relative wage levels of Black immigrants to be lower than observationally equivalent natives. The gap was larger the more work experience had been obtained in the origin country. He also shows that the earnings of these immigrants tend to assimilate towards those of natives, when cohort effects are controlled for (Borjas 1985). Among white immigrants, Bell (1997) finds an initial earnings advantage over similar natives, which declines with time spent in the UK. In addition, Gazioglu (1996) has demonstrated the importance of English language proficiency for the earnings of Bangladeshi and Turkish male immigrants in London.

A new analysis of earnings
Recently, Shields and Wheatley Price (1998) have investigated the earnings of 16-64 year old full-time male employees in the English labour market, using data collected for the Quarterly Labour Force Survey (QLFS) of the United Kingdom between December 1992 and November 1994. They separate native-born and foreign-born non-whites and isolate British, Irish, and other nationalities in their sample of white immigrants. They control separately for education and potential experience obtained in the UK and that undertaken abroad. Furthermore, they attempt to control for sample selection bias in the employment decision and take into account the large failure to report wage information exhibited in the dataset, using a generalized extension of the Heckman (1976, 1979) procedure (Behrman and Wolfe 1984; Tunali 1986). This 'double selectivity' problem is rarely investigated in the literature. Their findings suggest that neglecting the problem of missing wage information may lead to biased estimates of the true wage-offer distribution.

---

[47] Most of the discrimination studies also find this (see note 45).

[48] Non-whites have lower returns to potential experience according to the discrimination literature (see note 45).

Amongst the white native population, Shields and Wheatley Price (1998) report that an extra year of schooling yields a 5 per cent rise in wages (see also Blackaby, Leslie et al. 1998), holding other characteristics constant. For the immigrant groups the return is slightly lower (by 0.5–1 per cent), confirming Chiswick's (1980) finding. White (other nationalities) immigrants are the exception, receiving much higher returns (of 10.5 per cent), possibly due to their higher concentration of degree level qualifications. Each immigrant group receives smaller rewards from education received abroad, suggesting that the schooling received in the home country is of poorer quality than in the UK, or it does not transfer well (Chiswick 1980).

According to Shields and Wheatley Price (1998) the returns to potential labour market experience in England are 3.8 per cent for native-born whites (see also Blackaby, Leslie et al. 1998). As Chiswick (1980) found, all immigrant groups receive a smaller reward for potential UK experience than natives. However, this may be because immigrant workers have spent longer spells in unemployment (Blackaby, Drinkwater et al. 1997; Wheatley Price 2001b), are limited in their choice of occupation (Mayhew and Rosewell 1978; Stewart 1983; Shields and Wheatley Price 2002), are denied access to on-the-job training (Shields and Wheatley Price 1999a, 1999b) or have reduced promotional opportunities within occupations (Pudney and Shields 2000). Non-white native-born employees receive higher returns for years of UK education and greater rewards for potential UK experience than either white natives or non-white immigrants. These findings are not evident from the discrimination studies, which fail to distinguish between native and foreign-born ethnic minorities (e.g. Blackaby, Clark et al. 1994, 1995, Blackaby, Leslie et al. 1997, 1998).

With regard to years of potential experience abroad, white (other nationalities) immigrants receive higher rewards than they do for potential UK experience (Shields and Wheatley Price 1998). This suggests that they may have migrated to the UK on the basis of employer-desirable labour market skills acquired in their home country. British and non-white immigrants also receive significant, but lower, returns for potential foreign experience than for potential UK experience. These groups may then face difficulties transferring labour market skills acquired abroad from the UK. Differential returns for potential UK and foreign experience were not found by Chiswick (1980).

In Table 5.8 the predicted hourly wage rates, resulting from the separate effect of each characteristic, have been calculated for the different groups native and foreign-born male employees. The figures show that two more years of education carry a substantial wage premium for all groups, except

Table 5.8. Predicted hourly wage rates for white and non-white male employees in England, 1993–4 with mean characteristics

Variable	Native-born		Foreign-born			
	White	Non-white	White-British	White-Irish	White-other	Non-white
Average hourly wage	6.22	5.31	7.34	6.24	7.87	6.08
2 more years of education received abroad	–	–	7.62	7.03	9.18	6.29
2 more years of education received in the UK	7.11	6.08	8.00	7.14	9.61	6.44
5 more years of experience obtained abroad	–	–	7.53	6.70	9.27	5.77
5 more years of experience obtained in the UK	6.45	6.16	7.53	6.11	8.42	6.17
Single, never married	5.33	4.75	5.94	5.06	7.57	5.73
Married or living together	6.63	6.38	9.83	8.12	8.35	6.46
No longer married	5.96	2.49	7.16	7.47	6.80	7.22
Living in the Midlands	5.99	4.94	6.67	5.45	8.07	5.23
Living in the North	6.49	5.62	8.07	7.34	8.30	7.87
Living in the South	5.94	7.06	8.23	6.47	7.29	6.49
Living in Greater London	7.33	5.41	8.34	8.16	8.28	7.38
Construction/transport	6.08	6.86	4.45	7.45	8.04	3.38
Financial services	7.29	5.86	8.63	6.70	10.85	6.26
Manufacturing	6.34	4.91	7.77	5.94	7.65	6.70

Non-financial services	5.62	5.62	6.40	5.90	7.84	4.85
Public	6.05	5.39	8.20	6.22	6.66	7.34
>25 employees at workplace	6.69	5.70	7.20	7.10	8.89	6.00
<25 employees at workplace	5.63	4.43	7.70	4.48	5.55	6.31
Black	–	5.68	–	–	–	5.54
Indian	–	5.40	–	–	–	6.32
Pakistani	–	4.47	–	–	–	5.30
Mixed/other	–	4.72	–	–	–	6.09
Sample size	27,280	203	469	165	235	606

Source: Authors own calculations based on the estimated log earnings functions reported in Table A1 of Shields and Wheatley Price (1998).
Notes: The reported wage rates are gross hourly earnings expressed in 1990 prices. The sample consists of full-time men of working age (16–64).

the non-white immigrants. Five extra years of experience acquired abroad is valued more highly for Irish and white (other) immigrants while it carries a negative premium for non-white foreign-born employees, who also receive little reward for experience obtained in the UK.

Marital status and geographical location appear to be important influences on earnings for all groups, with being married and living in London increasing hourly wages for all white groups. Non-white natives earn the most if they live in the South, while their foreign-born counterparts receive the greatest rewards in the North. The highest wage rates exist in the financial sector for whites, except the Irish who, like the native-born non-whites, are paid more if they are employed in the construction and transport industries. Non-white male immigrants earn the highest wage in public sector employment while Pakistanis receive the lowest wage, among non-whites, irrespective of being native or foreign-born.

Sources of disadvantage and suggestions for future research
Existing work and the new results reported in this paper show that the major labour market problem for non-white males in the United Kingdom is in accessing employment rather than receiving low wages. They experience lower employment and higher unemployment rates, in comparison with white workers, even when characteristic differences have been controlled for. However, the assumption in many existing studies that discrimination is entirely to blame is questionable on theoretical grounds and in the light of recent empirical research. There are substantial differences among the various ethnic groups and between native-born and foreign-born members of the same ethnic group. In addition, there are wide variations in the employment and unemployment experience of non-white immigrants according to the country of birth. By contrast, the earnings of non-white males are more homogeneous and compare more favourably with white native men.

Interestingly, white foreign-born men are rewarded substantially, in terms of both employment and earnings, for the education and experience that they have acquired prior to immigration. Evidently the quality of the schooling they have received and the relevance of the labour market skills they have acquired make their human capital highly transferable to the United Kingdom labour market. In addition, the fact that most of these immigrants are fluent in the English language makes their human capital operational. By contrast, non-white immigrants receive little or no reward for their foreign educational qualifications and labour market skills. This may be because lack of language fluency reduces their productivity. Recent immigrants are significantly less likely to be employed regardless of ethnicity. However, this disadvantage is more severe and persists for much longer among non-whites.

There are some interesting differences in the labour market performance of non-white native-born and foreign-born men which are overlooked by studies focusing solely on ethnic differences. In particular, while non-white immigrants are concentrated in the lower occupational categories, non-white natives have an occupational distribution which closely mirrors that of white native-born men. Both groups experience similar employment rates but non-white natives receive much greater rewards for education gained in the United Kingdom than do non-white immigrants (and even white native males). Furthermore, regardless of country of birth, it is evident that Pakistanis and Bangladeshis fare worst in the labour market, both in terms of employment and earnings whereas Indians compare very favourably with whites. Differences in English language fluency are the most likely explanation.

Indeed, the role that English language fluency plays in immigrant labour market performance is probably the most important area for future work. Extensive analysis of the PSI data has investigated the determinants of English language fluency and its impact on employment and earnings for Black Caribbean and South Asian immigrants in the United Kingdom. The results suggest a large reward for language fluency in the United Kingdom labour market. Shields and Wheatley Price (2001) find that fluency is associated with a 20-30 per cent increase in employment probability compared with a similar individual with poor English speaking ability. Once employed both Shields and Wheatley Price (2002) and Dustmann and Fabbri (2003) find that fluent employees enjoy a 10–20 per cent wage advantage over non-fluent workers (see Blackaby et al. 2001 and Leslie and Lindley 2001 for additional evidence.

A second important area for study concerns the reasons behind the differences in labour market performance among the different ethnic minority groups. The separation of education and experience measures into pre- and post-migration human capital may be crucial in assessing what disadvantage may be due to differing characteristics and what may be attributable to discrimination. The performance of white Irish and EU nationality immigrants would also be an interesting and informative area for future research. In particular, the causes and consequences of return migration may become apparent if comparable datasets (e.g. Labour Force Surveys) are available in these countries. The results of such studies would be invaluable for the formation of future immigration policy in the United Kingdom.

In addition, for all these groups, other aspects of labour market activity have yet to be thoroughly investigated. For example, labour force participation, occupational distribution, self-employment, job tenure, job search activity, unemployment duration, promotion, training, sickness, absenteeism, and the take-up of social security benefits could all be examined with existing data sources. As more Quarterly Labour Force Surveys of the United Kingdom become available, further investigation of these issues will be possible, together with a more detailed study of the early years after immigration, which would shed much light on the immigrant adjustment process.

5.6. The Impact of International Migration

What have been the effects on the UK economy of the trends in international migration? Although immigration has been a controversial issue, its effects on the economy have been the subject of surprisingly little research. As a result, few comparisons can be drawn with the studies of the labour market impacts, particularly on wages and employment, that have been conducted for the United States and some European countries such as Germany. Some studies of the impact of migration focus on its effect, through altering the rate of labour force growth, on wages, capital intensity, sectoral change and per capita income using neoclassical general equilibrium models. Others concentrate on the direct labour market effects of the changing composition of the labour force as a result of migration, raising the following questions. Do immigrants and natives complement one another in production? Do immigrants compete directly with and displace natives in certain segments of the labour market? How does migration change the overall balance of human capital in the economy? There are also a range of other issues: short-term macroeconomic effects on demand and supply, impacts on the balance of payments, and effects on the government budget through differential tax contributions and benefit claims. For useful surveys of these possible impacts, see Greenwood and McDowell (1986, 1994), Borjas (1994, 1999), and on Britain, see Baines (1998).

There have been a number of recent studies of the effects of net emigration from Britain in the late nineteenth century. In the absence of international migration from 1870 the labour force in 1911 would have been 16 per cent larger than it actually was. The general equilibrium effect of this drain of labour was to raise the real wage of unskilled labour by 12.2 per cent by 1911 (O'Rourke et al. 1994). In the case of Ireland, which was still part of the UK at that time, the dramatic outflows from 1851 onwards had the effect of raising the wage by as much as 30 per cent above what it would otherwise have been in 1911 (Boyer et al. 1994). But there are two qualifications to these results. First, if capital is allowed to be internationally mobile then slower labour force growth as a result of emigration would tend to lower the marginal productivity of capital and induce capital outflows (or reduce the inflow). In the presence of capital mobility the wage effect for Great Britain in 1911 would be reduced to 6.6 per cent and for Ireland it would fall even further, to about 11 per cent. Second, these simple general equilibrium models do not distinguish different types of labour so that there is no scope for complementarity effects between migrants and those they left behind.

We do not have comparable studies for the more recent period but the potential effects seem likely to have been much smaller. Between 1951 and 1991 the UK population increased by a modest 15 per cent. Depending on the method of calculation up to half this increase can be accounted for by immigration.[49] Since a larger share of immigrants than of the receiving population are of working age their short-term impact on the labour force would be greater than the impact on population growth (see Table 5.2 above and Baines 1998: 21). But it seems more appropriate to evaluate the effects of *net* migration rather than of immigration alone. As Table 5.9 shows, in the 1960s and 1970s net immigration provided a small but increasing offset to the (declining) rate of natural increase. From 1981 net immigration accounted for between a third and a half of total population growth. Over the whole 35-year period the net contribution was close to zero. It also seems unlikely that effects on the age structure of the population have been very important since the demographic profile of immigrants and emigrants are rather similar. For both groups the proportion of males slightly exceeds that of females and about three-quarters of both

---

[49] One reason for this is that immigrants and particularly those from the NCW countries have higher birthrates (and therefore contribute more to population growth) than the indigenous population—although this difference is diminishing with the second and third generations. It has been estimated that by the mid-1980s about two-thirds of the growth in the ethnic minority population was due to net immigration and a third due to natural increase (Shaw 1988).

[50] Net immigration seems likely to make a larger contribution in the future. The latest projections made by the OPCS suggest a net immigration of 65,000 per annum over the years from 1996 to 2021 which would contribute about half the projected population increase (Shaw 1998).

Table 5.9. Population change and net migration, 1961-96

Years	Population growth (000s)	Population growth (%)	Net migration (000s)	Migration share (%)
1961-66	367	0.69	−8	−2.0
1966-71	257	0.47	−56	−21.0
1971-76	58	0.10	−55	−94.8
1976-81	27	0.05	−53	−120.2
1981-86	83	0.15	+43	+51.8
1986-91	188	0.33	+60	+32.8
1991-96	199	0.34	+76	+38.2

Source: Calculated from *Population Trends* (various issues).

immigrant and emigrant flows are aged between 15 and 45. Thus on purely demographic grounds the net effect of migration was small.[50]

It might be argued that the timing of migration is more important than the numbers involved. One possibility is that offsetting movements in migration could smooth out fluctuations in the natural increase of the population or in the labour force. There is little evidence of any consistent inverse movements of this kind. More important perhaps would be the sensitivity of migration movements to the domestic business cycle. In principle, such 'guest-worker effects' could add an element of flexibility to the labour force and smooth out fluctuations in unemployment. But although net immigration is positively correlated with the business cycle the year-to-year effects of increments to the labour force are negligible compared with the magnitude of the swings in employment. More important, as illustrated in Table 5.9, the medium-term impacts were the opposite of what the guest-worker model would predict. In the 1950s and 1960s when the unemployment rate averaged less than 2 per cent there was net emigration. By contrast, in the last two decades when the unemployment rate averaged 8 per cent there was net immigration.

It is possible that net international migration helped to ease the geographical relocation of the population and the labour force in response to the changing regional pattern of demand for labour within the UK. It has been widely observed that internal migration, while moving in the right direction, is rather unresponsive to regional unemployment and wage differentials (Pissarides and McMaster 1990). There is little evidence about the effects of regional differences on immigrants' choice of destinations within the UK. But the regional distribution of immigrants changed very little over time and remained concentrated in urban centres, particularly those where employment growth slowed after 1979.[51] The first destinations of immigrants, particularly those from the New Commonwealth, tend to be determined by the location of earlier immigrants through chain migration effects, and not necessarily by economic differences between regions.[52] But even if it could be shown that immigration did not ease the process of geographic relocation this would not necessarily be the case for net migration as a whole. In the absence of opportunities to emigrate, it seems likely that the most mobile section of the population would have migrated internally instead of emigrating.

Studies of other European countries suggest that low-skilled immigrants compete directly with low-skilled natives but are complementary inputs with higher skilled labour.[53] It has sometimes been argued that, in the early postwar years of buoyant labour demand, the inflow of immigrants had a key influence in certain sectors of the economy and that they took jobs that British-born workers would have avoided. From the late 1940s to the late 1960s NCW immigrants were readily accepted (and sometimes actively recruited) to work in low-wage, low-skilled sectors and those with particularly poor or harsh working conditions.[54]

The most important examples are the Lancashire textile industry and particularly service sectors such as London Transport and the National Health Service. (Baines 1998: 15). By the 1970s more than a quarter of all hospital employees were foreign-born and the building industry was dominated by Irish immigrants. The contemporary evidence suggests that NCW immigrants were received with hostility by low-wage native-born workers in sectors such as London Transport on the grounds that (among other things) they threatened wages and working conditions and weakened union bargaining power (Brooks 1975: 328–30). We have no estimate of such effects but it seems likely that in the absence of immigrant labour

[51] See Peach (1998: 1661). One study of NCW immigrants in the 1960s found that they 'replaced about a third of the indigenous inhabitants lost from the conurbations'. But it concluded there was little evidence that immigrants disproportionately entered the most rapidy expanding sectors (Jones and Smith 1970: 55, 62–3).

[52] Muellbauer and Murphy (1988: 9) found that immigrants settling predominantly in the southeast of England had some 'displacement' effect on interregional migration from the southeast. This is similar to the impact on the westward flow of population in the United States before 1914 as immigrants from Europe settled in the eastern cities (Hatton and Williamson 1998: 168).

[53] De New and Zimmermann (1994) find for Germany in the 1980s that a one percentage point increase in immigrant labour reduced the wages of blue-collar workers by 5.9 per cent but raised the wage of white collar workers by 3.5 per cent.

[54] For West Indians, the jobs they took and the conditions they experienced are discussed in detail by Peach (1968).

supply, wages would have risen to attract larger numbers of native-born workers. There is no evidence one way or the other about whether immigrants were complementary in production with native workers with different levels or sector-specific skills.

By the 1960s it was being argued that the key shortages in the economy were of skilled, and particularly highly skilled, labour. But again the evidence for a serious brain drain is not strong. The IPS figures record an net emigration of those with professional and managerial occupations between 1968 and 1982 of 190,000 but the net outward movement of manual and clerical workers was much larger. These figures largely reflect the overall outward balance, and at least by this crude measure the skill content of immigration was greater than the skill content of emigration (see Baines 1998, Table 3). From 1983 to 1993 the net balance of both the highly skilled and the low-skilled group were close to zero. But, as was highlighted in sections 5.4 and 5.5 above, immigrants, and especially non-white immigrants, evidently gain smaller returns in terms of access to jobs and the level of earnings than do the native-born. One interpretation of these findings would be that the skills embodied in immigrants are of lower value, either as a result of discrimination or because of lack of transferability than those embodied in the emigrant outflow.

Investigations of specific highly skilled sectors also failed to point to a serious brain drain. An international study suggested that in 1959–69 there was a small net outflow of university trained scientists and engineers. But there was no evidence that the quality of the inflow was inferior to that of the outflow. There was some evidence of downward mobility among scientists and engineers which suggested that supply was growing faster than demand (Fuborg ed. 1974: 139). An evaluation of international migration among university-based scientists and engineers over the period 1984–92 found a slight rise in immigration compared with the previous decade and no change in emigration. Furthermore there was no evidence of any quality differences between immigrants and emigrants. The conclusion was that 'there has not, in numerical terms, been a major exodus (or brain drain) from UK universities to other countries' (Ringe 1993: 63).

Among low-skilled workers, conditions in the labour market have deteriorated since the 1970s (see Nickell and Bell 1995). Structural shifts in the economy and technological change have reduced the demand for unskilled labour. While the allocation of work permits and leave to remain should have restricted the inflow of unskilled workers and those without pre-arranged jobs, its effects have been limited. Whereas immigrants in the 1950s and 1960s found it relatively easy to move into jobs, conditions in the last two decades have made this much harder. As we have seen from the analysis in sections 5.4 and 5.5 above, employment rates are especially low and unemployment rates especially high for the most recent immigrants. And these disadvantages are particularly marked for non-whites. But the important finding is that, in terms of employment, unemployment, and wage outcomes, immigrants very rapidly improve their labour market status. For non-white immigrants unemployment rates are halved in the first five to ten years and white immigrants also experience declining unemployment incidence with length of residence. The results for earnings also point in the same direction although not for non-white immigrants. Thus although lack of skills, or lack of transferable skills, put immigrants at an initial disadvantage and therefore provide limited economic benefit, the evident labour market mismatch is largely a temporary phenomenon.

Conclusion

In this survey of Britain's experience with international migration we have touched on a variety of aspects and we have drawn on a number of different literatures. Over the last half century, international migration has evolved from its traditional pattern of emigration to the white settler economies with the significant addition of immigration from NCW countries towards the present, increasingly diverse, pattern of immigration and emigration. While the bulk of migration is driven by economic incentives, the free flow of labour has been mediated or distorted by growing policy intervention. But, as we have emphasized, immigration policies have not been closely linked to labour market conditions or to economic considerations in general. They have been driven almost entirely by fears of deteriorating race relations and consequently have become inextricably linked with domestic race relations policy.

In our outline of the growth and structure of the ethnic minority population we drew attention both to its growth (despite increasingly restrictive immigration policy) and to the economic status of ethnic minorities. One of the key indicators is education and it is worth emphasising the rising educational levels of the ethnic minority population and in particular the strong drive to high standards of education among the second and subsequent generations. In considering education and labour market performance it is important to distinguish between immigrants and ethnic minorities and our presentation of recent research on labour market outcomes amply demonstrates this. Previous research has often interpreted labour market disadvantage as reflecting discrimination but the results presented above suggest that, in part, this disadvantage reflects the assimilation process whereby immigrants improve their labour market status with length of residence. Nevertheless, significant disadvantages remain, especially for non-whites (whether first or second generation) which are not accounted for by education, experience, or assimilation effects.

The final point we have briefly touched on is arguably the most important issue from an economic perspective but is the least studied: the impact of migration on the labour market and the economy as a whole. Here it is important to distinguish between the impact of immigration (which has most often been the focus of attention) and the net impact of immigration and emigration taken together. Given its overall magnitude and composition, the impact of immigration seems at most to have been modest—probably negative for workers in some low-skilled sectors of the economy but possibly positive in other respects. The overall impact of net migration to and from Britain would seem to have been smaller still. On any reckoning it seems likely that the social and political impacts of migration (especially immigration) vastly outweigh any conceivable economic effects.

REFERENCES

Anwar, M. (1986). *Race and Politics* (London: Tavistock).

Bailey, J. (1992). 'International Migration', *Population Trends*, **67**: 29–42.

Baines, D. E. (1998). 'Immigration and economic growth in Britain since 1945', unpublished paper London School of Economics.

Behrman, J. R. and Wolfe, B. L. (1984). 'Labor force participation and earnings determinants for women in the special conditions of developing countries', *Journal of Development Economics*, **15**: 259–88.

Bell, B. D. (1997). 'The performance of immigrants in the United Kingdom: evidence from the GHS', *Economic Journal*, **107**: 333–44.

Blackaby, D. H. (1986). 'An analysis of the male racial earnings differential in the UK using the general household survey', *Applied Economics*, **18**: 1233–42.

—, Clark, K., Leslie, D. G., and Murphy, P. D. (1994). 'Black–White Male Earnings and Employment Prospects in the 1970s and 1980s', *Economics Letters*, **46**: 273–9.

— (1995). 'The changing distribution of black and white earnings and the ethnic wage gap: evidence for Britain', *Department of Economics Discussion Paper*, 95-107 (Swansea: University of Wales).

—, Drinkwater, S., Leslie, D. G., and Murphy, P. D. (1997). 'A picture of male and female unemployment among Britain's Ethnic Minorities', *Scottish Journal of Political Economy*, **44**: 182–97.

— (1999). 'Explaining racial variations in unemployment rates in Britain', *The Manchester School*, **97**: 1-20.

—, Leslie, D. G., Murphy, P. D. and O'Leary, N. C. (1997). 'Differences in white and non-white hourly earnings in the 1970s and 1980s: a manual/ non-manual perspective', *Department of Economic Discussion Paper*, 97-104 (Swansea: University of Wales).

— (1998). 'The ethnic wage gap and employment differentials in the 1990s: evidence for Britain', *Economics Letters*, **58**: 97-103.

—, O'Leary, N. C., Murphy, P. D., and Drinkwater, S. (2001). 'English language fluency and the ethnic wage gap for men in England and Wales', *Economic Issues*, **6**: 21-32.

Borjas, G. J. (1985). 'Assimilation, changes in cohort quality, and the earnings of immigrants', *Journal of Labor Economics*, **3**: 463-89.

— (1987). 'Self-selection and the earnings of immigrants', *American Economic Review*, **77**: 531-53.

— (1994). 'The economics of immigration', *Journal of Economic Literature*, **32**: 1667-717.

— (1999). *Heaven's Door: Immigration Policy and the American Economy*, (Princeton, NJ: Princeton University Press).

Brown, C. (1984). *Black and White Britain: The Third PSI survey* (London: Policy Studies Institute).

Boyer, G. R., Hatton, T. J., and O'Rourke, K. (1994). 'The impact of emigration on real wages in Ireland, 1950-14', in T. J. Hatton and J. G. Williamson (eds.) *Migration and the International Labor Market, 1850-1939*, (London: Routledge).

Brooks, D. (1975). *Race and Labour in London Transport* (London: Oxford University Press).

Chiswick, B. R. (1978). 'The effect of Americanisation on the earnings of foreign-born men', *Journal of Political Economy*, **86**: 897-921.

— (1980). 'The earnings of white and coloured male immigrants in Britain', *Economica*, **47**: 81-7.

— (1982). 'The employment of immigrants in the United States', in Fellner, W. (ed.) *Contemporary Economic Problems 1982* (Washington DC: American Enterprise Institute).

—, Cohen, Y. and Zach, T. (1997). 'The labor market status of immigrants: effects of the unemployment rate at arrival and duration of Residence', *Industrial and Labor Relations Review*, **50**: 289-303.

— and Miller, P. W. (1995). 'Endogeneity between language and earnings: international analyses', *Journal of Labor Economics*, **13**: 246-88.

— and Hurst, M. E. (1998). 'The employment, unemployment and unemployment compensation benefits of immigrants', *Research in Employment Policy*, **2**.

Clark, K. and Drinkwater, S. (1998). 'Ethnicity and self-employment in Britain', *Oxford Bulletin of Economics and Statistics*, **60**: 383-407.

Clark, K. (2000). 'Pushed out of pulled in? Ethnic minority self-employment in England and Wales', *Labour Economics*, 7: 603–28.

Coleman, D. A. (1994). 'The United Kingdom and international migration: a changing balance', in H. Fassman and R. Münz (eds.) *European Migration in the Late Twentieth Century: Historical Patterns, Actual Trends and Social Implications* (Luxemburg, Austria: Edward Elgar).

—— and Salt, J. (1992). *The British Population: Patterns, Trends and Processes* (Oxford: Oxford University Press).

Daniel, W. W. (1968). *Racial Discrimination in Britain: Based on the PEP Report* (London: Penguin Books).

De New, J. and Zimmermann, K. F. (1994). 'Native wage impacts of foreign labour: a random effects panel analysis', *Journal of Population Economics*, 7: 177–92.

Dex, S. (1986). 'Earnings differentials of second generation West Indian and white school leavers in Britain', *Manchester School*, 54: 162–79.

Dobson, J., Koser, K., Mclaughlan, G., and Salt, J. (2001). *International Migration and the United Kingdom: Recent Patterns and Trends*, RDS Occasional Paper No. 75 (London: Home Office).

Dustmann, C. and Fabbri, F. (2003). 'Language proficiency and the labour market performance of immigrants in the United Kingdom', *Economic Journal*, 113: 695–717.

Fitzgerald, M. (1998). 'Race and the criminal justice system', in T. Blackstone, B. Parekh, and P. Sanders (eds.) *Race Relations in Britain: A Developing Agenda* (London: Routledge).

Fuborg, G. (ed.) (1974). *Brain Drain Statistics* (Stockholm: Committee on Research Economics, FEK).

Garvey, D. (1985). 'The history of migration flows in the Republic of Ireland', *Population Trends*, 39: 22–30.

Gazioglu, S. (1994). 'Assimilation: compensating differences and job disamenities by using life-cycle adjusted income', *International Review of Applied Economics*, 8: 157–73.

—— (1996). 'English language proficiency and the earnings of the Turkish and Bangladeshi immigrants in London', in S. Gazioglu (ed.) *Migrants in the European Labour Market* (Aberdeen: J-Net).

Greenwood, M. J. and McDowell, J. M. (1986). 'The factor market consequences of U.S. immigration', *Journal of Economic Literature*, 24: 1738–72.

—— (1994). 'The national labor market consequences of U.S. immigration', in H. Giersch (ed.) *Economic Aspects of International Migration* (Berlin: Springer-Verlag).

Hansen, R. (2000). *Citizenship and Immigration in Postwar Britain* (Oxford: Oxford University Press).

Hatton, T. J. (1995). 'A model of UK emigration, 1870–1913', *Review of Economics and Statistics*, 77: 407–15.

— (2001). 'Why has UK net immigration increased?' Unpublished paper, University of Essex.

— and Williamson, J. G. (1993). 'After the famine: emigration from Ireland, 1850–1913', *Journal of Economic History*, 53: 575–600.

— (1998). *The Age of Mass Migration: An Economic Analysis* (New York: Oxford University Press).

Heckman, J. J. (1976). 'The common structure of statistical models of truncation, sample selection and limited dependent variables and a simple estimator for such models', *The Annals of Economic and Social Measurement*, 5: 472–92.

— (1979). 'Sample selection bias as a specification error', *Econometrica*, 47: 153–61.

Howard, C. (1993). 'United Kingdom II: immigration and the law', in D. Kabat (ed.) *The Politics of Migration Policies: Settlement and Integration; The First World in the 1990s* (2nd edn) (New York: Center for Migration Studies).

Jones, C. (1977). *Immigration and Social Policy in Britain* (London: Tavistock).

Jones, K. and Smith, A. D. (1970). *The Economic Impact of Commonwealth Immigration* (London: Cambridge University Press).

Jones, T. (1993). *Britain's Ethnic Minorities: An Analysis of the Labour Force Survey* (London: Policy Studies Institute).

Kay, D. and Miles, R. (1992). *Refugees or Migrant Workers: European Volunteer Workers in Britain, 1946–1951* (London: Routledge).

Layton-Henry, Z. (1984). *The Politics of Race in Britain* (London: George Allen and Unwin).

— (1992). *The Politics of Immigration* (Oxford: Blackwell).

Leslie, D. and Drinkwater, S. (1999). 'Staying on in full-time education: reasons for higher participation rates among ethnic minority males and females', *Economica*, 66: 63–77.

—, Drinkwater, S., and O'Leary, N. C. (1998). 'Unemployment and earnings among Britain's ethnic minorities: some signs for optimism', *Journal of Ethnic and Migration Studies*, 24: 489–506.

— and Lindley, J. (2001). 'The impact of language ability on the employment and earnings of Britain's ethnic communities', *Economica*, 68: 587–606.

Mackay, D. (1996). 'The earnings determinants of immigrants and the native born in the UK labour market', *Department of Economics Discussion Paper*, 96-17 (University of Aberdeen).

Mason, D. (1995). *Race and Ethnicity in Modern Britain* (Oxford: Oxford University Press).

Massey, D. S. (1988). 'Economic development and international migration in comparative perspective', *Population and Development Review*, 14: 383–413.

Mayhew, K. and Rosewell, B. (1978). 'Immigrants and occupational crowding in Great Britain', *Oxford Bulletin of Economics and Statistics*, 40: 223–48.

McCormick, B. (1986). 'Evidence about the comparative earnings of Asian and West Indian workers in Great Britain', *Scottish Journal of Political Economy*, 33: 97–110.

McNabb, R. and Psacharopoulos, G. (1981). 'Racial earnings differentials in the U.K.', *Oxford Economic Papers*, 33: 413–25.

Metcalf, H., Modood, T., and Virdee, S. (1996). *Asian Self Employment* (London: Policy Studies Institute).

Muellbauer, J. and Murphy, A. (1988). 'UK house prices and migration: economic and investment implications', Shearson Lehman Hutton UK Economics Series (Oxford).

Modood, T. and Berthoud, R. (1997). *Ethnic Minorities in Britain* (London: Policy Studies Institute).

Nickell, S. J. (1980). 'A picture of male unemployment in Britain', *Economic Journal*, 90: 776–94.

— and Bell, B. D. (1995). 'The collapse in the demand for the unskilled and unemployment across the OECD', *Oxford Review of Economic Policy*, 11:40–62.

Oaxaca, R. (1973). 'Male–Female wage differentials in urban labour markets', *International Economic Review*, 14: 693–709.

OPCS (various issues), International migration, London: Office of Population, Censuses and Surveys.

O'Rourke, K., Williamson, J. G., and Hatton, T. J. (1994). 'Mass migration, commodity market integration and wage convergence: the late nineteenth century Atlantic economy', in Hatton, T. J. and Williamson, J. G. (eds.) *Migration and the International Labor Market, 1850–1913* (London: Routledge).

Paul, K. (1997). *Whitewashing Britain: Race and Citizenship in Postwar Britain* (London: Cornell University Press).

Peach, C. (1968). *West Indian Migration to Britain: A Social Geography* (Oxford: Oxford University Press).

— (1978). 'British unemployment cycles and West Indian immigration', *New Community*, 7: 40–3.

— (1998). 'South Asian and Caribbean ethnic minority housing choice in Britain', *Urban Studies*, 35: 1657–80.

Pissarides, C. and McMaster, I. (1990). 'Regional migration, wages and unemployment: empirical evidence and implications for policy', *Oxford Economic Papers*, 42: 812–31.

Pudney, S. and Shields, M. A. (2000). 'Gender, race, pay and promotion in the British nursing profession: estimation of a generalised ordered probit model', *Journal of Applied Econometrics*, 15: 367–99.

Rees, T. (1993). 'United Kingdom I: inheriting the empire's people', in Kabat D. (ed.), *The Politics of Migration Policies: Settlement and Integration; The First World in the 1990s*, 2nd edn. (New York: Center for Migration Studies).

Ringe, M. J. (1993). *The Migration of Scientists and Engineers, 1984–1992*, SEPSU Policy Study No. 8 (London: Royal Society and Royal Academy of Engineers).

Salt, J. (1995). 'Foreign workers in the United Kingdom: evidence from the labour force survey', *Employment Gazette*, 103: 11–19.

Shaw, C. (1988). 'Components of growth in the ethnic minority population', *Population Trends*, 52: 26–30.

— (1998). '1996 Based national population projections for the UK and constituent countries', *Population Trends*, 91.

Shields, M. A. and Wheatley Price, S. (1998). 'The earnings of male immigrants in England: evidence from the quarterly LFS', *Applied Economics*, 30: 1157–68.

— (1999*a*). 'Ethnic differences in British employer-funded on and off-the job training', *Applied Economics Letters*, 6: 421–9.

— (1999*b*). 'Ethnic differences in incidence and determinants of employer-funded training in Britain', *Scottish Journal of Political Economy*, 46: 523–51.

— (2001). 'Language fluency and employment prospects: evidence from Britain's ethnic minorities', *Applied Economics Letters*, 8: 741–5.

— (2002). 'The English language fluency and occupational success of ethnic minority immigrant men living in English Metropolitan areas', *Journal of Population Economics*, 15: 137–60.

Skellington, R. (1996). *'Race' in Britain Today*, 2nd edn. (London: Open University Press).

Sly, F. (1994). 'Ethnic groups and the labour market', *Employment Gazette*, 102: 147–59.

— (1995). 'Ethnic groups and the labour market: analyses from the Spring 1994 labour force Survey', *Employment Gazette*, 103: 251–61.

— (1996). 'Ethnic minority participation in the labour market: trends from the labour force surveys 1984–1995', *Labour Market Trends*, 259–70.

— Price, A., and Risdon, A. (1997). 'Trends in labour market participation of ethnic groups: 1984–1996', *Labour Market Trends*, 295–302.

Smith, D. J. (1977). *Racial Disadvantage in Britain: The PEP Report* (London: Penguin Books).

Spencer, I. R. G. (1997). *British immigration policy since 1939: Making of a Multi-Racial Britain* (London: Routledge).

Spencer, S. (1996). 'The implications of immigration policy for race relations', in Spencer, S. (ed.), *Strangers and Citizens: A Positive Approach to Migrants and Refugees* (London: Rivers Oram Press).

— (1998). 'The impact of immigration policy on race relations', in Blackstone, T., Parekh, B., and Sanders, P. (eds.) *Race Relations in Britain: A Developing Agenda* (London: Routledge).

Stewart, M. B. (1983). 'Racial discrimination and occupational attainment in Britain', *Economic Journal*, 93: 521–41.

Tunali, I. (1986). 'A general structure for models of double-selection and an application to a joint migration / earnings process with remigration', *Research in Labor Economics*, 8: 235–82.

Virdee, S. (1995). *Racial Violence and Harassment* (London: Policy Studies Institute).

Wheatley Price, S. (1998*a*). 'The employment adjustment of male immigrants in England', *Discussion Paper in Public Sector Economics*, 98/9 (Leicester: University of Leicester).

—— (1998*b*). 'The unemployment experience of male immigrants in England', *Discussion Paper in Public Sector Economics*, 98/10 (Leicester: University of Leicester).

—— (2001*a*). 'The employment adjustment of male immigrants in England', *Journal of Population Economics*, 14: 193–220.

—— (2001*b*). 'The unemployment experience of male immigrants in England', *Applied Economics*, 33: 201–15.

Woolford, C. (1994). 'Irish nationals in the British labour market', *Employment Gazette*, 102: 29–31.

6. The Netherlands: Old Emigrants—Young Immigrant Country

Jan C. van Ours and Justus Veenman

6.1. Introduction

In the course of the twentieth century the Netherlands changed from an emigrant to an immigrant country. After the Second World War in terms of immigration there are three distinct periods. The first period is characterized by the decolonization of Indonesia, as a consequence of which Moluccans and Dutch-Indonesian people came to the Netherlands. The second period is that of manpower recruitment, during which mainly Turks and Moroccans arrived. In this period the independence of Surinam also caused a large immigration. The final period of immigration is mainly connected to family re-unification and to (political) refugees and asylum seekers.

Now, at the beginning of the new millennium about 2.7 million people live in the Netherlands, who by their own birthplace or that of at least one of their parents are considered to be immigrants. Altogether they comprise approximately 17 per cent of the Dutch population of about 16 million. As counted in 1999 the largest groups of immigrants are the Turks (300,000), the Surinamese (297,000), the Moroccans (250,000), the Antilleans (99,000) and the people from (former) Yugoslavia (63,000). Those from the southern European countries comprise about 85,000 people, who have different nationalities. Even more diversity of nationality is found among the political refugees, who comprise about 180,000 persons. As far as immigrants are concerned we focus on Turks, Moroccans, Surinamese, and Antilleans.

On average, the labour market position of immigrant workers is not as strong as that of native Dutch workers. The immigration of the past decades originates from two rather different processes. The decolonization caused peaks in immigration in specific years while the hiring of immigrant workers—because of cyclical labour shortages—turned out to have a structural character. Current labour market problems are to some extent related to the shift in immigration from a business cycle phenomenon to a structural process. In the 1960s immigrant workers were hired because the Dutch labour market was booming. The immigrant workers got jobs in industries with low-paid labour. Since these industries were particularly hit by the economic recession of the 1980s, many immigrant workers lost their jobs to become long-term unemployed.

After a period of high unemployment in the early 1980s and a mild decline in the late 1980s, the Netherlands is among the few European countries that experienced a rapid decline of unemployment in the past few years. Whereas in the beginning of the 1990s the unemployment rate went up from 6.9 per cent in 1990 to 8.1 per cent in 1995, it went down at the end of the last decade, to 3.8 per cent in 2000. As we will describe in more detail below, unemployment rates of immigrant workers went down as well. However, since the level of the unemployment rates of immigrant workers is far above that of native Dutch workers, we think that there is still a need for specific labour market policies which target immigrant workers.

In this paper we give an overview of migration with a focus on immigration. We discuss immigration policy, the socioeconomic position of immigrants and the consequences of immigration for the Dutch labour market and labour market policy. The paper is set up as follows. In section 6.2 we give the stylized facts of population growth, migration and migration policies. In section 6.3 we describe the labour market position of immigrants in terms of education, earnings, employment, unemployment and mobility. In section 6.4 we discuss immigration policy, the economic effects of immigration and integration policies. Due to changing circumstances, the focus of government policy has changed substantially over time. Section 6.5 concludes.

6.2. Migration: Stylized Facts

6.2.1. Population Growth and Migration (1900–2000)

To put migration in perspective with respect to the population growth in the Netherlands we first discuss the evolution of the birth surplus. Table 6.1 presents an overview of population growth and migration in the Netherlands in the twentieth century. We distinguish four subperiods. The first period, pre-Second World War, has about the same annual number of births of approximately 180,000 as the last period, from 1976 onwards.

Table 6.1. Population growth and migration in the Netherlands, 1900–2000
(1,000 persons/year)

	1900–40	1946–63	1964–75	1976–2000
Births	174	241	225	187
Deaths	80	83	106	126
Birth surplus	94	158	119	61
Immigration	39	53	83	99
Emigration	38	60	60	60
Immigration surplus	1	−7	23	39
Population growth	95	151	142	101
Migration	406	474	637	585

Source: Netherlands Central Bureau of Statistics.

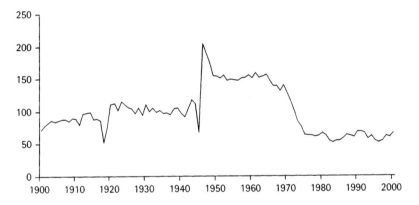

Figure 6.1. Birth-surplus in the Netherlands, 1900–2000 (1,000 persons)
Source: Netherlands Central Bureau of Statistics

The second period, from the end of the Second World War to the mid-sixties, has the highest annual number of births, with 240,000 about 35 per cent higher than the amount of the first and the last period. The period from mid-sixties to mid-seventies has an annual number of births of 225,000. With respect to the annual number of deaths there is not much change over time. Before the Second World War this number is smaller than thereafter, but this has to do with the much smaller population.

The annual birth surplus in the first decades after the Second World War is more than twice as high as the annual birth surplus before the war. After that, the birth surplus declines rapidly until, in the last two decades, it is just a little less than 40 per cent of the postwar decades. Figure 6.1 illustrates the evolution of the annual birth surplus over the century. There are clearly two dips during both world wars and there is a definite post-Second-World War baby boom in 1946. Probably the most striking elements of Figure 6.1 are the sudden major changes in the birth surpluses with a quite constant level before and after the change. The birth surplus before and after the Second World War is constant, but with a big difference in level. The high birth surplus of the 1950s and 1960s changes in a few years to a substantially lower level in the second half of the 1970s, the 1980s and the 1990s.

With respect to immigration, Table 6.1 shows that over time there is a gradual increase, while for emigration after the Second World War there is a steady level of about 60,000 per year. This combination causes the annual emigration surplus of 7,000 in the first decades after the Second World War to turn into an annual immigration surplus of 39,000 in the past two decades. Figure 6.2 shows there is an upward trend in the immigration surplus from 1960 onwards. The dips in this upward trend coincide with the periods of recession in the early 1980s and the early 1990s.

All in all, the demographic developments have caused the Dutch population growth to decrease from about 150,000 per year after the Second World War to about 100,000 per year in the past decades. Whereas the first number is fully due to a net birth surplus, 40 per cent of the latter number is due to an immigration surplus.

Migration within the Netherlands is somewhat higher after the Second World War than it was before, and substantially higher from the mid-sixties onward. Since then every year an average of about 600,000 families move from one municipality to the other.

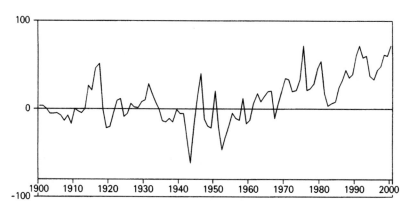

Figure 6.2. Immigration surplus in the Netherlands, 1900–2000 (1,000 persons)
Source: Netherlands Central Bureau of Statistics

6.2.2. Dutch Colonies Independence (1946–63)

Like many other European countries the Dutch colonies gained independence in the decades after the Second World War. In 1946, a first wave of about 70,000 immigrants came from Indonesia to the Netherlands, followed by a somewhat smaller second wave of 60,000 in 1950 after Indonesia became independent. A third wave of 40,000 immigrants came from Indonesia after this country nationalized its firms, many of which were until then owned by Dutchmen. Apart from Dutch people returning to the Netherlands, there are also many indigenous people from the colonies, especially Moluccans who served in the Dutch colonial army and who leave their home country. Figure 6.3 shows the evolution of the immigration from Indonesia over time.

6.2.3. Manpower Recruitment (1964–75)

After a period of modest economic growth in the 1950s, the Dutch economy booms in the 1960s, causing shortages in the labour market. The policy of the Dutch government and Dutch employers was to recruit workers from Mediterranean countries, especially Morocco and Turkey. Figure 6.4 shows the evolution of the immigration from these two countries. Heijke (1986 and 1987a) estimated an immigration equation on the basis of a cross-section of countries for the year 1974. He finds that immigration is positively influenced by the size of employment in the country of destination, the size of the population between 15 and 65 years in the country of origin, and the difference in income per head between the country of origin and the country of destination. The geographical distance between the country of origin and the country of destination negatively influences

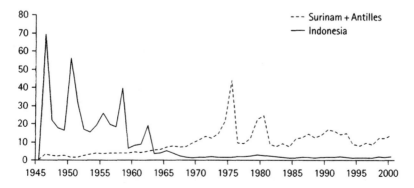

Figure 6.3. Immigration from former Dutch colonies, 1945–2000 (1,000 persons)
Source: Netherlands Central Bureau of Statistics

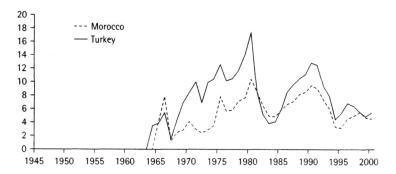

Figure 6.4. Immigration from Morocco and Turkey, 1945–2000 (1,000 persons)
Source: Netherlands Central Bureau of Statistics

immigration. According to Heijke in the 1960s it was hard to fill vacancies for unskilled workers due to the expansion of the Dutch economy. Heijke (1986 and 1987a) presents the results of a cross-section regression for Dutch industries in the year 1975. He finds that the percentage of immigrant workers from Mediterranean countries was higher in industries with a lower growth-rate, a higher percentage of unskilled workers, noisy working conditions and irregular working hours. So, immigrants are concentrated in low growth industries and have jobs with disamenities. As shown in Figure 6.3, in 1975 there was also a large immigration of about 40,000 people from Surinam, which became independent from the Netherlands in that year.

6.2.4. Chain Migration and Asylum Seekers (1976–2000)

Since the mid-1970s immigration is characterized by an additional inflow of people from Surinam in 1979–80 and people coming from Morocco and Turkey. Family re-unification and family formation increasingly determine the latter immigration. From Figure 6.4 it appears that there is a big decline of immigration from Morocco and Turkey in the early 1980s and an increase afterwards. The dip in immigration from these countries coincides completely with a sharp increase in Dutch unemployment in the early 1980s and a decrease in the second half of the 1980s. A recent phenomenon is the inflow of (political) refugees and asylum seekers.

6.2.5. Evaluation

In the first decades after the Second World War there is roughly a balance between immigration and emigration despite the large inflow of Dutch and (Dutch-)Indonesian people coming from Indonesia. Since the early 1960s there is an immigration surplus, mainly because of manpower recruitment in Mediterranean countries, people immigrating because of the independence of Surinam, and later on, family re-unification/formation. Part of the immigration is caused by external shocks. This also applies to the present immigration of political refugees. Part of the immigration is due to explicit policy because of labour market shortages in the 1960s.

There have been a few attempts to explain immigration and emigration using time series information on an aggregate level. Hartog and Vriend (1989) use annual data from the period 1948–79 and find that emigration is negatively influenced by the real national income per head. Heijke (1987b) did a similar time series analysis for the period 1948–85. He finds that the per capita net national product negatively influences emigration flows from the Netherlands. Hartog and Vriend (1989) find that immigration is affected negatively by the Dutch unemployment rate and positively by the real national income per head. So, there is a clear indication of economic variables driving emigration and immigration. The inflow of immigrant workers in the 1960s at the time was considered to be temporary. Of the first immigration wave (1960–7), annually about 30 per cent of the immigrant workers residing in the Netherlands returned to their country of origin. In the period 1967–72 this return migration percentage fell to 15 per cent, and thereafter, there was hardly any return migration (Hartog and Vriend 1989). Employers were actively recruiting immigrant workers, especially to fill vacancies for unskilled jobs. According to Hartog and Vriend (1989) hiring immigrant workers was a rational short-run strategy of Dutch employers, since it was much cheaper than paying higher wages for unskilled Dutch workers.

6.3. Immigrants in the Dutch Labour Market

6.3.1. Recent Developments in the Dutch Labour Market

Since the mid 1990s unemployment in Europe has slowly declined. The Netherlands is among the few European countries that experienced a rapid decline of unemployment in the past few years. As Table 6.2 shows, the registered unemployment rate went down from 8.1 per cent in 1995 to 3.8 per cent in 2000. Another frequently used indicator to characterize the usage of labour is the nonemployment rate, the share of the population that has no job. Whereas the unemployment rate is sensitive to government influence with respect to the classification of nonemployed, the nonemployment rate is not. The average nonemployment rate in the

Table 6.2. Unemployment rates (unemployed as per cent of labour force) and non-employment rates (employed as per cent of working age population)

	Unemployment rates			Non-employment rates		
	1990	1995	2000	1990	1995	2000
Total	6.9	8.1	3.8	44.8	42.2	35.5
Male	4.6	6.2	2.7	28.9	28.4	23.1
Female	10.9	11.1	5.4	61.2	56.5	48.1

Source: Ministry of Social Affairs and Employment, *Sociale Nota*, Tables 5.3 and 5.4.

Netherlands went down from 42.2 per cent in 1995 to 35.5 per cent in 2000. Although there are differences between males and females, the general pattern in the recent developments is the same. For males, unemployment went down from 6.2 per cent in 1995 to 2.7 per cent in 2000, for females these numbers are 11.1 per cent and 5.4 per cent respectively. The non-employment rate of males went down from 28.4 per cent in 1995 to 23.1 per cent in 2000, for females the decline was from 56.5 per cent in 1995 to 48.1 per cent in 2000.

Nickell and Van Ours (2000) indicate that the improvement of the labour market in the Netherlands originates from general policy measures and macroeconomic events. First, unions in the Netherlands have been very co-operative and they operate within a highly co-ordinated wage bargaining system. Second, the Dutch labour market is characterized by a large number of part-time jobs. These part-time jobs allow flexibility for both employers and employees and have enabled a rapid build up of female employment. Third, the gradual restructuring of the benefit system in the Netherlands has helped to reduce unemployment. In the course of the 1980s and 1990s benefits have been reduced and work test has been made stricter. As a complement to this, active labour market policies targeted on the long-term unemployed have been introduced.

As will be clear in the sections below where we describe the position of immigrant workers in the Dutch labour market, the labour market position is not equally good for every group.

6.3.2. Education

To compare the educational achievements of immigrants and native Dutch, one can use several indicators from examination performances in primary education, to the age at the end of this education, to the dropout rates in secondary education. All of these indicators give the same negative answer to the question of whether immigrants have educational achievements equivalent to those of the native Dutch. We shall use two indicators as an example: the educational qualifications of the population of working age; and the educational attainment of young people who are partly still at school.

The first column of Table 6.3 shows the average educational attainment of the population of working age (15–64 years). These averages are based on a five-level scale of education:

 0 = No education
 1 = Primary education
 2 = Lower secondary education (vocational or general)
 3 = Intermediate education (vocational, GCSE and A-levels)
 4 = Higher education (vocational and university)

As shown, the average educational level of the Turks is a bit above 1, while the average level for Moroccans is below 1, indicating that there are many Moroccans without even primary education. The average educational level of the two Caribbean groups is above 2, natives have an average level of about 2.6. Thus, although the Caribbean groups have higher educational qualifications than the Turks and Moroccans, they still lag behind the native Dutch. In each minority group women lag behind men as far as educational achievements are concerned. A higher percentage of women are on the lower educational levels, a lower percentage on the higher levels, although the differences are small among the Antilleans. They show more equality among men and women, just as among the native Dutch.

Given the majority in numbers that the first generation has in most of the immigrant groups, the aforementioned figures especially concern this generation, in particular the older people. This makes it interesting to describe the educational attainment of young people separately.

Table 6.3. Average educational attainment by immigrant status, 1998

	Age 15–64 years	Age 15–29 years
Turkish	1.31	1.83
Moroccans	0.98	1.72
Surinamese	2.16	2.30
Antilleans	2.21	2.42
Natives	2.63	2.80

Source: Van Ours and Veenman (2003), Tables 1 and 2, based on ISEO, Survey social position ethnic minorities, 1998.

As the second column of Table 6.3 shows, the educational levels of young people are higher than those of their parents. This is true of all groups including natives. It does not alter the fact that minority youths still lag behind their native peers. Neither does it change the pattern: Antilleans most closely approximate to Dutch education levels while the Turks and Moroccans are the most disadvantaged. Again, women lag behind men in all minority groups, with the greatest differences among the Surinamese and Antilleans.

Empirical research shows that several factors are of special significance in explaining differences in educational achievements. These factors are migration characteristics, socioeconomic status, cultural aspects, and school factors. Migration characteristics are connected with language problems of immigrants, their restricted knowledge of Dutch society in general and the formal educational system in particular, and also with the moment an individual arrives in the Netherlands. Young people, who do not participate in the Dutch educational system from the first year on, appear to have a difficult time 'catching up' at school. Many of them also have great difficulty in acquiring the Dutch language, which obstructs learning. But even those immigrants who speak Dutch well and are familiar with the school system still tend to lag behind the native Dutch.

A recent study by Van Ours and Veenman (2003) concludes that differences in the educational level of the parents are an important determinant of the difference in educational attainment of minority children and native Dutch children. Second generation minority children are worse off because their parents on average have a lower level of education. If these differences are taken into account the differences between second generation minority children and native Dutch children vanish to a large extent. This does not mean that the gap will close automatically. Educational decisions are also determined by factors such as language proficiency, social contacts, schooling ambitions, career planning, and orientation on return migration. Finally, there are strong indications that many schools are not really effective in combatting the educational arrears of minority children. Recent policy reforms are directed at improving the quality of these schools, by spending more money on them and by providing them with better equipment and facilities.

It is noteworthy that the aforementioned factors may explain the differences in educational achievement between immigrants and native Dutch, as well as those between the various immigrant groups. Turks and Moroccans, who lag behind most, have the lowest socioeconomic status, the 'largest cultural' distance, and the least acquaintance with Dutch society and the Dutch language (since Surinam and the Antilles are (former) Dutch colonies with the same educational system as in the Netherlands). Because of their residential distribution, Turks and Moroccans furthermore have the highest concentration in urban schools in the older centres of the largest Dutch cities, which may well be another harmful factor. Cultural aspects and possibly school factors are relevant for the explanation of the arrears of women compared with men among the immigrants.

6.3.3. Earnings

Netherlands' complex tax and subsidy system makes disposable income the best way to compare the *earnings* of individuals and groups. The 1998 survey of Turks, Moroccans, Surinamese, Antilleans, and native Dutch contains questions on net monthly income. The native Dutch enjoy the highest income level; their average disposable income is 3,510 Dutch guilders a month (1 Dutch guilder = 0.454 Euro). The average minority household has a monthly income of about 80 per cent of the Dutch average Surinamese (87 per cent), Turks (78 per cent), Antilleans (76 per cent), and Moroccans (68 per cent). Since the various groups differ widely with respect to family structure, it is interesting to compare the income of a household consisting of two adults and 1–2 children. Again, the Native Dutch enjoy the highest income level: 4,660 Dutch guilders a month. Turkish household now has a monthly income of not more than 61 per cent of the Dutch average, while for Moroccans this is 55 per cent and for the two Caribbean groups 87 per cent.

Labour income is the most important source of income for all groups, be it more for the native Dutch than for the immigrant groups. Although there are some differences in the level of support that various groups receive from the government when they are not working (induced by factors such as work history, family size, and family structure), minority groups do not appear to be in a disadvantageous position with respect to government assistance. Because minorities are more likely to have larger families and/or be part of a lone-parent household than native Dutch households, they are likely to qualify for relatively generous income support. Nevertheless, the average minority household has only about 50 per cent of the Dutch disposable income. This makes it all the more important to explain differences in labour income.

To explore the factors related to earnings differences, the labour income of heads of households working at least thirty hours a week were regressed on educational level, occupation, whether or not the job was a supervisory position, work experience, age, and the length of time in the Netherlands. These factors explain 98 per cent of the difference in earnings between native Dutch and Turkish, 87 per cent of the difference between Surinamese and Dutch, 81 per cent of the difference between Antilleans and Dutch, and 78 per cent of the difference between Moroccans and Dutch. These findings suggest that differences in human capital and in occupation explain most wage differences.

Kee (1993) investigated the labour market position of male household heads that directly emigrated from Turkey, Morocco, Surinam, or the Antilles to the Netherlands. He finds that the education of Turkish and Moroccans in their home country has no effect on their wages in the Netherlands. For immigrants from Surinam and the Antilles there is a positive effect of education in the home country on the wage in the Netherlands. Obviously, the educational system in the latter two countries has more resemblance to the Dutch educational system. Therefore, skills are more easily transferred. Kee (1993) also finds that the main contributor to differences in wages between immigrants and native Dutch workers is the difference in schooling acquired in the Netherlands. Differences in language abilities are another important determinant of differences in wages. In fact, in wage equations the number of years elapsed since migration has no longer a statistically significant effect once language skills are introduced as an explanatory variable. Hartog and Vriend (1990) investigated the labour market position of young Turkish and Moroccans who were older than twelve years at the time of arrival in the Netherlands. They find that in terms of earnings functions there is no difference between young Mediterraneans and young Dutch.

6.3.4. Employment and Unemployment

The *labour market participation* of ethnic minorities lags behind that of the native Dutch, as is shown in Table 6.4. This is partly due to differences in age structure, although this factor can hardly explain the large differences between the Turks and Moroccans on the one hand and the native Dutch on the other. Table 6.4 indicates that the labour market participation of most of the groups has increased in the period 1995–2000. Labour market participation of native Dutch went up from 63 to 67 per cent, especially because of a substantial increase in female labour force participation. Labour market participation of Turkish and Surinamese had an even bigger increase, also because of a strong growth of female labour force

Table 6.4. Labour market participation (as a percentage of population) and unemployment rate (as a percentage of total labour force) by immigrant status (15–65 years)

	Participation		Unemployment	
	1995	2000	1995	2000
Turkish	43	49	31	9
Moroccans	43	40	32	13
Surinamese	61	69	19	9
Antilleans	57	60	23	–
Native Dutch	64	69	7	3
Total	63	67	8	4

Source: Ministry of Social Affairs and Employment, Sociale Nota, Tables 5.3 and 5.4.

participation. Only the Moroccans had a decline in labour force participation over the period 1995–2000.

Given the educational differences mentioned earlier, one would expect certain minority groups to be especially disadvantaged in the labour market. Table 6.4 shows that *unemployment rates* (based on registration at the Employment Office) among minorities are several times as high as among the native Dutch. The pattern in 1995 is clear: Moroccans and Turks have the highest unemployment rates, while Antilleans and Surinamese still have higher rates than the native Dutch. As is the case with the unemployment rates of the native Dutch, the unemployment rate of all minority groups declined since 1994. In percentage-points the decline for all ethnic minority groups is even larger than that of native Dutch. The unemployment rates among Turks went down from 31 per cent in 1995 to 9 per cent in 2000, while among Moroccans the unemployment rate went down from 32 per cent in 1995 to 13 per cent in 2000. Also among Surinamese the decline in unemployment rate is substantial.

In distinct contrast to the situation among the native Dutch, for some minorities, men have higher unemployment rates than women. This does not necessarily mean that women have a better labour market position, since there are indications that their lower unemployment rate is related to their acceptance of low-level jobs. The decline in unemployment rate is most strikingly the case for Moroccan women, which might be due to the large increase of part-time jobs in the lower segments of the Dutch labour market. Women more than men benefit from this (Dagevos 1995). We add that among all ethnic groups, men have a higher percentage of long-term unemployed than women do. This is probably due to 'discouragement

Table 6.5. Job levels of employed workers by immigrant status, 1998

	Elementary jobs	Lower jobs	Intermediate jobs	Higher jobs	Scientific jobs	Total
Turkish	28	46	19	6	1	100
Moroccans	33	42	19	5	1	100
Surinamese	14	36	33	12	4	100
Antilleans	12	34	34	14	7	100
Native Dutch	6	27	33	24	9	100

Source: Martens (1999), Table 5.6, based on ISEO, Survey social position ethnic minorities, 1998.

effects', which may affect women more strongly than men, as a consequence of which women withdraw sooner from the labour market when their unemployment seems lasting.

The disadvantageous position of ethnic minorities in the Dutch labour market also appears from data on the *workers' position*. They more often have temporary instead of permanent jobs compared with the native Dutch; they have less job promotion opportunities and a lower quality of labour. Besides, there is a significant difference in job levels as is shown in Table 6.5. The pattern is well known: a high percentage of the Turks and Moroccans are on the lower job levels and a low percentage on the higher levels. The opposite holds true for the native Dutch, while the Surinamese and Antilleans are in between. It comes as no surprise that the data on wages shows much the same pattern (see section 6.1). The pattern described just now applies to women as well as to men, although Moroccan women distinguish themselves by a very high percentage on the lowest job levels. Antillean women most closely approximate to the pattern of the Dutch women.

6.3.5. General Explanations of Ethnic Minority Unemployment

The disadvantageous labour market position of ethnic minorities in the Netherlands, and especially their high unemployment rates, have been explained by several factors, from labour demand, to supply characteristics, to institutional aspects. With regard to labour demand, the relevance of general demand factors has been pointed out—such as slackening aggregate demand, and industry and occupation shifts—, as well as the selection practices of Dutch employers. Worker quality and reservation wages, in addition to social integration are considered to be relevant supply characteristics. Institutional factors such as labour market policies and the functioning of the Employment Office may also have some influence.

The essence of the aggregate demand explanation is that the supply of minority labour is at the back of an imaginary hiring queue, which implies that when aggregate demand decreases, the minority supply is disproportionately left without a job (see Thurow 1975). This hypothesis gains empirical support by the fact that there was indeed a slackening demand in the Netherlands, while at the same time ethnic minorities were disproportionately affected by unemployment (Dagevos 1995). What remains to be explained, is why ethnic minorities are at the end of the queue. We will turn to this question when we elaborate on supply characteristics.

The second type of demand-side explanation is a 'mismatch'-theory which posits that the minority unemployment problem is not (or not only) that of being last in line, but (also) of being in the wrong place on the labour market. The argument is that ethnic minorities are attached to particular industries, jobs or occupations, and that labour demand in these industries has decreased disproportionately. Analyses of the recent Dutch recessions have shown that some industries and jobs were affected more than others, while minority workers (even the younger ones) were concentrated in most of these market segments (Veenman 1998). This tallies with the theory, but a full explanation according to this theory requires an account of the immobility of negatively affected minority workers. Cultural factors and tradition may be at work here, but the attachment to certain labour market segments may also be due to little access to other segments. This leads us to a discussion of the selection practices of Dutch employers as well as to the relevance of a 'skills mismatch' hypothesis.

Explanations of massive minority unemployment that emphasise the importance of selection practices of Dutch employers, generally point to one of two phenomena: (a) direct racial discrimination, in the sense of Beckers' concept 'taste for discrimination', and (b) indirect, unconscious discrimination, in many cases a consequence of ethnocentrism (Veenman 1990). Whatever the exact reason of the discrimination may be, it is always to the immediate disadvantage of ethnic minorities since it limits access to (attractive) jobs; in other words: it sends ethnic minorities (further) back in the hiring queue. Empirical studies have concentrated much attention on finding out if labour market discrimination actually exists in the Netherlands, and in most cases the answer is in the affirmative (e.g. Bovenkerk 1977; Bovenkerk et al. 1995; Veenman 1990, 1995). For example, Beckers' decomposition method was used to indicate the degree to which discrimination actually determines the unemployment rates of minority groups (Niesing and Veenman 1990). However, the results are inconclusive about the exact degree, although several studies indicate that discrimination may have significant influence on minority unemployment.

The first supply-side explanation for massive minority unemployment emphasises that ethnic minorities generally have inadequate qualifications, and at the same time cling to reservation wages that impede them in finding a job (Niesing et al. 1994). This explanation finds some support in covariant data on educational achievements and language proficiency. In addition, it was shown that the reservation wages of ethnic minorities indeed have a negative influence on their employment opportunities, just as the theory predicts. From this we can conclude that the theory is also significant for the explanation of high minority unemployment, although multivariate analysis indicates that the educational level together with occupational identification, gender, age, and the regional labour market conditions explain only one-third of the difference between unemployment rates of the native Dutch and the respective minority groups (Niesing and Veenman 1990).

In terms of the Human–Capital theory, the former explanation involves 'economic capital'. Another supply-side explanation concerns—as the French sociologist Bourdieu puts it—'social capital' and 'cultural capital'. The essence is that ethnic minorities are not integrated (enough) into Dutch society, which implies (a) that they lack access to important social networks, and (b) that they are too oriented towards their own group and too little towards the Dutch social surroundings. This would impede success on the Dutch labour market. In a study on successful ethnic minorities, it was found that some immigrants who have an advantageous labour market position (high job level, high income), are not at all oriented towards the Dutch social surroundings (Merens and Veenman 1992). This at least means that social integration is not a necessary condition to find a job. Which, of course, is not to say that social integration might not help in acquiring an advantageous labour market position.

The analysis of minority unemployment in terms of institutional factors emphasises context variables rather than sheer labour market phenomena. Labour market policies in particular are discussed. For example, the disproportionate deterioration of the ethnic minority unemployment in the early 1980s has been explained by the fact that the Employment Office pursued a policy that was highly geared towards the preferences of employers. Although a rational choice (from the point of view of the Employment Office) in times of massive general unemployment, this policy has been to the benefit of those who are first in the hiring queue and to the disadvantage of those at the back.

We underline that the explanations mentioned above do not have the same significance for the different ethnic minority groups in the Netherlands. While using the aggregate demand theory, for example, we should not expect all ethnic minority groups to be at the same disadvantageous place in the hiring queue: some are better off than others are, because of higher worker quality and/or a higher degree of social integration. At the same time, such supply characteristics influence the selection practices of Dutch employers. This corresponds to the empirical findings that some groups are less wanted than others, mostly because of greater cultural differences (Veenman 1995). Furthermore, some groups more than others are attached to particular industries, jobs or occupations, which makes them more vulnerable to a decrease in unemployment in those sectors. And finally, policy measures (such as affirmative action) did not work out the same for the different minority groups. These are all reasons to say that the theories mentioned have a different significance for the explanation of unemployment in various minority groups, and probably also for minority men and women. In other words: these theories are more capable of explaining social diversity than sheer social deprivation among ethnic minorities.

6.3.6. Job and Geographical Mobility

In his dissertation Dagevos (1998) concludes that ethnic minority workers are restricted in their mobility because they have unfavourable labour market characteristics and because they are working in less favourable segments of labour organizations. At the moment the available data on *job mobility* of ethnic minorities are restricted to internal mobility and job stability, which are only two aspects of the more general phenomenon of job mobility. As far as internal mobility is concerned, we confine ourselves to three elements, analysed by Niesing (1993): (a) participation in courses to improve upward internal mobility; (b) actual internal promotions, and (c) expected promotional opportunities.

Contrary to the Surinamese and Antilleans, only a small proportion of the first generation Turks and Moroccans have taken courses to improve their opportunities for internal mobility. In this respect there is not much difference between the Surinamese, the Antilleans, and the native Dutch.

Turks and Moroccans have been promoted less frequently, and also expect fewer promotional opportunities, than the Surinamese and Antilleans who differ less from native Dutch workers in this respect. For ethnic minority workers problems with language proficiency decrease the probability of having been promoted, where as this probability increases with tenure on the job, more education, and age (that is to say up to middle age). For the native Dutch the probability of having been promoted depends more on personal characteristics than for the ethnic minorities. Therefore, it seems that the latter have been promoted more randomly than the Native Dutch, or due to factors not observed. For the Dutch, but even more so for ethnic minority workers, expectations of having promotional opportunities are affected positively and significantly by having been promoted. These expectations furthermore increase with education and age (again, up to a certain age), while they decrease with tenure.

As far as job stability is concerned, it was found that on average the native Dutch have filled a larger number of jobs than the ethnic minorities. Of the male Dutch workers, 40 per cent have filled more than 3 jobs, while this figure is 24 per cent for the Surinamese, 27 per cent for the Turks and Antilleans, and 36 per cent for the Moroccans. This is partly due to the fact that the Dutch have been longer present in the labour market than the ethnic minorities. Those Dutch who have had many jobs usually have a low degree of education, and frequently fill jobs at low job levels. In this sense they are comparable with ethnic minority workers with an unstable jobs.

There is not much information available on *geographical mobility* of ethnic minorities in the Netherlands. What is known, is that between 1986 and 1990 half of the ethnic minority households moved house versus one-third of the other households. In the period between 1990 and 1994, almost half of the Turkish and Moroccan households moved house and less than 30 per cent of the other households did. The Surinamese and Antilleans are in-between. The larger number of moves among ethnic minorities is partly due to a larger number of starters on the housing market, which is associated with the on average younger age of ethnic minorities. On the other hand, ethnic minorities are in general less satisfied with their home and therefore more inclined to move house independent of age (Van Dugteren 1993).

6.4. Immigration and Integration Policies

6.4.1. Immigration Policy

The Netherlands has one of the highest population densities in the world. Because of this and also to facilitate postwar rebuilding of the country, successive Dutch governments tried to encourage emigration.

Nevertheless, the Netherlands became an immigration country because of the influx of immigrant workers in the 1960s and beginning of the 1970s, and also because of the ongoing influx of people from (former) Dutch colonies and, more recently, of political refugees. Furthermore, chain migration in the form of family reunification and family formation among the second generation of immigrants adds to the fact that the Netherlands nowadays is an immigration country. Nevertheless, admission to the country is rather limited. Dutch citizens (among them the Antilleans who have Dutch citizenship) and other EU-citizens are free to move into the Dutch labour market. This freedom is denied to citizens of non-EU-countries. Who have limited possibilities to (temporarily) settle in the Netherlands. Examples of those who have such possibilities are: (a) labour migrants with a temporary labour permit according to the Law on Foreign Workers; (b) minor family members or partners of a native Dutch or legally settled non-Dutch person; (c) political refugees or asylum seekers; and (d) students who mostly come on the basis of bilateral treaties. Asylum seekers do not have access to the Dutch labour market during the period in which Dutch government has to decide on their status.

Nonetheless, the need for immigrant labour did not disappear after the recruitment of workers in Mediterranean countries stopped in 1973. This need for foreign labour was met mainly by immigrants arriving from Surinam in the years immediately before and after the independence of this former colony in 1975 and by immigrants from Turkey and Morocco admitted for family reunification. The liberal admission of those family members to the labour market is in sharp contrast with the persistent exclusion of asylum seekers from legal employment. The sole form of temporary employment of immigrant workers actively supported by the government was the secondment of Yugoslav workers from the 1960s until 1991. Since 1994 a gradual liberalization of the admission of foreign workers in seasonal jobs can be observed. This policy development coincided and was influenced to a large extent by the liberalization of the political regime in Poland and, after 1988, in the rest of Eastern Europe (Groenendijk and Hampsink 1995).

In a recent report, the Netherlands Scientific Council for Government Policy (WRR 2001) concludes that the Netherlands have become an immigration country. The council stresses that it is important that young immigrants and immigrant children get well educated with a focus on language skills. Furthermore the council indicates the important of increasing labour market participation among immigrant groups.

6.4.2. The Economic Effects of Immigration

There are no published studies which consider the overall effects of emigration and immigration on the Dutch economy. In an internal paper from the Dutch Ministry of Well-being, Health and Culture (Sociaal en Cultureel Planbureau (1988)), some estimates are presented with respect to the use by immigrants of government budgets such as education, and unemployment benefits. However, this exercise was never published. There is a study by the Dutch Centraal Planbureau (Bernardt 1993) that presents information about the use of the social security system by ethnic minorities and their contribution to the Dutch economy. However, there is no estimate of the overall effects. The Dutch Centraal Planbureau has made different scenarios for the future of the world economy from 1990 to 2015. The economic consequences of immigration depend heavily on the economic developments. In the case of a low growth economy the future will bring unemployment for a lot of immigrants. In the case of a high-growth economy, immigrants are expected to integrate more into the Dutch labour market. The differences in the labour market position are related to the type of immigrants that are expected to come to the Netherlands. In the low growth scenario most of the immigrants will come from poor countries, while in the high growth scenario most immigrants will come from other rich countries. A study by a consultant group (KPMG 1994) has similar conclusions with respect to the importance of economic growth on the labour market position of immigrants. As a reaction to discussions in Germany about immigration policy as an instrument to balance the ageing of the population there was a similar debate in the Netherlands. Since the Dutch demographic structure is very different from Germany increased immigration is not considered as an option in this respect.

6.4.3. Integration Policy

The Dutch policy with respect to immigrants changed over time, as the interpretation of immigration flows changed. Until the mid-1970s, immigrants, especially those hired for labour market reasons in the 1960s, were expected to return to their home country. It was the arrival of large numbers of Surinamese in the mid-1970s that caused a change in attitude. The initial policy towards immigrants was based on the idea that ethnic minorities should have the opportunity to participate fully in Dutch society but would not be asked to diverge too much from their own culture. This would enable the immigrants to return to their country of origin if they desired. Early 1980s there was a growing awareness that most immigrants did not return to their home country but stayed in the Netherlands. This shifted the focus of government policy to the integration of immigrants into Dutch society. The main ways to advance this integration were: (1) further the emancipation and participation of ethnic minorities in Dutch society; (2) prevent discrimination; and (3) diminish social and economic differences. Discrimination was legally prohibited, and laws were enacted to give minorities more equality and protection in such areas as suffrage and civil service employment. However, most emphasis was placed on the third goal of diminishing social and economic inequality, and the government became more concerned with ensuring equal access to the benefits of the welfare state. It was in this period that specific measures were chosen to achieve the goals of the integration policy.

In reaction to political developments (a growing support for right-wing movements in the larger cities) and as a consequence of cost-calculations, the Dutch government gradually abandoned the strategy of special targeted policies, in favour of emphasizing universal, general policies. From that moment on, special programmes for minorities were intended to supplement general policy measures. When in the early 1990s the Dutch government realized that migrants not only stayed in the Netherlands, but also kept coming, it started to emphasize policies oriented towards settling in newcomers in the Dutch society. Although these are by their character specific policies, the main idea remained that ethnic minorities had to profit from general policy measures.

6.5. Conclusions

Ethnic minorities in the Netherlands have a disadvantaged socioeconomic position. Data on educational achievements, labour market position, income and housing illustrates their relatively unfavourable situation. Migration characteristics, connected with language problems of immigrants and their restricted knowledge of the receiving society, help explain this situation. This implies that next generations, the children and grandchildren of those who are the true migrants, will have better chances to integrate into Dutch society. Nevertheless, migration characteristics are not the only relevant explanatory variables. As far as the ethnic minority groups themselves are concerned, cultural aspects, less functional social networks, and human capital factors add to the explanation. Furthermore, Dutch society seems to also contain some strong impediments to the improvement of the socioeconomic position of ethnic minorities.

One may wonder whether these impediments have a temporary character, and therefore might be seen as an anomaly in a modern, meritocratic society. In this view, Dutch society being a 'young' immigrant country, needs some time to adapt itself to the presence of relatively large numbers of migrants and their descendants.

To take a position in the discussion on the most effective labour market policy, we recall that the most important lesson from Dutch labour market research seems to be that there is no simple, monocausal explanation for the disadvantaged position of ethnic minorities. In recent years the labour market in the Netherlands has improved substantially. Labour market participation rates are rising and unemployment rates are declining. In this respect ethnic minority groups are not different from native Dutch workers. However for some minority groups participation is still low and for all minority groups unemployment rates are substantially higher that those of native Dutch workers. The policy implication of this finding is that an improvement of the labour market position of ethnic minorities can not be accomplished by general measures alone.

References
(In parentheses the translation of the Dutch titles)

Bernardt, Y. (1993). 'Migratie en de allochtone beroepsbevolking van Nederland, 1990–2015' (Migration and the immigrant labour force of the Netherlands, 1990–2015), *Research Memorandum* 100 (Den Haag: Centraal Planbureau).

Bovenkerk, F. (1977). 'Rasdiscriminatie op de Amsterdamse arbeidsmarkt' (Racial discrimination in the Amsterdam labour market), in J. J. van Hoof and A. Martens (eds.), *Arbeidsmarkt en ongelijkheid (Labour market and social inequality)* (Meppel: Boom, 58–76).

—, Gras, M. J. I., and Ramsoedh, D. (1995). 'Discrimination against migrant workers and ethnic minorities in access to employment in the Netherlands', *International Migration Papers*, 4, Employment Department, Geneve: International Labour Office.

Dagevos, J. M. (1995). *De rafelrand van de arbeidsmarkt (The Loose Ends of the Labour Market)* (Amsterdam: Boom).

— (1998). 'Begrensde mobiliteit; over allochtone werkenden in Nederland' (Restricted mobility, working ethnic minorities in the Netherlands), dissertation Erasmus University Rotterdam.

Groenendijk, K. and Hampsink, R. (1995). *Temporary Employment of Migrants in Europe*, (Nijmegen: University of Nijmegen).

Hartog, J. and Vriend, N. (1989). 'Post-war international labour mobility: the Netherlands', in I. Gordon and A. P. Thirlwall (eds.), *European Factor Mobility, Trends and Consequences* (London: Macmillan, 74–94).

— (1990). 'Young Mediterraneans in the Dutch labour market: a comparative analysis of allocation and earnings', *Oxford Economic Papers*, 42: 379–401.

Heijke, J. A. M. (1986). *Migratie van Mediterranen: economie en arbeidsmarkt (Migration of Mediterraneans: Economy and Labour Market)* (Leiden/Antwerpen: Stenfert Kroese).

— (1987a). 'The labour market position of migrants in selected European receiving countries', in *The Future of Migration* (Paris: OECD).

— (1987b). 'Internationale migratie en bevolkingsstructuur' (International migration and the structure of population), in *Demografische veranderingen en economische ontwikkelingen (Demographic changes and economic development)*, Preadviezen van de Koninklijke Nederlandse Vereniging voor de Staatshuishoudkunde (Leiden/Antwerpen: Stenfert Kroese), 125–56.

Kee, P. (1993). 'The Economic Status of Male Immigrants in the Netherlands', dissertation University of Amsterdam.

KPMG/Bureau voor Economische Argumentatie (1994). *De economische betekenis van minderheden voor de arbeidsmarkt (The Economic Contribution of Minorities to the Labour Market)*, (Hoofddorp).

Martens, E. P. (1999). *Minderheden in beeld (Minorities in Focus)* (Rotterdam: ISEO).

—, Roelandt, Th., and Veenman, J. (1991). 'Ethnic minority children in Dutch education: ethnic stratification, social class and migration', *Netherlands' Journal of Social Sciences*, 27: 92–108.

Merens, J. G. F. and. Veenman, J. (1992). *Succes en falen bij allochtonen (Success and failure among ethnic minorities)*, Den Haag: Organisation for Strategic Labour Market Research (OSA).

Nickell, S. J. and van Ours, J. C. (2000). 'The Netherlands and the United Kingdom: A European Unemployment Miracle?', *Economic Policy*, 30: 137–75.

Niesing, W. (1993). 'The Labour Market Position of Ethnic Minorities in the Netherlands', dissertation Rotterdam: Erasmus University Rotterdam.

—, van Praag, B. M. S., and Veenman, J. (1994). 'The unemployment of ethnic minority groups in the Netherlands', *Journal of Econometrics*, 61: 173–96.

— and Veenman, J. (1990). 'Achterstand en achterstelling op de arbeidsmarkt' (Deficits and discrimination in the labour market), in Veenman, J. (ed.), *Ver van Huis. Achterstand en achterstelling bij allochtonen (Far from Home, Deficits Among and Discrimination Towards Ethnic Minorities)* (Groningen: Wolters-Noordhoff), 41–69.

Sociaal en Cultureel Planbureau (1988). Kosten van de aanwezigheid van etnische groepen in de periode 1987–2000 (Costs of the presence of ethnic groups in the period 1987–2000), Internal paper Rijswijk: Ministry of Well-being, Health and Culture.

Thurow, L. C. (1975). *Generating Inequality* (New York: Basic Books).

Van Dugteren, F. (1993). *Woonsituatie minderheden, Achtergronden en ontwik-kelingen 1982–1990 en vooruitzichten voor de jaren negentig (Housing Conditions Among Ethnic Minorities, Backgrounds and Developments 1982–1990 and Prospects for the Nineties)* (Rijswijk: VUGA).

Van Ours, J. C. and Veenman, J. (2003). 'The educational attainment of second generation immigrants in The Netherlands', *Journal of Population Economics*, 16: 739–54.

Veenman, J. (1990). *De arbeidsmarktpositie van allochtonen in Nederland, in het bijzonder van Molukkers (The Labour Market Position of Ethnic Minorities, Particularly Moluccans)* (Groningen: Wolters-Noordhoff).

— (1995). *Onbekend maakt onbemind, Selectie van allochtonen op de arbeidsmarkt (Unknown and Unloved: The Selection of Ethnic Minorities in the Labour Market)* (Assen: Van Gorcum).

— (1998). *Buitenspel, Over langdurige werkloosheid onder etnische minderheden (Offside, A Treatise on Long-Term Unemployment Among Ethnic Minorities)* (Assen: Van Gorcum).

Wetenschappelijke Raad voor het Regeringsbeleid (2001). *Nederland als immigra-tiesamenleving (Netherlands as immigration society)* (The Hague: Staatsuitgeverij).

7. German Migration: Development, Assimilation, and Labour Market Effects

Thomas Bauer, Barbara Dietz, Klaus F. Zimmermann, and Eric Zwintz

7.1. Introduction

In 2001, for the first time in German legal history, the Federal Government had introduced a comprehensive immigration bill that contained a visible economic element. This ended a period of decades, where Germany was seen against all empirical evidence as 'no immigration country'. After years of political standstill, it seemed as if Germany was about to experience a sea change in migration policy at precisely a time when other nations were contemplating further restrictions on immigration in the face of international terrorism. After nearly four years of negotiations, the German government and the opposition agreed upon a new immigration law, which passed the German Federal Council in July 2004. The law allows legal immigration of workers only in the case of highly qualified foreigners, such as engineers, computer specialists, and scientists. In addition, self-employed people who offer a certain number of jobs to natives will be allowed to immigrate, and the law makes it easier for responsible officials to deport hate preachers and terror suspects.

This is related to two aspects of the German labour market, which are currently characterized by two seemingly contradicting trends. On the one hand, employers have for a number of years complained about an insufficient supply of skilled labour. On the other hand, German unemployment has remained high and was even increasing again recently. High unemployment when skilled labour seems to be short suggests co-ordination deficiencies in the labour market. There is excess demand for skilled workers and a falling need for low-skilled people. A large number of the less qualified or wrongly qualified job seekers are unfit for employment in the professions in which labour supply is short and will remain unfit and unemployed even in the long run. This characterizes not only the situation in Germany, but also in other European countries.

The situation is much different and significantly more complex than the situation in the 1960s, when the German economy was operating under conditions of full employment and blue-collar immigrants were badly needed to keep businesses running. The worries about the costs and benefits of migration have created demands for research into the economics of the process. What have been the migration flows into Germany over the last decades and how were they related to economic conditions? What type of systematic migration policies have been undertaken? How well did the immigrants assimilate or integrate into the German economic system? How were natives affected by the new members of the labour force? These questions fit well in the standard research programme of migration economists. Zimmermann and Bauer (2002) have documented the major research output in this area, which contains many important findings for Germany. Faini, de Melo and Zimmermann (1999) and Brücker et al. (2002) have recently collected international evidence on these issues in a European setting. Bauer et al. (2000) deal with the important issue of natives' sentiments about migrants.

It is the purpose of this chapter to provide a coherent picture of the major facts and a systematic summary of the relevant research findings in the German context. The review is divided into three general parts: (i) migration statistics and policies; (ii) assimilation and integration issues; and (iii) the effects on the natives. Section 7.2 deals with migration to Germany since the Second World War. After an overview, this part identifies and documents the situation in four phases: war adjustment; manpower recruitment; consolidation; and the aftermath of socialism. It ends with a subsection on internal German migration. It will become clear that Germany always has been a major immigration country, although the labour market consequences of this fact have been persistently ignored.

Section 7.3 covers the major research issues from the economic assimilation literature: Do migrant earnings adjust to the levels of comparative natives? What is the employment, unemployment and self-employment experience of immigrants? How is job and geographical mobility? Finally it is of interest to what extent migrants take up benefits of the welfare state and whether their contributions outperform the take-up. All in all, there is no strong assimilation evidence in the body of research for Germany.

Section 7.4 then studies the native labour market effects. Most evidence deals with the consequences for native wages. According to economic theory they depend on the type of interactions of migrant work with the qualifications of workers from the home country. Even more of policy relevance are the potential consequences for native employment, which has been the second important topic of research. Perhaps surprisingly for an outside observer, but consistently with the international evidence, there is no substantial evidence that migrants have threatened natives on the labour market at a relevant level. Section 7.5 ends the chapter with conclusions.

7.2. Migration to Germany since the Second World War

7.2.1. Overview

The German classification of migrants differs significantly from that in the United States. American statistics only distinguish between foreign-born (immigrants, refugees) and native individuals. German statistics differentiate between various groups of immigrants: foreign workers, refugees, and asylum seekers on the one hand, and immigrants of German descent or former citizenship on the other. The main distinction between these immigration groups is their citizenship status. Foreign workers, refugees, and asylum seekers do not receive German citizenship easily, and their right to migrate to Germany is subject to regulation.

Immigrants of German descent or former citizenship can be separated into 'Übersiedler' and 'Aussiedler'. 'Übersiedler' are Germans from the former German Democratic Republic (GDR) who left their home country to live permanently in the Federal Republic of Germany. This type of migrant ceased to exist upon German reunification in 1990. Aussiedler are ethnic German immigrants from Central and Eastern Europe (CEEC), whose immigration to the Federal Republic of Germany is legitimized by the postwar German constitution (Basic Law, paragraph 116). Because ethnic Germans had suffered as subjects of revenge for the aggressions of Nazi Germany during and after the Second World War, they are allowed to immigrate to Germany and are granted German citizenship (Kurthen 1995). This privileged acceptance has its roots in the German citizenship regulation, which gives priority to the criteria of descent (Jus sanguinis). (See Bauer (1998), Bauer and Zimmermann (1997a), and Velling (1995) for a description of the institutional regulations regarding the immigration of the different groups of migrants.) From other viewpoints such as social and cultural differences or integration, however, all migrant groups share a lot of commonalities. Depending on their place of origin, differences in language knowledge and cultural tradition can be substantial. Schmidt and Zimmermann (1992) even argue that Germans originating from the CEECs might find it more difficult to integrate into the German labour market than workers from fairly industrialized market economies in Southern Europe.

According to Schmidt and Zimmermann (1992), four phases of migration streams to Germany can be differentiated: war adjustment (1945-54), manpower recruitment (1955-73), consolidation or restrained migration

(1974–88), and the dissolution of socialism and its aftermath (since 1988). The overall immigration and emigration flows in Germany since the Second World War are displayed in Figure 7.1. A detailed breakdown of migration statistics for further reference are given in Table 7.1, where the migration streams for foreigners, Germans, ethnic Germans and asylum seekers for the different periods are provided.

In the period of war adjustment, 11.5 million Germans left the eastern part of Europe; 8 million went to the Federal Republic of Germany (Schmidt and Zimmermann 1992). After expulsion and forced migration had come to an end, there were an estimated four million ethnic Germans still living in CEECs (mainly Poland, Romania, and the former Soviet Union, see Harmsen 1983). Some of them already tried to move to Germany in the 1950s but because of the restrictive emigration policies by the countries of origin and the ongoing political tensions between their home countries and Germany, very few ethnic Germans were allowed to leave. The low emigration figures of ethnic Germans in that period can be further explained by the emigration policy of the CEECs, which allowed emigration only on the basis of family reunification. Between 1950 and the construction of the Berlin Wall in 1961, about 2.6 million Germans moved from East to West Germany.

The second phase (1955–73) can be seen as a period of labour migration. Like some other European countries such as France, Germany faced a shortage of low-skilled labour, which induced the establishment of an active recruitment policy. Between 1955 and 1968 recruitment offices of German firms were opened in several South-European countries, soon

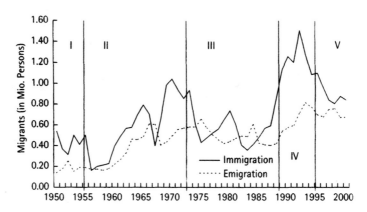

Figure 7.1. Immigration and emigration, 1950–2000 (in 1,000)
Source: Statistisches Bundesamt, Fachserie Gebiet und Bevölkerung, several volumes (I: War Adjustment, II: Manpower recruitment, III: Consolidation, IV/V: Aftermath of Socialism).

Table 7.1. Immigration and emigration, 1950–2001 (in 1,000)

Year	Foreigners[1]			Germans[2]			Total			Ethnic Germans	Asylum Seekers
	In	Out	Net	In	Out	Net	In	Out	Net		
War adjustment											
1950	91	38	53	60	80	−20	151	118	33	47	−
1951	94	41	53	60	82	−23	154	123	31	21	−
1952	95	43	53	61	80	−19	156	123	33	4	−
1953	99	46	53	60	84	−23	159	130	29	8	−
1954	100	44	56	57	85	−27	157	129	28	10	−
Manpower recruitment											
1955	60	36	24	68	101	−34	128	137	−9	13	−
1956	82	48	34	76	120	−43	158	168	−9	25	−
1957	107	59	48	93	114	−21	200	173	27	108	−
1958	118	64	54	94	98	−4	212	162	51	130	−
1959	146	81	65	82	98	−17	227	179	49	27	−
1960	317	124	193	77	94	−17	395	218	176	18	−
1961	411	182	230	78	85	−7	489	267	223	16	−
1962	495	248	247	72	79	−7	566	327	240	16	−
1963	506	384	122	71	79	−7	577	463	114	15	−
1964	625	371	254	73	86	−13	698	457	241	20	−
1965	716	413	303	76	77	−1	792	490	302	24	−
1966	632	535	97	70	74	−4	702	609	934	28	−
1967	330	528	−198	68	77	−8	398	604	−206	26	−
1968	589	333	257	68	72	−4	658	405	253	23	−
1969	910	369	541	71	68	3	981	437	544	30	−
1970	976	435	542	67	61	6	1043	496	547	19	−
1971	871	500	370	66	54	12	936	554	382	33	−
1972	787	514	273	65	54	11	852	568	284	24	−
1973	869	527	342	63	53	10	932	580	353	23	−
Net consolidation											
1974	539	580	−41	62	55	7	601	636	−35	24	8
1975	366	600	−234	63	53	10	429	653	−224	19	9
1976	387	515	−128	89	54	35	476	569	−93	44	11
1977	423	452	−29	100	54	46	523	506	17	54	19
1978	456	406	50	104	53	50	560	459	101	58	31
1979	545	366	179	105	53	52	650	419	231	55	51
1980	631	386	246	105	54	51	736	440	297	52	108
1981	501	416	86	104	55	49	605	471	135	69	49
1982	322	433	−112	82	60	22	404	493	−89	48	37
1983	273	425	−152	81	62	19	354	487	−133	38	20

(*continued*)

Table 7.1. (*Continued*)

Year	Foreigners[1]			Germans[2]			Total			Ethnic Germans	Asylum Seekers
	In	Out	Net	In	Out	Net	In	Out	Net		
1984	331	545	−214	79	60	19	410	605	−194	36	35
1985	398	367	32	83	59	24	481	426	55	39	74
1986	478	348	131	89	59	30	567	407	160	43	100
1987	472	334	138	119	65	55	591	399	193	78	57
1988	648	359	289	213	60	153	861	419	441	203	103
Aftermath of socialism											
1989	767	438	329	367	102	265	1134	540	594	377	121
1990	836	465	370	421	109	312	1257	574	682	397	193
1991	925	497	428	274	99	175	1199	597	602	222	256
1992	1211	615	596	291	105	86	1502	720	782	230	438
1993	990	711	279	288	105	183	1277	815	462	219	323
1994	776	629	148	305	138	167	1083	768	315	223	127
1995	793	567	225	303	131	173	1096	698	498	218	128
1996	708	559	149	252	118	133	960	678	282	178	126
1997	615	637	−22	225	110	115	840	747	94	134	123
1998	606	639	−33	197	116	81	803	755	47	103	122
1999	674	556	118	200	116	84	874	672	202	105	138
2000	649	563	86	192	111	81	841	674	167	95	118
2001	685	497	188	194	110	84	879	607	272	98	118

[1] Foreigners include Asylum Seekers.
[2] Germans include Ethnic Germans.
Source: Statistisches Bundesamt, Fachserie Gebiet und Bevölkerung, several volumes, Bundesamt für die Anerkennung ausländischer Flüchtlinge, several volumes, Infodienst Deutsche Aussiedler, several volumes, own calculations.

attracting thousands of migrants. Bauer and Zimmermann (1997*a*, *b*) describe the organization of the recruitment of guest workers in this period. The number of *Aussiedler*, who came to Germany during that time, was still comparatively small. Again the restrictive emigration regulations of their countries of origin prevented them from moving to Germany.

All over Western Europe, a period of restrained migration began at the end of 1973, lasting until 1988. Facing increasing social tensions and fears of a recession following the first oil price shock, active labour recruitment halted. It turned out, however, that it is difficult to induce return migration. Due to family reunification, a higher fertility rate of the foreign population, and the admission of refugees and asylum seekers, the foreign population actually increased. According to Zimmermann

(1994) the number of illegal immigrants also rose significantly in this period.

The last period, dissolution of socialism and its aftermath, was dominated by East–West migration and a heavy inflow of asylum seekers and refugees. According to the *Bundesamt für die Anerkennung ausländischer Flüchtlinge* (Federal Office for Asylum Seekers) almost half a million refugees migrated to Germany in 1992 alone. A large portion of East–West migrants were ethnic Germans. In 1988 immigration by this group rose sharply, up to nearly 400,000 individuals in 1989 and 1990. This development can be attributed to the fall of the Iron Curtain and the relaxation of emigration conditions in the sending countries. Beginning in 1991, immigration by ethnic Germans stabilized at a lower level and eventually decreased in the years 1996 and 1997. Various restrictive administrative regulations by the German government were responsible for the decline of the *Aussiedler* immigration (Münz and Ohliger 1998).

In 1992, when immigration reached its historical peak, Germany received 1.5 million new immigrants; net immigration was 782,000; and the number of new asylum seekers and refugees was more than 400,000. In order to understand the magnitude of this inflow to Germany, consider the fact that US immigration inflow in the first decade of the twentieth century was large enough to increase the population in 1900 by 1.2 per cent per year. In relative terms, this is the largest immigration stream in US history. The recent inflows to Germany have been close to these levels. Immigration to Germany increased the population at an average annual rate of 1.4 per cent from 1962–73, 2.5 per cent in 1989, and 1.8 per cent for each year from 1990–92. Hence, Germany should be considered the key European country of immigration.

Separating migration in push and pull migration (see Zimmermann 1995a) allows for the following conclusion: while migration to Germany was driven by pull-factors in the manpower recruitment phase, push-factors dominated in the other phases of migration to Germany. This can also be seen in Figure 7.2 which shows the number of foreigners living in Germany according to their labour force status. While non-labour force immigration was almost irrelevant in the 1960s, it was dominated by family migration after 1973, with increasing numbers since the late 1980s. Hence, beginning in the 1970s a lower and lower share of the migrants was working. In the following four sections we will give a detailed description of the different immigration periods defined above.

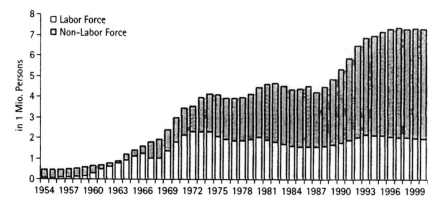

Figure 7.2. Immigration, labour force, nonlabour force (in 1,000), 1954–2000
Source: Statistisches Bundesamt, Fachserie Gebiet und Bevölkerung, own calculations.

7.2.2. War Adjustment

The first immigration movement to Germany after the Second World War consisted mainly of German expellees from the eastern parts of the former German Reich, from Eastern European countries, and from the Soviet Union. Already in the final months of the war, a large number of Germans, living east of the Oder and Neisse rivers, fled to the West. At the Potsdam conference in August 1945, the Allies agreed to the expelling of German citizens and of ethnic Germans from Poland, Czechoslovakia, Hungary, Yugoslavia, and the USSR (mainly East Prussia and the Baltics). This started a large migration movement, which defines the first of four periods of immigration to Germany, the phase of war adjustment (1945–1954).

The first population census in Germany after the Second World War (October 1946) registered 9.5 million German expellees: 5.9 million in the three Western zones and 3.6 million in the Soviet zone (Benz 1985). When the forced resettlements came to an end in 1950, 7.9 million refugees and expellees were living in West Germany and 3.6 million in the GDR. Compared to the total population, 15.7 per cent of West Germans and 19.6 per cent of East Germans were immigrants (Benz 1985). Rural areas in both German parts received a disproportionately large share of immigrants, mainly due to the destruction of urbanized and industrialized areas in mainland Germany. According to the 1950 census, 42.5 per cent of the population of rural Mecklenburg (GDR) were immigrants whereas only 12 per cent of the population of the urbanized Saxony were expellees. While there was very little immigration to Baden (4.4 per cent), about

21 per cent of the population of Bavaria and 33 per cent of the population of Schleswig-Holstein were expellees (Schmidt 1994a, 1996).

The settlement of expellees was determined by the housing situation and by the search for relatives and for work. The economic position of the German immigrants was unfavourable, even compared to the native population. Most of them came without physical assets and had lost proof of their insurance and pension claims, which was especially problematic for the retirees (Schmidt 1996). The housing situation of expellees was inadequate. In 1948 almost 400,000 immigrants lived in camps, 1.5 million in poor housing, and 2.3 million stayed in shared housing (Reichling and Betz 1949). Despite these facts and the impact of the currency reform in 1948, which resulted in a conversion of all savings, the war adjustment period was characterized by high economic growth and a decrease of the unemployment rate from 10.4 per cent in 1950 to 5.5 per cent in 1954. Although the integration of expellees did not succeed without frictions during the war adjustment period, it is usually seen as an integration miracle paralleling the economic miracle, which caused the recovery of the German economy after the Second World War (Schmidt 1996).

The year 1950 defines the end of the forced migration and the expulsion of Germans in the CEECs. It is estimated that in 1939, nine million Germans had been living in the German provinces east of the Oder and Neisse rivers (for example in Silesia, East Brandenburg, Pomerania, and East Prussia) and another 8.6 million in CEECs. In 1950 only four million ethnic Germans remained in these areas. They primarily lived in Poland (1.7 million), the Soviet Union (1.2 million), Romania, and other East European countries (1.1 million). Although many of these Germans wanted to leave their countries of origin because of ethnic discrimination, only a small number was allowed to move to Germany during that time. Since the beginning of the 1950s, ethnic German re-settlers from Eastern Europe and the Soviet Union were called *Aussiedler*, and their admission was regulated by the German constitution (basic law, paragraph 116). According to the German legislation, ethnic German minorities in Eastern Europe and the Soviet Union were still suffering from the consequences of the Second World War. Therefore, they had the right to immigrate to Germany and were granted German citizenship.

The war adjustment period in Germany was not only characterized by a large immigration movement. The Federal Republic also faced a remarkable out-migration of Germans, which was mainly caused by the decision of emigrants to escape from the destroyed country in search of a better life.

Another part of German emigration consisted of German wives and relatives of allied soldiers following them to their home countries.

7.2.3 Manpower Recruitment

The period of active manpower recruitment already started in the early 1950s and ended after the first oil price shock in 1973. High economic growth caused a shortage of low-skilled workers, which could no longer be compensated by the inflow of ethnic Germans from Eastern Europe. The German government therefore decided to pursue an active recruitment policy. The German guest worker system was characterized by recruitment treaties with Italy (1955), Spain and Greece (1960), Turkey (1961), Morocco (1963), Portugal (1964), Tunisia (1965), and the former Yugoslavia (1968). According to these treaties, 400 recruitment offices of the German Federal Labour Office operated in these countries on behalf of German firms.

The recruitment was organized as follows: the firms filed contract offers, which were approved and sent to the recruitment offices in the respective countries. These offices then chose workers on the basis of qualification, health, and employment record. Wage offers had to equal those for similar Germans. For the recruitment and mediation of a foreign guest worker, the firms had to pay a fee. Until September 1973 this recruitment fee amounted to 300 DM per worker. Furthermore, firms had to provide housing for the recruited employees. In addition, there was the possibility of a 'second way' of immigration: foreign employment seekers were allowed to apply directly at the German embassy in their home country.

In general, active recruitment policies require a decision on permanent versus temporary migration. The basic idea of a guest worker system is that the foreign workers are needed only temporarily and will leave the guest country after a predetermined period. Temporary migration also allows for an easy adjustment of the stock of labour according to the business cycle by importing workers in boom phases and exporting unemployment in periods of recession. An active recruitment policy can be organised either by the state, as in Germany, or by private companies. Information policies and assistance can also be offered in the home country of the emigrant or in the host country at the time of the guest worker's arrival. Assistance can take the form of payments for moving and recruitment costs, help with housing, and the provision of language courses. Furthermore, native firms can be allowed to use foreign firms as subcontractors in certain businesses that involve foreign workers. Policy instruments include quotas, limiting the duration of stay, and granting work permits only for specific industries.

Table 7.2. Foreign population and foreign labour force, 1955–73

Year	Foreigners		Employed foreigners	
	Total	Share[a]	Total	Share[b]
1955	466,675	0.9	79,607	0.4
1956	475,379	0.9	98,818	0.5
1957	480,598	0.9	108,190	0.6
1958	520,365	1.0	127,083	0.6
1959	604,378	1.1	166,829	0.8
1960	654,823	1.2	279,390	1.5
1961	723,145	1.2	507,419	2.5
1962	853,198	1.4	629,022	3.1
1963	935,671	1.6	773,164	3.7
1964	1,235,678	2.1	902,459	4.3
1965	1,458,364	2.4	1,118,616	5.3
1966	1,682,632	2.7	1,243,961	5.8
1967	1,806,653	3.0	1,013,862	4.7
1968	1,924,229	3.2	1,018,859	4.9
1969	2,381,061	3.9	1,365,635	6.5
1970	2,976,497	4.9	1,806,805	8.5
1971	3,438,711	5.6	2,128,407	9.8
1972	3,526,568	5.7	2,284,502	10.5
1973	3,966,200	6.4	2,285,564	10.0

Notes: [a] on total population, [b] on all employed persons.
Source: Amtliche Nachrichten der Bundesanstalt für Arbeit, Jahreszahlen, several volumes, Statistisches Jahrbuch, several volumes, own calculations.

Table 7.2 shows that during the phase of manpower recruitment in Germany the employment share of foreign workers increased from 1.5 per cent in 1960 and 5.3 per cent in 1965 to 10.0 per cent in 1973. The foreign population in Germany increased from half a million individuals in 1955, which was equal to 0.9 per cent of the total population, to almost four million foreigners in 1973, a share of 6.4 per cent of the total population in Germany.

Figure 7.3 allows a more quantitative analysis of the migration streams of foreign workers. As early as one year after the recruitment treaty with Italy, the number of employed Italians in Germany doubled. While in 1955 a total of 7,461 Italians worked in Germany, which corresponded to a share of 9.4 per cent of all foreign workers, this number increased to 18,597 workers (a share of almost 19 per cent of all foreign workers) within one year. Similar statements can be made for all individuals from countries

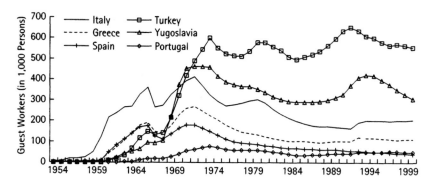

Figure 7.3. Guest workers by country of origin, 1955–2000 (in 1,000)
Source: Amtliche Nachrichten der Bundesanstalt für Arbeit, Jahreszahlen, several volumes, own
calculations.

with recruitment treaties. Foreign workers from Greece in particular
showed a strong movement to Germany. In 1960 the number of employed
individuals with Greek nationality increased from 13,005 to nearly 44,000
within one year. The upward trend in the employment share of foreign
workers continued until 1973, when it peaked with a share of 10.0 per cent.
At 30 per cent of all guest workers, Italian nationals constituted the main
share of the foreign workers. However, since 1972 the share of Italian
nationals has decreased in favour of foreign workers from Turkey,
who have become the largest group of employed foreign workers since
that time.

The *Einschaltungsgrad*, which shows the share of the foreign workers
migrating to Germany as a result of recruitment by the German Federal
Labour Office, serves as an indicator for the efficiency of the German active
recruitment policy. The *Einschaltungsgrad* increased from 17.1 per cent in
1957 to 45 per cent in 1972. However, it is important to realize that the
Einschaltungsgrad did not increase permanently for all countries during
the manpower recruitment period. For instance, following the regulations
of the European Community, the recruitment activity of the Federal Labour
Office in Italy decreased significantly after 1962, while migration of foreign workers from other countries still showed an *Einschaltungsgrad* of 40
to 90 per cent (see Bauer 1998).

Especially during the period of active recruitment policy and the following period of consolidation, the relation between immigration, on the one
hand and political and economic conditions on the other hand warrants
analysis. Despite the high quantity of immigrant labour, the unemployment rate in Germany decreased from 2.6 per cent in 1959 to 0.8 per cent

in 1971. Without the increase in the supply of labour caused by immigration of foreign workers, Germany would have been confronted with a
strong excess demand for labour between 1955 and 1973.

In general, work and residence permits were issued for one year in
order to keep immigration temporary. This fact explains the strong out-
migration of foreign workers during the manpower recruitment phase.
Overall, the foreign population increased from half a million individuals in
1955 to almost four million individuals in 1973.

Analysing the economic conditions for immigration also needs an
exploration of the cyclical sensitivity of immigration from the recruitment
countries. According to Figure 7.4, the employment of foreign workers
shows a strong sensitivity to the business cycle during the period of active
recruitment policy. The GNP growth and the growth of foreign employment
almost move parallel. This becomes most obvious in the short recession of
1967, where GNP growth and the growth of foreign employment decreased
strongly. In fact, the annual immigration of foreign workers decreased
from about 500,000 to 220,000 individuals in 1967, but began to rise to
the former level in the subsequent boom phase. According to these facts,
a parallel development of immigration from the recruitment countries
and the business cycle can be seen as characteristic for the manpower
recruitment phase of migration to Germany.

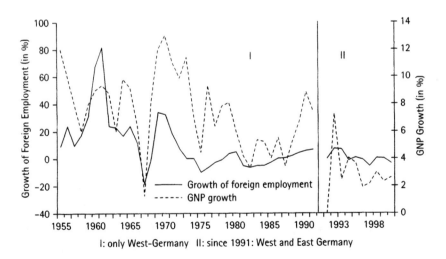

Figure 7.4. GNP growth and growth of foreign employment, 1955–2000
Source: Amtliche Nachrichten der Bundesanstalt für Arbeit, Jahreszahlen, several volumes, Statistisches
Jahrbuch, several volumes, own calculations.

In contrast to the immigration of foreign workers, the influx of ethnic Germans during the manpower recruitment phase was not sensitive to the business cycle. The development of the immigration figures of ethnic Germans can first of all be explained by the emigration policies of their countries of origin and by the political relations between these countries and the Federal Republic of Germany. Overall, a number of 709,000 *Aussiedler* came to Germany between 1950 and 1973, most of them originating from Poland. Besides a sharp increase in the number of ethnic German immigrants from Poland in 1957 and 1958, the immigration of ethnic Germans was rather stable (see Table 7.1 and Figure 7.5). On average, 31,000 *Aussiedler* moved to Germany every year during that period. The large number of ethnic German immigrants from Poland in 1957 and 1958 can be attributed to a special agreement between the Red Cross and the Polish government, allowing 216,000 *Aussiedler* from Poland to come to Germany on the basis of family reunification during these two years. After 1958, the Polish government readopted its restrictive emigration policy, partly because of political tensions between the Polish and German governments and partly for fear of losing workers.

While the immigration of Germans and ethnic Germans was comparatively stable during the manpower recruitment period, the outmigration of Germans decreased constantly after 1959. This can be explained by a large outflow of Germans escaping the destroyed country after the Second World War and the outmigration of German wives of allied soldiers.

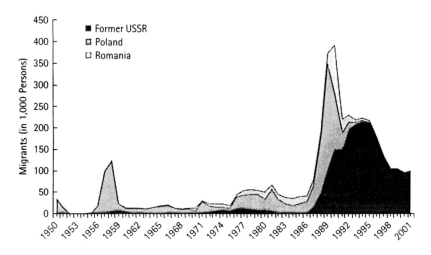

Figure 7.5. Inflow of ethnic Germans by country of origin, 1950–2001 (in 1,000)
Source: Infodienst Deutsche Aussiedler, Zahlen, Daten, Fakten, several volumes.

This trend ended with the beginning of the '*Wirtschaftswunder*' and the decreasing number of allied soldiers in Germany after 1955.

7.2.4 Consolidation

The active recruitment policy was terminated in 1973. On 23 November 1973, the Federal Labour Office was ordered by the German government to stop immediately any recruitment of foreign workers. Facing increasing social tensions and fears of a recession following the first oil price shock, this abrupt halt in recruitment started the period of consolidation or restrained migration which lasted from 1973 until 1988. This period was characterized by migration through family reunification. Although labour recruitments were stopped, family members of guest workers continued immigrating, and the foreign population increased even further due to high fertility rates.

The recruitment halt in 1973 changed the inflow of foreign workers significantly. While 869,109 foreign individuals immigrated in 1973, only 541,121 immigrated in 1974 and 366,095 in 1975. This size of inflow remained rather stable until the late 1970s; it began to increase again after 1980. The emigration of foreigners shows constant rates both in the recruitment period and in the consolidation period and tends to range between 300,000 and 550,000 individuals per year. Figure 7.3 shows the stock of guest workers by country of origin. In the consolidation period, individuals from Turkey contributed the largest share of foreigners; the share of individuals from other recruitment countries decreased slightly over the entire period.

In the years following the recruitment halt, Germany experienced negative net-migration, but by 1977 net-migration turned positive again. This is caused by the fact that the recruitment halt for foreign workers is not equal to a general immigration halt. With regard to family reunification, relatives of foreign workers in Germany were still allowed to migrate to Germany and to supply labour. Furthermore, foreign workers of Italian nationality did not suffer from the recruitment halt due to European Community regulations. Table 7.3 shows that the employment share of foreigners on total employment of around 10 per cent just after the recruitment stop decreased slowly to 9.2 per cent in 1981 and 7.6 per cent in 1988. Meanwhile the share of foreigners in the total population in Germany increased from 6.6 per cent in 1974 to 7.3 per cent in 1988.

According to Table 7.4, the unemployment rate in Germany increased sharply to about 5 per cent after 1973. However, until the late 1970s both

Table 7.3. Foreign population and foreign labour force, 1974–88

Year	Foreigners		Employed Foreigners	
	Total	Share[a]	Total	Share[b]
1974	4,127,366	6.6	2,286,625	10.0
1975	4,089,594	6.6	2,060,507	10.2
1976	3,948,337	6.4	1,924,730	9.6
1977	3,948,278	6.4	1,872,206	9.4
1978	3,981,061	6.5	1,857,488	9.3
1979	4,143,836	6.8	1,924,420	9.3
1980	4,453,308	7.2	2,018,382	9.6
1981	4,629,729	7.5	1,911,957	9.2
1982	4,666,917	7.6	1,787,316	8.7
1983	4,534,863	7.4	1,694,354	8.4
1984	4,363,648	7.1	1,608,501	8.0
1985	4,378,942	7.2	1,567,526	7.7
1986	4,512,679	7.4	1,569,667	7.6
1987	4,240,532	6.9	1,576,924	7.5
1988	4,489,105	7.3	1,609,820	7.6

Notes: [a] on total population, [b] on all employed persons.
Source: Amtliche Nachrichten der Bundesanstalt für Arbeit, Jahreszahlen, several volumes, Statistisches Jahrbuch, several volumes, own calculations.

foreign and domestic workers shared the same unemployment experience. After 1980, following a sharp rise in the overall unemployment rate, the unemployment rate of foreigners was significantly higher than the overall unemployment rate. This is especially interesting because the foreign workers' share of total employment decreased only slowly during this period.

Furthermore, one can observe an increasing gap between the number of foreign individuals and employed foreign individuals in Germany after 1973. This gap started to exist in the late 1960s and widened sharply in the early 1970s, remaining rather stable thereafter. As can be seen from Figure 7.4, the parallel development of GNP growth and foreign employment growth, which was typical for the manpower recruitment phase, does not continue in the consolidation period after 1973. During this period, migration streams developed independently from the business cycle. This is mainly caused by the family reunification character of migration to Germany after 1973.

Table **7.4.** Unemployment rates, Germans and foreigners, 1970–2002

Year	Unemployment rates								
	Total	Germans	Foreigners	Italians	Greeks	Spaniards	Turks	Portuguese	Yugoslavs
1970	0.7	0.7	0.3	0.3	0.2	0.2	0.3	0.1	0.2
1972	1.1	1.1	0.7	0.9	0.9	0.6	0.9	0.3	0.5
1973	1.2	1.2	0.8	1.1	0.9	0.6	1.0	0.3	0.6
1975	4.7	4.7	6.8	8.9	8.1	5.3	7.8	3.2	6.2
1976	4.6	4.6	5.1	7.1	5.8	4.3	5.2	2.4	4.1
1977	4.5	4.5	4.9	6.1	4.6	3.6	4.9	2.0	3.3
1978	4.3	4.3	5.3	6.1	4.6	3.6	5.5	2.1	3.4
1979	3.8	3.8	4.7	5.3	4.3	3.5	5.1	2.1	3.1
1980	3.8	3.8	5.0	5.4	4.2	3.4	6.1	2.2	3.2
1981	5.5	5.5	8.2	8.8	6.7	5.1	9.9	3.9	5.6
1982	7.5	7.5	11.9	12.8	10.0	6.8	14.6	6.6	9.3
1983	9.1	9.1	14.7	15.3	12.6	9.3	17.6	9.6	11.6
1984	9.1	9.1	14.0	15.3	12.5	9.5	17.1	9.7	11.1
1985	9.3	9.3	13.9	15.8	11.9	9.1	15.4	8.1	11.0
1986	9.0	9.0	13.7	15.9	11.8	9.0	14.9	7.9	10.0
1987	8.9	8.9	14.3	16.8	12.2	9.3	15.4	8.0	10.0
1988	8.7	8.7	14.4	16.8	13.4	9.5	15.1	7.6	9.8
1989	7.9	7.9	12.2	14.5	12.0	8.6	12.6	6.5	8.0
1990	7.2	7.2	10.9	12.5	10.2	7.3	10.3	5.5	6.6
1991	6.3	6.3	10.7	12.2	10.2	6.7	10.0	5.2	6.4
1992	8.5	6.6	12.2	13.9	12.3	8.2	12.2	6.4	7.7
1993	9.8	8.2	15.1	15.3	14.2	10.2	16.5	8.2	9.9
1994	10.6	9.2	16.2	16.6	16.3	11.9	19.6	10.7	10.9
1995	10.4	9.3	16.6	16.6	16.5	11.6	19.8	12.0	9.8
1996	11.5	10.1	18.9	18.1	17.7	11.8	21.9	13.5	10.4
1997	12.7	11.5	18.9	18.0	17.9	12.1	22.1	13.7	10.5
1998	12.3	11.3	18.8	18.1	17.7	11.9	22.3	13.5	10.5
1999	11.7	12.3	20.9	18.2	18.4	12.6	23.8	13.2	10.5
2000	10.7	14.6	19.2	16.2	16.5	11.9	21.7	12.2	11.8
2001	10.3	14.4	20.1	15.7	15.6	11.9	21.9	12.5	13.7
2002	10.8	13.9	19.1	17.1	16.7	12.6	23.3	13.4	14.5

Source: Amtliche Nachrichten der Bundesanstalt für Arbeit, Jahreszahlen, several volumes, own calculations.

In line with the recruitment halt, a discussion began about how to encourage return migration. As early as 1972, Germany signed a bilateral treaty with Turkey to create incentives for return migration, which included special aid for returning individuals such as education, financial consultancy, and investment support for business foundations in their home country (Frey 1986). Due to the negative impact of the second oil price shock on the labour market in the early 1980s, an increase of the foreign population caused by continued family reunification, and the growing number of asylum seekers since the late 1970s, the discussion grew in favour of an active return policy, which included the question of whether return migration should be fostered by financial measures (Dustmann 1996).

It took until 1983 for the new conservative government to propose such a law, which was subsequently accepted by parliament. The programme included financial incentives, measures to reduce mobility barriers, and guidance to foreigners who intended to remigrate. Foreigners from countries with a recruitment treaty were eligible if they were unemployed or in short-time work. The financial incentive was 10,500 DM plus 1,500 DM for each child leaving the country with the worker. Interested individuals had to apply within eight months. The government had expected 19,000 applications. In the end, 17,000 applications had been submitted, most of them from Turkish guest workers. Approximately 14,000 were accepted. However, this programme only showed short-term success. Emigration by foreigners increased in 1983 and 1984, but by 1985 net-immigration was once again positive.

During the period of consolidation, immigration by ethnic Germans increased after 1975, peaked in the early 1980s, and decreased again afterwards (see Table 7.1). The most important sending country during this time was Poland, followed by Romania and the former Soviet Union. At the Conference on Security and Co-operation in Europe (CSCE) in Helsinki in 1975, the Polish and German governments signed an agreement, which allowed between 120,000 and 150,000 ethnic Germans from Poland to migrate to Germany in the subsequent four years. Although it was agreed upon to prolong this arrangement, emigration restrictions from the Polish side let the emigration figure decrease again. In the case of Romania, the German and Romanian governments concluded an agreement, which allowed 10,000 to 15,000 ethnic Germans per year to move to Germany (January 1978). As a precondition, the German government had to pay a fixed amount per immigrant. For each ethnic German who left Romania, the German government invested 5,000 DM; in 1983, this sum was increased to 7,800 DM (Gabanyi 1988).

Aussiedler from the former Soviet Union did not play an important role in the seventies and the early eighties, although the ratification of the treaties with the USSR (Ostverträge 1972) increased their number for a short period. In the beginning of the eighties, relations between Germany

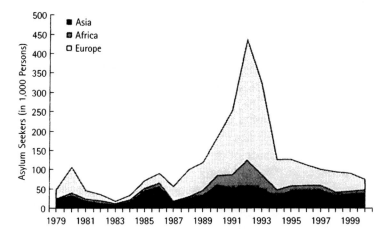

Figure 7.6. Asylum seekers by continent of origin, 1979–2000 (in 1,000)
Source: Statistical Yearbook, several volumes.

and the former Soviet Union worsened, which made it more difficult for ethnic Germans to leave the country. All in all, the immigration of ethnic Germans during the period of consolidation was mainly influenced by the political relations between the sending countries and the Federal Republic of Germany.

The out-migration of Germans seems to be rather constant at about 55,000 individuals per year during the consolidation period. This can be explained by the outmigration of retired individuals (*Rentnermigration*) to countries south of Germany (Austria, Italy, and Spain) and by the migration of students or other career-related migrant streams. Table 7.1 also shows an increasing number of asylum seekers in Germany starting in the early 1980s. As Figure 7.6 documents, this development was mainly driven by refugees from Asia, who escaped the war in Afghanistan, or from Tamils, who left Sri Lanka during the civil war. This process slowed down in 1987 and started to accelerate again at a later stage.

7.2.5 Migration in the Aftermath of Socialism

The political changes in the East, beginning in the late 1980s, triggered a new period of migration in Germany, which was characterized by a strong inflow of asylum seekers, a substantial East–West migration caused by ethnic Germans and to a smaller extent by foreign workers from former socialist countries.

According to Table 7.1, an increasing inflow of foreign individuals started in 1988. This inflow peaked at almost 1.2 million individuals in

1992 and slowed down afterwards. Table 7.1 further shows an increasing outflow of foreigners, which peaked in 1993 with more than 700,000 individuals and stabilized at a high level thereafter. This was caused by return migration of foreign individuals as well as by the reduction of allied troops after the German reunification.

Table 7.5 shows that the foreign workers' share of total employment increased slightly from 1989 until 1993 and remained stable on a level of 9.4 per cent from 1993 to 1997 before decreasing to around 7.2 per cent in 2001. The foreigners' share of the total population in Germany increased from 7.7 per cent in 1989 to 8.9 per cent in 1995 and subsequently stayed relatively constant. The earlier peak of the development of the foreign employment share when compared to the share of foreigners in the population is mainly due to the inflow of asylum seekers during this period and is not caused by family reunification aspects as during the period of consolidation.

Figure 7.2 shows that the gap between the total foreign population and employed foreigners in Germany, which started to open up in the late 1960s and tended to remain stable during the 1970s and the early 1980s, widens sharply after 1988. This provides strong evidence for the change

Table 7.5. Foreign population and foreign labour force, 1989–2001

Year	Foreigners		Employed	Foreigners
	Total	Share[a]	Total	Share[b]
1989	4,845,882	7.8	1,677,981	7.7
1990	5,342,532	8.4	1,774,732	7.9
1991	5,882,267	7.3	1,891,232	8.1
1992	6,495,792	7.8	2,030,253	8.6
1993	6,878,117	8.5	2,169,233	9.4
1994	6,990,510	8.6	2,141,365	9.4
1995	7,173,866	8.8	2,121,434	9.4
1996	7,314,046	8.8	2,067,782	9.4
1997	7,366,000	8.9	2,022,586	9.5
1998	7,320,000	8.9	2,030,266	7.5
1999	7,343,600	8.9	1,922,424	7.0
2000	7,296,800	8.8	1,963,090	7.1
2001	7,318,600	8.9	2,002,990	7.2

Notes: [a] on total population, [b] on all employed persons.
Source: Amtliche Nachrichten der Bundesanstalt für Arbeit, Jahreszahlen, several volumes, Statistisches Jahrbuch, several volumes, own calculations.

from labour migration in the 1950s and 1960s to family migration in the 1970s and early 1980s and refugee migration thereafter. Furthermore, Table 7.4 shows that the gap between the overall unemployment rate and the unemployment rate of foreign workers in Germany seems to have widened since the early 1990s. This is particularly interesting as the overall unemployment rate has increased since the end of the post-unification boom period; the unemployment rate of foreign workers, however, has seen an even higher increase.

Finally, Figure 7.4 documents that the growth of foreign employment is not sensitive to the business cycle in the period after the fall of the Iron Curtain. This is an expected result, since immigration to Germany changed from pull to push migration after 1973. According to Table 7.1 and Figure 7.6, the number of asylum seekers in Germany increased sharply after 1987. This development, however, was mainly driven by refugees from Europe and not by Asian asylum seekers as during the period of consolidation.

According to Art. 16 of the German constitution, political refugees have the right to asylum in Germany. Between 1953 and 1978 only 7,000 individuals per year took advantage of this law, and only political incidents such as the suppression of the revolt in Prague in 1968 caused a temporary increase in the number of applicants for political asylum. In the early 1980s, the yearly number of applicants seeking asylum was far below 50,000, yet since 1986 it had strongly increased and peaked at about half a million applicants in 1992. While Asia was an important source region in the 1980s due to the war in Afghanistan and the Islamic regime in Iran, the number of African asylum seekers increased significantly in the late 1980s, following diverse conflicts in Central and Western Africa. The shift from labour migration to refugee migration in migration streams to Germany becomes especially evident in the fact that the share of asylum seekers on immigration to Germany was a mere one per cent in the early 1970s, while it was over 30 per cent in 1990 (Münz and Ulrich 1996).

Several factors caused the increased migration stream of asylum seekers from Europe: the political confusion in the former socialist states of Eastern Europe, induced by the fall of the Iron Curtain, the war in the former Yugoslavia, and the clashes between Turks and Kurds in the southeast of Turkey. However, these conflicts on the edges of Europe were not only followed by an increasing stream of asylum seekers but also by increased family reunification, since many foreign workers from the endangered areas brought their relatives to Germany. The development of the inflow of asylum seekers and refugees between 1988 and 1992 caused an intense discussion about tightening the asylum law. In 1993 Art. 16a was added to the German constitution in order to make it more difficult to apply for political asylum. This alteration of the German constitution allowed for immediately sending back those asylum seekers who had immigrated from member states of the European Union or other so-called safe countries as defined by the law. The fact that Germany is surrounded by safe countries, in the sense of the law, limits the possibility of immigration by asylum seekers to Germany by air or sea. In addition, Germany signed treaties with Romania and Poland (1993), Switzerland (1994), Bulgaria, and the Czech Republic (1995) regarding the rebound of asylum seekers.

Obviously this change in the constitution achieved the desired effect. The number of asylum seekers decreased from over 320,000 to 120,000 individuals within one year and remained at this relatively low level. However, the new law may have caused a restructuring of migration in favour of illegal immigration. According to the Ministry of the Interior, 27,000 illegal migrants were caught in 1996, most of them trying to cross the Polish–German border. Naturally, exact figures on illegal migration to Germany are not available.

While these migration streams were characterized by push-factors, the boom period after the German reunification also caused some pull migration in 1990 based on bilateral agreements between Germany and some CEEC-countries. Especially Polish and Czech workers migrated as contract workers or seasonal workers across the eastern borders of Germany. The following goals were at the core of the bilateral agreements between Germany and the CEEC-countries concerning temporary migration: (i) to bring the CEEC countries up to Western European standards; (ii) solidarity with CEEC countries; (iii) to impart skills to firms and workers with modern technology in order to foster economic development in the countries of origin; (iv) to decrease the immigration pressure from these countries; and (v) to promote economic co-operation with these countries. In pursuit of these goals Germany created three different categories, under which workers from CEEC countries could temporarily work in Germany.

Germany has signed bilateral agreements with several Central and Eastern European countries regarding the immigration of *Werkvertragsarbeitneh-mer*. According to these bilateral agreements, Eastern European firms are allowed employment of their own workers in project-linked work arrangements co-ordinated under contracts with German firms. The workers immigrating under this category are allowed to stay until the project is finished but no longer than three years. After a worker has stayed in Germany as a *Werkvertragsarbeitnehmer*, he must stay in his country of origin at least as long as he has been in Germany in order to return to Germany again. The wage of the *Werkvertragsarbeitnehmer* must be the same as that of similar German workers. However, since the social security contributions of these workers are paid by their firm from the country of origin according to the rules of this country, the wage costs of *Werkvertragsarbeitnehmer* are lower than those of comparable Germans. The number of workers who can work under these treaties is limited by quotas, which are adapted each year according to the labour market situation in Germany. If the number of *Werkvertragsarbeitnehmer* from a particular country exceeds the respective quota, Germany does not allow the immigration of additional workers, and the quota will be blocked the following year. Furthermore, work permits are not granted in districts in which unemployment is significantly higher than the national average.

The employment of *Werkvertragsarbeitnehmer* increased sharply from 14,500 in 1988 to 95,000 in 1992. After 1992, the number of *Werkvertragsarbeitnehmer* decreased to about 46,000 in 1996. This decrease is mainly a result of the continuing cutbacks of the quotas. In most years, Polish *Werkvertragsarbeitnehmer* constituted almost 50 per cent of all workers employed in Germany under these bilateral agreements, followed by workers from Hungary and the former Yugoslavia.

In addition to the *Werkvertragsarbeitnehmer*, Germany initiated *guest worker* programs with several CEECs. These are also regulated under bilateral agreements. The aim of this programme is to improve the professional and linguistic skills of the participants. The participants have to meet the following requirements: (i) completion of vocational training; (ii) basic knowledge of the German language; and (iii) age between 18 and 40 years. These guest workers can stay in Germany for a maximum of 18 months. They need a work permit even though the programmes are not dependent on the labour situation in Germany. They must be paid the same wage as a similar German worker and, in contrast to the *Werkvertragsarbeitnehmer*, their social security requirements follow the German standards. From 1991 to 1993 the number of guest workers increased from 1,570 to 5,771 and then slightly decreased to 4,341 in 1996. Most of the guest workers come from Hungary and the Czech Republic, followed by guest workers from Poland and Slovakia.

Since 1991 foreign workers may obtain a German work permit for a maximum of three months. The requirement to get such a seasonal work permit is again a bilateral agreement between Germany and the worker's home country. Foreign seasonal workers are only allowed to work in agriculture, hotels, restaurants, and as showmen. They must be employed under the same wage and working conditions as German workers, and their employment requires payment of social security contributions according to German standards. In addition, the employer has to provide accommodation for seasonal workers. In general, there is no quota on this type of employment. However, the German Labour office must check whether similar unemployed native workers are available. Since 1992 the employment of seasonal workers has ranged between 130,000 and 220,000 per year. The decrease in seasonal workers in 1993 and 1994 can be explained by the introduction of an employment prohibition in 1993 of seasonal workers in the construction sector. Despite the poor employment situation on the German labour market, the employment of seasonal workers reached its peak in 1996 with about 221,000 workers. Most of them came from Poland; in 1996, for example, Polish nationals constituted almost 90 per cent of all seasonal workers.

In addition to the inflows discussed thus far, East–West migration has been dominated by a large immigration of ethnic Germans. With the political changes in Poland, Romania, and later in the former Soviet Union, and with the dissolution of the socialist block, the immigration of ethnic Germans began to rise sharply in 1988. This influx reached its peak with the immigration of nearly 400,000 *Aussiedler* per year in 1989 and 1990. Since 1991 the immigration of ethnic Germans stabilized at a lower level of approximately 120,000 re-settlers per year (see Table 7.1). Because the German government was increasingly concerned with the consequences of *Aussiedler* immigration, restrictive administrative regulations were introduced to control this migration movement. To begin with, a new admission procedure was installed (July 1991), which required re-settlers to apply for immigration in their countries of origin (Ronge 1997). With the enforcement of a new law (*Kriegsfolgenbereinigungsgesetz* 1993), the immigration of ethnic Germans was finally regulated by a quota system. From then on an annual maximum of 225,000 *Aussiedler* were allowed to come to Germany.

In 1996 the total number of ethnic German immigrants decreased by 18 per cent and by 23 per cent in 1997 and 1998. This must be attributed, first of all, to a newly introduced German language test (May 1996) for ethnic Germans who apply for admission to Germany. According to this new regulation, ethnic German immigrants must prove a certain command of the German language as a confirmation of their German descent (*Volkszugehörigkeit*) in the country of origin. Since Germans in the former Soviet Union, who are the most important *Aussiedler* group in recent years, were forbidden to speak German in public during the 1950s and

1960s, many of them—especially the younger ones—have lost all ties to the German language. Therefore, it is not surprising that between July 1996 and April 1999, out of the 133,817 ethnic Germans who applied for admission to Germany and were required to take the language test, almost two-thirds (62.6 per cent) failed (according to data provided by the Federal Administration Office).

Looking back at the composition of the ethnic German immigration to Germany, it becomes clear that its main source had switched from Poland and Romania to the former Soviet Union in the 1990s (see Figure 7.5). This development must be attributed to the new law of 1993 (*Kriegsfolgenbereinigungsgesetz*) regarding ethnic German re-settlers. The law allows only Germans from the former Soviet Union to come to Germany without individually proving that they had been discriminated in their countries of origin because of their German descent. In addition, the potential for ethnic German emigration appears to be more or less exhausted in Poland and Romania. Since 1993 almost 95 per cent of ethnic German immigrants have come from the successor states of the USSR, mainly from Kazakhstan and Russia.

The immigration of *Aussiedler* has been characterized by both push and pull factors. While ethnic discrimination has been the most important push-factor up to the end of the 1980s, political instability and economic crisis in the countries of origin became of growing importance in the 1990s. The rights for admission into Germany, family ties, and the political and economic stability in Germany have been strong pull-factors throughout the period of *Aussiedler* immigration. Furthermore, Table 7.1 documents an increasing outflow of Germans, which may be caused by the fact that many ethnic Germans follow a scheme of step migration: they stop in Germany to receive German passports only in order to move to Canada, the USA, or South Africa (Münz and Ulrich 1996). Another reason could be the out-migration by German husbands or wives of allied soldiers leaving Germany according to the treaties of German reunification.

7.2.6 Internal Migration

The data situation on internal migration in Germany has been quite satisfactory for the past twenty years. The Statistical Office supplies data on internal migration, which can be separated into German and foreign individuals as well as into labour force and nonlabour force, again distinguishing between German and foreign individuals. As Greenwood (1997) points out, there is a problem of regional differentiation of internal migration. This problem is also valid for Germany. Three different approaches are possible: data exist on internal migration between the states (*Bundesländer*), including movements between communities within these states but excluding movements within communities of the states. However, these data cannot be separated by different subgroups of the population (e.g. Germans and foreigners). Hence, one has to rely on data which describe the internal migration between states, excluding the movements between communities. A third data source, which we do not rely on, is a dataset of the German Federal Research Institute for Regional Geography and Regional Planning (*Bundesforschungsanstalt für Landeskunde und Raumordnung*), which separates Germany into 328 counties ('Federal Planning Regions') and thus provides data on movements between these regions. For an analysis of internal migration employing these datasets, see *Bundesforschungsanstalt für Landeskunde und Raumordnung* (1992) and Friedrich (1990).

The historical development of migration within Germany starts with the inflows of Germans from former German territories in the East (e.g. Silesia) to the Western territories after the Second World War. These movements are described in Section 7.2.2. These postwar migration streams are followed by a strong internal migration to industrial regions in North Rhine-Westphalia and the Saarland, which were the strongest growing regions in Germany in the 1960s. These migration streams are sufficiently described in Adebahr (1969) and Mackensen, Vanberg and Krämer (1975).

As for many other economic circumstances, the first oil price shock can be seen as a turning point for the development of internal migration in Germany. Beginning with the early 1970s, the traditional manufacturing areas, such as the Ruhrgebiet, faced negative net-migration. This development is caused by the growth of high-tech industries located in Southern Germany. While Adebahr (1969) differentiates between high-wage and low-wage states and clearly assigns Bavaria and Baden-Württemberg to low-wage and North Rhine-Westphalia to high-wage states, Hippmann (1983) shows that this relation changed completely in the 1970s. Generally speaking, destination areas of internal migration have changed from areas with mainly manufacturing industries to areas with growing high-tech industries.

Since specific characteristics of internal migrants and causes and motivation of internal migration in Germany are already examined elsewhere (see Friedrich 1990), the contribution of this section is to provide a quantitative picture of internal migration streams in Germany and to analyse its sensibility with respect to specific macroeconomic variables

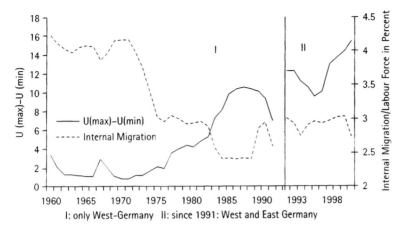

Figure 7.7. Internal migration and unemployment, 1960–2000
Source: Statistisches Bundesamt, Fachserie Gebiet und Bevölkerung, own calculations.

such as unemployment, vacancies, or GNP growth. This is partly motivated by recent contributions for some other European countries (Antolin and Bover 1997; Bentolila 1997; Faini et al. 1997; and McCormick 1997). In this context, a specific problem widely discussed in the literature is the German east-west migration shortly before and after the fall of the Iron Curtain (Burda 1993; Raffelhüschen 1992; and Wendt 1993).

Figure 7.7 shows a steady decline of internal migration relative to the labour force in Germany, which was only interrupted by the large east-west-migration streams due to German reunification in the late 1980s and early 1990s. This becomes especially interesting, taking into consideration the strong increase of unemployment since the 1970s. Thus, Figure 7.7 shows internal migration relative to the labour force in Germany and the difference between the highest and the lowest unemployment rate within the states of West Germany. The regional disparities of unemployment rates have widened in the 1980s, while internal migration decreased. This is the empirical puzzle mentioned by Faini et al. (1997), who also provide some explanations: supporting government payments may negatively affect the preference for moving as well as problems with housing transactions, or the fact that the older individuals' willingness to move is generally rather small. This becomes especially problematic in countries with ageing populations such as Germany.

In line with Figure 7.7, Figure 7.8 shows the development of vacancies and internal migration. Internal migration seems to decrease whenever vacancies decrease. This may be explained by a risk aversion argument

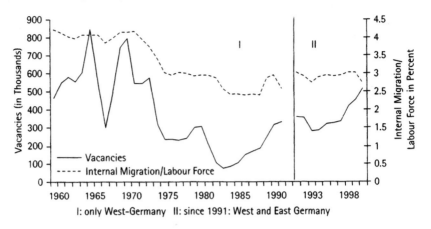

Figure 7.8. Internal migration and vacancies, 1960–2000

Source: Statistisches Bundesamt, Fachserie Gebiet und Bevölkerung, own calculations.

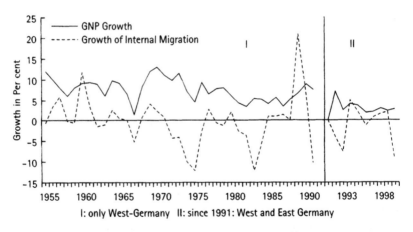

Figure 7.9. GNP growth and growth of internal migration

Source: Statistisches Bundesamt, Fachserie Gebiet und Bevölkerung, own calculations.

employed by Decressin (1994). When vacancies are scarce, the probability of finding a job after moving declines, thus inducing risk-averse individuals to stay. This became especially evident in the recession of 1967. While the number of vacancies increased again in 1968, internal migration did not increase until 1969. The same pattern appears during the first oil price shock. Figure 7.9 plots the development of GNP growth

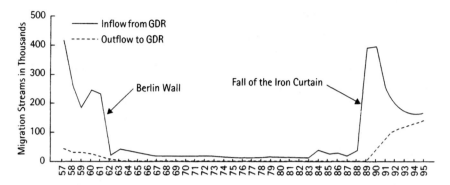

Figure 7.10. Migration streams between East and West Germany, 1957–1998
Source: Statistisches Bundesamt, Fachserie Gebiet und Bevölkerung, own calculations.

against the growth of internal migration. It suggests that internal migration has been rather sensitive to the business cycle since the early 1960s.

Migration streams between East and West Germany can be separated into three periods: (i) the period before the construction of the Berlin Wall in 1961; (ii) the period of the Cold War (1962–88); and (iii) the aftermath of socialism (since 1989). Before the construction of the Berlin Wall, thousands of individuals left the Soviet sector, which later became the German Democratic Republic, in order to move to the West. This development was abruptly halted in 1961 with the construction of the Berlin Wall. During the Cold War period, there were only negligible migration flows between East and West Germany, mainly induced by per-head premiums paid by the West German government.

Starting with the mass exodus of East Germans via Hungary and Austria in August 1989 and the opening of the borders between East and West Germany on 9 November 1989, a very strong migration stream from East to West Germany started, peaking in 1990 with over 400,000 movers. Since 1990, East–West migration has tended to consolidate, and migration from West to East Germany has increased (see Figure 7.10). The future quantity of migration between the old and the new states of Germany will depend on the economic development in the former GDR. In view of an average unemployment rate of 18.1 per cent in the eastern states (20.5 per cent in Saxony-Anhalt) and 9.7 per cent in the western states (7.0 per cent in Bavaria) in July 1997, theoretically, one would expect strong East–West migration streams. In the face of these differences, the actual mobility is rather low.

7.3. Assimilation and Integration of Immigrants

Since Chiswick's (1978) seminal article, the dominant microeconomic topic in the migration literature has been the assimilation of migrants into the labour market and the society of the receiving country. (A survey of the assimilation literature is given by Borjas (1994). Schmidt (1994b) provides an overview of some German studies. Zimmermann (1995a, 1995b) reviews the German and other European empirical literature.) The key issue of this research area is the speed of migrant assimilation to comparable natives in terms of earnings, unemployment experience, employment structure, or the utilization of the welfare system. The empirical specification used in this part of the migration literature overwhelmingly follows the strategy originally introduced by Chiswick (1978). Following Schmidt (1994a), a general formal description of this strategy is:

$$Y_i^* = \beta_1 X_i + \beta_2 M_i + \beta_3 M_i T_i + \varepsilon_i$$
$$Y_i = F(Y_i^*) \tag{1}$$

Y_i^* denotes a latent independent variable, X_i is a vector of the demographic characteristics including the constant, and M_i is a dummy variable indicating whether an individual is a migrant. The vector T_i includes measures of the time of residency of a migrant in the receiving country. Usually, these measures are the years since migration and its squared or a set of dummy variables indicating an immigration cohort. Using the observation rule F(.), the latent variable Y_i^* is translated into a dichotomous variable when analysing the unemployment experience, job and geographical mobility, or welfare utilization of the migrant and is left unchanged when analysing earnings assimilation.

The coefficient of the dummy variable M_i indicates the difference between migrants and comparable natives in their labour market position at the time of immigration. Following the human capital theory of migration, this differential depends on the ability of an immigrant to transfer pre-immigration skills to the necessities of the receiving country (Chiswick 1978). The more similar the sending and receiving countries are with respect to language, culture, structure, and institutions of the labour market as well as the development of the economy, the smaller the problems of transferring human capital between the two countries should be (Chiswick 1986).

A second important determinant of immigrants' labour market performance is the time of residency in the receiving country. It is argued that immigrants invest in the country-specific human capital of the receiving country, which increases their productivity with time of residency. Due to the returns from improvements in the ability to transfer human capital accumulated in the sending region, a shortening in the planning horizon and the opportunity costs, which increases with an improved labour market position, the incentives to invest in country-specific human capital should decrease with the time of residency in the receiving country. Furthermore, the incentives to invest in country-specific human capital should be higher, the lower the transferability of human capital accumulated in the country of origin. Since natives have no need to acquire country-specific human capital, the age-earnings profiles of immigrants investing in the country-specific human capital of the receiving country should be steeper than that of natives. This assimilation in the labour market position of immigrants to comparable natives is measured by the estimated coefficient β_3. It should be noted that we will not deal explicitly with some of the concerns with Chiswick's (1978) specification, like the influence of cohort and time effects, as outlined in Borjas (1994).

So far, the German Socio-Economic Panel (GSOEP) has been the primary data source for most studies of immigrants' assimilation in Germany. This is because the GSOEP has been for a long time the only available dataset providing valuable information on immigrants. Since 1984 this dataset has been collected annually to resemble the US Panel Study of Income Dynamics (PSID). Until 1994 the GSOEP sampled individuals in two subsamples. One subsample contains only individuals living in households whose head is German, the other subsample contains individuals living in households whose head is a foreigner originating from one of the five major sending countries of German guest workers. Since 1994 a third subsample has been added to the GSOEP, containing individuals whose household head migrated to Germany no longer than ten years ago. This new immigration subsample consists mainly of ethnic Germans who immigrated from the former GDR or Eastern Europe. A detailed description of this dataset is given by Bauer and Zimmermann (1996). Schmidt (1994a, 1997) has used the *Allgemeine Bevölkerungsumfrage der Sozialwissenschaften (ALLBUS)* which resembles the General Social Survey in the United States. This dataset, which has been collected every two years, samples only German nationals and contains information on the duration of residency of ethnic Germans, who immigrated since 1939.

In the following subsections, the literature on the assimilation and integration of immigrants in the German society with regard to their earnings, employment and unemployment experience, job and geographical mobility, and utilization of the welfare state is summarized. Within the framework discussed above, we survey existing empirical studies on the assimilation and integration of German immigrants with regard to different labour market outcomes. However, the review here ignores the new literature on educational attainment of migrants (Gang and Zimmermann 2002; Riphahn 2003; and Constant and Zimmermann 2003).

7.3.1 Earnings

Studies on the earnings assimilation of permanent migrants in Australia, Canada, and the United States have shown that an initial earnings gap between immigrants and native labour narrows considerably over time, indicating the willingness of foreign labour to invest in country specific human capital (Greenwood and McDowell 1986; and Borjas 1994). Table 7.6 summarizes the studies on the earnings assimilation of German immigrants. It appears that the results on the earnings dynamics of guest workers in Germany are more obscure. Dustmann (1993), Schmidt (1997) and Constant (1998) did not confirm the results for the classical immigration countries for the earnings adjustment of guest workers in Germany.

Depending on the model specification, the empirical results of Dustmann (1993) indicate an earnings disadvantage of guest workers of 13–19 per cent at the time of immigration. Immigrants are not able to narrow this initial earnings gap with duration of residency in Germany. Using entry cohort dummies instead of a continuous measure for the time of residency, Schmidt (1997) obtained similar results. Controlling for age and marital status, he estimates an average initial earnings differential between foreign guest workers and natives of 20 per cent, which appeared to be stable with time of residency. Schmidt (1997) further demonstrates that most of the initial earnings gap could be explained by persistent differences in the education endowment between foreign guest workers and natives. Controlling for education and occupational status, the earnings gap becomes negligible, without changing the results with regard to the effect of residency duration. The lack of earnings assimilation of German guest workers has been explained by the temporary character of this group. Since the size of investments of immigrants in country-specific human capital of the receiving country depends, among other things, positively on the expected duration of stay, temporary migrants should show a lower earnings increase, due to human capital

Table 7.6. Earnings assimilation of German immigrants

Study	Dataset	Immigration groups	Initial earnings gap (β^2)	Earnings Assimilation (β^3)per year
Bauer and Zimmermann (1996, 1997)	GSOEP	Ethnic Germans	No	0.04–0.07%
Constant (1998)	GSOEP	Guest workers, Men	No	No
	GSOEP	Guest workers, Women	Yes	Yes
Dunn et al. (1997)	GSOEP	Ethnic Germans	No	No
Dustmann (1993)	GSOEP	Guest workers	13–19%	No
Licht und Steiner (1994)	GSOEP	Guest workers	–	1.0%
Pischke (1992)	GSOEP	Guest workers	No	No
Seifert (1996)	GSOEP	Ethnic Germans Foreigners	No	Yes
Schmidt (1992a)	GSOEP	Guest workers	12%	0.7%
Schmidt (1992b)	GSOEP	Guest workers		
Schmidt (1994a)	ALLBUS	Ethnic Germans		0.6%
		Übersiedler	17%	
		Aussiedler	9–20%	
Schmidt (1997)	ALLBUS	Ethnic Germans	No	Unsystematic pattern
	GSOEP	Guest workers	No	No

Notes: With the exception of Bauer and Zimmermann (1996, 1997) and Seifert (1996) the reference group are natives. Bauer and Zimmermann (1996, 1997) and Seifert (1996) defined Übersiedler to be the reference group.

investments, than permanent migrants. This lower incentive to invest in country-specific human capital results in a permanent gap between the earnings of guest workers in Germany and comparable natives (Dustmann 1993).

These findings were contradicted by Pischke (1992), Schmidt (1992a, b); and Licht and Steiner (1994). Using the first six waves of the GSOEP, Pischke (1992) estimated pooled cross-section and fixed effect panel models. The results from the pooled cross-section indicate an initial average earnings disadvantage for guest workers of about 23 per cent with no significant earnings growth in subsequent years. The fixed effects estimation results do not differ much from the pooled cross-section findings. Investigating different subgroups, Pischke (1992) finds that there is no difference between the experience-earnings-profile of unskilled and blue-collar guest workers and comparable natives. For guest workers who immigrated after 1976, however, he confirms the typical assimilation pattern found in classical immigration countries. Restricting his analysis to blue-collar workers, Schmidt (1992a, b) finds that the average guest worker suffers an initial earnings disadvantage of about 12 per cent of comparable natives. His estimate of a linear assimilation coefficient β_3 implies that with each year of residency in Germany, immigrants' earnings rise 0.7 per cent faster than those of natives, implying that guest workers reach earnings parity with natives after about seventeen years of residency. Controlling for possible sample selection bias, which may occur due to return migration and the employment status of guest workers, Licht and Steiner (1994) obtained positive assimilation rates about one per cent, or 8 per cent during the first ten years in Germany.

Constant's (1998) study on the earnings assimilation of men and women guestworkers is based on the first ten years of the GSOEP. She employed a two-way fixed effect model that controled for unobserved heterogeneity and attrition and utilized the fixed effects to determine whether there were any significant cohort effects. With regard to the male samples, her results show significant and persistent wage disparities between natives and guest workers with the latter earning considerably less. Contrary to other studies, she finds an initial immigrant earnings advantage that is, however, shortlived and consistent with the labour market segmentation hypothesis. Whereas human capital played a major role in determining earnings, her results refute the assimilation hypothesis and emphasize a deterioration of male earnings with additional time in Germany. Her analysis on the female samples, however, reveals that guest-worker women earn more than their German counterparts. Whereas she finds evidence of assimilation—in the sense that immigrant women start with an earnings disadvantage but they catch up and outperform German women within ten years of migration—the human capital theory's applicability is not compelling. Her results are better explained by the labour market segmentation theory. Still, she finds a large gender wage disparity whereby immigrant women perform worse than immigrant men in the labour market.

The explanation of these puzzling differences in findings seems to be that the guest workers in Germany are relatively low-skilled. Furthermore, the results suggest that they are not able to climb the occupational ladder, that is, they remain in blue-collar occupations. Whether immigrants are found to adjust is, therefore, a consequence of the choice of the native reference group. Because Dustmann (1993) included all natives in the analysis, whether blue- or white-collar workers, his nonconvergence is understandable. A fundamental problem with all studies using the GSOEP as data base for their analysis is that the foreigners in the sample have already been in Germany for a long time (most of the foreigners in the GSOEP entered Germany before 1977), resulting in problems in identifying assimilation effects.

Some other interesting estimation results of the studies reviewed thus far are worth noting. Pischke (1992), Schmidt (1992a) and Constant (1998) also analyse the role of country of origin for the convergence of native and immigrant earnings. Using dummies for the nationality of the immigrants, Schmidt (1992a, b) reveals that there are significant differences between the initial earnings of guest workers from different sending countries. In particular, Schmidt (1992a) estimates that Spanish workers earn about 6 per cent less than Greek, Italian, and Turkish workers, while workers from the former Yugoslavia earn 5 per cent more. This is quite similar to the results obtained by Pischke (1992). Those ethnic groups with the largest initial earnings disadvantage realized the highest wage growth (Schmidt 1992b). Constant's (1998) study with regard to ethnicity, finds only mild wage differentials among the five guest-worker nationalities. For men, she finds that Greeks and Yugoslavs earn 12 and 8 per cent more than Turks respectively, and for women, Greeks earn 12 per cent more than Turks. However, German citizenship is not a significant determinant of their earnings.

Licht and Steiner (1994) show that sample selection bias due to the return migration of guest workers seems to be unimportant in the case of Germany. Similarly, Constant and Massey (2003) find that, although there is pronounced selection with respect to return migration, this selective emigration does not appear to distort cross-sectional estimates of earnings assimilation for men and women immigrants in Germany. Investigating the issue of language, Dustmann (1994) shows that proficiency, especially in writing, considerably improves the earnings of migrants. Finally, the empirical results of Dustmann (1996) imply that social assimilation, measured by dummy variables indicating the guest workers' feeling of national identity, does not affect the earnings of guest workers.

An innovative approach has been taken by Bauer, Pereira, Vogler, and Zimmermann (2002) to evaluate the performance of Portuguese migrants in the German labour market. They have merged German data from the *Beschäftigtenstichprobe* (the labour force survey) of the German Labour Office with Portuguese data from the *Quadros de Pessoal* (employees records) of the Portuguese Ministry for Employment and Social Security.

This enables them to study more deeply the selection mechanism of migrants and to compare the relative performance of Portuguese in Germany and in Portugal. The econometric evidence suggests that Portuguese workers who stayed in Portugal would have received higher wages if they had migrated to Germany than those who actually did, whereas those who migrated to Germany would have earned less in Portugal than their Portuguese counterparts. Portuguese migrants to Germany are negatively self-selected with regard to observed characteristics if compared to those who stayed at home. However, for the low-skilled blue-collar workers, a positive selection is observed with respect to Germans. A comparison of the wages of German natives and Portuguese guest workers using an Oaxaca decomposition suggests that the remuneration is higher for the migrants. This implies that Portuguese guest workers in Germany are positively self-selected in terms of unobserved skills if compared to the same German subgroup in the labour force. Hence, while the measured skills of migrants were below the market needs, unobserved characteristics like motivation have been positive.

Compared to research on foreign guest workers, only a few studies of the earnings assimilation of ethnic Germans exist, which can be attributed to the limited availability of data. A basic problem here is that ethnic Germans are not separately registered in public statistics after they have gained residence status in Germany because they are now considered to be German. The available findings are also mixed: using two cross sections from the ALLBUS, which were sampled in the years 1982 and 1990, Schmidt (1994a) analyses the labour market performance of ethnic Germans, who primarily immigrated before 1962. Regarding the earnings dynamics of these immigrants, his results imply an initial earnings disadvantage at the time of entry of about 9 per cent for migrants from the former German Democratic Republic (GDR) and of 16 per cent for migrants from Eastern Europe. It is further found that the earnings of these immigrants rise by about 0.5 per cent per year of residency, suggesting that *Übersiedler* reach earnings parity with comparable natives after about twenty-one years of residency and *Aussiedler* after about twenty-six years. However, similar to his results for foreign guest workers, most of the initial earnings gap and parts of the subsequent assimilation disappear when controlling for the job status of individuals.

Using a slightly different specification but the same dataset, Schmidt (1997) confirms his earlier results. Controlling for the education and the occupational status of the *Aus-* and *Übersiedler*, he could not reveal a significant earnings disadvantage of ethnic Germans at the time of entry.

Schmidt (1997) also finds numerically important and significant earnings assimilation of different entry cohorts. Across different entry cohorts, however, the earnings growth shows an unsystematic pattern, which cannot be explained by the standard human capital approach of migrant assimilation.

Bauer and Zimmermann (1996, 1997a) use the first wave of the immigration sample of the GSOEP to study the earnings growth of ethnic Germans, who have migrated to Germany since 1984. Their estimations reveal no significant differences between the earnings of *Aussiedler* and *Übersiedler* at the time of entry, with *Aussiedler* having a steeper age-earnings profile than *Übersiedler*. This result suggests that, due to the relative disadvantage of *Aussiedler* with regard to their knowledge of the German language and a greater similarity of the East and West German culture, *Aussiedler* need to invest more in the country-specific human capital of West Germany than *Übersiedler*. Bauer and Zimmermann (1996, 1997a) also show that the utilization of ethnic networks has a significant positive effect on the earnings of immigrants. Using the same dataset, but a categorical instead of a continuous specification of years since immigration, Seifert (1996a, b) obtains similar results.

Dunn et al. (1997) use the same dataset as Bauer and Zimmermann (1996, 1997a) but combine this dataset with the information of the GSOEP from the 1994 sample of natives in order to be able to study the earnings assimilation of ethnic Germans compared to natives. Their estimation results imply that no earnings differential exists between ethnic Germans and comparable natives at the time of entry. Different to Bauer and Zimmermann (1997a) and Schmidt (1994a, 1997), they find a U-shaped effect of years of residency in Germany on the wages of ethnic immigrants. As the authors note, their estimation results regarding the effect of the years since migration is not robust against changes in the empirical specification. Finally, the results of Dunn et al. (1997) show that there are virtually no differences between the returns to schooling obtained in the former GDR and East Europe and the returns to schooling obtained in Germany. However, work experience obtained in the sending regions has no value in West Germany.

7.3.2 Employment and Unemployment

Compared to the number of existing empirical studies on earnings assimilation, much less attention has been paid to the assimilation of migrants in terms of their employment and unemployment experience. To our knowledge, only three studies of the unemployment experience of foreign guest workers exist. Using the 1984 wave of the *Beschäftigten-statistik* (see Bender et al. 1996, for a detailed description of this dataset), which is comparable to the Labour Force Survey in the United States, Cramer (1984) analyses the causes of the observed differences between the unemployment rates of foreign guest workers and natives. His empirical results reveal that most of these differences can be explained by the guest workers' comparably bad occupational training as well as their concentration in industries with a relatively high unemployment probability. However, even after controlling for education, industry, and other socio-economic characteristics, there remains a significantly higher probability for guest workers to become unemployed. Using the same data source for the year 1991, Bender and Karr (1993) confirm the results of Cramer (1984).

Winkelmann and Zimmermann (1993) study the frequency of unemployment spells for natives and guest workers in the period from 1974 to 1984 using a count data estimation technique. Their results show that guest workers are more frequently unemployed than natives, especially later in life. Robust Poisson estimates indicate that there is a U-shaped relationship between age and frequency of unemployment for both German workers and guest workers. Guest workers, however, face lower unemployment risks than natives in early stages of their employment career and higher risks in later stages. Applying a simulated probit estimator to the 1984 to 1989 waves of the GSOEP, Mühleisen and Zimmermann (1994) find no significant differences between guest workers and natives concerning their risk of becoming unemployed.

Despite the data limitations already discussed in the former section, several empirical studies concerning the employment assimilation of ethnic Germans exist. Using the 1982 and 1991 cross-section of the *ALLBUS*, Schmidt (1994a) studies the labour market performance of ethnic Germans with regard to labour market participation, self-employment, and unemployment. His results reveal that there are no significant differences between the labour market participation of German immigrants and natives. Migrants from the former German territories in Eastern Europe are demonstrated as having a lower probability of becoming self-employed and a higher probability of becoming unemployed than natives, whereas no significant differences exist between natives and immigrants from the former GDR and from other territories in Eastern Europe. Neither for labour market participation nor for the probability of becoming self-employed or unemployed years of residency shows a statistically significant influence.

Constant and Shachmurove (2002) investigate the occupational assimilation of the self-employed in Germany. Based on the GSOEP, they estimate probabilities of self-employment versus salaried work and unemployment for West Germans, East Germans, guest workers, and other Eastern immigrants. Comparing East Germans to West Germans they find that the former have a higher probability of becoming self-employed. Comparing other immigrants to guest workers their results show that the odds of becoming self-employed double for the latter. Whereas self-employment probabilities increase with age, at a decreasing rate, they decrease with years since migration, albeit at an increasing rate. This indicates that self-employment is a way of overcoming mounting structural and other barriers that are present in the beginning of their immigrant carrier. With additional time in Germany, however, they might choose salaried jobs. Nonetheless, their findings with respect to earnings assimilation reveal that self-employed immigrants in Germany earn more than salaried workers. Still, immigrants do not fare as well as their German counterparts.

Koller (1992) uses two cross-section datasets of *Übersiedler* from 1984 and 1990 in order to study the occupational integration of this subgroup of ethnic Germans. Her results reveal that those who immigrated in 1989 needed significantly less time to find their first employment than those who immigrated in 1984. According to Koller (1992), this result can be attributed to an improvement of the West German labour market after the German reunification in 1990. Furthermore, she finds that 44 per cent of the immigrants changed their occupational status and work activity. Using a panel dataset of 2,851 *Aussiedler*, who took part in a German language course, Koller (1993) shows that the labour market integration of immigrants from Eastern Europe crucially depends on their settlement pattern and their country of origin. *Aussiedler*, who settled in regions characterized by relatively low unemployment rates, and ethnic Germans originating from Romania needed less time to obtain their first employment. Occupational skills acquired in the country of origin are another important determinant of successful integration. Whereas mechanics, drivers, and electricians obtained employment after a relatively short period of time, the integration of clerks and migrants in social and teaching occupations was much more problematic.

Using the immigration sample of the GSOEP of 1995, Schulz and Seiring (1994) analyse the time ethnic Germans need to find their first employment. They conclude that *Übersiedler* have a higher probability of finding employment within the first two years after immigration than *Aussiedler*. Females need much more time to find employment than males since they were mainly educated in occupations that are either in excessive supply in

West Germany or require language proficiency. Similar to Koller (1992), Schulz and Seiring (1994) demonstrate that macroeconomic conditions in the year of immigration are important for successful labour market integration. Immigrants during years of high unemployment needed more time to find employment than those who came during an economic boom.

Bauer and Zimmermann (1996, 1997a) use the same dataset as Schulz and Seiring (1994) in order to study the assimilation of ethnic Germans with regard to their unemployment experience. Their results reveal that *Aussiedler* from Poland and the former USSR have a significantly higher probability of becoming unemployed than *Übersiedler*, whereas there is no statistically significant difference between *Aussiedler* from Romania and *Übersiedler*. The authors explain this result as the consequence of network migration. *Aussiedler* from Romania prefer to settle in the south of West Germany, which is characterized by relatively low unemployment rates. On the other hand, immigrants from Poland and the former USSR move predominantly to North Rhine-Westphalia, which has relatively high unemployment rates. Furthermore, different from ethnic Germans in Poland and the former USSR, ethnic Germans from Romania lived in enclaves, which enabled them better to maintain German culture and traditions and, therefore, improved their potential to transfer human capital obtained in the country of origin. Further, it appears that the risk of unemployment decreases with increasing years of residency in Germany. The respective estimations of the assimilation coefficient β_3 from equation (1) implies that the probability of becoming unemployed disappears after eight years of residency for *Übersiedler* and for *Aussiedler* from Romania. Ethnic Germans from Poland and the former USSR need about fifteen years to reach employment assimilation. Finally, network variables show no significant influence on the unemployment experience of ethnic Germans.

The immigration sample of the GSOEP has also been employed by Seifert (1996a, 1996b) in order to study the employment status of ethnic Germans and other migrants one year after immigration. His results reveal that *Aussiedler* and other immigrants have a lower probability of being employed one year after immigration than *Übersiedler*. The year of immigration plays no significant role in the probability of finding employment. Seifert's (1996a, 1996b) estimation further indicates that ethnic networks play an important role for the integration of immigrants in the German labour market. Immigrants who did not use the help of relatives and friends while looking for a job have a lower probability of finding employment within the first year of residence.

7.3.3 Job and Geographical Mobility

Schmidt (1994a) shows that German immigrants are less likely to become civil servants or white-collar workers than comparable natives. With years of residency, immigrants are able to improve their labour market position and achieve parity in terms of the distribution in labour market segments after about thirty years.

The study of Winkelmann and Zimmermann (1993), already described in the last section, also analyses the frequency of direct job changes of guest workers and natives. The results show that foreign guest workers on average change jobs more readily than natives. During their working career, natives change jobs less frequently as they grow older; foreigners change less frequently the longer they are in Germany. Mühleisen and Zimmermann (1994) could not confirm these results. Their analysis suggests that no significant differences exist between guest workers and natives for the probability of changing jobs.

The paper of Bauer and Zimmermann (1999a) utilizes the first three waves of the immigration sample of the German Socioeconomic Panel (GSOEP) in order to analyse the extent and the determinants of occupational mobility among recent immigrants in West Germany. Their empirical results reveal that *Aussiedler* and foreigners face a higher probability of changing their occupational status during the process of integration in the West German labour market than immigrants from the former GDR. Despite significant gender differences, the results further indicate that migrants with higher levels of schooling have a higher probability of changing their occupational status. Compared to their less educated counterparts, however, those with higher schooling levels also experience a faster decrease in the probability of changing occupational status with time of residency in Germany.

A more distinct picture of occupational mobility among immigrants is provided by the empirical analysis of the extent and the determinants of downward mobility. The results of an ordered probit model estimation demonstrate that *Aussiedler* and foreigners have a higher probability of experiencing downward mobility in occupational status than otherwise similar *Übersiedler*. The same pattern can be observed for females, if compared to males, and for those individuals who have been skilled or professional workers in their sending countries, if compared to their unskilled counterparts. At the time of immigration, individuals with a secondary schooling degree show a lower probability of suffering from downward mobility than those with primary schooling only, while migrants with a university degree show a higher probability. Migrants with a university degree, however, reach their original occupational status after about fourteen years of residency in Germany, compared to about twenty-eight years for migrants with primary schooling.

7.3.4 Contributions to the Welfare State

One of the most heated public debates connected with migration to Germany has been the utilization of the welfare state by migrants. According to official statistics, the expenditures for social security benefits in West Germany between 1985 and 1993 increased by more than 106 per cent, from 21 billion DM in 1985 to 43 billion DM in 1993 (Statistisches Bundesamt, 1986, 1995). During the same period, the number of individuals receiving social security benefits increased by 52 per cent, from 2.8 million in 1983 to 4.3 million in 1993. Most of the increase in individuals receiving social security benefits could be attributed to foreigners. The number of foreigners receiving benefits increased by nearly 300 per cent (*Statistisches Bundesamt*, various issues), whereas the number of Germans receiving social security benefits increased by only 20 per cent between 1985 and 1993. However, since the official statistics treat ethnic Germans as natives, these numbers understate the role of immigration for the

Table 7.7. Private households receiving social security benefits, West Germany, 1995

	Proportion of houeseholds receiving social security benefits	Average benefits of households receiving social security benefits in DM per month	Average size of households receiving social security benefits in persons
Natives	2.7	680	2.4
Guestworkers	5.5	598	3
Immigrants since 1984	9.4	932	3.5
among them:			
Übersiedler until 1990	3.6	848	3
Aussiedler	12.6	683	3.7
Guestworkers	4.5	1,058	3
Asylum Seekers, Refugees	52.1	1,165	3.9
Others	4.1	522	1.6
All households	3.3	727	2.7

Source: Büchel, Fricke and Voges (1996).

increase in social security expenditures. Table 7.7 gives a more detailed picture of the structure of households receiving social security benefits in 1995. It appears that all immigration groups show a higher proportion of households receiving social security benefits than native households. The proportion of households of foreign guest workers receiving social security benefits is 2.8 percentage points higher than that of natives, and that of recent immigrants is 6.7 percentage points higher. Among all individuals who immigrated since 1984, asylum seekers and refugees show the highest probability of receiving social security benefits. This result is hardly surprising since asylum seekers and refugees were not allowed to work until their application was approved or denied, which could last several years. Since 1993 they have been allowed to work, but their employment possibilities are restricted (see Section 7.2). Table 7.7 further shows that a high proportion of *Aussiedler* households receive social security benefits. Overall, these numbers indicate that a large part of the increase in social security expenditures can be attributed to immigration.

This impression is corroborated by the study of Buhr and Weber (1996). They compare a cohort of individuals in Bremen, who started to receive social assistance in 1983, with a more recent cohort of new recipients, whose first spell of assistance began in 1989. The comparison of these two cohorts reveals that immigration of ethnic Germans and refugees is responsible for a large portion of the increased number of new recipients. The proportion of natives and guest workers receiving social security benefits decreased between the two periods. Furthermore, ethnic Germans and refugees are also responsible for the observed decline in the total duration of social assistance. Social recipients in the subgroup of natives and guest workers of the 1989 cohort stayed slightly longer on social assistance than those in the 1983 cohort. To summarize, the official statistics and the analysis of Buhr and Weber (1996) indicate that most of the increase in social security expenditures in the last fifteen years can be attributed to the immigration of ethnic Germans and refugees.

Despite the importance perceived by the public, there are few studies on whether immigration has been a burden or a gain for the German social security system. (See Wagner 1994 and Ulrich 1994 for surveys on the available research.) This lack of studies can mainly be attributed to a lack of appropriate data which could enable a careful analysis of the relationship between immigration and the welfare state (Schmähl 1995). Most of the existing literature in this area relies on descriptive statistics or simulations to evaluate the short and longterm effects of immigration on the welfare state. Büchel et al. (1996) analyse the utilization of the social security system by immigrants. Controlling for important household characteristics such as gender, age, education, and the employment status of the household head as well as the household size, they conclude that only *Aussiedler* and the group of asylum seekers and refugees show a statistically significant higher probability of receiving social security benefits than natives, whereas no statistically significant differences appear between the other immigration groups and comparable natives. For asylum seekers and refugees, these results can be explained by their restricted opportunities to work. Compared with the other groups of the population, *Aussiedler* receive a lower amount of benefits, indicating that this group receives additional income from other sources. For all immigrants Büchel et al. (1996) could further reveal that the probability of receiving social security benefits decreases with the time of residency in Germany.

Using a panel data extracted from the GSOEP, Riphahn (1998) analyses the participation of immigrants in social assistance programmes relative to natives. Relying only on descriptive statistics, she shows that the probability of welfare dependency of foreign households exceeds that of native households by more than 25 per cent. The estimation results, however, indicate that foreign households are less likely to depend on welfare once socioeconomic characteristics are accounted for. Further, Riphahn (1998) does not find assimilation effects in the welfare dependency of foreign households. Among the determinants of welfare dependency in Germany, the status of the labour force appears to be the main factor. Overall, her results reveal that the relatively high welfare dependency of foreign households in Germany is based on their relatively unfavourable socioeconomic characteristics. In other words, a different behaviour of foreigners if compared to similar natives does not play a crucial role in explaining the welfare dependency of foreign households.

Some studies attempt to simulate whether immigration has been a gain or burden for the fiscal budget. Taking the unemployment of native unskilled workers into consideration, Bauer and Zimmermann (1997*b*) simulate that, depending on the composition of the immigrants with regard to their skills, immigration could result in gains for the German tax receipts and the unemployment insurance system of about 17–44 billion DM, or 1–2 per cent of the GNP in 1993. Gieseck et al. (1993) use macrodata to make some rough estimates of the effect of immigration on tax revenues and expenditures. Implicitly assuming that foreigners are homogeneous to Germans with regard to their average incomes, their labour force participation, and their unemployment rate, they conclude that immigration has a positive impact on public coffers.

In his analysis on the impact of foreigners on the German social insurance system, Ulrich (1994) shows that until 1973 guest workers paid proportionately more unemployment insurance contributions than they received. After 1973, the unemployment of guest workers increased and stayed above the unemployment rate of natives, indicating that they participated in unemployment insurance benefits more than in contributions. With regard to the health insurance and pension system, Ulrich (1994) concludes that foreigners have been net contributors. But as the foreign population in Germany grows older, these positive effects will decrease. Using the 1984 wave of the GSOEP, Ulrich (1994) also calculates the contributions to social security insurance, tax payments, and the per average transfers of native and guest-worker households. On the one hand, these calculations reveal that foreign households pay, on average, lower taxes but higher contributions to social security insurance than native households. Taken together, taxes and social security contributions paid by foreign households are higher than those of the average native household. On the other hand, total transfers received by foreign households have been on average 50 per cent lower than those received by native households, indicating that the immigration of guest workers resulted in net gains for the German social security system thus far. A closer look at the data shows that unemployment benefits, child allowances, and social security benefits received by guest-worker families are on average double those of natives. The result that foreigners receive in total fewer benefits than natives is driven mainly by the average amount of pensions received: guest worker households receive on average only 6 per cent of the pensions received by native households. As the guest workers grow older and become eligible for pensions, the calculated net gain for the German social security system could switch to a net loss.

The studies reviewed so far show only the short-term effects of immigration on the welfare state. They can not answer whether immigration can be a solution to the welfare state's looming problems, which will arise from an ageing population and a decreasing workforce. Overall, this question is very complex, since one has to consider the labour market effects of immigration, the assimilation of the immigrants into society, the educational and occupational structure of the immigrant population, their intended length of stay, as well as differences in the possibilities of utilizing the welfare state due to institutional regulations, in order to evaluate the longterm effects of immigration on the welfare state (Schmähl 1995). However, existing simulation studies on the long-term effects of immigration on the German pay-as-you-go social insurance system and

242   BAUER, DIETZ, ZIMMERMANN, AND ZWINTZ

tax-financed social transfers indicate that immigration has a relieving effect (Dinkel and Lebok 1993; Börsch-Supan 1994; and Felderer 1994). These simulations also show that a relatively high permanent immigration is required to stabilize the German social security system. For example, Börsch-Supan (1994) calculates that an annual immigration of 300,000 persons is necessary to halve the increase of the proportion of the population over the age of sixty-five.

Compared to Börsch-Supan (1994), the simulations of Felderer (1994) reveal much higher numbers. He simulates that in 1998 Germany needs an immigration of nearly two million people to stabilize the public pension fund. This number increases to over 2.5 million in the year 2000 and reaches a peak in 2041 with a necessary immigration of 4.15 million per year. Felderer (1994) obtains similar results for the number of immigrants needed to stabilize the public health insurance. Although these simulations strongly depend on the underlying assumptions regarding the future evolution of the German reproduction rate, the life expectancy, and the age structure of the immigrants, they nevertheless show that increased immigration represents no solution to the upcoming problems of the German social security system. However, the analysis of Zimmermann et al. (2002) also shows that immigration is the more successful tool in comparison with an increase of the retirement age or the increase in female work participation to moderate the consequences of population ageing for the labour market.

7.4. The Native Labour Market Consequences

The effects of immigration on wages and employment of natives has always been of major interest to migration research and to the general public. In the US as well as in Germany, there have been concerns that immigrants might have negative effects on the earnings and employment of natives. Even the simplest theoretical model cannot give a clear answer as to whether immigration leads to negative labour market effects for natives. Greenwood and McDowell (1986, 1994) and Bauer (1997a) provide an overview of the theoretical literature on the labour market effects of immigration. Friedberg and Hunt (1995) review the empirical literature for the US, Schmidt (1994b) for Germany and Zimmermann (1995a, b) for Europe.

In a simple framework, in which the country of origin produces a single good by means of capital and homogeneous labour, immigration would increase the labour supply and the wage rate in the immigration country would fall, whereas the price for capital would increase. Given a particular amount of immigration, the reduction of the wages would be the greater the more inelastic the labour demand and labour supply. However, since immigrants are also consumers, they may have positive effects on investment expenditures, technological progress, and entrepreneurial activity. Therefore, immigration could result in an outward shift of the labour demand curve. Whether immigration leads to lower wages depends on whether the positive wage effects of increased labour demand can compensate for the negative wage effects of the increased labour supply.

In the German context, it is important to consider imperfections in the labour market when analysing the effects of immigration. For example, wages may not be downwardly flexible due to the behaviour of unions. If union behaviour remains unaffected by immigration, then the new immigrants may cause unemployment to rise. On the other hand, the unions' wage-employment choice may be affected by the pressure of increased unemployment or by the possibility of giving different weights to the interests of groups of workers. If labour is heterogeneous, the key issue for the evaluation of the labour market effects of immigration is whether foreigners are substitutes or complements to natives. Then immigration will result in decreasing wages of natives who are substitutes to immigrants and increasing wages of natives who are complements to immigrants. (See Schmidt et al. 1994, for a general model considering heterogeneous labour and wage rigidities.)

In the following subsections, we study the existing evidence on the wage and employment effects of immigration in Germany. In addition to the existing econometric studies, the subsections also review simulation studies. Section 7.4.1 deals with wages, Section 7.4.2 with employment. Section 7.4.3 discusses the effects of immigration on the occupational and geographical mobility of natives. The evidence is summarized in Section 7.4.4. The review here does not cover the rising interest in the determinants of sentiments and attitudes towards migrants (see Brücker et al. 2002, chapter 5, and Bauer et al. 2000, as a recent example).

7.4.1. The Effect of Immigration on Native Wages

Beginning with Grossman's analysis (1982), a large number of empirical studies on the wage effects of immigration in the US has been conducted. A survey of this research is given by Borjas (1994). Most of these studies do not support the hypothesis that native Americans are strongly and adversely affected by immigration (Borjas 1994). Compared with the United States, the empirical evidence for the European labour market is relatively scarce and not as clear cut. However, the available studies conclude that the wage effects of immigration are negligible or non-existent and, in some cases, even positive. In this section we review the existing evidence for Germany. A summary is contained in Table 7.8.

The first contribution to the native wage effects of immigration was made by DeNew and Zimmermann (1994a, b) and Haisken-DeNew and Zimmermann (1999). They employ a reduced form model of the labour market by regressing the effects of the foreigner share in an industry on logged hourly wages. The sign of the estimated coefficient of this foreigner share variable determines whether immigrants are substitutes or comple-ments to native workers, that is, whether they have a negative or a positive effect on the wages of natives. To control for possible endogeneity, the foreigner share variable was instrumented by industry dummies, industry value-added growth rates, and an overall and industry-specific time-trend. Regressions further include a number of individual and industry-specific control variables together with a set of dummies to control for fixed industry effects. The resulting equation has been estimated for various occupational groups by a random effects two-stage GLS method using the German Socioeconomic Panel (GSOEP) from 1984 to 1989.

Overall, DeNew and Zimmermann (1994a) find that a one per cent increase in the employment share of guest workers decreases hourly wages of all natives by 0.35 per cent (see Table 7.8). They also obtain significantly different effects of immigration on different groups of native workers. According to their results, a one per cent increase in the share of guest workers results in a decrease in wages of native blue-collar workers by 0.45 per cent, whereas the wages of white-collar workers increase by 0.12 per cent. The estimated coefficient for the latter group, however, appears to be statistically insignificant. Examining the industry-specific effects of the foreigner share, it turns out that natives in some industries gain. Overall, positive elasticities are found for natives working in in the transportation (+0.07) and wholesale/retail (+0.023) industries, whereas large negative elasticities are found for natives in the investment sector (−0.56) and the primary sector (−0.43). DeNew and Zimmermann (1994a) conclude that immigration measured by the share of foreigners in different industries has an overall but small effect on German wages.

Using the same framework and dataset but restricting the analysis to blue-collar workers, DeNew and Zimmermann (1994b) find smaller effects (see Table 7.8). The estimated elasticity of −0.16 suggests that the wages of native blue-collar workers are reduced by 0.16 per cent if the employment share of guest workers increases by one per cent. Compared to the existing

Table 7.8. Elasticities of native wages with respect to a 1% increase in foreign employment

Study	Specifications	Elasticity	
DeNew/Zimmermann (1994a)	Wage equation in levels; foreigner share in industries; Germany	All natives–All guestworkers	−0.349
		Blue-collar natives–all Guestworkers	−0.455
		White-collar natives–all guestworkers	0
DeNew/Zimmermann (1994b)	Wage equation in levels; foreigner share in industries; Germany	Blue-collar natives–all guestworkers	−0.161
		Blue-collar foreigners–all guestworkers	−0.240
Bauer (1997a)	Wage equation in levels; foreigner share in industries; Germany	All natives–all guestworkers	−0.082
Pischke/Velling (1994)	Wage equation in differences; foreigner share in regions; Germany	All natives–all guestworkers	0.033
Hatzius (1994)	Wage equation in differences; foreigner share in regions; Germany	All natives–guestworkers	−0.579
		All natives–Aussiedler	0.018
		All natives–Übersiedler	0
Bauer (1997b)	Translog production function; Germany	6 groups of workers defined over education (skilled, unskilled), occupational status (blue-collar, white-collar), and nationality (foreigner, German)	0.035; −0.021
Winter-Ebmer and Zimmermann (1998)	Wage equation in differences; foreigner share in industries; Austria Germany	Austria	−0.164; 0
		Germany	0; 1.027
Gang/Rivera-Batiz (1994a)	Translog production function; 4 European countries	The Netherlands	0.022; −0.090
		France	−0.002; −0.018
		United Kingdom	0.021; −0.081
		Germany	0.114; −0.046

evidence in the US, even this elasticity is rather large. Furthermore, DeNew and Zimmermann (1994b) show that immigrants themselves experience the highest negative effects of immigration. Disaggregating the foreigner industry share by industry and region and using the first nine waves of the GSOEP (1984–92), Haisken-DeNew and Zimmermann (1999) have found significantly different effects in relation to their 1994 studies. Overall, the estimates exhibit a complementary effect of immigration. Looking at different occupational groups, Haisken-DeNew and Zimmermann (1999) find no significant immigration wage effects on native white-collar workers, but a significantly positive wage effect on native blue-collar workers with more than twenty years of labour market experience.

Bauer (1998) replicates the studies of DeNew and Zimmermann using the 1994 wave of the *Beschäftigtenstatistik*. As can be seen from Table 7.8, his estimation of the overall wage elasticity is much smaller than those obtained by DeNew and Zimmermann (1994a, b). Bauer (1998) further disaggregates native and foreign workers according to their occupational status and their skill level. The results of this analysis imply that native unskilled blue-collar workers are complements to all immigration groups. Native skilled blue-collar workers suffer from the immigration of foreign unskilled and skilled blue-collar workers and can expect increasing wages in the case of an immigration of white-collar workers. Bauer (1998) also reveals, however, that native white-collar workers are substitutes to all groups of foreign workers. From a theoretical point of view, the latter result is hard to justify.

Pischke and Velling (1994, 1997) adopt a rather different approach. Unlike the studies reviewed so far, they use an earnings function approach. They employ the change in wage level as the dependent variable and the change in the number of foreigners in relation to the entire local population. They use the age group fifteen to sixty-four in a labour market region as an exogenous variable. Pischke and Velling (1994) employ a dataset from the German Federal Research Institute for Regional Geography and Regional Planning (*Bundesforschungsanstalt für Landeskunde und Raumordnung*), which separates Germany into 328 counties (Federal Planning Regions).[1] Pischke and Velling (1994) estimate a positive and

---

[1] These county data are aggregated by the authors to 166 labour market regions for the years 1985 to 1989. In order to capture the composition of the local labour force, several variables are controlled for, such as the shares of employment in twelve different industries, the share of highly skilled workers, the share of unskilled workers, the share of part-time workers, the share of female workers, and the share of workers older than 55. Furthermore, dummies for seven different regions of the country and the log of the population density in a region are used. Finally, the change in the

significant wage effect of immigration. A one per cent increase in the share of foreigners leads to a maximum of a 3.29 per cent increase in the wage level, implying a complementary effect of foreign labour (see Table 7.8). A possible problem with these findings is that the dataset used also includes economically inactive foreigners such as asylum seekers, who generally have no work permit. Allowing for this, regressions for foreigners of Turkish nationality are estimated, yielding similar results as the estimation for all foreigners. A one per cent increase in the share of Turkish foreigners leads to a 1.88 per cent increase in the wage level. Pischke and Velling (1994) add to the understanding of the native labour market consequences of immigration by analysing local labour markets. They are not able to separate between low-qualified and high-qualified labour. This is important, however, since immigration is supposed to have a negative wage effect, particularly for low qualified labour. Furthermore, they study a boom period, which might bias their results.

For the period of 1984 to 1991, Hatzius (1994) applies a model similar to that of Pischke and Velling (1994) to a German regional panel dataset constructed from the GSOEP and other officially published data. In contrast to the studies surveyed thus far, he further controls for the state of technology, measured as the trend in total factor productivity and the stock of capital in a region. Hatzius (1994) also differentiates between foreign guest workers, *Aussiedler* and *Übersiedler*, whereas the former studies only considered foreign guest workers. According to his regression results, immigration does not seem to affect native unemployment. By contrast, native earnings are substantially affected. Hatzius's (1994) results imply that foreign guest workers have a substantially negative impact on the earnings of natives, whereas *Übersiedler* appear to complement natives. Ethnic German immigration from Eastern Europe is unrelated to native earnings (see Table 7.8).

Bauer (1997) bases his empirical work on the estimation of a flexible production function, which allows for the calculation of the overall technical relationship between natives and foreigners, that is, whether they are substitutes or complements. He treats foreigners and natives as different production factors and further differentiates natives and guest workers according to their occupational status and skill, i.e. he uses low-skilled blue-collar, high-skilled blue-collar, and white-collar natives and immigrants. The empirical results summarized in Table 7.8 show that

share of foreigners in a region is instrumented with its first period level, due to the fact that foreigners may settle in regions with above-average growing labour markets. This leads to an endogeneity problem and an upward bias in the wage equation.

white-collar immigrants are substitutes for low-skilled, blue-collar and white-collar natives. Highly skilled blue-collar natives tend to be adversely affected by the increase in the supply of low-skilled blue-collar immigrants. Between all other native and foreign groups, Bauer (1997) reveals a complementary relationship. Since all immigration wage effects are calculated to be numerically negligible, Bauer (1997) concludes that fears of negative immigration effects on natives' wages lack an empirical basis. He demonstrates, however a remarkable impact of immigration on foreign individuals' wages in the German labour market. Here, the elasticities range from a 1.78 per cent increase in the wages of white-collar foreign workers (caused by a 10 per cent increase in the inflow of high-skilled blue-collar foreign workers) to a 2.55 per cent decrease in the wages of low-skilled blue-collar foreign workers (caused by a 10 per cent increase in the inflow of low-skilled blue-collar foreign workers).

Similar to Bauer's study (1997), Gang and Rivera-Batiz (1994a) also apply the production technology in order to estimate the effects of immigration on the labour market. In contrast to the existing literature, the authors do not consider immigrants and native-born as separate production inputs. Rather Gang and Rivera-Batiz (1994a) suggest that the labour market impact of immigrants is related to the specific skills they bring to the receiving country's labour market.[2] Based on six waves (1986–89) of the Eurobarometer, they estimate the technological relationship between natives and foreigners for four countries: the Netherlands, France, the United Kingdom, and Germany. The results of Gang and Rivera-Batiz (1994a) imply slightly negative effects of immigration on the resident workers in the countries considered in the analysis.

The estimated effects are very different, however, depending on the specific immigration group being examined (see Table 7.8). For example, in the Netherlands a one per cent increase of the population would lower the wages of Dutch workers by 0.09 per cent, if this inflow consisted solely of Turks but would increase the wages by 0.02 per cent if the migrants came from Surinam. In France and the United Kingdom, resident workers suffer the highest wage losses when the migrants come from Asia. A one per cent increase in the population of these two countries, due to the

---

[2] The authors have used three steps to evaluate the factor price elasticities between natives and immigrants. In the first two steps, they estimate factor price elasticities, differentiating the inputs of education, low-skilled labour and experience using a translog production function. In the third step, the authors calculate composite elasticities of complementarity between natives and immigrants using the average qualification of both labour groups regarding the three human capital inputs.

immigration of Asians, would lead to a 0.11 per cent reduction in the wages of French workers and a wage reduction of 0.08 per cent in the United Kingdom. The immigration of Italians to France has nearly no effect on the wages of natives. In the UK and Germany, the immigration of Irish workers actually increases the wages of natives. The wages of German workers are adversely affected by the immigration of Portuguese migrants. Small substitution effects are found for immigrants from guest-worker recruitment countries (Turkey, Portugal, Spain, and Italy). Gang and Rivera-Batiz (1994a) conclude that native individuals with human capital endowments divergent from those of immigrants experience wage increases, while native individuals with human capital endowments similar to immigrating workers experience wage reductions.

In addition to the empirical studies reviewed thus far, there are several simulation studies dealing with the effects of immigration and the labour market position of natives. Barabas et al. (1992) use a macroeconomic simulation model to simulate the effects of immigration during the period from 1988 to 1991. The authors assume an immigration flow of 1.1 million migrants, approximately 4.1 per cent of the German employment in 1991. Their simulation results show that this inflow increased the German national income by approximately 5.4 per cent and resulted in a decrease of the German unemployment rate by 0.2 percentage points. Bauer and Zimmermann (1996) use aggregated data from 1993 to calibrate the model of Schmidt et al. (1994), which allows for heterogeneous work and rigid wages that lead to unemployment of unskilled natives. They calculate that the immigration of unskilled immigrants could result in a decrease of natives' earnings, which could be up to 5.5 per cent of the national income. However, in the case of skilled immigration, the income gains for natives could reach 4.2 per cent of the national income as of 1993. These gains are mainly due to the improvement of the employment possibilities of unskilled natives if they are complements to skilled workers.

Several reasons may explain the small wage effects found in the existing empirical studies. First, binding wage floors (i.e. minimum wages or social security levels) might prevent natives' wages from falling. In such a case, immigration would lead to increased unemployment of natives without affecting their wages. In the next subsection we will, therefore, review empirical studies on the employment effects of immigration. Second, immigration may induce natives to move out of the areas with a high percentage of immigrants into areas with a low share of foreigners. This would result in a decreased supply of native labour in those areas with a high foreigner share and an increased supply of native labour in regions with a low foreigner share. Overall, natives' wages would fall, but far less when compared to a situation in which natives do not move in response to immigration. There is not much empirical evidence on the influence of the immigration of foreigners on the migration behaviour of natives. Evidence from the US (Card 1990) and France (Hunt 1992), however, indicates that natives to a great extent do not move in response to the influx of foreigners.

7.4.2. Employment and Unemployment

The existence of rigid wages may be one reason for the small wage effects found in the empirical studies in the last section. If wages are rigid, it might be the case that immigration will actually increase the unemployment of natives without affecting their wages. According to the theoretical framework presented above, one might expect that the higher the substitutability of foreign workers for natives, the more likely an increase in immigration would lead to an increase in unemployment, if wages in the destination country are inflexible. Once again, using the reasonable simplification that skilled and unskilled workers are complements and that immigrants tend to be substitutes for low-qualified native individuals and complements to highly qualified natives, increased immigration of low-skilled individuals may increase unemployment of low-skilled workers and may induce the reverse effect for highly qualified workers. On the other hand, assuming that the labour market for highly skilled workers is flexible, immigration of highly skilled migrants may decrease unemployment of low-skilled natives without having employment effects on qualified natives. Similar to the existing studies on the wage effects of immigration, most European studies analyse the employment effects of immigration using German data. However, since such empirical studies are much more heterogeneous in their empirical approach and estimation methods than those surveyed in the last section, a summary of the results similar to Table 7.8 is not feasible.

A first attempt to analyse the employment and unemployment effects of immigration to Germany was made by Winkelmann and Zimmermann (1993). For the ten-year period 1974–84, they estimate the effects of individual characteristics and industry-level variables on labour mobility measured by the number of job changes and the frequency of unemployment. Their analysis is based on 1,830 males, 586 of whom are foreigners. Females are excluded from the analysis in order to avoid having to model family formation. Immigration is evaluated as an exogenous variable by the share of foreign labour in 34 industries in 1974.[3] The estimation results of Winkelmann and Zimmermann (1993) show a significant but small immigration effect on the unemployment frequency of German workers. In order to examine the effects of an increased presence of immigrants in the labour market on the unemployment frequency of domestic workers, they simulate an increase in the share of foreign labour in all sectors by factors 2 and 4. The results of these simulations indicate that, all other things being equal, unemployment would rise substantially with immigration. In contrast to the 1970s (Winkelmann and Zimmermann 1993), Mühleisen and Zimmermann (1994) find no evidence that foreign labour induced unemployment in the 1980s.[4] Their estimation results provide no significant indication that a larger share of foreigners in the labour force of specific industries causes unemployment.

Pischke and Velling (1994, 1997) offer two different ways of analysing the employment and unemployment effects of immigration. The first model follows their approach outlined in Section 7.4.1. According to this approach, increased immigration yields small but insignificantly negative effects on employment, while simultaneously yielding a large and significantly positive effect on unemployment. There is some evidence, however, for a spurious effect in these estimation results, because the immigrants' impact on unemployment is not fully reflected in reduced employment. Pischke and Velling (1994, 1997) calculate that a one per cent increase in the share of foreigners should increase the unemployment rate by two per cent, which means that 430,000 additional foreigners would cause 500,000 additional unemployed individuals. Applying a similar approach, Hatzius (1994), whose analysis was discussed in the previous section, could not find statistically significant effects of immigration on native unemployment.

In their second model, Pischke and Velling (1994, 1997) analyse flow data for migration between labour market regions between the years 1986

---

[3] Furthermore, years of schooling, schooling squared, dummies for family status, membership of a trade union, and the occupational status of the worker's first job (using the categories ordinary blue, qualified blue, ordinary white, and qualified white-collar workers) are specified as control variables. Differences in the sectoral employment trends are captured by a variable measuring the growth of employment between 1974 and 1984.

[4] Their empirical application are based on a subsample of 1982 male individuals of the German Socioeconomic Panel, who were at least nineteen in 1984 and at most fifty-nine years old in 1989, and were not selfemployed, in schooling, or civil servants. Transitions between states of employment and unemployment are modeled as outcomes of binomial probit processes, where standard demographic variables like age, nationality, physical condition, years of schooling, job status, and previous employment, or unemployment are contained.

and 1988. They examine the impact of foreign net-migration on employment and unemployment, distinguishing whether a foreign individual migrates from abroad or from another labour market region within Germany. For the years 1986 to 1987, the estimated coefficients on the foreigner-share variable in the employment and unemployment equation switch signs and tend to be insignificant. Apart from a significantly negative effect of gross foreign inflow from Germany in 1986, the coefficients on gross foreign inflow from abroad and gross foreign inflow from Germany are small and insignificant for the analysed period. To sum up, the results of Pischke and Velling (1994, 1997) on the impact of immigration on employment and unemployment in the 1980s is in line with the findings of Mühleisen and Zimmermann (1994), who also find no significant negative effects of immigration on unemployment. One has to keep in mind that both studies examine the impacts of immigration during a boom period in Germany, so an analysis of periods of recession would be a topic for future research.

Velling (1995) examines the impact of immigration on regional unemployment rates. Like Pischke and Velling (1994, 1997), he employs a dataset from the Federal Research Institute for Regional Geography and Regional Planning and supplements it with data from the German Federal Labour Office. This is a dataset with longitudinal character, thus allowing for a deeper analysis of the native labour market consequences of immigration. Velling (1995) distinguishes between regional employment effects caused by immigration of Germans (including ethnic Germans), immigration of individuals with EU nationality, and immigration of other foreign individuals. Furthermore, he separates the employment effects of increased immigration by seasonal workers or contract workers.

According to the estimated results, a one per cent increase in total immigration causes a 0.24 per cent increase in the average regional unemployment in Germany between 1988 and 1993, while a one per cent increase in the inflow of Germans causes an increase in the average regional unemployment rate of 0.19 per cent. The inflow of EU foreign workers or foreign workers with other nationalities causes unemployment effects smaller than 0.05 per cent. These small effects are especially remarkable in the face of the large net inflow of foreigners and ethnic Germans to Germany in the years after the fall of the Iron Curtain. The employment effects of immigration defined by work permit workers (seasonal workers, contract workers) are even smaller and tend to be insignificant. Differentiating the effects of immigration on low-qualified and highly qualified labour yields larger effects of immigration on the employment of low-qualified workers when compared to highly qualified workers. Separating migrants into low-qualified and highly qualified individuals results in the expected complementarity of both groups of workers. That is, the inflow of low-qualified workers results in an increase in the unemployment of domestic low-qualified workers and a decrease in the unemployment of highly qualified workers and vice versa in the case of an inflow of high-qualified workers. Velling's (1995) results of small employment effects of immigration are in line with other contributions. As with all other microeconometric examinations of the consequences of immigration on the native labour market, the datasets used only allow for the analysis of a rather short period of time.

Gang and Rivera-Batiz (1994b) utilize the West German subsample of the October/November 1988 Eurobarometer survey in order to study the influence of guest workers on the employment probabilities of natives. They estimate the likelihood that a German resident will be employed relative to being unemployed on the share of foreigners in a region. To capture foreign presence, the authors use two different measures. The first is defined as the percentage of the foreign population in the *Bundesländer*; the second is based on the respondent's self-reported presence of foreigners in his neighbourhood. The results of Gang and Rivera-Batiz (1994b) show that there is no statistically significant effect on the employment probabilities of natives based on the share of foreigners in a *Bundesland*. Using the self-reported measure of foreign presence, they find that people living in neighbourhoods with many foreigners are more likely to be unemployed. The latter results can be interpreted in various ways: either unemployed natives misperceive the number of foreigners in their neighbourhood; they live in neighbourhoods with more foreigners; or the more localized, self-reported measure of foreigner presence captures the labour market effects better than the more aggregated share of foreigners in a *Bundesland*.

Using industry data for Austria and Germany, Winter-Ebmer and Zimmermann (1998) find that immigration to Austria has negative employment effects on natives, that is, a one percentage point increase in the foreigner share in an industry decreases native employment growth by 0.13 per cent. For Germany, they find that the overall foreigner share in an industry has a slightly negative effect on native employment growth. However, they also show that the share of foreigners from Eastern Europe fosters native employment growth.

To summarize, even though the empirical evidence on the employment effects of immigration is more contradictory than those on wages, the bulk of the evidence indicates that the employment effects of immigration in Europe are very small. Using the results of Hunt (1992) as an upper benchmark, a one per cent increase in the share of foreign workers in the EU raises the unemployment rate in Europe by approximately 0.2 percentage points. Following Bauer and Zimmermann (1991*b*), one can assume that immigration from Eastern Europe will increase the proportion of the non-EU population in the first year after a potential enlargement from 1.86 per cent to 1.91 per cent or by 2.69 per cent. From these numbers, one can calculate that the expected immigration from Eastern Europe will increase the EU unemployment rate by 0.54 percentage points. In addition to the reasons pointed out by Bauer and Zimmermann (1991*b*), there are further arguments indicating that this number represents an upper bound of the employment effects of immigration. First, as Hunt (1992) notes, her estimates of the unemployment elasticity of immigration is upwardly biased, because there is evidence that this number is also picking up some business cycle effects. Second, as we know from the discussion in Section 7.2 of this study, most potential migrants from the East intend to migrate only temporarily, which suggests that the numbers reported above are probably too high.

7.5. Conclusions

The lesson from the empirical material presented in this chapter is that after the Second World War, Germany has been the largest immigration country in the Western world, at least relative to its population size. In the 1950s and 1960s, migration was largely attached to labour market activities. Since the 1970s and early 1980s this turned into a phase of family migration. The 1980s and later were finally dominated by refugee migration. This all implied that since the 1970s, migrants were mostly not working, and this occurred at a rising level. Policy measures like the stop of the guest-worker system in 1973, and the uncontrolled inflow of non-economic migration afterwards is responsible for this development. No migration policy is also a migration policy. It is not difficult to conclude that this was not beneficial to the German labour market. At the same time and measured by internal migration, the German labour force became less mobile, also because the number of available jobs was declining.

The available earnings studies suggest that there is no clear-cut assimilation picture for the guest-worker generation. This has to do with the particular reference groups that were chosen by the researchers, but also with the fact that the estimation often uses data of migrants that have been in the country for already long time. Also guest workers in the 1960s were originally chosen to be alike to blue-collar natives and they got paid equal to similar qualified natives. In that case, the assimilation question does not make sense. Ethnic Germans were generally found to assimilate, although at a slow rate. Individuals with foreign passports are more likely to be unemployed. However, this is largely the consequence of occupational status, and not of behaviour. Ethnic Germans largely behave in a similar way to the natives. Self-employment is a channel that helps migrants to integrate in the host society and often to obtain a salaried job later.

Finally, there are not many indications that migrants depress the wages of native workers. Mostly, effects are small or insignificant, or even positive which can be interpreted in the sense that migrants are complements to natives. This is in line with evidence in other European countries and the United States. Similarly, the attempts to trace negative consequences of immigration for the employment status of natives have not been very successful. The available estimates suggest small effect parameters at best. However, it is also evident that the likely effects depend largely on the competitiveness of the local labour markets. The less competitive they are, the larger are the risks for natives, at least in the short run.

References

Adebahr, H. (1969). 'Binnenwanderung und Lohnhöhe. Eine Analyse der Binnenwanderungen in der Bundesrepublik Deutschland in den Jahren 1957–1967 im Hinblick auf die Frage, ob Wanderungen "lohngerichtet" sind', *Schmöllers Jahrbuch für Wirtschafts- und Sozialwissenschaften*, 89: 557–78.

Antolin, P. and Bover, O. (1997). 'Regional migration in Spain: the effect of personal characteristics and of unemployment, wage and house price differentials using pooled cross-sections', *Oxford Bulletin of Economics and Statistics*, 59: 215–35.

Barabas, G., Gieseck, U., Heilemann, H. D., and von Loeffelholz, D. (1992). 'Gesamtwirtschaftliche Effekte der Zuwanderung 1988 bis 1991', *RWI-Mitteilungen*, 43: 133–54.

Bauer, T. (1997). 'Do immigrants reduce natives' wages? Evidence from Germany', *Münchener Wirtschaftswissenschaftliche Beiträge*: 97–05, Munich.

——(1998). *Arbeitsmarkteffekte der Migration und Einwanderungspolitik: Eine Analyse für die Bundesrepublik Deutschland*, Heidelberg et al. (Physica-Verlag).

——and Zimmermann, K. F. (1996). 'Arbeitslosigkeit und Löhne von Aus- und Übersiedlern', in L. Bellmann and V. Steiner (eds.) *Mikroökonomik des Arbeitsmarktes* (Beiträge zur Arbeitsmarkt- und Berufsforschung, 192) (Nürnberg: Bundesanstalt für Arbeit).

Bauer, T. and Zimmermann, K. F. (1997a). 'Unemployment and wages of ethnic German', *Quarterly Review of Economics and Statistics*, 37: 361–77.

— (1997b). 'Integrating the East: the labour market effects of immigration', in S.W. Black (ed.) *Europe's Economy Looks East—Implications for Germany and the European Union* (Cambridge: Cambridge University Press), 269–306.

— (1999a). 'Occupational mobility of ethnic Germans', *IZA Discussion Paper*, 58, Bonn.

— (1999b). Assessment of Possible Migration Pressure and its Labour Market Impact Following EU Enlargement to Central and Eastern Europe, *IZA Research Report No. 3*, Bonn. Report for the Department for Education and Employment, London.

—, Lofstrom, M., and Zimmermann, K. F. (2000). 'Immigration policy, assimilation of immigrants and natives' sentiments towards immigrants: evidence from 12 OECD countries', *Swedish Economic Policy Review*, 7: 11–53.

—, Pereira, P. T., Vogler, M., and Zimmermann, K. F. (2002). 'Portuguese migrants in the German labor market: performance and self-selection', *International Migration Review*, 36: 467–91.

Bender, S., Hilzendegen, J., Rohwer, G., and Rudolph, H. (1996). *Die IAB-Beschäftigtenstichprobe 1975–1990* (Beiträge zur Arbeitsmarkt- und Berufsforschung, 197) (Nürnberg: Institut für Arbeitsmarkt- und Berufsforschung).

— and Karr, W. (1993). 'Arbeitslosigkeit von ausländischen Arbeitnehmern: Ein Versuch, nationalitätenspezifische Arbeitslosenquoten zu erklären', *Mitteilungen zur Arbeitsmarkt- und Berufsforschung*, 2: 192–206.

Bentolila, S. (1997). 'Sticky labor markets in Spain', *European Economic Review*, 41: 551–98.

Benz, W. (1985). 'Vierzig Jahre nach der Vertreibung. Einleitende Bemerkungen', in W. Benz (ed.), *Die Vertreibung der Deutschen aus dem Osten. Ursachen, Ereignisse, Folgen* (Frankfurt a. M.: Fischer), 10 ff.

Borjas, G. J. (1994). 'The economics of immigration', *Journal of Economic Literature*, 32: 1667–717.

Börsch-Supan, A. (1994). 'Migration, social security systems, and public finance', in H. Siebert (ed.) *Migration: A Challenge for Europe* (Tübingen: Mohr), 119–47.

Brücker, H., Epstein, G., McCormick, B., Saint-Paul, G., Venturini, A., and Zimmermann, K. F. (2002). 'Managing migration in the European welfare state', in T. Boeri, G. Hanson, and B. McCormick (eds.), *Immigration Policy and the Welfare System* (Oxford: Oxford University Press), part I, 1–167.

Büchel, F., Fricke, J., and Voges, W. (1996). 'Sozialhilfe als Integrationshilfe für Zuwanderer in Westdeutschland', *DIW-Wochenbericht*, 48: 767–75.

Buhr, P. and Weber, A. (1996). 'The impact of social change on social assistance: two cohorts of German welfare recipients compared', *SFB 186 Arbeitspapier*, 31 (Bremen: Universität Bremen).

Bundesforschungsanstalt für Landeskunde und Raumordnung (1992). 'Informationen zur Raumentwicklung, Heft 9/10: Perspektiven der künftigen Bevölkerungsentwicklung in Deutschland, Teil 1'.

Burda, M. C. (1993). 'The determinants of East-West German migration. Some first results', *European Economic Review*, 37: 452–61.

Card, D. (1990). 'The impact of the Mariel boatlift on the Miami labor market', *Industrial and Labor Relations Review*, 43: 245–57.

Chiswick, B. R. (1978). 'The effect of Americanization on the earnings of foreign-born men', *Journal of Political Economy*, 86: 897–921.

— (1986). 'Human capital and the labor market adjustment of immigrants: testing alternative hypotheses', in O. Stark (ed.) *Research in Human Capital and Development: Migration, Human Capital and Development*, 4 (Greenwich, CT: JAI Press).

Constant, A. (1998). 'The earnings of male and female guestworkers and their assimilation into the German labor market: a panel study 1984–1993'. *Ph.D.* dissertation, Vanderbilt University.

— and Shachmurove, Y. (2002). 'The entrepreneurial endeavors of immigrants and natives in Germany', *Proceedings of the Academy of Entrepreneurial Finance*, 202–18.

— and Massey, D. S. (2003). 'Self-selection, earnings and out-migration: a longitudinal study of immigrants', *Journal of Population Economics*, 16: 631–53.

— and Zimmermann, K. F. (2003). 'Occupational choice across generations' *Applied Economics Quarterly*, 49: 299–317.

Cramer, U. (1984). 'Multivariate Analyse von Arbeitslosenquoten', *Mitteilungen zur Arbeitsmarkt- und Berufsforschung*, 3, 330–5.

Decressin, J. W. (1994). 'Internal migration in West Germany and implications for East-West salary convergence', *Weltwirtschaftliches Archiv*, 130: 231–57.

DeNew, J. P. and Zimmermann, K. F. (1994a). 'Native wage impacts of foreign labor: a random effects panel analysis', *Journal of Population Economics*, 7: 177–92.

— (1994b). 'Blue collar labour vulnerability: wage impacts of migration', in G. Steinmann and R. E. Ulrich (eds.) *The Economic Consequences of Immigration to Germany* (Heidelberg: Physica-Verlag), 81–99.

Dinkel, R. and Lebok, U. (1993). 'Könnten durch Zuwanderung die Alterung der Bevölkerung und die daraus resultierenden Zusatzlasten der Sozialen Sicherung aufgehalten oder gemildert werden?' *Deutsche Rentenversicherung*, 6: 388–400.

Dunn, T. A., Kreyenfeld, M., and Lovely, M. E. (1997). 'Communist human capital in a capitalist labor market: the experience of East german and ethnic German immigrants to West Germany', *Vierteljahrshefte für Wirtschaftsforschung*, 1: 151–8.

Dustmann, C. (1993). 'Earnings adjustment of temporary migrants', *Journal of Population Economics*, 6: 153–68.

— (1994). 'Speaking fluency, writing fluency and earnings of migrants', *Journal of Population Economics*, 7: 133–56.

— (1996). 'The Social assimilation of immigrants', *Journal of Population Economics*, 9: 37–54.

Faini, R., Galli, G., Genari, P., and Rossi, F. (1997). 'An empirical puzzle: falling migration and growing unemployment differentials among Italian regions', *European Economic Review*, 41: 571–9.

Faini, R., de Melo, J., and Zimmermann, K. F. (1999). *Migration. The Controversies and the Evidence*, (Cambridge: Cambridge University Press).

Felderer, B. (1994). 'Can immigration policy help to stabilize social security systems?', in H. Giersch (ed.) *Economic Aspects of International Migration*, (Berlin et al.: Springer-Verlag) 197–226.

Frey, M. (1986). 'Direkte und indirekte Rückkehrförderung seitens der Aufnahmeländer–Überblick', in H. Körner and U. Mehrländer (eds.) *Die neue Ausländerpolitik in Europa* (Bonn: Verlag Neue Gesellschaft).

Friedberg, R. and Hunt, J. (1995). 'The impact of immigrants on host country wages, employment and growth', *Journal of Economic Perspectives*, 9: 23–44.

Friedrich, K. (1990). 'Federal Republic of Germany', in C. B. Nam, W. J. Serow and D. F. Sly (eds.) *International Handbook on Internal Migration* (New York: Greenwood Press) 145–61.

Gabanyi, A. (1988). 'Die Deutschen in Rumänien', *Aus Politik und Zeitgeschichte*, B 50/88, 9. Dezember, 28–39.

Gang, I. N. and Rivera-Batiz, F. L. (1994a). 'Labor market effects of immigration in the United States and Europe: substitution vs. complementarity', *Journal of Population Economics*, 7: 157–75.

— (1994b). 'Unemployment and attitudes towards foreigners in Germany', in G. Steinmann and R. E. Ulrich (eds.) *The Economic Consequences of Immigration to Germany*, (Heidelberg: Physica-Verlag), 121–54.

Gang, I. and Zimmermann, K. F. (2002). 'Is child like parent? Educational attainment and ethnic origin', *Journal of Human Resources*, 35: 550–69.

Gieseck, A., Heilemann, U., and von Loeffelholz, H. D. (1993). 'Wirtschafts- und sozialpolitische Aspekte der Zuwanderung in der Bundesrepublik', *Aus Politik und Zeitgeschichte*, B7.

Greenwood, M. J. (1997). 'Internal migration in developed countries', in M. R. Rosenzweig und O. Stark (eds.) *Handbook of Population and Family Economics*, 1B, 647–720.

— and McDowell, J. M. (1986). 'The factor market consequences of US immigration', *Journal of Economic Literature*, 24: 1738–72.

— (1994). 'The national labour market consequences of U.S. immigration', in H. Giersch (ed.) *Economic Aspects of International Migration* (Berlin et al.: Springer-Verlag).

Grossman, J. B. (1982). 'The substitutability of natives and immigrants in production', *Review of Economics and Statistics*, 64: 596–603.

Haisken-DeNew, J. P., and Zimmermann, K. F. (1999). 'Wage and mobility effects of trade and migration', in M. Dewatripont, A. Sapir and K. Sekhat (eds.) *Trade* and *Jobs in Europe. Much Ado About Nothing?*, (Oxford: Oxford University Press), 139–60.

Harmsen, H. (1983). 'Die Aussiedler in der Bundesrepublik Deutschland, Forschungen der AWR Deutsche Sektion. 2. Ergebnisbericht. Anpassung, Umstellung, Eingliederung' (Wien: Braunmüller Verlag).

Hatzius, J. (1994). 'The unemployment and earnings effects of German immigration', *Oxford Applied Economics Discussions Paper Series*, 165, Oxford.

Hippmann, H. (1983). 'Binnenfernwanderungen und Arbeitskräftenachfrage– Eine empirische Analyse für die Bundesrepublik Deutschland', Krefeld: M+M Wissenschaftsverlag.

Hunt, J. C. (1992). 'The impact of the 1962 repatriates from Algeria on the French labor market', *Industrial and Labor Relations Review*, 43: 556–72.

Koller, B. (1992). 'Integration in die Arbeitswelt im Westen: Zur beruflichen Eingliederung von Übersiedlern aus der ehemaligen DDR', *Mitteilungen aus der Arbeitsmarkt- und Berufsforschung*, 2: 168–91.

— (1993). 'Aussiedler nach dem Deutschkurs: Welche Gruppen kommen schnell in Arbeit?', *Mitteilungen aus der Arbeitsmarkt- und Berufsforschung*, 26: 207–21.

Licht, G. and Steiner, V. (1994). 'Assimilation, labor market experience, and earnings profiles of temporary and permanent immigrant workers in Germany', *International Review of Applied Economics*, 8: 130–56.

Mackensen, R. M., Vanberg, M., and Krämer, K. (1975). *Probleme regionaler Mobilität. Ergebnisse und Lücken der Forschung zur gegenwärtigen Situation in der BRD* (Göttingen: Verlag Otto Schwartz and Co.).

McCormick, B. (1997). 'Regional unemployment and labour mobility in the UK', *European Economic Review*, 41: 581–9.

Mühleisen, M. and Zimmermann, K. F. (1994). 'A panel analysis of job changes and unemployment', *European Economic Review*, 38: 793–801.

Münz, R. and Ohliger, R. (1998). 'Long-distance citizens: ethnic Germans and their immigration to Germany', in P. Schuck and R. Münz (eds.) *Paths to inclusion. The Integration of Migrants in the United States and Germany* (New York, Oxford: Berghan Books), 155–202.

— and Ulrich, R. (1996). 'Internationale Wanderungen von und nach Deutschland, 1945–1994. Demographische, politische und gesellschaftliche Aspekte räumlicher Mobilität', *Allgemeines Statistisches Archiv*, 80: 5–35.

Pischke, J.-S. (1992). 'Assimilation and the earnings of guest workers in Germany', *ZEW Discussion Paper*, 92-17 (Mannheim: ZEW).

— and Velling, J. (1994). 'Wage and employment effects of immigration to Germany: an analysis Based on local labor markets', *CEPR-Discussion-Paper Nr. 935*.

— (1997). 'Employment effects of immigration to Germany: an analysis based on local labor markets', *Review of Economics and Statistics*, 79: 594–604.

Raffelhüschen, B. (1992). 'Labor migration in Europe. Experiences from Germany after unification', *European Economic Review*, 36: 1453–71.

Reichling, G. and Betz, F. H. (1949). *Die Heimatvertriebenen*. (Frankfurt/Main: Wolfgang Metzner).

Riphahn, R. (1998). 'Immigrant participation in the German welfare program', *Finanzarchiv*, 55: 163–85.

Riphahn, R. (2003). 'Cohort effects in the educational attainment of second generation immigrants in Germany: an analysis of census data', *Journal of Population Economics*, 16: 711–37.

Ronge, V. (1997). 'German policies towards ethnic German minorities', in R. Münz and M. Weiner (eds.) *Migrants, Refugees, and Foreign Policy. U.S. and German Policies Toward Countries of Origin*, (New York, Oxford: Berghan Books), 117–40.

Schmähl, W. (1995). 'Migration und soziale Sicherung–Über die Notwendigkeit einer differenzierten Betrachtung: das Beispiel der gesetzlichen Kranken- und Rentenversicherung,' *Hamburger Jahrbuch für Wirtschafts- und Gesellschaftspolitik*, 40, (Tübingen), 247–71.

Schmidt, C. M. (1992a). 'The earnings dynamics of immigrant labor,' *CEPR Discussion Paper*, 763 (London: CEPR).

—— (1992b). 'Country-of-origin differences in the earnings of German immigrants', *University of Munich Discussion Paper*, 92–29 (Munich: University of Munich).

—— (1994a). 'The economic performance of Germany's East European immigrants', *CEPR Discussion Paper*, 963 (London: CEPR).

—— (1994b). 'Immigration countries and migration research: the case of Germany', in G. Steinmann and R. E. Ulrich (eds.) *The Economic Consequences of Immigration to Germany* (Heidelberg), 1–19.

—— (1996). 'German economic growth after the demise of socialism: the potential contribution of East–West migration', *Jahrbuch für Wirtschaftsgeschichte*, 96/2: 109–26.

—— (1997). 'Immigrant performance in Germany: labor earnings of ethnic German migrants and foreign guest-workers', *Quarterly Review of Economics and Statistics*, 37: 379–97.

—— and Zimmermann, K. F. (1992). 'Migration pressure in Germany: past and future', in K. F. Zimmermann (ed.) *Migration and Development* (Berlin et al.: Springer-Verlag, 207–36).

——, Stilz, A., and Zimmermann, K. F. (1994). 'Mass migration, unions, and Government intervention', *Journal of Public Economics*, 55: 185–210.

Schulz, E. and Seiring, K. (1994). 'Integration deutscher Zuwanderer in den westdeutschen Arbeitsmarkt', *DIW Wochenbericht*, 35, 609–17.

Seifert, W. (1996a). 'Neue Zuwanderergruppen auf dem westdeutschen Arbeitsmarkt: Eine Analyse der Arbeitsmarktchancen von Aussiedlern, ausländischen Zuwanderern und ostdeutschen Übersiedlern', *Soziale Welt*, 47: 180–201.

— (1996*b*). 'Occupational and social integration of immigrant groups in Germany', *New Community*, 22: 417–36.

Statistisches Bundesamt (ed.) (various issues). *Sozialleistungen, Fachserie 13, Reihe 2* (Wiesbaden: Statistisches Bundesamt).

Ulrich, R. E. (1994). 'Foreigners and the social insurance system in Germany', in G. Steinmann and R. E. Ulrich (eds.) *The Economic Consequences of Immigration to Germany* (Heidelberg: Physica-Verlag), 61–80.

Velling, J. (1995). *Immigration und Arbeitsmarkt. Eine empirische Analyse für die Bundesrepublik Deutschland*, (Baden-Baden: Nomos-Verlagsgesellschaft).

Wagner, G. (1994). 'Sozialpolitik und Zuwanderung: Ein Überblick', *Diskussionspapier der Fakultät für Sozialwissenschaften*, 94-08 (Bochum: Ruhr-Universität Bochum).

Wendt, H. (1993). 'Wanderungen nach und innerhalb von Deutschland unter besonderer Berücksichtigung der Ost-West Wanderungen', *Zeitschrift für Bevölkerungswissenschaft*, 19: 517–40.

Winkelmann, R. and Zimmermann, K. F. (1993). 'Ageing, Migration, and labour mobility', in P. Johnson and K. F. Zimmermann (eds.) *Labor Markets in an Ageing Europe* (Cambridge: Cambridge University Press), 255–82.

Winter-Ebmer, R. and Zimmermann, K. F. (1999). 'East–West trade and migration: the Austro-German case', in R. Faini, R. De Melo and K. F. Zimmermann (eds.) *Trade and Factor Mobility* (Cambridge: Cambridge University Press), 296–327.

Zimmermann, K. F. (1994). 'Some general lessons for Europe's migration problem', in H. Giersch (ed.) *Economic Aspects of International Migration* (Berlin et al.: Springer-Verlag) 249–73.

— (1995*a*). 'European migration: push and pull', *Proceedings of the World Bank Annual Conference on Development Economics 1994, World Bank Economic Review*, and *World Bank Research Observer*, 313–42.

— (1995*b*). 'Tackling the European migration problem', *Journal of Economic Perspectives*, 9: 45–62.

— and Bauer, T. (2002). *The Economics of Migration*, I–IV, (Cheltenham/Northampton: Edward Elgar Publishing Ltd).

— Bauer, T., Bonin, H., Fahr, R., and Hinte, H. (2002). *Arbeitskräftebedarf bei hoher Arbeitslosigkeit. Ein ökonomisches Zuwanderungskonzept für Deutschland* (Berlin et al.: Springer-Verlag).

8. Immigrant Adjustment in France and Impacts on the Natives

Amelie Constant

8.1. Introduction

The study of migration has garnered increased attention by political advocates and social scientists as immigration is heavily debated in the political arena. In an era of increasing globalization of economies, migration has also become an integral part of international economics, and remains of the outmost concern among all countries that face immigration challenges. In Europe, the immigrant population has reached an all-time high competing with the so-called traditional immigrant countries such as the US, Canada, and Australia. In France—a longstanding country of immigration—every statistic shows that immigration will keep increasing. Given the recent incidents in France, migrants without documents occupying churches (*les sans-papiers*), the deportation and expulsion of illegal workers,[1] the popularity of the extreme right in the local and national elections, the heightened anti-migration sentiments[2] and complaints that discrimination against immigrants is on the rise, migration management appears to have become rather complex and has polarized debates on migration.

The latest French census of 1999 enumerated 4.31 million legal immigrants, who make up 7.4 per cent of the French metropolitan population, and 3 million of whom are of North African decent. In Paris, the capital of France, already one person in six is an immigrant. Whereas these statistics are often perceived as high, they are still below or comparable to the immigration figures in other European countries like Germany and the UK. Further, while it is unquestionable that a large part of the foreign population in France has ties to the former French colonies, in the new century,

---

[1] Nicolas Sarkozy, the Minister of Interior, has recently reinstituted a policy of group deportations by plane, which was abandoned several years ago under pressure from human rights groups. A new law approved by the government in April 2003 will toughen conditions for entry and residence in France and create a fingerprint database of visa applicants.

[2] Le Pen's National Front campaign both, in 1997 and 2002 accused Arabs and Africans to be responsible for France's high unemployment and crime, and classified them as a threat to French bloodlines.

the demographic picture of France shows that it has a large immigrant population with increasingly diverse ethnic profiles.

Officially, France refuses to recognize ethnic communities and insists that immigrants must fully embrace the French culture so that the Republican ideals and model be sustained. In France, ethnic identity was always viewed as an obstacle to national solidarity and to immigrant integration. The country's migration policy has always been to integrate foreigners into the nation by putting into practice the Enlightenment[3] and the Republican ideals as derived from the Revolution.[4] The Republican assimilation model aspires to efface ethnic and national origins in the second generation, so that immigrant children can hardly be distinguished from French children. The Republican ideal was strengthened by the relatively relaxed citizenship laws and the integrating institutions such as schools, the military, unions, the French communist party, and the Catholic Church. It aimed at inculcating both French and immigrant children a common civic culture and the pride of French values. In reality, however, the French assimilationist concept of citizenship and French identity often clashes with the 'ethnic minority' claims.

Driven by the notion of the unified French culture, integration measures have always played a crucial part in French migration policy. Hence, one would expect that integration into the French society should be much more advanced and successful than in other European countries. However, for the last thirty years the particular needs of the French labour market have not been met. Whereas some immigrant groups manage to perform well, it is not surprising that migrants often fail on the labour market and this is the basis for economic, social, and political tensions and disintegration in this unofficially multicultural society. A successful economic integration into the native labour market is a necessary, although not sufficient condition, for the functioning integration of immigrants into society. As long as immigrants perform well in economic terms, for instance they remain employed, earn a decent salary, and provide goods and services that are in demand, they can be integrated without having to resemble the natives. At the same time, the adaptation of the national culture may also help foster assimilation into the labour market.

Since France tightened its immigration law in 1974, almost all non-European immigration is due to family reunification, albeit clandestine

---

[3] Enlightenment denotes the liberal thought of Voltaire and Diderot, and emphasises reason, toleration, and natural law, plus a confidence in modern man and his achievements. Above all, they promoted the idea of change and progress as good things.

[4] The notion that all individuals are treated equally regardless of birth, class, race, or religion.

migration and refugees are also of the essence. Family linked migration continues to predominate immigrant flows, since no sufficient attempts have been made to develop a migration policy that directly accounts for economic motives. In reality, the integration of family related migration has not been accomplished. Moreover, the integration of the second generation migrants has not been as successful due to the inability of the education system to include, guide, and prepare them for the demands of the labour market in the new century.

The purpose of this chapter is to study the immigrant adjustment and its impacts on the natives from an economic viewpoint by drawing on research findings from the existing academic literature on French migration. Surprisingly and in spite of the great importance the issue of migration has for the French economy, there have only been very few studies by economists dealing with this topic. In this chapter, I will review a very small but growing body of research on immigrants in France, to assess the immigrants' labour market accessibility, their economic assimilation, their intergenerational progress, and impact on natives.

The research questions of this chapter will, therefore, be fourfold: first, how do the various groups of immigrants fare on the French labour market? Namely, how do they perform in terms of wages, unemployment, occupational choices, and self-employment? Are they performing in a similar way to equally educated natives, is there a longer-term adjustment process, and any prospect of convergence to natives' position in the labour market? Second, are immigrants in competition with natives, and do they harm or improve the labour market situation of natives? Do they take jobs away by competing with natives, or do they create jobs for the natives, as entrepreneurs or due to the fact that their employment ensures demand for native employment due to complementarities, or alternatively, do they operate in different markets and they never interact with natives? And, do immigrants cause a reduction or an increase in the income levels of the natives? Third, does the presence of immigrants alter the internal migration flows of the natives? That is, do natives move away from the areas with a high concentration of immigrants, are they drawn into these areas, or are they migrating irrespective of the immigrant flows? Fourth, I will appraise the question on the sentiments of natives vis-à-vis the immigrants and investigate the role of the business cycle on the immigrant flows.

The outline of the chapter is as follows: first, I will present an overview of the socioeconomic characteristics of the immigrant population in France, and second I will delineate the main phases of the immigration system in the postwar period and outline how the various immigration policies affected the quantity and 'quality' of immigrants. In the fourth and fifth sections I will review and evaluate the findings of the existing scientific literature on the economic assimilation and intergenerational mobility of immigrants, and the immigrant impact on natives as well as the natives' attitudes towards immigrants, and the role of the business cycle, respectively. Finally, I will draw my concluding remarks.

8.2. Current Statistics on the Immigrant Population

In this section, I will reveal major facts about the immigrant population in France. The emphasis is on presenting and describing the major characteristics of the migrants and their children as they pertain to the labour market and their social environment. The summarized characteristics are based on the 1999 census, and are compared with previous censuses to identify and depict the longterm developments of the immigrant groups in France.

According to the definition adopted by the High Council for Integration in 1991 (*Haut Conseil de l'Intégration*, HCI), an immigrant is a foreign-born person who entered the French territory under a foreign nationality, lives in France at least for one year, and has not acquired the French citizenship. Immigrants who have naturalized or the children of immigrants who are born in France are considered French citizens. However, a question on the country of origin has always been included in the census, and the French government knows, at least since 1962, how many foreigners have naturalized, or how many French are not born with a French nationality. There are three categories in the census questionnaire: French by birth, French by naturalization, and foreigner. Since the 1999 census, the French Statistical Office (*Institut National des Statistiques et Études Économiques*, INSEE), has established some clarifying statistical definitions between a foreigner and an immigrant. Accordingly, a foreigner is a person who declared a different than French citizenship, and an immigrant is a person born abroad who is a foreign national or has acquired the French citizenship. Both categories have in common the group of individuals who are born abroad and have foreign nationality (SOPEMI 2001: 82).

Currently, similar to the US and the UK, France defines citizenship by the *jus soli* principle according to which immigrants who are born in the country are automatically granted citizenship. In addition, the children of immigrants who grow up in France are automatically French citizens at the age of eighteen. The so-called second generation immigrants, thus,

Table 8.1. Population by nationality and place of birth

	Born in France	Born abroad	Total
French at birth	97.1	2.9	100
Naturalized citizens	34.0	66.0	100
Total French citizens	**94.4**	**5.6**	**100**
Foreigners	15.6	84.4	100
Immigrants	–	100	100
Total population	**90.0**	**10.0**	**100**

Note: As per cent of persons born in mainland France; 1999 Census.
Source: OECD (2001).

disappear easily from immigration records. Consequently, immigration statistics for countries like France and the UK might present lower numbers of foreigners than actual.

Table 8.1 depicts the distinction between foreigners and immigrants by place of birth and nationality. Clearly, the definition of foreigners is based on nationality, while the definition of immigrants on place of birth. Table 8.1 reveals this by stating that 100 per cent of all immigrants have been born abroad, while in 1999 only 84.4 per cent of the foreigners were not born in France. Among the total population, 10 per cent of the people have been born abroad. In international comparisons in Europe, the key measure is not the share of foreign-born but the 'share of immigrants in total population'. For France in 1999, this number (not included in Table 8.1) has been 7.4 per cent. The foreigners, on the other hand, have been 5.6 per cent of the population. Moreover, Table 8.1 states that from all of those who have been French at birth 2.9 per cent were born abroad. Only 34 per cent of the naturalized citizens but 94.4 per cent of all French citizens have been born in France.

Out of the 4.31 million legal immigrants enumerated in the 1999 census, immigrant men constitute 9.5 per cent and immigrant women 7.7 per cent of the respective male and female populations. In reference to the 'active' population[5] or the population in the labour force, immigrants occupy an 8.6 per cent. Figure 8.1 exhibits the stock of foreigners as enumerated over the last three censuses. This figure shows how the origin mix has changed over the years, and the largest group dominating the stock of foreigners

[5] The active population in France comprises all persons who have a job, or who are looking for a job, as well as those in the military.

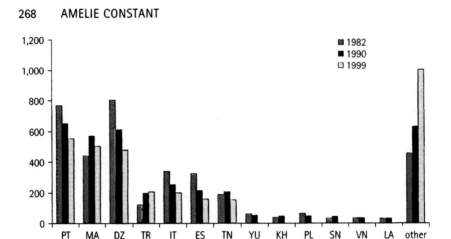

Figure 8.1. Stock of foreign population by nationality (in thousands)

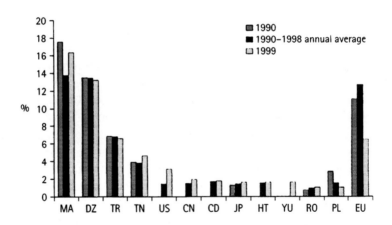

Figure 8.2. Inflow of foreign population by nationality as a per cent of total inflows

comes from Sub-Saharan Africa. While in 1982 Algerians were the leading country of origin, both in the 1990 and 1999 censuses the largest group were Portuguese, followed by Moroccans, Algerians, and Turks. Moreover, the stock of the European Union foreign population, e.g. from Portugal, Italy, and Spain, has been declining, and the presence of people from other non-EU countries has been increasing.

Figure 8.2 shows the inflow of the foreigners as per cent of total inflow into France from EU and from the major sending countries outside the EU over the last decade. Where data was available this figure depicts the annual inflows in 1990 and 1999, as well as the annual average inflows between 1990 and 1998. The numbers demonstrate the great gamut of foreign nationalities that is part of the French immigration experience. This figure also suggests that with the exception of the EU countries migration to France remains unabashed. Morocco, Algeria, and Turkey remain the major sending countries while the inflow from the EU countries has substantially decreased over the last decade. In fact, Moroccans account for the largest part of inflows because they are mainly seasonal workers, employed in agriculture, but also employed in tourism and the catering business.

Compared to the 1990 census, the immigrant population in France of 1999 has increased by 3.4 per cent but this increase is similar to the increase of the entire population. In general, since 1975, the immigrant population in France is rather stable. Although the number of immigrants from EU countries is 9 per cent lower than in 1990, the number of immigrants from non-EU countries is 38 per cent higher. Specifically, the number of immigrants from the Sub-Saharan Africa is up by 43 per cent compared to the 1990 statistics, and Turks constitute more than 2 per cent of the immigrant population. With regards to the age distribution, the immigrant population in France of 1999 is getting somewhat older. Only 8 per cent of the immigrants are less than twenty years old, while one-fifth of them are older than sixty. Finally, the 1999 census shows that men and women immigrants are almost equally represented (Glaude and Borrel 2002).

The immigrant statistics of the 1999 census also show a feminization of the immigrant workers, when compared to the sex composition of the immigrant workers in previous censuses. For example, whereas in 1982 only 22.3 per cent of the immigrant workers were women, in 1990 the female share had risen to 27.6 per cent, and by 1999 it had reached 35.3 per cent. However, this is not surprising given that the only venue of immigration to France is family reunion. The recent prominent presence of women migrants has also contributed to the overall increase in the labour force participation (LFP) of immigrants, while the participation rate of immigrant men has slightly decreased. Although immigrant women have tried to close the gap in LFP they are still less represented in the labour market and their LFP rates vary by nationality. Among the 15-64 year old immigrant women, only 57 per cent are active in the labour market, a percentage below the average of 63 per cent for all women. Immigrant women from Portugal and southeast Asia, namely Vietnam, Cambodia, and Laos, have the highest labour force participation while Turkish women have the lowest. In sharp contrast, immigrant men's LFP is higher than the LFP of all men (78.6 per cent against 74.9 per cent respectively, see Glaude and Borrel 2002).

In spite of the higher LFP, immigrant workers have been, and still are, concentrated in the lower rungs of the socioeconomic ladder. They comprise 18 per cent of the non-skilled blue-collar workers and 6 per cent of the employees without an education degree. Overall, 53 per cent of immigrant men and 20 per cent of immigrant women are manual workers, and tend to concentrate in labour-intensive and low-skilled industries. Immigrants are usually working under temporary contracts and often in part-time or dead-end jobs. While men are frequently in the construction, automobile or other heavy industry, women are in domestic services, hotels, and restaurants. Over the years, immigrants have remained in these jobs and a quarter of a century later, their children are also in these same jobs. It is clear that, contrary to popular beliefs, immigrants are not intruding on the jobs held by natives. They rather occupy jobs that are shunned by natives.

Along with their occupational segregation goes their geographic concentration. Immigrants are geographically concentrated in some areas of the country, usually in the poorer suburbs of big urban centres or 'banlieux'. More than one-third lives in the Ile-de-France region. On average, between 1993 and 1999, 40.5 per cent of the Portuguese, 29.9 per cent of the Maghrebiens, and 40.7 per cent of the Africans lived in the greater Paris area. Besides the Parisian area, immigrant prominence is found in the south-west and south-east French cities. Interestingly enough, the geographic concentration of immigrants does not necessarily imply a mingling among the various immigrant groups. Each immigrant group tends to stay among the same nationals. That is, the Spaniards mostly reside in the south of France, the Italians are in the Alps and Jura areas, the Maghrebians along the axis of Rhône-Saône, and the Turks in the East close to the German-Suisse borders (Jayet et al. 2001). Moreover, even within the immigrant localities the different nationalities remain distinctly apart. There is, for example, the 'Maghrebian' neighbourhood, the 'Jewish' neighbourhood, the 'black-African' neighbourhood, etc.

In general, unemployment and dire macroeconomic conditions affect workers adversely. In France, as in other immigrant countries, the immigrant population is more vulnerable to economic crises and more likely to be affected by unemployment. As declared by the 1999 census, the unemployment rate for immigrants is almost twice as high as that for natives (22 per cent versus 13 per cent respectively). This is higher by 18 per cent than the unemployment rate in the 1990 census. However, unemployment rates vary by gender and nationality. Within the immigrant population, women are affected by unemployment the most, with 25 per cent of women being unemployed versus only 20 per cent of men. Among all immigrant groups, Portuguese are the least affected by unemployment. Statistics also show that those naturalized immigrants are less affected by unemployment, compared to those who did not naturalize.

Another difficulty that immigrants in France face is job accessibility. In the 1990s, job perspectives for those entering the labour market have become worse, and are disproportionately tough for the younger immigrant workers. Not only immigrant youth faces the highest unemployment rates but once they are in unemployment the probability of returning to employment is much lower compared to natives. Moreover, even when immigrants have a job, their remuneration is much lower than that of the national average. On average, immigrant men earn 90 per cent less than the average salaries of all men. Immigrant women earn, on average, 76 per cent less than the average salaries of all women in part-time employment.

Because of the tight employment market, many immigrants in France choose to naturalize so they can have access to better jobs. According to the 1999 census, more than one-third of the immigrant population in France acquired the French nationality, a number higher by 19 per cent since the last census in 1990. Still, this is a low rate of naturalization compared to the US or Canada. Almost 50 per cent of the immigrants from South-East Asia, Poland, Italy, and Spain have acquired the French citizenship. In contrast, only a very small percentage of the immigrants from Algeria, Morocco, Turkey, and Portugal have acquired the French citizenship. For the first time in 2000, the number of naturalizations exceeded the symbolic number of 150,000 (Héran 2002).[6]

With the exception of European Union citizens, immigrants in France have no political rights, except the right to demonstrate and strike, and the freedom to create associations. On the other hand, immigrant workers in France have the same insurance benefits as the French (according to the social security code). Once matriculated in the French social security system, immigrants can receive health, disability, and life insurance, they can start accumulating pension rights, and can benefit from unemployment insurance similar to that of the French workers.

The 1992 Education Survey by INSEE showed that immigrant families had twice as many school age children as the rest of the families. However,

---

[6] One of the requirements for French citizenship is to have resided for at least five years in France.

this fact rather manifests the higher immigrant fertility of the 1970s. Immigrant fertility in the 1990s has somewhat declined as immigrants align their fertility with that of French natives the longer they stay in France (Héran 2002). However, immigrant children's education has not aligned with that of the French children. Immigrant children are under-represented in the general and technical education and over-represented in vocational education.

To complete the picture of the immigrant population in France, I turn to their real estate behaviour. Owning a house manifests the permanency of immigrants as well as their perception of regarding France as 'home'. Out of the 1,370,000 immigrant households in France enumerated in 1999, 30.7 per cent own their own house and 64.7 per cent rent apartments. Among the renters, 31.5 per cent live in HLM buildings, or low income– low rent housing, or workers' low-rise dwellings. Immigrant home ownership is still low, though, compared to about 60 per cent by the French. Overall, while the immigrant population in France has been living in France for at least twenty years, this section has shown that the immigrants in France do not resemble the native population vis-à-vis raw socio-economic statistics.

8.3. The Immigration System in France Since the Second World War

Clearly, the choice of immigration policy regimes affects both the quality and quantity of the immigration flows, the performance of immigrants in the host country, as well as the way natives perceive immigrants. In this section I will delineate the major changes in the French immigration laws in chronological order as they took place after the Second World War, and show how the changes in the immigration policy have affected the quantity and quality of the immigrants to France.

France has always been an immigrant nation for both economic and demographic reasons. In the nineteenth and early twentieth centuries, when most European countries were exporting immigrants, France was importing immigrants, pursuing expansionary immigration policies. The distinctive property of the French immigration system is that France is open to receive immigrants from both its former colonies for demographic reasons (thus resembling the US, Canada, and Australia), and immigrants from the Mediterranean region for purely economic reasons (thus, resembling demand driven migration as implemented by Germany, for example).

Although heavy recruitment of immigrant workers occurred during the Second World War, it was only after the second war, when France needed additional workers to meet the needs of the labour market, that immigration became the government's priority. The ordinance of 1945 created the National Office of Immigration (ONI), a neutral government agency, which has all the power to control, regulate, oversee, carry through, and ensure the smooth recruitment of immigrants and their families. A similar ordinance guaranteed liberal access to French nationality. Belgium and Germany, along with Poland, Italy, and Spain were the first countries to supply immigrant manpower to France. Some 430,000 immigrants were imported during this first five-year economic plan.

In the 1950s and 1960s the French government encouraged immigration under a 'laissez-faire' policy while upholding the nation's republican values. Immigration during this era was mainly due to decolonization from Algeria and Indo-China, culminating in the Algerian independence in 1962. In 1962, for example, 350,000 Algerians, or 'French Muslims' were enumerated in France. In parallel, during this period many foreign workers from Southern Europe also went to work in France. Whereas at times they entered without a work contract or outside the proper channels of the ONI they were able to regularize their status relatively easily once they were in France. Furthermore, until 1960 France was offering asylum to thousands of applicants who were welcomed to stay and were offered assistance for integration.

The years 1962–5 after the Algerian independence were the troubled years of immigration in France. There was a rise in immigration from Spain, and a decline in immigration from Italy, while immigration from Portugal started emerging. During that same period, immigration from Algeria developed strongly, and immigration from Sub-Saharan Africa marked its debut in France (Tapinos 1975). Naturally, the mass migration to France during this era created a shortage of housing. Thousands of immigrants lived together in overcrowded rooms often in run-down areas, in barrack-style housing, or self-built shacks and wooden settlements.

The year 1970 marked the beginning of the Turkish migration to France. Up to that time, France actively sought immigrant workers who were viewed as the cornerstone of economic recovery. However, emerging social conflicts coupled with the international economic crisis in the early 1970s, led the French government to start imposing regulations on immigration. The Ministry of Interior and Labour took several measures that aimed at controlling and suspending migration. Combined with higher productivity standards by French firms, these measures were successful in reducing the number of immigrants entering France by 44 per cent by

1972.[7] Still, in January 1973, the register of foreigners kept by the Ministry of the Interior, included: 789,000 Algerians, 742,000 Portuguese, 573,000 Italians, 571,000 Spaniards, 218,000 Moroccans, and 119,000 Tunisians.

The general recession of 1973 had serious effects on many European economies as energy prices quadrupled. Following other neighbouring countries with immigration issues, in July 1974, the French right wing government of d'Estaing officially suspended all labour migration with the exception of EU nationals.[8] Immediately, an upsurge of a diversified form of immigration took place, namely family reunification. The highest influx of immigrants occurred between the years 1962 and 1971 for men and between 1972 and 1981 for women. Overall, most of the immigrants in France today arrived between 1962 and 1974. By 1975, Algerians were representing the second largest group after the Portuguese.

The immigration halt of 1974 also caused the number of asylum seekers to skyrocket. As the number of asylum applications rose, so did the refusal rate, rising from 4 per cent in 1976 to 85 per cent in 1990. Still, in the 1970s, asylum applicants were allowed to work, and by 1981—under the socialist Mitterand government—they enjoyed an automatic right to work. It was often the case that applicants who had found employment could be legalized and they could obtain further housing assistance and help with integration (Wihtol de Wenden 1994).

In the mid-1970s, the French government (reflecting rising social tensions and frictions) also introduced several additional legislative measures. These measures aimed, mainly, to curb illegal immigration and even included sanctions on employers who hired illegal immigrants. In parallel, several measures were taken to induce return migration, although they were not successfully realized. Strict anti-immigrant legislation was later repealed and in 1978, the *Conseil d'État* cancelled these decrees so there are no more general restrictions for immigrants to enter France along with their families. However, family reunion, which has dominated the immigrant flows, has escalated the housing problems. Eventually, the government had to order additional reunification restrictive guidelines in order to alleviate the severity of housing issues.

In the 1980s, large immigrant populations settled in France in spite of the troubled French economy. Among them, political refugees and asylum

---

[7] A process of economic restructuring has started in the 1970s. Manufacturing and manual work has fallen and salaried, office related employment has increased. This has affected the plight and economic position of immigrants in France tremendously.

[8] However, the halt of recruitment exempted certain industries, such as construction and mining, and seasonal workers in agriculture.

seekers constituted the overwhelming majority. The socialist governments of the 1980s tried to ease the restrictions on migration. Since the 1980s the census numbers of the new immigrants to France showed a rather stagnant immigrant population. However, this appearance could conceal the fact that many of the new entrants have acquired the French nationality, and have thus vanished from the immigration statistics. Since the 1982 census, it is also evident that the national origin mix of immigrants had changed. Whereas the principal continent of origin of immigrants to France was Africa, especially Sub-Saharan Africa, there has been a considerable increase in the number of immigrants from Asia from 8 per cent in 1982, to 12.5 per cent in 2000. By the late 1980s, the number of asylum seekers had declined, only to rise sharply again from the mid-1990s on.

In the early 1990s there was a slight decline in migration, which can be related to the implementation of some very aggressive anti-immigrant legislation.[9] In 1991, the automatic right to work by asylees was abolished and employment authorization depended on the needs of the labour market. Further, in July 1993, Charles Pasqua, the French Interior Minister, announced a zero migration policy, and introduced the infamous Pasqua laws. According to these laws the police became more powerful in checking identities and deporting legal immigrants, the *jus soli* principle was modified so that immigrant children born in France were not automatically French, immigration for family reunification became more difficult to be realized, an increased waiting period was introduced, foreign students were not allowed to work in France, and asylum seekers lost their chances to appeal asylum rejections.

In spite of the rise of the far right, Le Pen and the anti-immigrant agenda, during the mid to late 1990s, about 12 per cent of the new entrants in the labour market were immigrants, constituting about 100,000 entrants per year. The majority of the new immigrants in the 1990s were from Africa (especially from Senegal and Mali), while the number of immigrants from the Maghreb[10] countries had diminished. Still, the main reason for justifiable immigration in France was family reunification. However, clandestine migration was also of the essence.

Paradoxically, French unions have adopted nuanced policy preferences in the recent years, in spite of high unemployment levels. In the 1980s and

---

[9] French migration policy had previously been more sympathetic: 'La France ne peut pas accueillir toute la misère du monde, mais elle doit savoir en prendre fidèlement sa part.' (Michel Rocard—former French Prime Minister—1990).

[10] Officially, the Maghreb Countries are: Libya, Tunisia, Algeria, Morocco, and Mauretania. The word Maghreb is Arabic and means 'Western.'

1990s, for example, unions have often opposed certain anti-immigration measures taken by various governments. Instead, they delved into organizing immigrant workers (Haus 1999). Assuming that the government cannot fully control migration flows, the unions' argument is that unorganized and irregular immigrant workers undercut unionized native workers.

Lastly, at the end of 1997, political refugees and asylum seekers represented about 4 per cent of the total foreign population living in France, and they were of diverse nationalities coming from Asia, to Europe, to Africa. By 1999, asylum applications had increased again, with Chinese nationals being the largest group of applicants. According to the Ministry of Foreign Affairs' Office for the Protection of Refugees and Stateless Persons (OFPRA), the volume of applications for asylum has increased by 272 per cent since 1996 and by 22 per cent compared to 2000. However, the rate of admission remained relatively low at roughly 12.4 per cent in 2001. Main countries of origin were China (12.9 per cent), Turkey (9.1 per cent) and the Democratic Republic of Congo (7.5 per cent)

An integral part of France's immigration policy has been granting amnesties to illegal immigrant workers.[11] Major amnesties occurred in 1968, 1974, 1981, and 1995. The amnesty of 1997 legalized about 87,000 illegal immigrants out of 150,000 applicants. The ratified new legislation and immigration law in 1998, which modified for the twenty-fifth time the 1945 ordinance, aimed to increase highly skilled immigration by giving scholars and scientists special immigrant status. The new law also extended the criteria for residence permits by emphasizing the rights of the person and the respect for family life, as well as it aimed to combat illegal immigration. Still, France lags behind the US and Germany in its pursuit for highly skilled labour while importance is still being given to family ties.

Up until the late 1990s, the French policy and public debate focused on immigration per se and little thought was given—even less action was taken—to the implementation of an effective integration. An affirmative action plan to battle discrimination against immigrants in the labour market was announced in 1998. The French government promised to: (1) end the practice of permitting employers to specify that they want French nationals when they request workers from a government employment office; and (2) re-examine current requirements that persons employed

---

[11] Illegal workers does not necessarily mean that they entered France illegally. The majority of them were entering legally under a tourist or student visa.

by state-run companies must be French nationals; one estimate is that 25 to 35 per cent of jobs in France require French citizenship (IGAS). In 2000, the Directorate of Population and Migrations adopted several regulations to facilitate the integration of foreigners. In particular, these regulations aimed at supporting young people having difficulty in entering employment, at implementing local contracts for reception and integration, and at introducing a single education support measure (SOPEMI 2001).

The booming period 1998–2000 of high employment has left the immigrant population in France untouched and marginalized. One of the reasons is that the labour market demand changed and required more qualified workers, who would speak the language fluently and possess more sophisticated skills. The emphasis was to employ individuals in strategic sectors such as information technology (IT), telecommunications, and health. French employers openly declared the need to recruit qualified workers and scientists from the non EU countries (Deneuve 2002). In 2000, the French authorities under pressure from the professional union of information technology issued about 1,600 residence permits to foreign qualified IT specialists. In 2001, they more than doubled the permits to 4,000. Amazingly, this new hiring under the so-called 'scientific visa' had been carried through under the maximum discretion and had even escaped the press and the media. Alternatively, the decline in demand for unskilled labour since the 1970s is mainly due to the change in the industry composition of domestic demand for goods and services and not so much to the technical progress per se (Goux and Maurin 2000).

In sum, over the last half century, France has received several waves of immigrants from diverse origins, and with distinctly different motives and aspirations. During the 'thirty glorious years', until the official stop to recruitment in 1974, immigration was an encouraged and welcomed phenomenon. Since then, immigration has continued under a different label, and has been perceived on and off as detrimental to the economy and as a threat to the social norms. Immigrants in France have access only to jobs in the private sector. With the exception of university and research and development jobs, immigrants do not work in the public sector, and can hardly be found in the freelance professions, such as lawyers and doctors. Nonetheless, immigration to France continues apace and French immigrants keep enduring transnational ties with their country of origin. The question to be answered in the next section is whether these immigrants and their children have successfully adjusted and assimilated in the French labour market.

8.4. Integration and Labour Market Assimilation

In this section, I survey the existing research on the labour market assimilation of men and women immigrants in France, as well as that of their children. First, I look at the philosophical, political, sociological, and economic distinction between, assimilation, insertion, and integration.

8.4.1. Definitions of Integration

In economics, assimilation has the meaning of becoming similar in monetary and occupational terms. A popular definition for assimilation is then, the rate at which the earnings of immigrants converge to the earnings of comparable natives[12] in a way that both groups are indistinguishable. Assimilation is a *process* of achieving similarity as immigrants are exposed to the host society's norms and rules and invest in human capital with additional years of residence in the host country. Similarly, occupational assimilation would mean that immigrants achieve to hold jobs of the same status and prestige as comparable natives. Besides wages and occupations, economic assimilation covers many other areas, such as unemployment, labour force participation, economic mobility, business ownership, and so on.

In France, assimilation implies the idea 'of unilateral[13] adaptation of the immigrant to the laws and the customs of France, the superiority of French culture and national identity, and the requirement that the immigrant renounce his or her identity and culture' (Weil and Crowley 1994: 111). This was the official motto by which the immigration system was functioning—at least until the mid 1970s—and has effectively acculturated and absorbed many waves of immigrants into the famous '*creuset français*' or the French melting pot.

Insertion is a term that was introduced in the mid-1970s by the intellectuals 'to designate the right to refuse assimilation, to defend and to preserve collective identity, and to refuse to adapt to dominant French culture' (Weil and Crowley 1994: 111). This term prevailed until 1984 and made people conscious of the right to be different. Later in the 1980s, the concept and parlance of integration became a priority in public discourse, and religion became particularly salient. The key feature of integration is

---

[12] Alternatively, assimilation is defined as the rate at which the earnings of newly arrived immigrants converge to the earnings of other ethnically similar immigrants residing in the host country for more than twenty-five years. Lastly, some researchers define earnings assimilation as the pure increase in wages through time.

[13] The idea being that assimilation affects only the immigrant group and has a minimal impact on the 'French society'.

tolerance—with moral, social, and legal dimensions—and accommodation. In sociology, integration derives from 'shared beliefs and practices, social interaction, and shared goals', while in political theory, 'integration may be seen as what makes standard majoritarian democracy possible' (Weil and Crowley 1994: 112). While integration still is the French legitimate term, it has come to denote, especially by politicians, an interactive process between cultures and the fact that immigration will continue.

Based on the theory of human capital, the economic theory on migration posits that newly arrived immigrants experience an initial disadvantage in the host labour market. During the initial shock of the move (one to ten years), even immigrants who possess higher human capital lag behind natives, due to the nontransferability of their human capital. Nonetheless, they are able to overcome this handicap, to reach economic parity with natives—thus, achieving economic assimilation—and to even surpass the natives. The mechanism of their success is through their additional investment in human capital as they stay longer in the host country along with their innate ability and will to succeed.

The labour market performance of immigrants is strongly influenced by the country of origin, as well as by the host country's admission criteria. At the same time, the labour market performance of immigrants is equally influenced by the host country's economy. During the upswing of the business cycle not only more immigrants will move to a country but this country will also have a strong absorptive capacity, since a prosperous booming economy can offer more opportunities for full participation, and advancement. One would, therefore, expect that the waves of immigrants that arrive during flourishing periods will achieve rapid economic assimilation. France, on the other hand, has always been characterized by rigid labour markets, a more centralized economy, relatively high minimum wages, strict regulations to layoffs, high unemployment rates, low labour force participation rates, and an extensive social welfare system. Under these circumstances, one would expect immigrant integration to be slow or not to take place at all.

8.4.2. Immigrant Assimilation and Intergenerational Mobility

One of the very first studies on the earnings of the immigrant groups in France was conducted by Butaud (1972). He carried out a survey on about 1773 men and 386 women workers who were actively involved in the labour market in 1970. His descriptive study revealed that there were substantial earnings differences among the various ethnic immigrant groups. Specifically, he found that Yugoslav immigrants ranked the highest. Not only the salaries of Yugoslav men and women were the highest among all groups but they also had the highest standard deviation. At the other end of the spectrum, Butaud (1972) found the Maghrebian men[14] who earned the lowest salaries (about 30 per cent less than Yugoslavs) while they had the lowest standard deviation as well. Spaniard men ranked second and Portugese men ranked third. Among women, Italians ranked second and Portuguese third. The Butaud study also found small earnings differences according to geographic location. Immigrants in the Paris region earned more and immigrants in Provence-Côte d'Azur earned less than in other areas. Nonetheless, Butaud (1972) found that the ethnic salary dispersion was consistently maintained geographically. In sum, already in 1970, a period of favourable economic conditions in France, this study showed that some immigrant groups did not fare as well as others in the French labour market. Butaud (1972) also declared that immigrants from Sub-Saharan Africa had low salaries and suffered from unemployment, with one in eight workers being unemployed. He concluded that cultural level disparities were the probable cause of low economic performance as every nationality was perceived by natives as being in a distant social scale.

Another one of the early studies on the earnings of immigrants in France was carried out by Granier and Marciano (1975). Based on a 1970 survey by the Ministry of Public Works and Housing and data by INSEE they studied the wages of individual men and women workers as well as the total family earnings of immigrants and tried to compare them to those of French nationals. They found that immigrant male workers were less skilled than native French workers, and heavily concentrated in manufacturing, especially automobile, and construction industries. In their analysis, they first compared the wages of the unskilled and semiskilled immigrants to those of similar French workers. From this exercise, they found that immigrant wages were quite close to those of French. However, when they compared skilled nonmanual immigrants to comparable French nationals the wage gap widened and became considerable. Similar to other studies, they found that the wages of immigrant men had a wide dispersion by ethnicity, with Yugoslavs earning 40 per cent more, on average, than North Africans. This result was also valid for the analysis on the wages of immigrant women. In general, immigrant women were concentrated in

---

[14] Maghrebian women were not in the labour force; only four women were in the sample and, thus, there is no reference to them.

domestic services, and in the textile and clothing industries. Women's labour force participation also varied by nationality with Yugoslavs, Spaniards, Portuguese, and Italians having the highest labour force participation rates. Still, compared to men, this study showed that immigrant women were poorly paid.

An idiosyncratic group of immigrants to France are the Algerian repatriates, or French refugees. Their migration to France was unprecedented, historic, and on a large scale. Some 500,000 refugees alone arrived in France in the summer of 1962. This group comprised the French,[15] the 'French Muslims', and many Jews. Among the first studies to examine the integration of the Algerian repatriates in France is Baillet (1976). Baillet studied the salaried and nonsalaried repatriates in both the private and public sectors. With regard to the salaried workers, he found that although about 80 per cent of them had to change job categories and professions once they moved to France, although they experienced lower salaries and lost the perks they were enjoying in Algeria, they managed to achieve a rapid economic integration through a process of professional mutation. Among the nonsalaried workers, he found that the workers in the independent professions—such as lawyers, doctors, and business men—were quite successful in the French labour market, but it was the farmers who had shown an exemplary reintegration. Overall, Baillet (1976) contended that the reintegration of the repatriates was relatively easy, was successfully realised and at a minimum cost. However, he found that there was pronounced differential integration by ethnicity, with Arabs and Berbers performing the poorest in the labour market. Out of all the repatriates in France, he found the Jewish to have experienced the fastest and most successful integration.

In 1992, Tribalat (1996) conducted an important survey on the integration of immigrants within the National Institute of Demographic Studies (*Institut National d'Etudes Démographiques, INED*) and INSEE. This survey-the *Mobilité Géographique et Insertion Sociale* (MGIS)—was based on samples drawn from the 1990 census and has since been the principal survey besides the census. The MGIS interviewed 8,900 immigrants from Algeria, Sub-Saharan Africa, South-East Asia, Spain, Morocco, Portugal, and Turkey, who were in France in 1990. This survey also included 2,500 young adults (20–9 years old) born in France of whom at least one parent was from Algeria, Spain, or Portugal, and a control sample of the indigenous population.

---

[15] They are the former colonists, who are French by birth, often called the *pieds noirs*. The closest analogy to this group is the ethnic Germans.

Tribalat's (1996) study concluded that the year of entry, the age at entry, years of residence in France, and professional experience were the key variables for the successful integration and assimilation of the immigrants in France. The striking result in that study was that the gap between the wages of immigrants and natives was the largest in the upper and lower ends of the distribution, while it was not particularly significant in the middle range.

Based on the same MGIS study, Dayan et al. (1996) studied the professional integration of immigrants in the French labour market as well as their professional and social mobility and compared them to the native population. In their longitudinal study that represents more than half of the immigrant population in France, they studied both men and women immigrants who were working during the interview. Overall, they found that immigrants were more often in temporary and precarious employment than the natives, and they were most often dilapidated by unemployment. Among all immigrants, they found women to be more vulnerable in the labour market and mostly hit by unemployment. On the other hand, they found that immigrant men suffered mostly from unstable and precarious employment.

Dayan et al. (1996) ran logistic regressions on the probability of being continuously in stable employment and found that age, years since migration, and years of schooling were the most important determinants of integration into the professional life. These key variables significantly increased the chances of having continuous stable employment. Knowing and speaking the French language fluently was the most significant determinant across all specifications. Surprisingly, they also found that the immigrants who kept close ties with the country of origin were better integrated than those who did not. With regard to the country of origin effect, they found that it was crucial for the integration of women only. In particular, Portuguese women were the most integrated into the labour market while women from the Maghreb and Turkey performed the worst. The number of children was also a significant determinant of the professional integration of women. Controlling for education, experience, seniority on the job, and language, they found that the wage differentials between immigrants and natives was minimal—about 5 per cent—and it was mostly due to the barriers of entry into the labour market. For example, when immigrants joined the labour market they were in the lower tier, working mainly as unskilled blue-collar workers. Further, while immigrants tended to stay in the same jobs they first started with, they were characterized by absence of promotions, a phenomenon indicative of labour market segmentation.

While young age at entry, years of schooling, French language, and no desire to return to the country of origin were positive determinants of upward mobility, Dayan et al. (1996) found that intergenerational mobility in France was very slow. Surprisingly, they found that intergenerational mobility was higher among women immigrants. Finally, Dayan et al. (1996) found that it was the young immigrants who were more often exposed to the risks and fickleness of the labour market. Depending on their country of origin, immigrants in France have different chances of entering the labour market and of succeeding. Echoing other studies, this study also found that immigrants from Algeria were performing the worst in the French labour market.

The Glaude and Borrel (2002) study looked at the difficulties that immigrants face when entering the labour market. Based on the latest data from the 1999 census their descriptive study only reinforced findings from previous studies. Among other findings, they also found that there are strong country of origin differences that are evident in every aspect of economic activity. In addition, when they examined the newly arrived immigrants to France and compared them to immigrants with a longer tenure in France they found that, although on average, immigrants who arrived after 1990 resembled the rest of the immigrants, there were substantial differences at the ends of the socioeconomic distribution. The newly arrived immigrants who were at the lower end were worse off than the other immigrants, while those at the upper end were better off than the other immigrants.

The next natural question is whether these findings also apply to the children of immigrants. The incorporation of the second generation immigrants from North Africa resulting from decolonization of Algeria, Morocco, and Tunisia was studied by Alba and Silberman (2002). Analysing microlevel data from the censuses of 1968, 1975, 1982, and 1990, they examined the integration of the second generation born in France in the period 1958–90. Based on the characteristics of the parents they were able to distinguish the children of the *pieds noirs*[16] from the children of the Maghrebians and compare them to the native French. Their findings demonstrate that there were different trajectories of integration by nationality. While the *pieds noirs* and their children exhibited signs of rapid integration, the Maghrebians (Arabic or Berber) and their children remained detached from the labour market. Resounding other studies they concluded that there is a sharp social distinction between the two

---

[16] The Muslims who fought on the French side in the Algerian war of independence and suffered exile, the *harkis*, are in this group as well.

groups as well as between the two groups and the mainland native French population.

The intergenerational mobility of immigrants was studied by Silberman and Fournier (1999). Their longitudinal study is based on the *Entrée dans la Vie Active* (EVA) survey, that targets the children of immigrants, especially the children who finished lower level schooling (level 5 and 6; below the baccalaureate level).[17] In 1989, EVA interviewed the children of immigrants from the moment they finished school or apprenticeship and followed them for four years as they experienced the transition from school to work, and began their careers and professional trajectories into the labour market. The study only looked at immigrant children from the Maghreb (especially Algerians) and Portugal. They paid attention to whether these children had actually left school with a degree (diploma) or not, and tried to capture sheepskin effects. In France, apprenticeship is a way to make up for not having a diploma; still few of the immigrant children have followed that track. One explanation is that immigrant children are not properly guided by their parents. Once again, this explanation may not hold for all different national origin groups. Whereas it is true for Algerian children it is not true for Portuguese children. In general, Algerian parents do not have the social capital to help their children enter the labour market. They are usually unskilled blue-collar workers, or unemployed, or already inactive and out of the labour force by the time their children are ready to join the labour market. Portuguese fathers, on the other hand, are usually working in small enterprises and have the appropriate connections to help their children in the beginning of their careers.

In sum, Silberman and Fournier (1999) found that Portuguese children have better opportunities than Algerian children mainly due to the social and ethnic capital of their parents, as well as to their parents' connections. They found that Algerian children had less often finished the apprenticeship, were more often unemployed, and benefited less from the familial network. Of great concern is the fact that Algerian youth were more often frustrated with their plight and discouraged from participating in the labour market, than other ethnic youth. The study argued in conclusion that social origin is a very important determinant of any kind of success in France while it could not rule out the role of discrimination in the labour market. In effect, discrimination affects male youth more than female youth. Obviously, it is easier for a daughter to escape the blue-collar job of the father, than it is for a son. As a last point of reflection Silberman and

[17] Roughly this is the equivalent of a US high-school diploma.

Fournier (1999) discussed the role of residential location of immigrants and their children. They found that part of the difficulty immigrants face in penetrating the professional life is their isolated residential location in the suburbs and the lack of transportation means, whether mass or individual. It is also often the case that immigrants lack the financial means necessary to relocate and take advantage of greater employment opportunities.

In the same period, Richard (1997) analysed the Permanent Demographic Sample (*Echantillon Démographique Permanent* EDP) to measure the intergenerational labour market progress of immigrants. The EDP is a census-based panel survey that, on average, comprises a 1 per cent sample of all immigrant groups. It has information on a person's nationality in relation to his/her labour market position. It also contains valuable information on parents and sons with a sample of 15,345 children, who were four to eighteen years old in 1975. Controlling for age and educational attainment, he examined the wages of immigrants and compared them to those of natives. Based on this panel study, he found that the poor performance of the young immigrants in the labour market is undoubtedly due to their ethnic background, which is negatively correlated with labour market opportunities. Richard (1997) found considerable divergence in performance between immigrants from EU and from other countries. Especially, he found that young workers with a Maghreb background often face labour market discrimination as they encounter unequal employment opportunities and permanent difficulties in penetrating the labour market.

France has a national education system, whereby the teachers are federal employees of the Ministry of Education, and education is based on four principles: equal access, nondiscrimination, neutrality, and secularity. However, in practice, the educational system has affected immigrant children disproportionately. In the 1960s a segregated system resulted in only 10 per cent of the working-class children going to the *collège* (the first four years of secondary education) and only 6 per cent to the university. The 1975 reform made it possible for all children to go to college, but still only 6 per cent go to university (Weil and Crowley 1994).

Over the years, it appears that French schools have lost their power to 'assimilate' immigrant youth, to ensure their upward socioeconomic mobility, or at least to even out socioeconomic differences between immigrant and native children, leading some immigrant youth to drop out of school and turn to crime, and others to assert their religious/cultural identity. Some fear that this may lead to the loss of identification as 'French'. Loss of French identity coupled with the change in the French law that requires youth to choose to become French nationals between the age of sixteen and twenty-one, could increase isolation and intensify identity crises. Others caution that even several programmes initiated to help youth have not succeeded in facilitating the transition from school to work. While buildings have been allocated for that purpose and teachers assigned to special neighbourhoods, immigrant and disadvantaged children have not benefited (IGAS 2002).

Vallet and Caille (1999) studied the scholastic achievements of the immigrant children. In their panel study they followed children during their high school years until they received their baccalaureate. Controlling for parental background, social origin, and size of the family, they found that immigrant children performed as well as French children and they even outperformed French children in mathematics. This finding lead them to conclude that it is the inequality of the conditions of being brought up in an environment with social handicaps and not the individual ability that makes a difference in the scholastic performance of children. Within the frame of intergenerational research, the Héran (1996) study also found that, everything else equal, the children of immigrants perform at least as well as the other native children. In fact, they proved that the observed inequalities (or gaps in performance) were due to the inequality of the living and social conditions as well as to a discriminatory educational system. Although the latter is rather hard to prove, it often happens that if the teachers anticipate that the immigrant children will fail in certain fields, they will try to dissuade them from pursuing these fields. Children who have no proper guidance from home find themselves in limbo unable to attain their full potential.

8.4.3. Diverse Immigrant Groups in France and the Self-Employment of Immigrants

Even though migration to France is mostly tied to its former colonies, migration from South-East Asia (Vietnam, Laos, Cambodia, and China) along with Lebanon and Turkey is becoming very prominent. In addition to the traditional immigrants from the ex-colonies and the Southern European labourers, the country-mix has shifted over the last two decades. In general, these diverse groups bring diverse skills and attitudes. Some groups exhibit a higher proclivity to entrepreneurship, for example. The argument is that immigrants are more likely to start their own business, because they are more willing than natives to assume risks. For many immigrants, self-employment is a way of economic and social upward mobility, a way to avoid discrimination, as it also gives them the satisfaction of being one's own boss. By starting out a small business, immigrants can create jobs in addition to occupying them, and by hiring other people for their companies they can even lower unemployment.

Dayan et al. (1996) studied the probability of immigrants going into self-employment. They found that among all immigrant groups, Turks had the highest propensity to become self-employed. Among the immigrant groups that are well represented in the self-employment category are the Chinese. Chinese migration to France became important in the 1980s. Currently, about 200,000 Chinese immigrants live in France. The performance of the Chinese immigrants in France is studied by Ma Mung (2002). He found that Chinese immigrants are well represented in the small-scale entrepreneurial sector. In 1990, the Chinese enterprises in the Parisian area alone employed 40 per cent of the active Chinese population in that area and constituted an important economic circuit. Chinese enterprises are usually of a small and familial setting and are characterized by being transnational. In his study, Ma Mung (2002) showed that Chinese entrepreneurs know the market, and know where to open a business; they know how to circulate the necessary capital to open a business; and they know how to circulate merchandise beyond country boarders. Finally, they have a great capacity to react swiftly to the macro fluctuations by changing and adjusting their import–export endeavours. Overall, Chinese entrepreneurs in France are faring quite well.

While in the 1970s immigrant women were practically invisible, and forgotten by social scientists, by the end of the last century 45 per cent of the immigrant women aged between fifteen and sixty were active in the labour market. At the same time, however, these women were affected by long-term unemployment three times more than the French women. Immigrant women also suffer from various obstacles—financial, cultural, social, institutional, and legislative. A study on immigrant women's employment and the creation of employment was conducted in 2000 by Hükum and Le Saout (2002). Creating employment in this study means that these women either form an enterprise, an independent profession, or an association. The Hükum and Le Saout (2002) study focused on 158 women from the Maghreb countries, Turkey, and Sub-Saharan Africa, who were in France for more than twelve years. They concluded that immigrant women are capable of transferring their professional knowhow into a variety of economic activity. These immigrant women are characterized by an entrepreneurial ethos, which distinguishes them by their superior ability to mobilize their social, ethnic, and personal resources in order to succeed in an often-fragile labour market. For these immigrant women, becoming self-employed was a way of achieving a respectable social status even though it does not necessarily mean that they become wealthy.

Baillet (2003) studied the occupational sorting of Algerians in Paris and the Parisian region. After the 1982 census, it is clear the number of Algerians in Paris has decreased. While this might reflect their becoming French and disappearing from the statistics as immigrants, they still remain the second largest immigrant group after the Portuguese. Baillet (2003) found that there has been a shift in their occupations from blue-collar workers to employees to small businesses. Especially after 1984, Algerians, and Kabyles in particular, are increasingly sorted into the commerce and craft occupations. When they are in the trade-business sector, they own small hotels, restaurants, and coffee shops. However, even those who are in the blue-collar or labourer occupations are mostly skilled and are in the iron and steel industry. In sum, for Paris and the Parisian region, Algerians (especially after the halt on immigration) are increasingly moving away from the blue-collar labourer milieu and moving into the *petite bourgeoisie en declin*, or the lower middle class in decline.

8.4.4. Remigration Bias

All studies on immigrant integration and assimilation are based on the immigrant population that is living in the host country at the time of the survey, ignoring the characteristics of those immigrants who have left the host country before the census or the survey. Estimations of this kind might suffer from remigration bias and draw the wrong conclusions; the rational being that the degree of assimilation of the return migrants remains unknown. France does not have population registers and immigrant departures are not recorded in the French statistical system.[18] This makes it extremely difficult to accurately measure the exits of immigrants. Some crude estimates on return migration in the 1970s show that the number of immigrants who left France to return to their home country was as high as 60,000–70,000 per year. Later, these numbers decreased mainly due to the increase in family immigration.[19] For the Algerian repatriates, in particular, some estimates show that 24 per cent of those who arrived in France during 1962-8 returned to Algeria during 1968-75.

---

[18] Only forced and assisted departures are recorded.

[19] Since 1975 the French government has given monetary incentives to immigrants so they return to their home country. More than 230,000 have taken advantage of this aid and have returned home (Le Moigne and Lebon 2002).

Based on the EDP, the INSEE (1999) published a study on the emigration patterns of immigrants in France. The EDP started in 1968 and, thus, contains information on the last five censuses. In this study return migration was defined as an absence from two consecutive censuses. This study found that from the immigrants who arrived in France between 1962 and 1968, one in four immigrants has returned back home within the first ten years of their arrival in France. Naturally, return migration rates varied substantially by nationality with more Spaniards returning home than Italians or Portuguese. This study also found similar return rates for the immigrants who arrived in France before 1962. For example, 28 per cent of the Portuguese who arrived in France before 1962, returned to Portugal during the period 1975–82. In contrast, return rates declined for those who arrived between 1968 and 1975. Less than 20 per cent of Algerians and Moroccans returned home, while return migration by EU nationals was appreciably higher (INSEE 1999).

A parallel attempt to account for the return migration rates when studying the immigrant population was carried out by Rouault and Thave (1997). They used longitudinal data of the EDP that have information on the entry and exit of the same immigrants from one census to the next since 1975. Their estimation of return migration rates is of the order of 30–40 per cent, which is quite considerable. The Thierry (2001) study on return migration focused on the renewal frequency of one-year residence permits. These permits were issued to foreigners authorized to enter France during the period 1994–6 by the Department of Interior. Based on the non renewal of permits, he estimated an average emigration rate of 35 per cent during that first year and this rate varied strongly by nationality. This rate was higher for the immigrants from other EU countries and lower for the immigrants coming from developing countries (54 per cent versus 21 per cent respectively). However, these estimates might be inflated due to the inclusion of foreign students in the data.[20]

An innovative approach to calculate remigration rates was undertaken by the HCI. This study focused on retirement pensions data. The study found that many immigrants return to their home country when they retire. During the 1990s, an impressive number of 90,000 retired Algerian immigrants returned home. Spaniard and Portuguese retirees also reached a high average annual return, with 8,100 returnees and 3,800 returnees respectively. Italians had the lowest number of returnees (1,300 per year),

[20] In 1997, foreign students from outside the EU comprised about 11 per cent of all university students enrolled in France.

probably because not many Italians lived in France in the 1990s. The calculated average annual departure number for Moroccans was also low at 1,400 immigrants. In all likelihood this is because Moroccans are more 'recent' immigrants and are a younger group far from retiring age (Héran 2002).

The review of the aforementioned studies leads to the following conclusion. It appears that immigrants in France are not as socially or as economically integrated as it was expected or desired. Moreover, they are often faced with unequal employment opportunities as well as with an unprecedented rise in unemployment. Immigrant assimilation in France varies considerably by nationality, and most studies argue that this is rather the result of integrating factors. For certain groups—such as the Maghrebians—assimilation is rarely realized. In the new century, immigrants from the Maghrebian countries, face even fewer prospects of social and economic assimilation. Whereas some studies show that self-employed immigrants fare well, most studies agree that there is no actual intergenerational mobility. Still, the sample of studies is too small and suffers from several biases: cohort effects, remigration bias, selection bias, etc.

8.5. Impact on the Labour Market

The crux of the debate of the impact of immigrants on the labour market centres upon the following question: does the arrival of immigrants in the host country and in a particular area depress the wages of the natives or of other immigrant residents, and does it increase their unemployment level? Inflated by rightwing politicians, there is a growing sentiment that immigrants are stealing away jobs from natives. In France, a country with chronic unemployment rates around 10 per cent, immigration has come to be equivalent to unemployment, and immigrants in France have become the scapegoat.

8.5.1. Impact on Employment, Income Levels, and Internal Mobility

The argument here centres upon the degree of substitutability or complementarity between the skills of immigrants and natives. However, the impact also depends on the flexibility of wages, the consumption behaviour of immigrants, and so on. In the US, the vast literature on the impact of immigrants on the wages and employment opportunities of natives does not provide support to the popular belief that there are adverse effects from immigration (Friedberg and Hunt 1995).

Brücker et al. (2002) studied this question for Europe. Their study was based on the European Community Household Panel (ECHP) of all EU country members. Looking at most European countries—including France—they found, at best, a negligible impact of migration on wages and on the employment of natives. Another interesting finding of the Brücker et al. (2002) study is that they could not confirm the popular belief that the more generous countries in terms of social welfare systematically attract the less qualified and less educated immigrants.

Angrist and Kugler (2002) estimated the effect of immigrant flows on native employment in Western Europe by focusing on the role of the labour market institutions. They examined the extend to which labour market flexibility—such as employment protection, high replacement rates, firing costs, rigid wages, and business entry costs—affects the employment consequences of immigration in the host labour markets. Their analysis is based on panel data for eighteen countries' labour-force surveys, including France, for the period 1983–9. Their OLS and IV estimates showed that a 10 per cent increase in the foreign share would reduce the employment rates of the natives by 0.2–0.7 of a percentage point. They concluded that while in the short-run restrictive labour market institutions might protect native workers, in the long-run they fail to protect them from job loss and can aggravate job losses due to immigration.

Specifically for France, only a handful of studies has looked at the impact of immigrants on the labour market. Among the first researchers to study the phenomenon of the labour market impact and internal migration patterns was Puig (1981). By examining, among other groups, the presence of young repatriates in France, the question he tried to answer was where do people move to, and why do people move away from some regions. Looking at the interregional migration of the active population of France's 21 regions, he examined this question for the periods 1962–8, and 1968–75. He studied the impact of the repatriates from Algeria for the period 1962–8 only. By decomposing the active population by age—with a cut off at thirty years of age—and by estimating gross immigration equations, he found that people move to areas where average salaries are higher and employment vacancies exist, and they move away from areas with a high percentage of young workers. Moreover, he found that people move away from areas where the repatriates live. He concluded that the repatriates engendered unemployment and discouraged internal immigration to regions where repatriates were concentrated.

Taking advantage of the natural experiment of the Algerian independence in 1962, Hunt (1992) also studied the impact of the Algerian repatriates on the French labour market. In particular, she estimated the impact of repatriates on unemployment, labour force participation, and wages of the nonrepatriates, as well as on the migration decisions of other groups. Based on census data, she estimated cross-sectional regression models and controlled for education, age, and industrial and regional differences. She found that the repatriates, who represented 1.6 per cent of the labour force in 1968, were over-represented in skilled occupations, and chose to locate in regions with a similar climate to Algeria, and regions where previous repatriates form Algeria were already located. Although within a couple of years of their arrival the repatriates suffered a high unemployment, she found that the repatriates caused only a small increase in the unemployment of non repatriates (an increase of 0.3 percentage points at the most). With regard to the impact on the wages, her estimates from several specifications showed only weak evidence that wages fell in response to the arrival of the repatriates. At most, average annual salaries were lowered by 1.3 per cent. The presence of repatriates had no effect on the labour force participation of the nonrepatriates either. Lastly, with regards to the effects on the migration decisions of other groups, she found that the presence of repatriates in a region had no significant effect on internal migration decisions, but exerted a positive and strong effect on international migration decisions. However, all things considered, the total impact of the repatriates was seen to be about zero, meaning that the arrival of immigrants in an area hardly affected the salaries or employment levels of the natives.

A more recent study, Gross (1999), investigated the effects of the flows of immigrant workers in the French labour market. This study focused on the period from the mid-1970s to mid-1990s. In a macroeconometric setting and using a Keynesian model of disequilibrium he estimated equations on unemployment, real wages, and labour force participation. His findings revealed that, in the short run, the arrival of immigrants can raise aggregate wages through the complementarity of immigrants and natives and, thus, increase unemployment. However, this effect is shortlived and similar to an increase in domestic labour force participation. In the long run, immigrant workers and their families lower the unemployment rate permanently, suggesting that the demand for goods and services by immigrants creates more jobs than they occupy. Gross (1999) also found that this result holds for immigrant workers, amnestied immigrants, and the flow of immigrant families. Finally, and contrary to the economic theory, he found that using amnesties as a channel for immigration is not detrimental to the labour market. All in all, he found little evidence for displacement effects due to migration, concluding that immigrant flows are not responsible for France's high unemployment rates.

A later study on the immigrant evolution on the French labour market by Brun (2003) also showed that a small sample of legalized or amnestied immigrants performed a lot better after they were granted amnesty. These amnestied immigrants were able to find better jobs and increase their wages. For example, whereas before amnesty 44 per cent of these immigrants had incomes below 610 euros per month and only 18 per cent earned more than 915 euros per month, the situation was almost reversed after amnesty with 14 per cent earning less than 610 euros and 37 per cent earning more than 910 euros.

These findings warrant a further comment on amnestied immigrants. The general presumption—dictated by economic theory—is that because economic migrants are selected according to their skills they have a higher probability of succeeding in the host country's labour market and achieve an accelerated economic assimilation. Obviously, illegal migrants do not seem to qualify for this theory. However, amnesty is typically given to successful illegal migrants, e.g. those who have found work over a particular period of time[21] and have proven that they are desirable participants of the labour force. Consequently, amnestied immigrants are de facto selected by the labour market forces. This type of selection should, thus, be more efficient than if imposed by a public bureaucracy that has insufficient knowledge about the labour needs of the economy. It is, therefore, quite possible that a strategy of allowing illegal migration with a policy to provide amnesty can be efficacious and efficient under certain circumstances, and France has often used amnesties as a means of selecting immigrants into the labour market.

Studying the period 1990–7, Jayet et al. (2001) estimated the effects of immigration on the probability of employment and the wage levels of natives. They employed data from the Employment Survey, and estimated a Heckman-2-step model of selection while conducting a separate analysis for men and women immigrants. They tested their model on the French born and on five separate groups of immigrants—naturalized French, Southern Europeans (including Italians, Portugese, and Spaniards), other Europeans, Maghrebians, and the rest of all other foreigners. They further considered five levels of professional qualification: upper administrative and managerial positions, intermediate professions, employees, skilled

---

[21] For France, one of the requirements for eligibility for amnesty in 1983 was to have worked in France for at least a year.

workers, and unskilled workers. Their results on the probability of employment for the male samples showed that the presence of immigrants in a locality had no effect on the probability of employment of the natives. For the female samples, they found that there was an effect but this effect depended on the nationality of the immigrants. In particular, the presence of the group labelled other foreigners had a positive impact while the presence of Maghrebians had a small negative impact on the probability of employment of women in France.

With regard to the impact on the incomes of natives, Jayet et al. (2001) showed that, in general, for both men and women, there were small effects. Looking closer at the socioprofessional categories, they found that, for men, there was a significant effect on income but only for the skilled workers and the intermediate professionals. In contrast, they found no effect for the categories of unskilled workers and employees. For women, they found some significantly positive effects that were related to the presence of the other Europeans group, and to the presence of other foreigners group. For women only, and for the years 1994–6, Jayet et al. (2001) obtained negative effects on the incomes of natives attributed to the presence of Maghrebians. In sum, this study showed that the presence of immigrants did not cause the incomes of the natives to decline for neither men nor women, and that the migration patterns of immigrants and natives in France are similar to those results for the United States.

8.5.2. Natives' Sentiments and Business Cycle Effects

With the exception of the poor performance of the Maghrebians, the leitmotiv of the previous section has been that over the last forty years, immigrants in France do not constitute a threat to the labour market or to the social fabric of French society. This finding holds true for both legal and illegal workers, and for immigrants who migrated for work or family reasons. However, natives' sentiments towards immigrants are often negative.

Based on data from national surveys from 1970 through 1995 Simon and Lynch (1999) tried to link public opinion towards immigrants and immigration policies. They found that public opinion about immigration policy varies over time and that the desire to restrict migration through policy is not consistently related to negative sentiments against immigrants. While in 1988, 64 per cent of French felt that France is a country that welcomes foreigners, in 1991, 64 per cent complained that there are too many Arabs in France. In 1993, 67 per cent of French ascertained that

France risks losing its national identity and something must be done about immigrants. At the same time, 76 per cent of French acknowledged that immigrants do not take jobs away but they do the work the French refuse to do. Among immigrant groups, northern Europeans were the most liked by French while Maghrebians, Turks, Persians, and Black Africans were the least favoured. Overall in this study, the French expressed at best ambivalent sentiments towards immigrants and when they were vociferous against a specific ethnic group it was because of the social and cultural distance between them.

Fetzer (2000) used public-opinion surveys on opposition to immigration and polls on support for the French *Front National* to examine the natives' sentiments towards immigrants in France in the late 1980s and mid-1990s. His analysis involved multivariate regression models and Tobits employing interesting demographic, economic, and cultural variables. He tested two hypotheses: (1) the economic self-interest belief that if the natives are unemployed, if they suffer declining personal finances, and they lack advanced education, then they oppose migration reflecting their narrow, material self-interest, and (2) the theory of marginality according to which, if natives feel marginalized and alienated they are more likely to be sympathetic to immigrants in the spirit of solidarity of the likes and reduce anti-immigration sentiments. His results provide minute support for the economic self-interest theory, and small support for the economic marginality theory. Namely, he found that individual unemployment did not have any effect on nativism. Nevertheless, he found confirmation of the cultural interpretation of the marginality theory.

In general, Fetzer (2000) found that being a racial, ethnic, or religious minority decreases anti-immigration sentiments. Moreover, he found that females and individuals of foreign origin have weakened anti-immigration sentiments. In his conclusion Fetzer (2000) stated that opposition to immigration 'has as much to do with symbolically delegitimating the values and cultures of immigrant minorities as with preventing the foreign-born from taking **natives' jobs** (p. 18). Lastly, this study emphasized the role of culture in nativism.

Based on individual data from twelve OECD countries, Bauer et al. (2000) found that natives favour immigration in countries that are positively selecting immigrants according to economic motives. This led them to conclude that an effectively selective migration policy can attenuate natives' xenophobia and hostility against immigrants, while it can allow politicians to increase the number of humanitarian immigrants without risking re-election failure.

The last question I examine in this review essay is whether it is the migration policy or the business cycle that determines the flow of immigrants and their employment patterns in the host country. Zimmermann's (1996) study on European migration showed that migration is strongly driven by business cycle effects as it occurred both in France and Germany from the 1950s until the halt in recruitment in the early 1970s. However, he also found that after the recruitment of immigrants ended, migration from most home countries responded less to the business cycle. Surprisingly, and contrary to general expectations, he found that humanitarian migration was also affected by the business cycle in the host countries.

Moreover, not only migration per se is related to the host country's business cycle, but the performance of immigrants is also affected by the stage of the business cycle they face at the time they enter into the host country labour market. It is also true that immigrant performance continues to be influenced by the macroeconomic conditions in the host country during their stay. The rationale is that immigrants are more vulnerable and more cyclically sensitive to the macroeconomic conditions than the native-born. Entering the host country during a period of high unemployment has adverse effects on the earnings of immigrants but these effects are temporary and disappear with additional years in the USA (Chiswick and Miller 2002).

For France, Hollifield (1990) tested the argument that immigration and foreign employment are a function of changes in labour market conditions, employers' hiring practices, and policy. In his time-series analysis with a one-year lag, he considered economic migrants, seasonal workers, and family reunion migration. He found that both changes in labour market conditions and in the hiring practices of employers have had substantial impact on the levels of permanent worker migration. On the other hand, he found that changes in policy had a very marginal impact on worker migration. With regard to seasonal migration, he found that although the social and economic conditions had some effect, the policy measures had contributed to a loss of state control over seasonal migration. Lastly, with regard to family migration, he found that family members do eventually join the labour force and their flows are, thus, very sensitive to employers' hiring practices. Family reunification levels are also contingent upon social and economic conditions in France. Overall, the policy changes in France have had only marginal effects on migration while labour market conditions had a substantial impact on migration.

8.6. Conclusions

Over the last fifty years, France has received numerous waves of immigrants with different origins, cultures, aspirations, and motives. French immigration policy has been to accept people that either had accepted or were willing to accept French language and culture. Such a policy seemed easy to implement, since the major source countries of immigration were the former colonies. However, while immigrants typically migrated from the former French colonies, there were also economic migrants actively recruited by the French government over some periods. The French *creuset* has functioned efficaciously until the last third of the twentieth century. In the seventies, when economic conditions in France changed and became more difficult, immigration policy became increasingly tight. After the halt of recruitment, family unification became a major channel of immigration to France albeit illegal immigrants and refugees became also important.

The socioeconomic portrait of the migrants in France by the year 2000 dictates that they have fewer skills than the natives and their occupational status is below that of the natives with comparable skills. The labour market performance of certain nationalities, in particular, persistently lags behind that of natives. Even when some nationalities manage to perform well in monetary terms, their insertion into the social hierarchy is minimal. Immigrants often live in poor areas of large cities, are disproportionately affected by unemployment, and are more vulnerable to economic crises. The majority of the immigrant population in France is manual workers and there is only minute intergenerational mobility.

Looking back at the French historical experience with regard to migration, it appears that economic assimilation has not taken place to a full extent. Economic integration is a necessary although not sufficient condition for full integration. It denotes opportunities, fairness, and smooth functioning of the labour market that lead to success. Whereas some studies have shown that some immigrant groups have achieved success, most studies showed that immigrants in France are performing very poorly compared to natives. Looking at the income distribution, it is noteworthy that while the middle class is performing in a comparatively similar way to French natives, immigrants in the upper and lower ends are doing much worse than their French counterparts. Moreover, there are often substantial earnings differences among the various immigrant groups, with the Portuguese, the naturalized, and even the amnestied immigrants faring well and the Algerians faring badly. From the surveyed studies in this chapter, it is clear that the socioeconomic position of immigrants, who are not from EU countries, is problematic. Immigrants suffer from high unemployment and when they are employed they occupy unstable, low-wage jobs with low possibilities of advancement.

With regard to the children of immigrants most studies have shown that immigrant children consistently lag behind French children. However, controlling for social, ethnic, and cultural background, immigrant children would have the same academic performance and labour market success as the French children. With the exception of the Portuguese children, there is no sufficient intergenerational mobility. Whereas some studies alluded to discrimination as the culprit, all studies concluded that Algerian youth were more often frustrated with their plight and discouraged to participate in the labour market, than other ethnic youth.

Most empirical findings on the impact of immigration on natives suggest that immigration is not harmful but, at the same time, immigrant contribution to economic growth is rather modest. This review showed that there is no consistent evidence that immigrants crowd out natives from the labour market. The few studies on this theme, confirm that there are no significant displacement effects, that there is no correlation between immigration and unemployment, and that the wages of natives do not decline due to the presence of immigrants. Nonetheless, natives' sentiments towards immigrants are often negative. Whereas these sentiments can be inflated and exacerbated by rightwing politicians, some studies point to the social and cultural distance between immigrants and natives as a possible reason. Lastly, immigration and economic integration are interlinked to the business cycle.

A recurrent theme of the surveyed studies is the allusion to widespread discrimination and geographical segregation in France. Unlike the USA, it is not the skin colour that interferes with the acceptance and embracing of immigrants in the French society; it is rather the different culture. Racial discrimination is a key factor for the poor labour market performance of immigrants and their children as 'an estimated 30–60 per cent of immigrant children face acute socioeconomic marginalization' (Hargreaves 1996: 612). In addition, some sort of operating statistical discrimination hinders the full potential of immigrants and their children. Some argue that this second-class status bolsters the longing and the languishing of the home country's culture and the appealingness of the Islam (where they can find consolation) and further contributes to their marginalization and isolation from mainstream society. Although the results of most studies on young immigrants are consistent with the possibility of discrimination it could also be that other labour market mechanisms are at work. Many studies point to the fact that a better selection and integration of immigrants by the French government would have boosted the economic performance of immigrants, would have alleviated labour market stagnation, and would have eased social and political tensions. However, as Angrist and Kugler (2002) argued, it is the reduced labour market flexibility that 'makes immigrant absorption more painful' (p. 29).

Migration remains both a political phenomenon, and an institutional construct. Contrary to the spirit of the French migration policy, this review has revealed that immigrants in France have multiple cultural identities. Since the early 1970s, both the right and the leftwing governments in France have unsuccessfully tried to control migration. Part of this failure might stem from a weak implementation of integration policy. While alternating between a laissez-faire and a restrictive immigration policy, there has been a systematic oversight of the needs of the labour market resulting in a significant gap between policy goals and outcomes. The inability to incorporate migrants successfully in to the economy and the labour market is probably more of the reason of failure.

France is inextricably bound to its immigrant force, and immigrants continue to arrive in France. Many immigrants and their descendants continue to live in France and are ready and willing to contribute to France's economic prosperity. However, they often experience forms of social stigmatization. Even worse, oftentimes, newly arrived immigrants are treated with disdain and fear by the previous waves of immigrants. Can France in the new century succeed in integrating its minorities of foreign origin in a way to take advantage of this vibrant and promising manpower in the labour market and to benefit from this younger and high fertility foreign population?

The lesson from the French experience is that assimilation through cultural and political venues is not enough. The low economic possibilities of the French labour market since the early 1970s were not conducive to the economic integration of immigrants. Cultural and economic integration should be intertwined to be successful. France should understand the power of ethnic networks and exhibit more religious tolerance as she should recognize the social embeddedness of the immigrants and their families. France should take pride in her multicultural society, embrace this 'mosaic' and make the French national identity compatible with the other forms of identity.

Immigration management is a very sensitive issue. The challenge ahead for France is to encourage and foster the economic and social integration of all its immigrants. France should reorient its policy in a way that it is beneficial to all. As Zimmermann (1995) pointed out 'immigration was largely beneficial in the past' and it can be advantageous in the future. France is a developed country with the ability and flexibility to absorb its foreign newcomers, and has proven to do so in the past with the repatriates.

In conclusion, there is substantial need for further studies on immigrants in France. First, while there is some research on the assimilation and integration of migrants and their effects on the natives, the findings need further support and often better treatment by using advanced econometric techniques and more appropriate data. Second, there are a few questions that have been completely overlooked by the French literature: Does immigration have fiscal implications, e.g. does immigration increase or reduce the public deficits? How do migrants affect the social welfare system and income redistribution? How can we understand the political economy of immigration?

References

Alba, R. and Silberman, R. (2002). 'Decolonization immigrations and the social origins of the second generation: the case of north Africans in France', *International Migration Review*, 36 (4): 1169–93.

Angrist, J. and Kugler, A. (2002). 'Protective or counter-productive? European labour market institutions and the effect of immigrants on EU natives', CEPR Discussion Paper, 3196 (London: CEPR).

Baillet, P. (1976). 'Les rapatriés d'Algérie en France', Notes et Etudes Documentaires, 4275-6 (Paris: La Documentation Française).

Baillet, D. (2003). 'Le travail des Algériens à Paris depuis 1945', *Migration Société*, 15 (85): 78–98.

Bauer, T., Lofstrom, M. and Zimmermann, K. F. (2000). 'Immigration policy, assimilation of immigrants, and natives' sentiments towards immigrants: Evidence from 12 OECD countries', *Swedish Economic Policy Review*, 7 (2): 11–53.

Brun, François (2003). 'Les immigrés et l' évolution du marché du travail en France', *Migration Société*, 15 (85): 67–78.

Brücker, H., Epstein, G. S., McCormick, B., Saint-Paul, G., Venturini, A. and Zimmermann, K. F. (2002). 'Managing migration in the European welfare state', in T. Boeri, G. Hanson and B. McCormick (eds.) *Immigration Policy and the Welfare System*, (New York: Oxford University Press).

Butaud, J.-P. (1972). 'Les resources des travaileurs étrangers', *Hommes et Migrations*, 827: 3–24.

Chiswick, B. R. and Miller, P. W. (2002). 'Immigrant earnings: language skills, linguistic concentrations and the business cycle', *Journal of Population Economics*, 15: 31–57.

Dayan, J.-L., Echardour, A. and Glaude, M. (1996). 'Le parcours professionnel des immigrés en France: une analyse longitudinale', *Économie et Statistique*, 299, 1996-9: 107-29.

Deneuve, C. (2002). 'Besoins de main-d'œuvre des entreprises et recours à l'immigration: quelles perspectives?', in F. Héran (ed.) *Immigration, marché du travail, intégration* (Paris: Commissariat Général du Plan).

Fetzer, J. S. (2000). 'Economic self-interest or cultural marginality? Anti-immigration sentiment and nativist political movements in France, Germany and the USA', *Journal of Ethnic and Migration Studies*, 26 (1): 5-23.

Friedburg, R. and Hunt, J. (1995). 'The impact of immigrants on host country wages, employment, and growth', *Journal of Economic Perspectives*, 9: 23-34.

Glaude, M. and Borrel, C. (2002). 'Les immigrés et leurs descendants sur le marché du travail: un regard statistique', in F. Héran (ed.) *Immigration, marché du travail, intégration*, (Paris, France: Commissariat Général du Plan).

Goux, D. and Maurin, E. (2000). 'The decline in demand for unskilled labour: an empirical analysis method and its application to France', *Review of Economics and Statistics*, 82 (4): 596-607.

Granier, R. and Marciano, J. P. (1975). 'The earnings of immigrant workers in France', *International Labour Review*, 111 (2): 143-65.

Gross, D. M. (1999). 'Three million foreigners, three million unemployed? Immigration and the French labour market', International Monetary Fund Working Paper, WP/99/124 (Washington DC: IMF).

Haus, L. (1999). 'Labour unions and immigration policy in France', *International Migration Review*, 33 (3): 683-716.

Hargreaves, A. G. (1996). 'A deviant construction: the French media and the "Banlieues"', *New Community*, 22 (4): 607-18.

Héran, F. (1996). 'L'école, les jeunes et les parents', *Économie et Statistique*, 296: 5-15.

—— (ed.) (2002). *Immigration, marché du travail, intégration* (Paris: Commissariat Général du Plan).

Hollifield, J. F. (1990). 'Immigration and the French state: problems of policy implementation', *Comparative Political Studies*, 23 (1): 56-79.

Hükum, P. and Le Saout, D. (2002). 'Les femmes migrantes et la création d'activité', *Migrations Etudes*, No. 104.

Hunt, J. (1992). 'The impact of the 1962 repatriates from Algeria on the French labour market', *Industrial and Labour Relations Review*, 45 (3): 556-72.

IGAS (2002). 'Le rapport annuel de l'IGAS 2002', L'inspection générale des affaires sociales, La Documentation Française: Paris.

ILO (1998). 'The effectiveness of integration policies towards immigrants and their descendants in France, Germany, and the Netherlands', Geneva: ILO.

INSEE (1999). 'Regards sur l'immigration', *Synthèses*, 30 (Paris: INSEE).

Jayet, H., Ragot, L. and Rajaonarison, D. (2001). 'L'immigration: quels effets économiques?' *Revue d'Économique Politique*, 111 (4): 565-96.

Le Moigne, G. and Lebon, A. (2002). L'Immigration en France (Paris: Presses Universitaires de France).

Ma Mung, E. (2002). 'La complexité des migrations des populations d' origine chinoise', in F. Héran (ed.) *Immigration, marché du travail, intégration* (Paris, France: Commissariat Général du Plan).

Puig, J.-P. (1981). 'La migration régionale de la population active', *Annales de l'INSEE*, 44–1981: 41–72.

Richard, J.-L. (1997). 'Unemployment among young people of foreign origin in France. Ways of measuring discrimination', in *On the way to a multicultural society?* The Siena Group Seminar on Social Statistics (Bern: Bundesamt für Statistik).

Rouault, D. and Thave, S. (1997?). 'L'estimation du nombre d'immigrés et d' Enfants d' immigrés', INSEE Méthodes, 66 (Paris: INSEE).

Silberman, R. and Fournier, I. (1999). 'Les enfants d' immigrés sur le marché du travail: Les mécanismes d'une discrimination sélective', *Formation-Emploi*, 65: 31–55.

Simon, R. J. and Lynch, J. P. (1999). 'A comparative assessment of public opinion towards immigrants and immigration policies', *International Migration Review*, 33 (2): 455–67.

SOPEMI (2001). 'Trends in international migration: continuous reporting system on migration, Annual Report' (Paris and Washington, DC: OECD).

Tapinos, G. (1975). *L'immigration étrangère en France: 1946–1973* (Paris: Presses Universitaires de France).

Thierry, X. (2001). 'La fréquence de renouvellement des premiers titres de séjour', *Population*, 56 (3): 451–68.

Tribalat, M. (1996). *De l'immigration a l'assimilation: Enquête sur les populations d'origine étrangère en France* (Paris, La Decouverte/INED).

Vallet, L.-A. and Caille, J.-P. (1999). 'Migration and integration in France: academic careers of immigrants' children in lower and upper secondary school', Paper presented at the European Science Foundation Conference in Obernai, France.

—— (1995). 'Les carrières scolaires au collège des élèves étrangers ou issus de l'immigration', *Education et Formations*, 1995–40: 5–14.

Weil, P. and Crowley, J. (1994). 'Integration in theory and practice: a comparison of France and Britain', *West European Politics*, 17 (2): 110–27.

Wihtol De Wenden, C. (1994). 'The French response to the asylum seeker influx, 1980–93', *The Annals of the American Academy of Political and Social Science*, 534: 81–90.

Zimmermann, K. F. (1995). 'Tackling the European migration problem', *Journal of Economic Perspectives*, 9 (2): 45–62.

—— (1996). 'European migration: push and pull', *International Regional Science Review*, 19 (1–2): 95–128.

9. Italian Migration

Daniela Del Boca and Alessandra Venturini

9.1. Introduction

Italy is a country with a long history of emigration and a very short experience of immigration. Mass emigration started with Italian unification: during the period 1861–1976 over 26 million people emigrated, half of them towards other European countries, the rest towards North and South America. Two-fifths of all these emigrations originated from the regions in the south of Italy.

The reasons were, on the one hand, the slow and difficult development of the Italian economy and, on the other, the economic expansion which characterized other countries between the second half of the nineteenth century and the First World War. After the Second World War, Italians emigrated mostly towards Europe, especially Germany. In the same years, the development of the industrial north stimulated mass internal migration from the south to the north west.

Emigration declined sharply in the period 1970–80. In spite of the high unemployment rate (especially among young people), the higher level of income of Italian households allowed them to bear the long periods of unemployment of their members. Now only a few highly skilled and specialized workers leave the country in search of better job opportunities.

During the same period, Italy changed from being a sender country into a host country, receiving immigrants largely from developing countries and Eastern Europe. While the effects of immigration are still difficult to grasp and interpret thoroughly, there is wide consensus about the crucial role that emigration has played in the history of the Italian economy.

In this chapter we analyse the facts, motivations and effects of emigration and immigration in the Italian experience. Section 9.2 analyses the facts of emigration and its motivations and effects; Section 9.3 illustrates the more recent phenomenon of immigration to Italy. Section 9.4 provides some conclusive remarks.

9.2. Emigration

9.2.1. The Facts

The history of Italian emigration started after the period of unification and has characterized the Italian economic history for over a century. During the period 1861–1985, over 26 million people emigrated, with an average of 3.4 million emigrants per decade between 1875 and 1928 and two million between 1929 and 1975 (approximately one Italian out of four emigrated).

Table 9.1 summarizes the emigration and migration rates (in thousands). These data show that emigration is not a steady flow, but it is characterized by periods of growth and stagnation.

As Figure 9.1 shows there are increasingly sharp fluctuations after the turn of the century. Between 1875 and 1928 emigration from Italy reached its peak with about 17 million emigrants abroad, between 1929 and 1985 about 9 million left the country.

The period of most intense emigration was the 1880s when flows from the northern areas of Italy were integrated and replaced by flows from the southern areas. The first period of Italian emigration was dominated by emigrants from agriculture as a result of the economic crisis and the poverty levels of central and southern areas, the industrialization process being concentrated mainly in the northwestern regions.

Table 9.1. Emigration and migration rate (per 1,000), 1876–1985

	Emigration	Migration rate
1876–1885	1,315	4.56
1886–1895	2,391	7.76
1896–1905	4,322	13.06
1906–1914	5,854	20.60
1876–1914	13,882	11.01
1915–1918	363	2.44
1919–1928	3,007	7.70
1929–1940	1,114	2.20
1941–1945	4,121	0.32
1946–1955	423	5.24
1956–1965	3,166	6.28
1966–1975	1,714	3.20
1946–1975	7,351	4.86
1976–1985	861	1.53
Total	26,595	

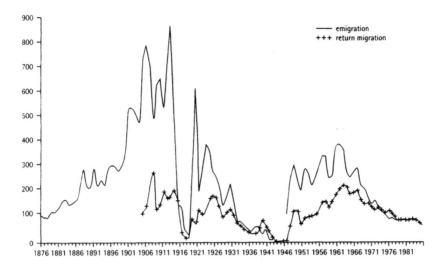

Figure 9.1. Italian migration abroad (thousands), 1876–1981
Source: Golini and Birindelli (1990).

Table 9.2 shows the regional contribution to emigration and its direction. Emigration from the industrial regions of the north was particularly evident only until the Second World War. Already in 1913, only 39 per cent of total emigrants came from the north, while 47 per cent were from the south and only 14 per cent from the centre against a population distribution of 45 per cent, 38 per cent and 17 per cent respectively. In the north itself, most emigrants came from the north-eastern regions: 33.3, while only 23.4 came from the north-west, due to the differing stage of industrial development.

Table 9.2. Regional contribution and direction (per cent national migration)

	1876–86	1887–1900	1901–14	1915–18	1919–31	1931–42	1932–42
Continental							
North	87.4	88.4	76.8	76.6	79.0	66.0	21.8
Central	8.3	6.4	15.5	15.1	12.2	11.7	
South	4.3	5.2	7.7	8.3	8.8	22.3	
Transoceanic							
North	46.0	32.8	17.6	13.6	24.6	24.2	
Central	5.7	8.9	11.2	9.5	10.0	10.0	
South	48.3	58.3	71.2	76.9	65.4	65.8	

Source: Vitali (1974, 8–9) in Sori E.

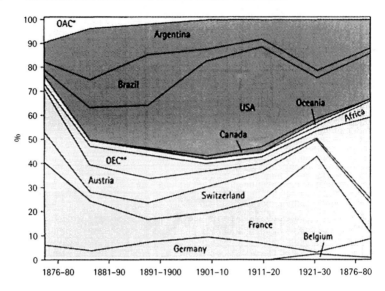

Figure 9.2. Emigrants by main destination, 1870–1940 (percentages)
*Other American countries; ** Other European countries
Source: Sori 1979 p 31.

Table 9.2 shows that the contribution from northern regions to continental migration decreased from 87 to 66 per cent of national migration, while the southern contribution increased from 4.3 to 22.3 per cent. A similar trend is evident for transoceanic emigration in which the contributions of the north and south are initially more equally distributed. While the north decreased its contribution from 46 to 24 per cent, the south increased its contribution from 48 to 65.8 per cent.

Emigration from the north of Italy was mostly European, while the emigration from the southern regions was mostly transoceanic, directed to the United States, Latin America, and Australia. The geographical position and the cost of transportation played an important role in explaining the different initial destinations. Figure 9.2 shows that Europe received 75 per cent of total Italian outflows in 1880, declined to 45 per cent during the boom of Italian emigration and regained the majority of the flows later on. In the years of the emigration peaks, a crucial role was also played by the earlier settlements of relatives and friends.[1] However, the region that

---

[1] Sori (1979) shows how the proportion of Italians leaving with their families increases after 1886 and starts declining after 1905 to start again after 1930.

had most emigrants was the Veneto, the region which has become the most important labour importer in recent years (Bacchetta, Cagiano de Azevedo 1990). The characteristics of emigrants are well identified by statistical analyses: they were usually male, of working age, and tended to be economically active. In terms of skills and occupation characteristics, the agricultural sector would appear to have been dominant, with most emigrants having low skills. Italian emigrants were largely hired in sectors such as construction, railways, and mining, all sectors characterized by a very high level of instability. However, these characteristics as well as the composition of emigration changes in the course of time.

Before 1886, the great proportion of emigrants were males of prime age (80–85 per cent male). Sori (1979) shows how the proportion of Italians leaving with their families increased after 1886 and started to decline after 1905. It began to rise again around 1930. The workers who emigrated in the first phase had fewer skills. The first group was formed of labourers (*braccianti*) from the agricultural sectors and unskilled manual workers. After 1900, workers with higher level of skills as well as craftsmen emigrated. Not all Italian emigrants settled permanently abroad. While, during the first period of prevalently transoceanic emigration, the proportion of returns was relatively small, in a second phase, in which emigration was largely towards Europe, returns tended to be of sizeable number (Table 9.3).

The data show a higher proportion of returns among emigrants to Europe than among emigrants to the US and Latin America. The trends in return migration seem to be coherent with emigration patterns: the two curves are closer at the lowest level of emigration (Figure 9.1).

Table 9.3. Return migration

Years	Total	Migration rate
1905–14	1,800	5.65
1915–18	229	0.15
1919–28	1,302	3.33
1929–40	835	1.65
1941–45	67	0.30
1946–55	898	1.90
1956–65	1,853	3.67
1966–75	1,453	2.70
1976–85	904	1.61

Source: ISTAT.

According to Giusti (1965), during the period 1811–1911, net emigration was about one-third of the gross flow. An implication of these estimates is that instead of an increase in the first decade of the century there was actually a fall in the net emigration rate. According to Hatton and Williamson (1988), the big surge in gross emigration after the 1890 was not matched by a big surge in net migration, but was mainly the spurious result of a change in passport regulations. When adjustment for defective official statistics is taken into account, the upsurge in Italian emigration is similar to that in northern Europe.

The understanding and measurement of migration flows and stocks are in fact severely limited by the lack of definition of emigrants, especially in a country like Italy, which is characterized by vulnerable frontiers. Until 1913, a person was considered an emigrant if he/she left because of poor economic conditions; later the definition was extended to include manual labourers and those emigrating to join other family members. In 1921, a special passport (with coupon for return migrants) was introduced for labour emigrants. From 1926 to 1958 ISTAT[2] collected data on emigrants every year, using the coupons attached to the passports as a unit of observation. Only in 1958 did ISTAT revise emigration statistics, while local authorities continued to register emigrants, classifying them by motives of migration (Golini 1987).

9.2.2. Policies Affecting Italian Emigration

Only during the late 1860s and 1870s did the Italian government start to show concern about emigration. The first laws controlling emigration are the 1868, 1873, 1876 circulars allowing the emigration of individuals who already had an employment contract or could demonstrate that they had sufficient income to support themselves. The first legislation, ratified in 1888 with the vague intention of controlling the relationship between recruitment agencies and emigrants, reflected different political and economic interests. On the one hand, mass emigration solved the problems of restructuring the agricultural sector in the south and relieving poverty. On the other, employers in the industrial area saw emigration favourably only if developed coherently with the economic growth (Golini and Birindelli 1997).

Several periods can be identified. A growing pressure for control and protection of emigrants, which gradually gave the state a more important role,

[2] ISTAT is the Italian central statistical office.

characterized the first period, 1869–1925 (years of growing emigration). During these years numerous laws were introduced to control and protect emigration and emigrants' remittances. This effort was also accompanied by measures to provide the emigrants training support to facilitate integration. A General Commissariat for Emigration was established under the Ministry of Foreign Affairs. In 1924, the National Congress of Emigration and Immigration was held in Rome with the important goal of coordinating the actions of several sender and recipient countries (Canistraro and Rosoli 1979).[3]

The second period (1926–39) is characterized by a new international and national situation. Internationally, the outbreak of the Second World War limited the entry of foreigners, and nationally, the Fascist regime restricted emigration. Restrictive legislation was introduced to limit permanent emigration (with the exception of family reunions) and encourage returns. The Department of Italians Abroad, which was set up to control emigration, encouraged returns in order to increase the population in Italy as well as populate Italian colonies in Africa.

The third period, which began in 1946, was dominated by the protection and promotion of emigration, and various issues such as family reunion, remittances and social security were better organized. In 1947 the Department of Emigration was set up to replace the Department of Italian Abroad.

Finally, the 1960s saw a more active involvement of various actors such as labour offices, trade unions and employers who acted explicitly to ensure better coordination and protection of Italian emigration and the Italian community abroad.

However, Italian emigration policies have had limited effects on the flows and directions of emigration. More important factors would appear to be the changes in the economic activities and the migration policies implemented in the countries of destination. One example of this was the 1902 law banning emigration to Brazil, which failed to have the expected effect in view of the coffee boom and substantial subsidies offered to Italians by the Brazilian government (Merrick and Graham 1979). Very important in reducing and redirecting flows to South America were the USA immigration barriers. In 1917, the U.S. prohibited entrance to the illiterate reducing the eligible immigrants from southern Italy, and in 1924, they introduced the quota system restricting the right to a limited

---

[3] The National Congress of Migration and Immigration was the first attempt at coordination of receiving countries and sending ones to define guidelines and co-ordinate actions.

number (about 5,000) of Italians.[4] Moving to more recent flows, it is worth recalling the much negotiated migration to France, Belgium, and Germany, which was organized through Government agencies.

9.2.3. Determinants of the Decision to Migrate

The reasons for Italian emigration reside in the poverty and lack of jobs and income opportunities caused by poor agriculture, which pushed Italians from both the north and the south to look for better chances abroad.

The traditional model of migration based on the human capital theory interprets the decision to move as an investment of the individual physical and monetary resources into a risky but probably better future life.

$$M_{(iod)} = f(W_d - W_o - C) \qquad f > 0 \tag{1}$$

The individual decision to emigrate (M_i) from the area of origin (o) to the area of destination (d) is a positive function of the expected income differential in countries of destination (W_d) and origin (W_o), net of migration costs (C). Thus, the larger the expected income benefit from migration, the more likely the move.[5] This equation is frequently tested with aggregate data, where the gross emigration rate—emigration flows over population in country of origin—is explained by the expected wage differentials between origin and destination—namely real wage differentials—plus labour market variables which proxy the probability of finding a job in the labour markets of origin and destination—usually proxied by the employment or unemployment rate or the participation rate—and a demographic variable which proxies the labour market pressure of demographic origin in departure areas—usually the population growth lagged twenty years. In such a model, a lagged dependent variable is usually introduced to capture the inertia. This interpretation implies that if income in the country of origin increases—*ceteris paribus*—the income differential decreases and migration would decrease.

Faini and Venturini (1994) have questioned this interpretation arguing that the willingness to migrate is constrained by inadequate human and physical capital and, for a given wage differential, an increase in income per capita in poor countries encourages individual to migrate and favour

[4] An interesting analysis on the emigration to Argentina see Moreno J. L., (1995), (Le donne in Banca: rimesse e famiglie di emigranti meridionali in Argentina prima del 1930). Il caso di Molfetta, Studi Emigrazione 32 n.118: 289–320.

[5] For a complete model see for instance Hatton T. (1995), 'A model of UK emigration, 1870–1913', *The Review of Economics and Statistics*: 407–15.

Table 9.4. Time series regression for Italian emigration, 1878–1913

	Faini and Venturini I	Faini and Venturini II	Hatton and Willliamson III	Hatton and Williamson IV
Dependent variable	LnM/Pop	M/Pop	M/Pop	M/Pop
Log W_f/W_h	0.55(2.14)	0.31(1.51)	9.67(1.31)	9.23(2.91)
Log W_h			6.19(0.52)	1.56(0.21)
Log Y_h	1.13(3.9)	1.21(3.51)		
LF/Pop$_f$	5.37 (3.27)	12.3 (4.18)	45.1 (3.0)	39.7(3.03)
LF/Pop$_h$	− 0.84(2.26)	− 0.58(1.14)	− 12.2(1.30)	− 7.27(0.90)
GrowthPop$_{t-20}$	− 0.001(1.0)	− 0.001(0.84)	1.07(1.58)	0.72(1.16)
Trend	0.01(2.36)	0.09(2.96)	0.19(0.95)	
Stock Mig.$_f$				0.13(2.75)
Dummy for 1901–1913			5.91(3.32)	4.85(2.95)
Lagged emigration rate(t-1)	0.72(12.5)	0.70(10.8)	0.25(1.56)	0.06(0.04)
Lagged emigration rate(t-2)			− 0.49(3.24)	− 0.55(4)

Dependent variable M/Pop migration rate, W wage, LF/Pop activity rate in f foreign or h home country, Growth Pop population growth in home country and Stock Mig in foreign country.

outflows.[6] At a given 'threshold', income per capita stops being a pushing factor and becomes a restraint factor when people have achieved enough wellbeing to prefer to stay home rather than to leave.[7] Faini and Venturini (1994) test this hypothesis to explain the Italian migration hump of the beginning of the 1990s and add the income per capita variable to the already mentioned variables to capture their hypothesis which is supported by the results (see Table 9.4 column I).

Wage differentials as well as the labour market variable coefficients have signs which are coherent with the theory (in sender and recipient countries). However, population growth lagged twenty years as proxy of demographic pressure is not significant, while the time trend to proxy transportation costs in American flows is significant with the expected sign. The income per capita variable is significant with the expected sign, supporting the view of a 'push' effect of income growth or, as Hatton and Williamson (1998) argue, a poverty-trap effect on migration. Had Italy's

[6] For a detailed exposition of the theoretical model see Faini R. Venturini A. (1994), "Migration and growth: the experience of Southern Europe", Working Paper CEPR. n. 964.
[7] When the income effect dominates the substitution one.

income per capita remained unchanged from its 1900 value, emigration in 1913 would have been almost 27 per cent lower than its fitted value.

Hatton and Williamson (1998) discuss this interpretation on two grounds: first, they underlay an overestimate of the gross migration flows of the beginning of the century, which determines an oversize of the hump. They correct it by introducing a dummy for the period 1901–13, and then they attribute an important role to the migrants' stock to explain the rapid emigration growth at the beginning of the century. They also introduce the real wage variable to capture the poverty-trap effect.

Equation II for Faini Venturini (F–V) and equation III for Hatton–Williamson (H–W) in Table 9.4 present comparable specifications which are not the best specifications for either of the two teams; the first is a fixed effect estimate of the Italian migration rate to France, Germany and the USA,[8] while the second is an aggregate estimate of the total emigration rate toward the previous destination, plus Argentina and Brazil.

In both specifications wage differential, labour market variable in sender country and population growth are not significant, while the proxy for the 'poverty-trap effect' is significant in the F–V case and not in the H–W one, just as the time trend is significant in the first case and not in the second. H–W argue that the income variable significant in the F–V test captures the remittance effect, which is better captured by the stock of immigrant variables used in their best specification (equation IV), while the income differential also becomes significant.

H–W (1998) also find support for their interpretation in their regional analysis. Cross-sectional analyses show that large wage gaps and lower levels of economic development drove emigration up. They also show that some of the forces driving migration were regionally different. Urban development in the north reduced emigration while agricultural under-development in the south raised it. These factors raised southern above northern migration.

The debate is still open. The income per capita variable is likely to capture other phenomena, not only the increase in domestic human and monetary resources that released the constraint and allowed more Italians to invest in emigration. However, H–W use two proxies for the chain mechanism, the lagged dependent variable following Gould (1980) and also the stock, and they do not question the negative sign of the lagged one.

---

[8] Results presented are from Table 4.6 where F–V use as dependent variable the migration rate for comparative purposes while in Table 4.7 F–V they test an aggregate estimate of gross emigration rate.

As a concluding comment on both best specification equations (Table 9.4 columns I and IV), wages and labour market variables and a lagged dependent variable are important for understanding migration dynamics, while demographic pressure seems to be not statistically significant and intercontinental and European emigration rates follow the same interpretation.

The same conclusion is reached by T. Straubhaar (1986, 1988) in his empirical analysis of the Italian emigration flows to Germany and France in the more recent period 1963–84. Income differential, labour market variables and lagged dependent variables are significant with the expected sign, while the income growth in the origin country has a 'pulling' effect (positive and significant coefficient) in the Italian–German flow, and is not significant but with the expected negative sign in the Italian–French one.

In another very interesting paper, Daveri and Faini (1997) analyse the choice between internal and international migration as alternative means for risk diversification. The empirical test for the Italian southern regions after the Second World War shows that in addition to the variables already mentioned above, the risk-related variables play a significant role in shaping migration decision.

9.2.4. Social and Demographic Effects of Emigration

The social and demographic impact of emigration is certainly difficult to measure because of the lack of knowledge of the real dimensions of the phenomenon. Some evidence emerges concerning the working-age population as well as the sex structure. Demographic studies show that the effect is particularly strong in small areas where the emigration rate was higher than the natural population growth rate, such as the region of Basilicata and Abruzzo-Molise, where there was a reduction of total population during the big hump of 1910-11, −0.98 per cent in the first case and −3.58 in the second. At the aggregate level, the net migration rate never reached more than 50 per cent of the natural population growth rate and more sizeable effects are found in the sex and age distribution of the population.

In 1887, for every 1,000 females there were 1,005 males, 1,026 in the north and 984 in the south. After the big hump in emigration of 1911, the national average fell to 967, with 979 in the north and 948 in the south. The percentage of males of working age (20-50) in the same period dropped on average to 36.6 per cent, while it was even lower in Abruzzo-Molise and Calabria—29 per cent (Sori 1979). This transformation of the

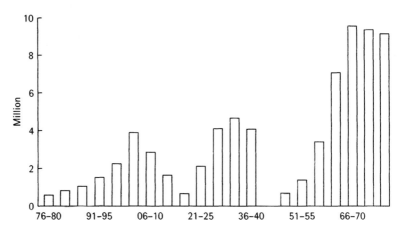

Figure 9.3. Remittances of Italian emigrants, 1876–1980 (5-year mean values)
(in 1938 liras)
Source: Golini and Birindelli (1990) p 163.

population and of the working-age population pushed women, children and the elderly to substitute for the males in their work, which was, however, mainly subsistence agriculture and did not induce any sizeable social change.

However, the important benefits of emigration are worth considering. The saving sent back by emigrants to the country of origin played a crucial role. The amount of remittances was lower before the Second World War, when migration was largely permanent, and increased after the Second World War, when migration was temporary and families did not follow the emigrants, but stayed in their place of origin (Figure 9.3). According to Sori (1979), remittances were very important for the rest of the families who remained in the region of origin being the resources to pay off debts and support the members of the family, but also had an important role in the national budget where the banking system was used.

During the big emigration hump of the beginning of the century, remittances were vital for the current account of the Italian balance of payments (Zamagni 1990), which, thanks to workers' saving inflows, was in equilibrium[9] and represented a positive exception for a country which was developing through domestic demand. During 1960–80, the total

[9] In 1911–14, the Italian current account has a surplus of 77 millions of lira at current price which resulted from the deficit of the goods balance (−910), the surplus of the services balance (+386) and the surplus of the factors' income balance which includes remittances inflows and interests on capital outflows of 510.

flows of remittances increased, especially from Germany and the United States where Italians had achieved greater economic outcomes (Bacchetta, Cagiano de Azevedo 1990). The data on remittances provide just an idea of the dimension of the flows. The introduction of a banking network in the areas of emigration strongly encouraged flows, avoiding the frauds that previously oppressed low-income migrants.

Data are a serious limitation for the assessment of the effect of emigration on the sender country. According to some studies on the effects of remittances (e.g. D'Amore et al. 1977), 45 per cent were used to buy land or houses, 34 per cent were used to buy durables and 12 per cent were deposited in bank accounts. Their effect was also important for the short-term reduction of local poverty, but did not contribute to any form of economic development. A social change was instead introduced by the new role played by women, who were now holders of bank accounts and could take decisions on the use of the savings (Moreno 1995).

Research on the effect of return migration shows a discouraging scenario, which indicates the various constraints to start-up new enterprises and the limited contribution to develop the local economies. Only in the northeast where returns have been encouraged as well as supported, it seems easier to identify the positive effect of returns.

In the south, where the labour market was still characterized by excess labour supply, the returning migrants face harsh difficulties in finding a job or in finding support available for their investments. Moreover, several other economic constraints on the environment severely limited the possibility of improvement, while little support was provided by local residents. Cerase (1967), in his research on return migration from the USA, finds out that 19 per cent returned because their migratory project failed, 40 per cent because their saving objectives were reached, 26 per cent came back for retirement and only 16 per cent with the intention of investing in the country of origin. The last-mentioned, however, were unable to implement their plans partly because of the hostility of the local bureaucracy and partly because of the disregard of the central one.

There can be no doubt that remittances released many Italians from their consumption constraints, but an aggregate balance on the benefit of emigration on the longer term economic development of the areas of departure seems negative, especially for the southern regions. The latter received a large amount of funds which they failed, however, to use in productive activities. Furthermore, the human capital drain from those regions has worsened the economic situation. Even if the emigrants from the south were unskilled and frequently illiterate, they were self selected: their risk-prone attitude testified to their willingness to learn and to work, which is a vital component to implement economic and social development.

9.3. Italy as a Country of Immigration

9.3.1. The Facts

Italy became a country of immigration during the 1970s. The number of foreign residents increased from 143,838 in 1970 to about 300,000 in 1980, and by the mid 1980s it had reached half a million (1985). In the 1990s, the foreign population increased further and workers were most concentrated.

Even if the stock of foreigners with a residence permit in absolute value increased substantially, it still represents a small percentage of the population, just a little above 2 per cent. The percentage of foreigners employed in the total labour force is still low on average, and it never reaches a value of over 7 per cent, the sectors where foreign workers are most concentrated (Table 9.5).

The composition of the immigrants changed remarkably in the 1980s and 1990s. The incidence of immigrants who came from the European Union declined, while the proportion of immigrants from outside the European Union increased and in the late 1990s accounted for 86 per cent of the total. Among the non-Europeans, in spite of the increase in African and Asian immigrants, their relative incidence declined in relation to Eastern European immigrants from Yugoslavia, Albania, and Rumania, who became the fastest growing group.

The growth of the African and Asian communities is clearly seen from the data emerging from the legalisation procedure. Where the African and Filipino nationals accounted for the most important groups in the first and second legalization procedures, the Yugoslavian, Albanian, and Rumanian were more important in the third and last.

The new immigrants tend to locate where demand for work is higher and more facilities make immigrants' integration possibilities easier and faster. According to the territorial distribution of residence permits, in 1998, 30.4 per cent of the legal foreigners are in the north-west, 29.4 per cent in the centre and 22.3 per cent in the north-east. During the 1990s, the northeast area is the one which has most increased its inflows, especially for Eastern European immigrants, but also for Africans. The south, with

Table 9.5. Stock of foreign resident population in absolute value, as share of domestic population and by area of origin and most important nationality of origin

Year	Value	Share	By Area of Origin %					By Main Nationality of Origin				
			Africa	Asia	(Europe)	East-EU	LatAm	Total	Morocco	Philippines	Yugoslavia	Albania
1970	143.834	0.27	3.3	7.8	61.3			100	—	—	—	—
1975	186.415	0.33	4.7	8.1	60.5			100	—	—	—	—
1980	298.746	0.53	10.0	14.0	53.2			100	0.2	0.2	3.9	0
1985	423.004	0.74	10.5	15.4	52.1			100	—	—	—	—
1990	781.100	1.37	30.5	18.7	33.5	5.6	8.4	100	10.3	4.5	3.8	0.3
1993	987.400	1.76	29.1	17.5	36.9	15.5	8.1	100	9.9	4.6	6.8	3.1
1995	991.419	1.85	26.7	16.6	40.8	21.0	8.0	100	9.5	4.3	5.2	3.5
1998	1250.214	2.01	28.8	18.3	38.5	22.5	8.4	100	11.7	5.4	3.3	7.3
2000	1500.200	2.20	29	18.6	38.0	27.1	8.3	100	11.6	5.0	6.9	9.9

11.2 per cent and the islands with 5.5 per cent are much less important.[10] Among the urban areas, Milan and Rome have respectively 13 per cent and 17 per cent of total resident permits, but the fastest growing provinces—Brescia, Vicenza, and Verona—are in the north-east. The north-east is more appealing on many dimensions. First, there is an excess demand of labour. The industrial and service structure is dominated by small firms in which labour legislation is less strict, and it allows an employment relationship which is more flexible and more favourable to the immigrants, who care less for employment stability and higher wages.

The gender composition indicates a small imbalance in favour of male immigration; in fact, 54.7 per cent (2,000) of the total number of foreign residents are male. Data show a prevalence of female immigrants among some Asian groups—e.g. Filipinos—where only 33.8 per cent are male, Latin American groups (Brazilian 27.8 per cent, Peru 28.3 per cent), while male immigrants prevail among the African groups (72.3 per cent among Moroccans, 78 per cent among Tunisians, 92.9 per cent among Senegalese) and East Europeans, namely ex-Yugoslavia (65 per cent), and Albania (70 per cent). Among these two groups where the male component prevails, there are exceptions, such as Rumanians and Poles, where female immigrants are prevalent and among Africans, Somalis, and Ethiopians.

In terms of age and household composition, young adults (18–39 year) constitute by far the most important share with 65.2 per cent of total presence. Most of them, whether married (48.6 per cent) or not (46.4 per cent), do not have children (75 per cent). This shows that Italian immigration is still in an initial phase of migration in which one family member alone usually immigrates. However, according to Caritas report data, the number of family reunifications are increasing at a fast rate. On the total new inflows in 1999, 40 per cent were family reunion permits while this type of permit represents only 21 per cent of total stock of permits.

Among the immigrants from outside the European Union, 61.8 per cent hold a residence permit for work reasons of whom 93.1 per cent are regular employees and 6.9 selfemployed, while 13 per cent hold a permit to look for job.[11]

---

[10] The dataset derived from Anagrafe residency registers is a subset of total permits because not all foreigners holding permits are registered at the Anagrafe but they show the same territorial distribution.

[11] In Italy the following information is available: (1) information derived from the residence permits issued by the Ministry of the Interiors. This document specifies the reason for which it was granted (family reunion work, tourism, study, asylum etc.) and work is the most important reason given (about 50 per cent). The figures are revised each year by the National Statistical Office and so

The Census data from 1991 show the distribution of immigrants by sectors: about 36 per cent in the industrial sector of which 18 per cent in the construction industry, 17.6 per cent in the agricultural sector, 30 per cent in trade and service and 16 per cent selfemployed. A degree of ethnic specialization exists: in fact, Africans are concentrated in agricultural, construction, and selfemployed activities, while Asians work mostly in services and agriculture and Eastern Europeans in construction and family services.

Since then Social Security data (covering only employees) has shown an increase in total foreign employment which reached 563,000 in 1998, 17 per cent as family workers, 9 per cent as agricultural workers and the remainder (74 per cent) in the private industrial (roughly 42 per cent) and service sectors (32 per cent).[12]

In terms of occupational characteristics, 73 per cent are registered as manual workers. This is due to a combination of two causes: their relatively low education level and the difficulty of finding a job on a par with their education and training. The information available regarding the education of foreigners serves little, given the educational differences which exist between schooling systems. When it is based on their declarations, there is an overvaluation of their education, when it is based on recognition of their degrees—the difficulties in comparing different schooling systems may induce an underevaluation of their education. Thus, given this provision, the educational level based on degree recognition among those registered at employment offices has fallen in the course of the 1990s. The proportion of immigrants with no education was 75 per cent in 1995 and increased to 85 per cent in 2000.

9.3.2. Illegal Immigration

The spontaneous flow of immigrants and the initial difficulty of controlling the phenomenon create the impression of a largely illegal[13] phenomenon. On account of the work they do as street vendors, windshield cleaners and

the permits which expire during the year (about 25–30 per cent of total permits) are excluded; (2) census for 1991 carried out by the Central Statistical Office, ISTAT; (3) local registry offices (Anagrafe); (4) legalization procedure dataset; (5) only for employees, the Italian Social Security Dataset (not available in detail up to now); (6) the National Placing Office dataset where foreigners have to register to enter the labour market.

[12] As mentioned before, data on recent foreign employment are derived from administrative sources which do not collect data on that purpose, and Venturini and Villosio in their 2000 paper present a different way of selecting migrants and a much higher value.

[13] The illegal presence of a foreigner is either due to his/her clandestine entry or to him/her remaining in the country after the permanency right has expired.

prostitutes, a small number of foreigners is highly visible and contributes to the impression that illegal immigration is growing at a rapid rate.

The results of the legalization procedures, however, seem to have brought some realism to the size of the illegal phenomenon. The foreigners who were regularized were limited in number and much fewer than expected; 118,000 with the first measure (1987), 234,841 with the second (1991) and 247,500[14] with the third (1996) and 219,000 with the last (1998). The illegality rate—namely, the number of immigrants regularized over the number of residence permits—was 30 per cent with the first procedure, 45 per cent with the second and 27 per cent with the third and 18 per cent with the last one. It is quite constant over time and the very limited decline suggests that only a small percentage of the total number of illegal immigrants can take advantage of the legalization procedure, that its frequency may determine repeated legalization by the same foreigners, and may attract additional flows of illegal immigrants.[15]

Estimates of the number of illegal residents have been made on many occasions using different sources.[16] The most recent survey of the estimates made by Strozza (2000) stresses the use of information drawn from the legalization procedures in the calculation of the share of illegal immigrants. In 1994, the lowest estimate was 465,000 while the highest was 564,000; in 1998 it ranged between 176 and 295,000.

The changes in the immigration flows that resulted in illegal Polish immigrants being replaced by illegal Moroccans and Filipinos, then illegal Albanians, and then illegal Kurds and illegal Rumanians, increase the difficulties in monitoring the phenomenon and make it more difficult to produce reliable estimates of the number of illegal immigrants present.

The national statistics office (ISTAT) provides time-series data (estimates) concerning the work done by illegal or legal foreigners in the underground economy.[17] The total work measured in standard unit of labour amounts to about 700,000 units, which represents 3 per cent of the total units of work and 7.6 per cent of total non-regular units of labour and 25 per cent of total non-regular units of labour among employees.

---

[14] The Caritas Report gives a smaller number 202,000 while the number reported is derived from the OCDE SOPEMI Report.

[15] See Caritas 2000 *Immigrazione Dossier statistico '96*, (Anterem, Roma and Natale and Strozza 1997).

[16] For a survey of the different methods used and of the different estimates see Natale M., Strozza S. (1997), *Gli immingrati stranieri in Italia* (Cacucci Editore 1997 and Strozza 2000).

[17] The ISTAT estimates of foreign non-regular 'work' are based on information regarding overstays when residency permits expire, police controls but there is no detailed description available.

The sectors where they work are the same as those of regular employment but with a different intensity, mainly services (70 per cent), agriculture, and construction.

9.3.3. Determinants of Immigration

The immigration phenomenon and its timing is partly explained by the closure of several Northern European labour markets at the beginning of the economic recession in 1974, which pushed foreign immigrants to search for new countries of destination. During that period the conditions enabling Italy to become an immigration country were already set. Wages for manual workers were higher in Italy than in France and income per capita had increased to reduce the gap from Northern European countries. Contrary to the 1960s experience, where migration was pulled by the demand in the countries of destination, in the 1980s immigration was initially pushed by supply factors, high fertility rates, lack of jobs in the country of origin, low wages, and poor working conditions and, given the proximity, relatively low transportation costs (Table 9.6).

Some available job openings were found in sectors such as family services, in the agricultural, in construction and in many small industries as well as in the informal economy. Then a chain mechanism was triggered and additional flows joined the stock of immigrants (the flow stock ratio is on average 12 per cent with a higher value in the more attractive regions).

The lack of an appropriate (restrictive) immigration law and the long and pouring frontiers caused the flow to start and the chain effect brought in additional immigrants, even though the law became more restrictive and economic opportunities diminished. During the 1990s, the collapse of the

Table 9.6. Determinants of immigration

Country	GDP per capita $ ppp 1995	Fertility rate	Share of employment in agriculture 1990	Share of GDP in agriculture 1995	Rural population 1995
Italy	19,890	1.2	9	3	33.4
Morocco	3,320	3.4	45	14	48.1
Philippine	2,850	3.7	45	22	46.0
Albania	670	2.6	55	56	62.8
Rumania	4,360	1.4	24	21	44.1

Source: World Bank, Social Indicators.

former Yugoslavia and Albania put Italy even more under the pressure of illegal flows. 'Boat people' came in from Albania and other nearby Mediterranean countries, but also from as far away as Kurdistan. All these people initially entered as asylum seekers and only after bilateral agreements were some nationalities, Albanians first and foremost, repatriated without accepting their application for demand asylum. Only 25 per cent of applications have been accepted (Caritas 1996: 122).

The fact that individuals know they fail to possess the appropriate prerequisites and prefer to enter anyhow, even at the risk of being and remaining irregular, may be one of the causes of the decline in total number of applications. Even if East European immigration does not have the traditional characteristics of labour immigration (in the Yugoslav and Albanian cases for instance, radical political changes took place), the push factors are still economic, with immigrants looking for better labour opportunities and higher income prospects. The country tried to regulate the flows, but the political disruption of neighbouring areas increased the pressure.

9.3.4 The Effect of Immigrants on the Domestic Economy

One of the main reasons for the opposition to immigration is found in the state of the Italian labour market, characterized by one of the highest unemployment rates in Europe. Italians were afraid that immigrants working in the formal or informal economy could compete with the natives and 'steal' their jobs.

There is no empirical evidence to support this assertion, but some preconditions that favoured complementarity between natives and foreigners in previous experiences were lacking in the Italian case. If the high internal mobility of the native labour force favoured the complementary role of foreign labour in the USA and a selective immigration policy guaranteed complementarity in the Australian, Canadian, and Swiss cases, Italy with its four ex-post legalizations and its very immobile labour force was a potential case of strong competition between different segments of the labour market, both in terms of wages and employment. This expectation does not seem to be confirmed by closer analysis of labour market variables.

First, we examine potential direct competition between natives and foreign workers in the regular labour market.

Three arguments can be provided against foreign regular workers, having a noticeable effect on the wages of domestic labour. First, in Italy wages are the result of national bargaining with strong trade unions and regular foreign labour is only 3 per cent of total employment, and in few branches reaches 7 per cent. Second, the number of regular foreign workers increased recently after the 1991 and 1996 amnesties and it was too early for their presence to have had a significant effect on the wages of domestic workers. Third, decentralized bargaining was introduced only in 1995 and there was no noticeable effect on wage differentials for the weakest categories of domestic labour—the young and the women—due to the presence of foreign workers.

A more formal analysis has been carried out by Gavosto, Venturini et al. (1999). First, they extracted from the Social Security Administrative Archive an individual dataset on foreign workers. The dataset covered only employment in private firms, which was 60 per cent of total employment for natives, but 76 per cent of total regular foreign employment—hence quite representative.

The results of empirical analysis[18] (using repeated cross-sections from 1989 to 1995) by branch and region show that the share of immigrant flows out of the native ones (F) after controlling for changes in demand (ΔY) and fixed years (t) and branches (b) and regions (r) effects, has a positive effect on the growth of the native's wage. This complementarity effect is larger if we focus solely on blue-collar workers, on small firms and on Northern Italy (see Table 9.7) where migrants are more numerous, where unemployment is very low and where there are open vacancies.

The same complementary effect remains if a different measure of foreign intensity, namely the share of the stock of foreign employment on total native employment (S) and its square (S^2) since 1989 is used. It has a positive but declining effect, which suggests that, *ceteris paribus*, as the share of foreign workers increases—at about 10–14 per cent of native branch and region employment—it will shift from a complementary to a competitive role. Many provisos can be applied to these results and to this last interpretation because the dataset is probably too short for this type of longterm analysis. However, at the moment a general complementarity effect prevails.

Let us now examine the effect on native employment. The territorial distribution of foreigners is uneven. More than 53.9 per cent of the foreigners holding a valid residence permit are in Northern Italy, and

---

[18] Following Moulton's objection in the first stage the native wage changes are regressed against individual characteristics and branch regions dummy variables, while in the second stage the dummies' coefficients and the explicative variables are divided by the dummies standard error.

Table 9.7. Wage competition between natives and foreigners

	I a Total	I a Manual workers	I a Firm size 0–50	I a North	II b Total	II b Manual workers	II b FirmSize 0–50	II b North
$\Delta Y_{t,b,r}$	0.03	0.027	0.08	0.04	0.03	0.027	0.08	0.04
	5.3	4.55	6.2	2.3	5.3	4.55	6.1	2.3
$F_{t,b,r}$	0.09	0.118	0.15	0.19				
	1.8	2	2	1.9				
$S_{t,b,r}$					0.22	0.48	0.80	0.73
					3.1	6	7.6	4.7
$S^2_{t,b,r}$					−0.034	−0.008	−0.10	−0.08
					−3.4	−5	−4.86	−3.7
Fixed effect:								
Branch	yes	yes	yes	yes	yes	yes	yes	yes
Region	yes	yes	yes	yes	yes	yes	yes	yes
Years	yes	yes	yes	yes	yes	yes	yes	yes
R2	0.87	0.86	0.93	0.95	0.87	0.87	0.83	0.95
n.obser.	1,983	1,917	1,839	780	1,983	1,916	1,834	780

Dep.Variable: $(\hat{y}/se_y)_{b,r,t} =$ Average rate of growth of wages of the natives by branch and region
$\Delta Y_{t,b,r}$ change of value added by time, branch and region
$F_{F,b,r}$ flow share of foreign, $S_{t,b,r}$ stock share of foreign employed since 1989 by time, branch and region
a OLS estimates, b IV instrumented cumulative inflow of foreign workers (stock) by share of blue-collar workers, share of woman and lagged dependent variable.

29.4 per cent in the centre, 70 per cent of the workers found a job in the north, and 21 per cent in the centre. These areas are, however, the ones in which the unemployment rate is below the national average.

A simple correlation between unemployment and the foreign labour rates among Italian regions yields a high, negative figure of −0.7. Given the different territorial distribution of the labour demand, this correlation suggests that foreigners are employed where the labour demand is high and domestic unemployment is low. The main concern is, however, the possible reduction of the probability of finding a job or a possible longer duration of the search process or also on a possible disincentive in intensive investment. A more fomal test has been done by Venturini and Villosio (2000c). They use the ISTAT's quarterly labour force survey dataset (from 1992 to 1996) to analyse what effect the percentage of foreigners in employment has on three cases: the probability of those employed losing their job and of those unemployed looking for a first job or with previous employment experience to find a job with annual probit cross-section estimates. The percentages of foreigners and the other aggregate

Table 9.8. The results of the probit regression of the probability of moving from unemployment to employment for those looking for their first job

Relative coefficient of the share of foreigners employed (*t-statistics in brackets*)

Probit estimate and exploited variable probit (a)	1993	1994	1995	1996	1997
Aggregate probit	−0.28 (−3.8)	−0.17 (−2.6)	−0.12 (−1.4)	−0.08 (−1.2)	−0.05 (−0.7)
Aggregate probit IV	−0.49 (−3.8)	−0.18 (−2.6)	−0.15 (−2.0)	−0.18 (−2.2)	−0.002 (−0.2)
Centre north probit	−0.35 (−2.5)	−0.03 (−0.3)	0.01 (0.1)	0.2 (1.3)	0.27 (1.9)
Centre north probit IV	−0.72 (−2.6)	−0.06 (−0.5)	−0.09 (−0.6)	0.29 (1.2)	0.24 (1.3)

(a) instruments used: share of foreigners employed in the earlier period, share of women employed, share of workers employed in the region, average wage in the region received by employed foreigners.

Source: Venturini and Villosio (2000c).

variables are respectively fixed at regional and sector levels in the former case and only at a regional level in the latter.[19]

When the probability of natives becoming unemployed is considered it is found that the effect of the percentage of foreigners on the regions and sectors in which natives are employed is either negative, that is to say, the probability of losing a job is reduced, or it is not significant. Similarly the effect on unemployed workers looking for a new job, usually adults, does not appear to be competitive, while there is a slight competitive effect on young people looking for a first job in the first few years. Looking more closely at a territorial distribution, there is no trace of such an effect in the north or centre of Italy, and in fact it turns into a complementary effect (see Table 9.8).

Other less direct competition between foreigners and regular domestic labour exists in the *irregular labour market* where the lower wages that foreign workers are willing to accept might attract capital from the regular sector and therefore indirectly displace regular labour (Dell'Aringa Neri 1987). There is a further area of competition between native regular workers and immigrants working irregularly. In fact, irregular migrants could favour the growth of the irregular economy at the expense of the regular one.

An empirical analysis using Italian data (where available ISTAT estimates exist) (Venturini 1999), shows that migrants working in the irregular

---

[19] To solve for the aggregation bias (different levels of aggregation were present in the equation: individual, sector and region) in the probit equation an heteroskedasticity consistent estimator has been used. To control for the endogeneity of the migrant location choice the share of foreigners was instrumented by lagged foreign share, the share of women employed, the share of blue-collar workers employed in the region and average wage among immigrants.

sector are also not very competitive with native regular workers. The long run aggregate elasticity between native and foreign labour is −0.1, and only in the agriculture sector reaches a higher value, (−3.5). The latter value, however, overvalues the competition of migrants because it understates the decreasing national supply of labour in that sector.

Another important aspect of the comparison between immigrants and native employment relationship concerns the wage differentials. Are foreigners paid the same wages as natives? Villosio and Venturini (2000a, 2000b) analyse wage differentials between foreign as well as native employment using Social Security Administrative data. The average wage differential between natives and foreigners is 1.15 (log 0.130) which is not surprising given the higher level of education of natives and their higher tenure. When the Oaxaca decomposition is used to distinguish between the wage differential explained by the different workers' characteristics and the unexplained one, over the years the latter is never more than 34 per cent. The male–female differential computed by Bonjour and Pacelli (1998) on the same dataset shows that the gender differential is almost double that of the native-foreigners[20] and the unexplained part is on average 75 per cent, more than double of the foreign-native one.

Another recent research focuses on the gender differential among foreigners (Strozza, Gallo, Grillo, 2002).[21] The survey dataset used by the authors is much more informative than the administrative one used in the previous research, but limited to foreigners. It includes important information such as years of education, proficiency in the Italian language, and number of relatives. Taking all this information into account, the log wage gender differential is 0.182 for the Moroccans, 0.341 for the former Yugoslavs and 0.288 for the Poles.[22] It is higher than in the native-foreigners case shown before, but very similar to the native gender wage differential mentioned above. In addition, the different national employment behaviour is reproduced in the male–female differential: in the former Yugoslav and Polish groups, the wage differential is mainly due to

---

[20] The log wage differential is 0.225 in the male–female case and 0.130 in the foreign-native case.

[21] The survey covers 1440 immigrants belonging to three communities: Moroccan, former Yugoslav, and Polish with an employment rate of 70 per cent among the Moroccans and 82 per cent in the other ethnic groups. Female employment behaviour is uneven among the groups: Moroccan women have the highest duration in longterm unemployment (more than four months), and the lowest employment rate, while the former Yugoslav have the shortest longterm unemployment duration and the Polish the highest employment percentage.

[22] The authors use the Olsen correction to take into account the different participation rate.

differences in human capital; the unexplained part is about 10 per cent, while, in the Moroccan case, the differential is totally unexplained.

From another dataset, the result of another survey[23] conducted in the 1993–4, foreign immigrants in two regions (Latium and Campania) with a much larger number of ethnic groups, Baldacci et al. (1999) estimate the legal–illegal wage differential which results in log 0.246 for male and 0.192 for female immigrants in both cases, indicating low economics for illegal work.

The illegality of some immigrants suggests that public goods are consumed as well as some social benefits (hospital, assistance) without any fiscal contribution to them and this gives rise to widespread protests. A research study by the Brodolini Foundation (1992) predicted the cost for the national welfare of regular immigration for the next ten years through six items of expenditure–compulsory education, training or adults education, university, housing, health assistance, police–and the fiscal benefits drawn by income taxes and social contributions.[24] The balance is negative if social contributions (mainly pensions) are not included, while it becomes positive if they are included. This balance is, however, positive only if regular immigration is considered. If illegal immigration persisted, its use of public utilities without any contribution to their financing would make a final evaluation impossible. Needless to say, immigration cannot be considered a long run solution for the pension funding deficit,[25] and the intertemporal pension distribution scheme needs to be revised (Vitali 1991).

The degree of integration of foreigners can also be indicated by the employment and unemployment rate of foreigners. Unfortunately, the ISTAT Labour Force survey is unable to get appropriate information on immigrants because they are still difficult to sample. The unemployment rate among the extra–European union immigrants and the share of foreigners registered at the employment bureau on the total residence permits reached 13.3 per cent in 2000. The number of foreigners registered at the employment offices increased from about 100,000 in 1995 to 205,000 in 1999, but more importantly by, 50 per cent of the registered were registered in the North, the area with a lower unemployment rate. Registration at the employment registers does not necessarily mean poverty in these cases,

---

[23] The survey covers 1574 immigrants in working age, 1052 employed during the survey with a much larger ethnic group from less developed countries.

[24] Dolado, Ichino, Goria (1994) show that immigrants holding an amount of human capital below the average of natives will reduce the income per capita growth rate.

[25] Gesano 1994.

but arises mainly from irregular forms of work, though the high level registration at the placement offices shows that the greater demand for regular economic integration was not completely achieved.

Other indicators of more widespread integration are available. One is the incidence of the family reunion entrances over total entrances which represents a growing share of total residence permits (about 21 per cent in 1998). We find a different trend by nationality, where 75 per cent of the 1998 inflow of Africans entered under the family reunion programme against only 15 per cent among the East European immigrants. This difference would suggest that immigration was at a more mature stage among the Africans.

Data on the number of arrests show the increase of their role in deviant behaviour; in fact 26 per cent of all those arrested are foreigners. They represent a large share of the foreign population, 21 per cent of the estimated foreign population and 39 per cent of the foreign residence permits (Natale and Strozza 1997). The African community is also the most important in this respect due to its incidence on the total stock of immigrants, but also to some deviant behaviour. The East European community shows a lower number of arrests, but its share is increasing rapidly (Natale and Strozza 1997).

9.3.5. Italian Migration Policy: Laws and Legalizations

As was stressed earlier, when immigration started in any sizeable way the Italian institutional infrastructure was not prepared to cope with it. The legislation was not adequate, the administrative structure insufficient and the financial support for the necessary activities was not even planned. The legislation tried to adapt the institutions to the new phenomenon. The asylum law was revised and extended to all other countries, a visa to enter the country was requested from countries of potential immigration, and an expulsion policy was improved and financed.

Even though Law 59/1990 established a 'planned number' of new entrants each year, the number was not decided upon, and it thus remained at zero, with immigrants continuing to enter the country illegally by the 'back door'. The existence of a large shadow economy contributed to attracting immigrants who came solely to earn money for a short time, and the expectation of a legalization procedure attracted not only temporary migrants, but also the ones who wanted to change their country of residence. The large inflow of Albanians in the 1990s induced the Government to rethink its immigration policy and its role in Europe and the

Mediterranean with a more restrictive law (DL489/1995). The initial feeling of a country of emigration is to behave differently toward immigrants—so as to treat them more favourably than Italian immigrants were treated in the past—but this sentiment has now been replaced by the feeling that Italy is a country of immigration, part of a broader area in which there is freedom of movement, the Schengen area, and the country now has the duty to think more in terms of the integration of foreigners.

Regularizations are emergency interventions. From the beginning, the Government wanted to abandon them as policy instrument. However, it is difficult to succeed in a country with a large underground economy—about 25 per cent of total activity—and with long frontiers which are difficult to police to prevent illegal immigration (similar to the US experience). The Government under the pressure of illegal immigrants always implemented the last legalization for foreign already integrated in the labour market. Table 9.9 reports the four legalisations by countries of origins from 1987 to 1998. The abolition of possible regularization procedures for the future together with a clearer definition of the possibilities for legal entry from abroad with a quota system, supported by more controls at the frontiers and stricter persecution of organized clandestine flows are the backbone of the Italian immigration policy.

Furthermore, to discourage illegal entrance in search of jobs, the sponsor institute has been introduced; as in Australia, a native, a legal foreigner, or an organization can sponsor the entrance of foreigners in search of jobs for a limited number of months.

The Italian migration regulation is not only focused on the entrance of the foreigners. Since the mid-1990s the Government has provided support for foreign integration. A number of interventions have been implemented

Table 9.9. Legalizations by countries of origin (millions)

I	1987–8	II	1990	III	1995	IV	1998
Morocco	21.7	Morocco	49.9	Morocco	42.3	Albania	39.4
Philippines	10.7	Tunisia	25.5	Albania	34.9	Romania	23.4
Sri Lanka	10.7	Senegal	17.0	Philippines	29.9	Morocco	22.5
Tunisia	10.0	Ex-Yugoslavia	11.3	China	14.9	China	19.1
Senegal	8.4	Philippines	8.7	Peru	14.9	Nigeria	11.6
Ex-Yugoslavia	7.1	China	68.3	Romania	10.0	Senegal	10.8
Others	50.1	Others	97.1	Others	102.1	Others	97.2
Total	118.1	Total	217.7	Total	247.0	Total	218.2

Source: Sopemi 1997, Caritas 1998, Annual Report.

in the field of education (training and language courses) as well as in the field of social services (mainly housing subsidies and childcare).[26]

9.4. Conclusions

In this chapter we have summarized and interpreted Italian emigration and immigration patterns and discussed the role of migration policies. While it is difficult to predict the future of Italian immigration given the early stage of the process, it seems easier to consider the emigration process. International emigration no longer seems to be an option for young southern European workers. Income differentials among European countries have shrunk through time and in some cases have reversed its sign.[27] In addition, unemployment is a very widespread phenomenon; thus there is a shortage of work opportunities everywhere. International emigration is no longer a rewarding investment for Italian workers.

A possible stream of emigration could involve skilled workers who represent an increasingly important source of labour demand in many advanced countries. However, in Italy the proportion of higher education workers is among the lowest in Europe.

The limited increase in the level of education and wealth in the south has not increased the international and internal mobility of workers but contributed to some extent to its immobility by increasing job expectations of young people and the length of search (financed mainly by the family and frequently by occasional work in the black economy). While in the north of Italy (especially in the north-east) labour demand for all skill levels is growing, a low cross-regions mobility is observed. In this mismatch between supply and demand, immigrants from abroad fill the gaps left by the domestic labour force. If migrants are not directly competitive with native workers, they could have an indirect competitive effect by increasing production in the labour intensive and traditional sectors. Such a process would slow down modernization, which would create more jobs for qualified natives. At present, none of these effects is apparent (that is there is no evidence of direct or indirect competition), but in the future the scenario could change.

---

[26] A complete review of the new policies and their effects are in the newly published Ministry Report edited by the Commission on Foreigners' Integration (chaired by Giovanna Zincone) (2000).

[27] In the Franco–Italian case for instance according with the Swedish Employer Confederation data the wage differential became −6 per cent in 1985; see Venturini 2001, 2004.

The aging of the labour force may create a generational demand for additional young workers. By 2010, young male workers will find one and a half jobs available in the centre and north of Italy because of generational factors. In the south of Italy fertility is higher and the demographic demand for immigrants is simply postponed.[28] Thus, if internal mobility does not increase, in the first five years of the twenty-first century in Northern Italy the explicit demand for foreign workers will amount to 30 per cent of new entrants. The immigration policy should comply with the short and long-term evolution of southern European labour markets. This objective can be achieved if the immigration policy is selective and flexible so that it can on one hand discourage clandestine flows, and on the other hand cope with the many changes in the labour market that take place.

References

Attanasio O., Padoa Schippa F. (1991). 'Regional inequalities, migration and mismatch in Italy, 1960–86', in Padoa Schioppa F. (ed.) *Mismatch and Labour Mobility* (Cambridge: Cambridge University Press).

Bacchetta, Cagiano de Azevedo (1990). *Le comunita' italiane all'estero* (Turino: Giappichelli).

Baldacci E., Inglese L., Strozza S. (1999). 'Determinats of foreign workers' wages in two Italian regions with high illegal immigration', Labour, 13–3: 675–710.

Blanchet D., Marchand O. (1991). 'Au-delà de l'an 2000, s'adapter à une pénurie de main-d'oeuvre', *Economie et Statistique*, 243: 61–7.

Bonifazi C. (ed.) (1999). *Mezzogiorno e migrazioni interne* (IRP, monografie n.10).

Bonjour D., Pacelli L. (1998). 'Wage formation and gender wage in italy and Switzerland', UCL Discussion paper, 12/98.

Brücker H., Epstein G., McCornick B., Saint-Paul G., Zimmermann K. (2002). *Managing Migration in the European Welfare State* (Oxford: Oxford University Press).

Bruni M. (ed.) (1994). *Attratti, Sospinti, Respinti*, (F. Angeli).

—— and Venturini A. (1995). 'Pressure to migrate and propensity to emigrate', *International Labour Review*, 134–3: 377–400.

Cannistraro P.V., Rosoli G. (1979). *Emigrazione Chiesa e Fascismo. Lo scioglimento dell'Opera Bonomelli (1922-1928)* (Roma: Studium).

Caritas diocesana di Roma (1994). *Immigrazione, Dossier Statistico '94*, (Roma: Anterem Edizioni Ricerca).

---

[28] Bruni, M. (ed.), 1994.

Caritas diocesana di Roma (1996). *Immigrazione, Dossier Statistico '96*, (Roma: Anterem Edizioni Ricerca).

— (1999). *Immigrazione, Dossier Statistico '99*, (Roma: Anterem Edizioni Ricerca).

Caritas diocesana di Roma (2000). *Immigrazione, Dossier Statistico '2000*, (Roma: Anterem Edizioni Ricerca).

Cerase F. (1967). 'Sulla tipologia di emigranti ritornati: il ritorno di investimento', *Studi Emigrazioni* 10: 327–49.

Chillemi O., Gui B. (1977). 'Fattori determinanti le rimesse dei lavoratori migranti: uno schema metodologico ed una applicazione al caso dei lavoratori italiani nella Repubblica federale tedesca (1964-1975)' *Rivista di Politica Economica*, LXVII, serie III, fasc.XII, December.

Cornelius W. A., Martin P. L., Hollifield J. F. (ed.) (1994). *Controlling Immigration. A Global Perspective* (Stanford: Stanford University Press).

Daveri F., Faini R. (1999). 'Where do migrants go? Risk-aversion, mobility costs and the locational choice of migrants', *Oxford Economic Papers*: 595-622.

Dell'Aringa C., Neri F. (1987). 'Illegal immigrants and the informal economy', *Labour* 1,2: 107-26.

Dolado J., Goria A., Ichino A. (1994). 'Immigration and growth in the host countries', *Journal of Population Economics*, 7-2: 193-215.

Faini R. (1994). 'Workers remittances and the real exchange rate', *Journal of Population Economics* 7: 235-45.

— and Venturini A. (1993). 'Trade, aid and migration, some basic policy issues', *European Economic Review*, 37: 435-42.

—(1994a). 'Italian emigration in the prewar period', in Hatton T., Williamson J. (eds.) *Migration and the International Labour Market, 1850-1913* (London: Routledge).

— (1994b), 'Migration and growth: the experience of Southern Europe', Working Paper CEPR. n. 964.

—, Galli G., Rossi F. (1996). 'Mobilità e Disoccupazione in Italia: un'analisi dell' offerta di lavoro, in Galli G. (eds.) *La Mobilità della Società Italiana*, (Roma: Centro Studi della Confindustria, SIPI).

Fondazione Giacomo Brodolini (1992). 'Stima dell'onere sinanziario pubblico connesso al fenomeno migratorio: il costo dell'integrazione', in Ministero degli Affari Esteri-Fondazione Giacomo Brodolini, in *Rapporto sulla cooperazione e le politiche migratorie*, (Roma).

Frey L., Livraghi R., Venturini A., Righi A., Tronti L., Giubilaro D. (1997). *L'immigrazione dai paesi del Maghreb in Europa*, ILO (Geneva).

Gavosto A., Venturini A., Villosio C., (1999). 'Do immigrants compete with natives'? *Labour*, 13-3: 603-22.

Gesano G. (1994). 'Nonsense and unfeasibility of demographically based immigration policies' *GENUS*, 3-4: 47-63.

Giusti F. (1965). 'Bilancia demografica della popolazione italiana dal 1861 al 1961', *Annali di statistica*, 8,17, ISTAT, Roma.

Golini A., Birindelli A. M. (1990). Italy, Serow W. J., Nam C. B., Sly D. F., Weller R. H. (eds.) *Handbook on International Migration*. Westport, CT: Greenwood Press.

— (1987). 'Population movements typology and data collection, trends, policies', *European Population Conferences 1987 Plenaries*, (Helsinki: Central Statistical Office).

— (2000). 'L'emigrazione italiana all'estero e la demografia dell'immigrazione straniera in Italia', in Zincone G. (ed.), *Primo rapporto sull'integrazione degli immigrati in Italia* (Bologna: Il Mulino).

Gould J. D. (1979). 'European inter-continental emigration, 1815-1914: patterns and causes', *Journal of European History*, 8: 593-679.

— (1980), 'European inter-continental emigration. the road home: return migration from USA' *Journal of European History*, 9: 41-112.

— (1980). European inter-continental emigration: the role of 'diffusion' and green', *Journal of European History* 9: 267-315.

Hatton T. (1995). 'A model of U.K. emigration, 1870-1913', *The Review of Economics and Statistics*: 407-15.

—, Williamson J. (eds). (1994). *Migration and the International Labour Market, 1850-1913* (London: Routledge).

— (1998). Italy, in Hatton T., Williamson J., *The Age Of Mass Migration* (New York: Oxford University Press).

ISTAT (1995). *National Accounts*.

— (1996). *Rapporto Annuale 1996, La situazione del paese* (Roma).

— (1996). 'Statistiche sui permessi di soggiorno degli stranieri', *Notiziario*, serie 4, fo 41, VII, n.1.

Johnson P., Zimmermann K. F. (eds.) (1993). *Labour Markets in an Ageing Europe* (Cambridge: Cambridge University Press).

Lianos T., Sarris A. and Katseli L. (1995). 'The impact of illegal immigrants on local labour markets: the case of northern Greece', paper presented at the CEPR Workshop, Halkidiki.

Livi Bacci M., Abbate M., De Santis G., Giovannelli C., Ricci R. (1996). 'Mobilità e territorio', in Galli G. P. (ed.) *La mobilità nella società italiana: le persone, le imprese, le istituzioni* (SIPI, Roma).

— (ed.) (1867). *La migrazione interna in Italia*, (Scuola di Statistica, Firenze).

Merrick T. W., Graham D. H. (1979). *Population and Economic Development in Brazil* (Baltimore, MD: John Hopkins University Press).

Moreno J. L. (1995). 'Le donne in banca: rimesse e famiglie di emigranti meridionali in Argentina prima del 1930. Il caso di Molfetta.' *Etudes Migrations*, 32, n.118: 289-320.

Natale M., Strozza S. (1997). *Gli immigrati stranieri in Italia. Quanti sono, chi sono, come vivono?* (Bari: Cacucci Editore).

OECD (1991). *Employment Outlook* (Paris).

— (1995). *Employment Outlook* (Paris).

— (1994). The OECD Jobs Study: Evidence and Explanations, part I, Paris.
— (1985). *Labour Force Statistics* (Paris).
OECD (1995). *Labour Force Statistics* (Paris).
Reyneri E. (1979). *La catena migratoria* (Bologna: Il Mulino).
— (1998). 'The role of the underground economy in irregular migration to Italy: cause or effect?' *Journal of Ethnic and Migration Studies*, 24, n. 2, April.
Rosoli G.(ed.) (1978). *Un secolo di Emigrazione Italiana 1876-1976* (Roma: Centro Studi Emigrazione).
Signorelli A., Tiriticco M. C., Rossi S. (1977). *Scelte senza potere. Il ritorno degli emigrati nelle zone dell'esodo*, (Roma: Officina Edizioni).
SOPEMI (1995). Trends in International Migrations. Annual report (OECD, Paris).
Sori E. (1979). L'emigrazione italiana dall'unità alla seconda guerra mondiale Bolonga: Il Mulino.
Straubhaar T. (1986). 'The causes of international migration–a demand determined approach' *International Migration Review*, 20/4, 835–55.
— (1988). *On the Economics of International Labor Migration* (Bern: Haupt).
Strozza S., forthcoming (2002). 'Foreign immigrations in Italy: estimates of legal and illegal presence', *International Migration Review*.
— (2000) 'La presenza straniera illegale in Campania: alcune congetture', in Pane A., Strozza S. (a cura di), *Gli immigrati in Campania. Un difficile percorso di integrazione tra precarietà e clandestinità diffusa* (L'Harmattan Italia, Torino, 2000), pp. 51-71.
—, Gallo G., Grillo F. (2002). 'Gender and labour market among immigrants in some Italian areas: the case of Moroccans, former Yugoslavians and Poles' in the Proceedings of the IUSSP Conference on *Women in the Labour Market in Changing Economies: Demographic Issues* (Oxford: Oxford University Press).
UN (1979). *Labour Supply and Migration in Europe*.
Venturini A. (1991). 'Italy in the contest of European migration', *Regional Development Dialogue*, 12/3 (1996). 'Extent of competition between and complementarity among national and third-world migrant workers in the labour market: an exploration of the Italian case', in Frey L., Livraghi R., Venturini A., Righi A., Tronti L., *The Jobs and Effects of Migrant Workers in Italy. Three Essays* (ILO, International Migration Paper n.11).
—(1999). 'Do Immigrants working illegally reduce the natives' legal employment? Evidence from Italy', *Journal of Population Economics* 12/1, 135-54.
—(2001) *Le migrazioni nei paesi del Sud Europa* (Torino: UTET Libreria).
—(2004). *Post-War Migration in Southern Europe. An Economic Approach* (Cambridge: Cambridge University Press).
—, Villosio C. (2000a) 'Foreign workers in Italy: are they assimilating to natives? are they competing against natives? An analysis by the SSA dataset' with C. Villosio, *Einwanderungsregion Europa?*, 33. Arbeitstagung der Deutschen Gesellschaft für Bevölkerungswissenschaft in Zusammenarbeit mit dem Institut für Migrationsforschung und Interkulturelle Studien der Universität Osnabrück.

—(2000*b*) 'Are immigrants assimilating in the Italian Labour Market? The role of Big town', CHILD W.P.11/2000.

—(2000c). 'Disoccupazione dei lavoratori nazionali: effetto dell'immigrazione', with C. Villosio, Working Paper n.10. della Commissione per l'integrazione degli immigrati, Vicepresidenza del Consiglio, Roma. The english version presented at the ESPE Annual Conference 2001.

Vitali L., (1991). 'Alcune considerazioni sulla previdenza dei lavoratori extra-comunitari in Europa', Proceedings of the International Conference, 13–16 March, Presidenza del Consiglio dei Ministri-OECD, Editalia, Roma.

Vitali O. (1974). 'Le migrazioni interne: una sintesi storico-statistica', *Affari Sociali Internazionali*, 12.

Zamagni V. (1990) *Dalla periferia al centro* (Bologna: Il Mulino).

Zincone G. (ed.) (2000). *Primo rapporto sull'integrazione degli immigrati in Italia*, Commissione per le politiche di integrazione degli immigrati (Bologna: Il Mulino).

—(ed.) (2001). *Secondo rapporto sull'integrazione degli immigrati in Italia* (Bologna: Il Mulino).

10. Greek Migration: The Two Faces of Janus

Nicholas P. Glytsos and Louka T. Katseli

10.1. Introduction

Migration movements from and to, or via Greece, are an age-old phenomenon. Situated at the crossroads of three continents (Europe, Asia, and Africa), Greece has been, at different historical times, both a labour-sending and a labour-receiving country. Both its history and economic development have been affected by migration flows, as Greece has completed about a century-long cycle of emigration and repatriation and has entered a new era of net immigration.

During the twentieth century, Greeks emigrated initially to the United States and Australia and subsequently to the rest of Europe. The first waves of overseas emigrants headed to transoceanic destinations. They departed from the rural areas of the country where income was low and the prospects bleak, at a time when domestic alternatives for making a living outside the farm were limited. This was also the time when the national boundaries of Greece were gradually widening as previously occupied territories were reannexed (Ionian Islands 1864; Thessaly 1881; Macedonia and Epirus 1914; and Thrace 1920) expanding the Greek population and labour force. Employment opportunities were scarce, especially after the entry of 1.2 million Greek refugees from Asia Minor in 1922. Pressures in the labour market increased further, after the 1929 economic crash, when more than half of the migrants from the USA returned home. Overall, during the period 1910–40, migration reached a break-even point, with emigration flows equalling repatriation flows.

In the aftermath of the Second World War, overseas emigration was resumed and Greek emigrants headed mostly to Europe, especially to Germany, where jobs were created as a consequence of postwar reconstruction. At the same time, Greece itself began to grow fast via mechanization

Assistance by Dr E. Markova is gratefully acknowledged.

and the restructuring of its own economy, partially financed by transfers under the Marshall Plan. Postwar emigration thus coincided with rapid domestic economic transformation and urbanization, highlighting the complex interrelationship between migration and economic development. In contrast to the more permanent nature of emigration to transoceanic countries in the early twentieth century, migratory flows to and from Germany in the postwar period were temporary and repetitive. In fact, after 1974, annual return migration exceeded emigration.

After the collapse of the communist regimes in Eastern and south-eastern Europe in the 1990s, increasing flows of legal and illegal migrants from these countries entered Greece in search of jobs and better living standards. Today, the emigration–repatriation cycle of Greek migrants has practically come to a standstill, and an ongoing process of foreign immigration is well under way. Greece is now a labour-importing country, with legal and illegal immigrants coming from neighbouring countries, such as Albania and Bulgaria, as well as from countries situated as far away as the Philippines and Pakistan. Over the two years 2000–1 in particular, illegal immigrants mostly from Asian destinations, fleeing war and poverty, attempted to enter the country by sea with a view towards settling in Greece, Italy, or other European countries.

In the mid-1990s, the stock of illegal immigrants residing in Greece was estimated to be around 500,000 people (Lianos et al. 1996). These immigrants, mostly Albanians, have occupied relatively low-paid, unskilled jobs in various sectors of the economy both in the urban and in the rural areas. They have been sending remittances back home, exactly as Greek emigrants used to do from Germany and other countries only a few decades ago.

After trying unsuccessfully to curtail illegal immigration flows through administrative and law-enforcement measures, the Greek government initiated, in 1998, a major legalization programme that was repeated in 2001. Approximately 370,000 illegal immigrants filed applications in 1998 and 351,000 in 2001. Green Cards, granting residence and working permits, were extended to 220,000 people.

The continuous flow of illegal immigrants into the country and the net costs associated with their smooth integration into the host labour market and into Greek society have raised concern over the scope and effectiveness of immigration policies. The policy debate is increasingly becoming a European one, as European integration has deepened and national borders have increasingly become European borders. The design of effective migration and integration policies, both at the national and European levels, has to take into account the changing characteristics of the migrant population and the interlinkages between migration and development. This chapter attempts to probe into some of these basic issues, by studying the Greek experience.

Section 10.2 of this study analyses the characteristics and trends of migrants and remittances from and to Greece. Section 10.3 presents an overview of the successive policy regimes pertaining to migration. Section 10.4 presents the available empirical evidence on the causal factors of Greek emigration-repatriation and of foreign immigration and remittances. Section 10.5 probes into the interlinkages of migration and development. Finally, Section 10.6 concludes with an overall evaluation of the rich experience of Greece and of the role of migration and integration policies in the context of future European enlargement and south-eastern European integration.

10.2. Overview of Migration Movements: Trends and General Characteristics

10.2.1. Overall Trends after the Second World War

In the postwar period, one can distinguish two migration phases. The first phase spans roughly the period 1960–85, when many Greeks emigrated mostly to Western Europe and subsequently returned home for either temporary or permanent repatriation. The second phase starts in the 1990s, when Greece became a labour-importing country, attracting economic migrants from south-eastern Europe, Africa and Asia.

The emigration-repatriation phase

The emigration phase began in 1960 and ended in 1984–5. Net migration, defined as the difference between the total population at the beginning and the end of a calendar year minus the difference between births and deaths, was negative till 1974. It turned positive in the second half of the seventies when repatriation exceeded emigration flows (Figure 10.1).[1] Following Greece's signing of the Treaty of Rome in 1957 and the Association Agreement between Greece and the European Common Market in 1963, emigration to Europe increased abruptly from 28.8 per cent of total emigration in 1959, to 70.0 per cent in the early 1970s. Approximately 1,200,000

---

[1] The numbers corresponding to the figures are presented in the Appendix. Table 10.A.1 pertains to Figure 10.1.

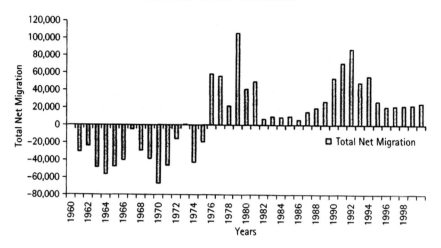

Figure 10.1. Greek total net migration, 1960–99[1]

[1]Net migration is defined as the difference between the total population on 1 January and 31 December for a certain calendar year, minus the difference between births and deaths. Therefore the numbers in this figure include corrections and may differ between immigration and emigration. *Source*: Eurostat Demographic Statistics. 1997, p. 192; 1999, p.184; 2000, p.117.

people left Greece during this period. Among European countries, annual emigration flows to West Germany tripled between 1960 and 1964, reaching 81,000 persons. In 1970 alone, 94,000 people headed to Germany. During this period, the size of net emigration to West Germany approximated the natural rate of population increase (see Appendix, Table 10.A.1).

The emigration–repatriation cycle of the post-1960 period between Greece and West Germany is depicted in Figure 10.2. Between 1960 and 1985 about one million Greeks emigrated to West Germany, corresponding to 11.5 per cent of Greece's total population in 1971. On an annual basis, both emigration and repatriation to and from Germany fluctuated widely. Emigration flows peaked in 1964 and 1970 and repatriation in 1967 and 1975. These humps point to a two-phase emigration–repatriation process and demonstrate the temporary and repetitive nature of migration. This is also supported by evidence from 878,000 return migrants from Germany, during the period 1960–85. Emigration flows to West Germany continued at lower annual rates of growth until 1987 and resumed their strength in the early 1990s (see Appendix, Table 10.A.2).

The first peak of repatriation coincided with the 1967 economic recession in West Germany. The second peak occurred in 1974, when the seven-year long dictatorship ended and growth resumed in Greece. During the period 1975–9, the average annual growth-rate of non-agricultural output

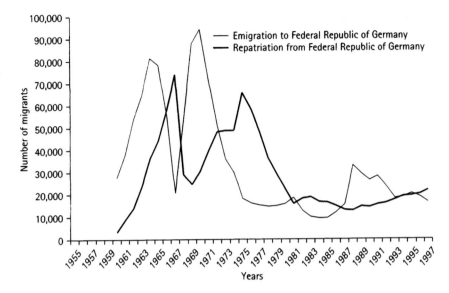

Figure 10.2. Emigration and repatriation of Greeks to and from Germany, 1955–97
Sources: For emigration (inflows to Germany) and repatriation (outflows from Germany), 1960–82, German Federal Office of Labour. For inflows and outflows, 1983–88, SOPEMI, 1990 (original source Statistiches Bundesamt). For inflows and outflows, 1989–97, SOPEMI, 1999.

increased to 5.9 per cent and employment grew at 3.9 per cent per year. In 1974, repatriation exceeded emigration for the first time. During that same year, the German government banned new immigration. Thus, repatriation from Germany, after 1974, appears to have been motivated by both push and pull factors. It started declining in the 1980s, as the Greek economy entered a long period of recession. During the period 1980–92, non-agricultural output in Greece grew at an annual rate of 1.9 per cent and non-agricultural employment at an annual rate of 1.5 per cent. Survey estimates confirm that, during the 1980s, migrant movements were not very significant and net immigration was negligible (Dogas 1993). As Figure 10.2 demonstrates, emigration appears to have resumed in 1987, with emigration exceeding considerably repatriation at least up to 1992.

In a large nation-wide microcensus, conducted in 1985, Petropoulos et al. (1992) analysed 105,000 questionnaires of repatriates of the period 1971–85 and compared their responses to those of non-migrants. The survey found that around 627,000 emigrants returned to Greece during that period, one-third of whom were born abroad. Apart from repatriates from West Germany and other countries, returnees included ethnic Greeks from the former Soviet Union (Pontians) as well as refugees and their families who had fled to the communist block during the Greek civil war (1946–9) and had been refused entry until the mid-1970s. In the early 1990s, approximately 37,000 Pontians settled in Greece (OECD 1993). No working permits were required for these immigrants. Between 1989 and 1996, about 70,000 permanent repatriation visas and 100,000 temporary ten-month visas were issued to Pontians (Tinguy 1997). Out of the 40,000 political refugees who returned to the country, only 30 per cent were born in Greece.

Another category of legal immigrants, who entered Greece at that time, consisted of political refugees. Until 1991, 61,000 foreign nationals were granted political refugee status in Greece and 20,729 work permits were issued (OECD 1993). Finally, during the same period, repatriates also included Greek students who had studied at foreign universities as well as skilled workers who had sought temporary employment in construction activities in the Middle East or in international organisations.

According to the National Statistical Service (NSS), between 1980 and 1990, the number of residence permits remained stable at around 220,000 a year, with 2 per cent of the population being legal resident aliens (namely foreign citizens). In the early 1980s, a significant number of these permits (around 62 per cent) concerned foreign nationals of Greek descent. By 1990, this share declined to 20 per cent (Lianos et al. 1996). During the same period, the number of work permits was much lower (approximately 28,000).

The character of migration flows changed dramatically after 1990, when immigration flows increased significantly. Legal and illegal immigrants from various countries entered Greece in large numbers. The same phenomenon was observed, in varying degrees, in most other southern European countries (Italy, Spain, Portugal), which underwent similar transitions from emigration to immigration countries (Venturini 1994).

The immigration phase

The bulk of immigrants in the 1990s constituted of illegal immigrants. From different official and unofficial sources, it is estimated that in 1992, approximately 280,000 foreign nationals out of a total of 500,000 were residing illegally in Greece. By 1994, the number of illegal immigrants was raised to 350,000, half of whom were estimated to be Albanians. Survey evidence (Lianos et al. 1996) indicates that illegal immigrants in the mid-1990s amounted to 470,000 people, that is up to 4 per cent of the Greek population and 13 per cent of the Greek labour force, offering about 157,000 full-time person years of labour input (ibid., p. 457).

Continuous political turmoil and the worsening economic conditions in many neighbouring developing countries create favourable conditions for illegal immigration waves into Greece. Thus, at the turn of the twenty-first century, as Greece joins the Euro-zone, it faces the dual challenge to curtail illegal immigration flows and to effectively integrate immigrants into the host economy and society.

10.2.2. Characteristics of Migration Flows

Geographic distribution

During the period 1955–77, the border regions of Greece to the north and east were heavy contributors to emigration, sending over 30 per cent of their labour force abroad (Figure 10.3). Out of the total number of emigrants, approximately 500,000 people—around 42 per cent of the total—emigrated from Macedonia and Thrace. The Attica region, most notably Athens, was another home region of heavy emigration, followed by Lakonia, in the southern tip of Peloponnessos. Emigration from Central Greece, the Aegean Islands, and the eastern part of Crete was relatively low, affecting less than 10 per cent of the population. In between these extreme cases, the remaining regions exported between 11 and 30 per cent of their labour force. Among them, the Ionian Islands and the central regions of Peloponnessos appear to be relatively high emigration areas (Figure 10.4).

Emigrants from these regions were relatively unskilled with the exception of emigrants from Kastoria who were previously employed in the fur industry and had developed specialized skills. These workers were in great demand for highly paid work in Germany (Kanetakis 1990: 32–3).

Correlation analysis of data from 52 geographic departments (prefectures) of Greece shows that the exodus of population, during the 1970s, was relatively high from places with relatively large households, low literacy rate, high unemployment, and a high proportion of employment in agriculture (Unger 1981).

Upon repatriation, almost half of all returnees settled in the two major cities of Athens and Thessaloniki and their surroundings (Petropoulos et al. 1992). Repatriates from overseas countries, who had lived longer abroad and had acquired skills in services, settled mostly in Athens, Peloponnessos and the Aegean Islands, where they could find more suitable jobs in commerce, business services or tourism. More than half of the returnees from West Germany, on the other hand, settled in their home region of Macedonia (Table 10.1). The survey also found that the overall unemployment rate of returnees was 10.4 per cent, as compared with 6.9 per cent for nonmigrants.

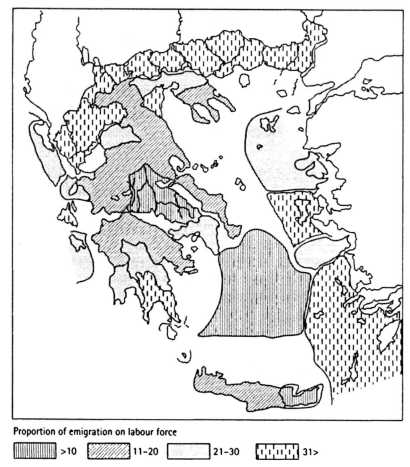

Proportion of emigration on labour force

>10	11-20	21-30	31>

Figure 10.3. Greek emigration areas, 1955-77
Source: Kanetakis (1990).

In the 1990s, the geographic distribution of immigrants followed a similar pattern of settlement to that of earlier repatriates, with a strong preference for residence in the urban areas. According to a survey by the Greek Employment Observatory (Ependitis 1999), more than 51 per cent of the illegal foreigners who took part in the first legalisation programme registered in Thessaloniki and/or the Attica regions. More than 38 per cent of the registered immigrants—making up 4.4 per cent of the city's population—settled in the Athens area, thus changing the economic and social characteristics of the capital city. The same happened in all areas with large concentration of immigrants, such as in the rest of Attica, where the

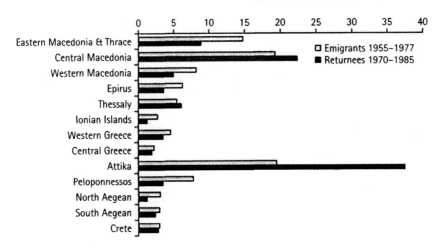

Figure 10.4. Regional shares of emigrants (1955–77) and returnees (1970–85)
(Greece = 100)

Source: Elaboration from Glytsos, 1991: 189–92 (for emigrants). Elaboration from Petropoulos
et al. (1992), vol. b: p. 72 (for returnees).

Table 10.1. Number of emigrants (1955–77) and returnees (1970–85) by region

Regions	Number of emigrants 1955–77	Number of Returnees 1970–85	Proportional shares (%)	
			Emigrants 1955–77	Returnees 1970–85
Eastern Macedonia and Thrace	168,929	56,066	14.8	8.9
Central Macedonia	219,921	140,626	19.3	22.4
(Thessaloniki)	(69,205)	(82,609)	(6.1)	(13.2)
Western Macedonia	94,054	31,575	8.2	5.0
Epirus	71,769	22,805	6.3	3.6
Thessaly	62,863	38,472	5.5	6.1
Ionian Islands	31,304	7,682	2.7	1.2
Western Greece	52,773	21,791	4.6	3.5
Central Greece	24,890	11,551	2.2	1.9
Attika	223,195	234,998	19.5	37.5
(Athens)	(215,047)	(223,530)	(18.8)	(35.6)
Peloponnessos	89,200	21,622	7.8	3.5
North Aegean	35,148	7,700	3.1	1.2
South Aegean	34,279	14,945	3.0	2.4
Crete	34,224	17,792	3.0	2.8
Greece	1,142,549	627,625	100.0	100.0

Sources: Elaboration from Glytsos 1991: 189–92 (for emigrants) and Petropoulos et al. (1992), vol. b: 72
(for returnees).

fraction of foreigners in total population exceeded 5 per cent or in Viotia, a region adjacent to Attica, where immigrants in the post-legalisation period constituted around 6 per cent of the total resident population. The high concentration of immigrants in or near the major urban areas was also evident after the second wave of legalization in 2001. Thus, more than 50 per cent of registrations took place in the Greater Athens area and only 17 per cent in Thessaloniki and Central Macedonia.

Sex and age distribution

About half of the emigrants who left Greece for West Germany in the 1960s and 1970s were young in age. One particular category of young emigrants consisted of students in foreign universities, many of whom returned to Greece after the completion of their studies. According to the OECD (1997), out of 50,000 Greek students abroad, a quarter did not choose to return home.

Among Greek workers going to West Germany, young workers (ages 25-44) accounted for 55.5 per cent in 1964, 45.3 per cent in 1971, and 45.0 per cent in 1977. The share of older workers (ages 45-64) increased over time from 4.8 per cent in the 1960s to 14.1 per cent in 1977. This evidence, coupled with evidence on family migration, which was low in the early migration period when compared to the mid and late 1970s,[2] is consistent with the hypothesis of repetitive migration that also involved family reunification. Even though, this hypothesis cannot be verified from aggregate data, it is confirmed by micro-evidence from a sample of 288 repatriates (Papademetriou 1985).[3]

In the 1990s, immigrants to Greece, were predominantly male and young in age. According to the survey of the Greek Employment Observatory (1999), the majority of illegal immigrants who applied for legal status in 1998 were between twenty and thirty years of age (44 per cent), while an additional 38 per cent consisted of migrants between thirty and forty years of age. There were, however, significant age differences across gender and nationality. Men tended to be younger than women. Furthermore, whereas more than 70 per cent of the registered Albanians were male, women accounted for a significant share of total immigrants from Bulgaria and Ukraine.

---

[2] Female emigration to European countries as a fraction of total emigration to Europe increased from 19.9 per cent in 1960 to 34.2 per cent in 1964, 43.2 per cent in 1971 and 40.7 per cent in 1977. The share of children (age 0-14) in the number of emigrants increased from 7.6 per cent in 1960 to 18.0 per cent in 1971.

[3] Out of 288 repatriates interviewed in Northern Greece, 64, i.e. 22 per cent answered that they had returned and re-emigrated to West Germany at least once.

Table 10.2. Occupational composition of the Greek–German migration

Year	Emigration to W. Germany as % of total emigration	Emigrants by major occupational classification (per cent)		Repatriation from W. Germany as % of total repatriation	Repatriates by major occupational classification (per cent)		
		Farmers	Craftsmen, Workers, Labourers		Farmers	Craftsmen, Workers, Labourers	Scientific and Technical Personnel
1960	45.1	23.5	56.4				
1961	52.9	11.8	72.5				
1962	58.9	10.3	78.1				
1963	64.6	10.3	72.3				
1964	69.5	44.7	43.1				
1965	68.8	44.0	45.8				
1966	52.4	52.7	31.6				
1967	22.8	35.5	39.2				
1968	39.7	44.4	37.3		4.0	68.0	6.4
1969	64.9	61.7	25.3	50.1	3.7	66.4	8.4
1970	70.4	56.3	31.1	51.0	5.2	67.7	7.3
1971	64.9	49.2	33.7	47.8	2.6	73.1	6.4
1972	61.1	49.1	31.9	49.2	2.3	72.5	6.7
1973	46.6	39.1	34.3	51.8	4.6	70.3	5.6
1974	33.8	28.7	38.3	63.0	3.4	76.5	5.5
1975	36.1	29.1	42.6	71.7	1.4	84.6	4.4
1976	33.5	30.1	42.1	70.0	1.6	81.0	4.7
1977	44.1	36.4	42.3		2.8	71.0	6.9

Sources: National Statistical Service of Greece, Bank of Greece (unpublished data).

Occupational structure and skill formation

The occupational distribution of economically active Greek emigrants to West Germany, during the period 1960–77, for which data are available,[4] appears to have shifted over time. As emigration to West Germany peaked in 1964, the occupational distribution changed in favour of farmers as opposed to craftsmen, workers or labourers, who had composed more than 70 per cent of the economically active emigrants in the period prior to 1964 (Table 10.2). The predominance of farmers among emigrants continued till the early 1970s. As emigration to West Germany fell below 40 per cent in 1973, the share of farmers declined sharply. These trends suggest that the Greek emigration–repatriation experience can be decomposed into distinct sub-phases of emigration–repatriation involving migrants of different age, family structure and occupational characteristics.

[4] The collection of migration data by the National Statistical Service of Greece (NSS) was terminated in 1977. No official data are available since that time either for in- or for out-migration.

Table 10.2 also provides interesting evidence on the occupational classification of migrants at the time of their repatriation. Upon their return,
more than 65 per cent of migrants classified themselves as craftsmen,
workers, or labourers as opposed to farmers. This largely reflects the
changing occupational characteristics that took place through emigration
due to the acquisition of new skills by migrants in the host country. In fact,
upon repatriation, between 4.5 and 7 per cent of repatriates chose to
classify themselves as scientific or technical personnel.

The Petropoulos et al. survey of repatriates (1992) also sheds some light
on skill acquisition in the host country and the changing occupational
structure across migrants and repatriates. The educational level of
repatriates, as a whole, was higher than the educational level of natives,
with 17.3 per cent stating that they have acquired third-level education,
compared to only 8.6 per cent for non-migrants. This difference can be
partly explained by the composition of repatriates, since, as was mentioned
before, the sample also includes a large number of people who acquired
education in the host country prior to their return. It also includes Greek
students from foreign universities and skilled workers with temporary
contracts in the construction industries of the Middle East. Nevertheless,
repatriates born in Greece appear to have had a much lower educational
level, than those born abroad, with only 6.7 per cent of them holding
higher educational degrees.

Foreign immigrants into Greece, especially from neighbouring countries,
appear to be more educated than Greek emigrants to Europe. Among
registered immigrants, the majority of them have completed high school
(49.2 per cent), while an additional 37.1 per cent have completed secondary
school. Approximately 8 per cent hold university degrees (Ependitis 1999).

These workers have sought employment mostly in agriculture, construction activities, or commercial and domestic services, filling vacancies
left over by Greeks who seek higher-status and higher-paid jobs. It appears,
therefore, that whereas Greek emigration to the Northern European markets, mostly to Germany, brought about new skill acquisition, recent
immigration to Greece is often associated with a deskilling process driven
by the migrants' urgent needs to secure employment and income.

10.2.3. Remittance Flows

Greece has as long a history of migrant remittances as it has of migration.
Such flows were always a substantial source of foreign exchange, covering
a large part of import payments and financing a growing trade deficit.

In the post First World War period (1914–28), migrant remittances covered about half of the trade deficit and represented about three-fifths of Greece's exports proceeds (Emke-Poulopoulou 1986: 298, referring to Tournakis 1930: 100–1). In 1921 and 1922, remittances actually exceeded the trade deficit.

The increasing flows of emigration in the 1960s gave rise to substantial remittance flows during the 1970s (see Appendix, Table 10.A.3), especially in 1979, which was a peak year (1,169 million US dollars). Remittances continued unabated in the second half of the 1980s, with a very rapid upward trend after 1987 (Figure 10.5). More specifically, between 1960, the first year of mass emigration to Europe and 1972, the last year of Greece's postwar rapid economic growth, migrant remittances covered between 30 and 36 per cent of the trade deficit, around a quarter of import payments and between 50 to 60 per cent of export receipts (Figure 10.6). In particular, during the period of intense emigration, i.e. between 1965 and 1973, remittance flows amounted to about 57 per cent of total export receipts, providing a very important source of foreign exchange for the country and sustaining incomes, consumption and saving for domestic residents.

The significance of remittances as a source of balance-of-payments financing has been reduced over time. After the 1973 oil crisis, and at least till 1985, remittances ceased to be a stable and significant source of financing of Greece's international transactions. Thus, whereas remittances covered 26 per cent of total import payments in 1972, they covered

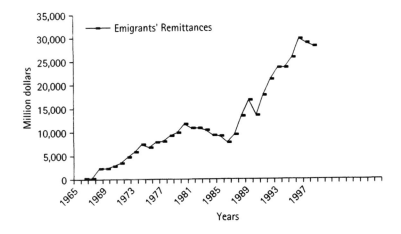

Figure 10.5. Total emigrants' remittances (in million dollars), 1965–97
Sources: Bank of Greece, *Monthly Statistical Bulletin*, March 1975 and 1996; December 1981; February 2001; Bank of Greece, *Annual Reports*, for different years. IMF, *International Financial Statistics Yearbook*, 1987 and 1992; 1993 (pp. 34–5 and 60–1); 1995 (pp.13–14 and 47–8).

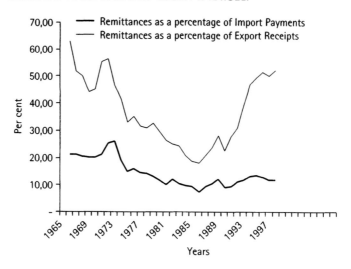

Figure 10.6. Emigrants' remittances as a percentage of import payments and
export receipts
Sources: Bank of Greece, *Monthly Statistical Bulletin,* March 1975 and 1996; December 1981;
February 2001; Bank of Greece, *Annual Reports,* for different years. IMF, *International Financial
Statistics Yearbook,* 1987 and 1992; 1993 (pp. 34–5 and 60–1); 1995 (pp.13–14 and 47–8).

only 7 per cent in 1985. This deterioration could have been potentially
very serious, had imports not declined during some of these years, as a
result of recession and low investment activity in Greece. Remittances
regained their significance as a source of finance for the Greek economy
during the second half of the 1980s, largely in response to improved
economic conditions and rising domestic interest rates. Their contribution continued to be significant in the 1990s. By the second half of
this decade, remittances represented around 13 per cent of imports (see
Appendix, Table 10.A.3).

10.3. Changing Policy Regimes and Policy Challenges

Apart from the underlying economic and political conditions motivating
migration, policies of both host and home countries have influenced migration movements. Migration policies have tended to reflect each government's
perceptions of the economic, social, and cultural impact of emigration or
immigration on its economy and society and more specifically on its
labour market. As these effects have been strongly influenced not only
by the political and economic cycle but also by the stage of development

of the home and host countries, policy stances on migration have shifted over time.

From a political point of view, emigration is usually facilitated at times of domestic political turmoil or distress, and restrained as political conditions normalize. From an economic point of view, emigration policies tend to be more liberal at early stages of development, especially in labour-abundant countries where productivity of labour is relatively low. They tend to become tighter as development proceeds, when shortages of relatively skilled labour appear and the negative implications of 'brain drain' become apparent. Migration policies also tend to shift over the economic cycle, serving the role of implicit effective stabilizers for national income. At times of high domestic unemployment, governments tend to offer direct or indirect incentives in favour of emigration while, at the same time, they tighten immigration laws and procedures. The opposite happens when growth resumes and employment prospects improve. Emigration and immigration policies concerning Greek emigrants or foreign immigrants into Greece are no exception to these rules.

10.3.1 Immigration Policies of the Destination Countries

Attracting foreign population for permanent settlement has been an integral part of immigration policy for most developed transoceanic countries, including Australia, Canada, and the United States of America. It has led to the early development of a legal framework for regulating the size and the national origin of population flows as well as the early formulation of policies to integrate immigrants into the economy and society of these countries. In sharp contrast to these policies, most Western European countries, including Germany, have sought to attract guest workers for temporary employment in response to the requirements of their home labour markets. This stance has dictated in the mid-1960s the formulation of a legal framework suited to the pursuit of this objective, as well as the implementation of stop-go policies which responded to the changing labour market needs of the economic cycle (Glytsos 1997: 412).

In the pre-1965 period, the USA, the major overseas destination country for Greek emigrants, controlled immigration through a national origin quota system that gave priority to inflows from Germany and the United Kingdom (Zolotas 1966; Borjas 1994). After 1965, the Amendments of the Immigration and Nationality Act and their subsequent revisions increased the number of visas granted and made family reunification a key policy priority. Canada adopted in the 1950s a similar policy for the admission of residents' dependants, favouring, in general, immigrants from the United Kingdom (Atchison 1988; Borjas 1994). By 1962, the national origin restrictions were repealed in Canada, widening the preferential treatment in favour of European over non-European immigrants and allowing the sponsorship of a wide range of relatives (Atchison 1988).

Australia, on the other hand, designed its immigration policy in the post Second World War period on the basis of two requirements: additional population for defence and for economic development. As it was formally articulated, 'the central plank of Australia's immigration programme was permanent immigration' (OECD 1989). To satisfy these requirements, Australia adopted for three decades (1952–82) a policy of 'assisted passages' for immigrants. Approximately 75,000 Greeks took advantage of these incentives for settling in Australia (Glytsos 1997: 412).

All three countries adopted, in the late 1960s and early 1970s (USA in 1968, Canada in 1967, and Australia in 1973), more non-discriminatory immigration policies with respect to ethnic origin preference (Atchison 1988). At least for the USA and Canada this policy shift resulted in a higher inflow of Greeks. By 1971, one out of ten European immigrants to Canada was Greek, setting a record high for the entire postwar period (Papanikos 1991).

A year later, Canada reduced the annual intake of immigrants by 21.4 per cent, but Greek immigration was not affected as much. Emigration to Canada practically ceased in 1986, affected by the restrictive immigration policies, which were initiated in the mid-1970s. Most of the Greek emigrants to Canada, the US and Australia settled permanently there, and integrated themselves successfully in these countries. Employed initially in the service sector and/or starting their own small businesses, they saw their children occupy important positions in all sectors of the host countries' economies. Second or third-generation Greeks in these countries make up today a well-educated and dynamic Hellenic Diaspora.

In contrast to this experience, the 'guest-worker policy schemes' adopted by Germany and other European countries, provided incentives for the temporary settlement of Greek emigrants and were subjected to frequent amendments due to changing labour market conditions. In 1960, a bilateral agreement was signed between Germany and Greece, establishing recruitment centres, through which about 381,000 Greeks moved to West Germany (Sava 1989). As has already been noted, the first wave of Greek emigrants to Western Europe consisted of 'Gastarbeiter' who went to Germany to fill particular posts. By the early 1970s, family reunification took place. Greeks were among the first foreign nationals in Germany to bring over their spouses and children (Patiniotis 1991). During the period of economic recession, namely between 1966 and 1967, the German government put a break on new immigration flows. It banned entirely the inflow of new workers in 1973, allowing only family reunification.

By 1980-1, the German government, with the consent of the Greek government, sought to reduce the overall migrant stock by offering financial incentives for repatriation (Schmidt and Zimmermann 1992). Thus, in 1980, a bilateral agreement was signed by the two governments that provided financial support to returning emigrants, especially to those establishing companies in Greece. Till the end of the year, five such companies started operating in Crete and Thrace (Sava 1989). On 25 November 1981, a Federal law was passed expanding the range of financial incentives offered to returning migrants and improving the information capabilities of the government (Schmidt and Zimmermann 1992).

10.3.2. Integration Policies in Destination Countries

In sharp contrast to Australia and Canada, Germany did not develop a coherent policy for the integration of migrants. This was partly due to the fact that 'rotation' was considered a desirable feature of the German immigration model. Measures to foster integration such as language courses were considered superficial and contrary to the short-term economic interest of the host country. Immigrants did not acquire political rights. Their employment in low-skilled manufacturing or service jobs limited the need to develop appropriate educational and training programmes (Manfras 1994: 41).

In light of these developments and in accordance with their perceived status as temporary workers, Greek emigrants organized their efforts around the establishment and sponsorship of Greek schools funded by the Greek government. In Bavaria, for example, Greek schools covered both the primary and secondary educational levels. These programmes—often of disputed quality—soon became controversial, as graduates faced severe difficulties in pursuing their studies further in either Germany or Greece or in integrating themselves successfully in the labour market of either country (Katseli et al. 2000). By the end of the 1980s, the Greek government initiated a series of policy measures to direct Greek children into German schools (Sava 1989). In the 1990s, educational policy shifted towards the establishment of intercultural, bilingual programmes and schools that aimed to expand the options of their graduates and to promote the mobility and integration of second-generation migrants into a unified European labour market (Katseli et al. 2000).

10.3.3. Greek Emigration Policies

Greek emigration policy originally developed in the context of the 1950–3 Development Plan. Temporary emigration of Greek nationals was considered to be beneficial for the workers themselves and the country as a whole. It was stated that emigration would be organized and directed towards countries with 'suitable conditions' for the Greek people. The Greek government encouraged the exodus of workers as part of an active employment policy and as a means of meeting external balance constraints. This was a time of significant rural–urban labour flows within Greece, of serious underemployment in agriculture and of rising urban unemployment.

Several bilateral agreements were signed with various European countries, with a view towards enhancing workers' assimilation capabilities through the extension of vocational and language training programmes, as well as for ensuring the transfer of social security rights in the host countries (Glytsos 1995). The Greek government assisted the German government in its recruitment efforts through the operation of the Recruitment Centres mentioned above. Active policies were also undertaken to attract worker remittances, including the relaxation of controls on foreign exchange transactions by emigrants and the offer of relatively attractive interest rates on long-term currency deposits. Within a decade, however, the Greek Government's liberal policy stance towards emigration changed considerably.

The 1966–70 Economic Development Plan identified emigration as a serious potential problem. The Plan aimed to reduce gross annual emigration to the level of 60,000–70,000 persons. At the same time, it recommended that emigrants should be directed to Europe as opposed to transoceanic countries (Zolotas 1966). By the mid-1970s, repatriation was in fact encouraged through sizeable reductions of taxes and import duties on consumer durables especially cars brought in by repatriates, as well as through special credit provisions for the purchase of assets and land that were financed by imported foreign exchange.

Finally, in the 1990s, the existence of a sizeable stock of Greeks still residing abroad prompted official and non-governmental organisations to co-ordinate their efforts in order to develop active networks across the Greek migrant communities. The Council of Expatriate Greeks, established in the early 1990s, created, for the first time, an operative network linking emigrants with their home country.

With the benefit of hindsight, some of the critics of Greek migration policies have claimed that while the early efforts of alleviating unemployment through emigration were sensible, the exodus of workers acquired its own self-sustained dynamics with detrimental effects on overall economic development. The Greek government has also been criticized for failing to create appropriate incentives for the channelling of migrant savings to productive uses or to develop a coherent policy for the effective reinteg-ration of repatriates (Dikaiou 1994; Fakiolas 1995; Fakiolas and King 1996). Even though these criticisms appear valid, nonetheless, migration has sustained incomes of Greek nationals and has contributed positively both to physical and human capital formation.

10.3.4. Greek Immigration Policies

As an immigration country, Greece finds itself under different economic conditions today from those prevailing in the host countries during the 1960s. In the early 1990s, when immigration started, there was no per-ceived or pressing need for the permanent settlement of foreigners in Greece either for demographic or for labour-market reasons; nor was there an acute labour shortage problem that could have been alleviated via immigration. This is perhaps the reason why, until very recently, no suitable legal framework for immigration was developed.

The opening of the borders and the liberalization of passport regulations in the former Communist countries in the early 1990s, facilitated immi-gration of foreigners into Greece. At the same time, oppressive regimes and conflicts in various parts of the world tended to enhance the pressure for refugees. Partly in response to this situation some new legislation was initiated in Greece.

A Presidential Decree was issued in 1993 for the determination of refugee status. Until 1990, the Greek government was unwilling even to consider applications for refugee status, except only for refugees coming from Turkey. By the end of 1992, only 3,243 refugees were recognized. They consisted mainly of Iraqis, Iranians, Turks, Ethiopians, Lebanese, Somali, and Sudanese (OECD 1995). The thrust of policy was to discourage per-manent settlement and allow only a transitory stay in the country. Thus, the granting of refugee status remained negligible, with only 2 per cent of the applications accepted (Black 1992).

On the other hand, immigration policies for returning ethnic Greeks either from the Pontos region who were residing in the former Soviet Union or from Southern Albania, continued to be liberal. Immigrants were offered diplomatic and legal protection, were not required to have work permits and were very easily naturalised. Despite these efforts, the integration of these immigrants did not prove easy, despite various subsidy schemes concerning education and housing (Kassimati et al. 1992).

As opposed to the liberal legislation concerning ethnic Greeks, the early legislation concerning foreigners was in fact considered to be one of the most restrictive in Europe (Fakiolas and King 1996: 186). The 1991 Greek Immigration Law (L. 1975/91) established a series of provisions dealing with the legal stay of aliens, family reunification and work permits (Petrinioti 1994) and included a series of aliens' obligations. For combating illegal immigration, the new law stipulated increased policing of border areas and allowed administrative deportations on grounds of public policy. The Law was, in fact, more oriented towards deterring immigration and left unregulated the stock of illegal immigrants in Greece (Baldwin-Edwards 1994: 8).

According to this law, a worker from non-EU member states could work legally in Greece only by invitation from an employer. Such an invitation could be extended, however, only if Greeks (native or ethnic) or European union nationals could not be found to fill the vacancy for which the foreign worker was invited. The worker received a one-year residence and work permit that could be renewed annually for a period of five years. At the end of the five-year period, if the priority criteria for hiring him/her continued to be valid, the permit could be renewed for a maximum of fifteen years, after which the foreigner could stay indefinitely in Greece. Family reunification was rather difficult and required a minimum legal residence of five years. Naturalization was even more difficult and required ten years of legal residence for filing an application, after which it took another five years for the application to be examined. (Glytsos 1995: 168). The 1991 law also put severe limits on the extension of public services, while positive integration measures were applied only in the case of ethnic Greeks.

Despite the restrictions imposed by this legislation, illegal immigrants continued to arrive in Greece in large numbers. After a long period of inertia and hesitation, the Greek government initiated two consecutive legalisation programmes aimed at regulating the stay and work of illegal immigrants.

10.3.5. Legalization Policies

Two Presidential Decrees (358/1997 and 359/1997) that granted 'amnesty' to illegal immigrants were published in the Government Gazette on 28 November 1997. The registration phase started on 2 January 1998 and ended on 31 May 1998. Registration took place at the local offices of the Organization for the Employment of Human Resources. Illegal immigrants, who registered during the five-month period and submitted the necessary certificates, were issued an alien's temporary residence card, the so-called 'White Card'. The White Card was due to expire on 30 April 1999 and was to be replaced by a 'Green Card' granting temporary legal status. However, only few migrants managed to submit all the necessary papers by 30 April 1999, so as to become eligible for the Green Card.

According to data provided by the Organisation for Employment (OAED) under the above first legalization programme, 373,196 applications were submitted. Albanians constituted 64.91 per cent of all the registered foreign workers, followed by Bulgarians (6.53 per cent), Romanians (4.52 per cent), Pakistanis (3.17 per cent), Ukrainians (2.64 per cent), Poles (2.25 per cent), Georgians (2.01 per cent), Indians (1.77 per cent), Egyptians (1.67 per cent), Filipinos (1.5 per cent), Moldavians (1.16 per cent), and Syrians (0.92 per cent). The remaining 6.95 per cent consisted of all other nationalities. The total number of applications under the first legalization programme was lower than most existing estimates for illegal residents in Greece. Lianos (1999) attributes the reluctance of many immigrants to register and to obtain legal status to employers' opposition towards paying social security contributions and taxes. Uncertainty on the part of immigrants as to the prospects of their legalization also contributed to the relatively low registration turnout.

Only 60 per cent of the registered applicants (220,000 persons) met the legalization requirements and further satisfied the minimum of forty working days covered by social security contributions for obtaining the Green Card. Most of the Green Cards granted were valid only for one to three years. The duration of the work permit depended on the type of occupation of the migrant, the duration of his/her stay and work in Greece and the overall conditions in the labour market. It could be renewed for another two-year period depending on the state of the Greek economy. Registered immigrants meeting the requirements for a Green Card who could prove that they had been living in Greece for at least five years covering their living expenses, were eligible for a five-year permit. These 'old' immigrants could apply to have their immediate families join them in Greece or in the case that they were already living in Greece, to prevent their deportation. On 9 September 1998, a supplementary law came into effect lowering significantly contributions to the Government Social Security Fund for those foreigners employed in household services. The reduction amounted to 50 per cent of normal social security payments. This was the first time Greek immigration policy provided special incentives for specific type of employment (Markova 2001a).

As expected, the legalization programme did not abolish illegal residence and work. In fact, illegal immigration kept rising after the closure of the programme in May 1998. Some have argued against the 'moral hazard' effects of legalization, noting that the problem was aggravated by these policies since legalization fostered expectations of further amnesty programmes. By the year 2000, the stock of illegal immigrants in Greece was estimated to be once again 400,000 persons (Fakiolas 2001).

The legalization programme of 1998 gave rise to a series of discussions and political debate on the need for a new aliens' law to replace the existing one. A new law (L. 2910/2001) finally appeared in the Government Gazette on 2 May 2001 and came into effect a month later. Due to problems with its implementation, amendments were brought to Parliament in December 2001 (Markova 2001b) and further amendments are expected today.

According to the new law (L. 2910/2001), Green Cards and residence permits that expired before 31 December 2001 became automatically extended for another six months. Green Cards and residence permits expiring after that date would fall under the provisions of the new law. The law also contains new arrangements for the regularization of immigrants under illegal status and extends temporary residence permits to various categories of illegal immigrants (e.g. holders of expired Green Cards who have not applied for their renewal, or whose application for renewal has been rejected, holders of a White Card, illegal migrants who have appealed their case to the competent authorities, applicants not satisfying the regular requirements for a Green Card on humanistic grounds, persons that can prove continuous residence for a period of one year until June 2001 etc.). Bills of public utilities and mobile phones as well as insurance contracts are accepted as legal proof of residence. For immigrants, residing in local communities with less than 20,000 inhabitants, a confirmation of residence by the municipal council is sufficient.

The new law has slightly relaxed some of the stricter provisions of the previous legalization scheme. An invited foreign worker is not anymore attached to a specific employer, and is free to move within Greece. The maximum stay of legal residence safeguarded through consecutive permit renewals, prior to acquiring a residence permit of indefinite duration, has been reduced to ten instead of fifteen years. Concerning family unification, the minimum legal residence for inviting a family member (spouse, children under eighteen) has been reduced from five to two years and the invited member can acquire the right to work.

The new law on aliens also sets up a decentralized mechanism for granting residence and work permits, delegating a decisive role to regional prefectures and municipalities. The regional services of OAED are expected to prepare an annual assessment of regional labour-market needs together with an evaluation of the extent to which these can be covered by available Greek workers, ethnic Greek immigrants, EU nationals or legal migrants. Only vacancies that cannot be filled by the above are open to invited foreign workers.

Despite the two legalization programmes, Greece continues to face an immigration problem as flows of illegal immigrants and the cost of integration continue to rise. The limited effectiveness of immigration and integration policies has prompted Greek authorities to seek ways to contain emigration from the border regions of neighbouring countries. This is particularly evident in the case of Pontians and ethnic Greeks from Southern Albania. Recent legislation (L. 2790/2000) allows, for example, ethnic Greeks to apply for Greek citizenship at the Greek consulate authorities at their place of residence, thus enabling them to acquire Greek citizenship without having to emigrate. In case of restrictions imposed by the country of residence, ethnic Greeks are extended a Special Identity Card, which is valid both as a residence and work permit in Greece. The Greek citizenship or the Special Identity Card has also been granted to ethnic Greeks who came to the country on a visa, irrespective of the date of expiration of the passport or the visa as well as to parents and children of ethnic Greeks coming to the country (Article 76, L. 2910/2001).

10.4. Causal Factors of Migration

10.4.1. Theoretical Underpinnings

The most widely known framework for analysing migration movements is provided by human capital theory, developed in the 1960s by T.W. Schultz (1961) and G.S. Becker (1962), and elaborated by many other economists (Sjaastad 1962; Cebula 1979). According to it, migration is related to the difference between the expected benefits and costs of working in another country. The rate or probability of migration, defined as the percentage of people migrating from a particular population group, is thus positively associated with the present value of the stream of expected income differences between host and home countries, summed over the expected working life of the prospective emigrant. Since expected incomes depend not only on wages but also on employment conditions, the relative probability of finding a job in the two countries is an important determinant of the decision to migrate. Another important factor that determines not only the decision to migrate but also the length of stay in the destination country is the amount of savings that can be accumulated there.

Furthermore, personal and socioeconomic characteristics, such as age and education, are also expected to have an impact on the self-selection process of migration. Thus, the existence of a wage income differential between countries is not a sufficient condition to induce migration, even if it exceeds transportation and relocation costs, unless the prospects of moving provide an excess of expected benefits over costs. Conversely, current wage equalisation cannot deter migration if expectations of favourable future income prospects outweigh expected costs. Thus, individual rational actors make intertemporal decisions to migrate or repatriate based upon cost–benefit calculations over the net return to migration (Katseli and Glytsos 1989).

Temporary migration, as opposed to permanent relocation, is more difficult to explain, as the optimal duration of foreign stay needs to be determined. The length of stay abroad, the timing of repatriation and the amount of transfers remitted to family members back at home are, in this case, integral parts of the migration decision. Subjective personal or family factors, in addition to prevailing economic conditions, play an important role in explaining the migration–remittance–repatriation cycle. Recent work on migration underlines family (i.e. group) strategies to diversify sources of income, to minimize risks to the household, and to overcome barriers to credit and capital as important determinants of these decisions. In this strand of literature, international migration is viewed as a means of compensating for the absence or failure of markets in developing countries (Stark 1991).

These factors may explain some migrant actions that are unexplained by the accepted economic wisdom of one-way emigration. Thus, the emigration-remittance-repatriation cycle involves a series of family decisions, taken before the migrant's departure and during his stay in the foreign country. This cycle can be decomposed into five major decisions: the decision to emigrate; the timing of movement; the amount of remittances sent to the family; the decision to return, and the timing of return. These decisions may be contemporaneous and combined or distinct in time. For example, the decision to emigrate and to return may be taken, contemporaneously, before the departure of the emigrant to another country, subject to revisions, when the migrant and his family come face to face with the new reality in the host country (Glytsos 1991: 51). Such revisions concern alternative scenaria regarding the length of stay, the prospects for family reunification, the saving target, the use of savings, and the amount and regularity of remittances.

The decision to emigrate or not and the series of the subsequent decisions cited, can be formally cast as endogenous nonlinearly interconnected variables in an intertemporal utility maximization framework. For instance, income generation and the accumulation of savings are expected to be positively related to the length of stay abroad up to a certain level of income. Then, as in the case of a backward sloping labour supply curve, higher incomes and saving may shorten the length of stay and expedite return, while an economic slowdown may prolong the duration of stay. This seems to have been one of the reasons, why, after the 1973 oil crisis, the recession in the German economy induced Greek immigrants to lengthen their stay abroad from an average of about three years in the early 1960s to five years in the 1970s (Katseli and Glytsos 1989). This evidence is also consistent with different behavioural characteristics of 'early' as opposed to 'late' migrants.

According to Glytsos (1991), early Greek migrants tended to move alone and were more 'impatient quick savers', with a shorter time horizon, as opposed to late migrants who could be characterized as 'sensible savers' with a more comfortable time horizon. As better and more accurate information became available through repatriates and migrant networks, emigrants tended to be older and moved together with family members for a longer period of time.

This evidence is consistent with more recent theoretical work on networks and their impact on migration. According to this strand of literature, migrant networks serve to reduce the costs and the risks of international migration and thus tend to increase the probability of movement (Russell 1997). The reduction of costs and risks is also achieved via the development of institutions, such as private and/or voluntary organizations, which support and sustain the movement of migrants providing transport, housing, legal, and other services.

The importance of financial and informational costs on migration helps explain the migration 'hump', i.e. the observed tendency for migration to increase with development (Schiff 1996). Low-income workers in low-income countries are often unable to afford the costs of migration and of relocation, despite favourable migration incentives. As wages and incomes rise as a result of either trade expansion, foreign investment, or foreign aid, migration pressures rise despite weak incentives (Schiff 1996). This would explain why, in the mid-1960s, high rates of emigration from Greece coincided with relatively high domestic growth-rates, or why the expansion of Greek trade and investment with Balkan countries in the 1990s, appears to have fostered expanded immigration from these countries. As migration continues and migration-networks get established, informational costs are reduced sustaining further emigration. Thus, a cumulative process is established where international migration flows create 'feedbacks' that make additional movements more likely.

Overall, there are four groups of factors that shape migration decisions:

(a) demand-pull factors that draw migrants into richer countries;
(b) supply-push factors that encourage migrants to leave poorer countries;
(c) financial and informational costs determined by distance, social networks, institutions and/or policies;
(d) institutional factors and more specifically market failures, especially in the sending countries that affect the overall emigration–remittance–repatriation cycle.

Within this framework, remittances are jointly determined, along with other variables in the migration–repatriation function. Lucas and Stark (1985: 906), analysing rural–urban migration, argue that migrants are motivated to remit out of 'tempered altruism', or 'enlightened self-interest' vis-à-vis their families in the rural sector in the context of an 'implicit contract' signed between the migrant and his own family. The amount of remittances depends on both supply and demand factors. On the supply side, remittances depend on actual and expected savings. The migrant maximises these savings, by minimizing leakages, such as migrant consumption in the host country or remittances for consumption purposes.

On the demand side, the amount of remittances that the migrant is obliged to send depends on the need for sustaining a decent living for the family. This is determined not only by family size and subsistence requirements but also by educational needs for children as well as by the family's desired social prestige and relative standing in the community. Thus, 'neighbourhood effects', are often created as families of migrants attempt to maintain living standards which are higher than the standards of living of nonmigrant neighbours. The minimum level of required remittances is thus often influenced by the relative size of family income from domestic activities in relation to the average income of neighbours (Glytsos 1988: 527–32).

Naturally, not all remittances are of the kind described, i.e. 'required' income for family support. Some remittances are transferred for the purpose of investment, motivated by the relative return on investment and the safety of the transferred funds. Such remittances, which can be described as 'desired' remittances, can be explained in the framework of a simple portfolio model, as developed by Katseli and Glytsos (1989).

10.4.2. Empirical Findings

In accordance with the theoretical arguments presented in the previous section, various econometric studies (Botsas 1970; Sapir 1975; Lianos 1980; Katseli and Glytsos 1989; Glytsos 1991) and survey evidence from either Greek repatriates (Petropoulos et al. 1992) or from illegal immigrants in Greece (Lianos et al. 1996; Markova and Sarris 1997), have confirmed that income, employment opportunities, and expected savings have been the principal determining factors of emigration. Specifically, according to the econometric estimates presented in Table 10.3 on Greek–German migration, a significant positive association of emigration and of the probability of emigration with per capita income in Germany and a negative association with per capita income in Greece is found. When both income and employment variables are jointly included in the estimated equations, employment in the host country appears to be strongly significant, absorbing some of the income effects. This is expected due to multicollinearity between income and employment. Lagged values of the dependent variable are positively associated with current values, confirming the phenomenon of chain emigration and the importance of social networks in reducing the costs of emigration. A significant dummy variable provides also some indication that the 1973 restrictive migration policy in Germany restrained emigration.

Similar factors seem to determine the inflow of immigrants to Greece. In a survey conducted among 100 illegal Bulgarian workers in Greece, almost 45 per cent quoted as their primary reason for leaving Bulgaria the 'lack of money that made them unable to survive', while another 13 per cent gave as their primary reason for departure the lack of actual employment (Markova and Sarris 1997).

The cost of moving and the burden of financing migration expenditures seem to be significant determinants of the choice of destination. Thus, Filipinos appear to have chosen Greece as a host country because employers have covered the initial transportation costs, while Bulgarian

Table 10.3. Determinants of emigration to Germany (selected studies)

Author	Year of Publication	Dependent Variables		Independent Variables						
		Period Covered		Real Income of the Host Country	Real Income of Greece	Employment Rate of the Host Country	Employment Rate of Greece	Relative Income (Host-Home)	Relative Unemployment Rate (Host-Home)	Emigration Lagged
Botsas	1970	1958–1966	E/LF					0.889* (8.631)	NO EFFECT	
Sapir	1975	1956–1971	E					0.460* (2.674)	−4.792* (−3.027)	
Sapir	1975	1956–1971	LnE					1.473* (5.356)	−1.643* (−8.647)	
Lianos	1980	1959–1976	E					STATISTICALY INSIGNIFICANT	−17.900* (−2.265)	STATISTICALY INSIGNIFICANT
Katseli and Glytsos	1989	1961–1983	WE/LF	0.30 (0.81)	−0.99* (−2.48)	0.110 (1.76)	−0.093* (−2.87)			
Katseli and Glytsos	1989	1961–1983	E/N	0.57* (2.11)	−0.58 (−1.91)	0.178* (3.89)	0.096* (3.91)			
Glytsos	1991	1962–1985	LnE	5.62* (2.231)	−4.453* (−2.607)					0.705* (4.092)
Glytsos	1991	1962–1985	LnE	0.793 (0.302)	0.715 (0.630)	10.250 (4.649)	−2.711 (−1.036)			0.169 (0.973)

Notes: The numbers in parentheses represent t-ratios.
* Statistically significant at the 5% level.

List of Variables

E = Number of Greek Emigrants
LF = Labour Force
WE = Working Age Emigrants
N = Population
1/In Lianos relative unemployment is home–host.

immigrants prefer Greece because of low transportation costs (Markova and Sarris 1997).

The presence of friends and relatives in Greece have been found to have significantly reduced housing and installation costs, to have facilitated adaptation and to have enhanced the probability of finding employment. According to Glytsos (1991) and Markova and Sarris (1997), cost reducing migration networks have facilitated migration. The friends and relatives could explain why the majority of Pontians are settled in Athens and Thessaloniki (Glytsos 1992) as well as the concentration of immigrants of the same ethnic origin into specific neighbourhoods or areas. These 'institutional' factors have also contributed to chain migration, both at the national and regional levels. Glytsos (1991) for example, has found that in the case of 51 geographic departments of Greece, during the period 1960–76, the intertemporal correlation coefficient of emigrant flows across consecutive years is high. A particularly high correlation is observed between current flows and the level of emigration 2–4 years earlier, suggesting that emigration during the recent past affects positively current emigration.

Increased migrant savings covered not only the costs of family reunification to West Germany in the 1960s, but also paid for the relocation of Greek migrants to other destinations. Savings accumulated in Greece also financed the relocation of aliens from Greece to the US and Canada during the 1990s.

The reasons for repatriation have been classified by some into three categories: attainment of target, disappointment on expectations, and unforeseen employment developments (Lianos 1980: 22). Survey evidence indicates that, contrary to emigration, return migration was not prompted so much by economic as by personal and family reasons, such as aged parents, education of children, health problems, homesickness etc. (Bernard and Ashton-Vouyoucalos 1976; Bernard and Comitas 1978; Unger 1984, 1986; Dikaiou 1994).

Repatriation was substantial and roughly equal in numbers both in times of rapid economic growth in Germany (1963–70) as well as in times of slow growth (1971–82). The reasons for the return of emigrants as well as the characteristics of returnees differed, however, across the two periods. In the first period, returnees were young and moved from a fast-growing German economy to an even faster growing Greek economy; in the second period, returnees moved from a low-growth German economy to a relatively high-growth Greek economy. In both periods, the prospects in Greece were promising and moving costs between Germany and Greece were relatively low.

Glytsos (1997: 415) argues that those who left Germany at a time of a growing economy very likely consisted of 'weak' and 'quick' savers, i.e. those who could not adjust to the new conditions of work and life in Germany and those that had a limited time horizon of migration. In the second period, the main factors contributing to repatriation included inter alia, the rising standards of living in Greece whose growth-rates exceeded an annual 5 per cent, the restoration of democracy in the home country and the restrictive policy stance in Germany. Between 1975 and 1979, 61 per cent of the total number of Greek migrants living in Germany returned home. Repatriation from West Germany to Greece appears in fact to have been retarded by the higher growth-rates in the host country. Glytsos (1991) has estimated that the income elasticity of repatriation was −4.6. In other words, a 1 per cent rise in German per capita GDP postponed the repatriation of about 2,000 persons per year.

During the same period, only 3 per cent of Greek migrants from Australia returned, highlighting the importance of transportation costs and the different nature of migration processes in the two countries (Glytsos 1997: 415). As has been noted earlier, migration to Germany was perceived to be temporary and of a relatively short duration while migration to Australia was perceived to be more permanent. There are however, indications that emigration to Germany gradually shifted in the 1980s from temporary to more permanent (Glytsos 1991: 71–4).

Econometric analysis on remittance flows by Glytsos (1988, 1991, 1997) and Katseli and Glytsos (1989) have used as explanatory variables, among others, lagged values of remittances and per capita income in both the home and host countries (Table 10.4). These variables captured the past behaviour of migrants and their families and its adjustment over time. The rate of inflation and nominal interest rates were also used as explanatory variables in order to capture the expected purchasing power of remitting and the real yield of migrant savings. The evidence produced indicates that per capita income in Germany had a positive and statistically significant effect on remittances per migrant, while per capita income in Greece had a negative but relatively weaker effect. The rate of inflation in Greece, which not only determines the expected purchasing power of remittances but also captures economic uncertainty had the expected negative sign. Finally, increases in the German nominal interest rates affected positively remittances since they provided additional income to the migrant on his/her saving. Increases in Greek nominal interest rates had no statistically significant effects probably due to the dominant effect of inflation (Katseli and Glytsos 1989).

Table 10.4. Determinants of remittances

Author	Year of Publication	Period Covered	Host Country	Dependent Variables	Per Capita GDP in the Host Country	Per Capita GDP in Greece	Rate of Inflation in Greece	Foreign Exchange Rate	Interest Rate in the Host Country	Interest rate in Greece	Remittances lagged one year	Remittances lagged two years	Time	Number of Returning Immigrants	Per Capita GDP in Greece Squared
Glytsos	1988	1960–82	Germany	ln (REM/M)	1.556* (2.552)	−3.928* (−3.012)					0.229 (1.499)	−0.306* (−3.124)	0.537* (3.931)		
Glytsos	1988	1960–82	U.S.A.	ln (REM/M)	1.068* (3.007)	0.621 (1.016)					0.521* (2.090)	0.151 (0.563)	−0.215* (−4.153)		
Katseli and Glytsos	1989	1961–82	Germany	ln (REM/M)	5.135* (11.674)	−1.047* (−4.349)	−4.204* (−4.811)		0.080* (4.506)						
Glytsos	1997	1960–93	Germany	ln (REM/M)	5.317* (7.968)	−0.879* (−3.847)	−3.264* (−3.696)	−0.032 (−0.071)	0.027 (0.795)	−0.007 (−0.156)	−0.021 (−0.185)			−0.088 (−1.140)	
Glytsos	1997	1960–93	Australia	ln (REM/M)	1.106* (2.310)	4.345* (2.394)	−1.280 (−1.187)	1.607* (3.683)	−0.066* (−1.937)	0.193* (2.848)	0.513* (3.793)			−0.843* (−3.983)	−0.197* (−2.679)

Notes: The numbers in parentheses represent t-ratios.
* Statistically significant at the 5% level.
List of Variables
REM = Volume of Remittances in GDR.
M = Migrant.
REM/M = Per Migrant Remittances.

Remittances from the US and Australia were also positively related to the host country's per capita income, with an elasticity of approximately unity. The estimated elasticity was lower compared to the German case. Furthermore, increases in per capita incomes in Greece had a positive and strong effect on remittances from Australia, but not on remittances from the USA (Glytsos 1988, 1997).

A time variable, standing for the duration of stay abroad, was positive and significant for West Germany, implying that the migrant continued to remit over time, as long as he continued to perceive his stay as temporary. This 'return illusion' disappeared in the case of the US, where migrants perceived themselves as permanent residents. For them, an extension of their stay abroad reduced remittances as a result of a 'permanent settlement syndrome' (Glytsos 1988: 533).

Independently of these estimates, there is evidence that the policy of attracting migrant savings through special tax allowances, especially for the purchase of housing was successful (Glytsos 1991: 118). Other evidence shows that, in the late 1970s, more than half of Greek emigrants put their savings into banks in Germany, and only one-fourth into banks in Greece. The rest divided their savings between banks in both countries.

Other studies, using different models, have reached sometimes similar and sometimes different results. In a cross-section analysis of Mediterranean countries (Faini 1994), remittances were found to be positively associated with the real exchange rate, and negatively with domestic family income, confirming the altruistic motive of remitting behaviour. In contrast to Glytsos' estimates, Faini found that a longer duration of stay in Germany reduced remittances. Finally, Swamy (1981) confirmed the finding that fluctuations in the host country's wages and the volume of migrants jointly determined 90 per cent of remittance changes in various countries including Greece.

10.5. Migration and Development Interlinkages

Migration, growth, and development are interdependent processes. Migration affects development and growth, but it is also affected by them. Rarely have sending countries designed an overall development strategy that incorporated the effects of migration on the economy and society in the short and medium run. In fact, it is usually the migrants themselves who make countries realise that they are 'needed', because of their contribution to production, labour market flexibility or skill formation.

In view of the importance of migration flows for the development of the Greek economy, this section concentrates, initially, on labour market adjustment, taking into account factor substitution and income effects. It then proceeds to survey evidence on trade competitiveness and growth and to underline the potential migration, trade, and investment interlinkages that underpin development efforts. Finally, it reviews the effectiveness of policy measures adopted recently from a developmental point of view.

10.5.1. Migration and Labour Market Adjustment

The shortrun effects of migration on labour markets do not depend only on initial labour market conditions but also on the skill composition of the migrant flows as well as on the flexibility of the labour market to substitute these resources. These factors play a crucial role in determining whether emigration constitutes a 'drain' of workers, sufficient to hinder the development process. Emigration of unskilled workers from agriculture or industry is expected in the short-run to reduce output of the relevant sector, due to the limited substitutability among workers in the agricultural sector. It is also expected to increase the trade deficit due to the reduction of agricultural exports. Over the medium-run, however, labour shortages are expected to increase pressures for factor substitution, enhancing productivity and growth.

Emigration from Greece absorbed the most dynamic and productive part of the active population (Zolotas 1966), thus reducing the available labour supply, at least in the high emigration areas. This contributed to a slow-down in agricultural production and in agricultural exports. In the medium-run, however, the introduction of labour-saving equipment, partly financed through remittances, induced the mechanization of Greek agriculture and the sustainability of agricultural production.

The speed of mechanization and the restructuring of agricultural production that coincided with emigration has differed substantially across regions. Melas and Delis (1981) found that, in 1976, a nationwide surplus of man-days in agriculture existed, with vast seasonal fluctuations across the 52 geographic departments (prefectures) of Greece (Table 10.5). In thirteen high-emigration prefectures, from which more than 16 per cent of the population had emigrated between 1960 and 1976, agricultural labour shortages reached 25.2 per cent of man-days available. However, in another group of sixteen high emigration prefectures, from which 19.5 per cent of the population had emigrated during the same period, labour surpluses amounting to 25.6 per cent of total man-days appeared. In the remaining

Table 10.5. Surpluses and shortages of agricultural labour and proportion of emigrating population, 1976

Groups of Geographic department	Number of geographic departments	Share in the size of emigration 1960–76	Number of emigrants 1960–76 as a proportion of 1961 population	Shortage (−) or surplus (+) of mandays as a proportion of available mandays 1976	Simple correlation coefficient between emigration and labour balances
Group I	13	28.7	16.3	−25.2	−0.729
Group II	5	3.3	4.9	−51.9	−0.173
Group III	16	45.5	19.5	+25.6	−0.262
Group IV	16	22.5	7.7	+15.0	−0.278
Greece*	50	100.0	13.0	+9.2	−0.090

* Attika (Athens) is excluded because of its insignificant agricultural production.
Sources: NSSG, Greek Yearbook of Statistics (various issues); Melas and Delis (1981) for labour shortages and surpluses.

prefectures, the situation was mixed. In some cases, low emigration coincided with high labour shortages; in others, low emigration went hand in hand with high labour surpluses.

In a more recent study, Glytsos (1991) has confirmed a positive and statistically significant association between emigration and labour shortages in thirteen prefectures (Glytsos 1991: 134). The evidence, however, is less clear in all other prefectures, in which no such correlation is observed. These figures demonstrate that only in areas with a very high loss of workers have labour shortages in fact appeared.

In an earlier study, based on a survey of migrant and non-migrant families (1,699 in number) in seven prefectures across the country and on interviews with local officials in 56 communities and municipalities conducted in 1966, Filias (1974: 233) found no evidence of an emigration effect on agricultural production. Farm workers who emigrated were substituted by local labour while the peak seasonal (2–4 months) demand was covered by an inflow of workers from other communities. According to the same author, emigration may even have accentuated agricultural underemployment by inducing the introduction of more capital-intensive techniques that rendered many workers redundant.

From a longer-term perspective, migration seems to have retarded urbanization in Greece. Emigrants leaving the rural areas postponed their movement to the Greek urban centres to which they eventually returned following their repatriation. As was mentioned earlier (Figure 10.4), half of the repatriates who settled in Athens and Thessaloniki had emigrated originally from rural areas. Calculating a 'return migration index' (returnees per 100 emigrants) from survey data, Unger (1986) has found that the index was higher for the more urbanised regions, the regions with better social infrastructure, higher rates of literacy, lower unemployment, and a higher proportion of employment in industry and services.

The delayed movement of farmers to the cities, following a short or longer period of stay abroad, suggests that these people became urbanized in the foreign countries while they also accumulated capital and skills which they brought back to their home country. Their settlement and integration into the Greek cities became, therefore, smoother and was distributed more evenly over time than would have been the case had they moved directly from the farm to the city. Were it not for external migration, the problem of urban unemployment would have become more serious than it was actually the case, especially in view of the concentration of industrial activity in the Greek cities and the tripling of capital intensity in industrial production (Glytsos 1994: 168).

In the 1990s, the inflow of unskilled foreign labour into the Greek rural sector has contributed to the expansion of agriculture. According to a recent study by Lianos et al. (1996), illegal immigrants alone have supplied, in the mid-1990s, about 31 per cent of all hired labour in agriculture and 12 per cent of all farm labour. According to that same study, the productivity-adjusted wage level for legal immigrants in the mid 1990s was approximately 4 per cent lower than that of Greeks with the same skill levels. The productivity and social security–adjusted wage for illegal immigrants was 60 per cent lower than the corresponding Greek wage. Evidence is provided that foreign workers largely covered pre-existing vacancies and even generated their own jobs.

Other econometric estimates corroborate, more or less, these findings, indicating that immigration did not raise the overall unemployment of natives (Tsamourgelis 1996: 4). According to a report by Linardos-Rylmon (1993), which is consistent with the views of the General Federation of Greek Labour, illegal immigrants induced an increase in the unemployment of Greek workers only in selected industries, such as construction, services, and handicraft.

The immigration of unskilled labour in the Greek economy, during the 1990s, expanded production not only in agriculture but also in construction and services. It also contributed to the expansion of consumption and of income through multiplier effects. Given the importance of agriculture in Greek trade, immigration also produced, through its dampening effects on wages, positive trade effects.

Using an amplified General Equilibrium Model for the Greek economy, Sarris and Zografakis (1997) found that the influx of illegal aliens contributed to a 1.5 per cent increase in real GNP coupled with a 47,000 man-year decline of total employment for Greeks. This estimate is considerably less than the 130,000 man-years contributed by illegal immigrants, implying that about one third of the illegal immigrant labour is net displacement of Greeks, while the rest is net addition to the Greek labour market. According to the same authors, the inflow of illegal immigrants resulted in major gains for thirteen classes of households among the fifteen modelled and losses for two. These include poor and middle-income households, which make up 37 per cent of the Greek population.

The impact of migration flows on the labour markets of the home and host countries depends critically, as we have seen, on the skill composition of migrants relatively to non-migrant workers. The out-migration of skilled workers, whether employed or not, is expected to incur substantial costs. As Bohning (1984) states, "it hits at the heart of the sending country's development efforts", where the crucial dilemma is the shortage of qualified workers and the abundance of unskilled ones.

The home country is supposed to benefit from any skills that farmers or unskilled workers acquire during their stay abroad. This does not appear to be fully the case for repatriating Greek migrants from Europe, especially from West Germany. This might be due to the fact that Greek migrants were employed primarily as unskilled workers in industry and services. Their educational level remained low and eagerness to attain their goals as soon as possible and to return home did not give them the possibility and time for adequate training (Unger 1984: 96; Papademetriou 1984: 265). Even those who underwent some training acquired skills which were not suitable for the low-level productive technology in Greece, aside from the fact that returnees were not willing to work in the industry. A microsurvey from the region of Macedonia revealed that only 6 per cent of the returnees chose to work in the manufacturing sector (Fakiolas 1984: 40). Even though, 16 per cent of repatriates from Germany had acquired vocational training, only 40 per cent of them could put this training into productive use in Greece (Unger 1984).

A more recent survey of 100 repatriates in five villages with 1,000–2,000 inhabitants in the heavy emigration prefecture of Drama in Northern Greece found that 72.4 per cent of returnees were 30–50 years of age; 65.5 per cent had only primary schooling and had not acquired any additional education in Germany; 13.7 per cent had acquired a third grade secondary education; only 5.8 per cent held high school diplomas and 6.8 per cent had secondary technical education (Dikaiou 1994: 33). Only 12.7 per cent of these returnees were working upon their return as skilled workers and 6.8 per cent held white-collar jobs. Among repatriates, 11.7 per cent remained unemployed and 8.8 per cent returned to farming.

Repatriates in general have suffered from high unemployment, partly because of their high reservation wages and the quality of jobs they wanted to accept (Fakiolas 1984: 41). McLean and Kousis (1988) and Petropoulos (1998) provide evidence that employment opportunities have in fact been limited for returnees regardless of their qualifications. A special survey in Athens, Thessaloniki, and Serres, in 1980, based on interviews with 574 repatriates, demonstrates that 58.4 per cent of those employed were salaried workers, 35.9 per cent self-employed, and 5.6 per cent were employers (Unger 1984: 93). Of the self-employed, 9.7 per cent worked in construction, 14.0 per cent in trade, 17.9 per cent were taxi-drivers, 12.6 per cent worked in grocery stores, and 20.8 per cent were managing a café or a restaurant. The same survey also found that 95 per cent of the respondents were working in semi-skilled and unskilled jobs.

One may conclude from all this evidence, that emigration to Europe was not really an opportunity for training and skill acquisition. This potential advantage of emigration was lost for Greece. Nonetheless, the repatriates' role in rural development has probably been more important than what is actually documented due to their contribution to local government, to the tourism and trade industry, to business services and to the establishment of international networks. In addition, emigration sustained family incomes and financed schooling and skill formation of younger family members with long-run positive effects on development.

10.5.2. Factor Substitution, Income Effects and Growth

Turning to the impact of migration on Greek productive restructuring, one should highlight the importance of the interdependencies between migration and rural development. Emigration is expected to influence growth. The deprivation of agriculture from its efficient young workers will tend, as we have seen above, to reduce agricultural production. The exodus of workers will tend eventually to raise wages and to induce mechanization and capital–labour substitution, partly financed by remittances (Glytsos 1998). The resulting growth in agricultural output and productivity on the other hand, may lead to labour redundancies, pushing more workers to emigration.

In Greece, following the massive exodus of workers between 1960 and 1964, the growth of agricultural production decelerated, largely because of the limited substitutability among workers in the agricultural sector. The subsequent introduction of labour-saving equipment, however, contributed to the mechanisation of agriculture and to substantial increases in productivity. Agricultural production increased at an annual rate of 3.4 per cent during 1964–72, offsetting any loss of output, which occurred as an immediate consequence of emigration. According to the Glytsos (1991) cross-section study of 50 prefectures quoted earlier, the marginal product of labour increased by 22 per cent between 1971 and 1977, while the marginal product of capital decreased by 58 per cent. One can infer that these were the results of reduced labour/land and labour/capital ratios, brought about by emigration.

Similarly, in the 1990s, the significant inflow of unskilled immigrants into the rural sector expanded agricultural production. Lianos et al. (1996) found that illegal immigrants have contributed considerably to agricultural GDP, raising it at least 3 per cent higher than what it would have been, had it not been for illegal immigrants.

It should be noted that whereas Greek emigrants had made a positive contribution to agricultural production through substitution of capital for labour and enhanced labour productivity, immigrant workers contributed to the expansion of agricultural output by raising unskilled labour supply, thus retarding the necessary restructuring in the agricultural sector of the economy.

Remittances have provided an important source of foreign exchange for most home countries. Official global remittances rose to 71 billion dollars in 1990, up from just over 43 billion dollars in 1980. If remittance flows through informal channels are included, this figure becomes considerably higher. Apart from the provision of foreign exchange and savings, remittances can have a structural impact on the economy, affecting both the domestic pattern of consumption as well as the composition of investment. Furthermore, they provide partial finance for education and skill acquisition of nonmigrant family members thus contributing to sustainable development.

There is, however, a view that remittances could widen the economic gap between home and host countries, if they are used to finance either the consumption of imports and of nontradable goods and services or investment in land, housing, etc., which do not generate direct foreign exchange. In such cases, the expansion of liquidity and the rising demand for nontradables is likely to bring about a deterioration in trade competitiveness with detrimental effects on net export earnings (Stahl 1982).

Analysing the overall contribution of migration to development, Papademetriou (1985) claims only a 'tentative relationship' between Greek labour migration and development. He argues that even though migration relieved unemployment and remittances had beneficial income and balance of payment effects, emigration depopulated the Greek countryside. In addition, Greece was deprived from its most efficient workers, whereas remittances, spent mostly on housing, distorted the Greek real estate market and increased inflationary pressures. Papademetriou claims that emigration had redistributive effects in a way that added "a new layer to the middle class: the remittance supported household" (ibid., p. 217). His overall conclusion is that Greece's 'investment' on migration was not generally profitable and its advantages of unemployment relief and the flow of remittances played "only a minor and essentially passive role in Greek growth" (ibid., p. 218). This view, however, appears to be rather extreme.

Transfers from abroad, including remittances, have sustained income and demand in the Greek economy throughout the 1960s and 1970s (Maroulis 1986; Katseli 1990, 2001). According to Glytsos (1993), in the early 1970s, remittances alone contributed to a 3 per cent increase in consumption and a 4 per cent increase in production. The multiplier of GDP with respect to remittances was estimated to be 1.7. Remittances contributed by 4.7 per cent to nonagricultural employment and expanded by 8 per cent the installed horsepower capacity in manufacturing. On the other hand, continuous transfers contributed to a deterioration of trade competitiveness, through the expansion of imports, of liquidity and of the demand for nontradables, including housing and land (Maroulis 1986; Katseli 2001).

Regressing private consumption expenditure on remittances in a cross-section study of 36 industries, estimated over two selected years (1964 and 1974), Glytsos (1991: 168) finds an approximately unitary elasticity for each year. In other words, a 10 per cent increase in remittances generated a proportional 10 per cent increase in private consumption expenditures. Glytsos (1993: 144) also found that, in the early 1970s, remittances in fact doubled the consumption expenditure of recipients, with a relatively stronger effect on education and durables. In the high emigration rural regions of northern Greece, remittances changed the consumption pattern of recipients towards the average consumption pattern of semi-urban areas and increased greatly the demand for beverages, apparel, footwear, and durables.

The author also produces evidence on the controversial issue of remittance leakages to imports. He finds that 21.5 per cent of remittances were directly or indirectly spent on imports. Only 26.6 per cent of these imports were imports of investment goods.

10.6. Adjustment and Development through Migration: Lessons from South-eastern Europe

As we have seen, emigration from Greece to West Germany and other European countries took place at a time of a rapidly growing Greek economy. Migrants were attracted to West Germany by better prospects, supported by the great differences in wages and by the practically 'unlimited' demand for unskilled workers. Repatriation to Greece took place both in times of growth and in times of recession.

Emigration curtailed rural unemployment and underemployment and retarded urbanisation. The departure of workers from agriculture reduced, initially, agricultural production and exports especially in those rural areas which experienced heavy emigration of their most productive workers. However, any loss of output, was soon recovered by the intensification of employment of the remaining workers and by the substitution of capital for labour. Mechanization of agriculture and more effective capacity utilisation raised agricultural productivity and released additional labour from agriculture creating incentives for more emigration. This process retarded further urbanization and prevented the rise of unemployment in the urban centres.

Emigration has not contributed much to the acquisition of skills by Greek migrants as they served mostly in unskilled jobs and did not have the incentives to expand skills. On the other hand, emigration has financed skill formation of dependants either in the host country or in the Greek countryside.

Remittances are an important source of foreign exchange and have sustained incomes, saving and domestic spending, boosting growth and employment, despite their detrimental effects on trade competitiveness.

More importantly, returnees themselves have undergone a process of cultural transformation, and have acquired in the process 'middle-class attitudes'. Relying upon their accumulated savings, families have invested in the education of their children and have emulated higher income patterns of consumption. Moreover, as is evident from the empirical survey by Collaros and Moussourou (1978), the mentality of returnees concerning social issues, including the role of women changed, in the process of migration. The same survey also confirmed the hypothesis that migration made returnees more politically conscious and more actively involved in their local communities.

Overall, migration flows have helped to propel Greece towards modernity. There have been advantages and disadvantages in that change, but the overall effects have been rather positive (Fakiolas 1984: 43). The benefits from migration, however, have not been as widespread as expected, largely due to the complementarity of the home and host countries, which has prevented repatriates to use effectively in Greece skills they have acquired abroad. Evidence from Greece suggests that migration between two countries appears to be more beneficial when the productive structures of the countries concerned are competitive, so that skills can be easily transferred and the benefits of migration can be exploited to the fullest. If skills are not transferable to the home country, then 'emigration fails to provide "a discernible development impetus" (Papademetriou 1984: 266). This argument is analogous to the conclusion reached in customs-union theory, where it is shown that a custom-union between two countries is beneficial when the countries are presently competitive in their trade structure and aspire to become complementary. In that case, free trade allows countries to specialise in the sector where they possess a comparative advantage and thus reap the full benefits of expanded trade.

The compatibility of productive structures across Southern European countries makes them presently 'competitive', thus rendering temporary migration potentially beneficial both for the sending and the receiving countries (Katseli and Markova 1999). On the one hand, the inflow of foreign immigrants in Greece has provided a 'substantial subsidy' to Greek agriculture, to exports and output and has contributed to an amelioration of price competitiveness through its dampening effect on wages and non-wage labour costs. The influx of labour in the rural sector has expanded agricultural output and GDP. On the other hand, foreign immigrants find employment and increase their income despite the fact that they do not usually acquire new skills. More importantly, foreign immigrants from neighbouring countries can continue to be active participants in the development process at home. They do not only send remittances at home but they tend to return, periodically, to look after the family, till the land, mend their homes or invest their earned incomes into small businesses. In the meantime, family and kinship ties are maintained and family members often choose to join the principal migrant for few months at a time. Thus, migration has tended to facilitate domestic adjustment and development through the gradual integration of neighbouring countries' labour markets.

Because of the temporary nature of migration movements, the inter-linkages between migration, trade and investment have been strengthened. Many migrants, while residing and working abroad, purchase domestic goods and export them back home or set up more permanent trading networks in collaboration with partners in the home and host countries. Others find investment partners with whom they set up businesses back home. These interlinkages produce permanent effects on trading and investment patterns and complementarities between trade, investment, and migration activities. Thus, temporary or seasonal migration of relatively unskilled workers not only affects positively growth in both home and host countries, but also helps develop trading and informational networks contributing to the gradual integration of the region.

Today, after the collapse of the planned economies of South-eastern Europe and the upsurge in migration movements across the area, migration, trading and investment networks are developing throughout the area. Trade diversification is taking place. Greek exports to the neighbouring Balkan countries soared to 10 per cent of the country's total exports in 1998, while some ten years earlier the corresponding share was only 5 per cent. Similarly, cross-country investment activity has expanded significantly. Greece ranks fifth among foreign investors in Bulgaria, with invested capital flows between 1 January 1991 and 30 September 1997 of around US$12 billion. A similar dynamic trend is observed in Romania and Albania (Pelagidis 1999). According to available information on registered activity, foreign direct investment in these countries takes the form of joint ventures between foreign companies and local partners, often to be financed or supported by international institutions and/or foreign banks.

Increasing transactions and rising demand for financial services has motivated Greek banks to extend their services to the region, primarily in Bulgaria, Albania, Romania, and the former Republic of Yugoslavia. They are opening up local branches and participating in investment and venture capital funds, set up in collaboration with private investors and international financial institutions. The establishment of banks in the region has been prompted, to a large extent, by the presence of migrants and has facilitated remittances and their channelling into productive investment at home. South-eastern Europe is thus, once again, slowly but steadily, integrating its labour, capital, commodity, and financial markets. If this integration process continues unabated, an enlarged market will eventually be created that could expand further to include other neighbouring countries and finally become incorporated into the European Union.

Policies have to take into account this emerging reality and to facilitate the progressive integration of these markets. This requires a shift in policy direction from policies focusing exclusively on combating illegal immigration to policies favoring integration and regional development, through the enhancement of temporary migration, trade, and investment.

Greek migration policies are still exclusively designed with a view towards combating illegal immigration through three sets of policy instruments:

(a) *Prevention through law enforcement.* This involves patrolling the extended Greek borders, tightening up visa procedures, using internal policy controls to prevent overstaying and launching media campaigns and/or police operations to discourage illegal immigrants from coming and staying.

(b) *Expulsion of immigrants.* Through extended and costly police operations, the government continues to expel illegal immigrants, largely to appease domestic residents. Immigrants, however, especially from neighbouring countries tend to return only after a few months of deportation.

(c) *Regularization.* The legalization programmes adopted in 1998 and 2001 have provided temporary solutions to the 'illegality' issue, but have not resolved the fundamental economic and social problems associated with immigration. On the one hand, regularization has entailed moral hazard effects, as it has tended to create positive incentives for increased illegal immigration. On the other hand, legalization, by narrowing the productivity adjusted wage differential between domestic and migrant workers, eliminates the beneficial subsidy effect resulting from immigration.

A desired policy shift is needed towards measures that facilitate temporary migratory movements as an integral part of regional development policies. These measures can be designed on the basis of bilateral immigration agreements for seasonal work, contract, or project-tied work and should include inter alia:

(a) *Seasonal work schemes.* If administered efficiently, seasonal schemes could serve as a very effective policy tool for facilitating temporary movements.

(b) *Project-tied work schemes.* These are schemes that encourage immigration and work in specified activities undertaken for a fixed period of time in conjunction with specific projects.

(c) *Contract work.* The admission period under contract work is strictly fixed in the foreigner's contract. The time of stay allowed can span a year or more. Renewal can be granted for a limited number of times.

These types of policies would be extremely useful and effective in South-eastern Europe, given the seasonal characteristics of employment in the rural areas of the host countries, the project-specific nature of construction activities and the contract-work character of home-based services and trading. They would preserve the beneficial effects of legalization without creating incentives for permanent settlement. More importantly, these special agreements would preserve the necessary flexibility in the foreigners' working conditions, by maintaining the cost-advantages in contracts and by securing employment.

Bilateral agreements could also be extended to include investment or trading stipulations benefiting the home country. Thus, migration policies could be supplemented by a number of economic, financial or structural measures to facilitate adjustment and growth. In the integrated and enlarged market of South-eastern Europe such policies could be mutually beneficial as they would create synergies and give rise to economies of scale and scope.

Investment in infrastructure of the sending countries would thus facilitate trade and investment activity and help to contain migration pressures. The same would hold true for the modernization of transportation and telecommunication networks and for entrepreneurial investment. The extension of financial and banking services throughout the area would not only promote trade and investment activities but would also permit the rational management of migrant workers' saving with mutual benefits for both sending and receiving countries.

Policies to facilitate temporary migration movements should also be supplemented by social and educational policies that would underpin integration and be consistent with migrant workers' needs. Educational exchanges, training programmes, bilateral or multilateral agreements for the transfer of social security and of insurance, and health benefits are some of the policy measures that would facilitate temporary migration flows and promote integration and development.

Appendix

Table 10.A.1. Greek total net migration*

Year	Net migration	Year	Net migration
1960	−30,475	1980	50,105
1961	−23,861	1981	7,008
1962	−48,201	1982	9,870
1963	−56,039	1983	9,078
1964	−47,477	1984	10,073
1965	−39,978	1985	6,005
1966	−4,804	1986	15,199
1967	−28,966	1987	19,801
1968	−38,532	1988	27,142
1969	−66,847	1989	53,852
1970	−46,222	1990	71,135
1971	−15,501	1991	87,246
1972	−636	1992	48,878
1973	−42,479	1993	56,025
1974	−19,269	1994	27,302
1975	58,550	1995	20,859
1976	55,871	1996	21,558
1977	22,004	1997	22,070
1978	105,900	1998	22,500
1979	41,417	1999	25,000

*In this table net migration is the difference between the total population on 1 January and 31 December for a certain calendar year, minus the difference between births and deaths. Therefore, the figures in this table include corrections and may differ between immigration and emigration.

Source: Eurostat, Demographic Statistics, 1997, p. 112; Eurostat, European Social Statistics: Demography 1999, p.184; 2000, p.117.

Table 10.A.2. Emigration and repatriation of Greeks, 1955–97, selected regions

Year	Emigration to transoceanic countries*	Emigration to Federal Republic of Germany	Repatriation from transoceanic countries	Repatriation from Federal Republic of Germany
1955	19,766			
1956	23,147			
1957	14,783			
1958	14,842			
1959	13,871			
1960	17,764	27,469		3,198
1961	17,336	37,986		8,791
1962	21,959	53,656		14,002
1963	24,459	64,583		23,894
1964	25,327	81,109		36,369
1965	29,035	78,233		44,137
1966	33,093	55,396		58,093
1967	26,323	20,589		73,828
1968	25,891	53,107	4,734	29,043
1969	28,425	87,884	5,156	24,394
1970	24,153	94,307	7,112	30,259
1971	18,690	71,064	8,226	40,119
1972	13,239	51,083	8,484	48,060
1973	11,706	36,102	6,326	48,807
1974	12,380	29,960	4,793	48,732
1975	8,806	18,196	2,254	65,709
1976		16,004		58,200
1977		15,276		48,000
1978		14,400		36,300
1979		14,787		29,247
1980		15,811		22,318
1981		18,536		15,782
1982		12,838		18,137
1983		10,000		18,900
1984		9,300		16,800
1985		9,500		16,400
1986		11,800		15,000
1987		15,500		12,900
1988		33,000		12,800
1989		29,500		14,600
1990		26,500		14,300
1991		28,300		15,400
1992		23,600		16,200
1993		18,300		17,500
1994		18,900		19,200
1995		20,300		19,300
1996		18,800		20,100
1997		16,400		21,800

*Including USA, Australia and Canada.

Sources: Column 1 and 3: Statistical Yearbooks of Greece, different years. Column 2 and 4: Federal Office of Labour (Germany) (for Emigration–Repatriation, 1960–82). Emigration (inflows to Germany) and repatriation (outflows from Germany), 1983–88, SOPEMI, 1990 (original source Statistiches Bundesamt). Emigration (inflows to Germany) and repatriation (outflows from Germany) 1989–97, SOPEMI, 1999.

Table 10.A.3. Total emigrant remittances, 1965–97 (in million dollars)

	Emigrant remittances	Import paym. $	Export Rec. $	Remittances as a percentage of import paym.	Remittances as a percentage of export rec.
1965	207.0	978	328	21.16	63.10
1966	235.0	1,103	403	21.30	51.99
1967	232.0	1,125	452	20.62	50.0
1968	234.0	1,167	464	20.05	44.15
1969	277.3	1,363	530	20.34	45.31
1970	344.6	1,613	612	21.36	55.22
1971	469.7	1,840	624	25.52	56.25
1972	575.3	2,208	835	26.05	46.77
1973	735.4	3,869	1,230	19.00	41.45
1974	673.5	4,509	1,774	14.93	33.19
1975	781.5	4,836	2,029	16.16	35.09
1976	803.5	5,552	2,227	14.47	31.85
1977	924.8	6,401	2,522	14.44	30.84
1978	985.4	7,408	2,998	13.30	32.86
1979	1169.0	9,931	3,931	11.77	29.73
1980	1083.0	10,592	4,093	10.22	26.45
1981	1080.1	8,956	4,316	12.06	25.02
1982	1043.0	10,021	4,308	10.40	24.21
1983	931.0	9,673	4,477	9.62	20.79
1984	917.0	9,672	4,842	9.48	18.93
1985	774.5	10,561	4,293	7.33	18.04
1986	942.3	10,198	4,512	9.24	20.88
1987	1333.8	12,556	5,613	10.62	23.76
1988	1675.0	13,564	5,933	12.34	28.23
1989	1349.6	15,115	5,994	8.92	22.51
1990	1774.2	18,693	6,364	9.49	27.87
1991	2115.0	19,105	6,797	11.07	31.11
1992	2366.4	19,902	6,008	11.89	39.38
1993	2359.8	17,615	5,034	13.39	46.87
1994	2576.0	18,741	5,218	13.74	49.36
1995	2981.7	29,929	5,783	13.00	51.56
1996	2894.5	24,135	5,770	12.00	50.16
1997	2816.0	23,644	5,373	11.91	52.41

Sources: Bank of Greece, Monthly Statistical Bulletin, March 1975 and 1996; December 1981; February 2001; Bank of Greece, Annual Reports, for different years.
IMF, International Financial Statistics Yearbook, 1987 and 1992; 1993 (pp. 34–5 and 60–1); 1995 (pp.13–14 and 47–8).

References

Atchison, J. (1988). 'Immigration in two federations: Canada and Australia', *International Migration*, 26.

Baldwin-Edwards, M. (1994). 'Immigration and border control in Greece', Workshop Police et Immigration: Vers l'Europe de la Securite Interieure, European Consortium for Political Research, mimeo.

Becker, G. S. (1962). 'Investment in human capital: a theoretical analysis', *Journal of Political Economy*, Supplement 2, 70.

Bernard, H. R. and Ashton-Vouyoucalos, S. (1976). 'Return migration to Greece', *Journal of the Steward Anthropological Society*, 8.

Bernard, H. R. and Comitas, L. (1978). 'Greek return migration', *Current Anthropology*, 19.

Black, R. (1992). 'Livelihood and vulnerability of foreign refugees in Greece', King's College Dept. of Geography *Occasional Paper*, 33 (London: King's College).

Bohning, W. R. (1984). *Studies in International Migration* (London: Macmillan).

Borjas, George J. (1994). 'The economics of immigration', *Journal of Economic Literature*, 32.

Botsas, E. L. (1970). 'Some economic aspects of short-run Greek labour emigration to Germany', *Weltwirtschaftliches Archiv*, 105.

Cebula, R. J. (1979). *The Determinants of Human Migration* (Lexington Massachusetts: Lexington Books).

Collaros, T. A. and Moussourou, L. M. (1978). *The Return Home: Socioeconomic Aspects of Reintegration of Greek Migrant Workers Returning from Germany* (Athens: Reintegration Center for Migrant Workers).

Dikaiou, M. (1994). 'Present realities and future prospects among Greek returnees', *International Migration*, 32.

Dogas, D. (1993). 'Migration, return migration and population changes in Greece during the last twenty five years', mimeo.

Emke-Poulopoulou, I. (1986). *Problems of Immigration and Repatriation* (Athens: Institute for the Study of the Greek Economy (in Greek)).

Ependitis (1999). Greek Weekly Newspaper, 17–18 April.

Faini, R. (1994). 'Workers' remittances and the real exchange rate', *Journal of Population Economics*, 7: 235–45.

Fakiolas, R. (1984). 'Return migration to Greece and its structural and socio-political aspects', in D. Kubat (ed.) *The Politics of Return. International Return Migration in Europe* (Rome: Centro Studi Emigrazione).

— (1995). 'Migration from and to Greece during the last four decades', in G. Alogoskoufis et al. (eds) *Essays in Honor of Constantine Drakatos* (Athens: Papazissis (in Greek)).

— (2001). 'Socioeconomic effects of immigration in Greece', mimeo.

— and King, R. (1996). 'Emigration, return, immigration: a review and evaluation of Greece's postwar experience of international migration', *International Journal of Population Geography*, 2.

Filias, V. (1974). 'Emigration of farmers and structural impact on agriculture', in V. Filias (ed.), *Problems of Social Transformation* (Athens: Papazissis Publishers).

Glytsos, N. P. (1988). 'Remittances in temporary migration: a theoretical model and its testing with the Greek-German experience', *Weltwirtschaftliches Archiv*, 124, Heft 3.

— (1991). *Theoretical and Empirical Analysis of Migration Movements and of Remittance Flows between Greece and Germany*, Studies Series, 7 (Athens: Centre of Planning and Economic Research (in Greek)).

— (1992). 'Insertion of Pontians in the Greek labour market', in K. Kassimati (ed.) *Pontian Immigrants from the Former Soviet Union* (Athens: General Secretariat of Greeks Abroad and Panteion University (in Greek)).

— (1993). 'Measuring the income effects of migrant remittances: a methodological approach applied to Greece', *Economic Development and Cultural Change*, October.

— (1994). 'Greek labor market adaptability in the EC integration', in L. Nicolau-Smokoviti and G. Szell (eds) *Participation, Organisational Effectiveness and Quality of Work Life in the Year 2000* (Frankfurt am Main: Peter Lang).

— (1995). 'Problems and policies regarding the socio-economic integration of returnees and foreign workers in Greece', *International Migration*: 155–96.

— (1997). 'Remitting behavior of temporary and permanent migrants: the case of Greeks in Germany and Australia', *Labour*, 11(3).

— (1998). 'La Migration comme moteur de l'intégration regionale: l'exemple des transferts de fonds', in OCDE, *Migrations, Libre-échange et Intégration Régionale dans Le Bassin Méditerranéen* (Paris: OCDE).

— (2001). 'Determinants and effects of migrant remittances: a survey', in S. Djajic (ed.) *International Migration: Trends, Policies and Economic Impact* (London: Routledge).

Kanetakis, M. (1990). 'Regional behaviour of migration', in N. Petropoulos (ed.) *Research Project of Migration–Repatriation*, vol. A (Athens: General Secretariat of Greeks Abroad (GSGA) (in Greek)).

Kassimati, K., Maos, B., Glytsos, N. et al. (1992). *Pontian Migrants from the Former Soviet Union: Social and Economic Accession* (Athens: Panteion University (in Greek)).

Katseli, L. T. (1990). 'Economic integration in the enlarged European Community: structural adjustment of the Greek economy', in C. Bliss and B. de Macedo (eds) *Unity with Diversity in the European Economy: The Community's Southern Frontier* (Cambridge: Cambridge University Press).

— (2001). 'The internationalisation of Southern European economies', in H. Gibson (ed.) *Economic Transformation, Democratisation and Integration into Europe: The Case of Southern Europe* (Hampshire: Palgrave Publishers).

Katseli, L. T. and Glytsos, N. P. (1989). 'Theoretical and empirical determinants of international labour mobility: a Greek-German perspective', in I. Gordon and A.P. Thirlwall (eds) *European Factor Mobility: Trends and Consequences* (London: Macmillan).

— and Markova, E. (1999). 'A South-Eastern model of structural adjustment through migration', PHARE ACE Project, P 96-6070-R, mimeo.

—, Magoula, H., and Markova, E. (2000). 'Educational choices for second generation migration: is there a role for a European educational policy?', Paper presented at the Euresco Conference on Migration and Development: Second Generation Immigrants and the Transition to Ethnic Minorities, Acquafredda di Maratea, Italy, 12–17 May, mimeo.

Lianos, T. (1980). 'Movement of Greek labor to Germany and return', *Greek Economic Review*, 2 (1).

— (1999). 'Illegal migrants to Greece and their choice of destination', Discussion Paper, 111 (Athens: University of Economics and Business).

Lianos, T. P., Sarris, A., and Katseli, L. (1996). 'Illegal immigration and local labour markets: the case of Northern Greece', *International Migration*, 34 (3).

Linardos-Rylmon, P. (1993). *Foreign Workers and Labor Market in Greece* (Athens: Institute of Labour Studies 1 (in Greek)).

Lucas, R. E. B. and Stark, O. (1985). 'Motivation to remit: evidence from Botswana', *Journal of Political Economy*, 93.

Manfrass, K. (1994). 'Migration policy in Germany', in OECD, *SOPEMI: Migration and Development* (Paris: OECD).

Markova, E. (2001a). 'The Economic performance of Bulgarian illegal and legalized immigrants in the Greek Labour Market', PhD Dissertation, Department of Economics, University of Athens.

— (2001b). 'Greek government policy response towards managing migration flows in the 1990s', mimeo.

— and Sarris, A. (1997). 'The performance of Bulgarian illegal immigrants in the Greek labor market', *South European Society and Politics*, 2 (2).

Maroulis, D. (1986). *Economic Development and the Structure of the Balance of Payments*, Studies Series, 18 (Athens: KEPE).

McLean, El. and Kousis, M. (1988). 'Returning migrant characteristics and labor market demand in Greece', *International Migration Review*, 22 (4).

Melas, G. K. and Delis, D. I. (1981). *Agricultural Wages and Employment in Agriculture* (Athens: Agricultural Bank of Greece (in Greek)).

OECD (1989, 1993, 1995, 1997). *SOPEMI* (Paris: OECD).

Papademetriou, D. G. (1984). 'Return to the Mediterranean littoral: policy agendas', in D. Kubat (ed.) *The Politics of Return: International Return Migration in Europe* (Rome: Centro Studi Emigrazione).

— (1985). 'Illusions and reality in international migration: migration and development in post World War II Greece', *International Migration*, 23(2).

Papademetriou, M. (1990). 'Occupational composition and mobility of Greek migrants and their participation in the labour market of host and home countries', in N. Petropoulos et al. (1990), vol. A.

Papanikos, G. (1991). 'Greek emigration to Canada: economic or political?', in J. Fossey (ed.) *Proceedings of the first International congress on the Hellenic Diaspora from Antiquity to Modern Times. From 1453 to Modern Times,* vol. II.

Patiniotis, N. (1991). *Dependence and Migration: The Case of Greece* (Athens: National Center for Social Research, (in Greek)).

Pelagidis, T. (1999). 'The Economic address of Greece in the Balkans', *Project* (Athens: Institute of International Economic Relations).

Petrinioti, X. (1994). *Migration towards Greece,* (Athens: Odysseas).

Petropoulos, N. (1998). 'Migration de retour et integration dans la societe Grecque: approche comparative migrants/non-migrants', in OECD, *Migrations, Libre-Echange et Integration Regionale dans le Bassin Mediterraneen,* Series Conference de l'OCDE (Paris: OECD).

— et al. (1992). *Research Project of Emigration–Repatriation of Greek Population,* vol. B (Athens: General Secretariat of Greeks Abroad (in Greek)).

Russell, S. S. (1997). 'International migrations: implications for the World Bank', HRO Working Paper, 54 (Washington, DC : World Bank).

Sapir, A. (1975). 'A Note on short-run Greek labour emigration to Germany', *Weltwirtschaftliches Archiv,* 111 (2).

Sarris, A. and Zografakis, S. (1999). 'A computable equilibrium assessment of the impact of illegal immigration on the Greek economy', *Journal of Population Economics,* 12.

Sava, N. (1989). 'The immigration of Greeks in West Germany and its consequences', *Economikos,* July (in Greek).

Schiff, M. (1996). 'South–North migration and trade: a survey', Policy Research Working Paper, 1696 (Washington DC : World Bank).

Schmidt, C. M. and Zimmermann, K. F. (1992). 'Migration pressure in Germany: past and future', in Klaus F. Zimmermann (ed.) *Migration and Economic Development* (Berlin: Springer-Verlag).

Schultz, T. W. (1961). 'Investment in human capital', *American Economic Review,* 51.

Sjaastad, L. A. (1962). 'The costs and returns of human migration', *Journal of Political Economy,* 10, Supplement.

Stahl, C. W. (1982). 'Labor migration and economic development', *International Migration Review,* 16.

Stark, Oded (1980). 'On the role of urban-to-rural remittances in rural development', *Journal of Development Studies,* 16.

— (1991). *The Migration of Labor* (Cambridge, MA: Basil Blackwell).

Swamy, G. (1981). 'International migrant workers' remittances: issues and prospects', World Bank Staff Working Paper 481 (Washington DC: World Bank).

Tinguy, Anne, de (1997). *Repatriation of Persons Following the Political Changes in Central and Eastern Europe*, Report to the Council of Europe, CDMG (97), 13E (Strasbourg : Council of Europe).

Tournakis, I. (1930). *International Migration Movements and Migration Policy*, Book I, Part 1 (Athens (in Greek)).

Tsamourgelis, Y. (1996). 'The impact of migration on employment, wages and unemployment of the host country: the case of Greece and Portugal', Paper presented at a CEPR Conference, Halkidiki, Greece, mimeo.

Unger, K. (1981). 'Greek emigration and return from West Germany', *Ekistics*, 290.

— (1984). 'Occupational profile of returnees in three Greek cities', in D. Kubat (ed.) *The Politics of Return: International Return Migration in Europe* (Rome: Centro Studi Emigrazione).

Unger, K. (1986). 'Return migration and regional characteristics: the case of Greece', in R. L. King (ed.) *Return Migration and Regional Economic Problems* (London: Croom Helm).

Venturini, A. (1994). 'Changing patterns of labour emigration in Southern Europe', Paper presented at the conference on Economic Change in Southern Europe, Social Science Research Council, mimeo.

Zolotas, X. (1966). *International Labor Migration and Economic Development* (Athens: Bank of Greece).

11. Migrations in Spain: Historical Background and Current Trends

Olympia Bover and Pilar Velilla

11.1. Preliminaries

11.1.1. Introduction

Spaniards have historically moved in large numbers in response to economic incentives. At the beginning of the twentieth century the outflow to South America was massive and later, from the 1950s through the 1960s and 1970s, emigration to Europe was impressive. At the same time, during the 1960s and 1970s, inter-regional mobility inside Spain was also substantial.

However, since the mid 1980s we witness in Spain what may seem a migration puzzle: despite persistent unemployment differentials, high unemployment regions are not any more net outmigration regions while rich and low unemployment ones are no longer net immigration regions. Since this is the currently important migration issue in Spain, in this chapter more attention will be devoted to internal migration and its determinants. Nevertheless, we also aim at describing the different migration episodes in recent Spanish history relying on various pieces of empirical work that have tried to identify the economic factors behind them.

In Section 11.2 we will examine migrations abroad, first for the 1900–50 period and then for the 1950–73 period. Spanish emigration at the beginning of the twentieth century was very significant and headed basically to South America. This mass migration was triggered by the crisis in the European agricultural sector but mainly by activity and growth in the destination countries. The First World War and the Spanish Civil War put an end to those flows. Over the 1960–73 period more than 100,000 workers

We wish to thank Manuel Arellano for useful comments and Samuel Bentolila for providing us with some of the data and for comments.

were emigrating per year to Germany, France, and Switzerland due to excess supply of labour in Spain, and the need for nonqualified workers in Europe. This outflow stopped with the 1973 crisis.

In Section 11.3 we will study internal migrations, distinguishing between two different inter-regional migration periods: 1960–82 and 1983 onwards. Inter-regional migrations during 1960–73 were very intense given strong economic growth with substantial regional imbalances at the time. People left rural and poor areas like Andalusia and Extremadura towards richer and more industrial zones like Madrid, Catalonia, or the Basque Country.

However, since the early 1980s and continuing during the 1990s net inter-regional flows declined substantially despite the persistence of regional differentials and sustained high unemployment. High aggregate unemployment is precisely to blame for this drop in inter-regional migration according to Bentolila and Blanchard (1990), Bentolila and Dolado (1991), and Bentolila (1997). However, after 1982 and up to 1999, despite persistent high aggregate unemployment, gross inter-regional migration flows have increased to levels above the ones prevailing in 1960–73, while net flows have dramatically fallen. Following the work of Antolin and Bover (1997) we present evidence supporting the idea that the profile of the migrant in the late 1980s and early 1990s has changed with respect to the 1960–73 period. People who move between regions are educated people, moving in search of cheaper housing and better quality of life. High regional unemployment does not trigger any more migrations to more prosperous regions. Registered unemployed (probably reflecting unemployed receiving benefits) living in regions with high unemployment rarely change regions.

In the second part of Section 11.3 we consider intra-regional migration, which has not received much attention so far, in spite of the fact that it has increased spectacularly since 1982 and represents 1.76 per cent of the population in 1999. Remarkably, this unprecedented increase has taken place in all the Spanish regions. These are obviously short-distance moves, nontheless, we believe it is interesting to study the forces that have driven such an increase. Results in this paper and in Bover and Arellano (2002) support the view that part of this increase in intra-regional migration responds to the increased employment opportunities in the services sector in all regions since the late 1970s, which has prompted (mainly within region) moves, mostly of skilled workers, towards larger towns where the new jobs are.

Finally, in Section 11.4 we will briefly discuss foreign immigration. For the first time in modern times, Spain is now a net immigration country.

However, foreign immigration is a small proportion of the population, but it is growing very fast. Understandably, therefore, it has not been a very important economic issue in Spain, in contrast to other countries, but it is rapidly gaining attention. In this section we will describe the work by Dolado et al. (1996) who study the impact on some labour market variables of the lifting of some restrictions on immigration policy in 1991.

Before turning to the main body of the chapter we would like to describe briefly which are the data at our disposal for studying migration issues in Spain.

11.1.2. Spanish Data Sources on Migrants

The official data for Spanish emigration abroad are widely agreed to under-represent the level of migration, but more dramatically so for the most recent period. Until 1971 an emigrant (or immigrant) was defined as a passenger travelling third class from (or to) a Spanish port. From 1972, only emigrants 'assisted' by the 'Instituto Español de Emigración' (IEE) (or estimated to be an immigrant by the IEE) were counted as emigrants (or immigrants). For the period 1882–1930 Sanchez Alonso (1995) constructed a new time series using data on destination countries and concluded that although in the official data the migration level is clearly under-estimated, they capture correctly the fluctuations and trends. Again, for the migrations to Europe during 1950–73, official data appear to capture fluctuations adequately when compared to data on Spanish immigrants from France and Germany.

Since the early 1980s there is much more precise information on foreign immigrants to Spain through the Residential Variation Data ('Estadística de Variaciones Residenciales') which has traditionally registered new arrivals (and departures) at the municipality level. For the earlier period there is census information and information on foreign residents from the Ministry of the Interior.

To study internal migrations in Spain there are two main data sources aside from census data. The first one is the Residential Variation Data we mentioned above. Its drawback is the very scarce information on the characteristics of the migrants. On the other hand it is the only source on migration flows inside Spain since the 1960s and has therefore being the main source for work on aggregate internal migration. It should be noted that around the years when the municipal census was renewed, migrations dropped artificially because, during the months the census takes place, migrants were considered as new registers to the census and not as immigrants.[1] In this chapter we have interpolated the values for those years when referring to series from this source. The second source is the Migration Survey, included in the second quarters of the Labour Force Survey, which takes as migrants those persons whose municipality of residence is different from the one a year before. This information is very rich in individual characteristics but is available only since 1987, the year in which a general break in the Labour Force Survey methodology took place. Due to the short time span, together with the small number of migrants and the sample size, the Migration Survey may be subject to sampling errors for certain purposes. From 1980 to 1986 the Internal Migrations Survey was conducted, also as part of the Labour Force Survey. In contrast to the new Migration Survey which takes place only every second quarter, this would take place every quarter.

11.2. Mass Migrations Abroad (1900–73)

11.2.1. The South American Experience and its Decline (1900–50)

After having pioneered mass migration to America in the sixteenth century, Spain was, together with Italy and Portugal, a latecomer to the European mass migrations of the last part of the nineteenth century. However, when Spanish emigration started at the beginning of the twentieth century (see Figure 11.1) it grew distinctively more than in the rest of the Latin countries. Between 1900 and 1913, the rate of growth of Spanish emigration was almost 12 per cent, compared to 4.7 per cent for Italy and 9.9 per cent for Portugal (see Sanchez Alonso 1995). The chosen destinations were overwhelmingly South-American countries (Argentina, Brazil, Cuba, and Uruguay particularly) and also North Africa (Argelia). Note, however, that, in common with other Latin countries, return migration was significant (see Figure 11.1) and higher than for previous mass migrations from Northern Europe (see Hatton and Williamson 1994).

Among the factors that may explain this important emigration in the early 1900s, it has often been cited how the arrival of agricultural products (cereals particularly) from America triggered a crisis in the European agricultural sector, which was unable to compete. This crisis had significant effects on the rural population, inducing it to migrate. Like in most European countries, tariff barriers were introduced. Additionally, a depreciated exchange rate played an extra protectionist role in Spain

---

[1] Years ending in 1 or 6 usually.

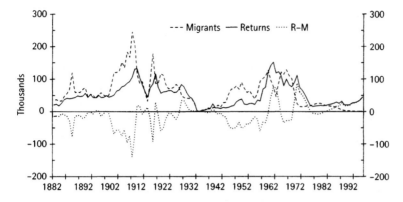

Figure 11.1. Spanish emigration, 1882–2000
Source: Ministry of Labour and Social Affairs.

(see Sanchez Alonso 1995). This double protection kept people attached to their land for a while, through an artificially sustained agriculture. Therefore, when the peseta started appreciating in 1903–4 the increase in migration was spectacular. However, even more important than the internal push factors was economic activity and growth in the destination countries. As an example, in her econometric work Sanchez Alonso (1995) shows how the building sector in Argentina, with a high demand of non-qualified workers, is the most influential factor in Spanish migration during the period 1882–1913, together with fluctuations in Argentina's GDP. On the basis of their econometric evidence, Hatton and Williamson (1994) emphasize the widening of the wage gap between Spain and the destination countries, and, more generally, the much more pronounced economic failure at home relative to other countries, as the main force driving the rise in Spanish emigration at the time. They note that, in contrast with other Latin countries, the increase in emigration did not follow from an increase in the proportion of the population in prime emigration age group which, on the contrary, experienced a fall in Spain. At the time, migration legislation in Spain was basically of a protective nature towards the emigrants (both the 1853 Order and the 1907 Law).[2]

However, migrants in the early twentieth century in Spain came from a reduced number of regions (namely Galicia, Asturias, and the Canary Islands) and hence, to complete the aggregate factors at play, attention should be paid to regional differences as well. Sanchez Alonso (1995) in a

[2] A full historical index on emigration legislation in Spain is provided as an annex in *Revista de economia y sociologia del trabajo*, September 1990, n1° 8–9, 164–240.

cross-section analysis for 49 Spanish provinces in 1911–13 stresses some factors that would explain why some regions stayed out of that migration process. From her results migration would be undertaken in regions where the land surface per agricultural worker was small and also where the increase in literacy allowed access to information. Agricultural wages played a double role. On the one hand, high wage levels in the preceding years induced migration by allowing people to afford the cost of migrating, while wage increases had the expected negative effect on migration. Finally, differences in urbanization across provinces also played a role. Developed cities in some provinces stood as an alternative to migration abroad.

The First World War brought to a halt migration towards those that had been so far the traditional destinations. However, important flows of migrants headed towards France which was very much in need of workers given the war. These migrations declined in the second part of the 1920s due to economic recession in France. On the other hand, at that time we should mention that there was an increase in internal migrations given Spain's role as an international supplier of various goods during the war period. Eventually, while for the period 1901–10, 61 per cent of migrants went abroad, for 1921 to 1930, only 6 per cent did so.

The Spanish Civil War was the last blow to migration outwards. However, although migrations for economic reasons diminished, migrations for political reasons were notorious. In Spain, the Civil War induced a revival of rural activity, with the number of people working in agriculture increasing between 1930 and 1940. However, this meant a surplus of badly paid people in agriculture which would lead eventually to a massive exodus from the rural areas during the 1940s, and continuing through the 1950s and 1960s.

11.2.2. The European Experience (1950–73)

The flow of workers from agriculture to manufacturing intensified due to the growing importance of the manufacturing sector and to the increase in agricultural mechanization. It was a period of very high migration both abroad and inside Spain. During the 1950s alone a million workers left agriculture (seventeen times more than during the previous decade).

Migrants to other countries started heading to South America again but restrictive immigration policies against nonqualified workers stopped migration to those countries in the second part of the 1940s. France, short of workers after the European and the Argelian wars attracted Spanish emigrants, together with Germany and Switzerland, over the 1960s and early 1970s. Over that period it is estimated that more than 100,000 workers per year were emigrating to France, Germany, and Switzerland. On average, from 1962 to 1970, around 42 per cent of the Spanish migrants to Europe were heading to Germany, 23 per cent to France, and 28 per cent to Switzerland. In Spain these migrations were particularly welcomed as a source of finance for imports. Transfers from migrants abroad covered between 17 and 30 per cent of the trade deficit over 1960–73 (see Rodenas 1994*b*). In 1956 the Spanish Migration Institute was created and it acted as the basic instrument of employment policy at the time. All along, the period, as we can see in Figure 11.1, return migration was significant. An indication of the 'temporary' nature of migrations abroad could be the very

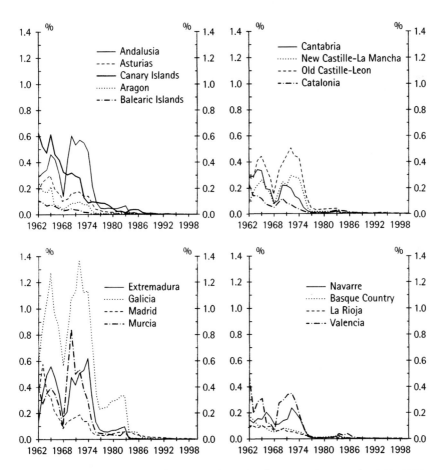

Figure 11.2. Spanish emigration by origin region (in per capita terms), 1962–2000
Source: Spanish Statistical Yearbook, Migrations by regions, and Residential Variations (INE).

high proportion of males, around 80 per cent, both during this period to Europe and to America at the beginning of the century.[3]

The sharp drop in the migration series in 1967 corresponds to the German economic recession of 1967–8. But this was shortlived and emigration to Europe picked up again. However, from 1973 emigration abroad ceased to be a significant phenomenon. Indeed, the 1973 crisis hit the destination countries as well. Furthermore, technological progress reduced their need for manual workers. Finally, the economic gap between Spain and Europe would diminish over the 1970s and 1980s. Antolin (1992) using French and German data on Spanish immigrants for the years 1960 to 1988 shows how migration over this period responded as expected to differentials (between Spain and Germany and France) in income, wages, housing costs, and unemployment, as well as to the unemployment rate in the destination countries.

Migration abroad was a much more relevant phenomenon in certain regions (see Figure 11.2). In Galicia, *per capita* emigration was double than in any of the also poor and heavily migrant regions (e.g. Andalusia and Extremadura).

11.3. Internal Migrations

11.3.1. Inter-Regional Migrations (1960–82)

The period from 1960 to 1973 is seen as a very intensive period for internal migration as well as for emigration abroad. It was a period of strong economic growth but with very substantial regional differentials. People left rural and poor areas towards the richer industrial towns. As we can see in Figure 11.3, Andalusia, New Castile-La Mancha, Old Castile-Leon, and Extremadura were net emigration regions, while Catalonia, Madrid, and the Basque Country[4] were net immigration ones (see Table 11.1 for regional unemployment rates).

Santillana (1981) analyses the economic determinants of migrations between Spanish provinces[5] for different years during the 1960–70 period.

---

[3] The existence of difficulties by the destination countries in Europe in accepting dependants might have induced some illegal migration of women and children.

[4] Note that Valencia, despite appearing as a net immigration region, had a substantial emigration abroad at the time.

[5] Continental Spain is administratively divided into 17 regions (or 'Comunidades Autónomas') and fifty provinces.

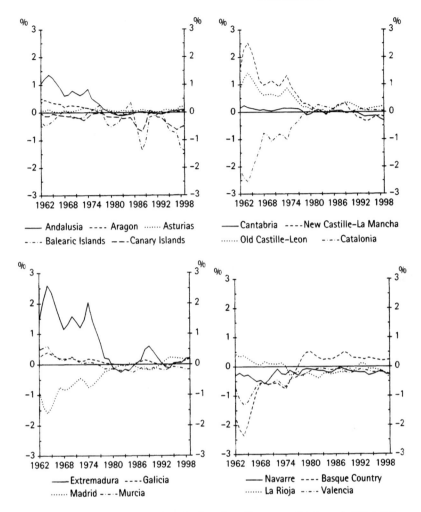

Figure 11.3. Net inter-regional migrations (in per capita terms), 1962–99
Source: Spanish Statistical Yearbook, Migrations by regions, and Residential Variations (INE).

In particular, his dependent variable is defined as the number of migrants from province i to province j and the explanatory variables capture characteristics of both the origin and the destination provinces. The estimated effects of these explanatory variables go in the expected direction. The stock of previous migrants and distance to destination confirm the importance of social interactions and uncertainty in the decision of migrating. Importantly, people respond by migrating to wage and employment opportunities, measured by income, size of the labour market and employment. Along the same lines, Rodenas (1994*a*) studies the

Table 11.1. Regional unemployment rates

	1962	1971	1975	1980	1985	1990	1995	2000
Andalusia	3.4	4.3	13.5	17.5	29.7	25.6	33.9	24.5
Aragon	0.2	1.4	2.8	8.6	17.6	9.5	15.9	7.2
Asturias	0.3	1.0	2.9	8.5	18.4	17.3	20.2	17.0
Balearic Islands	0.4	0.3	2.3	7.7	13.9	10.5	14.3	6.3
Canary Islands	1.1	0.7	9.3	12.3	25.7	23.0	23.7	13.5
Cantabria	0.5	1.6	2.7	7.3	15.5	16.8	22.3	13.7
New Castile-La Mancha	0.5	1.1	8.5	10.6	16.6	13.0	20.2	12.6
Old Castile-Leon	0.3	1.4	3.0	8.4	18.1	15.3	20.5	13.9
Catalonia	0.8	1.2	2.8	12.0	22.7	12.7	19.9	8.8
Valencia	1.2	1.9	3.7	9.7	20.8	14.3	22.4	11.6
Extremadura	1.7	2.7	7.6	14.8	27.3	24.5	30.6	23.6
Galicia	0.3	0.8	4.4	4.8	12.8	12.0	17.6	14.8
Madrid	1.1	2.4	4.5	12.9	22.1	12.5	20.9	11.7
Murcia	1.4	5.2	8.0	10.0	20.1	15.8	23.7	12.8
Navarra	0.1	1.9	5.3	11.6	18.9	11.7	12.9	5.9
Basque Country	0.2	0.7	2.4	12.8	23.6	18.8	23.0	12.2
La Rioja	0.3	0.4	1.6	5.1	17.3	8.4	16.1	8.1
NATIONAL	1.4	1.9	5.6	11.4	21.6	16.2	22.9	14.1

Source: Labour Force Survey (INE) and Banco Bilbao Vizcaya.

determinants of region to region migration for 1973 and her results confirm the relevance of distance and previous migration stock and the expected effect of wage and employment differentials on migration.

During the late 1970s and early 1980s there was a considerable decline in inter-regional migration in Spain (see Figure 11.4). From the 0.62 per cent average during the 1962–73 period, with a 0.91 per cent peak in 1964, it declined to its through in 1982, 0.32 per cent. This decline cannot be justified in terms of reductions in differentials across regions. Although wage differentials have declined (see Bentolila and Dolado 1992), the absolute differences in unemployment rates across regions have greatly increased over the period, as reported by Bentolila and Dolado (1992). Bentolila and Blanchard (1990) argued that it is the rise in overall unemployment that has been responsible for inhibiting labour mobility in Spain.[6] On this basis, Bentolila and Dolado (1991) estimated an econometric model of inter-regional migration using data from 1964 to 1986. They

---

[6] Although causation here may go both ways, since the decrease in labour mobility is also seen as resulting in an increase in equilibrium unemployment.

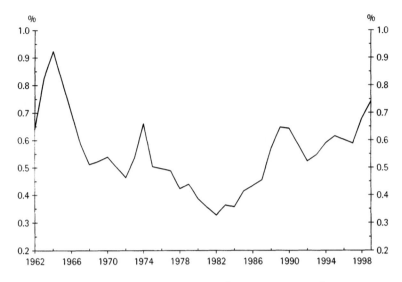

Figure 11.4. Inter-regional migrations (in per capita terms), 1962–99
Source: Spanish Statistical Yearbook, Migrations by regions, and Residential Variations (INE).

chose net migration as their explanatory variable because they consider net and gross flows to be very similar over that period. In order to capture the effect of the overall unemployment rate, they allow for their regression coefficient to depend inversely on the level of the unemployment rate. They find that net inter-regional migration responds to unemployment and wage differentials but with long lags and low elasticities. In particular, their estimate of the unemployment differential elasticity depends inversely on the aggregate unemployment rate, both in the short and in the long run.

11.3.2. Inter-Regional Migration (1983–99)

Since 1982, after the prolonged fall of the earlier years and despite consistently high aggregate unemployment rates, gross inter-regional migrations started to increase. In fact, for 1999 the gross inter-regional per capita migration rate is at 0.74 per cent higher than the 1962–73 average (see Figure 11.4). However, as Bentolila (1997) reports, absolute net migration[7] fell by 90 per cent from 1962–4 to 1990–4. Additionally, in contrast to the pattern in the previous two decades, following the expansion of the welfare state, the traditionally poor and high unemployment regions (Andalusia and Extremadura) have become net immigration regions, while the better-off ones (like Madrid and Catalonia) have become net

---

[7] Absolute net migration taken as the sum of the absolute values of net inflows to regions divided by population.

outmigration regions. Furthermore, for the period 1987–91, only 31.2 per cent of the unemployed would accept a job implying a change of residence.[8] In this section, following the work of Antolin and Bover (1997) we will explain which have been the factors behind the migration decision in the late 1980s and early 1990s in Spain, what is it that has made people stay in or move from regions in Spain. Indeed, since the early 1980s and compared with the 1960–73 period it is not so much the number of inter-regional migrants that has changed but their profile.

In Antolin and Bover (1997) the focus is on identifying which regional economic factors influence male migration decisions, taking into account personal characteristics. Individual data from the Labour Force Survey are used, pooling cross-sections from 1987 to 1991. The sample includes men, aged 16 to 70, who are in the labour force both at the time of the survey and a year before. Women were excluded because their migration behaviour could be quite different from that of men and, in particular, they are more likely to move for family reasons. In that paper only push factors from the origin region (and differentials with respect to the national average) were considered due to the small number of inter-regional migrants in the sample. The proportion of migrants is 0.295 per cent (664 out of 224,714 individuals). This is a very small probability. With the Residential Variation Data the probability for the whole population is 0.58 per cent. One possible reason for the discrepancy is that the Labour Force Survey compares the place of residence with the one a year before and therefore it may miss other moves within the year. However, Pissarides and Wadsworth (1989) have a 1.2 per cent of migrants using a single cross-section of the British Labour Force Survey.

One contribution of Antolin and Bover (1997) is the emphasis on the importance of interactions between individual characteristics and regional variables. Personal characteristics not only have an important direct effect on migration but also alter the effect of regional economic variables on migration. Many migration studies report a lack of significance of area economic variables, in particular unemployment, in explaining migration (Hughes and McCormick 1989; Pissarides and Wadsworth 1989; Greenwood 1975, 1985). Da Vanzo (1978) finds, for the US, that unemployment is relevant only for unemployed persons. For Spain it turned out to be very important to distinguish between persons that are registered as unemployed at the Official Employment Office (INEM) and the unregistered unemployed.

---

[8] Information from the Labour Force Surveys.

We reproduce in Table 11.2 the final estimated inter-regional migration equation from Antolin and Bover (1997) and the predicted probabilities in Table 11.3. Only nonregistered unemployed respond to their own unemployment. Without distinguishing by the registration variable, being unemployed did not appear to be significant for the migration decision. Employed people have a higher probability of migrating than the registered unemployed but lower than the unregistered unemployed. Among the employed most move probably with jobs (on that point see also Gil and Jimeno 1993). That would explain the much higher probability of public sector employees.

One reason by which registered people tend to migrate less is because of unemployment benefits since registration is a necessary condition for receiving benefits and the official register is not seen to perform well as an employment agency. Furthermore, registration is also found to alter the effect of regional unemployment.[9] Higher than average unemployment in the individual's region will only have a positive effect on the probability of migration if the person is a nonregistered unemployed but will have an important negative effect if the person is registered. Some estimates in Antolin and Bover (1993) suggest different impacts on the same lines for the national unemployment rate, a negative effect for registered unemployed, a barely significant positive effect for unregistered unemployed, and no effect for the employed.

Some of the other personal characteristics have effects on migration that are worth mentioning. Being single and not head of household reduces significantly the probability of migration, which reflects the strong family bonds in Spain. On the contrary, higher education does not only increase directly the probability of migrating but individuals with higher education tend to be sensitive to their region's unemployment. The positive effect of education on migration is important and it is an indication of the different profile of migrants as compared to the 1960–73 period.

House prices are among the most important items in the cost-of-living calculations when migration is envisaged. Furthermore, substantial increases took place in the second half of the 1980s in some of the Spanish regions. In Antolin and Bover (1997), given that owner-occupied housing involves an investment decision, an asymmetric effect of house price differentials was allowed for.[10] The results show that people who would

---

[9] Rodenas (1994a) finds a positive effect on migration of the unemployment in the destination region using aggregate inter-regional data for 1985 and 1989 (but not for 1973).
[10] Owner occupation is around 82 per cent in Spain and includes subsidized housing.

Table 11.2. Final estimated migration equation using pooled cross-sections for 1987–91[1]

	logit
Constant[2]	−4.382 (20.58)[3]
Aged 16 to 24	0.404 (2.72)
Aged 25 to 34	0.512 (4.83)
Aged 50 to 70	−1.035 (6.14)
Primary education	−0.451 (5.15)
Higher education	0.416 (3.23)
Children	−1.027 (10.07)
Not head of household, single (nhhs)	−1.331 (11.76)
Married with working wife	−0.630 (4.76)
Unemployed	0.587 (2.76)
Registered at INEM	−1.511 (6.07)
Tenure ≥ 3 years	−0.980 (9.92)
Employee in public sector	1.366 (8.01)
Employee in private sector	0.945 (6.04)
Agriculture	−0.719 (3.33)
Industry	−0.891 (5.94)
Services	−0.238 (1.96)
Unemployment differential	−0.121 (0.08)
Unempl.diff. *unemployed	3.698 (1.59)
Unempl.diff. *registered	−13.641 (2.85)
Unempl.diff. *higher education	4.055 (1.61)
Unempl.diff. *children	−5.210 (2.81)
Unempl.diff. *nhhs	−8.367 (4.01)
Participation rate growth differential	0.125 (4.56)
Partic. rate growth differential*higher education	−0.106 (1.43)
House price differential	0.665 (3.32)
House price differential	1.698 (6.12)
Real Wage differential	2.426 (5.34)
D88	−0.136 (1.09)
D89	−0.359 (2.73)
D90	−0.261 (2.08)
D91	−0.343 (2.72)
Association of predicted prob. and observed responses	
concordant	73.8%
tied	14.1%
− log likelihood	3970.70

Notes:
[1] Sample size = 224,714. Migration frequency = 0.295%.
[2] the constant term will determine the probability of migrating for individuals with the following characteristics: head of household single or married to nonworking wife (or not head, but married), aged between 35 and 49, with either no schooling or secondary education, no children, self-employed in the construction sector with less than three years in the current job, and living in a hypothetical region where the value of the relevant regional variables equals the national average.
[3] t-ratios in brackets.
Source: Antolin and Bover (1997).

Table 11.3. Predicted probabilities (%)

	Employed				Unemployed	
	Agriculture	Construction	Industry	Services	Registered	Not registered
Standard[1]	0.35	0.69	0.28	0.55	0.30	1.30
BUT						
Age 35–49	0.21	0.41	0.17	0.33	0.18	0.78
Working wife	0.18	0.37	0.15	0.29	0.16	0.69
Children	0.13	0.25	0.10	0.20	0.11	0.47
Not head, single	0.09	0.18	0.07	0.14	0.08	0.34
Higher education	0.82	1.63	0.67	1.29	0.70	3.02
Tenure <3 years	0.91	1.80	0.75	1.43	–	–
Self-employed	0.14	0.27	0.11	0.22	–	–
REGIONAL DIFFERENTIALS						
House Prices = (i)+0.5235 (e.g. Madrid 1989)	1.07	2.11	0.88	1.68	0.91	3.90
(ii) – 0.3842 (e.g. Aragon 1989)	0.47	0.94	0.39	0.75	0.40	1.76
Participation rate of change *100 = 1.3 (e.g. Catalonia 1989)	0.41	0.82	0.34	0.65	0.35	1.53
Unemployment rate = 0.1 (eg. Andalusia 1989)	0.35	0.69	0.28	0.55	0.11	1.85

Notes:
[1] Standard: head of household, age 25–34, wife not working, no children, primary education, employee private sector, tenure over three years, average region.
Source: Antolin and Bover (1997).

normally migrate are more likely to do so if they lived in a region with above-average house prices. This ties up with the effect of real wage differentials. Real wage differentials show the opposite sign to what one would expect if wage differentials were to correct regional disequilibria by encouraging migration from low-wage regions.[11] An appealing explanation is the quality-of-life motive: people leaving high-wage regions because of an increased demand for a better quality of life, once a certain income threshold is reached (Greenwood 1985).

The conclusion in that study is that reasons that make people migrate to another region in Spain in the 1980s and early 1990s are probably different from the reasons that made people move in the 1960s and 1970s. People who move now between regions are people with higher education and they seem to do so in search of cheaper housing, better quality of life,

[11] Also found by Rodenas (1994a) in her 1985 estimation.

and perhaps professional promotion.[12] High regional unemployment or own unemployment do not trigger substantial migration from people in poor regions. Unemployment will only increase the probability of migration if the individual has higher education or is unemployed and not registered as such. Registered unemployed with low education and living in high unemployment regions have the lowest probability of moving to another region.

These factors seem to be behind what we observe in Figures 11.5 and 11.6, namely that people are leaving regions like Madrid, Catalonia, or the Basque Country and staying in or moving to regions like Andalusia or Extremadura.

11.3.3. Intra-Regional Migration, 1983–99

Until the early 1980s inter-regional migration and total internal migration moved together. Per capita intra-regional migration was from 1967 higher than inter-regional migration, but it evolved around a more or less constant level since 1962 until 1982. However, from 1982 this has changed dramatically, but has surprisingly not received much attention (it was first noted by Olano 1990). As we can see in Figure 11.7, intra-regional migration has been climbing very rapidly since 1982 and was in 1999 at an all-time high: 1.76 per cent, taking overall internal migrations at their highest level ever and representing over 70 per cent of them. Most of these moves are obviously short-distance (intra-provinces) ones (see Figure 11.7) but it is interesting to try and see what are the forces behind such a steady and unprecedented increase in short distance moves. It is noteworthy that this increase in intra-regional movements is a feature shared by all the Spanish regions (see Figure 11.8). Furthermore, it has been accompanied by an important movement from rural areas to cities, as can be seen in Table 11.4 where we decompose intra-regional migration according to size of town of origin and destination.

Below we associate part of the increase in intra-regional migration with changes in the composition and location of employment. In particular, employment opportunities have increased substantially in the services industry since the late 1970s. Employment in services climbed from 42 per cent in 1977 to 62 per cent in 1999. While from 1964 to 1978 it grew at an annual rate of 0.79 per cent, from 1980 to 1993 the annual rate was

---

[12] They do not seem to reflect return migrations of individuals who originally migrated from the poor regions of origin in the 1960s and 1970s.

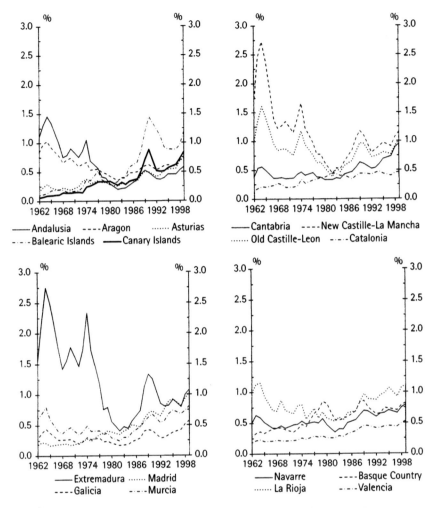

Figure 11.5. Inter-regional migrations: emigrants (in per capita terms), 1962–99
Source: Spanish Statistical Yearbook, Migrations by regions, and Residential Variations (INE).

1.12 per cent, the highest among OECD countries together with Portugal. This increase in the service share of employment has taken place in all regions, opening up new employment opportunities inside the regions but usually in large towns.

In Table 11.5 we report some results on the estimation of per capita intra-regional migration equations, using pooled data for the seventeen Spanish regions, over the 1978 to 1995 period. As explanatory variables we include regional unemployment, regional real house prices, as well as

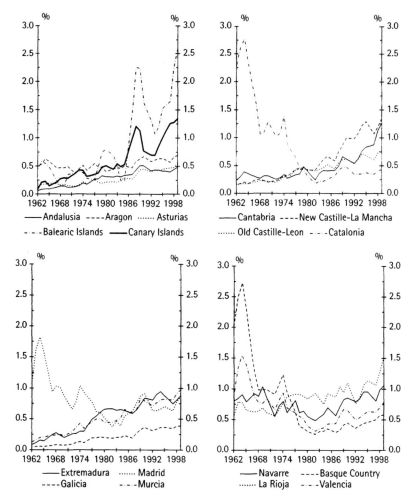

Figure 11.6. Inter-regional migrations: immigrants (in per capita terms), 1962–99
Source: Spanish Statistical Yearbook, Migrations by regions, and Residential Variations (INE).

the percentage of employment in the services sector in the region.[13] All explanatory variables refer to $t - 1$.

The effects of the region's unemployment and house prices change over our sample period. They are both negative at the beginning and positive

---

[13] We have constructed a regional house price variable for our sample period from regional housing CPI data available for the whole period (but not comparable in levels across regions) and the level regional house prices data from 'Sociedad de Tasación', available since 1985. The resulting variable has been deflated by the national general CPI and will therefore be capturing other differences in cost of living across regions aside from house prices.

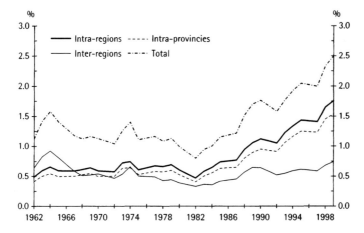

Figure 11.7. Intra-regional migrations (in per capita terms), 1962–99
Source: Spanish Statistical Yearbook, Migrations by regions, and Residential Variations (INE).

later. We model these varying effects by allowing the coefficients of these variables to vary with log t and its square.[14] This change in the effect of the economic variables after the mid-1980s may be part of the explanation of the increase in intra-regional moves. For instance, high unemployment in the region would not induce moves within the region during the 1960s and 1970s; it would rather prompt migration to other regions with lower unemployment (see results cited in previous section, e.g. Rodenas 1994*a*). After the large increase in the service sector, however, high unemployment may be inducing people to move within their own region, probably to larger towns. It would have been nicer to be able to explain these across time variations in the effect of regional unemployment and house prices with economic variables, but tried and failed, probably due to the lack of sufficient information in our dataset.

As for the proportion of employment in the service industry, we obtain an important and significant effect, which is stable along our sample period. We do not include variables like wages due to the impossibility to obtain real measures of these variables that are comparable across regions. We have, however, included the log of real regional wages in the specification that includes regional dummies to see if it helped explain the time-series evolution of intra-regional migration but it was not significant.[15]

---

[14] Similar results were obtained using bounded trends of the form log $(1+T/t)$ and $[\log (1+T/t)]^2$ where T is the total number of periods in the sample.

[15] Note that in this case the different unobservable base year CPI levels in each region would be captured by the regional dummies.

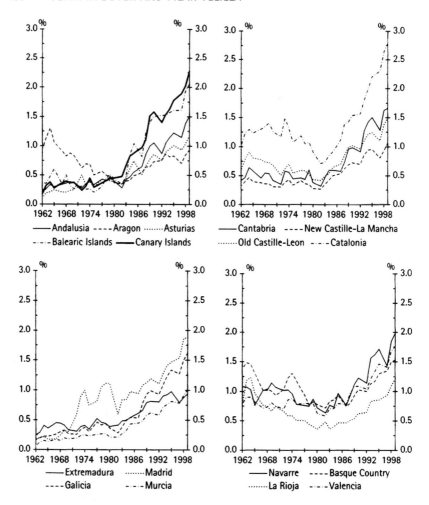

Figure 11.8. Intra-regional migrations (in per capita terms), 1962–99
Source: Spanish Statistical Yearbook, Migrations by regions, and Residential Variations (INE).

Bover and Arellano (2002) use individual migrants records from the Residential Variations Data, for the years 1988, 1989, 1990 and 1992, to study the determinants of within region moves distinguishing by size of town of origin and destination.[16] The effect of the proportion of regional employment in the service sector is found to double the probability of moving to large towns when the share of services is changed from the

---

[16] Identification is achieved by comparing the distribution of characteristics of the migrants with the distribution of characteristics in the population.

Table 11.4. Intra-regional migration, by size of town of origin and destination
(as a percentage of the population in the corresponding size of town of residence)
Men aged 20 to 64

Origin	Destination			Total
	Small	Medium	Large	
1988				
Small[1]	0.49	0.46	0.29	1.24
Medium	0.31	0.45	0.30	1.06
Large	0.29	0.43	0.25	0.97
1995				
Small	0.74	0.71	0.45	1.90
Medium	0.57	0.68	0.45	1.70
Large	0.58	0.75	0.32	1.65

[1] Small, medium and large are defined as less than 10,000 inhabitants, between 10 and 100 thousand inhabitants, and over 100,000 inhabitants, respectively.
Source: Authors' calculations from Residential Variations Individual data and Labour Force Survey.

Table 11.5. Equations for intra-regional migration using pooled data for the
17 Spanish regions, over the 1979–95 period

Dependent variable: Per capita intra-regional migration	Pooled OLS	Pooled OLS with regional dummies
Unemployment rate$_{(t-1)}$	−0.023 (3.14)[1]	−0.020 (2.68)
Unempl. rate$_{(t-1)}$ * log t	0.010 (3.24)	0.009 (3.14)
Real house prices$_{(t-1)}$	0.003 (5.28)	0.001 (0.67)
Real house prices$_{(t-1)}$ * log t	−0.003 (5.88)	−0.002 (5.64)
Real house prices$_{(t-1)}$ * (log t)^2	0.001 (5.59)	0.001 (5.36)
Services as a proportion of total employment (t − 1)	0.013 (5.80)	0.021 (4.50)
Regional dummies	no	yes
R2	0.70	0.98
Test for autocorrelation^2	−0.001 (.02)	−0.009 (.19)

Notes:
[1] t-ratios in brackets, from heteroskedasticity consistent standard errors.
[2] As a test for autocorrelation we report the coefficient and the t-ratio of the lagged residuals in a regression of the residuals on lagged residuals and the rest of the variables in the original equation.
Source: Authors' calculations from Residential Variations, Labour Force Survey (INE), and Sociedad de Tasación.

average to the maximum value observed in the sample period and reaches its highest value for the more educated. House prices are also found to have a very sizeable effect on within region migration but in the opposite direction, pushing people from larger cities towards smaller towns, where house prices are usually lower. House prices at their peak treble the probability of these large to smaller moves, as compared to mean value house prices.

The available empirical evidence therefore supports the view that part of the unprecedented increase in intra-regional migration in all Spanish regions is in response to the increased employment opportunities in the services sector in all regions since the late 1970s, which has prompted moves, mostly of skilled workers, towards larger towns where the new jobs are.

In conclusion, our picture about internal migration in Spain is that in contrast to the extended view of low mobility, many Spaniards move nowadays in response to economic incentives, in particular, in search of better employment prospects. However, those who move are different from the low educated, manual worker migrants of the 1960s and 1970s. Furthermore, these moves in search of better employment prospects are not necessarily inter-regional moves, as they used to be, since employment opportunities in the services, nonmanual sector have increased substantially within all regions, but mainly in large towns.

11.4. Foreign Immigration

Until the late 1980s the number of foreign immigrants per year was less than 10,000, which amounts to less than 0.02 per cent of the population (see Figure 11.9). Numbers increasing very rapidly subsequently, but still the percentage over the population of foreign immigrants was 0.25 per cent in 1999. These numbers refer to legal immigrants and not much information is available on illegal migration. Izquierdo (1992) estimates the number of illegal immigrants in 1989 to be between 18 and 28 per cent of the legal ones.[17] In Figure 11.10 the total number of foreign residents in Spain is represented. Again we can see a substantial rise from the mid-1980s and nowadays they account for 2.0 per cent of the population. Most foreign immigrants have traditionally come from Europe and Latin

---

[17] Some information on illegal migrants and their characteristics could be also found in that reference, as well as explanations about legislation on residence and work permits in Spain.

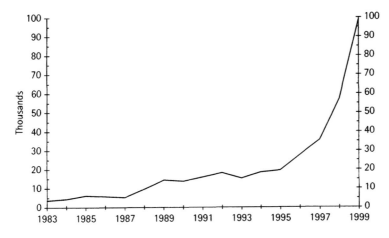

Figure 11.9. Foreign immigration, 1983–99
Source: Residential Variations (INE).

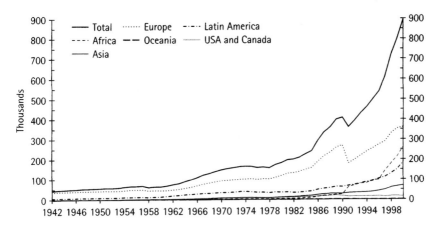

Figure 11.10. Foreign residents in Spain: total and by origin, 1942–2000
Source: Ministry of Interior.

America, although from the end of the 1980s immigration from Africa has increased more than from other parts of the world and accounts in 1999 for around 20 per cent of the total (see Figure 11.11). The preferred destinations are mainly Catalonia and Madrid followed well behind by Andalusia and Valencia.

Given this situation, not much effort has been devoted so far to study the labour market consequences of foreign migration in Spain but more research will be needed. There is, however, a study by Dolado, Jimeno, and Duce (1996) where they try to measure the effects on the labour market of

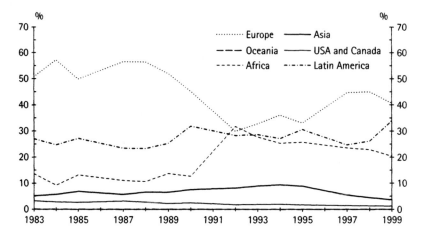

Figure 11.11. Foreign immigrants, by origin, as a percentage of the total, 1983–99
Source: Residential Variations (INE).

an increase in the number of work permits following the lift of some restrictions on immigration policy in 1991. In that work, along the lines of Altonji and Card (1991) and using data disaggregated at the provincial level (50 provinces), they regress the change between 1990 and 1992 of the variable of interest (total and unskilled employment, skilled and unskilled wages) against the change over the same period in the number of work permits (from the Ministry of Employment) and in the other conditioning variables. For all the variables of interest the reservation wage (as the minimum bargained wage in each province) and the sectoral composition of employment in each province are included as control variables. As additional controls, they use the ratio of skilled to unskilled wages for the total employment equation and the provincial unemployment rate for the rest. The equations are estimated both by OLS and by instrumenting using lagged unemployment and migration changes. They find a small positive elasticity for wages and total employment to the migration change, and a negative one for unskilled employment. It should be noted, however, that the number of work permits variable over that period is mostly the result of policy action and does not reflect any underlying evolution of the number of foreign workers. Furthermore, it is not clear that the sort of endogeneity present in these equations could be solved using lagged values of the endogenous variables.

In any case, and to summarize this section, we should note that in Spain the number of work permits has until now accounted at the most for 1.5 per cent of employment.

References

Altonji, J. and Card, D. (1991). 'The effects of immigration on the labour market outcomes of natives', in J. Abowd and R. Freeman (eds) *Immigration, Trade, and the Labor Market* (Chicago: University of Chicago Press).

Antolin, P. (1992). 'Labour market and international migration flows: the case of Spain (1960-1988)', IVIE Discussion Paper, 9209.

— and Bover, O. (1993). 'Regional migration in Spain: the effect of personal characteristics and of unemployment, wage and house price differentials using pooled cross-sections', Banco de España Working Paper 9318, Madrid.

— (1997). 'Regional migration in Spain: the effect of personal characteristics and of unemployment, wage, and house price differentials using pooled cross-sections', *Oxford Bulletin of Economics and Statistics*, 59(2): 215-35.

Bentolila, S. (1997). 'Sticky labour in Spanish regions', *European Economic Review*, 41: 591-8.

— and Dolado, J. J. (1991). 'Mismatch and internal migration in Spain 1962-86', in F. Padoa Schioppa (ed.) *Mismatch and Labour Mobility* (Cambridge: Cambridge University Press).

— and Blanchard, O. (1990). 'Spanish unemployment', *Economic Policy*, 10: 233-65.

Bover, O. and Arellano, M. (2002). 'Learning about migration decisions from the migrants: an exercise in endogenous sampling and complementary datasets', *Journal of Population Economics*, 15: 357-80.

Da Vanzo, J. (1978). 'Does unemployment affect migration? Evidence from microdata', *Review of Economics and Statistics*, 60: 504-14.

Dolado, J. J., Jimeno, J., and Duce, R. (1996). 'The effects of migration on the relative demand of skilled versus unskilled labour: evidence from Spain', FEDEA Working Paper 9620, Madrid.

Gil, L. and Jimeno, J. (1993). 'The determinants of labour mobility in Spain: who are the migrants?', FEDEA Working Paper 9305, Madrid.

Greenwood, M. J. (1975). 'Research on internal migration in the United States: a survey', *Journal of Economic Literature*, 13: 397-433.

— (1985). 'Human migration: theory, models, and empirical studies', *Journal of Regional Science*, 25: 521-44.

Hatton, T. J. and Williamson, J. G. (1994). 'Late-comers to mass emigration: the Latin experience', in T. J. Hatton and J. G. Williamson (eds) *Migration and the International Labor Market: 1850-1939* (London: Routledge).

Hughes, G. and McCormick, B. (1989). 'Does migration reduce differentials in regional unemployment rates?', in Van Dijk et al. (eds) *Migration and Labor Market Adjustment* (Kluwer Academic Publishers).

Izquierdo, A. (1992). *La inmigración en España 1980-1990* (Informes, Madrid: Ministerio de Trabajo y Seguridad Social).

Olano, A. (1990). 'Las migraciones interiores en fase de dispersión', *Revista de Economía y Sociología del Trabajo*, 8-9: 86-98.

Pesaran, M. H. and Smith, R. (1995). 'Estimating long-run relationships from dynamic heterogeneous panels', *Journal of Econometrics*, 68: 79-113.

Pissarides, C. A. and Wadsworth, J. (1989). 'Unemployment and the inter-regional mobility of labour', *The Economic Journal*, 99: 739-55.

Rodenas, C. (1994a). 'Migraciones interregionales en España, 1960-1989', *Revista de Economía Aplicada*, 2(4): 5-36.

— (1994b). *Emigración y Economía en España* (Madrid: Editorial Civitas).

Sanchez Alonso, B. (1995). *Las Causas de la Emigración Española* (Madrid: Alianza Editorial).

Santillana, I. (1981). 'Los determinantes económicos de las migraciones internas en España. 1960-1973', *Cuadernos de Economía*, 4(25): 381-407.

12. International Migration from and to Portugal: What Do We Know and Where Are We Going?

Maria I. B. Baganha, Pedro Góis, and Pedro T. Pereira

12.1. Introduction

At the beginning of the 1990s, official sources (IAECP 1991) estimated[1] that there were more than four million Portuguese citizens living abroad. In that same year, the *Serviço de Estrangeiros e Fronteiras* (Portuguese Immigration Service, hereinafter SEF) had records on 113,978 foreign nationals residing legally in Portugal. Adding this figure to the number of residency requests that were processed in the following year,[2] we arrive at a total number of foreigners residing within the Portuguese borders (both legally and illegally) of about 150,000—which is to say, in 1991, foreigners accounted for 1.5 per cent of the resident population of Portugal, and Portuguese living abroad amounted to more than 40 per cent of the resident population. Despite what these numbers appear to tell us, it is common to find assertions in academic works and the press that Portugal has undergone a transformation from 'emigration country' to 'immigration country'. Although paradoxical on the surface, there may in fact be some truth to these claims when we consider that the elevated number of Portuguese living abroad are there as a result of earlier migrations.

However, our reading of the evidence (looking beyond the mere numbers cited above), leads us to the belief that emigration does in fact remain a hallmark of the overall Portuguese society. Whether legal or extra-legal, Portuguese emigration continues at a strong pace,[3] while remittances from

The authors thank John Huffstot for helpful comments and editing of the text.

[1] The estimate refers to May of 1991.

[2] During the programme of *Regularização Extraordinária* (Special Legalization) which took place in 1992, 39,166 illegal immigrants came forward and requested official authority for their residence. (SEF informative publication (no author), cited in Baganha 1998a).

[3] More than 170,000 (permanent and temporary) between 1986 and 1988 (Baganha 1993).

abroad continue to exert a powerful social and economic impact at home.[4] At the same time, immigration remains important—not so much in terms of numbers, but rather in the socioconomic imprint it has left in some locations (and not others), and gaining a high-profile in Portuguese society from the 1980s on. This phenomenon has drawn evermore attention from researchers in recent years.

Since the mid-1980s, this attention has been focused mainly on the immigration process and its consequences for the Portuguese society. Three factors have come together in this regard:

> (1) a falling rate of permanent emigration between 1974 and 1985, coupled with a strong wave of returning nationals in the late 1970s and early 1980s— prompting some researchers to declare an end to the emigration cycle to Europe;
> (2) the fact that the official source of data, the *Instituto Nacional de Estatística* (INE—National Bureau of Statistics), continued mistakenly to promulgate improbable emigration figures—a result of the Bureau's chronic inability to develop observation instruments capable of accurately measuring the exit movements and characteristics of the emigrants;
> (3) the high visibility that foreigners (immigrants and nonimmigrants, alike) have been attaining since 1975, especially in the Lisbon Metropolitan Area.

This heightened visibility is in part the result of a widespread confusion between the so-called *retornados*[5] of dark skin and bona fide immigrants from African countries where Portuguese is the official language ('PALOP's, *Paises Africanos de Lingua Official Portuguesa*).

The goal of this article is to make a survey of the Portuguese published research which deals specifically with the issues of emigration from and immigration to Portugal since the Second World War. We shall pay special attention to those works which have been published within the last twenty years. It is not our intention to provide a review of the literature on this subject,[6] but rather, to shed light on what is known and not known about the two major themes, to detect and expose the main lines of research that have been pursued by Portuguese investigators, and in light of that, to offer some suggestions for further research—thereby adding to our knowledge of the Portuguese society.

---

[4] 10 per cent of Portuguese GDP during the 1980s, up from 8 per cent during the 1970s (Baganha 1993).

[5] A nickname for individuals residing in the one-time Portuguese colonies.

[6] Portuguese emigration has fallen under the scrutiny of researchers from many fields, including history, demography, anthropology, geography, psychology, sociology, literary studies, communication science, political science, economy, etc. The reader will discover that the greater part of the contributions considered herein are from the perspective of history, sociology, and economy.

12.2. Emigration

As noted above, 30 per cent of the Portuguese population lived and/or worked abroad at the beginning of the 1990s. This figure is simply the remnant of a longstanding fact. According to Magalhães Godinho (1978), emigration is nothing less than a structural constant in Portuguese history—a constant which, for Joel Serrão (1970), has its roots in the colonization of Madeira (c. 1425), and which has grown, ever since, evermore integral to the Portuguese psyche. Drawing upon the perspective of another discipline and paraphrasing the classic formulation of W. Petersen (1958), we could say that since the fifteenth century, the exit movements have become progressively integrated into the lifeways of several social groups, which have developed their value systems so as to support those lifeways.[7] Clearly, this does not mean that migration has run at a constant rate over time. Nor does it mean that all regions of the country have participated equally. This system of values that sanction and legitimize emigration is found in some regions, and not others. These values tend, by the same token, to occur in the absence of exogenous factors which would impede their materialization.

Such exogenous factors reduce the exit flows only temporarily, as it happened in the 1930/40s and again between 1974 and 1985. The slump in emigration did not spell its death, however. It meant only that during both periods, emigration fell dormant in the face of a discouraging 'winter' in the international environment, ready to awaken anew upon the 'spring's' return. This is of particular interest to the Portuguese case, as we find no structural ruptures in the value systems of the groups which have produced emigrants—rather, emigration has resumed as soon as the situation in the destination countries has allowed.

The social framework that gave rise to Portuguese emigration[8] came into being earlier than the phenomenon itself. Until about 1820, Portuguese migration was essentially linked to the mercantile and imperial objectives of the Portuguese Crown. Prior to the independence of Brazil (1822), for example, those who left the homeland were either in direct service to the Crown or seeking personal advance in other parts of the Empire. Thereafter, the character of migration changed, becoming more of what we see it

---

[7] Thus, one might better say that a social group in motion (e.g. nomads), tends to remain so unless impelled to change; for with any viable pattern of life a value system is developed to support that pattern' (Petersen 1958: 258).

[8] Herein, emigration is considered to be the move, for an uncertain amount of time, of workers and their relatives, from one sovereign country to another.

as today—international labour mobility—which is based on imbalance in the geoeconomic system, and Portuguese emigrants sought destinations which were now outside of their own colonial Empire.[9]

Whether representing international labour mobility or the quest for a new life, Portuguese emigration falls into three well-defined cycles. The first lasted throughout the nineteenth century and can even be said to have stretched all the way into the 1960s. During this cycle more than two million left Portugal for the new world—principally Brazil. The second cycle starts in the 1950s and begins to fade out in 1974. This cycle saw about the same number of individuals emigrate, and as it happened over a much shorter time span, represents a far greater intensity. This exit wave left mostly for destinations elsewhere in Europe—principally France and Germany. The third cycle got under way around 1985 and continues to date. Europe remains the destination of preference—Germany, still, but now Switzerland more than France.[10]

As noted above, intercontinental emigration shows a sharp decrease beginning in the 1960s. Although greatly reduced, it remains detectable to this day. However, given the objectives of this article and the marked decline of impact that these residual trans-Atlantic flows have in recent emigration dynamics, they will not be treated in great depth, and the remainder of this section will be centred on Portuguese emigration to Europe.

12.2.1. Intra-European Labour Movements:
the Portuguese Case, 1950–74

12.2.1.1. The European context[11]
Between 1953 and 1973, the (then) six countries comprising the EEC issued the first eight million foreign-work authorizations, illustrating the massive transfer of labour from the peripheral south to the industrialized north during the phase of sustained postwar growth. During that same period,

---

[9] Although this shift in nature emerged in its present form only in the middle of the nineteenth century, we can identify earlier instances which show similarities, such as the Portuguese emigration to the Spanish colony of Santo Domingo in the fifteenth and sixteenth centuries (D'Esposito 1998), and the migratory flows to Spain and the United States beginning at the end of the eighteenth century (Baganha 1990).

[10] We prefer to speak of a new intra-European cycle, as either the country of destination or the conditions of the migration show a specificity that was not present earlier.

[11] A great deal of literature exists on this subject. The synthesis presented here relies heavily on the following works: Piore 1976; Kritz et al. 1983; Bohning 1984; Bruneau 1984; Seccombe and Lawless 1985; Werner 1986; Salt 1987 and Castles and Miller 1993; and one of the present authors, Baganha 1994 and 1998a.

which J. Fourastié called the 'thirty glorious years', industrialized Europe implemented a systematic policy to recruit workers from abroad, triggering the arrival of several million noncommunity migrants with their families. Settling these 'guest-labour' immigrants was encouraged by the need for labour, by the economic and social mobility it afforded the citizens of the host country, and by the widespread belief that the situation was only temporary and could be easily changed as soon as the crisis of imbalance in the economic-labour market became rectified, or as soon as the immigrants lost their jobs in the host country or saved enough money to return home.[12] In turn, the labour market became sharply divided, and demand in the secondary market came to be satisfied by the foreign labour (Piore 1979).

The oil crisis of 1973-4, the economic downturn that proceeded from it, and the restrictive immigration policies that came into place, marked the beginning of a new phase in the European migratory processes. Until then, the immigration policies of the leading European countries could be characterized as 'open door' or even 'actively seeking', while after 1974 we see the policies grow ever more restrictive–to the point of serving as barriers to further immigration.

During the 1980s–in full economic recession–industrialized Europe woke up to the fallacy of the 'return myth' they had created, and simultaneously discovered that within its borders Europe had provoked the creation of highly concentrated communities which were clearly suffering sociocultural exclusion. The exclusion ills were compounded by the working and living conditions and pay scales, all of which were substantially lower than the respective national averages.

From the political point of view, the collapse of Eastern Europe and the reunification of Germany neutralized the decisions that by then already appeared to be inevitable. In the economic field, the transfer of labour-intensive industries from Western Europe to South-East Asia, the partial substitution by capital-intensive industries, and above all, sharp growth in the tertiary sector, have sent the immigrant communities farther down the slippery slope toward poverty–and created an arena where many voices can be heard to claim that Europe needs no more immigrants. This polemic permeates the scholarly and political discourse of our day.

In response to this crisis, since the mid-1970s the European countries have sought to set migratory policies into motion which simultaneously

---

[12] Beginning in the late 1950s, and especially following the construction of the Berlin Wall (1961), the areas that supplied labour were progressively enlarged to Turkey, North Africa and, in general, to all of the areas in which Europe had previously maintained colonial relationships.

promote the integration of earlier-formed immigrant communities and their relatives into the respective social fabrics of their host countries while discouraging further labour-motivated immigration. In other words, the goal of the policies is to allow for the reunification of families, but prohibit economic emigration.[13]

12.2.1.2. The place of Portuguese emigration in Europe

It is estimated that 1,815,000 emigrants left Portugal between 1950 and 1974. Table 12.1 presents the Portuguese emigration, broken down by destination and five-year periods from 1959 to 1988. The data can be summarized in the following way: Portuguese emigration showed strong, steady growth from 1950 (22,000 registered departures) to 1970 (183,000 departures); a downturn from 1971 to the late 1980s; and a postwar peak between 1965 and 1974, with an annual average of departures standing at around 122,000.[14]

As one can see from the table, the human drain upon the Portuguese demographic fabric intensified when Europe became a primary destination. In fact, in the 1965–74 period alone, 1,218,000 people left the country. Of these, 775,000 (63 per cent) went to France and 175,000 (14 per cent) went to Germany[15] (Baganha 1994, 1998a).

Just as we find in the trans-Atlantic cycle, the typical emigrant of this period comes from a rural area. Within the intra-European cycle, on the other hand, we can detect a growing number of departures from larger urban and industrial concentrations. We can also detect change in the fact that the coastal area of Lisbon yields up more and more emigrants, and of legal emigrants from 1955 to 1988, 26 per cent from 1955–59, 38 per cent from 1960–9, and 50 per cent in the 1970s originated in the secondary sector of the economy.

It is particularly risky to make conclusions about changes in the gender, age and/or family status of the migrants (see note 15). However, it seems

---

[13] Currently, only the purposes of family reunification are explicitly worded in the policies of European governments. For more on this, see, e.g. Kubat 1993 or Baldwin-Eduards and Schain 1994.

[14] Many sources exist for data on this period. We draw special attention to Stahl et al. 1982; Arroteia 1983; Baganha 1993 and 1998a; Rocha-Trindade (ed.) 1985; and Baganha et al. 1998.

[15] Between 1950 and 1988, about 777,000 Portuguese appeared in France and Germany who were not counted in the Portuguese statistics. A comparison between Portuguese and French figures indicates that Portuguese authorities underestimated the exits by 48 per cent during the 1960s and 81 per cent during the 1970s. Migration to Germany was underestimated by 27 per cent from 1962-9 and 42 per cent during the 1970s. Earlier studies (Antunes 1981; Stahl et al. 1982) considered only the illegal and clandestine migration to France, and their totals may be different from those presented here (cf. Baganha 1998a).

Table 12.1. Portuguese emigration for selected countries, 1950–88

Year	Brazil	USA	Canada	Total Trans-atlantic	France	Germany	Other Europe	Total Europe	Total	Europe (%)
1950–4	145,867	5,569	–	180,636	2,824	11	995	3,830	184,466	2.1
1955–9	91,460	10,624	11,350	145,899	18,929	19	644	19,592	165,491	11.8
1960–4	58,289	15,997	18,463	120,040	115,235	8,613	3,639	127,487	247,527	51.5
1965–9	14,978	50,677	31,942	133,804	352,830	51,358	12,102	416,290	550,094	75.7
1970–4	5,646	43,839	39,410	112,656	416,848	123,930	14,380	555,158	667,814	83.1
1975–9	3,485	39,574	19,398	82,731	68,013	27,834	4,360	100,207	182,938	54.8
1980–4	963	16,271	7,601	51,188	42,600	11,900	1,668	56,168	107,356	52.3
1985–8	276	10,242	10,818	27,557	6,800	11,400	745	18,945	46,502	44.6
Total	320,964	192,793	138,982	854,511	102,4079	235,065	38,533	129,7677	215,2188	60.3

Source: Taken from Baganha 1994: 975.

reasonable to allow that the migratory flow to Europe shows two waves: a first in the 1950s and mid 1960s, which was dominated by isolated departures of men in their prime working years; and a second beginning in the late 1960s and lasting throughout the 1970s, resulting in a significant number of family reunions, as is suggested by the rising number of children less than fifteen years of age and married women departing in the 1970s.

Portuguese emigration to Europe followed the same pattern observed in the trans-Atlantic wave: men seeking work, followed in the late-1960s by their families. This was easier in the case of Europe, due to the geographic proximity, additional means of transportation and increasing employment opportunities for women in the host countries (Brettell 1978, 1986).

In the early 1970s, the principal destination countries of Portuguese emigrants unilaterally suspended authority for any further work-seeking migration. This was followed by a number of incentives aimed at encouraging the existing migrant communities to return to their countries of origin (Poinard 1983; Stahl et al. 1982). For most of those who returned, the entire emigration episode–at least at the personal level–ended on a note of success. Gains often included a home, a car, savings in the bank, even a small business or restaurant, and moreover, the possibility, if desired, for the wife to become a homemaker. Other benefits which are more difficult to measure are the satisfaction of returning to one's homeland and the potential for upward mobility derived from savings.

At the macro level, on the other hand, their contributions and gains are perhaps less than what they could have been. Fully 92 per cent of those who returned were either illiterate (12 per cent), possessed no formal education (24 per cent), or had completed only the first grade (56 per cent). Specialization acquired abroad—in those rare instances when it occurred at all—was not easily transferable to the home country, nor were the returnees even interested in many cases in continuing in the same type of work they had been engaged in abroad. It is essential to recognize that only 59 per cent of those who returned even went back to work—and that most of these returned to agriculture or set up an independent small trade.

It is undeniable that the returning emigrants contributed in a decisive way to regional development in Portugal, namely, in promoting the banking system, improving housing conditions and propelling small trade. However, these contributions have not been appraised in an overly positive light, as we find in the works of Caroline Leite (1989, 1990), nor have they been deemed particularly favourable by those who remained at home, if we accept the findings of Albertino Gonçalves (1996) on this theme.

An examination of the Portuguese experience in France, which typifies the emigration phenomenon, serves well to illustrate the overall process and its phases during the first intra-European cycle. In 1961, the number of Portuguese migrants in France still stood below 10,000,[16] accounting for only 10.5 per cent of all new immigrants into that country. From this year until 1970, Portuguese immigration skyrocketed, reaching 136,000 in 1970 (the largest influx of Portuguese migrants to France in any single year), and 111,000 in 1971—53 per cent and 51 per cent, respectively, of all new immigrants (according to French sources) for those two years (Antunes 1973: 73, 109). We thus regard 1970 as the turning point from the expansion phase (1950-70) to the retraction phase (1971-85). Even though this turning point came in 1970/1, it was only after the oil crisis of 1973/4 that we see the truly marked decline of Portuguese emigration to France (Baganha 1994, 1998a).

This decrease of migratory flow to France which began in the early years of the 1970s would have less importance had it not occurred in conjunction with a change in the composition of the flow. Until this time, men seeking work had made up the bulk of emigrants. Now, however, the greater part of the flow is comprised of relatives of those men who had gone ahead, as well as a surprising number of people returning to Portugal. Despite the appearance of retraction, the work component did continue to be an important element between 1972 and 1977. From 1978 to 1985, though, the flow was consistently dominated by the family component.

[16] According to official French figures, 10,492 Portuguese immigrants entered France in 1961 (Antunes 1973).

From 1987 to 1989, the work component reasserted its dominance, representing 74 per cent of the registered immigrants, according to French sources.[17]

Michel Poinard (1983) estimated the average annual number of definitive returns from 1960–80 to be between 25,000 and 30,000, and that in the following decade the figure dropped to 24,000. The period of greatest return seems to be the first half of the 1980s. The research team coordinated by Manuela Silva (Silva et al. 1984: 59) estimated that there were 209,000 returns from 1980–5, which is to say an annual average of 42,000 returns. This calculated annual average is greater than the 25,000 to 30,000 returns that occurred during the previous decade.[18] These three factors come together to form the end of a migratory cycle. This end, in fact, marks a terminus in the minds of those who had gone: half had emigrated and returned home to Portugal; half had emigrated and established new homes, along with their families, in France.

Given that the number of Portuguese immigrants who resided legally in France was 759,000 in 1975, 767,000 in 1982, and 650,000 in 1990 (Sopemi 1993: 193), the end of the migratory project seems to point up that far more Portuguese settled permanently than left France.

The socioeconomic characteristics and the integration of Portuguese immigrants into French society are treated in M. Tribalat (1995) and Pereira and Tavares (1999, 2000). From the first work we have extracted a number of indicators on these subjects (Tables 12.2 and 12.3).

As we can see in Table 12.2, there is a clear decrease in the rate of Portuguese endogamy by the age of arrival in France. The evidence apparently falls right into line with the so-called 'Chicago School' theory of assimilation regarding the process of adaptation of immigrants to their host society, which was first advanced by Milton Gordon (*Assimilation in American Life*, 1964), and came to dominate migration studies during the 1980s. This theory postulates that continued marriage outside of the immigrant group (i.e. with members of the host society) will assure the progressive mélangement (mixing) of the immigrant population and its descendants. In the long run, this mixing will make it impossible to distinguish the various subgroups in the population.

Regarding the emigrant males' socio-professional categories, neither the age nor date of entry (though relevant) seem to affect the structure very greatly (see also, Pereira and Tavares 1999, 2000). However, the sub-group

[17] In the three-year period from 1969–71, 65 per cent of entrances were work-related—falling to 45 per cent over the next three years—and 20 per cent from 1975–7 (ONI data cited in Stahl et al. 1982: 52). For data after 1980, see (Sopemi 1985, 1988 and 1990).
[18] On the theme of return, see (Stahl et al. 1982); (Silva et al. 1984); and (Baganha et al. 1998).

Table 12.2. Origin of Portuguese immigrants' spouses and the children of Portuguese origin (%) spouses

	Spouse's origin		
	French nationality	Immigrant	Born in France from immigrant parents
Men			
Who arrived aged 16 or more	15	82	3
Who arrived aged 15 or less	42	46	14
Born in France from immigrant parents (Portuguese nationality)	59	13	28
Women			
Who arrived aged 16 or more	6	93	1
Who arrived aged 15 or less	31	61	8
Born in France from immigrant parents (Portuguese nationality)	47	36	17

Source: Tribalat 1995: 69.

Table 12.3. Socioprofessional category of immigrants of the male sex according to age and dates of entrance and of the male individuals born in France of Portuguese origin

	Portugal		
	Who arrived aged 16 or more, before 1975	Who arrived aged 15 or less, before 1975	Born in France
Farmers	0	0	0
Agricultural workers	2	3	1
Other blue-collar workers	80	63	67
Technicians, managers	6	14	5
Employees	1	4	12
Workers in services	2	1	3
Artisans, merchants, directors	6	10	3
Liberal and intermediate professionals	3	5	10
Total	100	100	101

Source: Tribalat 1995: 160.

of those who arrived in France at a younger age seems to show a slight increase over those arriving at sixteen or older in the category of 'Technicians and managers'.[19][20] In relationship to those born in France compared to those who arrived aged sixteen or more, the socioprofessional structure shows a higher percentage of tertiary occupations and a relative weight (10 per cent) of liberal and intermediate professionals, revealing a clear pattern of upward socioeconomic mobility across the whole distribution (Table 12.3).

12.2.1.3. Main trends in Portuguese research up to the 1980s

Whether due to the magnitude of its numbers, its economic impact or the sociocultural transformations which it provoked, since the 1960s the migration of Portuguese labour and families has attracted the attention of more and more researchers. Bear in mind that within a mere ten years (1965-74) more than a tenth of the Portuguese population emigrated. The economic consequences of this fact cannot be overstated, but have been summarized succinctly by Baganha (1994): the value of remittances from the Portuguese work force abroad during this period established Portuguese labour emigrants as the nation's leading 'export good'. From a sociocultural perspective, the journalist Nuno Rocha observed in work done between 1963 and 1965 some of the effects of Portuguese emigration to France:

> The first emigrants—the pioneers—have now returned, and are already cultivating their lands, once again (...) In Castro Laboreiro, there are now more 'French houses' (...) the emigrants now buy vitamins for their children and the women use perfume. The doctor attends to the sick more often (...) the people are more developed, cultivated from the contact abroad—they go to the doctor at the first sign of illness. As a result, the next generations are getting healthier (...) there are movies, the stores are full, the men dress in nice clothes and the women cook in front of modern stoves... (Rocha 1965: 162-3)

One of the themes that caught the eye of Portuguese researchers early on was the size and composition of the Portuguese migratory flow, leading to a good many studies during the 1950s, 1960s, and 1970s. During this period,

[19] Just as with Italian immigrants, previously, and Spanish immigrants, subsequently, Portuguese immigrants worked in sectors which did not demand professional qualifications: civil construction, public works, domestic services, maintenance, agriculture, etc. (Stahl et al. 1982; Kritz et al. 1983; Bohning 1984; Branco 1986). A breakdown of the labour market by workers' nationality (French and immigrants) reveals segmentation in the fact that certain occupations were routinely filled by immigrant labour, particularly in the areas of civil construction and public works.
[20] In the early 1980s, the percentage of unqualified Portuguese workers was 45 per cent of the total, which was similar to other groups of immigrants. For the French population, however, the percentage of unqualified workers did not exceed 29 per cent (Branco 1986: 70-1).

investigators were particularly interested in correcting and filling in the gaps, where they existed, in the official Portuguese records about emigration. Much attempt was made to establish data on illegal emigration, either by studying the records of the host countries or by making indirect estimates based on other national demographic statistics. The work of João Ferreira de Almeida, published in *Análise Social*, 1964, was the pioneer in this subject. Others having the same objective followed: Antunes (1970, 1973, and 1981) and Stahl et al. (1982).[21] The reasons underpinning Portuguese emigration also drew the attention of several sociologists and historians, who concluded that the principal motivations for migration in the 1960s and 1970s were the duality of the Portuguese society and the fluctuation of the national economic structure (Sedas Nunes 1964; Almeida and Barreto 1976; Serrão 1977; Godinho 1978). Economists stressed other factors, namely the difference in wages between Portugal and the host countries (M. Murteira 1965; Pintado 1967; A. Murteira and Branquinho 1976; Ferreira 1976). There is an interdisciplinary consensus on, at least, one thing: during the 1960s, changes in the production structure triggered high unemployment which, when added to the chronic underemployment rate in the farming and trades sectors, prompted a growing number of Portuguese to opt for emigration (Pereira and Barosa 1989: 8).

These works mentioned above all conform to the mainstream analytical tradition that has dominated scholarship in this area—that is, the model that explains migration through push factors in the society of origin and pull factors in the society of destination. In our overview of research from the 1960s to date, when expressed in terms of the 'push–pull' model, we find a clear division in the scholarly opinions: historians and sociologists tend to find the motive(s) for emigration in the push factors, while economists tend to favour pull factors.

Portuguese scholars have, for the most part, traditionally aligned their methods and views to the French School in matters of the social sciences and political studies. This, coupled with the fact that academic preparation in sociology has only recently become possible in Portugal, left the field of sociological study of the Portuguese in France largely to the researchers there. In 1973, M. Beatriz Rocha-Trindade published *Immigrés Portugais* [Portuguese Immigrants], which became, even within Portugal, the seminal work regarding the adaptation of the Portuguese immigrants to France. A few years later, in 1978, a Canadian anthropologist, Caroline Brettell,

---

[21] Projections regarding migratory flow, published after 1984 (for example, Straubhar 1984; Barosa and Pereira 1989; Pereira 1994), complement the available information on the number of exits.

published *Já Chorei Muitas Lágrimas, Una História de Vida de una Mulher Portuguesa Imigrada em França* [I Have Already Cried Many Tears, A History of the Life of a Portuguese Woman in France]. These works lent voices for the first time to the immigrants, and were followed up in later years with additional works by these same authors, as well as others: Cordeiro and Soares (1987); Leandro (1987); and Valagão (1989), to name a few.

Still other researchers, however, analysing the eating practices, support groups and leisure activities (forms of expression of the Portuguese identity of the immigrant families) tend to emphasize the maintenance of bonds and practices transplanted from the society or community of origin over the temporary adaptive processes in the host society, within or without the immigrant group(s), or to the changes in the socioeconomic structures.[22]

Scholarship in the 1980s was marked by two other veins of research: the impact of emigration on the society or community of origin; and the analysis of the characteristics of the returning emigrants and their impact on Portuguese society. A number of works in this decade following one or the other of these lines have addressed the cultural ethos, the adaptation strategies, and the ways and means of social reproduction in the community of origin. Notable here are: the collection of studies undertaken by Maria Beatriz Rocha-Trindade, published in 1981 in the *Revista de História Económica e Social. Cadernos 1–2: Estudos sobre a Emigração Portuguesa*; and a work which is, in our opinion, a milestone study in this field, (whether for the thoroughness of empirical research methodologies, or for its recourse to documentary sources which until then had been little used by other anthropologists and sociologists, or for the influence it had on Portuguese academics), by anthropologist Caroline Brettell (1986), Men Who Migrate, Women Who Wait.

The impact of emigration on the Portuguese economy has been addressed, for example, by Rocha (1982); Chaney (1986); Leeds (1983); Baganha (1993); Pereira and Barosa (1988); Pereira (1989) and Pereira (1994). At the macro level, the last assessment (written in the 1980s) of the impact of emigration on the Portuguese economy summed it up in the following way:

Past emigration is projected to have positive welfare effects in the Portuguese economy under status quo. That means that the positive effect of a steady flow of remittances overrides the negative welfare effect of depopulation. (Pereira 1989)

---

[22] Which is at odds with the conceptual models of the Chicago School, which dominated the scholarly research in this area from the 1960s to the 1980s.

The return/reintegration of the emigrants into Portuguese society was, perhaps, the topic which received the most attention during this period. The Volkswagen Foundation generously supported two enormous projects—the results of which were published in 1984. The first of these projects was organized by a team from the *Instituto de Estudos para o Desenvolvimento* (IED–Institute of Developmental Studies), co-ordinated by Manuela Silva. This project focused on measuring the volume of returns between 1960 and '70, estimating the returns for the 1980s, and describing the socioeconomic profile of the returnees, including work before, during and after the emigration experience. The second project was conducted by a team from the *Centro de Estudos da Dependência* (CED–Centre for Economic Dependency Studies), organized by Eduardo Sousa Ferreira. This project was centred on the evaluation and enumeration of regional development policies aimed at maximizing the economic benefits of the returnees in the areas in which they settled.

In the year following the publication of the results of these two projects, a new project was undertaken by the *Universidade Aberta* (Open University) which was linked, although only partially, to the theme of returning migrants. This project sought to evaluate the impact of formal education on the Portuguese emigrants and of former emigrants' children in Portugal. The project was financed by the IAEC and the Ministry of Education, and was coordinated by Maria Beatriz Rocha-Trindade. Its results were published in 1988. Based upon information gathered in a national sample of public-school students, aged twelve to eighteen, the team described the students' school experience, their main difficulties, and the migratory path of their parents.

Compared with the works on the determinants of emigration, or on the return to the society of origin, the impact of the economic and migration policies of the *Estado Novo* ('New State', the dictatorial regime in Portugal, 1926–74) on the composition and direction of migratory flows deserved much less attention. Even so, the *Estado Novo* question has been investigated: Cassola Ribeiro (1986); Almeida and Barreto (1976); Sousa Ferreira (1984); E. Leeds (1983). From this period, there are, in addition, several collections of studies and special editions of magazines and journals, resulting from congresses and seminars: *Análise Social*, 19 (77, 78, 79), (1983)–Actas of the Colloquium, *A Formação de Portugal Contemporâneo*: 1900–1980 [The Making of Modern Portugal: 1900–1980]; *Análise Social*, 21 (87, 88, 89), (1985)–*Actas* of the Colloquium, *Mudanças Sociais no Portugal de Hoje* [Social Change in Today's Portugal]. These readings illustrate some of the variety of themes that have drawn more and more attention from Portuguese investigators.

12.2.2. Portuguese Emigration in the 1980s and 1990s

Based upon the findings of the 1991 census, it is clear that Portuguese emigration has increased, once again. Recognizing this fact, since 1992 the INE has undertaken to apply new methods for measuring the phenomenon. With due respect for the difficulty of the task, the fact is that since that date the INE has not been able to hone their tools to the point of satisfaction. As a result, the figures promulgated continue to depict the true situation tenuously, at best. Actual emigration is surely far greater than what the official figures would lead us to believe. This is the current reality, and the one which is likely to continue for some time.

In earlier works, one of the current authors argued that since the last century, Portuguese emigration has been an international labour flow, meaning that its direction has been determined essentially by the supply of opportunity in the international labour market of the geo-political macro-system in which Portugal is situated. This same author has also contended that although economic reasoning may explain the individual decisions, the evolution of the migratory flow depended not so much upon the evaluation that the 'potential' emigrant was making about the gains to be had from the sale of his work abroad, as it did upon the political sanctions of those countries involved (Portugal and the various host countries), as well as upon the force and degree of the structuring of the migratory nets[23] at both ends (Baganha 1990, 1993, 1994, 1998a).

This conceptualization led the author to evaluate, in 1991[24] and again in 1992,[25] a decrease in the emigration phenomenon which was evident between 1974 and 1985 as a lag in the time needed for the formation of new nets, sufficiently structured to exhaust the existing migratory potential for new destinations, and consequently, to attribute the observed slow-down to the lack of migratory nets for alternative destinations in the wake of restrictions to the entrance of Portuguese labour emigrants, unilaterally

---

[23] We use the concept of 'net' that it received in MacDonald and MacDonald (1964) and Tilly and Brown (1967), which is, the informal structures of information and support derived from the migrants, themselves.

[24] Portuguese Emigration: Current Characteristics and Trends. Communication presented at Cost Workshop, Migration: Europe's Integration and the Labor Force. Louvain, October, 1991.

[25] Communication presented at the III Congress of Sociology. Lisbon 1992. Published in the Minutes of the Congress. See Baganha (1993).

imposed by France and Germany. In these same works, an attempt was made to provide an initial correction to the official figures for the exit flows during the 1980s and early 1990s. What was advanced at that time, based upon the scant data then available, later came to be confirmed in the work of João Peixoto (1987, 1993) and especially in the monograph (1997) by José Carlos Marques regarding Portuguese emigration to Switzerland. Although these works leave no doubt that there is a new emigration flow underway from Portugal to various European countries,[26] the truth is that we still know little about the volume, types of flows, and the characteristics of the migrants.

On the economic dynamics of the process, we know more—based upon the works which were carried out in conjunction with the MIGRINF project,[27] which allow us to show the interrelationship between the actual exit and entrance movements that occurred in Portugal. Early findings of this project were published in 1998, in which it was defended that Portugal's entrance into the European Community, in 1986, provoked a profound change in the civil construction sector—a change that had an enormous impact on both the exit flow of Portuguese workers abroad, and the entrance flow of foreign workers immigrating to Portugal. This change was felt in two ways: firstly, Community adhesion allowed Portuguese companies to subcontract their manpower within the European Community's space (CE), in competition with their Community counterparts—an opportunity which Portuguese companies took advantage of by adapting their work strategies to the new situation. These strategies included—especially following the fall of the Berlin Wall and reunification—the dislocation of several thousand Portuguese construction workers to Germany, reducing the available labour supply in Portugal. Secondly, at the same time that demand for construction labour was growing abroad, Portugal's Community adhesion channelled a very substantial amount of structural funds to the country, of which a great deal was applied to various communication infra-structures and public works—increasing, if only temporarily, the domestic demand for labour in this sector.

The combination of these two factors opened vast opportunities to the Portuguese companies working in this sector. In order to take maximum

[26] Notice, for example, that the number of Portuguese immigrants in Switzerland has gone from 10,700 in 1980, to 39,900 in 1985, to 85,600 in 1990, and 134,800 in 1995. The annual average of seasonal entrances in the 1980s stood at 33,000 (Marques 1997).

[27] MIGRINF, Migrants' Insertion in the Informal Economy, Deviant Behavior, and the Impact on the Receiving Societies. Project coordinated by Emilio Reyneri. TSER-programme, CE/DG XII-ERBSOE2.CT95-3005. This project pertaining to Portugal was undertaken by a team to which Baganha and Góis belonged.

advantage from this boom situation, many Portuguese companies hired immigrant labour and workers of African origin on a temporary basis, either directly or through subcontracting firms operating in the informal market, and at the same time sent their permanent staff and workers, or Portuguese workers hired formally and expressly for the purpose, to other community countries. The most recent work that we are aware of that treats these emigration and 'detachment' exit flows has this to say about Portuguese emigration in the 1980s:

Considering the data from the host countries, even if the estimates of the number of emigrants is far below that of the preceding decades, the 1980s witnessed a new impetus in the Portuguese migratory process. This new phase exhibits a new character, however, in the form of 'irregular' and 'temporary' migration. Moreover, the opening of the community borders promoted new forms of mobility within Europe that do not fit the 'classical' definition of emigration. (...) From the mid-1980s on, emigration continues to grow, gradually, due to the following factors: the creation and structuring of nets in the new destination countries, as is the case in Switzerland; the revival of existing nets, as is the case with trans-Atlantic migration; new conditions regarding international mobility, derived from Portugal's adhesion to the European Community; and Community law regarding the employment of workers from other countries, as is the case of the 'detachment of workers' in Germany. (Baganha, Ferrão, and Malheiros et al. 1998: 49)

12.2.3. Conclusion

Portuguese scholarship about Portuguese emigration is scarce. This scarcity is evident in the work *Bibliografia da Emigração Portuguesa* [Bibliography of Portuguese Emigration], by Maria Beatriz Rocha-Trindade and Jorge Arroteia (1984). Despite being exhaustive—covering all historical periods and including, along with the scholarly works, novels and administrative documents of both Portuguese and foreign origin—the corpus, in A8 format (which is half that of A4), covers the subject in just 71 pages.[28]

This scarcity is probably attributable to a number of reasons, not the least of which is the fact that Portugal has the smallest scholarly community in the European Union. Another reason is to be found, we feel, in the embarrassing fact that emigration continues to be for the country's political elite. This phenomenon is more understandable when we recall that emigration is, as Zolberg observed (1983: 7), 'voting with your feet'.

---

[28] Even when we added those works which we know of which have been published in Portugal since 1984, the number of references falls short of 600.

In spite of the scarcity of publications, there are some themes about which we know more than others. Some of the areas best understood are those of volume and direction of Portuguese migratory flows and the characteristics of returning emigrants in the early years of the 1980s. As to those who leave, and especially, clandestine immigrants, we continue in near total ignorance.

We can say with fair certainty—based upon studies of the illegal component of the Portuguese migratory flow in other historical periods (Baganha 1990), or upon available information about illegal departures for Europe following the Second World War—that the clandestine flow is substantially different from the legal flow (Almeida 1964; Antunes 1970, 1973, 1981; Stahl et al. 1982). Our knowledge pertains mostly to the legal flow, but it must be borne in mind that the picture rests on data which are suspect and almost certainly flawed. Notwithstanding that awareness, the characteristics of the legal emigrants continue to be cited as if no one realized that more than 48 per cent and 81 per cent of all emigrants, 1960–9 and 1970–9, respectively, left Portugal clandestinely, and that the evaluation of their demographic and socioeconomic profiles very probably bears little resemblance to reality.

Correctly ascertaining the profile(s) of Portugal's clandestine emigrants continues, therefore, to be a research priority—and not just at the level of the individual's characteristics. We also need to determine what support nets were used by these emigrants, what kind of work (by sector) they entered into or developed (at their own expense), and whether their migratory experiences coincide with or diverge from those of their legally emigrating counterparts.

Further study of the returnees is also needed. Sofia Afonso has recently concluded (1997) a work of interest, *A segunda geração e o regresso— A geografia do actor de fronteira* [The second generation and the return— The geography of the border actor]. A return to this line of research is laudable, but it should go hand in hand with the research initiated by Manuela Silva and Eduardo Sousa Ferreira and their respective collaborators, but now for the period after 1985.

The impact of emigration upon the communities of departure, on the other hand, has been the target of excellent investigation in recent years. Special note is made in this regard to the efforts of Manuel Ribeiro (1998).

In light of its importance, the continuation of studies into the migratory flow to France and the process of Portuguese immigrants' adaptation to French society are completely justifiable. Along these lines, the recent works of Engrácia Leandro (1995*a*, *b*) are an important landmark in the profound treatment of these themes. This is so, first, because they are enriched by a comparison of various residential areas, allowing us to better comprehend the phenomenon of adaptation in differing sociocultural contexts. Second, the research traces three nuclear-family histories, allowing for an analysis of three different settings, and capturing the transformation of values and expectations at the personal level, as well. In our opinion, these two works serve as a benchmark from which future investigations should be measured, not only in the case of emigration to France, but to other destinations, as well.[29]

We still lack descriptive monographs for various other European countries in which Portuguese immigrants have settled, notably Germany and Luxembourg. Regarding Portuguese immigrants in Spain, we can turn to the work of Spanish researcher, Lopez Trigal (1995, 1996). For the new flow of immigrants to Switzerland, there is the first monograph by José Carlos Marques (1997). Aside from these publications, however, there are no comparative works either about the several Portuguese flows to different European countries or about the Portuguese migration compared to other currents—those originating in other southern European countries, for example.

The migratory nets have various roles and goals according to the phase of the migratory project and the structural mode. As information channels and for logistic support, they are excellent facilitators for the vast majority of immigrants, both to the act of immigration and in the initial phase of adaptation in the host society. These two 'net' aspects have been pointed out time and again in the Portuguese scholarly literature regarding Portuguese immigration. In latter phases, these two nets can become powerful traps, 'hooking' the immigrants and their children to cultural values and social practice that hinder their integration into the host society or upward mobility within it. This 'hooking' aspect has received little or no attention from Portuguese investigators. The interfacing of the nets with respect to the host societies, themselves, has likewise received no attention. Indeed, the effectiveness of the nets in promoting adaptation to the

---

[29] We extend our thanks to Sofia Afonso for drawing our attention to the work *Les Migrations Portugaises—bibliographie francophone* [The Portuguese Migrations—French bibliography]. As the title indicates, it is a bibliography of French research in the area of Portuguese migration, by Kohot-Piot, with collaboration of G. Dubus, published by CCPF (Coordination des Colectivités Portugaises de France) and MIGRINTER (a team of researchers associated with CNRS and the University of Poiters), no date (but includes references up to 1997). This work is particularly important for listing many works of interest to English-speaking investigators who wish to gain insights into French scholarship in this field. It is also a valuable complement to the bibliography assembled by Maria Beatriz-Trindade and Jorge Arroteia (1984).

host society beyond the initial phase has evaded the scrutiny of investigators, as well.

Renewed study of the impact of political sanctions of the *Estado Novo* on the composition and evolution of migratory flows came in the 1990s (Maria I. Baganha 1994, 1998*a*). This followed earlier research, on the years following the 1974 revolution. For work on this earlier period, notable authors include Baganha and Peixoto (1996); Jorge Malheiros (1996); Baganha (1998*b*) and Baganha et al. (1998).

The relationship between the current exit and entrance flows in the Portuguese territories have attracted the increased attention of scholars—for example: Pires and Saint-Maurice (1994);[30] Malheiros (1996); Baganha (1996, 1998*b*, 1998c); and Baganha and Peixoto (1996). Recently, a team led by Baganha, Ferrão, and Malheiros has looked at this relationship, focusing their attention on the economic insertion of the emigrants and detached workers in the leading European countries, and on immigrants in the domestic labour market (Baganha et al. 1998).

12.3. Immigration

12.3.1. International Context

During the 1980s, for the first time in recent history, Southern Europe became attractive as a destination for emigrants. These emigrants originated principally in Eastern Europe and Africa. This was an entirely unfamiliar situation in the region, as for more than a century it had found itself at the sending end of the migratory stream. The traditional role of Southern Europe, which was to furnish labour for the countries that were more economically advanced, was turned on its head in the 1980s. During this decade, Southern Europe was a major migratory destination, even when compared to those countries which served as traditional hosts.

As a result, while the foreign population grew at an average annual rate of 2 per cent in the European Community at large, from 1981–91, this growth rate stood at 10 per cent in the Southern European countries.[31] At the beginning of the 1990s, the number of legal immigrants in Italy, Greece, Portugal, and Spain stood at 1.4 million, and estimates for illegal immigrants

---

[30] Communication presented in the Workshop Cost A2 'Immigration in Southern Europe', Coimbra, November 1994.

[31] Only ten countries are considered here. Data for 1981 and 1991 are from Sopemi (1994); Eurostat (1994); and Baganha (1996).

in the same countries range from 1.3 to 1.5 million.[32] Three million immigrants—half of them illegal—raised social, judicial, and economic problems that had no precedence in the region.

The novelty, urgency, and political implications of this situation led researchers and politicians to seek consul and guidance in the experience of traditional immigration countries. As some may expect, the outcome was less than what had been hoped for, due largely to the fact, as pointed out by Kingsley Davis (1974), that although migration is an historical constant, the flows are themselves temporary and specific to their own time—reflecting the world in which they occur.

The world of the 1980s and 1990s was very different from the world of the 1950s and 1960s. Political upheavals, social unrest and grave ethnic conflicts in the East; and bloody religious strife, poverty and war in Africa are some of the factors that have put a new face on the world and turned Southern Europe into an attractive migratory destination, for economic immigrant and refugee, alike.

It is not only the geoeconomic gap between Europe, the East, and the South that is altering the global landscape. The very globalization process amounts to a deep restructuring of industries, relocation of labour supplies, redirection of capital flows, and new patterns of international competition. All of these factors go in, and what comes out are new processes, new social politics and alterations in the mining of labour and the structure of labour markets in Western and Southern European countries.

Added to this were the successive enlargement of the European Common Market, followed by the early steps in the building of the European Union—both of which stirred even more innovation into the pot. In the course of these changes the borders within the EU space dissolved, but no common migratory policy was put into place regarding the 'nationals of third countries'.[33] In fact, full attainment of consent regarding EU migratory policies continues to be blocked by geo-economic and political interests, adherence to nationalistic historical traditions, and ethnic lobbies.

The recent evolution of Southern Europe is largely determined by the evolution of this 'new world', marked by geo-economic inequalities, the intensification of globalization, and the construction of the economic and political bloc (the EU) in which the countries find themselves. But, as all of these processes are still 'under construction', the recent migrations into the Southern European countries are also a result of the way(s) in which each

---

[32] Diário da *Assembleia da República*, series I, 44, March 1992: 1365.

[33] An exception being the harmonization of visas inside the Shengen Agreement countries.

Table 12.4. Legal foreign residents, 1980-97

Year	Africa	North America	South America	Asia	Europe***	Others	Total
1980	27,748	4,821	6,403	1,153	17,706	260	58,091
1981	27,948	6,018	8,123	1,394	18,931	278	62,692
1982	28,903	6,855	10,481	1,663	19,924	327	68,153
1983	32,481	8,520	13,351	2,219	22,053	391	79,015
1984	37,128	9,887	15,394	2,860	23,896	460	89,625
1985	34,978	7,987	11,567	2,564	22,060	438	79,594
1986	37,829	9,047	12,629	2,958	24,040	479	86,982
1987	38,838	8,623	13,009	3,124	25,676	508	89,778
1988	40,253	8,338	14,645	3,413	27,280	524	94,453
1989	42,789	8,737	15,938	3,741	29,247	559	101,011
1990	45,255	8,993	17,376	4,154	31,410	579	107,767
1991	47,998	9,236	18,666	4,458	33,011	609	113,978
1992*	52,037	9,430	19,960	4,769	34,732	621	122,348
1993	55,786	10,513	21,924	5,520	37,154	696	136,932
1994**	72,630	10,739	24,815	6,322	41,819	748	157,073
1995	79,231	10,853	25,867	6,730	44,867	768	168,316
1996	81,176	10,783	25,733	7,140	47,315	765	172,912
1997	*81,717*	10,573	25,274	7,192	49,797	760	175,263

Sources: 1980-94: Demographic statistics 1980-94; 1995: SEF, Statistical Report 1995, 1996, 1997; *statistics of 1994 include the process of special legalization of 1992/3; *The values for 1992 and 1993 change depending the statistical sources; **About 95 per cent of the original resident foreigners of Africa are from Palop; ***In Europe, about 90 per cent come from an EEC country (*apud* Baganha 1996).

of these countries were positioned and inserted into the processes. In this sense, the recent migratory history of Southern Europe is the sum of the specific national cases that reflect their respective historical pasts and their geo-economic and political interests.[34]

12.3.2. Immigration in Portugal in the 1980s and 1990s

In 1960, there were 29,428 foreigners residing in Portugal (Esteves et al. 1991), of which 40 per cent were Spanish and 22 per cent Brazilian. Fifteen years later the situation had not changed much, as the number of legal foreign residents was 31,983 in 1975.[35] We have synthesized in Table 12.4

[34] The works of Malheiros (1996); Esteves et al. (1991); Pires (1993); and Baganha et al. (1998) include conceptualizations that either explore some of the dynamics that are referred to here in greater depth, or introduce interpretive aspects.   [35] Demographic Statistics, INE, 1995.

the evolution of the number of legal foreign residents in Portugal between 1980 and 1997.

As we can see in Table 12.4, the stock of the foreign population in Portugal grew steadily from 1980 to 1997, albeit with some variation in the rate.

Following strong growth in the second half of the 1970s (an average annual growth of 11.9 per cent, 1975–81),[36] the pace of foreigners settling in Portugal slows during the 1980s, but then picks up again in the 1990s. It was not only the absolute number of arriving foreigners that grew; the composition by nationality and socioeconomic profiles also show some very radical shifts—pointing clearly to an increasing complexity of the foreign population residing in Portugal. This complexity is illustrated very well indeed by the growing number of immigrants coming from countries with which Portugal has never had any trade links or historical privileges to speak of, who asked for residency permits during the 'Special Legalization' period in the 1990s.[37] (See Table 12.5.)

From the sociodemographic point of view, on an aggregate level the flow of legal immigrants to Portugal is typical of the international flows, at large. In Portugal we find poorly qualified labourers concentrating in the well-known, densely populated greater Lisbon area (AML, *Área Metropolitana de Lisboa*) having the following characteristics: a male/female ratio of 1.4 to 1 (1990–5–Baganha 1996); a weighting of ages between 25 and 45; and job-taking principally in 'production and transformation in the extractive industries' and 'drivers of fixed machines and transport' (Baganha 1996, 1998*b*).

However, when we disaggregate these characteristics by nationality, we find a clear, bipolar, division of the foreign population in Portugal. One group is made up mostly of citizens of other European countries and Brazil. Elements of this group show a settlement and residential pattern which tends to extend beyond the AML concentration, and a higher per capita rate of employers, selfemployed, scientific professionals, technicians, directors, and senior management executives than do the native Portuguese, themselves. This group of individuals is located right at the top of the Portuguese socioprofessional structure.

The second group comprises, for the most part, citizens of PALOP countries and (still few in number, but rising) citizens of countries such as

---

[36] Demographic Statistics, INE, 1995.

[37] For the characteristics of the foreign residents in Portugal, there are several sources. The pioneer work in this matter was (Esteves et al. 1991). More recent works include (Malheiros 1996; Baganha 1996, 1998*b*, 1998*c*; Pires and Rocha-Trindade 1993; and Baganha et al. 1998).

Table 12.5. Requests for residency permits, by nationality (Special Legalization Programme, 1992/3 and 1996)

Countries	1992/3	%	1996	%
Angola	12,525	32	9,255	26.4
Cabo Verde	6,778	17.3	6,872	19.6
Guiné-Bissau	6,877	17.6	5,308	15.1
Mozambique	757	1.9	416	1.2
S. Tomé e Príncipe	1,408	3.6	1,549	4.4
Total Palop	28,345	72.4	23,400	66.7
Senegal	1,397	3.6	672	1.9
Morocco	98	0.3	520	1.5
Brazil	5,346	13.7	2,330	6.6
China	1,352	3.5	1,608	4.6
Pakistan	286	0.7	1,754	5.0
Índia	261	0.7	915	2.6
Bangladesh	139	0.4	752	2.1
Other Nationalities	1,942	5.0	3,803	10.9
Total	39,166	100	35,082	100

Source: Serviço de Estrangeiros e Fronteiras (Immigration Service).

Zaire, Senegal, Pakistan, Romania, and Moldavia. By virtue of its numbers, this second group defines the over-riding profile of the foreign population, at large. By itself, it exhibits the characteristics outlined two paragraphs above in their extreme. This group is clearly situated at the foot of the Portuguese socioprofessional structure.

12.3.3. Main Trends of Research

One of the principal hurdles to overcome in studying immigrants in Portugal is knowing who, exactly, should be considered an immigrant. This problem stems from Portugal's recent colonial past, and is still far from gaining the consensus of those who are interested in the matter. The dramatic surge in the number of foreigners in the country—doubling in only six years (1975-81)—comes as the result of a complex array of factors that are difficult, in fact, for anyone to sort out, including: first, the entrance and settlement of Portuguese citizens of African descent who had already resided in Portugal, but had been retroactively stripped of their

Portuguese nationality (Legal Decree 308-A/75); and second, the entrance of relatives who joined these same individuals between 1976 and 1981.[38]

Can it be considered correct to categorize Portuguese citizens of African descent (who had lived in Portugal since the 1960s) as 'immigrants', or for that matter, the so-called *retornados* of African descent who came to Portugal between 1975 and 1981, or their families who followed them?

According to the definition most commonly adhered to in the literature on international migration, an 'immigrant' is the citizen of a sovereign country (and that individual's descendants) who voluntarily abandons that country, to settle in another sovereign country, in order to undertake an economic activity, without any regard to the issue of seeking citizenship in the host country.[39] In light of this, applying the term 'immigration' to the 'involuntary return' of Portuguese passport-holders of African ancestry (and their descendants) seems to the authors to be conceptually flawed. This may lead to erroneous perceptions of social realities and/or the scholarly legitimization, albeit without intent, of political decisions.

Having said this, it is equally evident that between 1975 and 1981, there were also genuine immigrants, in the truest sense of the word, originating in the PALOP nations, and coming to Portugal. Were these sufficiently high in number, however, to offset the doubts expressed above?

If we accept the estimates for the numbers of Euro-Caucasians and *retornados* in the former colonies in (Pires et al. 1984. *Os retornados—um estudo sociográfico*)—particularly the data found in Annex 1—we arrive at a figure of 25,000–35,000 persons of African descent coming to Portugal between 1975 and 1981. Adding this to the official number of grants (8,069) of new or maintained citizenship (under Article 5 of Legal Decree 308-A/75 of 24 July—see Esteves et al. 1991: 133), the indication emerges that the residency of 27,287 PALOP individuals in Portugal can be attributed to the simultaneous occurrence of:

> the final dissolution of the Portuguese Empire into sovereign states;
> the retreat of the colonial population to the Motherland;
> the loss of Portuguese nationality imposed retroactively by Legal Decree 308-A/75 of 24 July.

The difficulty of knowing how to categorize these foreign residents has been pointed out by a number of investigators, and is made patent in the

---

[38] If we discount the number of PALOP citizens residing legally (27,287), the average annual rate of increase falls to 1.7 per cent—quite a slow increase.

[39] This definition is adopted by the United Nations, as well (Recommendations on Statistics of International Migrations, Statistical Paper, Series M, 58, UN, New York, 1980).

definition advanced by Maria do Ceu Esteves: '... in rigour, the immigrant population includes the majority of resident foreigners and the (many) Portuguese born in other countries and regions' (Esteves et al. 1991: 27). This definition illustrates the frustrating imprecision inherent to this (probably insoluble) problem—taking recourse to such phrases as 'includes the majority' and 'in other countries and regions'.

Further complicating the challenge of distinguishing between PALOP-citizen immigrants and Portuguese nationals who had been stripped of their passports, the 1981 and 1991 censuses (the first instruments of scrutiny available for overcoming the problem) are, in the opinion of the authors, at best useless, and at worst totally misleading. One example will suffice to illustrate the point.

Based upon the findings of the 1981 census, the team coordinated by Maria do Ceu Esteves estimated the foreign population in Portugal to be 154,980, subdivided in the following way: having a legal status and known nationality, 94,251; stateless,[40] 202; grantees of asylum, 527; having an illegal status, 60,000 (Esteves et al. 1991: 29). To obtain these figures, the IED investigators assumed that the information regarding 'persons from other nationalities', collected by the INE, was more rigorous than the foreign registers of customs officers (Ministry of Internal Affairs MAI-SEF). This assumption led the team to estimate the number of illegal immigrants, in 1981, to be approximately 60,000—which is to say, the difference between the number of individuals categorized as foreigners by the INE (108,526), and foreigners of legal residence according to the MAI-SEF (62,692), increased by 14,166 based on other sources (Esteves et al. 1991: 29, 161). This estimate and the assumptions that support it seemed reasonable at the time they were made. However, were the methodology underpinning this estimate to be adopted, we would have to accept the belief that there were no illegal immigrants in Portugal in 1991 (since in that year the number of foreigners registered in the census was 106,519, and the number of foreign legal residents registered by the MAI-SEF was 113,978). We know this to be false because of the number of applications for legalization presented by illegal immigrants in the following year.

Taking into account the figures of these two sources (the INE and the MAI-SEF) in 1981 and 1991, along with the evidence gathered from the programm of Special Legalization, the following conclusions seem to be more reasonable to the authors: first, the 1981 census greatly exaggerated the number of foreigners residing in Portugal (due to an inability to

---

[40] A person who has lost his or her nationality for any reason.

distinguish between 'place of birth' and 'nationality';[41] and second, the 1991 census failed to detect a significant number of foreigners residing in the country, thus erring in the opposite direction.

All of this leaves us with the belief that we sadly know very little about the immigrants in Portugal because the only source which demonstrates any internal consistency[42] has and imposes serious limitations (first, because the number of immigrant characteristics both collected and released by the MAI–SEF is small, and second, because it began to systematically collect (more) in-depth data only in 1990).

From what the authors have been able to learn through contacts with the documentation centre in the SEF, until 1990, there is little more available than the series of foreign population broken down by nationality and residency. From this date on, we know in addition, age, gender, professional status, occupation, and the date of exit and/or entrance.

The scholarly research that has been undertaken over the last decades has resorted to the expedient of considering all foreigners as immigrants,[43] or has adopted the definition proposed by the IED team, which combines 'ethnic minorities' with 'immigrants'.

Bibliography remains scarce.[44] Early studies focused on the people from Cape Verde and include (Amaro 1986a, 1986b and 1986c; Menezes and Pinto da Cunha 1987; Guerra et al. 1992; França et al. 1992). One of the most recent works on this subject, *Identidades Reconstruídas: Cabo-verdianos em Portugal* (Identities Reconstructed: Cape Verdians in Portugal) by Ana Saint-Maurice (1993), provides a detailed and multi-level examination of the first and most important group of immigrants in Portugal, and is especially important for an understanding of this group.

In later years more attention has been devoted to other ethnic groups, such as the people from Guiné-Bissau (Machado 1992, 1994a and b), the people from India (Ávila and Alves 1993; Malheiros 1994, 1996) or, in a generic sense, to the immigrant communities in Portugal (Esteves et al. 1991; CEPAC 1995a, 1995b; Cordeiro, 1997). Still lacking is a systematic

---

[41] The IED team was aware that this failure might lead to exaggerated figures in the case of the PALOP countries, but felt that the possible bias resulting from it was of little significance.

[42] The information contained in the *Inquéritos ao Emprego* (Labour Survey, INE) are neither an alternative nor a supplement to the information released by SEF, due to the sampling error for this population (Baganha 1996).

[43] Such is the case in the statistics of the SEF and the current work, as well.

[44] The remarks made earlier about scarcity of bibliography on emigration apply equally well to the subject of immigration. For the themes of immigration, ethnicity and ethnic minorities in Portugal, in 1994 we found, according to the search efforts of Fernando Luís Machado (1994b) only 67 references.

study of immigrant groups coming from countries such as São Tomé e Príncipe, Brazil, Mozambique, Angola, China and, in a general way, all the communities made up of European immigrants in Portugal. We should underscore that nearly all of the studies of immigration undertaken within the last two decades follow the logic of characterization of the integration in the socioeconomic region of greater Lisbon.

During the 1990s, studies of immigration branched out—a response to the growing visibility of the immigrant communities in Portugal. New themes were developed, notably those concerning the labour integration of the immigrants (Freire 1991). Many studies have emerged from this line of research which have addressed the different kinds of jobs accepted by the immigrants. These works were preceded—all too sparingly, as it were—by similar studies in the case of Cape Verdians (Amaro 1986b).

In the same vein, a pioneering (and very detailed) series of works by João Peixoto (1994, 1996a, 1996b, 1998) has followed the settlement pattern of highly qualified immigrants. The last of these works focused on, among other things, the entrance ways, motivations, and migratory experiences in Portugal of personnel attached to multi/transnational enterprises, allowing valuable comparisons between this privileged subgroup of immigrants and the other immigrants. One team of the CES (Centre for Social Studies—Universidade de Coimbra)—part of the MIGRINF Project—has attempted to capture the economic insertion of immigrants in the domestic labour force from a vast group of indirect indicators, supplemented by 45 interviews of 'privileged informers' and 51 immigrants residing illegally in 1996. Based on information from these sources, an obviously incomplete typology of illegal immigrants and a matrix of entrance motivations of the informal labour market for employers, employees and workers (immigrants and nonimmigrants) was constructed (Baganha, 1996, 1998c). Along these lines of investigation, we believe that the work undertaken by the team coordinated by Baganha, Ferrão, and Malheiros (1998) is one of the most recent studies that exists pertaining to the economic insertion of immigrants in the Portuguese economy.[45]

The ethnicity of earlier immigrant populations has gained interest, as well, and is the topic of several works, including (Castro and Freitas (1991); Bruto da Costa (1991); and Alves (1994). This interest has highlighted the need for clarifying the concept, itself, of ethnicity—a task which has been admirably treated by Fernando Luís Machado (1992a, 1992b, 1994a).

---

[45] See note 27.

Recently, even more themes of interest have emerged. Examples are: the role of feminine immigration (Machado and Perista 1997; Perista 1997); sociographic studies about immigrants residing in degraded areas or involved in re-location processes (Castro and Ferreira 1991; Craveiro and Menezes 1993; Marques et al. 1998; Malheiros 1997); and the social rights of immigrants (Palma Carlos, 1993; Gourjão Henriques 1996; and the obligatory references on this subject, by Pierre Guibentif 1995 and 1996).

The theme of the so-called 'second generation', regarding the impact of the migratory experience on the children of immigrants and the respective adaptation process of the Portuguese society has too been the object of various approaches (Paes 1993; Cortesão and Pacheco 1993; Cortesão 1994; and Justino et al. 1998).

Non-traditional settlement areas outside of the greater Lisbon area-Oporto (Luvumba 1997) or, in a particularly interesting case, immigrants from Guiné settling in Águeda (Pereira 1998)—have also received attention. Although slow, the dispersion of immigrant groups in Portugal is gaining visibility. The works of Luvumba and Pereira mentioned here focus on very specific situations, and we do not yet have a comprehensive picture of this developing phenomenon.

12.3.4. Conclusion

As mentioned above, there exist today important studies of immigrant 'communities' and 'ethnic' minorities in Portugal. Problems of theory regarding conceptualization and the useful transformation of variables are especially complex. This may be because it is not always clear what the theoretical affiliation is that is being followed, or because while moving from one theoretical model to an empirical application, an additional theoretical model is seen to intrude.

The majority of investigators working in the area of migration are self-affiliates of the schools of social theory nonsubstantiality and, in particular, constructivism.[46] Some of the investigations in which the articulation between theoretical framework and empirical application is particularly secure are those of Fernando Luís Machado on ethnicity (1992a, 1992b, 1993, 1994). The last of these works is of special interest for the purposes of this article as it addresses the concepts of immigration and the Luso-Africans:

this last designation brings two main groups together. One, the older, has to do with the Africans of Portuguese nationality, of an average or above average social

---

[46] For the schools and currents see (Maritinello 1995; Guibernau and Rex 1997; Oommen 1997; Machado 1992a, 1992b, 1993).

condition and often of mixed race, who decided during the decolonization process to move to Portugal. The other, that is starting to appear now, is that of the children of the immigrants—born and/or raised in Portugal. While different, these two groups have in common the very thing that differentiates them from all the other immigrants: the degree of integration in the Portuguese society and the lack of intention to return to the countries where they were born. (Machado 1994: 111)

The historical context and motivations that determine the settlement of 'Luso-Africans', until the end of the 1970s, show several things:

> socio-economic characteristics of high professional position and qualification;
> nets of sociability (they do not establish direct and regular social relationships with the immigrants of their respective countries (Machado 1994: 117);
> one social identity ('It is clearly the class identity that is superimposed over the ethnic identity', Machado 1994: 117);
> one ancestry that clearly distinguishes them from the 'new Luso-Africans'.

The new Luso-Africans show the characteristics typically described in the literature on this subject for children of immigrants, the so-called 'second generation'. The usefulness of this is not, in the opinion of the authors, the label attached to the concept, but rather the fact of having a clear cleavage between the population of African descendants that resided in Portugal in 1974 (or settled there between 1975 and 1980), and the population of African descendants which came to Portugal after 1980.

It seems to the authors that these aspects have not received enough attention from the Portuguese scholarly community, but there are at least three good reasons why they should:

> (1) this population does not result from voluntary international migration;
> (2) there existed alternatives to the political decisions that were made (recall that the Netherlands politically recognized the minorities resulting from the end of their own empire (Entzinger 1994; Münz 1996), so the decision and its consequences must be taken into account;
> (3) because, as Zolberg affirms, in line with the thoughts of Horowitz:

> ethnicity is not only a projection or a re-birth of traditional links, but [also] a social construction of today that is used as an organizational resource in conflicts about the allocation of resources and power. (Zolberg 1989: 417)

Several authors have pointed out the change in the composition and motivation of the PALOP citizens who came to Portugal in the 1980s (see, for example, Saint-Maurice 1997).[47] To our way of thinking, this change

---

[47] Saint-Maurice observes that the people of Cape Verde concur with this change.

was accompanied by institutional changes which were sufficiently important that we should consider 1981 as a turning point for immigration to Portugal.

Our reason for this has to do with the legal framework that went into effect in that year, created by Legal Decree 264-B/81 of 3 September, regulating the entrances, duration of stay, exits, visas and residency permits of foreigners (citizens of the—at that time—EEC Member States), and by the newly created 'Nationality Law' (Law no. 37/81 of 3 October), which abandoned the principle of *jus soli* in favour of *jus sanguinis*. As a consequence of this shift to *jus sanguinis*, it became more difficult for children of noncitizens to acquire Portuguese citizenship simply by being born within Portuguese borders, or for any foreigner to gain citizenship through marriage to a Portuguese citizen. At least as important as the changes in the letter of the law, in our opinion, was the perception of these changes on the part of the political elite then in power.

We further believe that Portugal must redefine its own identity *vis-à-vis* its own history and its current position in Europe, whereby the principle of *jus sanguinis* will allow the nation to preserve and transmit its *real politik* to future generations, even if doing so demands some hard concessions. The 'Portuguese identity' advanced by the political elite in the 1981 legislation (essentially one of ethnic affiliation, 'by blood', to its European roots) witnessed some consolidation in the following years through Portugal's EC adhesion, its enrolment in the Schengen Treaty, and then through its ratification of the Amsterdam Treaty.[48] In our reading of the events, therefore, 1981 marks the watershed between 'Portugal: Homeland of Colonial Empire' and 'Portugal: European State'.

Having said this, we remind the reader of our awareness that Legal Decree 308-A/75 of 24 July was revoked only in 1988, and that from 1982 until 12 May 1989, 16,261 persons kept or received Portuguese citizenship under Article 5 (Esteves et al. 1991: 133)—which is to say that the impact of the end of the Empire upon the settling of foreigners in Portugal continued to be felt well beyond 1981. The point to be made is that we recognize that 1981 saw the first steps in the political sphere toward Portugal's self

---

[48] We believe that the address of the Internal Affairs Minister, Dias Loureiro, delivered in Parliament in March of 1996 (see *Diário da Assembleia da República* (DAR), srie, no. 53), exemplifies this new national identity very well. The remarks of government members and the PDS (Social Democratic Party) regarding the proposal for a programme of Special Legalization of Immigrants, and the debates surrounding the alteration of the 1981 Nationality Law (see *Diário de República, I série, no. 57*, 14 April 1994), perfectly illustrate this thinking as well (see Baganha 1998c).

image as an immigration country, and its labelling, largely through the media, as 'immigrants', PALOP citizens, and Portuguese nationals of African descent.[49] If we accept this as a working hypothesis and reconsider the contributions of Fernando Luís Machado in that light, the identification of 'Luso-Africans' as an ethnic group may be confined to its real historical context—a consequence of the fragmentation of the Portuguese Empire in Africa, and the migratory flows, beginning in the 1980s, that came out of it. This labeling, and the collective representation demanded by the 'Luso-Africans', themselves (which served as a lobby group and lent logistical and information support), have led to discrimination in the Portuguese legal environment against PALOP immigrants, compared to immigrants coming from other countries.

It may be fair, therefore, to view the PALOP immigration to Portugal, beginning in the 1980s, within the overall international context of 1980s and 1990s immigration, and to analyse movements of labourers and their families alongside 'forced' re-locations. As mentioned above, this new context would reflect, in a profound and fundamental way, the processes of economic globalization and legal restrictions on economic immigration.

As discussed above, the international migrations we consider here are essentially flows of labour, which presupposes that the direction of flow is a response to the demand for labour in the international market.[50] The economic determinant of international labour movement is refuted and viewed differently, depending on several factors. These factors include the political sanctioning that the EU can exercise (at the national or supra-national levels) over some of the involved countries, and the strength and structure(s) of the active migratory nets at both ends of the migration path. These factors are often construed in such a way that results are at odds with what an economic analysis alone might suggest (Baganha 1990, 1991, 1997). The globalization processes demand that our analytical framework be adapted to accommodate the range of factors that affect international migration.

Economic globalization processes have greatly influenced the organization of national labour markets. These influences are filtered through many types of regulations in those markets and through the social value systems that underlie them, respectively.[51] These filters (which are not limited to institutions) go a long way to explaining why in some markets

---

[49] For more on this, see (Guibentif 1991).

[50] This does not mean that there is or is not forced international migration (flows of refugees and asylum-seekers) towards Portugal—only that our work focuses on voluntary migrations.

[51] The Danish case illustrates this well. See (Hjarno 1996).

there is a tendency for precarious and informal work situations to direct immigrants into self-employment–principally in large metropolitan areas.[52]

This tendency is particularly reinforced in the EU by the migratory policies adopted after 1973 and 1974, that impede the entrance of economic migrants and/or the change of legal residency status, for example, from 'tourist' to 'immigrant'. In response to this 'double punch' (economic globalization coupled with the new institutional framework), sophisticated nets of illegal traffic in people have emerged (Salt and Stein 1997)–a traffic which is extremely lucrative (estimated at 3 to 4 billion dollars annually–just to the EU), and which moves about 400,000 persons into Europe every year.

These entrances, which depend on those traffic nets, can be legal, can appear to be legal (through the use of forged documents), or can be in the form of clandestine immigrants taking advantage of loop holes in the various national legal frameworks (in the EU). These legal loopholes, as is well known, differ tremendously from country to country. As economist George Borjas points out, however, all of the migratory policies share one thing in common. Their primary objective is to answer two questions: 'how many immigrants should the country allow in?' and 'who should those immigrants be?' (Borjas 1996).

The same author also points out that since policy-setting is in the hands of the nationals, the answers normally proposed for those questions are the same: 'whatever maximizes the well-being of the nationals'. Such a maximization should in theory lead to an 'open door' policy on economic immigration, since their entrance would increase the per capita internal product, or as Borjas says, 'would increase the size of the cake'. The problem is that the 'division of the cake would become particularly biased' to the detriment of the national workers who are poorly qualified. Now, as economic distribution has fundamentally one economic response, it is exactly there that the answers to the initial questions will be found.

As the benefits derived from immigrants' entrances are concentrated (they revert to some economic agents usually the immigrants, themselves, because the corresponding costs are deferred and diffused), the political answers to the two questions for the most part reflect the interests of certain economic groups and the interests of previous immigrant groups (perhaps their own) who have already settled in the country. It is evident that aside from the migratory policies in and of themselves (that regulate

---

[52] See (Burgers and Engbersen 1996; S. Sassen 1994, 1996, 1998; Hjarno 1996).

the volume and kind of entrances, as well as permanency), in exercising their own sovereign rights, the countries, too, regulate who it is who can 'belong', and the way in which 'belonging' should occur.

The regime of 'immigrant incorporation' in the welcoming society can be illustrated by two extremes: the Swedish model, which since 1975 has been defined as multicultural, and where the representation of interests is 'corporatist'; and, on the other hand, the French model, which was defined as assimilative, and in which the representation of interests is individual (Kubat 1993; Soysal 1994; Bauböck 1998).

As mentioned above, both the immigration/labour market and the adaptive processes of immigrants to the Portuguese society have been approached by numerous Portuguese investigators, but studies regarding 'immigration as a business', which is gathering interest, and the triad of 'globalization/EU migratory policies/national politics' are still forthcoming.

The impact of economic globalization and the determinants of political sanctioning of the migrations in Portugal (Baganha 1996, 1998b, c) in the EU space have led us to visualize Portugal as a turntable, distributing and absorbing labour according to the parameters of the political space in which it is situated, and the needs of the domestic and international labour markets.

In the Centre for Social Studies other investigations are underway (emigration and detachment of Portuguese workers to Germany, seasonal emigration to Spain, insertion of immigrants in the Portuguese civil construction sector and Cape Verdian immigrants in various European cities). We know that other institutions are carrying on similar or supplemental works, as well. Published findings will advance our knowledge about the migrations across Portuguese borders, in both directions. Based upon a more-informed view, we will be able to formulate a better picture of where the Portuguese worker is going in this new millennium.

References

Afonso, Sofia Isabel Coelho (1997). 'A segunda geração e o regresso—A geografia do actor de fronteira'. Master's Thesis in Sociology, Faculdade de Economia da Universidade de Coimbra.

Almeida, Carlos and Barreto, António (1976). *Capitalismo e Emigração em Portugal*. 3rd edn. (Lisboa: Prelo).

Almeida, J. C. Ferreira de (1966). 'Dados sobre a emigração portuguesa em 1963–65: alguns comentários', *Análise Social*, 4 (13): 116–25.

Alves, Manuel Rodrigues (1994). 'As minorias étnicas do concelho de Loures–que comunicação?', in *Dinâmicas Culturais, Cidadania e Desenvolvimento Local*, Actas do Encontro de Vila do Conde da Associação Portuguesa de Sociologia, APS (Lisboa), 201-10.

Amaro, Rogério Roque (1986a). 'Emigração e desenvolvimento em Cabo Verde–algumas reflexões', *Economia e Socialismo*, 10, 69/70: 129-142.

— (1986b). *Caracterização dos Cabo-verdianos residentes em Portugal, a partir dos dados do recenseamento de 1981* (não publicado).

— (1986c). 'Mercado de trabalho e franjas marginalizadas–o caso dos imigrantes cabo-verdianos', in *O Comportamento dos Agentes Económicos e a Reorientação da Política Económica*, II Conferência do CISEP, vol. II (Instituto Superior de Economia, Lisboa), 355-78.

Antunes, M. L. Marinho (1970). 'Vinte Anos de Emigração Portuguesa: alguns dados e comentários', *Análise Social*, 8 (30-1): 299-385.

— (1973). 'A Emigração Portuguesa desde 1950. Dados e comentários', GIS, Caderno no. 7.

— (1981). 'Migrações, Mobilidade Social e Identidade Cultural: Factos e Hipóteses sobre o Caso Português'. *Análise Social*, 19 (65): 17-37.

Arroteia, Jorge C. (1986). 'A Emigração Portuguesa: Características e Perspectivas Recentes', *Povos E Culturas*, 1: 129-47.

Ávila, Patrícia, Alves, Mariana (1993). 'Da Índia a Portugal–trajectórias sociais e estratégias colectivas dos comerciantes indianos', *Sociologia–Problemas e Práticas*, no. 13, pp. 115-33.

Baganha, Maria I. B. (1990). *Portuguese Emigration to the United States, 1820–1930* (New York: Garland Publishing Inc.).

— (1991). 'Uma imagem desfocada? A emigração portuguesa e as fontes portuguesas sobre emigração', *Análise Social*, 26 (112/113): 277-302.

— (1993). *Principais Características e Tendências da Emigração Portuguesa*. Estruturas Sociais e Desenvolvimento. APS (ed). vol. I (Lisboa: Fragmentos), 819-35.

— (1994). 'As correntes emigratórias Portuguesas no Século XX', *Análise Social*, 31 (128): 959-80.

— (1996). *Immigrants' Insertion in the Informal Market, Deviant Behaviour and the Insertion in the Receiving Country*, In Relatório (Centro de Estudos Sociais, Coimbra) (mimeo).

— (1997). 'Economic opportunities for illegal immigrants in Portugal', Paper Presented to the CEPR Workshop *On The Economics Of Illegal Immigration*, Athens (February).

— (1998a). 'Portuguese emigration after the First World WarI II', in A. Costa Pinto (ed.) *Modern Portugal*, Palo Alto, The Society for the Promotion of Science and Scholarship: 189-205.

— (1998b). 'Immigrant involvement in the informal economy: the Portuguese case', *Journal of Ethnic and Migration Studies*, 24 (2): 367-85.

Baganha, Maria I. B. (1998c). *Immigrants Insertion in the Informal Market, Deviant Behaviour and the Insertion in the Receiving Country*, 2nd Relatório (Centro de Estudos Sociais, Coimbra. (mimeo)).

— and Góis, Pedro (1999). 'Migrações internacionais em Portugal: o que sabemos e para onde vamos', Revista Crítica de Ciências Sociais, no. 52–3, pp. 229–80.)

— and Peixoto, João (1996). 'O estudo das migrações nacionais', in J. M. C. Ferreira et al. (org.) *Entre a Economia e a Sociologia* (Celta edn., Oeiras): 233–9.

— (1997). 'Trends in the 90s: the Portuguese migratory experience', in Baganha, M. I. (ed.) *Immigration in Southern Europe* (Celta Ed., Oeiras).

—, Ferrão, João, Malheiros, Jorge, et al. (1998). *Os Movimentos Migratórios Externos e a sua Incidência no Mercado de trabalho em Portugal*, Instituto do Emprego e Formação Profissional UUC/Oefp, Lisboa.

Baldin-Edwards, M., Schain, Martin A. (eds) (1994). 'Special Issue on The Politics of Immigration in Western Europe', *West European Politics*, 17 (2).

Barosa, José P. and Pereira, Pedro T. (1988). 'Economic Integration and Labour Flows: the European Single Act and its Consequences', Working Paper N. 123. FE–UNL, 1988.

Bauböck, Rainer (1998). 'International migration and liberal democracies: the challenge of integration', 3rd International Metropolis Conference (Zichron Yaakov, Israel).

Böhning, W. R. (1984). *Studies in International Labour Migration* (London: Macmillan).

Borjas, George (1996). 'The new economics of immigration', *The Atlantic Monthly*: 72–80.

Branco, Jorge P. (1986). *A Estrutura da Comunidade Portuguesa em França* (Porto, SECP).

Brettell, Caroline (1978). *Já chorei muitas lágrimas* (Lisboa: Universidade Nova de Lisboa).

— (1986). *Men Who Migrate, Women Who Wait* (Princeton, N.J.: Princeton University Press).

Bruneau, Thomas, et al. (ed.) (1984). *Portugal in Development. Emigration, Industrialization, The European Community* (Canada: University of Ottawa Press).

Bruto da Costa, A., Pimenta, M. (org.) (1991). *Minorias Étnicas Pobres em Lisboa* (Lisboa, Dep. de Pesquisa Social do Centro de Reflexão Cristã).

Burgers, J., Engbersen, G. (1996). 'Globalization, migration and undocumented immigrants', *New Community*, 22, 84.: 619–35.

Carlos, Leonor Palma (1993). 'Imigração e Integração', in *Emigração–Imigração em Portugal*, Actas do Colóquio Internacional sobre Emigração-Imigração em Portugal nos séculos 19 e 20, ed. Fragmentos (Lisboa), 392–406.

Castles S. and Miller, M. J. (1993). *The Age of Migration: International Population Movements in the Modern World* (London, Macmillan).

Castro, Paula, Freitas, Maria João (1991). *Contributos para o Estudo de Grupos Étnicos Residentes na Cidade de Lisboa–Vale do Areeiro, um estudo de caso*, Grupo de Ecologia Social do Laboratório Nacional de Engenharia Civil (GES/LNEC), Lisboa.

CEPAC (1995a). 'Imigração e Associação: Associações Africanas, Outras Associações e Instituições Ligadas à Imigração na Área Metropolitana de Lisboa', *Cadernos Cepac*, Lisboa.

— (1995b). 'Os números da imigração africana. Os imigrantes africanos nos bairros degradados de Lisboa e Setúbal', *Cadernos Cepac/2*, Lisboa.

Chaney, Erick (1986). *Regional Emigration and Remittances in Developing Countries. The Portuguese Exprerience* (New York/London, Praeger).

Cordeiro, A. and Soares, F. (1987). *Les Portugais de France*, in 'Nouveaux Comportements Immigrés dans la crise' (Paris: Mire, Ministère des Affaires Sociales).

Cordeiro, Ana Rita (1997). 'Immigrants in Portuguese society. Some sociographic figures', *SOCINOVA Working Papers*, 4, Lisbon.

Cortesão, Luiza (1994). 'Quotidianos marginais desvendados pelas crianças', *Educação, sociedade e Culturas*, 1: 63–82.

— and Pacheco, Natércia (1993). 'O conceito de educação intercultural. Interculturalismo e realidade portuguesa', *Forma*, 47. 54–61.

Craveiro, João, Lutas, Menezes, Marluci (1993). 'Ecologia Social de um bairro degradado de Lisboa: a Quinta da Casquilha nas vésperas da mudança', in *Estruturas Sociais e Desenvolvimento, Actas do 2.º Congresso Português de Sociologia*, vol. II, ed, Fragmentos, Lisbon: 139–55.

Davis, Kingsley (1974). 'The migration of human population', *Scientific American*, 231 (3): 96–105.

D'Esposito, F. (1998). 'Portuguese settlers in Santo Domingo in the sixteen century (1492–1580)', *The Journal of European Economic History*, 27 (2): 315–29.

Entzinger, H. B. (1994). 'Shifting paradigms: an appraisal of immigration in the Netherlands', in H. Fassmann and R. Münz (eds) *European Migration in the Late Twentieth Century* (Aldershot: Edward Elgar), 93–112.

Esteves, Maria do Céu et al. (1991). *Portugal, País de Imigração* (IED, Lisbon).

Ferreira, Eduardo S. (1976). *Origens e Formas da Emigração* (Lisbon: Iniciativas Editoriais).

— (1984). *Reintegração dos Emigrantes Portugueses: Integração na CE e Desenvolvimento Económico* (CEDEP/AE ISE, Lisbon).

França, Luís de [coord.] [et al.] (1992). *A comunidade cabo verdiana em Portugal* (Instituto de Estudos para o Desenvolvimento (IED), Lisbon).

Freire, João (1991). 'Imigrantes, capatazes e segurança no trabalho da construção civil', *Organizações e Trabalho*, 5–6: 147–53.

Godinho, Vitorino Magalhães (1978). 'L'Émigration portugaise (xve.-xxe. Siècles). Une constante structurale et les résponses aux changements du monde', *Revista de História Económica e Social*, 1: 5–32.

Gonçalves, Albertino (1996). *Imagens e clivagens—Os Residentes face aos Emigrantes* (Edições Afrontamento, Porto).

Gorjão-Henriques, Miguel (1996). 'Aspectos gerais dos Acordos de Schengen na perspectiva da livre circulação de pessoas na União Europeia', separata da revista *Temas de Integração*, 1: 47–95.

Guerra, Isabel et al. (1992). A Comunidade Cabo Verdiana em Portugal, *Cadernos IED* 23 (Instituto de Estudos para o Desenvolvimento, Lisbon).

Guibentif, Pierre (1991). 'A opinião pública face aos estrangeiros', in Esteves, Maria do Céu et al. (1991) *Portugal, País de Imigração*, IED (Lisbon): 63–74.

—(1995). La Pratique du Droit International et Communautaire de la Sécurité Sociale. Étude de Sociologie du Droit à l'Exemple du Portugal, Thèse no. 701, Doctoral dissertation in Law, Geneva and Lisbon.

—(1996). 'Le Portugal face à l'immigration', *Revue Européenne des Migrations Internationales*, 12, (1): 121–39.

Guibernau, M., rex, John (1997). *The Ethnicity Reader Nationalism, Multiculturalism and Migration* (Cambridge: Polity Press).

Hjarno, Jan (1996). 'Global cities in two ways: a comment on Saskia Sassen's global city hypothesis', *Paper Immigration*, 18, Danish Centre for Migration.

IAECP (Instituto de Apoio à Emigração Comunidades Portuguesas) (1991). Documento Avulso.

Justino, D. et al. (1998). 'Children of immigrants. A situation in flux between tension and integration', SOCINOVA, *Working Papers*, FCSH, UNL, 7.

Kohot-Piot (1998). *Les migrations Portugaises—Bibliographie Francophone*, CCPF/ MINGRINTER, Poitiers.

Kritz, Mary et al. (ed.) (1983). *Global Trends in Migration: Theory and Research on International Population Movement*. 3rd printing (New York: CMS).

Kubat, Daniel (ed.) (1993). *The Politics of Migration Policies- Settlement and Integration The First World into the 1990s* (New York, Center for Migration Studies).

Leandro, Maria Engrácia (1987). 'Alimentação e relações interculturais dos emigrantes Portugueses na Região Parisiense', *Cadernos do Noroeste*, I-I: 31–40.

—(1995). *Familles Portugaises Projets et Destins* (Paris, CIEMI, Éditions L'Harmattan).

—(1995). *Au-delà des Apparences Les Portugais Face à l'Insertion Social* (CIEMI, Éditions L'Harmattan).

Leeds, Elizabeth (1983). 'Industrialização e emigração em Portugal: sintomas inevitáveis de uma doença estrutural', *Análise Social*, 19, (77-78-79): 1045–81.

Leite, Carolina (1990). *Ironias de Sempre: Casas de Emigrantes e Discursos sobre o Gosto* (Relatório de Síntese para provas de APCC, Universidade do Minho, Braga).

—(1989). 'Casa de emigrantes: gosto de alguns, desgosto de muitos', *Sociedade e Território*, 8: 67–71.

Luvumba, Felícia Marta (1997). 'Minorias Étnicas dos PALOP's Residentes no Grande Porto (Estudo de Caracterização Sociográfica)', *Cadernos REAPN*, Porto.

MacDonald, J. S., MacDonald, L. D. (1964). 'Chain migration, ethnic neighborhood formation, and social networks', *Milbank Memorial Fund Quarterly*, 42: 82–97.

Machado, Fernando Luís (1992a). *Etnicidade em Portugal–Aproximação ao caso guineense* [Provas de Aptidão Pedagógica e Capacidade Científica], ISCTE, Lisbon. (mimeo)

— (1992b). 'Etnicidade em Portugal–Contrastes e Politização', *Sociologia–Problemas e Práticas*, 12: 123–36.

— (1993). 'Etnicidade em Portugal: o grau zero da Politização', in *Emigração/Imigração em Portugal*, Actas do 'Colóquio Internacional sobre Emigração e Imigração em Portugal' (séc. 19–20), ed. Fragmentos, Algés, 407–14.

— (1994a). 'Luso-Africanos em Portugal: nas margens da etnicidade', *Sociologia–Problemas e Práticas*, 16: 111–34.

— (1994b). 'Imigração, etnicidade e minorias étnicas em Portugal', *Sociologia–Problemas e Práticas*, 16: 187–92.

— (1997). 'Contornos e especificidades da imigração em Portugal', *Sociologia–Problemas e Práticas*, 24: 9–44.

—, Perista Heloísa (1997). 'Femmes Immigrées au Portugal–identités et différences', *Migrations Societés*.

Malheiros, Jorge Macaísta (1994). 'Comunidades Indianas na Área Metropolitana de Lisboa. Geografia de um reencontro, Master's Thesis, Universidade Nova de Lisboa, Lisbon.

— (1996). *Imigrantes na Região de Lisboa. Os anos da Mudança*, ed. (Colibri, Lisbon).

— (1997). 'Urban restructuring, immigration and the generation of marginalised spaces in the region of Lisbon...or a returning to Poço(s) dos Negros', Conference on military aspects of security in Southern Europe: *Migration, employment and labour market* (Santorini, Greece).

Marques, José Carlos Laranjo (1997). 'A emigração portuguesa para a Suíça'. Master's Thesis in Sociology, Faculdade de Economia da Universidade de Coimbra.

Marques, M. M. et al. (1998). Realojamento e Integração Social–A população do Vale de Algés perante uma operação de requalificação urbana, col. SOCINOVA, 1, FCSH, UNL.

Martinello, Marco (1995). *L'Ethnicité dans les Sciences Sociales Contemporaines*, (Paris, col. Que-sais-je?, PUF).

McNeill, William H. (1984). 'Human migration in historical perspective', *Population and Developement Review*, 10 (1): 1–18

— (1978). 'Human migration: a historical overview', *Human Migration: Patterns and Policies*. William McNeill and Ruth s. Adams (eds) (Indiana University Press), 3–19.

Menezes, Manuela, Pinto da Cunha, Conceição (1987). 'Cabo-verdianos em Portugal', *Terra Solidária*, 6.

Münz, Rainer (1996). 'A continent of migration: European mass migration in the twentieth century', *New Community*, 22 (2): 201–26.

Murteira, Aurora e Isilda Branquinho (1969). 'A mão-de-obra industrial e o desenvolvimento português', *Análise Social*, 12 (46): 315–62.

Murteira, Mário (1965). 'Emigração e política de emprego em Portugal', *Análise Social*, 3 (11): 258–78.

Murteira, Mário, et al. (1969). *Recursos Humanos em Portugal* (Lisboa, Fundo de Desenvolvimento da Mão-de-Obra).

Nunes, A. Sedas (1964). 'Portugal, sociedade dualista em evolução', *Análise Social*, 2 (7/8): 407–62.

Oommen, T. K. (1997). *Citizenship, Nationality and Ethnicity* (Cambridge, Polity Press).

Paes, Isabel Sasseti (1993). 'Migrações e Multiculturalidade', in *Escola e Sociedade Multicultural*, Ministério da Educação, Secretariado Coordenador dos Programas de Educação Multicultural, Lisbon: 76–90.

Peixoto, João (1987). 'Migrações e Mobilidade: as novas formas da emigração portuguesa a partir de 1980', in *Emigração/Imigração em Portugal: actas do 'Colóquio Internacional sobre Emigração e Imigração em Portugal (séc. 19–20)*, Ed. Fragmentos, Algés.

—— (1993). 'Migrações e mobilidade: as novas formas de emigração portuguesa a partir de 1980', in M. B. Silva et al. (org.) Emigração/Imigração em Portugal, Algés, Ed. Fragmentos/APS: 278–307.

—— (1994). 'As migrações de profissionais altamente qualificados no espaço europeu: do "brain drain" ao "skill exchange" ', *Socius Working Papers*, 1/94, (Lisbon, ISEG).

—— (1996a). 'Livre circulação e reconhecimento de diplomas–Políticas e realidades na União Europeia', *Socius Working Papers*, 6/96, (Lisbon, ISEG).

—— (1996b). 'A mobilidade de quadros nas empresas transnacionais–o caso de Portugal', Relatório de pesquisa (ISEG, Lisbon (mimeo)).

—— (1998). 'As migrações dos Quadros Altamente Qualificados: Mobilidade e Transferências Intra-Empresariais em Portugal e no Espaço Internacional', Doctoral. dissertation (Lisbon, ISEG).

Perista, Heloísa (1997). 'Mulheres imigrantes em Portugal: um estudo de caso relativo à migração intra-comunitária', comunicação ao colóquio *As Mulheres e o Estado* (Associação Portuguesa de Estudos sobre as Mulheres).

Pereira, A. M. (1989). 'Trade-Off between emigration and remittances in the Portuguese economy', W. P, 129, Faculdade de Economia (Universidade Nova de Lisboa), September.

Pereira, Margarida M. (1998). *O Universo dos Outros–Dissertação sobre a imigração guineense em Águeda*, (Seminário de Licenciatura em Sociologia, Faculdade de Economia da Universidade de Coimbra) (não publicado).

Pereira, Pedro T. (1994). 'Portuguese emigration 1958–1985: some empirical evidence', *Empirical Economics*, 647–57.

Pereira, Pedro T., Tavares, Lara, (1999). 'Portuguese population in France: a snapshot 25 years after their arrival', Working paper 375, Faculdade de Economia, Universidade Nova de Lisboa.

— (2000). 'Is Schooling of Migrants' Children more like that of their Parents, their Cousins or their Neighbours?', *Journal of International Migrations and Integration*, 1/4, fall 2000, 443–59.

Petersen W. (1958). 'A general typology of migration', *American Sociological Review*, 23: 256–66.

Pintado, Xavier (1967). 'Níveis e estruturas de salários comparados: os salários portugueses e os europeus', *Análise Social*, 5 (17): 57–89.

Piore, M. J. (1979). *Birds of Passage: Migrant Labour and Industrial Societies.* (Cambridge, Cambridge University Press).

Pires, Rui Pena, et al. (1984). *Os retornados–um estudo sociográfico* (IED, Lisbon).

— (1993). 'Immigration in Portugal: a typology', in Rocha-Trindade, Maria Beatriz, (ed.) *Recent Migration Trends in Europe (Europe's New Architecture)* (Universidade Aberta/Instituto de Estudos para o Desenvolvimento (IED), Lisbon), 179–94.

—, Saint-Maurice, Ana (1994). 'Da emigração à imigração: o caso português', comunicação ao 'Cost A2 Workshop Immigration in Southern Europe', Coimbra, Novembro 1994. (mimeo).

Poinard, Michel (1983a). 'Emigrantes portugueses: o regresso', *Análise Social*, 19 (75): 29–56.

— (1983b). 'Emigrantes retornados de França: a reinserção na sociedade portuguesa', *Análise Social*, 19 (76): 261–96.

Ribeiro, F. G. Cassola (1986). *Emigração Portuguesa. Aspectos relevantes às políticas adoptadas no domínio da emigração portuguesa, desde a última guerra mundial. Contribuição para o seu estudo* (Porto: Secretaria de Estado das Comunidades Portuguesas/Centro de Estudos).

Ribeiro, Manuela (1998). 'Moving into the frontline–women and emigration in less-favoured areas', in *Shifting Bonds, Shifting Bounds–Women, Mobility and Citizenship in Europe* (Virginia Ferreira, Teresa Tavares and Silvia Portugal (eds), Oeiras, Celta Editora).

Rocha, Edgar (1982). 'Colónias e exportação de mão-de-obra como fontes de divisas: considerações sobre a contribuição dos emigrantes para o subdesenvolvimento económico português', *Análise Social*, 18 (72–4): 1053–75.

— (1987). *'Emigração Portuguesa'. Regulamento emigratório: do Liberalismo ao fim da Segunda Guerra Mundial. Contribuição para o seu Estudo.* (Porto: Secretaria de Estado das Comunidades Portuguesas/Centro de Estudos, 1987).

Rocha, Nuno (1965). *França. A Emigração Dolorosa* (Edi. Ulisseia, Lisbon).

Rocha-Trindade, Maria Beatriz (1973). *Immigrés Portuguais: Observation psycho-sociologique dun groupe de portuguais dans la banlieue parisienne (Orsay)* (ISCSPU, Lisbon).

— (1988). *População Escolar Directa e Indirectamente Ligada à Emigração* (Universidade Aberta, Lisbon).

Rocha-Trindade, Maria Beatriz, Jorge Arroteia (1984). *Bibliografia da Emigração Portuguesa* (Instituto de Ensino Português a Distância, Lisbon).

Salt, John (1987). 'Contemporary trends in Mediterranean labour migration study', *International Migration*, 25 (3): 241–50.

— and Stein, J. (1997). 'Migration as a business: the case of trafficking', *IOM*, 35 (4): 467–94.

Saint-Maurice, Ana de (1993). 'Cabo-Verdianos Residentes em Portugal–Imagens a Preto e Branco', in *Emigração/Imigração em Portugal*. Maria Beatriz Nizza da Silva et al. (eds.) (Lisbon, Fragmentos), 392–406.

— (1997). *Identidades Reconstruídas: cabo-verdianos em Portugal* (Celta Ed., Oeiras).

Sassen, Saskia (1994). *Cities in a World Economy* (London, Pine Forges Press).

— (1996). 'New employment regimes in cities', *New community*, 22: 579–95.

— (1998). 'Whose city is it? Globalization and the Formation of New Claims', in Kristine Dösen (ed.) *Proceedings from the Metropolis Inter Conference. Divided Cities and Strategies for Undivided Cities* (Sweden, Götemborg University), 27–47.

Seccombe, Lawless (1985). 'Some new trends in Mediterranean labour migration: The Middle East connection, *International Migration*, 23 (1): 123–48.

SECP (Secretaria de Estado das Comunidades Portuguesas) (1986). *Emigração. Acordos e Convenções Internacionais* (Lisbon).

Serrão, Joel (1970). 'Conspecto histórico da emigração portuguesa', *Análise Social*, 8 (32): 597–617.

— (1977). *A Emigração Portuguesa–Sondagem Histórica*. 3rd edn (Lisbon: Livros Horizonte).

SEF (Serviço de Estrangeiros e Fronteiras). Relatórios Anuais.

Silva, Manuela et al. (1984). *Retorno, Emigração e Desenvolvimento Regional em Portugal* (Lisbon: Instituto de Estudos para o Desenvolvimento).

Sopemi, Annual Report, OECD, vários anos.

Soysal, T. N. (1994). *Limits of Citizenship Migrants and postnational Membership in Europe* (University of Chicago, Chicago).

Stahl, H.-M. et al. (1982). *Perspectivas da Emigração Portuguesa para a CEE, 1980–1990* (Lisbon: Moraes Editores/IED).

Straubhaar, T. (1984). 'The causes of international labour migration–a demand determined approach', *International Migration Review*, 20 (4): 835–55.

Tilly, C. and Brown, C. H. (1967). 'On uprooting, kinship, and the auspices of migration', *International Journal of Comparative Sociology*, 8 (2): 139–64.

Tribalat, Michèle (ed.) (1995). *Faire France: Une Enquête sur les Immigrés et leurs Enfants* (La Découverte, Paris: Milton Gordon).

Trigal, L. Lopez et al. (1995). *La Migracion de Portugueses en España* (Universidade de Leon).

— (1996). 'La Migration Portugaise en Espagne', *Revue Européenne des Migrations Internationales*, 12 (1): 109-19.

Valagão, Maria Manuel (1989). 'Práticas alimentares dos emigrantes. Mudança ou continuidade', *Sociedade e Território*, (8): 81-91.

Werner, H. (1986). 'Post-war labour migration in Western Europe: an overview', *International Migration*, 24 (3): 543-57

Zolberg, Aristide R. (1983). 'International Migrations in Political Perspective', *Global Trends in Migration*, Kritz, M. et al., CMS, NY: 3-27.

— (1989). 'The next waves: migration theory for a changing world', *International Migration Review*, 23 (5): 403-29.

13. Aliyah to Israel: Immigration Under Conditions of Adversity

Shoshana Neuman

13.1. Introduction

A snapshot at figures of immigration (*Aliyah*) to the Land of Israel
(Palestine) and to the State of Israel reveals the following: between 1882
and 1947, in successive waves of immigration, some 543,000 Jews
immigrated to Palestine, joining the 24,000 who lived there. During the
first three years of statehood (1948–50) the average annual growth-rate of
the Jewish population was about 24 per cent, and between 1948 and 1952,
mass immigration of 711,000 supplemented a population of 630,000.
During the last decade of the 20th century, Israel witnessed a massive
influx of Soviet immigrants. During 1990–98 the Israeli population of 4.56
million was enriched by 879,486 immigrants—a growth-rate of 19.3 per
cent. In 1991, 15,000 Jews were airlifted in one single day in 'Operation
Solomon'.

What were the factors that drove this unprecedented migration of Jews
from around the globe to Israel? Many of the major international migration movements were largely economic in nature (the push of poverty or
the pull of expected enhanced standards of living) or have been in response
to persecution. While all these factors have played some role in immigration to Israel, the Israeli case is unusual in that its origins are essentially
ideological, triggered by the emergence of the Zionist Movement in Eastern
and Central Europe in the last quarter of the nineteenth century. The early
immigrants were motivated by a commitment to resettle and rebuild the
land of Israel, neglected by centuries of Jewish dispersal round the world;
this was paralleled by the intention to create a new socioeconomic order
which would reverse the narrow occupational base allowed to Jews in the
diaspora. These ideological motivations were inherited by their successors;
while economic and political considerations also played a minor role, the
major incentive for immigration remained ideological.

Israel has always encouraged and assisted the immigration and absorption process as part of a pro-immigration ideology and policy. Its *raison d'être* was and remains the ingathering and retention of Jewish immigrants and the forging of these diverse elements into a unified nation. Israel is a country established for and administered by immigrants from diverse countries and origins. The Declaration of the Establishment of the State of Israel (14 May 1948) states:

The State of Israel will be open to Jewish immigration and after the Ingathering of the Exiles will develop the country for the benefit of all its citizens; will be based on the principles of equality, justice and peace in light of the vision of the prophets; will credit equal social and political right to all its citizens no matter what their religion, race or gender; will ensure rights of religion, consciousness, education, and culture; will keep the religious sites of all religions; and will be faithful to the principles of the United Nations.

Israel is legally committed to the absorption of *any* applicant of Jewish origin. The 'Law of Return' which was passed in 1950 states that:

each and every Jew has the right to immigrate to Israel... He will be given an Immigration Certificate by the Minister of Interior... unless he is: acting against the Jewish people; might endanger the health of the public or the security of the country; or has a criminal record which might endanger the safety of the public.

In 1970 this law was amended and the right to immigrate extended to the children, grandchildren, spouse and spouses of children and grandchildren of a person who is Jewish. A person is defined as Jewish if he has a Jewish mother or had converted to Judaism.[1] Indeed, the application of the Law of Return resulted in the growth of the Jewish population from 1.37 million in 1950 to 4.86 million at the end of 1998.

In most cases of rapid population growth, per capita income declines. This is due to adjustment problems, low productivity of immigrants and infrastructure bottlenecks. Israel was an exception. Immigration was accompanied by accelerated growth-rates even though large public funds were devoted to housing, employment and social services to facilitate the

[1] Immigrants may choose to enter the country on an A-1 visa or as full citizens. The latter have the right to vote, as well as the obligation to serve in the Israeli Defence Forces. Apart from this, there is no difference between the two categories of immigration. For example, entitlement for absorption subsidies is not affected. Normally, A-1 immigrants are expected to become full citizens after three years but may renew their A-1 status, if so desired. Although Israeli law permits dual or multiple nationality, immigrants from certain countries are deprived of their original citizenship on emigrating (e.g. from the USSR) or fleeing from their original country (e.g. from Iran). In those cases they are required to become full Israeli citizens and thus the A-1 visa is not an option. Non-Jews, too, may immigrate, but in common with international practice, this right is restricted (Beenstock 1993).

direct absorption of mass immigration. As a result, per capita income which was $3,500 in 1950 surged to $17,000 in 1996—an annual growth-rate of 3.5 per cent.[2] Israel now comes close to the per capital GDP of the high-income economies and is well above the figures of the middle-income economies (World Bank 1995). As an illustration, in 1950 per capita income (adjusted to purchasing power) in the US was 260 per cent larger than in Israel. In 1995 the difference shrank to 65 per cent. Comparing Britain and Israel, a difference of 114 per cent in 1950 dropped to 15 per cent in 1995. There is no parallel in economic history of rapid economic growth going hand in hand with massive immigration and population growth.

While Jewish immigration and the establishment of the State of Israel created the opportunity to achieve the Zionist Movement's goals, it also intensified the historical Jewish–Arab conflict. As the Jewish community grew, conflict with the Arab population escalated. When independence was declared, the new state was already engaged in the first of a series of wars (others following in 1956, 1967, 1970, 1973, and 1982) with neighbouring Arab countries. The War of Independence established the borders of the new state and led to the departure of a significant portion of the Arab population.

At the end of 1997, the Israeli population of 5.9 million was composed of 4.7 million Jews (80 per cent), 868 thousand Moslems (15 per cent), 126 thousand Christians (2 per cent) and 97 thousand Druze (close to 2 per cent). About 108 thousand were not classified by religion.

While millions of Jews left their country of origin to settle in Israel, at the end of 1995 only 34.8 per cent of world Jewry lived in Israel and some 8.5 million still reside all over the world. The largest Jewish community lives in the United States (5.69 million, 43.6 per cent of world Jewish population). Other major countries of residence, with more than 100,000 Jewish residents are the former USSR (660,000; 5.3 per cent), France (525,000; 4 per cent), Canada (362,000; 2.8 per cent), the United Kingdom (292,000; 2.2 per cent), Argentina (206,000; 1.6 per cent) and Brazil (100,000, 0.8 per cent) (Della Pergola 1997).

There is a strong and lasting relationship between Israel and Jews worldwide. These ties translate into material as well as moral support and thus carry concrete implications for the availability of national resources and the balance of payments. Transfers from world Jewry have been

[2] Growth-rates varied during the period 1950-96; from 5 per cent in the 1950s and 1960s, they declined to 2 per cent in the 1970s and 1980s and then increased a little to 2.5 per cent in the 1990s.

a major source of external financing. This aid, which is especially responsive in times of emergencies, provides a unique economic safety net.

The present chapter is organized as follows: the following section describes the major waves of immigration, starting from 1882 up to the present. For each immigration wave, its size, composition, origin, and characteristics are documented.

The third focuses on the process of immigrants' assimilation in the local labour market and addresses three main questions: how well do immigrants adapt to the Israeli economy?; what are the effects of immigration on employment opportunities and are they paying their way in the welfare state? and, are population and production growth interrelated?

The fourth section attempts an overall evaluation of the immigration process and considers what may be learned from past experience to improve the absorption process. In particular, return migration, which reflects failure to absorb, is discussed and the very different absorption policies of the 1950s and the 1990s are contrasted and compared. Suggestions for changes in immigration policies are discussed. An evaluation of the contribution of immigration to economic growth and of the importance of Hebrew language acquisition conclude the section. The last section provides a summary and conclusions.

13.2. Jewish Immigration to Israel: Facts and Policies

The Land of Israel (Palestine) was under foreign occupation for many centuries. Between 1517 and 1917 it was under Ottoman rule. The British occupation, which began in 1917, became a British mandate in 1924. In November 1947 the UN Partition Resolution was accepted by a majority vote, and the State of Israel was established on 14 May 1948.

Jewish immigration to Palestine began in the last quarter of the nineteenth century, accelerated in 1882 after the emergence of the Zionist Movement and has continued ever since. The period 1882–1996 can be decomposed into five subperiods: 1882–14.5.1948, 15.5.1948–51, 1952–66, 1967–89 and 1990–98.

13.2.1. Immigration Streams: Size, Origin, and Dispersal

Table 13.1 presents Jewish immigration figures for each of the subperiods, as well as the average annual number of Jewish newcomers and their

Table 13.1. Waves of Jewish immigration, 1882–1998

Period	Jewish population at beginning of period	Number of Jewish immigrants	Number of immigrants per year	Annual population growth-rate stemming from immigration only
1882–14/5/1948	24,000	542,857	8,293	4.9
15/5/1948–1951	649,500	687,624	194,244	22.7
1952–1966	1,404,400	587,472	39,165	2.4
1967–1989	2,344,900	558,909	24,300	0.9
1990–1998	3,717,100	879,486	97,721	2.5

Calculations based on: *Annual Statistical Abstracts*, various issues; The labour Market in Israel in Recent Months, various issues.

contribution to population growth. Table 13.2 looks at two other sources of population growth as well: fertility and emigration. It also documents the share of net migration (immigration minus outmigration) out of the total population increase.

Table 13.1 reveals that in each of the five periods, more than half a million Jewish immigrants arrived in the country. Dividing the numbers relating to the totals by the different timespans yields annual figures. The most impressive average belongs to the first three and a half years after statehood—199,244 immigrants settled in Israel per year, adding each year 22.7 per cent to the Jewish population. Second comes the most recent wave of immigrants who came, predominantly, from the former Soviet Union—97,721 newcomers arrived every year, thereby causing a population growth at an annual rate of 2.5 per cent. Immigration was more moderate during 1952–66 and 1967–89. During the 1952–66 period immigration was responsible for an annual increase of population by the size of 2.4 per cent and this figure dropped to only 0.9 per cent during 1967–89. Before statehood the annual number of immigrants was relatively low—8,293. However, as the Jewish population at the beginning of this period numbered only 24,000, immigration led to an annual growth-rate of 4.9 per cent.

Table 13.2 provides a closer look at population growth and immigration after statehood. Considering the entire time period (15.5.1948—end of 1996, detailed data for 1997/8 have not yet been published), we see that the Jewish population grew at an annual rate of 4.1 per cent and net migration was responsible for 49.6 per cent of population growth-rates. More than

Table 13.2. Sources of population growth: Jewish and non-Jewish population, 15/5/1948–96 (thousands)

Period	Population at beginning of period	Natural increase	Migration balance		Total growth	Population at end of period	Annual growth-rate	Per cent of immigration balance out of total growth
			Total	Immigrants				
Jewish population								
15/5/1948–1996	649.6	2022.3	1988.0	2590.4	4011.2	4637.4[1]	4.1	49.6
15/5/1948–1951	649.6	88.4	668.4	687.6	754.8	1404.4	23.7	88.3
1952–1966	1404.4	546.7	432.5	587.5	979.2	2344.9	3.5	46.0
1967–1989	2344.9	1042.3	314.5	558.9	1356.8	3717.1	2.0	22.9
1990–1996	3717.1	344.9	575.4	756.4	920.3	4637.4	3.2	62.5
Non-Jewish population								
15/5/1948–1996	156.0	815.2	81.9	84.7	897.1	1122.0[1]	4.3	9.1

[1] Including census adjustments. The non-Jewish population includes the addition of the Arab population in East Jerusalem and in the Golan.
Note: Data for 1997 and 1998 have not been published yet.
Source: Annual Statistical Abstracts, various issues.

two and a half million Jews immigrated to Israel and half a million (both former immigrants and natives) emigrated.

Major differences in immigration measures, in the different subperiods, result in differences in population growth-rates and in the share of migration out of total population growth. Immediately following statehood (1948–51), mass immigration led to an annual growth-rate of 23.7 and net immigration accounted for 88.3 per cent of total population growth. Shortly after (1952–66) these figures dropped respectively to 3.5 per cent and a share of 46 per cent. The decline continued and during 1967–89 annual growth-rates fell to 2 per cent and emigration was responsible for only 22.9 per cent of total population growth. A dramatic change in this trend has been observed since 1990–population grows at an annual rate of 3.2 and net migration now explains 62.5 per cent of population increase.

The Arab population, which totalled 156,000 in 1948, grew mainly as a result of natural growth, at an annual rate of 4.3 per cent. Only 9.1 per cent of total growth stems from migration flows.

Now that we have had a general overview of population and immigration trends, a closer examination of each of the subperiods will lead to a better understanding of immigration patterns.

13.2.2. Period I: 1882–14 May 1948

In 1882 the Jewish population in Palestine which numbered 24,000 was concentrated in four cities: Hebron, Jerusalem, Safed, and Tiberias. The Jewish community shared the land with about one million Arab inhabitants. The land was therefore very sparsely populated and based mainly on subsistence agriculture. At the end of the British Mandate (14 May 1948) Jewish inhabitants in Palestine numbered 649,500 and composed about one-third of the total population of 1.950 million. They lived in six cities, 22 smaller urban settlements and 302 agricultural settlements (Bein 1976). Many of the Jewish settlers were members of the Zionist Movement which emerged in Eastern Europe at the end of the nineteenth century with the goal of resettling the Jewish people in Palestine.

The immigrants arrived in five waves of immigration. Table 13.3 documents their sizes. Each wave had its particular characteristics and influence on the settlements and population. In general, the first three waves (1882–1903, 1904–14, 1919–23) known respectively as the First, Second and Third Aliyah (immigration) originated mainly from Russia, Rumania and Poland, following the Russian pogroms of 1881 and

Table 13.3. Jewish immigration waves, 1882–May 1948

Waves of Aliyah (immigration)	Volume (thousands)
First Aliyah (1882–1903)	20–30
Second Aliyah (1904–14)	35–45
Third Aliyah (1919–23)	35
Fourth Aliyah (1924–31)	82
Fifth Aliyah (1932–38)	217
The Second World War (1939–45)	92
Post-the Second World War (1947–May 1948)	61
Total (1882–May 1948)	542–562

Source: Sicron, M., *Immigration to Israel: 1948–1953*, Jerusalem: The Falk Center for Economic Research in Israel and the Central Bureau of Statistics, 1957, p. 14, table 1.

the organization of new social movements. Each wave numbered some 35,000 immigrants who established new types of agricultural settlements, such as the *Moshava* (private agricultural settlement) and the *Moshav* and *Kibbutz* (both collective agricultural settlements).

In contrast, the 82,000 newcomers from the fourth (1924–31) wave and the 217,000 newcomers from the fifth (1932–8) wave of immigration, who came from Poland and Germany in the wake of the Second World War and the Holocaust, contributed significantly to the development of the cities in the center of the country (Eisenstadt 1973). These immigrants imported capital, human capital, and socioeconomic modernity into the country, helping toward its rapid development and modernization, particularly after the 1930s. They preferred the urban centers of the country as they were the locations of employment and finance (Eisenstadt 1967, 1973). Many of the country's political leaders and high-ranking officials, at that time, after statehood, and even today, belong to this wave of immigration.

During the Second World War (1939–45) about 92,000 Jewish immigrants entered the country, many illegally, as the British Mandate restricted the total number of immigrants to 75,000 over five years (The White Paper, 17 May 1939). This was done in a period when immigration to Israel was, for many European Jews, the only means of escaping the Holocaust and its aftermath.

After the Second World War, 61,000 Jews entered the country. The restrictions of the White Paper were still valid and many of the immigrant ships were seized at sea by the British Navy and the passengers were deported to refugee camps in Cyprus. The obstruction of landing in Israel to immigrants who survived the Nazi concentration camps and their internment in refugee camps aroused anger and residence among the Jewish population in Palestine. The British government appealed to the UN for help in solving the problem. In the summer of 1947 a UN committee visited Palestine, and based on its recommendations, the UN Partition Resolution of November 1947 was passed. It gave the Jewish people national rights over parts of Mandatory Palestine.

In 1947 about 80 per cent of the Jewish population in Palestine lived in the three capital cities: more than half of the population lived in Tel-Aviv (founded in 1909), about 20 per cent in Haifa and close to 10 per cent in Jerusalem. At the same time 20 per cent inhabited 260 agricultural settlements. Sixty per cent of these settlements were located at the geographical periphery of Israel (Lipshitz 1991). The great majority of Jews were of European origin as the number of immigrants from oriental countries was very small during this period.

The funds devoted to immigration and to the development of the Jewish community in Palestine came from Jewish organizations from outside the country. They collected and distributed them, and controlled the absorption process and land acquisition. The chief organization was the World Zionist Movement, replaced in 1929 by the Jewish Agency. The Keren-Kayemet, a second organization closely related to the Jewish Agency, was responsible for land acquisition and bought land for Jewish settlements. Land purchase and agricultural settlements were at the core of Zionist policies and about 40 per cent of all expenses were devoted to this purpose. The British Mandate authorized the Zionist Movement, and later the Jewish Agency, as the main representative of the Jewish interests in Palestine (Bein 1976).

13.2.3. Period II: 15 May 1948–51

The establishment of the State of Israel on 14 May 1948 created a major fundamental change in immigration policies. While during the Ottoman and British rule the size of immigration and land acquisition were dictated by the foreign administrations and in many cases tough restrictions were imposed on immigration, this changed altogether. The Israeli government declared the development of the country as its ultimate goal, which aimed at the absorption of a huge wave of immigration. The gates of the nascent country opened widely and the goal of 'Ingathering of the Exiles' was declared as the mission of the state. Such a mission was unprecedented in the history of the Jewish nation and even in that of other nations. Moreover, it began while war against Israel was declared by the neighboring

Arab countries and was executed by an inexperienced administration with restricted resources which took upon itself the two huge tasks of winning the war and absorbing the many newcomers who fled into the country.

This immigration wave, which began on 15 May 1948, differed from the previous ones in size and composition. (1) *Size*: Between May 1948 and August 1951 the *monthly* number of immigrants was 15,000–20,000. This means that in about three years the Jewish population of 649,500 (on 14 May 1948, at statehood) doubled. At the end of 1951 the Jewish population totalled 1,404,400 which means an annual growth-rate of 23.7 per cent. (2) *Composition*: The first to immigrate were Jews who survived the Holocaust and shortly afterwards they were joined by immigrants from Asian and North African countries. Large communities from North Africa, Turkey, Yemen, and Iraq left their countries of origin and arrived in Israel. Most of them came for ideological reasons or because they felt insecure in their mother countries. The proportions of immigrants by continent were the following: 49 per cent from Europe, 35.4 per cent from Asia, 15 per cent from Africa and 0.6 per cent from the Americas and Oceania.[3] The basic ethnic composition of the Israeli population was formulated at this time. The two major ethnic groups being Westerners (*Ashkenazim*)–Jews originating from European and American countries and Easterners (*Sepharadim*)–those who came from Asian and African countries.

The great majority of the immigrants had no capital or property. Their transportation, accommodation and living expenses (at least for the first few months) were covered in part by international Jewish organizations (e.g., the American Joint Committee and the Jewish Agency) and by the Israeli government (Bein 1976). There also was the urgent need to provide the newcomers with shelter, food, education, and social services, and build the infrastructure of administration, defense, health, education, and social services. The economic burden was very heavy. Funds and loans were provided by the American government, by world Jewry and by the German government (Eban 1972: 76–82).

The authorities which provided the immigrants with low-cost or free housing designated their location. They used the settlement process as

---

[3] The figures of immigrants (followed by their percentage in parentheses), by country of origin, between May 1948 and the end of 1952 are the following: Eastern Europe: Poland–106,727 (18). Rumania–121,535 (17.6), Bulgaria–37,703 (5.5), Czechoslovakia–18,811 (2.71), Hungary–14,517 (2.1), Yugoslavia–7,737 (1.14), other East European countries–6,171 (0.7); Central and Western Europe: Germany–8,350 (1.2), France–3,120 (0.5), Austria–2,671 (0.4), Italy–1,321 (0.2), The Netherlands–1,163 (0.2); Asia: Yemen–45,127 (6.7), Turkey–34,647 (5), Iraq–124,225 (18), Iran–25,971 (3.8), Syria and Lebanon–3,162 (0.5), Eden–3,320 (0.5); Africa: Morocco, Tunisia and Algeria–52,565 (7.7), Libya–32,130 (4.6) (Keren-Hayesod 1953).

a means for population dispersal. Most of the immigrants originating from North Africa and Asia were directed to the new development towns (many of which had begun as *mabarot*) and to *moshavim* (agricultural settlements).[4] They were established by the State and located primarily on the national periphery of Israel (the Galilee in the north and the Negev in the south). The industries established in these towns were based on textiles and food, which do not demand skilled labour and pay relatively low salaries. Later this periphery became socioeconomically inferior. At the same time the large cities (Tel-Aviv, Haifa, Jerusalem), the smaller cities in the core of the State (Ramat-Gan, Netanya, Petach Tikva) and the *moshavot* extended significantly. The polarization between Israel's core and its periphery had grown.

13.2.4. Period III: 1952–66

Following the early years of mass immigration right after statehood, the rate of Jewish immigration declined after 1951 and varied between low and moderate levels. During the period 1952–66, 587,200 Jews immigrated to Israel and at the same time 155,000 emigrated—an addition of about 30 per cent to the population of about 1.4 million at the beginning of the period. Consequently, the mean annual growth-rate of the Jewish population decreased from about 23.7 per cent (during 1948–51) to 3.5 per cent (during 1952–66) (see Table 13.2). This was still an impressive rate by international standards but small compared to the early years of the state. Most of the immigrants during this period came from the traditional countries of Eastern Europe (excluding the USSR) and from North Africa.

During the fifteen years between 1952 and 1966 a cyclical behaviour of immigration can be observed with similar cycles of ups and downs. During 1952–4 immigration dropped very dramatically, net migration totaled 20,200 and immigration accounted for only 17 per cent of the population growth. Moreover, 1953 was the only year since statehood (until today) when the net migration balance (immigration-emigration) was negative. During 1955–7 immigration accounted for 58 per cent of population growth, the share dropped to 32 per cent during 1958–60, increased again to about 59 per cent in 1961–4 and dropped again to 30 per cent during

---

[4] The *mabara* was a new experimental type of settlement. It was a large extended camp, usually in proximity to cities or existing settlements. People were housed in tents or huts of wood and tin. Public services such as health, education, day-care centers, employment centers, etc. were provided by the government. By the end of 1952, 250,000 immigrants lived in 113 *mabarot* (Naor 1986; Eban 1972).

1965–6. For the entire period of fifteen years the migration balance was responsible for 46 per cent of total Jewish population growth.

The non-Jewish (Arab) population grew almost exclusively as a result of natural growth, based on high fertility rates. The annual growth-rate is around 4 per cent and at the end of 1966 the non-Jewish population accounted for 12 per cent of the total population. It is composed of 223,000 (8.4 per cent) Moslems, 58,500 (2.2 per cent) Christians, 31,000 (1.1 per cent) Druze and others (*Annual Statistical Abstracts*, various issues; Rabi 1968).

13.2.5. Period IV: 1967–88

The Six Day War in June 1967 united the city of Jerusalem and reawakened the desire of Jews all over the world to immigrate to Israel.

After a sharp decrease in the number of immigrants during 1965–6, when immigration dropped to about 15,000 annually, the trend changed again in the second half of 1967.[5] In 1967 the number of immigrants rose to 18,056 and in the following year it was 24,107.

The sources of this immigration wave were different from the previous two waves—more than half of the immigrants now came from Australia, Canada, Latin America, South Africa, and the United States.[6] Others came from Western Europe. There were still immigrants from Asia and North Africa, but now they were of a higher socioeconomic status compared to their counterparts from those countries who left during 1948–67 (Achiram 1969, 1971, 1973). Many of these immigrants left family and property in their countries of origin and were willing to try life in Israel while retaining the option for return. This is indicated by the preference of the majority of them for the status of Temporary Resident or Tourist rather than full citizenship.[7] A survey conducted by the Ministry of Absorption in 1970 reveals that 50 per cent of the temporary residents who arrived in Israel between June 1969 and October 1970 returned; most of them were unmarried and the main problem they reported was housing.[8]

---

[5] This shrink in immigration was one of the reasons for a two-year depression in 1966–7 when growth ceased and the share of unemployed surged to about 10 per cent of the labour force.

[6] During each of the years 1969, 1970 and 1971 some 5,000 American Jews immigrated to Israel (Bein 1982).

[7] For example, in 1970, 64 per cent of the immigrants from Western countries and 84 per cent from North Africa refused citizenship and preferred a legal status of Temporary Resident. More indicators: 70 per cent of potential immigrants (age 18+) visited Israel at least once before moving. Nevertheless, two months after arrival, one-third were not certain about the prospects of applying for full citizenship (Central Bureau of Statistics, Absorption Survey 1970).

[8] There was a shortage of houses and apartments (partly caused by the economic depression in 1966–7) and prices rose significantly. Potential immigrants had difficulties in raising funds for high-standard housing.

These changes imply that immigration is no longer exogenous to the social and economic climate of Israel, but rather becomes an endogenous factor. The size and composition of immigration depends on absorption opportunities which, in turn, are related to economic and social/political prospects. For example, unemployment or the high prices of housing depress immigration. High demand for specific occupations (e.g. engineers in the late 1960s) encourages people in those fields to immigrate.

In the 1970s a new source of immigration opened up—the USSR. The three million Jews who lived in the USSR had been denied the right to immigrate to Israel. The Six Day War reawakened their national Jewish identity and their desire to come to Israel. In November 1969 an appeal was submitted to the UN committee for Human Rights, signed by eighteen Jewish families from Georgia, Russia, declaring their desire to join their ancient nation in the State of Israel. It was an enthusiastic, heart touching appeal which received the support of the international community. Russia was torn between its policy of a closed society and close relations with the Arab countries on the one hand, and public opinion on the other hand, and reached a compromise; tens of thousands of Jews were given a permit to immigrate (Eban 1972). As a result, about 150,000 Russian Jews immigrated to Israel.

The immigrants during this time period, most of whom had higher education, technological skills and capital, were less dependent on government aid and were able to decide for themselves the location of their homes. Approximately 70 per cent of the immigrants of the 1970s chose the metropolitan areas of the country: Jerusalem, Tel-Aviv, and Haifa; a minority settled in development towns and contributed to their intensified development (Lipshitz 1991).

A totally different source of immigration which opened up in the mid-1980s (1984–5) was Ethiopia. Confidential diplomatic efforts led to 'Operation Moses' which brought 16,965 Ethiopian Jews to Israel. Although small in size, this operation has an emotional pioneering significance. These immigrants who came from a very different culture and society suffered cultural shock upon arrival and many of them are still dependent on public services and assistance.

During the twenty-three years between 1967 and 1989, over half a million Jews immigrated and 244,000 outmigrated, most of them former immigrants. As a result, the share of net migration in population growth was as low as 22.9 and the share of outmigration was about half of immigration. Population growth dropped to 2 per cent annually.

At the end of 1989, the Jewish population totalled 3,717,100 and the Arab population 842,500. The annual rate of increase of the Arab population at around 3 per cent (stemming from natural growth) resulted in a decrease in the share of the Jewish population to 81.5 per cent, down from 88 at the beginning of the period (*Annual Statistical Abstract* 1968).

13.2.6. Period V: 1989–98

A dramatic change in the moderate inflow of immigrants started at the end of 1989. Triggered by Glasnost and as a response to worsening political and economic conditions in the former USSR, Israel witnessed a massive influx of Soviet immigrants. Between the beginning of 1990 and the end of 1998, the Israeli population of 4.56 million was supplemented by 879,486 immigrants—a growth-rate of 19.3 per cent. The Jewish population increased by 23.7 per cent. The numbers were very high during the first two years: 199,516 in 1990 and 176,000 in 1991 and then slowed down to 70–80 thousand per year, during the years 1991–8 (Israel, Labour Ministry, various issues). For the next coming years the estimates run around 50,000 annually. While in the 1980s the annual growth-rate of the Jewish population was between 1.4 and 1.8 per cent, the 1990–1 wave of immigration increased the Jewish population by 10 per cent, in two years. The reduced immigration flow between 1992 and 1998 has contributed about 2 per cent a year to population growth. Compared with immigration into the USA and other receiving countries, this wave still stands out in its magnitude.

The inflow of Ethiopian Jews also continued in the 1990s. Between 1990 and 1993, 28,646 Ethiopian Jews arrived in Israel, 15,000 of them were airlifted in a single day in 'Operation Solomon'. They were later joined by smaller numbers of Ethiopians and recently by the Falasha Mura people. The Falasha Mura tribe advocates a Jewish origin which had to be denied at some stage due to religious persecution.

The absorption of the immigrants of the 1990s is marked by a new policy concept known in Israel as 'direct absorption'. This change began in the 1980s and is a reversal of the centralized policy which was applied in the first three decades of the State, when the government intervened directly and vigorously in all aspects of immigrant absorption.

Absorption is now directed by market forces and free choice of immigrants. Upon landing in Israel, immigrants now receive an 'absorption basket' from the government, with a certain sum of money meant to last for a limited period of time. With this sum they may do as they see fit in all areas of life: housing; employment; education; consumption; etc. Direct absorption thus lets immigrants decide for themselves, based on their own personal considerations, how they wish to be absorbed. The declared goal of the government's direct-absorption policy was to lessen the immigrants' dependence on national and local authorities, to streamline the absorption process itself and make it more flexible; and to speed up the immigrants' ability to begin functioning in housing, employment, and social and cultural life.

While most of the Soviet immigrants took advantage of this new policy, this was not the case for Ethiopian immigrants. Being equipped with low levels of human capital and with skills which are not compatible with the requirements of the more modern Israeli economy and society, they are more dependent on government assistance. Many of them still reside in public absorption centres or caravan sites and did not integrate into the native labour market and society. This is mainly true for the older newcomers. The younger ones are better integrated into the educational system, the army and various vocational training programmes which prepare them for the labour market.

About 63 per cent of the immigrants of the 1990s settled in the core districts (Tel-Aviv, Central, and Haifa), 10 per cent in the Jerusalem district, 24 per cent in the national periphery: the Northern and Southern districts, and 2 per cent in Judea and Samaria (Lipshitz 1997).

At the end of 1996 the Israeli population totalled 5,759,400 Israelis, of whom 80.5 per cent were Jewish and 19.5 per cent were Arab. The share of the Arab minority increased during the 1990s, despite massive Jewish immigration, due to high fertility rates.

13.2.7. Immigration Streams: Education, Age, and Profession

The immigrants of the various waves originated from various educational, social, and professional backgrounds. Each stream added another building block, as well as a finishing touch, to the Israeli society and economy.

The characteristics of the pre-state immigrations shaped the image of the Jewish community in Palestine. Many of the political leaders of the nascent State of Israel originated from these streams. The immigrants were young, well educated and driven by a social Zionist ideology. Less than 16 per cent of the immigrants (between 1929 and 1948) were older than 44 years and about half were 15–29 years old. As a result, over half of the population in Palestine (between 1931 and 1947) belonged to the age interval of 15–44. Their youth and ideology facilitated a relative smooth adjustment to the different and difficult conditions in the host country.

The newcomers were highly educated. There are no systematic data of educational attainments; however, there are many indicators: in 1931, 93.4 per cent of Jewish men aged 7+ and 78.7 per cent of Jewish women (same age) were literate. There is evidence that this share did not drop until 1948 (Halevi and Klinov-Malul 1968). Studying did not stop after arrival in Palestine. High schools, universities, and cultural centres which were established during this time period enabled the population to flourish intellectually. Easterlin (1961), who did a comparative study of educational attainments of populations of various countries found that in the late 1940s Israel stood out significantly. For example, in 1948 almost 10 per cent of the male Jewish population had a full academic education. This was higher than in the US and more than double compared to many countries for which he had data. Another striking feature of pre-state Israel's educational level is that, in contrast to the usual pattern, the average level of education was higher for the older age groups. An examination of figures of veteran population of 30 and over in 1954 (24 and over in 1948) shows that the percentage of higher education graduates for groups of 30–34, 45–59, and 60 and over were 7.5, 11.4, and 10.9 respectively. While in most countries educational attainments drop significantly with increasing age, the opposite was true in Israel where the level of the two older age groups was noticeably higher than that for the youngest. This fact was relevant for the possibility of successfully assuming the wide variety of tasks involved in the establishment of a national state and the operation of a modern economy. Easterlin (1961) concludes, 'It is no exaggeration to say that in 1948 the educational level of the Jewish population in Israel was close to the highest in the world' (p. 71).

Most of the immigrants had a profession when they entered the country: 15 per cent of the household heads among the newcomers (between 1919 and 1947) were trained for agricultural jobs, 36 per cent for industry, 4 per cent were clerks and 12 per cent had academic and professional positions. Only 13 per cent were unskilled workers (Halevi and Klinov-Malul 1968). The relatively high proportion of agricultural professions was due to the special importance accorded to the return to agriculture in Zionist thinking; this was seen primarily as a means of changing the occupational structure of the Jewish community which hitherto had focused on commerce, finance, and brokerage which were perceived as nonproductive and even exploitative occupations. From 1882 until the outbreak of the First World War, some 49 Jewish agricultural colonies were established in Palestine with about 13 per cent of the Jewish population living in them (Eliav 1978; Katz and Neuman 1996).

The high socioeconomic status also led to improved health standards. Life expectancy rose in less than twenty years (between 1926 and 1944) by about ten years, and reached the level of 64.1 years for men and 65.9 for women (Department of Statistics, *Statistical Abstract of Palestine, 1944–45*, p. 24).

While the pre-state immigrants laid the solid foundations for the Israeli society and economy, the various floors were built after statehood. The main floor was constructed between 1948 and 1951 when the Jewish population more than doubled in three years.

Immigrants of this time period had a lower socioeconomic background than the veteran population and among them there were differences between the Easterners and Westerners. The former were less educated, more traditional, had larger families, less economic resources, and lower skills (Rabi 1968). These differences were responsible for the gap in employment and income between the various groups of immigrants. The reason for these differences was rooted in the cultural, social, and economic natures of the countries of origin. The Asian and African countries were culturally and technologically underdeveloped and the Jews living there, like their native neighbours, were not equipped with modern education and skills. Upon arrival in Israel they had to adjust to the more modern society of the veteran population which originated from Europe and America (Achiram 1973). Unfortunately, the gap in education, standards of living and professions did not close.

Immigration during the third time period of 1952–67 also originated from both Western and Eastern countries and socioeconomic differences between the ethnic groups persisted. According to the 1961 census, 69 per cent of the Asian and African immigrants were literate, compared to 97 per cent of the Americans and Europeans. Data for the academic year 1965/6 show that in the age group of 14–17, 60 per cent of the native Israelis attended school, compared to 50 per cent of immigrants from Europe and America (Westerners) and 30 per cent of immigrants from Asia and Africa (Easterners). At the academic institutions, 60 per cent belong to the first ethnic group, 30 per cent to the second and only 10 per cent to the third. Education gaps combined with other background differences led to gaps in their standard of living. Labour force surveys and income surveys conducted by the Central Bureau of Statistics in the 1950s and 1960s show that while housing and the standard of living improved constantly, the ethnic gap persisted, partly as a result of educational and professional differentials. For example, in 1965, 80 per cent of Western families had living conditions of less than two persons per room, compared to only

35 per cent of the Eastern families. In 1963/4 the average income of an Eastern family was about 65 per cent of that of a Western family. As Eastern families were larger than Western families (average family size of 4.8 and 3.1 respectively) meaning that the differences in income per person were even larger (Rabi 1968).

The immigrants of the 1970s and 1980s were very different from those who came in the first two decades of statehood. They came from Western countries and from the USSR and the majority of them were equipped with high levels of human capital and trained in professional occupations.

Table 13.4 presents educational attainments of Soviet immigrants in comparison to the Israeli Jewish population. Over 50 per cent of them had a post-secondary education compared to 20 per cent of the Israelis. About one-quarter had completed more than sixteen years of schooling, compared to less than 10 per cent of the Israelis. Only 0.1 per cent of the immigrants of this wave had no schooling at all, as opposed to 6.6 per cent of the Israelis.

Table 13.5 gives the occupational distribution of the 1970–9 immigration and the distribution of Israeli workers in 1977. The percentage of immigrants with academic and scientific professions is four times larger than the corresponding figure for Israeli workers (30 per cent and 7.5 per cent, respectively). About 15 per cent are engineers and architects and 5 per cent are physicians (Gur, Vinokur, and Bar-Chaim 1980). The percentage of service and agricultural workers is very low among the immigrants.

However, despite the high levels of human capital, the Soviet immigrants had major problems of adjustment to the Israeli labour market. The source of these problems was rooted in the Russian centralized economic

Table 13.4. Years of schooling: Soviet immigrants and the Israeli Jewish population, 1978

Years of schooling	Soviet immigrants			Israeli population		
	Men	Women	Total	Men	Women	Total
0	—	0.2	0.1	3.9	9.1	6.6
1–4	3.6	4.7	4.2	3.9	4.4	4.1
5–8	12.8	11.1	11.9	23.1	22.4	22.7
9–12	27.8	31.1	29.5	47.9	45.1	46.5
13–15	28.9	32.7	30.8	10.5	13.1	11.8
16+	26.9	20.2	23.5	10.7	5.9	8.3

Sources: Annual Statistical Abstract, 1979, p. 618/9, Survey conducted by the Central Bureau of Statistics, 1979, in Ofer, Vinokur and Bar-Chaim (1980).

Table 13.5. Occupational distribution: Soviet immigrants and the
local Jewish population

Occupation	Soviet immigrants (1970–1979)		Israeli population (1977)	
	Men	Women	Men	Women
Academic and scientific occupations	29.8	30.0	7.8	7.5
Technological occupations	14.6	24.2	8.6	22.5
Managers and clerical workers	3.9	16.4	19.8	31.9
Sales workers	5.0	5.4	8.3	6.9
Service workers	2.1	5.0	7.6	18.2
Agricultural workers	0.1	0.1	6.1	2.9
Skilled industrial workers and other workers	44.5	18.9	41.6	10.1

Source: Ofer, Vinokur and Bar-Chaim, tables 10 and 11.

Table 13.6. Occupation and schooling of Israeli workers (1990) and
immigrants[1] (%)

	Occupation[2]			Schooling		
	1	2	3	0–12	13–15	16+
Israeli workers	14.8	18.1	67.1	74.8	14.5	10.7
Immigrants in USSR	35.5	32.6	35.6	47.3	41.4	11.3
Immigrants in Israel	12.9	12.0	75.1			

[1] Occupation in USSR and education of immigrants is according to the distribution among those who arrived in 1991. Occupation of immigrants in Israel is according to the average distribution in 1991–95 for those who arrived in 1990–91 (Source: CBS Income Surveys, 1991–5).
[2] Occupation 1 includes engineers, physicians, professors, other professionals with an academic degree and managers; Occupation 2 includes teachers, technicians, nurses, artists, and other professionals; Occupation 3 includes blue-collar and unskilled workers.
Source: Eckstein, Zvi and Yoram Weiss, 1997, 'The absorption of highly skilled immigrants: Israel 1991–95', p. 41, table 2.

system and its technological inferiority compared to the West. Many of the newcomers needed some sort of training, retraining in a new profession, or downgrading.

The educational attainments and professional distribution of the recent mass immigration of Soviet Jews are similar to those of the previous wave. They too have an exceptionally high level of education and prior experience in academic jobs (Table 13.6). Over 55 per cent had post-secondary education, compared to about 25 per cent for the native-born population. More than half of them held academic and managerial positions before immigration: 15 per cent were engineers and architects; 7 per cent were physicians; 18 per cent were technicians and other professionals; and 8 per cent were managers.[9] The Soviet immigration contributed to a significant increase in the educational attainments of the Israeli population. Data from the most recent census of 1995, which were recently released, reveal that 70 per cent of Israelis aged 25–64 have a high school diploma, 35 per cent have post-secondary education, and 20 per cent have an academic certificate—up from 11 per cent from the previous census. This dramatic increase is largely due to the immigration from the former USSR. In an international comparison of university graduates, Israel ranks third, after the United States with 25 per cent academics and the Netherlands with 22 per cent.[10]

In contrast to the high quality of education and skills of the Soviet immigrants, the rather small Ethiopian group embodies low levels of human capital.

There is little systematic data on educational and professional attainments of the Ethiopians. The Brookdale Institute carried out a few surveys among Ethiopians who arrived during 'Operation Moses' in the mid-1980s and we can assume that the results would not be very different for the Ethiopian immigrants of the 1990s. A representative survey conducted among 1,200 immigrants, aged 16–30, reveals that over one-third (53 per cent of women and 23 per cent of men) lacked any formal education on arrival in Israel. Only a few were able to join Israeli high schools upon arrival and the great majority joined vocational and training courses funded by the Ministry of Labour, the Jewish Agency and the Joint. Eighty-five per cent of young male immigrants and 39 per cent of female immigrants were enrolled in vocational courses and another half took shorter courses of one year or less. The syllabi were planned to meet the special needs of these immigrants; to provide them with general education and Hebrew language knowledge, and at the same time give them a technical-vocational education to help them integrate in the labour market. Indeed, many of the course completers were later occupied in skilled professions and jobs. About one-third were employed as skilled workers in

---

[9] As an illustration, 57,400 of those who arrived until the end of 1993 defined themselves as engineers and 12,000 as physicians. These numbers should be compared with 30,200 engineers and 15,000 physicians in Israel, in 1989.

[10] In all other European countries the percentage of academics is significantly lower, e.g. Poland and Ireland, 10 per cent; Switzerland, 9 per cent; Italy and Turkey, 8 per cent; Austria, 6 per cent (OCED Statistics, *Ha'aretz*, 1 June 1998).

industry and construction, 13 per cent were technicians and another 13 per cent worked in skilled service jobs. Only one-third remained unskilled workers. The results are impressive given that in Ethiopia the great majority lived in rural areas and worked as agricultural labourers. They therefore had to undergo a complete occupational transformation (Lifshitz, Noam, and Segal 1993).

A comparison of the age distribution of Soviet versus Ethiopian new-comers shows that Ethiopian immigrants are much younger than immigrants from the former USSR. Over 30 per cent of the former are under the age of ten and over 60 per cent are under twenty. Only 5 per cent are older than sixty-five. Respective per centages for the Soviet immigrants are: 14 per cent aged 0-9; 29 per cent at the age of 0-19; and 13 per cent aged 65+. The major differences in the age distributions are due to the much larger families among Ethiopians and the higher life expectancy among Soviets. There is increasing sensitivity to the special problems of Ethiopian youth in coping both with the developmental process undergone by every adolescent, and with the special problems arising from immigration and the need to adjust to a new society. These problems are especially serious, given that most of the families arrived in Israel with very limited educational and financial resources, and that many live in peripheral towns, which are often characterized by limited resources and a shortage of services. Service personal cited a variety of problems among Ethiopian immigrant youth: problematic parent–youth relationships; academic difficulties; difficulties in parental communication with school staff; behavioral and identify problems; and severe economic difficulties. Recently, a number of changes have been made in the policies of the government and of public agencies concerning Ethiopian youth. Maximum effort is being invested in three directions: integrating youth into schools in their home communities; referring youth studying outside their home communities to high-level boarding schools and to matriculation programmes; and tracking down and treating youth at risk (Lifshitz, Noam, and Segal 1997).

It is worth noting that this overall trend of an increase in educational attainments of immigrants (since the 1970s) which is observed in Israel is not a worldwide phenomenon. In the US the relative educational levels of successive immigrant waves fell dramatically in recent decades; in 1970 the typical immigrants who had just arrived in the United States had 11.1 years of schooling, as compared to 11.5 for the typical native workers. By 1990, the typical immigrant had, upon arrival, 11.9 years of schooling, compared to 13.2 for natives. This also led to a corresponding decline in the relative wage of immigrants (Borjas 1994*b*). This trend of decrease in skills exists even in Canada, even though it encourages immigration of the highly skilled, and is screening about one half of an immigrant cohort for human capital characteristics. Although immigrants still tend to be more concentrated in the higher skilled sectors than is the case with the native-born, and less concentrated in more traditional sectors, the over-representation on the skilled occupations appears to decline across subsequent entry cohorts (Green 1995).

13.3. Immigrants' Assimilation and Effects of Immigration on the Local Economy

Many studies in the economics of migration explore the issue of how well immigrants have assimilated into the labour market of the receiving country, and what impact they have on economic growth and on employment opportunities for natives (Bailey 1987; Abowd and Freeman 1991; Borjas 1994*a*). The answers to these questions have clear policy implications, e.g. if the local population benefits from immigration, it may be cost-effective to subsidize it. The discussion of these questions has been debated heatedly in many countries and since the 1970s there has been a growing number of studies on these issues. The introduction and development of computers and computational methods facilitated such studies. Simultaneously, statistical methods have been improved and new procedures (e.g. for the use of panel data) have been proposed. This contributed to a sophisticated econometric analysis of the data, compared to the descriptive nature of data analysis used before.

The Israeli case is used in many of these studies, as Israel provides a large, rich and varied pool of immigrants to observe. They come from a wide range of countries and have vast educational and occupational backgrounds. The lesser degree of self-selection among immigrants to Israel also makes the Israeli experience well suited for such research. The availability of rich data bases such as the 1972 and 1983 censuses, many absorption surveys, and panel data of the last two waves of immigration from the Soviet countries, facilitates such studies.

Three questions will be addressed: (1) How well do immigrants perform in the Israeli labour market?; (2) What are the effects of immigration on employment opportunities and the welfare of the native population?; and (3) What is the relationship and causality between immigration and growth-rates of the local economy?

13.3.1. Immigrants' Assimilation in the Local Labour Market

When immigrants first arrive in a new country, they are at a disadvantage in the labour market, relative to natives with comparable demographic characteristics and skills. Typically, they start with lower wages and subsequently experience a relatively fast earning growth (Borjas 1994a; LaLonde and Topel 1991). This rise in earnings is a result of several factors: immigrants learn the local language and become familiar with local institutions and labour market conditions; they accumulate country-specific human capital and experience; and they find a better match for their occupational skills and move up the occupational ladder. As time since migration passes, this earning differential diminishes. Chiswick (1978) found in a pioneering study, that in the US in the 1970s, earning parity was reached about fourteen years after arrival, and thereafter immigrants earned more than natives.

In Israel this question has been studied mainly for the immigrants of the 1970s and of the last influx of the late 1980s and 1990s. Friedberg (1995) used the 1983 census to study wage-convergence of some 54,000 male, fulltime, salaried immigrants, aged 24–65, from all immigration cohorts. She found that upon arrival in Israel, the average immigrant earns about one-third less than a native-born Israeli with similar characteristics. This earning gap diminishes over time, but is eliminated only after thirty-five years. The assimilation rate of immigrants in Israel is therefore approximately 1 per cent per year.[11]

The innovation of Friedberg (1995) is to introduce to the analysis a distinction between human capital that was acquired abroad and that which was acquired domestically. Her study demonstrates that the most important factor determining the gap in the standard human-capital-corrected earnings of immigrants and natives is the source of their human capital. Foreign human capital earns a lower return than domestic, and this fact alone is sufficient to explain the residual earnings disadvantage of immigrants. Friedberg also found a difference in returns to education by country of immigrant origin—the return to education obtained abroad is higher for immigrants from Europe and the Western hemisphere than for immigrants from Asia and Africa. These patterns may reflect differences in educational quality across continents of origin, as well as compatibility of the education obtained abroad with the requirements of the host labour market.

[11] There is no consensus in the literature regarding assimilation rates in the United States. Most estimates fall in the range of 0–2 per cent (Borjas 1985, 1990; Chiswick 1978; LaLonde and Topel 1991).

Beenstock (1993) and Chiswick (1997) investigated the interdependence between employment absorption and Hebrew proficiency. Beenstock used panel data on immigrants who came to Israel in the 1970s. These immigrants were interviewed on arrival, after one year in Israel and after three years. The data are unique because they refer to different functions of language (understanding, speaking, reading) and record ability at different time points. Examination of panel data for 6,700 immigrants who arrived in Israel during the 1970s reveals that Hebrew proficiency tends to promote employment absorption. It enhances participation, reduces unemployment and promotes occupational convergence.[12] He also found that while Easterners were faster than Westerners at language absorption, the opposite was true for employment absorption. This was evident for participation, employment, and occupational convergence.

Chiswick used the 1983 census data to analyse the effects of Hebrew fluency on labour market earnings of male immigrants. By using census data he was able to refer to 56,000 male immigrants coming from a wide range of countries of origin with various lengths of duration in Israel. His analysis reveals that earnings increased monotonically with the ability to speak Hebrew. The patterns are very similar to relationships in English speaking immigrant receiving countries (Chiswick 1991b; Chiswick and Miller 1992, 1994, 1995).

Ofer, Vinokur, and Bar-Chaim (1980) studied the absorption process of Soviet immigrants who arrived in Israel between 1974 and 1976. They used panel data and absorption surveys and their results draw a picture of very successful economic integration. Immigrants' standard of living is higher compared to their standard of living in Russia, and in some cases even in comparison with the native population. Immigrants reported an increase in most personal consumption components, with the exception of culture only. The absorption of young immigrants was more successful than that of older ones and a positive correlation was observed between assimilation and education, professional status and gender (women were more easily integrated than men). However, occupational convergence took time and, at least during the first few years in Israel, immigrants form the Soviet Union 'traded downward', i.e. doctors became nurses, nurses became auxiliary help, etc. Similar results have recently been obtained by Amir (1993) for immigrants with higher education who belong to the same immigration stream.

---

[12] Wage data were not available and therefore wage-convergence could not be estimated.

Parallel to the Soviet Jewish immigration to Israel in the 1970s and the early 1980s, about a quarter of a million Soviet Jews migrated to the United States at the same time.[13] Chiswick's (1990, 1991a) comprehensive study of their economic integration into the US labour market facilitates a comparison between assimilation of similar groups of immigrants into two different labour markets. Chiswick's studies suggest that immigrants to the US faced greater problems than those met by their counterparts who migrated to Israel. According to the US census of 1980, Soviet immigrants were also less successful compared to other immigrant groups; their average income was 30 per cent lower than that of other immigrants and about 60 per cent lower than the income of immigrants from Europe. Only half of the migrants who had academic, technical or managerial professions were employed in their original job, and a substantial share of them were unemployed. One of the major reasons for the disadvantaged situation of the Soviet Jewish immigrants to the US was their poor command of the English language. In Israel immigrants acquire the language (Hebrew) faster and more easily due to public language schools (ulpan) which they may attend at no charge for six months.

Eckstein and Weiss (1997) have analysed occupational convergence and wage growth of the recent large wave of highly skilled immigrants from the former Soviet Union. Using panel data, their findings suggest that upon arrival immigrants receive no significant return on imported human capital (either schooling or experience); with more time spent in Israel, these returns increase but a gap between returns obtained by immigrants and those obtained by natives remains. This is reflected in returns of 0.03 to schooling acquired abroad, compared to returns of 0.07 that native Israelis receive. Immigrants eventually obtain the same return on experience as natives but convergence is slow. Occupational convergence is also slow, after fifteen years in Israel, the occupational distribution of immigrants tends to converge to that of Israeli workers but, in the short run, a significant downgrading is observed.

Immigrants start with low wages and experience rapid increases; in the initial five years following arrival, wages of immigrants grew at a fast rate of 6.4 per cent a year. Half of this growth can be ascribed to rising rates of return to skills. Occupational transitions account for growth of 3 per cent per year (among immigrants with 16+ years of schooling) and accumulated

---

[13] The US was one of the major countries of destination for Jews who migrated out of their countries of origin. Until the 1920s it hosted the majority of Jewish migrants. Since the 1930s and, significantly after 1948, Israel took the lead. All together, about 7 million Jews changed countries of residence in the last millennium (Della Pergola 1991).

experience in the local labour market accounts for about 1.6 per cent per year. As an illustration, an immigrant who arrived at the age of thirty with 16+ years of schooling initially earns, on average, only half the wage of a comparable native Israeli. By the age of fifty, the wage of this same immigrant will be 10–16 per cent lower than that of a comparable native worker.

A series of studies referred to wage differentials between immigrants from various continents and, in particular, between Easterners and Westerners. Following the mass immigration to the nascent state of Israel at the end of the 1940s and the beginning of the 1950s, large wage differentials between the two ethnic groups were observed. Subsequently these gaps narrowed. As Amir (1980, 1987) has shown, in 1957–8 a gap of 37 per cent was observed between earnings of heads of families who originated from Asia and Africa (Easterners) and those from Europe and America (Westerners). By 1963–4 the gap fell to 32 per cent. In 1968–9 the weekly income difference for family heads was 26 per cent, and in 1975–6 it dropped to 13 per cent. The wage difference between all employee immigrants (and not only heads of families) was larger; about 35 per cent in 1969, 17 per cent in 1976, and 16 per cent in 1982. The social and economic significance of these wage gaps can be related to the factors determining them. The respective roles of human capital differences and discrimination have also been examined. It was found, for example, that the mild decrease in the wage gap between 1957 and 1958 and 1963 and 1964 was comprised of similar decreases in each of the two components. With regard to the highly significant decrease between the end of the 1960s and the middle of the 1970s, two opposite conclusions were drawn; according to Weiss, Fishelson, and Mark (1979) the decrease is attributable largely to a decrease in the explained portion of human capital differences while Amir (1980) claims that the share of the unexplained component of discrimination is larger.

The more recent immigration waves (since the 1970s and up to the present date) are composed of Westerners (the great majority from the Soviet countries) with a negligible proportion of Easterners originating from Ethiopia. A distinction between assimilation of Westerners versus that of Easterners is no longer relevant. However, wage and occupational differentials still exist, stemming partly from differences in educational attainments and other socioeconomic background variables. These gaps result in social and political tension.[14]

[14] For more information on ethnic, economic, and social stratification see Cohen, Bechar, and Raijman (1987); Neuman (1994): Neuman and Silber (1996); and Neuman and Oaxaca (1998).

13.3.2. The Impact of Immigration on the Native Labour Market

A rapidly growing literature documents the impact of immigrants on the native labour market of the receiving country. A pioneering empirical paper on this issue was written in 1970 by Jones and Smith who explored the impact of immigration from the British Commonwealth to Britain, and found that it neither increased unemployment of natives nor overused state welfare funds. Most of the studies which were conducted thereafter investigated the following issues: do immigrants have an adverse impact on native earnings and employment opportunities? If so, how large is the loss in the economic welfare of the natives? Borjas (1994a) reports studies done in the US, Germany, and France in which correlations between native wages and the immigrant share in local labour markets are estimated. All these studies do not support the hypothesis that employment opportunities of native workers are adversely affected by immigrants. Zimmermann (1995) points to similar results for Europe. However, Borjas' appraisal of the literature suggests that 'we still do not fully understand how immigrants affect the employment opportunities of natives in local labour markets, nor do we understand the dynamic process through which natives respond to these supply shocks and reestablish labour market equilibrium' (Borjas 1994a: 1700).

In Israel, this question has been addressed by Simon (1976) who examined the Soviet immigration wave of the 1970s and by Hercowitz and Yashiv (1997) who looked at the last massive inflow of the 1990s.

Simon (1976) explored the effect of the Soviet immigration of the 1970s on the income of native Israelis. Whereas most studies of this kind looked at correlations and elasticities between wages and the share of immigrants, Simon employed a different estimation technique which considered the following elements: (1) the significant burden which immigrants impose on the State welfare system—Israel provides new immigrants, for a period of three years, with various services of housing, health, education, income maintenance, and social services. Subsidies for housing are particularly high with 50 per cent of the rent for the first three years and, in the case of purchase of an apartment, the immigrant receives inexpensive loans; (2) the increase in the size of the labour force results in a decrease in the capital/labour ratio and might also lead to economies of scale; and (3) immigrants who serve in the army and spend several years in mandatory service contribute to defense production. This is a very significant contribution in a state like Israel which, in the 1970s, devoted to defence 25 per cent of its national income. After netting out the first two negative

effects by the third very positive one, Simon came up with the following
estimates: the net effect is negative only for the first year after migration
(−10.75 per cent), close to zero (−0.8 per cent) for the second year and
then increases gradually up to 26 per cent seven years after migration and,
as much as 59 per cent fifty years later. Three years after migration the
immigrant pays back his absorption costs and from then on he contributes
to the welfare of the State. Returns to investment in absorption therefore
are very high, according to Simon's calculations.

As for employment opportunities, in the 1970s the Israeli economy
enjoyed full employment. Unemployment rates were around 3–4 per cent
for both natives and immigrants and immigration had no significant effect
on unemployment. In the 1990s unemployment rose to 5–7 per cent and
the last massive wave of immigration arrived into an economy with above
normal unemployment rates. In this case the effect of mass immigration on
employment rates is of special interest. Hercowitz and Yashiv (1997)
proposed a theoretical model dealing with several aspects of this process
and have tested it empirically. The model emphasizes the point that
immigrants are absorbed into the local labour market gradually and
therefore the effect on the employment opportunities of the native labour
force occurs with a lag. It also incorporates the phenomenon whereby
the immigrants first 'tradedown' their skills and only later they climb the
occupational ladder. The model caters for substitution and complementarity among the various skill groups and takes into account effects
from the markets for goods. The two main findings are: (1) the effect of the
immigration wave of the 1990s on natives' employment is for the most part
positive. This is explained by aggregate demand effects. This finding is
stronger than those of many other papers which found insignificant or
very small negative effects (e.g. Card 1990; Borjas 1994*b*; Zimmermann
1995); and (2) the effect of immigration differs for different native occupational groups. This is explained by the occupational convergence of
these highly skilled immigrants—they first enter low-skill occupations and
gradually work their way up.

13.3.3. The Entwined Growth of Population and Product

The third issue we examine are the growth-rates of the Jewish and then the
Israeli economy during one hundred years of immigration.

Under the British mandate a Jewish economy existed alongside an Arab
one. The Jewish population at the beginning of the century was so small
that it hardly constituted an economic entity. The rapid growth of that

population during 1919–48 (487,000 immigrants, see Table 13.3) with its own institutional structure, accompanied by a concurrent huge growth of product, created a distinct Jewish economy, separate but not completely isolated from the Arab sector (Metzer 1982). Since 1948, the Jewish economy and the economy of Israel have been synonymous, with only a small Arab sector integrated into the general economy.[15]

A full analysis of the performance of the Israeli economy and its interrelations with population growth is beyond the scope of our review.[16] We will concentrate on population as an engine of growth of product. As the estimates of product for the years 1882–1948 and the estimates for the first years of statehood are very rough, our discussion will not refer to these time periods and we will use 1950 as our starting point.

Table 13.7 documents annual population and product growth-rates (total product, per capita product and per capita consumption) for the period 1950 and up to the present date. The record of long-term growth in both product and in Jewish population is truly exceptional by world standards. It is at a record high for the first years of statehood. In 1951 GDP increased by 30.1 per cent and per capita GDP surged by 10.3 per cent. A significant share of GDP was government consumption; however, per capita private consumption also rose by 3.8 per cent. During the period 1952–66 the figures dropped to 10.3, 6.2, and 5.3 respectively. These figures are still very high by any international comparison.

Richard Easterlin (1961) was so impressed by the Israeli experience that he wrote in 1961:

Fortunately, despite the usual difficulties of statistical collection and organization in a newly founded state, reasonably acceptable estimates of real national product are available back to 1950. For the eight years since this date, these tell a story of remarkable accomplishment—a growth in total gross national product of around 140 per cent, an annual rate exceeding 11 per cent. While data for all nations are not available for comparison, it seems certain that no other nation attained a comparable rate during this period. Of course, one may point to the extraordinary addition to the nation's labour force, one of the major inputs into an economic system, as creating some presumption that total product would rise significantly. But, when one turns to the figures for growth of real per capita product, the result is still amazing—an increase of 50 per cent during the period, an annual rate of

---

[15] After the 1967 war, the West Bank and the Gaza strip became part of the Israeli market and the labour pool there both benefited from the higher wages in the Israeli market and served as a buffer to domestic fluctuations (Ben Portath 1986).

[16] For a more detailed analysis see Bein (1976) for the pre-State period; Gaathon (1964a, 1964b, 1971), Prop (1968), and Halevi and Klinov-Malul (1968) for the period 1948–66; Ben-Porath (1986) for 1922–82, and Hercowitz and Meridor (1991) for 1989–91.

Table 13.7. Growth-rates of product and population

Year	Annual growth-rate of GDP	Annual growth-rate of per capita GDP	Annual growth-rate of per capita personal consumption	Annual growth-rate of Jewish population
1922–32	17.6	7.8	–	8.0
1932–14/5/48	11.2	3.0	–	8.4
15/5/48–50	–	–	–	26.5
1951	30.1	10.3	3.8	3.3
1952–66	10.3	6.2	5.3	3.7
1967	2.3	−1.0	−0.9	1.7
1968–72	11.9	8.5	4.7	2.9
1973–80	3.1	0.9	1.5	2.2
1981–89	2.7	1.1	2.5	1.4
1990	6.1	2.8	2.3	6.2
1991	6.3	0.1	1.0	5.0
1992	6.6	2.9	4.1	2.4
1993	3.5	0.8	4.5	2.2
1994	6.8	4.0	6.4	2.4
1995	7.1	4.3	4.4	2.4
1996	4.7	2.5	2.6	2.4
1997	2.7	0.1	1.6	2.5
1998	2.0	−0.4	0.9	2.4

Sources: Ben-Porath (1986) for 1922–50. Calculations based on *Annual Statistical Abstracts*, various issues for 1951–96. Unpublished figures—The Ministry of Finance for 1997/8.

over 5 per cent. Though not the highest in the world during these years, such a rate would put Israel well up among the leaders and would be warmly welcomed by any nation seeking economic development. Moreover, few nations, if any, were confronted with equally adverse circumstances. For, if one harks back to classical stationary state reasoning, such growth in population in an economy of poor and limited resources would be expected, other things remaining unchanged, to lead not to a rising or even a stationary per capita product, but to a declining one. (p. 64)

An international comparison presented by Kuznets (1973) adds more perspective to the Israeli figures.

Table 13.8 shows growth-rates for various countries, for the period 1950–68.[17] Only Japan precedes Israel with an annual GDP growth-rate

[17] Communist countries are excluded due to their different economic/political system.

Table 13.8. Growth-rates—various countries, 1950–68

Country	GDP	Population	GDP per capita
Israel	9.2	3.9	5.1
Japan	9.7	1.0	8.6
Taiwan	8.5	3.4	4.9
South Korea	6.3	2.7	3.5
Austria	5.2	0.4	4.8
Germany	6.2	1.1	5.0
France	5.1	1.2	3.9
Italy	5.6	0.7	4.9
Greece	6.4	0.8	5.6
Spain	6.1	1.0	5.1
Portugal	5.4	0.8	4.6
Puerto Rico	6.3	1.1	5.1

Sources: Kuznets, S., 1973, 'Notes on the Economic Development of Israel', The Economic Quarterly: Yearbook of National Accounts Statistics, 1970, vol. II: International Tables, tables 4A and 4B, New York.

of 9.7 (compared to 9.2 in Israel). Taiwan comes close with a rate of 8.5. When per-capita growth-rates are compared, Japan stands out again (with a rate of 8.6) while Israel is close to seven other countries: Austria, Germany, Greece, Italy, Puerto Rico, and Spain, with growth-rates of around 5 per cent. Kuznets concludes that in 1965, out of 106 non-Communist economies with a population of one million or more, only very few reached growth-rates higher than Israel.

Kuznets (1972) also raises the question of causality between the influx of immigrants during the late 1940s and early 1950s and the very impressive growth-rates during 1951–66. He does not give a clearcut answer as there are counter observations. There are countries with similar demographic backgrounds and low productivity rates and also countries with similar demographic experience and yet low growth-rates. He felt that ideological and moral factors contributed to the phenomenal economic success; the strong belief that the Jewish state has to be rebuilt, the sense of unity both in the country and among world Jewry; and the existence of a hostile and isolated environment.

1966–7 were years of recession when per capita GDP and per capita consumption dropped by about 1 per cent. One of the traumatic lessons of this recession was the ensuing wave of emigration, which indicates that emigration responds to economic fluctuations. In 1968 the economy was back on track and between 1968 and 1972 GDP rose by 11.9 per cent annually while the population increased by 2.9 per cent. As a result per capita GDP grew more than 8 per cent each year. The two decades of the 1950s and the 1960s were therefore years of rapid economic growth in which gross domestic product rose about 10 per cent annually. There were relatively few changes in the average annual growth-rate of the population (around 3.5 per cent) and, as a result, product per capita increased by more than 5 per cent annually. By the late 1960s only several other countries (Hong-Kong, Korea, Singapore, Taiwan, and a few oil exporters) performed as well as Israel or better.

In the third decade a sharp downward trend set in. Between 1973 and 1980 the population grew at an annual rate of 2.2 per cent, GDP at 3.1 per cent and GDP per capita at 1 per cent only. After 1973, in addition to a slowdown in immigration, Israel underwent external shocks; the energy crises of 1973–4 and 1979 with associated changes, made the 1970s a period of slow growth worldwide. Rising defence expenditures after the 1973 war and the return of the Sinai oil fields to Egypt as part of the Camp David Accord exacerbated the problem.

This trend of slowdown of immigration and growth continued in the 1980s as well. Between 1981 and 1989 the Jewish population grew by less than 1.5 per cent annually, GDP rose by a yearly average of 2.7 per cent and per capita GDP by 1.1 per cent. This trend has changed altogether with the mass immigration of Jews from the former Soviet Union which started towards the end of 1989. This wave, which stands out in its magnitude, reached population growth-rate peaks of 6.2 and 5.0 per cent in 1990 and 1991, respectively, and then slowed down to an annual population growth-rate of 2.4 during each of the years 1993–8. The increase in population was accompanied by annual GDP growth-rates of over 5 per cent during 1990–5.[18] Per capita GDP growth-rates were less consistent and ranged between 0.1 per cent in 1991 and over 4 per cent in 1994 and 1995. The high growth-rates of 1994–5 are probably a result of the assimilation process and the increase in the productivity of the immigrants who arrived in 1990–1. The rate of growth of the Israeli economy, during the first half of the 1990s, has been one of the highest in the world, more than double the rate of the OECD countries, the G-7, Japan, the United States or the United Kingdom.[19] Only some newly industrialized Asian countries (Singapore, Korea) preceded the Israeli economy (International Monetary

[18] The Israeli GDP growth-rate figures (in percent) are: 1990–6.1, 1991–6.3, 1992–6.6, 1993–3.5, 1994–6.8, 1995–7.1 (Table 13.7).

[19] The G-7 includes Canada, France, Germany, Italy, the United Kingdom, and the US.

Fund, 1997, table A2, p. 148). Starting in 1996, the trend of high growth-rates has changed dramatically. In 1996 GDP growth-rates decreased to 4.7 per cent (from 7.1 in 1995) and per capita GDP growth-rate dropped to 2.5. During 1997–8 economic activity continued to decrease and the economy witnessed a recession. Annual GDP growth-rates plunges to 2.7 in 1997 and only 2 per cent in 1998 and per capita GDP grew by 0.1 per cent in 1997 and −0.4 per cent(!) in 1998. Per capita personal consumption also decreased significantly (Table 13.7). The recession was the result of several economic factors: the economic crisis in the Far East and in the former USSR; security instability in the Middle East; and a significant drop in the number of new immigrants.

13.4. What Have We Learned, What Should be Done?

13.4.1. Failure to Absorb—Return Migration of Immigrants to and from Israel

Immigration decisions are reversible and part of the immigrants into Israel out-migrated, either to their country of origin or to a third country.

Emigration from Israel is frequently stigmatized as unpatriotic. It evokes negative sentiments and even hostility on the part of government officials and the general public. While immigrants who come to Israel are described as *olim* ('going up'), those leaving the country are labeled *yordim* ('going down'). The attitude is more tolerant toward recent immigrants who are migrating back than towards native Israelis who emigrate. Yet, with a growing number of Israelis residing abroad, the social stigma of being a *yored* has significantly weakened. In any case, return-migration indicates failure to absorb and the identification of the factors leading to the phenomenon might lead to an improvement of absorption policies.

Table 13.2 includes figures of net migration and immigration. Calculation of emigration out of immigration reveals that the shares have changed over time: from 3 per cent right after statehood, to 23 per cent during 1952–66, up to 44 per cent at the period of 1967–89 and down again to 20 per cent during 1990–6. However, these figures include emigration of Israeli natives and return-migration of newcomers as well and it is not possible to distinguish between the two different outflows. Nonetheless, the motives for return-migration can still be explored using panel data described below, which follow immigrants up to five years after immigration to Israel.

The study of 'return-migration' has been relatively neglected in the economic literature. Yet the little evidence which is available suggests that the process is far from marginal. Jasso and Rosenzweig (1982) report that possibly as many as 50 per cent of legal immigrants to the US emigrated within eight years after arrival. In pre-state Israel, of the 13,000 Jews who arrived in Palestine in 1926, more than half left; in 1927, emigration, for the first time, exceeded immigration (Elizur 1980). This was also the case in 1966. Beenstock (1993) reports that among the immigrants of the late 1970s, the return migration rate among young single immigrants from North America reached 40 per cent within more than three years.

The literature offers three alternative hypotheses for return-migration: (1) Ramos (1992) presents a 'self-selection model' and claims that unskilled workers remain while the more skilled and educated workers migrate back to their country of origin and take advantage of the higher returns to skills in the native country. A sample of return-migrants to Puerto Rico supports his hypothesis. (2) Tunali (1986) argues that re-migration is an option that will be planned in advance if it enhances life-time earnings. He uses data on internal re-migration in Turkey and offers a very loose test for his theory. (3) The 'unfulfilled expectations hypothesis' suggests that the return migrant goes home because life in the host country did not turn out to be as good as expected (Beenstock 1993). This is probably a major reason in the Israeli case where many of the newcomers are ideological immigrants who may suffer from 'burn out' and a culture shock which drives them back home. Return-migration is also motivated by economic factors (such as unemployment or housing problems), although they played only a secondary role in the decision to immigrate to Israel. Moreover, most Westerners take a cut in living standards on arrival in Israel and economic considerations play a major role in the decision *not* to immigrate to Israel. This is the case for Western Jewry as well as for North African and Iranian Jews who preferred to go to France and North America. For similar reasons there has been a high dropout rate among Soviet Jews who received Israeli exit visas but opted for North American while ostensibly en route for Israel.

Until 1988 the American immigration policy was quite liberal and a large share of Soviet Jews preferred immigration to the US. The second hypothesis of lifecycle planning might apply to Soviet immigrants in the 1990s. Part of them chose Israel as a first stop with the plan of later migrating to North America.

There has been almost no empirical testing of the various hypotheses regarding return–migration due to lack of data–return migrants cannot normally be observed once they have left. Israel and Germany are two exceptions, in that data exist on immigrants who left. In Germany the German Socia Economic panel (GSOEP) contains such data,[20] and in Israel the Immigrant Absorption Surveys follows immigrants during various stages after arrival and makes it possible to determine whether return migration has occurred. Such surveys have been conducted in the 1970s–80s tracing the previous wave of immigration from the Soviet Union, and recently in the 1990s, following the last massive wave of Soviet immigrants. However, as this wave is still arriving the panel data collected so far is premature for the analysis of back-migration.

Two empirical studies by Blejer and Goldberg (1980) and by Beenstock (1993) investigated return migration of immigrants who arrived in Israel in the 1970s and the 1980s. Both used panel data from the Immigrant Absorption Survey (IAS) conducted by the Israeli Central Bureau of Statistics. This survey offers a rare look into the behavior of immigrants who subsequently re-migrated. The sampled immigrant households were interviewed three times; first two months after arrival when basic data on the immigrant and his family (both in the country of origin and in Israel) were collected. A second interview took place after a year when immigrants were questioned about their progress with language, employment, housing, and social integration. If an immigrant could not be located at this stage, Border Control Files were checked to see if he left the country. If he had, relations, neighbours, and friends were consulted to determine whether the departure from Israel was permanent or temporary. A similar interview was carried out three years after arrival. Here too, every effort was made to determine whether return migration occurred.

The IAS therefore offers a wealth of microdata on return migrants and enables an examination of whether experience in the first year had any effect on emigration decisions.

Blejer and Goldberg, using a subsample of the IAS, investigated return migration of Western immigrants to Israel (between 1969 and 1972) who migrated back within three years after arrival. They found that return migration was positively affected by economic factors of unemployment and housing density, but negatively affected by knowledge of Hebrew upon arrival, age, and family size. The economic hardships contributed to the frustration of unfulfilled expectations. The age effect can be interpreted in terms of the lifecycle model which suggests that older people have less to gain by reversing their initial decision to immigrate because they have

[20] See, for example, Licht and Steiner (1993) and Steiner and Velling (1992).

a shorter time horizon. Family size raises the cost of return-migration and knowledge of Hebrew upon arrival facilitates a softer and smoother integration process.

Beenstock (1993) used a subsample which covers a longer period, as well as non-Western immigrants. He made a distinction between immigrants who left the country within the first year and those who left during the second and third years and also between the holders of various visa types (A-1 versus full citizenship).

Beenstock's findings suggest that Soviet immigrants are less likely to emigrate while the opposite is true for immigrants from Western Europe and North America. Immigrants on full visas are less likely to re-emigrate compared to A-1 visa holders. Visa status may reflect intentions at the stage of immigration; absorption experience with language and housing appears to be relevant in predicting the propensity of re-migration while unemployment does not seem to affect it.

Overall, the research lends support to an 'unfulfilled expectations model', immigrants leave because they are dissatisfied with what they have experienced in their new country. Immigrants are more likely to remain if things go well for them.

These findings carry policy implications, some of which have already been recognized leading to changes in the absorption process of the immigrants of the 1990s. The government offered a limited amount of cheap housing and solutions but at the same time gave immigrants subsidies which enabled them to rent or buy apartments wherever they wished. Immigrants were offered training in many areas and employers who showed interest in employing immigrants were subsidized to encourage them to hire newcomers. Language schools (*ulpan*) took care of Hebrew acquisition. A future analysis of the IAS survey currently conducted will help us check of these steps contributed to the relatively smooth integration of this recent massive immigration flow.

Studies of emigration of native-born Israelis (Lamdani 1989) suggest that in this case emigration from Israel is motivated by economic factors such as unemployment and living standards. However, results of two samples of Israelis residing in the US (interviewed in 1972 and in 1977) presented by Elizur (1980), reveal that factors relating to personal development have the most significant effect on emigration. These include opportunities for higher education, professional training, and the utilization of talent, as well as the desire to experience life in other countries. Thus the motives of Israelis coming to the United States are more of a pull than a push nature. Being aware of that and of the fact that migration caused by pull forces has greater chances for return (Lee 1966), the Israeli authorities have recently changed their approach towards Israelis residing abroad. Israel has realized that they constitute a potential pool of immigrants and has employed various means to encourage them to return. Assistance in finding employing and housing, customs reductions, and loans for travel expenses are among the benefits to which returning Israelis are entitled. Elizur's (1980) study suggests that Israelis residing abroad should be encouraged to maintain their Israeli and Jewish identities (read Israeli newspapers, listen to Hebrew language broadcasts and send their children to Jewish schools). While this can not guarantee that Israeli immigrants will feel the need to return to Israel, it may considerably increase the chances. The estimates of native Israelis residing abroad are around 300,000 and they constitute a significant pool of potential immigrants. Other countries facing outmigration of natives might benefit from a similar strategy.

13.4.2. Comparison of Absorption Policies of the 1950s and 1990s

The absorption models used in the 1950s and 1990s are conceptually different. In the first three decades after statehood and especially in the 1950s, the Israeli government employed a highly centralistic model and intervened directly and vigorously in all aspects of immigrant absorption. This policy gradually changed in the 1970s and 1980s and the absorption of the immigrants form the former Soviet Union and Ethiopia in the past seven years has been marked by a completely new policy concept, known in Israel as 'direct absorption'. This policy constitutes a reversal in the manner of thinking regarding immigrant absorption; the newcomers are now given a sum of money and are free to choose how to allocate it, where to live, where and in which occupation to be employed, etc. Preferences and market forces are therefore responsible for the outcomes. Although, so far we have only a short perspective of this new policy, we can still draw some comparison and lessons.

The absorption process of the 1950s is considered as one of the largest in human history in terms of the ratio of immigrants to the native population. During a short time period of three to four years, each of the Israeli natives absorbed more than one immigrant. This was done in a nascent state with very limited resources, engaged in the War of Independence with neighbouring Arab countries. The absorption policy was centralistic; the state provided the newcomers with low-cost housing, employment, health, and educational services. At the same time other national goals were set as well: (1) Population distribution: The state designated the location of immigrants which was motivated by political, economic, and defence needs. Most of the immigrants were directed to development towns that had been established by the State and which were primarily located on the national periphery of Israel. (2) The development of an agricultural sector and basic industry. Given the centrality of agriculture in Zionist thinking, the Israeli government set an economic ideological goal of developing a strong agricultural sector and increasing the number of agricultural workers. Many of the newcomers were directed to agricultural settlements (*moshavim*) where the families owned their farms and cultivated them on an individual basis. At the same time, labour intensive industries have been established by the government in development towns. (3) The third goal was the creation of a homogenous society. The 'melting pot' policy was adopted with the idea that the immigrants would be socially and culturally assimilated into the native Israeli Western-style society. This meant a major cultural change for the Eastern immigrants.

The State of Israel mobilized its resources, power, and imagination to achieve these goals and, indeed, the absorption process was relatively short and successful in terms of the provision of employment, housing, and food and of the development of the periphery and an agricultural sector. However, it created some social and psychological problems: (1) Many of the newcomers were forced to change occupations and the human capital they acquired abroad was ignored. While the majority of them were employed in their countries of origin in commerce, finance, public services, or owned small businesses, here they had to switch to agriculture and industry and be employed as manual workers. Their preferences and backgrounds were not considered and the enforcement of jobs accompanied by steps taken towards cultural homogeneity led to a long-lasting crisis in family structure. (2) The centralistic absorption model led to the total dependency of immigrants on public services. (3) Many of the newcomers suffered from a severe cultural shock. The majority of them came from large cities or urban centres and in Israel were settled in isolated development towns and peripheral settlements.

It is difficult to tell whether, given the limited resources, there was a better alternative absorption model. It was probably the best policy under the difficult circumstances of that time. However, we know that most of the development towns never took off and are socioeconomically inferior. Many of the industries created to provide employment were inefficient and were heavily subsidized in order to keep them from closing. When some of them closed it resulted in intensified unemployment; unemployment in the periphery has always reached much higher rates than the rate for the core of the state.[21] A partial solution for the severe unemployment problems might be easy transportation and connection between the periphery and metropolitan areas. This can be achieved by investment in efficient transportation facilities (trains, subways, roads, etc.).

The agricultural sector gradually lost its centrality. It has been realized that Israel with its very limited land and water resources has no comparative advantage in agriculture (although it does have a comparative advantage in agricultural technology). The agricultural sector is constantly shrinking; the share of employed in agriculture which was 17.9 in 1954 dropped to 14.3 per cent in 1963, 7.5 per cent in 1973, 5.5 per cent in 1983 and mere 2.6 per cent in 1996.[22]

The romantic view that as time elapses social, political, and economic differences between immigrants and natives will fade and all ethnic groups will blend into one homogeneous uniform society has not materialized either. Moreover, it is no more perceived as a target of the absorption policy. Ethnic diversity is being more valued rather than robbing individuals of their cultural heritage. A multicultural, pluralistic society is no more a threat but rather a benefit of immigration.[23]

The absorption policy adopted in the 1990s was totally different. The only objective was a smooth and efficient economic and cultural adjustment of the immigrants. There were no other political, national, cultural, or economic goals. The immigrants were given free choice of settlement and occupation. The various ministries and the Bank of Israel were neutral regarding questions of spatial dispersion or preferred economic sectors, and were at the same time active in employing efficiency measures such as privatization, liberalization, and exposure to import. Investments in infrastructure and education have been made accompanied by a fiscal and monetary policy in order to facilitate the huge absorption process.

As a result, the massive immigration wave was integrated successfully in a relatively short time and at a low cost. Inflation decreased (compared to the 1980s) and is at a one-digit level. Unemployment increased for a while

---

[21] The newspapers of the last weeks are full of sad stories of desperate unemployed heads of households in places like Ofakim, Sderto, and Kiryat Malachi where unemployment reaches peaks of 20–30 percent.

[22] A survey conducted by the CBS reveals that 25,000 agricultural farms were active in Israel in 1997, down from 32,000 in 1981 (a decrease of 22 per cent); 16,000 growing fruits, 5,400 raising chickens, 2,000 raising cattle (some have more than one branch). Kibbutz farms are included in these statistics. The average annual volume of production is $70,000 for a private farm, and $3,000,000 for a kibbutz (*Ha'aretz*, 21 December 1997).

[23] A similar process is prevalent in the United States (Bjoras 1990: 97–9).

and at its maximum reached a level of 12 per cent which then decreased to 6–8 per cent. Output growth has almost doubled. GDP grew in the 1990–6 period at an average annual rate of 6 per cent and the output of the business sector had grown even faster, 7.4 per cent per annum. This was a result of the expansion of both demand and supply of goods and services. The immigrants demanded housing, food, services, and consumption goods and these market forces of demand led investors to increase their demand for investment goods in order to increase their production capacity to meet higher demand for their output. The main contributor to growth of supply was the increase in labour input. Capital growth was another contributor though of a lesser importance.[24] Market forces were therefore responsible for the very positive economic performance of the Israeli economy as well as for the well-being of the newcomers.[25]

The Soviet immigrants were well integrated socially as well, while preserving at the same time their own culture. All together, their landing in Israel is much softer than that of their counterparts of the 1950s.

The difference between the two absorption policies stems from differences in the overall conception which changed gradually and constantly from a centralistic, bureaucratic, and socialist ideology in the 1950s to a liberal one in the 1990s. From an orientation which favored enterprises owned by the Federation of Labour (*Histadrut*) or by large investors who had the ability to face government bureaucracy to a free market orientation which emphasizes entrepreneurship and private investment.

Although we are too close to this last wave to be able to learn the full lessons, there are already many indications that it has been a success story. The lesson that could be drawn is that a country which is facing the need to achieve a goal of absorption of a large volume of immigration, should concentrate on successful absorption only and should not try to concurrently achieve other social or economic goals (Gabaay, Yoram, 'The 1950s vis-a-vis the 1990s', *Ha'aretz*, 24 October 1997).

13.4.3. The Contribution of Immigration to Economic Growth

Neither Kuznets (1972) nor Ben-Porath (1986) were able to establish a clear-cut relationship between immigration and GDP growth-rates.

---

[24] Gross capital stock grew at an annual rate of about 4 per cent during 1990–6.

[25] A survey conducted recently shows that as a result of constant increases in immigrants' income, the gap between patterns between Soviet immigrants and native Israelis is closing and expenditures, e.g., an immigrant household spends on food 1,540 shekel per month compared to 1,730 shekel spent by a native Israeli household. Differences in per capita consumption are even smaller. Gaps in other consumption items (cosmetics, footware, furniture, electrical appliances, clothing, and toys) are also small (*Ha'aretz*, 15 December 1997).

Ben-Porath (1986) used causality tests and concluded that in Israel causality is complex and runs in two directions: at times from population growth to economic growth and at other times the opposite is true. He found strong evidence for causality from immigration to economic growth in the Mandate Period (1926–48). For the period from 1954–82 immigration responded to the growth-rate of per capita income or consumption. However, it is very clear from his study that immigration pushed the rate of increase of capital stock.

Zilberfarb (1996) analyses the factors responsible for the impressive growth-rates between 1990 and 1995 and argues that the main impetus for the increase in output has been the massive immigration inflow. The peace process, which gained momentum with the signing of the Oslo agreements in 1993, has helped reinforce the trend of income growth, but only to a limited extent. Following his argument, we can argue that decrease in the volume of immigration combined with the stagnation of the peace process (since the Likud Party came into power in May 1996) lead to an economic slowdown. Indeed, the growth-rate in 1997 was only 2.7 per cent for GDP and 0.1 per cent for per capita GDP, and in 1998 these two figures continually dropped to 2.0 and −0.4, respectively (unpublished figures–the Ministry of Finance).

The more appropriate test for causality between immigration and growth-rates is, probably, to look at future growth-rates using a large time lag. There is much evidence that when immigrants arrive in the host country their production is lower than that of the native population and it increases with residence in the country.[26] If the assimilation process is spread over twenty years (which is probably an upper limit) this means that immigrants' productivity will rise in the future faster than productivity of native workers. This will lead to a future increase in GDP growth-rates over a long time period. The benefits of immigration are therefore reaped in the future and accumulate for many years after the last immigrant has arrived in the country.

13.4.4. The Importance of Language Proficiency

Many studies conducted in Israel and other immigrant receiving countries testify to the significant role which native language acquisition has on

---

[26] For example, during the first year after arrival in Israel immigrants from the former USSR earned about 45 per cent of the wages of native Israelis with comparable characteristics. Five years after arrival the ratio increased to 71 per cent (Beenstock, M., 'Immigration of the Long Run', *Ha'aretz*, May 1997).

successful economic and social integration (e.g., Chiswick 1997; Beenstock 1993). These studies also indicate complementarity between the native language acquisition and other forms of human capital (such as schooling). As Chiswick (1997) points out, this has important implications for the understanding of expected Hebrew language experience of the recent waves of immigrants from the former Soviet Union and Ethiopia. Intensive Hebrew language training should be very productive for the Soviet immigrants. However, Hebrew language programmes for Ethiopian immigrants will need to overcome their low levels of formal education and literacy. Many of the Ethiopian immigrants still live in absorption centers and this isolation from Hebrew speakers also slows their progress in acquiring Hebrew language fluency.

Israel offers immigrants free language schools for a period of six months. Not only are the courses free, but students are paid some basic subsistence allowance which allows them to devote their fulltime energies to the study of Hebrew. This is one of the explanations why Soviet immigrants to Israel fare better than Soviet immigrants to the US, with similar characteristics. The lesson to be learned is that immigrant-receiving countries could benefit from allocating resources to the establishment of native language schools which will significantly improve immigrants' productivity and integration.

13.5. Summary and Conclusions

This chapter presented an overview of successive immigration waves of Jews into Israel, starting in 1882 and up to the present date. The characteristics of each of the inflows have been documented including size, composition, origin, education, and professional attainments. The integration process and the effects on employment opportunities of the local native population have been examined, as well as the contribution of immigration to economic growth.

Israel provides a large, rich, and varied pool of immigrants to observe. They come from a wide range of countries and have diverse educational and professional backgrounds. The Israeli experience is therefore well suited for the derivation of lessons regarding absorption policies. Some of these lessons have been outlined in the previous section in terms of comparing the different absorption policies employed by Israel, by looking into the return-migration phenomenon which signals failure to absorb, and by relating economic growth to immigration.

Finally, we should mention that much more needs to be explored and has been omitted, due to space limitations. While we have focused on economic assimilation, we have ignored other dimensions and effects of immigration and assimilation: the demographic impact of immigration (e.g., on the age structure, fertility, internal migration, the gender balance, household formation patterns); the impact of immigration on social cohesion and ethnic conflicts; the effects of drastic population pressures on the environment (e.g., deterioration of natural resources such as water, open spaces or ecosystems, pollution); and the effect on micro and macro economic variables, other than employment and growth (e.g., the housing market, the balance of payment, capital stocks, consumption and savings patterns, occupational and industrial structure, unemployment, inflation, public spending and the transfer system, income distribution).

We have not paid attention to other types of immigration which, while minor compared to permanent immigration, still exist in quite sizable magnitudes. These include Arab cross border commuters from Judea, Samaria, and the Gaza Strip working in the Israeli labour market since the occupation of these territories in 1967; and towards, the late 1980s, temporary labour migrants from countries such as the Philippines, Thailand, Portugal, Romania, and Poland. These immigration channels are partly illegal and emerged due to deteriorating Jewish–Arab relations, making Arab workers less attractive as a form of cheap unorganized labour. It is estimated that there are 250,000 labour migrants currently employed in the Israeli labour market, mainly in construction and agriculture.

The study of these and other subjects, all related to immigration, will be facilitated by the use of data from the recent population census conducted in 1995, and which has been released recently, as well as the panel data, derived from successive interviews of immigrants of the last wave.

References

Abowd, John M. and Freeman, Richard B. (eds) (1991). *Immigration, Trade and the Labor Market* (Chicago: University of Chicago Press).

Achiram, Ephraim (1969). 'Economic aspects of absorption of immigrants', *The Economic Quarterly* 62: 151–6 (Hebrew).

—— (1971). 'Lessons from immigration absorption after the Six Days War', *The Economic Quarterly* 69–70: 61–70 (Hebrew).

—— (1973). 'Immigration, absorption and the Israeli economy—past, present, future', *The Economic Quarterly* 79–80: 298–305 (Hebrew).

Amir, Shmuel (1980). 'The wage function of Jewish males in Israel, between the years 1968/9 and 1975/6', *Bank of Israel Review* 52: 3–14 (Hebrew).

— (1987). 'Wage differentials between Jewish males of different ethnic origins in the 1970s', *Bank of Israel Review* 63: 43–63 (Hebrew).

— (1993). 'The absorption process of academic immigrants from the USSR in Israel: 1978–84', Report of the Israeli International Institute for Applied Economic Policy Review (Hebrew).

Bailey, Thomas R. (1987). *Immigrants and Native Workers: Contrasts and Competition* (Boulder, CO: Westview Press).

Beenstock, Michael (1993). 'Failure to absorb: return-migration by immigrants into Israel', Discussion Paper No. 93.04, Jerusalem: The Maurice Falk Institute for Economic Research in Israel.

— (1993). 'Learning Hebrew and finding a job: econometric analysis of immigrant absorption in Israel', Discussion Paper No. 93.05, Jerusalem: The Maurice Falk Institute for Economic Research in Israel.

— (1997). 'Immigration of the long run', *Ha'aretz*, May (Hebrew).

Bein, Alex (1976). *History of the Jewish Settlement in Israel*, 5th edn. (Ramat-Gan, Massada Ltd) (Hebrew).

— (1982). *Immigration and Settlement in the State of Israel* (Jerusalem: Am Oved and the Zionist Library) (Hebrew).

Ben-Porath, Yoram (1986). 'The entwined growth of population and product, 1922–82', in Y. Ben-Porath (ed.) *The Israeli Economy: Maturing Through Crisis* (Cambridge: Harvard University Press).

Blejer, Mario I. and Goldberg, Itshaq (1980). 'Return migration–expectations versus reality: a case study of Western immigrants to Israel', *Research in Population Economics* 2: 433–49.

Borjas, George J. (1985). 'Assimilation, changes in cohort quality and the earnings of immigrants', *Journal of labour Economics* 3(4): 463–89.

— (1990). *Friends or Strangers: The Impact of Immigrants on the US* (New York: Basic Books).

— (1994a). 'The economics of immigration', *Journal of Economic Literature* 32: 1667–1717.

— (1994b). 'The economic benefits from immigration', NBER Working Paper no. 4955.

Card, David (1990). 'The impact of the Mariel boatlift on the Miami labor market', *Industrial and labor Relations Review* 43(2): 245–57.

Chiswick, Barry R. (1978). 'The effect of Americanization on the earnings of foreign-born men', *Journal of Political Economy* 86(5): 897–921.

— (1990). 'Jewish immigrant skill and occupational attainment at the turn of the century', *Explorations in Economic History*, January: 64–86.

— (1991a). 'Soviet Jews in the United States: a preliminary analysis of their linguistic and economic adjustment', *The Economic Quarterly* 148: 188–210 (Hebrew).

— (1991b). 'Speaking, reading and earnings among low-skilled immigrants', *Journal of labor Economics* 9(2): 149-70.

— (1997). 'Hebrew language usage: determinants and effect on earnings among immigrants in Israel', Discussion Paper No. 97.09 (Jerusalem: The Maurice Falk Institute for Economic Research in Israel).

Chiswick, Barry R. and Miller, Paul W. (1992). 'Language in the immigrant labor market', in Barry R. Chiswick (ed.) *Immigration, Language and Ethnicity: Canada and the United States* (Washington: American Enterprise Institute).

— (1994). 'Language choice among immigrants in a multi-lingual destination', *Journal of Population Economics* 7(2): 119-31.

— (1995). 'The endogeneity between language and earnings: international analyses', *Journal of Labor Economics* 13(2): 245-87.

Cohen, Yinon, Bechar, S., and Raijman, R. (1987). 'Occupational Segregation in Israel, 1972-1983', *Israel Social Science Research* 5(1.2): 97-106.

Della Pergola, Sergio (1991). 'Comment on: "Soviet Jews in the United States: a preliminary analysis of their linguistic and economic adjustment"', *The Economic Quarterly* 148: 225-31 (Hebrew).

— (1997). 'World Jewish population', in David Singer (ed.) *American Jewish Yearbook 1997* (New York: The American Jewish Committee), 513-44.

Easterlin, Richard A. (1961). 'Israel's development: past accomplishments and future problems', *Quarterly Journal of Economics* 75: 63-86.

Eban, Abba (1972). *My Country: The Story of Modern Israel* (Jerusalem: Weidenfeld and Nicolson and Tel-Aviv: Davar).

Eckstein, Zvi and Weiss, Yoram (1997). 'The absorption of highly skilled immigrants: Israel: 1991-95', Paper presented at the CEPR conference 'European migration: what do we know?' Munich, November.

Eisenstadt, Shmuel N. (1967). *Israeli Society* (London: Weidenfeld and Nicholson).

— (1973). *Israeli Society: Background, Development, Problems* (Jerusalem: Magnes Press, Hebrew University of Jerusalem).

Eliav, M. (1978). *Eretz Yisrael and its Yishuv in the 19th Century, 1917-1977* (Jerusalem: Keter Publishing House) (Hebrew).

Elizur, Dov (1980). 'Israelis in the United States: motives, attitudes and intentions', *American Jewish Year Book* (Philadelphia: Jewish Publication Society of American), 53-67.

Friedberg, Rachel M. (1995). 'You can't take it with you? Immigrant assimilation and the portability of human Capital: evidence from Israel', Discussion Paper No. 95.02, Jerusalem: The Maurice Falk Institute for Economic Research in Israel.

Gaathon, A. L. (1964a). 'Economic growth in Israel: 1948-1953', *The Economic Quarterly* 43: 13-30 (Hebrew).

— (1964b). 'Economic growth in Israel: 1954-1962', *The Economic Quarterly* 43: 205-16 (Hebrew).

Green, David A. (1995). 'Immigrant occupational attainment: assimilation and mobility over time', Discussion Paper No. 95-15, Department of Economics, The University of British Columbia, Vancouver, Canada.

Ha'aretz, daily newspaper, various issues (Hebrew).

Halevi, Nadav and Klinov-Malul, Ruth (1968). *The Economic Development of Israel* (Jerusalem: Academon) (Hebrew).

Hercowitz, Zvi and Meridor, Leora (1991). 'The macroeconomic effects of mass immigration to Israel', Working Paper No. 29-91, The Foerder Institute for Economic Research, Tel-Aviv University.

Hercowitz, Zvi and Yahsiv, Eran (1997). 'The effects of mass immigration on the employment of natives', Discussion Paper No. 5-97, Tel-Aviv University: The Pinhas Sapir Center for Development.

International Monetary Fund (1997). *World Economic Outlook* (New York).

Israel, Central Bureau of Statistics, *Annual Statistical Abstract*, various issues.

— (1970). *Immigration Absorption Survey* (conducted jointly with the Ministry of Absorption and the Institute for Applied Social Research).

Israel, Ministry of Labour, *The Labor Market in Israel in Recent Months*, various issues.

Jasso, Guillermina and Rosenzweig, Mark R. (1982). 'Estimating the emigration rates of legal immigrants using administrative survey data: the 1971 cohort of immigrants to the United States', *Demography* 19: 279–90.

Jones, C. and Smith, A. D. (1970). *The Economic Impact of Commonwealth Immigration* (Cambridge: Cambridge University Press).

Katz, Yossi and Neuman, Shoshana (1996). 'Women's quest for occupational equality: the case of agricultural workers in pre-state Israel', *Rural History: Economy, Society, Culture* 7(1): 32–52.

Keren-Ha'yesod (1953). in *Numbers—A Periodical for Statistics and Information*, 46 (Hebrew).

Kuznets, Simon (1972). 'The gap: concept, measurement, trends', in Gustav Ranis (ed.) *The Gap Between Poor and Rich Nations* (London: Macmillan).

— (1973). 'Notes on the economic development of Israel', *The Economic Quarterly* 78-79: 189–209 (Hebrew).

LaLonde, Robert and Topel, Robert (1991). 'Immigrants in the American labor market: quality, assimilation and distributional effects', *American Economic Review* 81: 297–302.

Lamdani, R. (1989). 'Emigration from Israel', in Y. Ben-Porath (ed.) *The Israeli Economy: Maturing Through Crisis* (Tel-Aviv: Am-Oved) (Hebrew).

Lee, Everett, S. (1966). 'A theory of migration', *Demography*: 47–57.

Licht, G. and Steiner, V. (1993). 'Assimilation, labor market experience and earnings profiles of temporary and permanent immigrant workers in Germany', Zentrum für Europäische Wirtschaftsforschung GmbH, Discussion Paper No. 93-06, Mannheim (February).

Lifschitz, Chen, Noam, Gila, and Segal, Eran (1993). 'A survey of young Ethiopian immigrants', Jerusalem: JDC-Brookdale Institute of Gerontology and Human Development.

— (1997). 'The absorption of Ethiopian immigrant youth–a multi-dimensional perspective', Research Report: RR-313-97, Jerusalem: JDC-Brookdale Institute of Gerontology and Human Development.

Lipshitz, Gabriel (1991). 'Immigration and internal migration as a mechanism of polarization and dispersion of population and development: the Israeli case', Economic Development and Cultural Change, 391-408.

— (1997). 'Immigrants from the former Soviet Union in the Israeli housing market: spatial aspects of supply and demand', Urban Studies 34(3): 471-88.

Metzer, Jacob (1982). 'Fiscal incidence and resource transfer between Jews and Arabs in mandatory Palestine', Research in Economic History 7: 87-132.

Naor, M. (ed.) (1986). Immigrants and Settlements (Ma'abarot): 1948-1952 (Jerusalem: Yad BenTzvi) (Hebrew).

Neuman, Shoshana (1994). 'Ethnic occupational segregation in Israel', Research on Economic Inequality 5: 125-51.

Neuman, Shoshana and Oaxaca, Ronald (1998). 'Estimating labour market discrimination with selectivity corrected wage equations: methodological considerations and an illustration from Israel', CEPR, Discussion Paper No. 1915.

Neuman, Shoshana and Silber, Jacques G. (1996). 'Wage discrimination across ethnic groups: evidence from Israel', Economic Inquiry 34(4): 648-61.

Ofer, Gur, Vinokur, A., and Bar-Chaim, Y. (1980). 'Absorption in Israel and economic contribution of immigrants from the Soviet Union' (Jerusalem: The Maurice Falk Institute for Economic Research) (Hebrew).

Prop, P. (1968). 'Twenty years of employment policy', The Economic Quarterly, 57-8: 72-85 (Hebrew).

Rabi, C. (1968). 'Demographic development of Israel: 1948-1968', The Economic Quarterly 57-8: 43-54 (Hebrew).

Ramos, F. A. (1992). 'Out-migration and return migration of Puerto Ricans', in G. J. Borjas and R. B. Freeman (eds) Immigration and the Workforce (Chicago: University of Chicago Press).

Sicron, Moshe (1957). Immigration to Israel, 1949-1953 (Jerusalem: Falk Project for Economic Research and Central Bureau of Statistics).

Simon, Julian L. (1976). 'Economic implications of Russian immigration', The Economic Quarterly 90: 244-53 (Hebrew).

Steiner, V. and Velling, J. (1992). 'Re-migration behavior and expected duration of stay of guest-workers in Germany', Zentrum für Europäische Wirtschaftsforschung GmbH, Discussion Paper No. 92-14, Mannheim (November).

Tunali, I. (1986). 'A general structure for models of double-selection and an application to a joint migration/earnings process with remigration', Research in labor Economics, 8 (Pt.B): 235-82.

Weiss, Y, Nili, M., and Fishelson, G. (1979). 'Male wage differentials by ethnic origin, 1969–76' in A. Arian (ed.) *Israel-The Formative Generation*, (Tel-Aviv: Zmora-Modan) (Hebrew).

World Bank (1995). *Word Tables* (Baltimore: The Johns Hopkins University Press).

United Nations (1970). *Yearbook of National Accounts Statistics*, vol. II (International Tables, New York).

Zilberfarb, Ben-Zion (1996). 'The Israeli economy in the 1990s: immigration, the peace process and medium-term prospects for growth', *Israel Affairs* 3(1): 1–13.

Zimmermann, Klaus, F. (1995). 'Tackling the European migration problem', *Journal of Economic Perspectives* 9(2): 45–62.

14. The New Immigrants: Immigration and the USA*

Barry R. Chiswick and Teresa A. Sullivan

14.1. Immigrants and the Census

From the colonial period to the present, and we can expect far into the future, immigration has posed persistent economic, social, and political issues for the United States. The nature of the concerns may change over time, but the issue is seldom far from America's consciousness. Three themes emerge sharply in an analysis of immigrants in recent decades.

- The increased numbers of immigrants and an increase in the proportion foreign-born in the population, especially since 1980.
- The increased diversity among immigrants and the foreign-born population in terms of country of origin, skills, and labor market adjustment, among other characteristics.
- Converging characteristics with duration of residence between the foreign-born and the native-born populations, although the gap may not be closed. Characteristics that converge include fertility, English language fluency, occupational status, and earnings.

14.1.1. Introduction

Immigration has played a vital role in the development of the American population, society, and economy. Since the start of recordkeeping in 1820, over 60 million people have immigrated legally to the United States. The total number since 1820 is even larger because the early data do not include those crossing the land borders with Canada and Mexico, and the data do not include illegal immigrants. Not all immigrants remained in the United States permanently, but without reliable data on emigration, it is difficult to estimate how many returned to their countries of origin. The flow of immigrants to the

* Chiswick, Barry R. and Teresa A. Sullivan "The New Immigrants." In *State of the Union: America in the 1990s*, edited by Reynolds Farley. © 1995 Russell Sage Foundation, 112 East 64th Street, New York, NY 10021. Reprinted with permission.

United States, adjusted for those who have left the country or have died, constitutes the stock of the foreign-born or immigrant population of the United States. According to the 1990 Census of Population there were about 20 million foreign-born persons in the United States (excluding those born abroad of American parents and those born in dependencies of the United States), comprising 8.0 percent of the total population.[1] In recent decades immigration has become an important national and local issue because of both perceptions and misperceptions regarding the immigrants' characteristics and their impact. This chapter uses data from the 1990 Census of Population to explicate the demographic, social, and economic circumstances of the foreign-born population of the United States.[2]

14.1.2. The Census as a Source of Immigration Data

Every decennial census since 1850 has included a question on place of birth that identifies those born outside the United States and classifies them by their country of birth. The decennial census is the best data source available for the study of the foreign-born population. Its nearly universal coverage of the population permits identifying relatively small nationality groups that would otherwise be difficult to survey. Other questions in the decennial census provide a wealth of information about the demographic, social, and economic characteristics of the foreign-born for describing them (e.g., by gender, country of origin, and duration of residence), and then for comparing them with the native-born population.

Yet, the 1990 census has limitations. Immigration is a dynamic process that involves adjustments over time at the destination. The census, however, provides information about individuals only at a single point in time. Although there are some retrospective questions in the 1990 census (e.g., where the respondent was born, where he or she was living in 1985, and if foreign-born, when the respondent came to the United States), they are rather limited.[3] As a result, some aspects of the dynamic adjustment process of immigrants must be inferred from the cross-sectional census data or by tracking cohorts of immigrants from one decennial census to another.

By its very nature the census focuses on measuring the characteristics of individuals and households. Thus, the empirical analysis of the macroeconomic impact of immigrants, and their impact on the distribution of income of either families or persons cannot be addressed here (see Chiswick, Chiswick, and Karras 1992). The absence of data on parental nativity (except for those living with their parents) and the inability to identify illegal aliens or recently legalized aliens pose additional limitations in using the census data.

Parental nativity, which had been asked in every census from 1870 through 1970, would provide information for analyzing the longer term adjustment and impact of immigrants in the first and second generations.

The administrative records of the Immigration and Naturalization Service (INS) provide additional information concerning the flow of immigrants and the characteristics of those entering during a year.[4] The INS data are, however, largely confined to the self-reported characteristics of legally admitted aliens when they apply for permanent alien status, and hence the reporting may be influenced by the applicant's desire to maximize the probability of obtaining a visa. There is no regular INS follow-up survey on immigrants, and so INS data are not directly useful for analyzing either the characteristics or impact of the foreign-born population or the adjustment process of immigrants. INS obtains data on the characteristics of illegal aliens at the time of apprehension, but these data are quite limited in terms of the information solicited.

Illegal immigration has returned as a major policy concern, in spite of the provisions of the Immigration Reform and Control Act of 1986.[5] The 1986 Act was intended to "wipe the slate clean" by offering amnesty to certain illegal aliens already in the United States and to discourage future illegal migration by imposing penalties on employers who knowingly hire illegal aliens.[6] It is reasonable to assume that most beneficiaries of amnesty were enumerated in the 1990 Census, but it is unclear to what extent the illegal aliens who could not satisfy the provisions of the 1986 Act or who arrived after 1986 appear in the 1990 census data. Census data are likely to include some, but not all, illegal aliens.

14.2. Immigration, Immigration Law, and Diversity

Anyone who walks the streets of Los Angeles today, or who walked the streets of Chicago or New York at any time in this century, would conclude that America's foreign-born population has grown rapidly and that they come from "everywhere." Just how true this observation is, and why it is prompted by visiting our largest cities, is the theme of this section.

14.2.1. Trends Over Time

Data from the INS indicate that after the great wave of immigration from the 1880s up to World War I, there was a period of decline and then very low immigration during the 1930s and early 1940s (Table 14.1). The difficulties in leaving Europe and the dangers of ocean transport during

Table 14.1. Immigration and proportion foreign-born in the United States, 1871–1998

Period	Number	Immigration Rate[a]	Percent Foreign Born[b]
1991–98	7,605,680[c]	3.7	10.0
1981–90	7,338,062[c]	3.2	8.0
1971–80	4,493,314	2.2	6.2
1961–70	3,321,677	1.9	4.7
1951–60	2,515,479	1.7	5.4
1941–50	1,035,039	0.8	6.9
1931–40	528,431	0.4	8.8
1921–30	4,107,209	3.9	11.6
1911–20	5,735,811	6.2	13.2
1901–10	8,795,386	11.6	14.7
1891–00	3,687,564	5.9	13.6
1881–90	5,246,613	10.5	14.7
1871–80	2,812,191	7.1	13.3

[a] Annual immigration in the period per 1,000 of the population in the census year preceding the period.
[b] Percent of the U.S. population that is foreign-born (excluding those born abroad of American parents) at the end of the period.
[c] Includes 1,329,209 former illegal aliens who received permanent resident alien status from 1991 through 1998 and 1,359,184 former illegal aliens who received permanent resident alien status in 1989 and 1990 under the Immigration Reform and Control Act of 1986. Some may have come to the United States to stay in an earlier decade.
Sources: *Statistical Yearbook of the Immigration and Naturalization Service*, 1998, Table 1, Statistical Abstract of the United States, 1992, Tables 1 and 45. *Historical Statistics of the United States: Colonial Times to 1957* (1960) Tables Series A 5, 53, 57, 62, 63, 68, 69.

World War I, the restrictive immigration legislation enacted in the 1920s, the Great Depression of the 1930s, and World War II limited immigration from Europe, which was until then the primary source of immigrants to the United States. Following World War II, and particularly following the relaxation in 1965 of immigration barriers enacted earlier against Southern and Eastern Europeans and Asians, immigration has increased decade by decade both in absolute numbers and relative to the size of the United States population.

Was immigration to the United States during the 1980s large by historical standards? The answer depends on the criterion selected—absolute numbers or the number of immigrants relative to the population. In terms of absolute numbers, the 7.3 million new immigrants in the 1980s is second only to the peak immigration in the first decade of this century (8.8 million), although relative to the population, the immigration rate of 3.2 per 1,000 population is only about one-quarter of the rate in 1901–10.

Table 14.2 Region of origin of immigrants, by period of immigration, 1921–1998 (per cent)

Period of immigration	Europe/Canada[a]	Mexico	Other America	Asia	Africa	Total number
1991–98[b]	17.0	25.4	22.2	30.9	3.7	7,605
1981–90[b]	13.1	22.6	24.6	37.3	2.4	7,338
1971–80	22.5	14.3	26.1	35.3	1.8	4,493
1961–70	47.0	13.7	25.6	12.9	0.9	3,322
1951–60	68.7	11.9	12.7	6.1	0.6	2,515
1941–50	78.0	5.9	11.8	3.6	0.7	1,035
1931–40	86.8	4.2	5.5	3.1	0.3	528
1921–30	82.7	11.2	3.2	2.7	0.2	4,107

[a] Includes Australia, New Zealand, Oceania, and countries not specified.
[b] Includes over 1.3 million and nearly 1.4 million former illegal aliens receiving permanent resident alien status in 1991–98 and 1989 and 1990, under the Immigration Reform and Control Act of 1986.
Source: Statistical Yearbook of the Immigration and Naturalization Service, 1998, Table 2.

Immigration in the past few decades has been characterized not merely by a rise in the numbers but also by a dramatic change in the source countries. Whereas, during the nineteenth century and the first half of the twentieth century, immigrants came primarily from Europe and Canada, immigration is now predominantly from Asia, Mexico, and other parts of Latin America, including the Caribbean (Table 14.2). The "new immigration" from Asia, Mexico, and other parts of Latin America is having a profound effect that perhaps rivals the effects on the United States of the "new immigrants" of a century ago, who were from Southern and Eastern Europe.

Changes in the flows of immigrants affect the proportion of immigrants in the population, but only after a time lag. For the three decades starting with World War I, while the large number of turn-of-the-century immigrants gradually died and new immigration flows remained small, the proportion of the foreign-born in the population dwindled from its peak of nearly 15 percent in 1910 to about 7 percent in 1950 and less than 5 percent in 1970. The proportion of foreign-born in the population has since increased to 8.0 percent in 1990 (Table 14.1). Despite the recent rise, however, the proportion foreign-born remains substantially below the levels recorded in the late nineteenth and early twentieth centuries.

Just over one-quarter of the total foreign-born population of the United States in 1990 was born in Europe and Canada, with another one-quarter coming from Asia (Table 14.3). Mexico and other parts of Latin America each account for one-fifth. Less than 2 percent of the foreign-born were

Table 14.3. Foreign-born population of the United States, by region of birth and period of immigration, 1990[a]

Period of immigration	Europe/ Canada[b]	Mexico	Other Latin America	Asia	Africa	Other[c]	Total	Number (1,000s)
1985–90	3.2%	6.5%	5.6%	7.8%	0.6%	1.2%	24.9%	4,895
1975–84	3.6	8.3	7.6	11.1	0.8	1.5	32.9	6,464
1965–74	4.2	4.2	5.0	4.2	0.3	0.7	18.6	3,662
1960–64	2.5	1.0	1.7	0.7	0.1	0.2	6.1	1,198
1950–59	5.3	1.0	0.8	0.8	0.1	0.2	8.1	1,588
Before 1950	7.3	0.8	0.4	0.5	0.0	0.4	9.4	1,841
Total	26.1%	21.9%	21.0%	25.0%	1.8%	4.3%	100.0%	19,649
Number (1,000s)	5,128	4,293	4,124	4,913	354	836	19,649	

Source: 1990 Census of Population, Public Use Microdata Sample.
[a] Excludes persons born abroad of American parents or born in U.S. territories.
[b] Includes Australia and New Zealand.
[c] Includes foreign-born with country not specified.

from Africa. Reflecting trends over the past few decades, among the most recent arrivals, those immigrating between 1985 and the 1990 census, only 13 percent were born in Europe and Canada, whereas 26 percent came from Mexico, 31 percent from Asia, 22 percent from other parts of the Americas, and only 2 percent from Africa. Thus, the foreign-born population is increasingly Asian and Latin American in origin.

A population of particular interest is the primary working-age population, those aged 25–64 years. This group of 12.5 million forms the core of the immigrant labor force and household decision makers. This group also shows the effects of changes in the flow of immigrants over time (Table 14.4). Among the adult foreign-born, those from Asia, Mexico, and other parts of Latin America are far more likely to be recent immigrants, while the European/Canadians have, on average, been in the United States for a longer period of time.

14.2.2. Where They Came From: Policy and Geography

Immigrants to the United States have not always come from "everywhere." Through the first two-thirds of the nineteenth century, the principal immigration to the United States came from the Northwest European countries of Great Britain, Ireland, Germany, Scandinavia, France, and the

Table 14.4. Foreign-born population aged 25–64, by region of birth and period of immigration, 1990[a]

Period of immigration	Europe/ Canada[b]	Mexico	Other Latin America	Asia	Africa	Other[c]	Total	Number (1,000s)
1985–90	12.6%	17.9%	19.7%	26.4%	26.5%	23.4%	19.7%	2,466
1975–84	17.6	40.7	37.2	45.0	48.6	38.8	35.6	4,462
1965–74	22.3	26.5	28.5	20.3	17.7	22.4	23.9	2,999
1960–64	14.0	6.7	9.7	3.7	3.4	6.5	8.3	1,037
1950–59	24.9	6.3	4.1	3.8	3.2	6.1	9.5	1,196
Before 1950	8.6	1.9	0.9	0.8	0.6	2.7	3.0	375
Total	100.0%	100.0%	100.0%	100.0%	100.0%	100.0%	100.0%	12,536
Distribution by Region of Birth	24.1	20.7	22.6	26.5	2.1	4.0	100.0	
Number (1,000s)	3,019	2,592	2,830	3,327	262	507	12,536	

Source: 1990 Census of Population, Public Use Microdata Sample.
[a] Excludes persons born abroad of American parents or born in U.S. territories.
[b] Includes Australia and New Zealand.
[c] Includes other areas not separately listed and country not specified.

Low Countries. The Constitution barred the importation of slaves after 1808 (although some were smuggled in illegally), and even voluntary immigration from Africa was virtually nonexistent until recently. Immigration from Eastern Europe and Asia was also very small.

After the Civil War, however, the immigrant flows changed in composition. On the West Coast, Japanese, Chinese, Korean, and Filipino workers came as contract laborers. On the East Coast, a shift occurred toward the so-called new immigrants from the city-states of the Italian peninsula, from Poland and Russia, from Greece and the Balkans. They differed from the earlier immigrants in language, religion, and appearance. Less likely to be literate or to be skilled laborers, they also came from countries with more autocratic forms of government (Lieberson 1980; Carpenter 1927). Fears mounted on both the East and West coasts that these immigrants could not be assimilated.

In a reaction to racial prejudice and economic competition in the West Coast states where most Asian immigrants lived, measures were taken by the federal government as early as the 1870s to exclude the Chinese, and in 1907 immigration from Japan was halted through diplomatic means (Bonacich 1984). To restrict Southern and East European immigration, legislation enacted in the early 1920s attempted to force the nationality composition of the immigrant population of the United States to be the same as the distribution of the origins of the white population. Throughout this time, however, immigration continued from Canada, Mexico, and the Caribbean. Immigrants from the Western Hemisphere were technically subject to the same qualitative restrictions that were applied to the Eastern Hemisphere—for example, the exclusion of criminals and persons with communicable diseases—but they were exempt from numerical restrictions (Cafferty, Chiswick, Greeley, and Sullivan 1983).

The National Origins Quota Act of 1924, which barred some nationalities entirely and subjected others from the Eastern Hemisphere to quotas, continued with some modifications until the major changes wrought by the 1965 Amendments to the 1952 Immigration and Nationality Act. An important feature of the 1965 legislation, which took effect in 1968, was to make people from all independent countries of the world eligible for visas. Although it was first applied only to the Eastern Hemisphere and then to all countries, there was an overall numerical quota and a uniform country limit for certain categories of immigrants, but admission of individual immigrants was determined by a preference system. Preference was given primarily to persons being reunited with family members already residing in the United States (i.e., spouse, parents, children, and siblings) and secondarily to persons based on their skills. Provision was also made for some refugees and for investors, persons making job-creating investments in businesses in the United States (Keely 1971 and 1975).

This legislation had three important ramifications. First, Asian and African immigrants were again permitted to enter the United States, and most of the initial entrants came under the skilled-worker preferences and the investor category because they did not have immediate relatives in the United States. They were now identified as the "new" immigrants. Second, Latin American immigrants came under numerical restriction for the first time. As a result, many workers who had previously migrated back and forth across the U.S.–Mexico border legally suddenly found themselves redefined as illegal immigrants. Third, to a much greater extent than had been anticipated, family reunification visas came to swamp the visas for skilled workers and investors. The framers of the legislation had anticipated that family reunification would apply principally to the European relatives of the now-aging immigrants already resident in the United States. By linking new visas to kin already residing in the United States, family reunification would merely replicate the countries of origin of the foreign-born population. Instead, family reunification was extensively used by the relatives of the newly arrived skilled workers, investors, and refugees, creating new patterns of chain migration (Jasso and Rosenzweig 1986). And, seemingly, the more immigrants admitted under family reunification provisions, the more new applicants there are for those family-based visas.

The pressures on the U.S. immigration system were intensified by a number of overwhelming pull and push factors. American higher education, reputed to be the world's best, attracted thousands of international students who were the best and brightest of their countries, and who received a first-hand taste of the world's most vigorous economy. Population pressures in the rapidly growing countries of Asia, Africa, and Latin America outstripped the abilities of many of their economies to generate good jobs and made emigration attractive to young adults. Wage rates for unskilled workers in the United States that might seem very low by U.S. standards seemed very attractive to those with even poorer labor market opportunities in their country of origin. Especially for Mexicans, an undetected entry across the southern border of the United States was easy, resulting in a large number of illegal entrants. Even for Asians and Africans, for whom the cost of air travel declined, overstaying a tourist or student visa proved easy to accomplish. Events abroad, such as government instability, wars, and revolutions, created streams of refugees, many of whom sought ultimate asylum in the United States.

Tensions over the illegal portion of the immigration stream led to a legislative compromise in the Immigration Reform and Control Act of 1986 (IRCA) (Bean, Vernez, and Keely 1989; Chiswick 1988). This legislation initiated sanctions against employers for knowingly hiring undocumented immigrants, while providing that legally resident workers, regardless of their origin or citizenship status, could not be legally discriminated against in hiring. The intent of these provisions was to dry up the demand for undocumented workers without harming legally resident workers with a similar national or ethnic background.

As a result of confusion over the employers' legal responsibilities neither to hire illegal aliens nor to discriminate against those with legal rights to work, minimal funding for enforcement of employer sanctions, and the virtual absence of any penalties against illegal aliens who are apprehended by the authorities, the illegal alien flow into the United States continues. By 1992, apprehensions of illegal aliens increased to 1.3 million, the level that had been attained prior to the 1986 legislation. The law has apparently failed to eliminate the flow of illegal aliens attracted by jobs and other benefits, although there is some indication that the flow would have been even larger in the absence of employer sanctions.

The 1986 Act provided for amnesty for undocumented workers who could prove that they had resided continuously in the country since January 1, 1982. An alternative provision permitted those who had worked at least 30 days in seasonal agriculture to apply for amnesty. As of 1992, over 2.6 million persons out of 3.1 million applicants had been granted legal permanent resident status under the 1986 Act. Of the remainder, about half have had their applications denied while the applications of the others are still pending. These amnesties have created the expectation of future amnesties, and some limited amnesty provisions have been written into subsequent legislation.

The Refugee Act of 1980 redefined the terms under which a person could be admitted to the United States as a refugee. Under the 1952 legislation a refugee had to be fleeing persecution in a communist country or be a refugee from certain parts of the Middle East. The 1980 Act required merely that the person have a well-founded fear of persecution for political, religious, ethnic, or other related reasons. Among its provisions was the requirement that the United States not be the country of first asylum. Almost immediately, the Mariel boatlift to Southern Florida challenged the first-asylum provision. Later in the 1980s, large numbers of Haitians entered the country claiming an "economic refugee" status because of the poverty in their country. Other novel claims of asylum have been made, including claims by Chinese nationals that their country's one-child policy is a form of persecution against them, a claim by a Nigerian woman that her U.S.-born daughters would be subjected to ritual genital mutilation if she were deported, and a claim by a Mexican national that he was persecuted for sexual orientation. The instability in Eastern Europe and the former Soviet Union that has followed the collapse of communism may generate new refugee flows.

The Immigration Act of 1990, which modified the provisions for issuing visas based on kinship and skills and opened other opportunities for new flows of immigrants, did not affect the characteristics of the immigrant population in the 1990 census. Nor is it likely that the 1990 Act will be the last major legislative initiative on immigration. Legislative controversies for the 1990s include the definition of refugees and the mechanisms for granting asylum. Moreover, the increased public interest in the economic dimensions of immigration is likely to keep open the debate on allocating visas on the basis of the applicant's own level and type of skill rather than on kinship. Illegal immigration has again become an important political issue, with many observers arguing that current enforcement mechanisms, at the border and in the interior, have been ineffective in stemming the flow of undocumented workers. More effective enforcement of employer sanctions and penalties against the illegal aliens themselves will be subject to legislative debate.

14.2.3. Geographic Diversity of Origins

The foreign-born population enumerated in the 1990 census is the most diverse in our history, and yet one out of every five immigrants comes from only one country, Mexico. The claim that Americans "come from everywhere" was by 1990 almost literally true. Table 14.5 shows the twenty sending countries that account for the largest number of the foreign-born population, excluding those born abroad of American parents and those born in U.S. territories. These twenty countries together accounted for 69 percent of the total foreign-born population of 20 million enumerated in 1990.

Mexico was the leading country of origin for immigrants in both 1980 and 1990, and the proportion of the total foreign-born who are from Mexico increased from 16 percent to nearly 22 percent over the decade. Journalistic accounts of immigration occasionally lose sight of the fact that Mexico is a major source of legal immigrants. According to INS data, nearly one in every four legally admitted immigrants during the 1980s were from Mexico. Many Mexicans seeking legal entry are already familiar with the United States (Portes and Bach 1985; Hirschman 1978). Moreover, the family reunification preferences, applied to the Western Hemisphere since 1976, have made many Mexicans eligible to immigrate legally to rejoin family residing on the U.S. side of the border. The Mexican migration stream is large for several reasons: the large gap in real wage rates and employment opportunities between the U.S. and Mexico; the long-standing circulatory movements of Mexican workers between the two countries; and the development of chain migration, as residents of Mexican villages learn more about life in the United States and receive migration assistance from friends and relatives who migrated previously (Massey et al. 1987).

An important issue in the census taking of both 1980 and 1990 was the extent to which the illegal immigrants were enumerated. Analysts claimed that substantial numbers of illegally resident Mexicans had been counted even in the 1980 census.[7] By 1990, some 2.3 million Mexicans had applied for legalization through the amnesty programme enacted in 1986, presumably reducing their hesitation to be counted. The issue remains, however, as to how many illegally resident foreign-born persons were

Table 14.5. Top twenty countries of birth among the foreign-born, and selected demographic characteristics, 1990[a]

Rank in 1990	Country[b]	Rank in 1980	Number (1,000s)	Percent distribution	Median age	Ratio males to females	Percent naturalized	Percent immigrated since 1985
1	Mexico	1	4,297	21.8%	29	123	23%	30%
2	Philippines	7	882	4.5	38	77	54	26
3	Canada	3	755	3.8	53	71	53	11
4	Cuba	6	735	3.7	49	94	53	7
5	Germany	2	713	3.6	53	53	74	6
6	United Kingdom	5	633	3.2	49	71	49	14
7	Italy	4	583	3.0	59	98	75	3
8	Korea	10	575	2.9	34	79	38	34
9	Vietnam	12	552	2.8	30	113	44	25
10	China	11	524	2.7	45	99	42	32
11	India	16	446	2.3	36	114	35	32
12	El Salvador	28	446	2.3	29	109	14	34
13	Poland	8	378	1.9	58	88	61	20
14	Jamaica	18	344	1.7	35	83	39	24
15	Dominican Republic	19	341	1.7	33	86	25	32
16	USSR	9	332	1.7	55	82	59	30
17	Japan	13	279	1.4	37	61	27	45
18	Colombia	23	277	1.4	35	85	29	28
19	Taiwan	33	244	1.2	33	87	40	33
20	Guatemala	39	228	1.2	30	104	19	39
—	All Others	—	6,160	31.2	38	98	42	26
Total			19,724	100.0%	37	96	40%	25%

Source: 1990 Census of Population, Public Use Microdata Sample.
Note: Native-born: median age 33; ratio males to females 95.
[a] All data refer to 1990, except rank in 1980.
[b] Germany includes East and West Germany, United Kingdom includes all constituent units, USSR includes all areas of what was the former USSR, China includes Hong Kong but not Taiwan.

missed in 1990. Ethnographic studies conducted in conjunction with the census suggest that illegal immigrants were missed in the census– Mexicans as well as undocumented entrants from other countries (De la Puente 1993).

The Philippines moved to second place on the list from seventh in 1980, accounting for 4.5 percent of the total foreign-born population in 1990 (Table 14.5). The Philippines is a country with direct ties to the United States since the Spanish-American War of 1898, and even when other Asians were barred from immigrating, some Filipinos could immigrate legally. The Philippines has many well-educated workers, and their admission both as skilled workers and as family members has led to a total foreign-born population of nearly 1 million people. The majority of the Filipinos reside in California (53 percent), with smaller numbers living in Hawaii (8 percent) and other states. The Philippines ranked second in the number of permanent resident alien visas received in 1992.

Three countries each account for about 3.5–4.0 percent of the foreign-born: Canada, perennially a major sending country; Cuba, a major source of refugees since the beginning of the Castro regime in 1959; and Germany, a traditional source of immigration since colonial times. Although these countries were major contributors to the stock of the foreign-born, they are less important in the recent flow; none of these three countries is among the top ten countries of origin for immigrants admitted to the United States in recent years. There is actually another group that could be considered the third-largest source "country": that is, the 856,000 foreign-born who reported only that they were "born abroad" or gave similarly vague answers as to their foreign birthplace, so vague that the Census Bureau could not code their country of birth.

Of the remaining countries listed in Table 14.5, many have contributed immigrants because of recent refugee streams. Entrants from Vietnam, El Salvador, the former Soviet Union, and Guatemala have sought asylum from political, religious, or ethnic persecution. For example, the persecuted ethnic Chinese of Vietnam and Jews from Russia received asylum. Many entrants from El Salvador and Guatemala seek refugee status because of armed violence in their home countries, although it appears that others from these countries are undocumented entrants (Hagan and Rodriguez 1992; Rodriguez 1987). The significance of these sending countries increased after the census of 1990. Among the countries of origin for immigrants admitted during 1992, Vietnam had moved to second place, the Soviet Union to fourth, and El Salvador to eighth.

Some of the remaining top 20 countries listed in Table 14.5 are there because immigrants survive from migrations that took place much earlier in this century. Their median age is therefore considerably older than the median age for more recent immigrant groups. For example, the median age of the Italian foreign-born is 59, and the median age of the Polish foreign-born is 58, in contrast to 37 years for all of the foreign-born. Between 1985 and 1990, only 23,309 foreign-born persons entered the United States from Italy and 69,209 from Poland. Italy's rank in Table 14.5 results principally from immigration earlier in this century, including survivors of the immigrants who arrived prior to the restrictive legislation enacted in 1924. Polish immigration is being renewed in the wake of the collapse of communism and the Iron Curtain. In 1992, over 25,000 immigrants were admitted from Poland. By contrast, median ages are much younger among the foreign-born from some of the newer sending countries, 36 for persons born in India, and 29 for El Salvador.

The degree of heterogeneity among immigrants may well be typified by the group born in Africa, of whom 45 percent reported their race as black or African, 44 percent as white, 7 percent as Asian, and 3 percent as other and mixed races. By region within Africa, 50 percent were born in Central Africa (of whom over two-thirds were black and 13 percent Asian), 36 percent in North Africa (three-quarters white), and 14 percent in Southern Africa (three-quarters white).

The evident diversity of the immigration stream is manifested by the great number of origins listed by nearly one-third of the remaining foreign-born. The Census Bureau coded the foreign places of birth that were reported on the census forms into more than 250 areas, including Antarctica. Some of the codes are subnational entities; for example, the Channel Islands, Guernsey, and Jersey are coded separately from England, and United Kingdom is yet a different code. On the other hand, with the breakup of the USSR, Czechoslovakia, and Yugoslavia, country categories would exist today that did not exist in 1990.

Sometimes, however, the respondents' self-identifications proved to be prescient of later political developments. In addition to country of birth the census asked for ethnic origin (ancestry). Of the nearly 140,000 people who listed Yugoslavia as their place of birth, only 30 percent claimed to be Yugoslavian by ethnicity or ancestry, 19 percent reported themselves Croatian, 13 percent German, 12 percent Serbian, 4 percent Slovak, 4 percent Slovene, 3 percent Macedonian, 1.5 percent Hungarian, and 14 percent reported other ancestries or did not respond to the question. Among the nearly 86,000 persons born in what used to be Czechoslovakia, only 17 percent identified their ancestry as Czechoslovakia while 30 percent reported themselves to be Slovak, 27 percent Czech, 19 percent Austrian, and 6 percent reported other ancestries or did not respond.

Perhaps most interesting of all are the 330,500 foreign-born who reported that they had been born in what was then the Union of Soviet Socialist Republics. They reported 71 different ancestries, and 15.5 percent were coded in one residual category that included any response that might reveal religion. The most numerous of the specific ancestries were Russian (45 percent), Ukrainian (15 percent), and Armenian (10 percent). By 1992, the former Soviet Union ranked fourth in the number of immigrants admitted; and the continued entry of immigrants from this multiethnic region seems likely.

These combinations of birthplace and ancestry data point to processes of ethnic identification and reidentification. Social scientists have previously documented the disappearance of ethnic identification, such as the replacement of Germans by "Austrians" in the Canadian census after World War I (Ryder 1955). But censuses also document the emergence of ethnic identification. For example, the idea of a unified Italy gained impetus from immigrants who, once in America, no longer considered themselves Sicilian nor Milanese but rather "Italian" (Glazer 1954; Greeley 1971; Lieberson and Waters 1990). As the political maps of the world change, the continuity of census data becomes more complex, but in the detailed coding categories may lie useful clues.

14.3. Where Immigrants Live and Their Citizenship

14.3.1. The Geographic Location of Immigrants

Immigrants are attracted to a locality for much the same reason that the native-born are, and so from the beginning of our history there have been distinctive geographic clusters of immigrants (Portes and Rumbaut 1990; Bartel 1989). The availability of jobs (or in earlier times, of farmland) and amenities attract migrants. Immigrants also tend to settle, at least initially, in ports of entry. Finally, they also tend to settle near earlier entrants from their place of origin. Explicit government policies to channel immigrants to specific areas have seldom been adopted in the United States, and when attempted, they have failed because of subsequent internal migration.

Americans are deeply interested in the local economic impacts of immigration, but these impacts are difficult to measure. Because these localities are often growing through internal as well as international migration, it is technically difficult to identify a separate effect of the foreign-born within a labor market. As the number of migrants attracted by jobs rises, local wages should fall and unemployment may rise, but this effect occurs whether the migrants were born in the United States or abroad. Some recent work indicates that the internal migration of native-born workers may slow, cease, or be reversed in response to international migration, even though immigrants and native-born workers tend to be attracted to areas with growing employment opportunities (Filer 1992).

Even if the effect on individual workers cannot be precisely determined, however, there remains a strong interest in the collective effect of immigration on the public sector. Admission to the United States is a matter of federal law; and as a matter of constitutional right, the states are not permitted to limit migration, neither into nor from their territory. This is not true in all receiving countries; in Canada, for example, a potential immigrant can receive extra "points" in the visa allocation process by promising to settle in a relatively less populous part of the country, and the Province of Quebec can apply somewhat separate immigration criteria. Earlier in American history some states sent recruiters to Europe to encourage the migration of workers with technical skills. Much like the native-born population, however, once immigrants have entered the United States they are entitled to settle and resettle at will, moving from city to city and from state to state. Indeed, federal government efforts to distribute Cuban and Vietnamese refugees throughout the country proved fruitless as they tended to concentrate themselves through secondary migrations within the United States.

Immigrants benefit from government infrastructure, such as highways, and from government services, such as public education and police protection, just as do the native-born. To the extent that immigrants cluster in only a few states or localities, the impact of immigration, both costs and benefits, will also be concentrated. Thus, while the federal government makes immigration policy, much of the impact may fall disproportionately on certain states and localities that have no control over the influx of immigrants into their areas. This imbalance between where policy is made and where the policy may have its largest impact has resulted in tension between the federal government and states and localities that have received the largest numbers of low-skilled immigrants.

Nearly three-quarters of the immigrants are clustered in only six states, with California the leading destination. One-third of the nation's foreign-born population lived in California in 1990. New York, which had been the leading destination in 1960, when 24 percent of the foreign-born lived there, was home to 14 percent of the immigrants in 1990, a distinct second place. Florida and Texas each accounted for about 8 percent of the foreign-born in 1990, and New Jersey and Illinois for 5 percent each. The remaining 27 percent of the foreign-born are scattered among the other 44 states and the District of Columbia.

Figure 14.1 shows the distribution of the foreign-born by county. The darkest shading represents counties with at least 16 percent of the population foreign-born, or twice the national proportion of 8 percent. Of the 3,141 counties in the nation, 95 percent of them have fewer than 8 percent foreign-born in their population, or less than the national average. Only 47 counties, or 1.5 percent of the total counties, have twice the national proportion of foreign-born; the highest proportion of foreign-born population, in Dade County, Florida, is 45 percent. The map concretely displays the uneven distribution of the foreign-born population.

Within California, the immigrants are concentrated in the largest metropolitan areas, particularly Los Angeles and the San Francisco Bay Area. Of all immigrants admitted to the United States in 1992, 129,000 or 13.3 percent intended to reside in the Los Angeles–Long Beach Area. Another 3.5 percent intended to reside in the neighboring Anaheim–Santa Ana Area; 2.4 percent in San Jose; 2.2 percent each in San Francisco and in San Diego. Among the top 20 metropolitan areas of intended residence, 8 were in California. California has attracted large numbers of immigrants from many different countries, including Mexico, Central America, China, Korea, the Philippines, Iran, and other parts of Asia and the Middle East.

Other major destinations included Miami, the fifth-ranked residence for those admitted in 1992, and Houston, which was seventh. Linguistic communities add to the appeal of these particular cities. In Houston, for example, the large Spanish-speaking community of Mexican origin helped attract new immigrant groups from Guatemala, El Salvador, and other Central American locations, even if the newcomers preferred to speak one of the indigenous languages of their home country rather than Spanish.

14.3.2. The Local Impact

Besides absolute numbers of the foreign-born, it is useful to consider the relative impact of immigration on the state and locality. California is, after all, the nation's most populous state, and thus it could be expected to absorb a large number of immigrants. Even in relative terms, however,

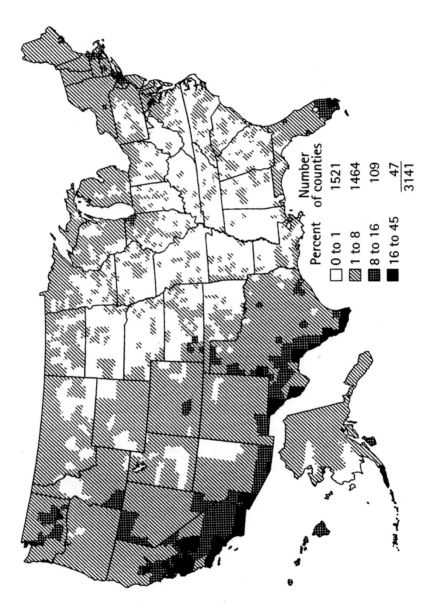

Figure 14.1. Percentage of foreign-born by country: 1990

Source: 1990 Census of Population, Summary Tape File, 3C.

Note: National percentage: 8 percent.

Percent	Number of counties
0 to 1	1521
1 to 8	1464
8 to 16	109
16 to 45	47
	3141

California stands out as a host state. Over 22 percent of the residents of California are foreign-born compared with 16 percent of New Yorkers. Inevitably, the fact that one of every five Californians is foreign-born has a profound impact on the social, economic and political life of the state.

Some states without large absolute numbers of immigrants nevertheless receive a large number in relative terms. In Hawaii, for example, 16 percent of the population is foreign-born, and in the District of Columbia almost 10 percent of the population is foreign-born. At the other end of the distribution, in 16 states fewer than 2 percent of the population are foreign-born. These states include Southern states, such as Mississippi (0.9 percent) and Kentucky (1.0); Midwestern Farmbelt states, such as Iowa (1.7 percent) and Nebraska (1.8 percent); Mountain states, such as Montana (1.9 percent); and Northern Plains states, such as South Dakota (1.2 percent). The political salience of immigration in the Farmbelt may be quite different from its salience in California, New York, and Florida.

One political issue is the expense borne by cities and states to provide services to immigrants. The cost of providing many public services may differ little for an immigrant or for a native-born migrant with the same level of income, age, and family structure (except perhaps for bilingual education for immigrant children); and the immigrants and migrants bear the costs of many of these services through sales taxes and user fees. There is little evidence that immigrants are able to avoid such taxes. Moreover, immigrants are specifically barred from receiving some types of welfare benefits until after some years of residence in the country (Jensen 1989).

The tension over providing services to immigrants is enhanced, however, in programs whose costs have been shifted to states and cities. When fewer federal dollars are available, states become concerned about the immigrant as a "free rider," especially for costly services such as Medicaid. Although the federal government disburses some impact payments for refugees and for immigrants legalized under the 1986 amnesty provisions, for the most part the states cannot recover the additional costs of providing public services for immigrants, except through their normal taxing mechanisms.

The impact that the immigrants have on state and local services varies according to how many immigrants there are—and with what characteristics. One important characteristic is age. Immigration has traditionally been undertaken by young adults. Although the host country has not clothed, fed, and educated them as children, the host country will reap the benefit of their productive years. Adults in their prime working years are usually self-supporting and taxpayers. Longer life expectancies, the family reunification policy, and the influx of refugees, however, have increased the likelihood that immigrants of all ages will inhabit American communities, and at some ages people are more likely to need government services. Children, for example, require public education, and the elderly are more likely to require medical care. We examine these groups in some detail because of the likelihood that their presence may increase the demand for government services.

14.3.3. Children and Education

More than 2 million children and teenagers were born outside the United States, or about 3 percent of those aged 19 and younger enumerated in 1990. California and New York also led the country in the proportion of children who are foreign-born. One in every nine children in California, and 1 in every 14 children in New York, was born in another country. Hawaii, Rhode Island, Nevada, District of Columbia, and Massachusetts, although not mentioned previously as having large numbers of immigrants, have a high proportion of children who are immigrants. In addition, immigrant parents may also have children born to them in the United States. They are native-born children, but they are the consequence of international migration. In the area of education, for which states and localities have responsibility, the uneven distribution of immigrants may be a problem.

One service that schools must provide, as a consequence of federal court rulings, is bilingual education. Consequently, schooling for immigrant children or the native-born children of immigrants may cost more than providing the same service to native-born children raised in English-speaking homes. This cost rises with the diversity of the immigrant stream. A school system whose immigrant population speaks many different languages faces a greater challenge than a school system whose immigrant children speak but one language other than English. These nuances are often lost in the debate, however, and immigration itself is seen as the driving force behind the need to provide bilingual (or multilingual) services in schools, courts, public hospitals, and other service agencies.

The magnitude of the bilingual education debate is illustrated by the fact that 1 in 7 school-age children speaks a language other than English at home. Along the Southwestern border (California, Arizona, New Mexico, Texas) and in New York, one-fifth or more of the school-age population can speak a language other than English (Pollard 1993). For two-thirds of these students, the home language is Spanish. But in areas such as Southern California, where the children have come from many different groups and speak many different languages, offering bilingual education and communicating with parents becomes problematic. In Los Angeles, for example, school children speak 80 languages at home. Emergency 911, fire and police dispatchers, and hospital trauma groups are among the services that need quick and accurate translations. And, when dozens of languages are routinely used, translation services can become a substantial public expense.

14.3.4. Senior Immigrants

At the other end of the life cycle, the distribution of the elderly immigrants may have policy significance. In the 1990 census, 13.2 percent of the foreign-born population were aged 65 or older, and 2.2 percent were aged 85 or older. As is the case with the native-born, there were fewer men than women among the aged. Among those aged 65 and older, there were 64 men for every 100 women among the foreign-born and 67 among the native-born.

Although some elderly immigrants have entered the United States recently through family reunification procedures, most have been residents for decades. Only 5.3 percent of the elderly foreign-born have entered the United States since 1985. Many of the states with the highest proportion of elderly immigrants, including Middle Atlantic and New England states (New York, New Jersey, Massachusetts, Connecticut, Rhode Island) and Illinois, have been destinations for immigrants for decades. The presence of older immigrants has potential implications for local health care and other services (Treas and Torrecilha 1994).

14.3.5. Naturalization and Politics

Naturalization is the process by which immigrants become citizens of the United States. The immigrant who wishes to become a U.S. citizen must apply for naturalization, which generally requires a 5-year residence in the United States as a permanent resident alien, demonstration of good moral character, and passing a simple test in English and U.S. history and civics. Naturalization confers many benefits on immigrants, including the right to vote, to hold elected public office (except president and vice president), and to serve on juries. Additional benefits include greater privileges for sponsoring the immigration of relatives (spouse, parents, children, siblings), the opportunity for employment in the Federal Civil Service and certain other government jobs (including police officers and teachers in many states), and certain government subsidies and transfers.

Among the foreign-born aged 18 and over in 1990, 43 percent were naturalized citizens. Naturalization rates vary systematically by demographic and other characteristics. For example, naturalization rates vary by duration of residence. It was very low (7 percent) among immigrants aged 18 and older who entered the United States between 1985 and 1990, largely because of the 5-year residency requirement for most immigrants. The rate was 31 percent for those who immigrated during 1975–1984, and the rate rose to 90 percent among those who immigrated before 1950. The increase with duration of residence arises, in part, because naturalization involves a waiting period and passing examinations on the English language and history/civics. More important, however, may be the delay until the immigrant decides to make the commitment to the United States, with the reduced ties to the country of origin that are implied by naturalization. Moreover, naturalization rates increase with duration because of the greater likelihood that those who have not made this commitment will return to their countries of origin.

But naturalization patterns differ sharply by region of origin. For example, among those in the United States 15–25 years in 1990, naturalization rates ranged from a high of 76 percent among Asian immigrants (for whom naturalization has been an important step in sponsoring relatives), to 65 percent for African immigrants, 53 percent for European/Canadian immigrants, 50 percent for non-Mexican Latin American immigrants, but only 31 percent for Mexican immigrants. The low rate among Mexican immigrants may be related to their higher-than-average rate of circular migration; that is, migration to and from Mexico and the United States. The ease of illegal immigration from Mexico may reduce the incentives for relatives legally in the United States to naturalize so as to serve as immigrant sponsors. Lower levels of schooling and English fluency may also account for the low naturalization rates among Mexican immigrants. Finally, compared with other source regions, the Mexican-born population in 1990 included a larger proportion of individuals whose status was recently legalized under the 1986 Immigration Reform and Control Act, thereby lowering the naturalization rate among the foreign-born from Mexico.

Naturalized immigrant voters may represent an important interest group in a ward or congressional district. To the extent that immigrants cluster within relatively few states and live within relatively few cities or neighborhoods within those states, their potential political power is enhanced. Even the immigrants who do not naturalize or who do not vote affect local politics through the redistricting process. One-person, one-vote requirements include all of the enumerated population, including the enumerated foreign-born, whether legally or illegally resident, and whether naturalized or resident alien. The Census Bureau was challenged in court because it attempts to enumerate illegal aliens in the census. Challengers argued that persons illegally residing within the country should not be given political influence through inclusion in the enumeration. The courts have so far agreed with the Census Bureau, stating that the Constitution requires the enumeration of everyone within the national boundaries.

During the earlier migrations of this century, Congress and the courts had not yet reformed the process of redistricting. In fact, there was no redistricting at all after the 1920 census, in part because of concern about how immigration had swelled the population of cities (Anderson 1988). In many states, the dramatically unequal distribution of the population among districts allowed rural areas to maintain control of state legislatures (and, of course, the redistricting process), even after the population had largely shifted to the cities. One-person, one-vote became the law in *Baker* v. *Carr* (1962), and subsequently Congress passed the Voting Rights Acts, the most recent version of which provides that redistricting does *not* dilute the votes of certain protected minority groups; such as blacks, Hispanics, American Indians, and Asian-Americans.

A large nonvoting population of immigrants can be useful to the existing voters in a district, for in effect their vote is enhanced. In California, for example, there are voting districts in which the majority of the population is Hispanic, but the majority of the voters are white (Clark and Morrison 1993). The reason for the apparent anomaly is that many of the Hispanic residents are immigrants who have not become naturalized, or if they are citizens they have not registered to vote or simply do not vote. As a result, the potential impact of the registered white voter is increased.

There has recently been a suggestion in California that permanent resident aliens (i.e., legal immigrants who have not become citizens) should have the right to vote, at least in local elections. There is precedent for this suggestion, but voting rights were usually offered by less populous states as a way to attract immigrants as settlers. For example, as recently as 1924, aliens could vote in Arkansas. The current context differs because it is not the less populous states with small numbers of immigrants, but rather the most populous state, where more than one in every five residents is foreign-born, where the issue of voting is being raised.

Although immigration policy is federal in scope, the patterns of geographic distribution have also affected public opinion differently in different parts of the country. Consensus about immigration policy has never been easy to reach in the United States: the geographic concentration and the increased diversity of the immigrant stream are likely to give the policy debate in the 1990s a distinctly regional and local flavor.

14.4. The Skills of Immigrants

The skills that immigrants bring with them or acquire while living in the United States affect not only many facets of their own lives but also the impact that their presence has on others.[8] Immigrants with more schooling and with greater English-language fluency in general have higher occupational attainments, higher earnings, lower unemployment, higher rates of internal geographic mobility, higher rates of naturalization, and lower fertility. It is, therefore, important to understand the level and temporal changes in the skills of immigrants.

The 1990 census provides data on the number of years of schooling and educational qualifications, current school enrollment status, language used at home, and English-language fluency. Data on other important dimensions of skill are, unfortunately, not available in the census. For example, there is no direct information on literacy in English or in another language, the place of the schooling, apprenticeship or other craft training, or investments in on-the-job training. Occupational attainment is sometimes perceived as a measure of skill and sometimes as an outcome of a labor market process that is influenced by skill level. In this chapter, occupational attainment will be treated as a measure of adjustment to the labor market and will be analyzed in the next section.

14.4.1. Educational Attainment

Possible answers to the question on educational attainment in the 1990 Census of Population are a mixture of years of schooling completed through grade 12 and, at higher levels, educational qualifications or type of degree completed. For simplicity of presentation, the categorical educational attainment data were recorded into equivalent years of schooling completed. Table 14.6 reports the mean and standard deviation of schooling among the foreign-born aged 25–64, by sex, country of birth, and period

Table 14.6. Schooling attainment among the foreign-born aged 25–64, by sex, region of birth, and period of immigration, 1990[a]

| Period of Immigration | Mean years of schooling | | | | | | | | | | | | Standard deviation | |
| | Europe/Canada[b] | | Mexico | | Other Latin America | | Asia | | Africa | | Total[c] | | Total[c] | |
	M	F	M	F	M	F	M	F	M	F	M	F	M	F
Mean														
1985–90	14.1	13.3	7.5	7.2	10.3	10.4	13.2	12.0	13.9	13.6	11.3	10.9	5.3	5.1
1975–84	13.4	12.8	7.1	6.9	10.8	10.5	13.4	12.2	15.3	13.7	11.1	10.7	5.1	4.9
1965–74	11.9	11.8	7.4	7.5	11.8	11.5	14.9	13.3	15.7	14.2	11.4	11.2	4.9	4.5
1960–64	12.7	12.2	8.3	8.1	13.1	12.5	15.1	13.1	15.3	13.2	12.3	11.8	4.5	4.0
1950–59	12.9	12.3	8.9	8.4	13.1	12.5	14.5	12.7	14.5	12.9	12.5	11.8	4.2	3.7
Before 1950	13.3	12.3	7.7	7.8	13.5	12.3	13.0	10.9	12.9	13.6	12.4	11.7	4.5	3.8
Total	12.9	12.3	7.4	7.3	11.3	11.1	13.8	12.4	15.0	13.7	11.5	11.1	5.0	–
Standard Deviation	4.0	3.5	4.7	4.6	4.4	4.2	4.4	4.6	3.5	3.5	5.0	4.6	–	–

Source: 1990 Census of Population, Public Use Microdata Sample.
Notes: M = Male, F = Female.
Native-born: Mean (standard deviation): Males 13.1 (2.9), Females 13.0 (2.6).
[a] Excludes those currently enrolled in school.
[b] Includes Australia and New Zealand.
[c] Includes other areas not separately listed and country not specified.

of immigration. Those currently enrolled in school are deleted from the analysis since many of them are in the United States on foreign student visas rather than as immigrants, and they cannot be separately identified in census data.

Several patterns emerge from these data. Immigrants have a lower mean and a greater dispersion (or variability) in their schooling than do the native-born. Adult foreign-born men have 11.5 years of schooling and the women 11.1 years, in contrast to 13.1 years and 13.0 years, respectively, for native-born men and women (Table 14.6). Among immigrants the proportion with 16 or more years of schooling is 24 percent for the men and 18 percent for the women, compared with 24 and 20 percent, respectively, for the native-born; that is, the proportion with college degrees is identical for native- and foreign-born men. While men have a wider dispersion in schooling attainment than women among both immigrants and the native-born, the dispersion in schooling is greater for immigrants than it is for the native-born, both within gender and overall.

A second important pattern is that the educational attainment of immigrants varies less by period of arrival within countries of origin than it varies across countries (Table 14.6). As a result, the change in the source countries of immigrants has had a profound effect on both the overall level and dispersion of the schooling distribution of immigrants. Mexican immigrants have the lowest educational attainment, around $7\frac{1}{2}$ years for both men and women, compared with nearly 14 years for Asian men and 15 years for very small groups of immigrant men from Africa.

The change in source countries of immigrants, with the European/Canadian component declining and the Asian and Mexican component increasing, among other factors, contributes to a decline in the level of schooling and a rise in the inequality of schooling among more recent immigration cohorts. Throughout the postwar period, among men, and since the 1960s among women, the level of schooling has declined with succeeding immigrant cohorts, except for the most recent group. Among male immigrants who arrived before 1960 the mean schooling level was nearly 12.5 years in contrast to only 11.1 years for those who arrived after 1975. Among female immigrants the schooling level declined from about 11.8 years (1950–1964) to about 10.8 years in the post-1975 cohorts. These declines in schooling level are not likely to be significantly mitigated by immigrants' attending school in the United States, because we are describing the population aged 25 and over. Postmigration schooling among adult immigrants is small and more likely among those who arrive with a higher level of schooling (Chiswick and Miller 1992).

Moreover, the shift over time in the countries of origin of immigrants has changed the shape of the distribution of schooling. Immigrants from Europe and Canada have a relatively high, homogenous schooling distribution (68 percent with 12–16 years of schooling and 11 percent with higher levels of schooling). Immigration is now heavily concentrated, however, in two other source regions, Asia and Mexico. Asian immigrants also have high educational attainments (66 percent with 12–16 years of schooling and another 15 percent with higher levels), but Mexican immigrants have a very low level (60 percent with 8 or fewer years, 27 percent with 12–16 years, and 1.4 percent with higher levels). As a result, recent immigrants are more diverse in that they bring both very high level and relatively sketchy educations to the United States.

The proportion of the foreign-born with very low educational attainment has increased sharply. Among the adult immigrants in the United States in 1990 who arrived in the 1950s, nearly one-quarter (23 percent) had 10 or fewer years of schooling, while among those immigrating from 1985 to 1990 over one-third (34 percent) had 10 or fewer years. Thus, at a time of increasing skills among the native-born population and when industrial restructuring requires greater schooling levels to compete successfully in the labor market, an increasing proportion of the immigrant stream has very low levels of schooling.

14.4.2. Language Skills

The 1990 census asked if a language other than English was currently spoken in the home. If so, respondents were asked to identify the language and to indicate their ability to speak English. The emphasis is on fluency, with no information on literacy in English or in another language. Figure 14.2 shows the English-language proficiency of immigrants aged 5 and over; that is, those who are school age and adult immigrants. Of these, 21 percent reported that they spoke only English at home, 32 percent lived in a home in which another language was spoken but reported that they spoke English very well, 22 percent reported that they spoke English well, 17 percent reported not well, and 8 percent reported that they did not speak English at all.

Among immigrants aged 25–64, 80 percent reported that a language other than or in addition to English was spoken in the home, This bilingualism was most common among immigrants from Mexico (96 percent) and Asia (92 percent), and less common among immigrants from Europe/ Canada (56 percent). Among those reporting a language other than English, Spanish was the language most frequently cited (47 percent).

Three Asian languages then followed—Chinese (7.0 percent of those reporting speaking a language other than English at home), Tagalog (5.3 percent), Korean (3.8 percent)—followed by German (3.3 percent), Italian (2.9 percent), French (2.7 percent), Vietnamese (2.6 percent), Hindi (2.2 percent), and Portuguese (1.8 percent). A total of 32 percent reported speaking these nine languages. The remaining myriad languages were reported by the 21 percent listing another language.

Reflecting the changing source countries of immigrants, the European languages, other than Spanish, were predominantly spoken by older immigrants who came to the United States in earlier decades. Spanish and the Asian languages, on the other hand, were more prevalent among newer cohorts of immigrants.

Retention of one's mother tongue may not be of much importance for understanding the social and economic adaptation of immigrants, although for some people retention might retard acquiring fluency in English. Speaking English is an important aspect and determinant of adjustment in the United States. Table 14.7 reports by period of immigration and country of birth the proportion of the foreign-born aged 25–64 who speak only English at home or who speak another language but speak English very well. The data are not reported by gender because the gender differences are very small.

English-speaking fluency varies by country of origin and duration in the United States, among other variables (Table 14.7). Among adult immigrants who lived in the United States 6–15 years by 1990 (i.e., immigrated 1975–1984), 68 percent of the European/Canadian immigrants spoke only

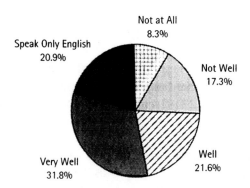

Figure 14.2. English-language proficiency of the foreign-born, 1990[a]

Source: 1990 Census of Population, Public Use Microdata Sample.

[a] Persons aged 5 and over were asked if they spoke a language other than or in addition to English at home and, if so, to report their fluency in English.

Table 14.7. English-language fluency of the foreign-born aged 25–64, by sex, region of birth, and period of immigration, 1990[a]

Period of immigration	Europe/ Canada[b]	Mexico	Other Latin America	Asia	Africa	Total[c]
1985–90	60%	15%	34%	34%	66%	36%
1975–84	68	20	44	45	80	42
1965–74	71	29	59	66	84	57
1960–64	83	42	68	73	89	71
1950–59	86	46	70	75	85	77
Before 1950	90	51	83	70	100	83
Total	76%	25%	50%	49%	78%	51%

Source: 1990 Census of Population, Public Use Microdata Sample.
[a] Proportion who speak only English at home or who speak English very well.
[b] Includes Australia and New Zealand.
[c] Includes other areas not separately listed and country not specified.

English or spoke English very well, as did 45 percent of Asian immigrants, 44 percent of other Latin American immigrants, and 20 percent of Mexican immigrants. The extent of exposure to English, whether it is a primary, secondary, or a language little used in the country of origin, is an important determinant of these differences by country of origin.

Exposure to English in the United States, measured in part by duration of residence, is another major determinant of English language skills. In general, fluency in English increases, but at a decreasing rate, with duration of residence. Among all immigrants, those who spoke only English or spoke English very well increased from 36 percent among immigrants in the United States 5 or fewer years to 57 percent among those here 16–25 years, to 77 percent for those in the United States 40 or more years. The increase with duration is also found when the data are disaggregated by country of origin: the increase with duration occurs for immigrants from all regions of origin.

The use of English and the degree of fluency in English are also influenced by other dimensions of exposure to English and efficiency in acquiring English-language skills (Chiswick and Miller 1992). The immigrant's demographic characteristics and other dimensions of skill can be proxies for exposure and efficiency factors. Other measured variables held constant, immigrants who arrive in the United States at an older age, with less schooling competed, who immigrate with a spouse with the same "mother tongue," or who live in an area where many others speak their "mother tongue" are all less likely to speak only English at home and are more likely to have poorer fluency in English. By contrast, immigrants who anticipate attaining greater labor market earnings from greater fluency in English have been found to become more fluent in English.

14.4.3. School Enrollment Rates

The 1990 census asked respondents whether they are currently enrolled in school. It is therefore possible to study the school enrollment of immigrants. Unfortunately, because there is no question on visa status it is not possible to identify those on student visas who may comprise a significant component of the foreign-born enrolled in college or university programs.

An alternative approach is adopted here. There are relatively few exchange students (e.g., youths on student visas) enrolled in secondary school. As a result, this factor is not likely to generate statistical bias in an analysis of school enrollment patterns among youths aged 15–18 years. Those aged 15–18 years in 1990 were born in 1972–1975; the more recently they immigrated to the United States, the older their age at immigration.

Overall, 81 percent of the foreign-born youths aged 15–18 in 1990 were enrolled in school, in contrast to 88 percent among the native-born.[9] The immigrant youths who arrived in the United States as infants or toddlers have enrollment rates comparable to those of the native-born. On the other hand, among the youths who arrived in the $3\frac{1}{4}$ years prior to the 1990 census (1987–1990); that is, as preteens and teenagers, enrollment rates were 66 percent for the males and 69 percent for the females, far below the comparable percentages for the native-born.

The school enrollment rates also varied by country of birth. Much of this disparity by country of birth is attributable to duration in the United States. In general, for the same period of arrival in the United States, enrollment rates for the foreign-born aged 15–18 are highest for those born in Asia (93 percent), followed by European/Canadian immigrants (89 percent), and lowest among those born in Mexico (64 percent). Although Mexican immigrant youth consistently have lower enrollment rates than youths from the other major source regions, the gap is small among those who arrived in the United States as toddlers and infants and is very large among the most recent cohort. For example, among those who immigrated in 1987–1990 the enrollment rate of 15–18 year olds born in Mexico was 40 percent, in contrast to over 87 percent for Asian and European/Canadian immigrants.

The lower enrollment rates of new immigrant teenagers may result from difficulties in adjusting to the language and curriculum of the American schools. Moreover, given the very low educational attainment of immigrants from Mexico, many of the new immigrant youths may have dropped out of school in Mexico prior to their migration. Additionally, economic factors may come into play among low-income immigrant families. It is not the out-of-pocket cost of secondary schooling so much as the foregone earnings of teenagers that may affect the decisions of low-income new immigrant families from Mexico.

14.5. Immigrants and the Labor Market

Immigrants play an important role in the labor market, and the labor market, in turn, has profound effects on the flow of immigrants to the United States and on their adjustment once they are here. Most immigrants come to the United States either because of their own (or some close relative's) labor market opportunities. Even refugees who may have noneconomic motives for leaving their country of origin choose among alternative destinations partly on the basis of labor market opportunities.

This section focuses on three key issues: employment status; class of worker, and occupational status.[10] Employment status refers to the classification of an immigrant as employed, unemployed, or not a member of the labor force. Class of worker refers to the status of the employer—private sector, government, or self-employment. Occupational status refers to the type of work that is performed. No single all-encompassing measure of adjustment in the labor market is available, but earnings are as close as one can get.

14.5.1. Employment Status

The 1990 census asked about the employment status of noninstitutionalized respondents aged 16 years and older during the week before the enumeration: employed, unemployed, or not in the labor force. The employed are working for pay (employees) or for profit (the self-employed), or are unpaid workers in a family-owned business, even if they were temporarily absent from work during the reference week. The unemployed are either workers who have a job but are on a temporary job lay-off, or those without a job who are available for work and have been looking for work during the past 4 weeks. Respondents are not in the labor force if they do not have a job and are either unavailable for work or have not looked for work during the past 4 weeks.

Our analysis of the employment status of immigrants is limited to those aged 25–64. Older immigrants are likely to be retired, and younger immigrants are often enrolled in school or job training programs, so that their employment status reflects a temporary situation. Employment analyses are most appropriately performed separately by gender, because women tend to have lower rates of labor force participation. For example, among native-born men and women (aged 25–64) in the 1990 census, 87 percent of the men but only 70 percent of the women were in the labor force.

Recent immigrants are similar to other new entrants to the labor market in many of their characteristics. Compared with native-born workers, new immigrants tend to have fewer skills that are specific to the U.S. labor market, their industry, and their employer. They have less experience, shorter job tenure, and lower job seniority than other workers. As a result, both the new immigrant worker and the employer may perceive a weaker attachment between the worker and the job, with the result that recent immigrants experience higher job turnover, higher rates of lay-off and discharge, and higher quit rates. This greater labor market turnover need not be dysfunctional, because the employment of new immigrants involves a learning experience for both the worker and the employer. Indeed, one effective way for new workers to learn about jobs is to experience several jobs, which involves job turnover. Job turnover may entail periods of unemployment from the time of the quit/layoff until the new job is found. New immigrants are also often making investments in school or in special language training programs to facilitate the transferability of the skills they acquired abroad to the U.S. labor market or to acquire new skills. These investments are sometimes made full-time, thereby reducing their labor force participation.

The labor force participation rates of immigrant men aged 25–64 are slightly higher than the native-born, 89 percent compared with 87 percent. Among women, the immigrant labor force participation rate of 63 percent was lower than the 70 percent among the native-born. Thus, while immigrant men are somewhat more likely to be labor force participants, immigrant women are less likely to be participants than their native-born counterparts. Immigrant men and women are similar to the native-born in having labor force participation rates that vary systematically with demographic and skill variables. Participation rates increase with level of schooling and vary by marital status. Marriage is associated with higher participation rates for men and substantially lower participation rates for women. Children living at home, particularly young children, are associated with lower female participation rates.

Of particular interest for understanding the labor market status of immigrants are the variations in labor force participation rates by duration in the United States, region of origin, and gender (Table 14.8). Immigrants in the United States for fewer than 5 years have lower participation rates than those of longer duration immigrants. Among men aged 25–64, for example, the participation rates of those entering the United States in 1985–90 was 84 percent, but it was 92 percent for the 1965–74 cohort. Among women aged 25–64, the participation rate was 53 percent for the most recent (1985–90) cohort, compared with 69 percent for the 1965–74 cohort. Labor force participation among the most recent immigrants may be reduced because they are making relatively larger investments in skills specific to the United States, such as schooling, job training, and language training. The immigrants who arrived before 1950 (the longest duration cohort identifiable in census data) also have lower labor force participation rates, but they are disproportionately in their 50s and early 60s, and many have taken early retirement.

Immigrants' labor force participation rates vary systematically by region of birth and by gender. Mexican-born men tend to have higher rates of

Table 14.8. Labor force participation rates of the foreign-born aged 25–64, by sex, region of birth, and period of immigration, 1990

Period of immigration	Europe/ Canada[a]		Mexico		Other Latin America		Asia		Africa		Total[b]	
	M	F	M	F	M	F	M	F	M	F	M	F
1985–90	84%	53%	92%	46%	89%	65%	78%	52%	83%	63%	85%	55%
1975–84	92	67	93	56	91	71	91	67	93	72	91	66
1965–74	92	69	91	57	90	73	94	76	95	81	91	69
1960–64	90	67	87	56	89	70	92	70	98	67	89	66
1950–59	87	58	85	52	88	66	90	60	88	56	87	59
Before 1950	79	51	76	56	81	56	80	45	77	60	78	51
Total	89%	62%	91%	54%	90%	70%	88%	64%	91%	70%	89%	63%

Source: 1990 Census of Population, Public Use Microdata Sample.
Notes: M = Males, F = females.
Native-born (percent in labor force): Males 87, Females 70.
[a] Includes Australia and New Zealand.
[b] Includes other areas not separately listed and country not specified.

participation than other immigrants, particularly during the first few years in the United States. On the other hand, Mexican-born women have lower rates than other foreign-born women in the same immigrant cohort, only in part because of their larger number of children.

Labor force participation includes both employment and unemployment, and immigrants experience higher unemployment than the native-born. In 1990 the economy was close to "full employment," where full employment means the lowest unemployment rate attainable at a low and nonaccelerating rate of inflation. The unemployment rate in the census data among the native-born (aged 25–64) was 4.8 percent for men and 4.7 percent for women. The foreign-born experienced higher unemployment rates, 6.1 percent for men and 7.8 percent for women.

Viewing new immigrants as new workers, not just to the labor market but in the country itself, puts their unemployment experience into perspective. It is therefore not surprising to find higher unemployment rates among the newest of immigrants; and this differential seems to be largely dissipated after a few years in the country. Among the adult immigrant men in 1990, the unemployment rate was 7.9 percent for those in the U.S. 5 or fewer years, compared with 6.2 percent for those in the U.S. 6–14 years, and 5.2 percent for immigrant men in the U.S. for more than 14 years. For women, the gap is larger: an unemployment rate of 12.2 percent for the recent cohort compared with 8.3 percent for immigrants in the U.S. 6–14 years and to the 5.7 percent for those in the U.S. for more than 14 years.[11]

The highest unemployment rates are experienced by the Mexican immigrants, both overall and controlling for periods of immigration. Among adult men, the Mexican immigrant unemployment rate of 8.3 percent exceeded the overall immigrant rate of 6.1 percent, while among women the rates were 14.3 percent and 7.8 percent, respectively. To some extent this higher rate arises from the larger proportion of Mexican immigrants in the U.S. for 5 or fewer years. Yet unemployment rates are higher for Mexican immigrants even for the same period of arrival. Among the Mexican men, the unemployment rate was 9.3 percent in the recent (1985–1990) cohort and 7.9 percent among those in the U.S. for 6–14 years. Among the Mexican women the rates were 19.2 percent and 14.7 percent, respectively. Unemployment rates vary systematically by level of education, with the least educated having the highest rates. The low level of schooling of the Mexican immigrants is partially responsible for their higher rates of unemployment for the same duration of residence in the United States, but some of the differential remains unexplained.

The employment-population ratio, perhaps the least understood of the three labor force statistics, is the proportion of the relevant population that is employed. Some labor market analysts view this as the most relevant labor force statistic because it avoids the perhaps arbitrary boundary between being unemployed and outside the labor force. The employment-population ratios for immigrant and native-born men (aged 25-64) are quite similar, 84 percent and 83 percent, respectively, compared with the ratios for women, 58 percent and 67 percent, respectively. As would be expected from the lower labor force participation rate and higher unemployment rate among the recent (1985-1990) immigrants, this group had a relatively low employment ratio, 78 percent for men and 48 percent for women. The employment-population ratio shows little variation by country of origin for men. Among women, however, there are larger differences. In particular, Mexican women have a very low employment-population ratio (47 percent compared to 58 percent for all immigrant women), reflecting their low labor force participation rate and high unemployment rate.

In summary, the employment status of immigrants reflects patterns similar to those of the native-born (e.g., with respect to the effects of schooling and marital status), but also reflects effects from two characteristics unique to immigrants, duration of residence and country of origin. In general, unemployment rates are higher and labor force participation rates and employment-population ratios are lower during the first few years in the United States as immigrants make formal (schooling and language training) and informal (on-the-job training) investments to increase their skills relevant for the U.S. labor market and to acquire information about the labor market through job searches and experiencing jobs. Many are also using this period to find out about employment opportunities and where they fit in best. This adjustment process seems to be complete by about 5 years in the United States. Thus, labor force statistics show little variation by duration among immigrants in the United States for more than 5 years.

There are few differences in the employment status data by country of origin among immigrants in the United States for many years. Differences do emerge among more recent immigrants. Mexican immigrants have higher unemployment rates than other immigrants, although the employment ratio is higher for Mexican men and lower for Mexican women than for other immigrants.

14.5.2. Type of Employer: Class of Worker

Another way of looking at the employment of immigrants is termed "class of worker" by the Census Bureau, which actually refers to the status of the employer. The 1990 census provides detail on whether an employed person is working for a private company, a private not-for-profit organization, a government agency (by level of government), is self-employed, or is an unpaid family worker in a family-owned business.

Employed immigrants are more likely than native-born workers to be working in the private sector (i.e., for a private company or a not-for-profit organization) than for a government agency, but are equally likely to be self-employed. Among those aged 25–64 who were employed, 78 percent of the immigrants, in contrast to 72 percent of the native-born, were private sector employees, with only a trivial difference by gender.

In the public sector, from the local level up through the federal level, many jobs require U.S. citizenship. For example, in many jurisdictions public safety jobs, such as police and fire-fighting, require U.S. citizenship, and by a Presidential Executive Order employment in the Federal Civil Service requires citizenship. Moreover, some government jobs require passing proficiency tests in English, which are not required in their private sector counterparts. As a result, whereas 18 percent of the employed adult native-born men and women (16 percent and 19 percent, respectively, by gender) work for the government at all levels, among immigrants only 11 percent (10 percent for men, 12 percent for women) are government employees.

There is, however, a very strong relationship between government employment and duration in the United States as well as region of origin. Among the most recent immigrants, those who arrived between 1985 and 1990, only 10 percent were employed by government, with the proportion increasing with duration until a peak of 16 percent for the pre-1950 cohort of immigrants. With a longer duration of residence, the two primary barriers to new immigrant employment in the government sector become less formidable–proficiency in the English language and U.S. citizenship.

Country of origin also matters. Although differences in government employment by country of origin are slight among immigrants who arrived before 1950, they are very large among more recent immigration cohorts, reflecting important differences in education, English language fluency, and U.S. citizenship. Among employed immigrants who arrived in the United States in 1975–1984, by 1990, 10.4 percent of the Asian, 9.6 percent of the European/Canadian, 8.6 percent of the Other Latin

American, and only 3.5 percent of the Mexican immigrants were in government employment. The small proportion of Mexican immigrants in government employment may arise from their low level of education and low proportion naturalized.

Among both immigrants and the native-born, 11 percent of the employed are self-employed. This similarity in overall rates masks important differences in self-employment patterns. Among the immigrants who are self-employed, 52 percent are in service, sales, and managerial occupations, and only 3 percent are in agriculture (including forestry and fishing), in contrast to 43 percent and 12 percent, respectively, for the native-born.

Rates of self-employment vary by duration of residence and country of origin. Overall, and for all country groups, self-employment increases with duration of residence. For immigrants aged 25–64 in 1990, it is 8 percent for the newest immigration cohort (immigrated 1985–1990), rising monotonically to 16 percent for the pre-1950 cohort. To some extent this reflects the rise in self-employment with age observed even for the native-born. It also reflects an independent effect of the exposure and experience that enhance self-employment opportunities through increased knowledge of the United States and easier access to capital from lending institutions. Presumably, many immigrants begin as employees, but after some years amass enough capital to start their own businesses.

As Tables 14.9 and 14.10 indicate, self-employment tends to be lower among Latin American immigrants (7 percent for Mexican immigrants and 9 percent for Other Latin American immigrants), and is higher for European/Canadian and Asian immigrants (14 percent each). Among Asian immigrants who arrived prior to 1950, one-fifth were self-employed in 1990.

14.5.3. Occupational Attainment

Occupational attainment is a measure of the outcome of the labor market process in which workers, with various skills and demographic characteristics, sort themselves out among the myriad types of jobs in the economy. The Census Bureau coded detailed occupational categories based on the information provided by the respondent on the type of work performed. The detailed occupations were then grouped into nine broad occupational categories used in this analysis. Data on the occupational distribution of those aged 25–64 are presented for the foreign-born

Table 14.9. Occupational attainment and self-employment status of men aged 25–64, by region of birth, 1990

Occupation	Foreign-born						Native-born	Foreign-born in occupation
	Europe/ Canada[a]	Mexico	Other Latin America	Asia	Africa	Total[b]		
Managerial	18%	4%	9%	15%	16%	11%	14%	8%
Professional	16	2	8	21	25	12	13	10
Technical	4	1	3	7	4	4	4	10
Sales	9	3	9	12	11	8	11	8
Clerical and Adm. Sup.	4	3	8	8	8	6	6	10
Craft	24	22	20	12	8	19	21	9
Service	9	14	17	12	14	13	8	15
Agriculture[c]	2	16	2	1	<1	5	4	14
Operative/Laborer	14	35	24	12	13	21	20	11
Total	100%	100%	100%	100%	100%	100%	100%	100%
Self-employed[d]	18%	8%	10%	16%	13%	13%	13%	

Source: 1990 Census of Population, Public Use Microdata Sample.
Notes: Detail may not add to total due to rounding. Index of dissimilarity between native-born and foreign-born = 7.8.
[a] Includes Australia and New Zealand.
[b] Includes other areas not specified and country not specified.
[c] Includes fishing and forestry and farm managers.
[d] Percent self-employed among those who are employed.

and the native-born for men and women in Tables 14.9 and 14.10, respectively.

The occupational distributions of foreign- and native-born men are quite similar. Fewer than 8 percent of the foreign-born men would have to change their occupation to have the same occupational distribution as the native-born men. The differences for the women are larger: nearly one in every five of the immigrant women workers would have to change her occupation for the foreign-born women to have the same occupational distribution as native-born women.

Not surprisingly, differences in occupational attainment reflect relative differences in education and levels of skill. Asian, African, and European/ Canadian male immigrants have a high occupational attainment, higher even than the native-born; that is, they are more concentrated in the prestigious professional and managerial jobs, while Latin American

Table 14.10. Occupational attainment and self-employment status of women aged 25–64, by region of birth, 1990[a]

| Occupation | Foreign-born | | | | | | Native-born | Foreign-born in occupation |
	Europe/Canada[a]	Mexico	Other Latin America	Asia	Africa	Total[b]		
Managerial	13%	4%	7%	11%	12%	9%	13%	8%
Professional	16	4	11	17	22	13	19	8
Technical	3	1	3	6	4	4	4	9
Sales	12	6	8	12	11	10	10	10
Clerical and Adm. Sup.	22	10	20	18	24	19	28	7
Craft	4	6	3	5	2	4	2	19
Service	19	30	31	18	19	23	14	16
Agriculture[d]	<1	8	<1	<1	<1	2	<1	20
Operative/Laborer	11	32	15	13	6	16	8	20
Total	100%	100%	100%	100%	100%	100%	100%	
Self-Employed[e]	10%	6%	7%	11%	11%	9%	8%	9%

Source: 1990 Census of Population, Public Use Microdata Sample.
Notes: Detail may not add to total due to rounding. Index of dissimilarity between the native-born and foreign-born = 19.8.
[a] Among women who worked in the previous year or in the reference week in 1990.
[b] Includes Australia and New Zealand.
[c] Includes other areas not specified and country not specified.
[d] Includes fishing and forestry and farm managers.
[e] Percent self-employed among those who are employed.

immigrants, particularly those from Mexico, have a very low occupational status. Among the men, the professional, technical, and managerial occupations employ 43 percent of the Asian immigrants (including 1 in 5 Asian immigrants in professional occupations), 45 percent of the African immigrants, 38 percent of European/Canadian immigrants, 31 percent of the native-born, 20 percent of non-Mexican Latin American immigrants, and only 7 percent of Mexican immigrants. Among women the proportion employed in professional, technical, and managerial occupations ranged from 38 percent of the immigrants born in Africa to 9 percent of those born in Mexico, with 36 percent of the native-born women reporting one of these high-level occupations.

The ranking is reversed at the lowest end of the skill distribution. Operative and laborer jobs outside of agriculture employ one-third of male Mexican immigrants, but only 12–14 percent of Asian and European/ Canadian immigrants. Including agriculture in the lower-skilled occupations, since most immigrants in agriculture are laborers, raises the proportion for Mexican immigrants to around one-half compared with only 13 percent and 16 percent, respectively, for Asian and European/Canadian immigrants. Similar patterns emerge for women, where 70 percent of women born in Mexico were in operative, laborer, agricultural, and service jobs, in contrast to 32 percent for Asian immigrant women and 30 percent for European/Canadian.

Another way of looking at the occupational attainment of immigrants is to consider their concentration in broad occupational categories. Although immigrants constitute 10 percent of all adult males reporting an occupation (Table 14.9), they are most heavily concentrated in service (15 percent) and agricultural jobs (14 percent) and have the lowest representation in managerial and sales jobs (8 percent each). Among the women, immigrants are most heavily represented in all of the lower-skilled jobs, particularly craft, service, and operative/laborer employment. Although one in five women in agriculture is foreign-born, relatively few women work in this sector.

Much of the public debate over immigration has centered on the issue of what kinds of jobs immigrants take. Are they clustered in the jobs that the native-born do not want, or are they dominating high-paid jobs in industry, universities, and health care? One reason that the debates are confusing is that, as the data indicate, these alternatives are not mutually exclusive. The diversity of the immigrants' impact on the occupational structure is shown by their dispersion across the occupational spectrum— because they take all sorts of jobs—as well as by their concentration in certain occupational groups.

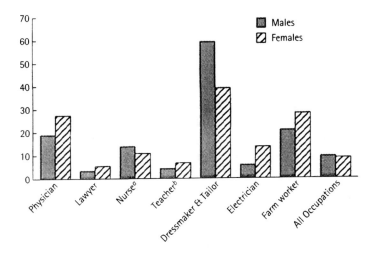

Figure 14.3. Proportion of foreign-born in selected occupations ages 25–64, by sex, 1990

Source: 1990 Census of Population, Public Use Microdata Sample; Employment and Earnings, Jan. 1991.
[a] Only registered nurses.
[b] Only primary and secondary educators.

To demonstrate this point, Figure 14.3 depicts graphically the proportion of workers in certain occupations who are foreign-born. Immigrants figure prominently in some professions, such as medicine (especially female physicians) and nursing, while they are much less likely to be found in the legal and teaching fields. Skilled craft jobs show much the same pattern, with immigrants comprising a very large proportion of some occupations, such as tailors and dressmakers, but much less numerous among others, such as electricians. Finally, as the preceding discussion indicated, immigrants are heavily concentrated in agriculture. Yet even within agriculture there is an uneven distribution, as immigrants are concentrated in farm laborer jobs for perishable crops (fruits and vegetables). Generalizations about the immigrant impact on the labor market must take into account both patterns, the general pattern of dispersion across the occupational spectrum and the concentration within certain occupational groups and specific occupations.

14.6. Household Structure, Marital Status, and Fertility

Immigration inevitably entails a transition period for the immigrant, followed by a reorganization of family and household. The family reunification preferences that affected immigration since the 1965 Amendments were intended to assist the reconstitution of families within the United States. The process of reorganization, however, is by no means uniform. Some immigrants come with the intention of sojourning for a limited period of time and then returning to their home countries; for others, the relocation to the United States is permanent. For some families, the dislocation is temporary and adjustment is quickly made; for others, the period of dislocation may be lengthy.

In the sojourner stage, for example, the characteristic household may be made up of unrelated individuals. An ethnographic study of Mexican immigrants in San Diego depicted this type of organization:

A total of eleven men, all undocumented Mexican immigrants, lived in this [one] unit. These men were all employed and worked different shifts, thus not all of them were in the housing unit at the same time. Their work schedule permitted them to sleep in shifts. [Velasco 1992]

In this type of household, the unrelated workers have not yet brought any family members to join them. Eventually, the entire family may be reconstituted within the United States. One of the incentives to naturalization offered by U.S. immigration law is the greater ability of citizens to sponsor relatives to enter the United States. Studies of the Mexican-origin population have indicated that by combining its efforts, the family experiences social and economic benefits from this reconsolidation (Briody 1987; Tienda 1980). Immigrants from other nationality groups may experience similar benefits.

During the family reunification process, various relatives may live together in extended families. The family reunification provisions in the 1965 Amendments tended to favor both generational extensions, through the immigration of the spouses, parents, and children of U.S. citizens and resident aliens, and horizontal extensions, through the immigration of brothers or sisters of U.S. citizens. It should be noted, however, that immigrants sponsored by their relatives need not live in the same household as their sponsor. Unfortunately, there are no data on the physical proximity of sponsoring relatives.

14.6.1. Diversity in Household Structure

The staging of family immigration over a period of years implies another type of diversity among immigrants: a diversity in the size and composition of their households. Complex households are further encouraged by the high rents typical of such large cities as Los Angeles and New York

City, in which many immigrants reside. Sharing living quarters may offer one means to economize while the family members adjust to labor market conditions and seek to earn a living.

An ethnographer who assessed census coverage in San Francisco describes one complex household:

Alejandro and his wife were Salvadoran immigrants employed in low wage service jobs. In order to meet the relatively high rent in the sample area Alejandro and his family rented a three bedroom apartment and took in nine other Salvadoran immigrants to help with the rent. ... Alejandro, his wife and two children shared one of the three bedrooms. The other bedroom was occupied by a woman in her 30's with her twenty-one year old partner, their six month old child, two children from the woman's previous marriage and the nineteen year old brother of her partner. Three recent Salvadoran immigrants occupied the remaining bedroom. Two were in their twenties and unrelated and the third was a man in his forties who was the father of Alejandro's partner. [De la Puente 1993]

This household, made up of both related and unrelated family groups and nonrelatives, is complex and difficult to enumerate. Only six of the thirteen residents of this apartment were reported in the 1990 census.

Table 14.11 illustrates some of the differences that can be found in household types using census data. Recently immigrated males have the most varied household structures, with nearly 1 in 5 living without any family members. Foreign-born males who are naturalized are more likely to be in married-couple households and less likely to be in nonfamily households than those who have recently immigrated. The prevalence of the male householder with no wife present also declines with length of residence. For women, the findings are quite different. Possibly because of family reunification, the most recent women immigrants are most likely to be living in married-couple households. Women who are naturalized citizens are most likely to be in nonfamily households. The female householder with no husband present is most likely to be an alien who immigrated before 1985. Mexican immigrants exhibit little difference from other immigrants in these household patterns.[12]

Table 14.12 investigates the extent to which family reunification among recent immigrants affects the composition of extended family households. Although the census does not provide information on the preference category used for obtaining a visa, it does have information on the relationship of each person to the householder, that is, the person who rents or owns the housing unit in which he or she resides. Parents and siblings are two groups of relatives who may be sponsored under the kinship

Table 14.11. Household type of persons aged 18 and over, by nativity and immigrant status, 1990

Household type	Males				Females			
	Alien		Naturalized citizens	Native-born	Aliens		Naturalized citizens	Native-born
	Immigrated 1985–1990	Immigrated pre-1985			Immigrated 1985–1990	Immigrated pre-1985		
Married couple	57%	71%	77%	72%	70%	69%	66%	63%
Male householder, No wife present	16	10	6	5	8	4	2	2
Female householder, No husband present	8	6	3	6	13	17	13	16
Nonfamily	20	13	13	17	9	10	19	20
Total	100%	100%	100%	100%	100%	100%	100%	100%
Number (1,000s)	1,682	3,125	3,405	79,875	1,583	3,277	3,940	87,214

Source: 1990 Census of Population, Public Use Microdata Sample.
Note: Totals may not add to 100 because of rounding.

Table 14.12. Recent immigrants residing with relatives, by relationship, age, and hemisphere of birth of the immigrant, 1960–90[a]

Hemisphere/Year	Parents of household head Ages			Siblings of household head Ages		
Eastern	45–54	55–64	65+	25–34	35–44	45–54
1960	3.5%	18.6%	51.5%	2.7%	2.2%	2.1%
1970	4.2	20.4	48.0	2.9	4.1	4.1
1980	7.8	30.2	55.4	5.2	3.9	4.5
1990	6.6	36.3	54.6	6.7	5.3	5.0
Western						
1960	5.4	20.2	40.9	4.3	4.1	5.4
1970	7.1	24.9	47.9	4.5	3.7	3.9
1980	10.2	25.0	50.4	8.3	7.5	6.7
1990	11.7	33.9	49.3	12.5	10.0	6.5

Sources: Adapted from Jasso and Rosenzweig, 1991: Table 5.2, pp. 204–205; 1990 Census of Population, Public Use Microdata Sample.
Note: Native-born respondents—1990.

	Parents of household head			Siblings of household head		
Age	45–54	55–64	65+	25–34	35–44	45–54
Percent	1.6%	3.0%	12.1%	0.01%	0.3%	1.4%

[a] Percentage of recent immigrants (i.e., immigrated in the 5 years prior to the census year) who are the parents or siblings, including parents-in-law and siblings-in-law of the household head, by age, in the census year. Data from decennial censuses, 1960 to 1990.

provisions. If the kinship provisions of the 1965 Amendments applicable to the Eastern Hemisphere and the extension a decade later of the preference system to the Western Hemisphere affected family-based migration, the proportions of parents and siblings living with household heads should rise with each successive census year. The data in Table 14.12 indicate that in 1990 over half the immigrants from the Eastern Hemisphere aged 65 and over were parents of householders, with a third of those aged 55–64 also parents of the householder. As expected, the proportions, especially for the 55–64 age group, have generally increased from 1960 to 1990. What is perhaps more revealing is the proportion of parents living with their children among Western Hemisphere immigrants. It increased from 41 percent in 1960 to 49 percent in 1990 among the older group (age 65 and over) and from 20 percent to 34 percent, respectively, among parents aged 55–64. Thus, for both hemispheres the proportion of elderly immigrants who are parents of householders has risen, suggesting that there are more older immigrants coming to the United States to be reunited with their adult children.

The pattern for siblings is not as startling as that for parents, but there has been a steady increase among the proportion of immigrants who are siblings of householders, particularly among Western Hemisphere immigrants in the 1980s. For example, 13 percent of the 1985–1990 cohort of immigrants from the Western Hemisphere aged 25–34 were living with a householder who was their brother, sister, brother-in-law, or sister-in-law. Of course, other siblings and parents have immigrated who do not live in the same household with their relatives.

Table 14.12 is revealing, not only because it shows the strength of family reunification policies, but also because it demonstrates the prevalence of extended family households for the most recent immigrants. These data undoubtedly also reflect the need of low-income immigrants to double up because of economic circumstances.

14.6.2. Marital Status and Fertility

Figure 14.4 shows the marital status of foreign-born and native-born adults in 1990. The two pie charts look remarkably similar except for the larger proportions of immigrants who report themselves married, spouse

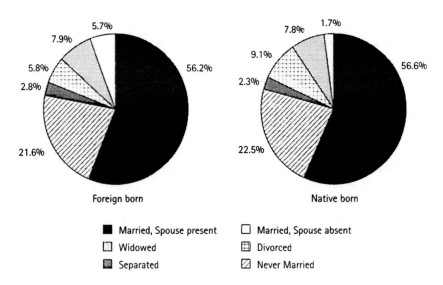

Figure 14.4. Marital status of the foreign-born and native-born populations ages 18 and over, 1990
Source: 1990 Census of Population, Public Use Microdata Sample.

absent and separated, presumably because one spouse has yet to move to the United States. Immigrants are slightly less likely than the native-born to be widowed or married, spouse present. The dislocation of the immigration experience may lead to delayed or disrupted marriages, although some marriages of foreign nationals to U.S. citizens occur to facilitate the legal immigration of the former.

One heated immigration issue is the extent to which immigrants increase population growth through high fertility. Although many recent studies have indicated that immigrant fertility converges, after several generations, to American norms, the concern has been renewed because so many of the sending countries have current high levels of fertility (Rindfuss and Sweet 1977; Bean and Swicegood 1985). The total fertility rate is a measure of the number of children a woman would have, on average, if current fertility rates persisted throughout her entire childbearing years; the current rate in the United States is about 1.85. A total fertility rate of about 2.1 is required for a population to remain at about the same size. In major sending countries, such as Mexico, the total fertility rate is about 3.3 children per woman; in El Salvador the figure is 3.9, and in Guatemala it is 4.9. In other sending countries the fertility level is either low or it has been dropping. For example, in China the total fertility rate is 1.9, and in Korea it is only 1.6.[13] The question then arises, will the immigrants' fertility be typical of their home country, or will it be more typical of the United States?

Recent studies in both the United States and Canada of female immigrants from high-fertility countries have found their overall fertility rates to be very close to those of native-born women (Blau 1992; Sullivan 1992). The explanation for this finding may be found in the selectivity of immigration. Men and women who are better educated and have more "modern" attitudes are more likely both to migrate and to have lower fertility. Furthermore, migration is less expensive in terms of out-of-pocket costs and nonmoney (psychic) costs if there are fewer children in the family. Those anticipating immigration may delay childbearing; those with large families may be less likely to move. Moreover, just as immigrants adapt to the United States in other dimensions, they may also adjust their fertility in response to the same incentives that affect the native-born population. Thus, even immigrants who come from high-fertility countries may converge to the low-fertility norms of the United States.

Data on completed fertility confirms the reduced fertility of immigrant women. Completed fertility is the average number of children born per woman for a birth cohort of women at the end of their childbearing years.

For U.S. native-born women over the age of 45 in 1990, the mean completed fertility (i.e., total number of children ever born) was 2.7. For the 2.4 million immigrant women over the age of 45 who were naturalized citizens, the number was *lower*, 2.4 children per woman. For 1.6 million immigrant women over the age of 45 who were not naturalized citizens, the number was higher, 3.3 children per woman. The lower fertility for naturalized citizen women, compared with alien women, can be attributed to the differences in their age structure, duration in the U.S., education, labor market opportunities, and other characteristics.

Table 14.13 presents detailed data on completed fertility and on childlessness by region of birth and by period of immigration. The data indicate that the immigrant women of European/Canadian origin have consistently low completed fertility (2.1 to 2.3, depending on period of immigration). The Mexican women present the strongest contrast to this pattern; their completed fertility is an average of 4.6 children, with a still higher number for the most recent immigrants, 5.5.

Table 14.13. Fertility of foreign-born women, by region of birth and period of immigration, 1990

Period of immigration	Europe/ Canada[a]	Mexico	Other Latin America	Asia	Africa	Total[b]
A. Mean number of children ever-born for women Aged 45 and Over						
1985–90	2.2	5.5	3.7	4.0	3.9	3.8
1975–84	2.1	5.2	3.2	3.8	2.9	3.5
1965–74	2.2	4.6	2.4	2.5	2.5	2.7
1960–64	2.2	4.1	2.2	2.3	2.2	2.5
1950–59	2.3	4.1	2.2	2.5	2.4	2.5
Before 1950	2.3	4.5	2.3	3.2	2.3	2.5
Total	2.3	4.6	2.6	3.2	2.7	2.8
B. Percentage of women aged 15–30 who are childless						
1985–90	72%	48%	59%	71%	65%	62%
1975–84	64	39	54	69	61	55
1965–74	64	46	54	76	78	69
1960–64	43	28	42	52	46	40
Total	66%	44%	56%	70%	65%	58%

Source: 1990 Census of Population, Public Use Microdata Sample.
Note: Data for native-born women: panel A, 2.7 children ever-born; panel B, 65 percent childless.
[a] Includes Australia and New Zealand.
[b] Includes other areas not specified and country not specified.

Immigrant women from Latin America, Asia, and Africa also show the highest completed fertility among the recent immigration cohorts. It would, however, be erroneous to assume any implication of a little baby boom among the foreign-born. These women are unusual because, having immigrated within the past 5 years, they must have entered the United States at age 40 or older. Their childbearing, therefore, was largely completed in their home countries. As the data in Table 14.5 showed, the median age at immigration for the largest sending countries is much younger, and so these women are atypical in the timing of immigration, and perhaps more than others they reflect the fertility norms in their origins rather than in the United States.

The distribution of women by the number of children they have borne seems quite similar for the native-born and the foreign-born. Foreign-born women as a group are somewhat less likely to be childless, and somewhat more likely to have had a larger number of children. Of the foreign-born women aged 15 and over, 38 percent had no children compared with 48 percent of the native-born, and 18 percent had one child versus 16 percent of the native-born. Another 23 percent had two children, compared with 20 percent of the native-born. Fully 21 percent reported three or more children, compared with 16 percent of the native-born.

The lower panel of Table 14.13 provides a closer view of childlessness. Although not quite as likely as the native-born to be childless, a relatively high proportion of immigrant women aged 15–30 are childless. This figure is significant because a delay in childbearing past the age of 30 will result in a low completed fertility. Mexican women are the least likely to be childless, but 44 percent of them, and 48 percent of the most recent Mexican women immigrants under the age of 30, are still childless. Over half the Mexican immigrants are below the age of 29, and so this proportion of childlessness could have a significant impact on eventual completed fertility. The figure for Asian women rises to 70 percent being childless, including 71 percent of the most recent immigrants. These women, because of their age, are more typical of all immigrants in the timing of their immigration as young adults.

The long-term effects of immigrant fertility on population growth are difficult to project. First, not all of the immigrants' children may be in the United States, so the population growth may occur in another country. Because the average age at migration is often in the young adult years, it is likely that young children will accompany (or follow) their immigrant mothers or be born in the United States. Family reunification preferences make it possible for children born abroad to rejoin their mothers in the United States. Second, the effect that these children will have on future growth depends on how rapidly they adopt the prevailing American fertility norms.

To summarize, census data indicate that immigrant households are likely to be larger and more complex than the households of the native-born, although the differences may diminish with duration of residence. There are substantial variations in fertility by duration in the United States and region of birth. Although immigrant fertility is somewhat higher than native-born fertility, the 1990 census data confirm findings from earlier censuses of a convergence in fertility to the U.S. norms. Mexican immigrant fertility shows high variability, with the most recent immigration cohorts having high completed fertility among the older immigrants, but nearly half of the younger immigrants are still childless.

14.7. Earnings and Income

The incomes of immigrants are of interest for two fundamental reasons.[14] Data on income (including income transfers) provide information on the economic well-being of immigrant households, including the extent to which they are in poverty, as well as being strong indicators of the productivity of immigrant workers.

The decennial census contains separate questions on various sources of money or cash income, but it lacks direct information on the value of in-kind benefits, including the economic value of food stamps, public housing, Medicaid, Medicare, and employer-financed health insurance. Moreover, the reliability of reporting of money income in the census varies by type of income. Wage and salary incomes have been shown to be accurately reported in census data, but there is substantial underreporting of self-employment income, rental and investment (interest and dividends) income, and public and private transfer income. In the aggregate, wage and salary disbursements (and other labor income) were nearly 65 percent of total personal income in 1990 and 76 percent of personal income from sources other than income transfers.[15] Thus, the largest component of income and the primary source income for most households are well reported in census data.

14.7.1. Labor Market Earnings

Labor market earnings constitute an important measure both of immigrant adjustment and of their economic well-being. Earnings are defined in the 1990 census as the sum of wage, salary, and self-employment income in the previous year, 1989. Annual earnings are the product of two factors: units of time worked during the year and remuneration per unit of time worked. Among men aged 25–64 with earnings, most variations in earnings are due to variations in rates of pay. Among women, on the other hand, the variations in time worked are substantial and are dominant causes of differences in earnings. Because of the greater complexity of the analysis for the determinants of earnings among women, including variations in past and present labor market experience, the discussion of earnings that follows focuses on foreign-born men.

As indicated in Table 14.14, among adult immigrant men who had earnings, the mean earnings were $27,600, 14 percent less than the $32,100 earned by native-born men. Immigrant earnings increased with duration in the United States, rising from $20,000 among those being in the United States for 5 or fewer years to nearly $38,900 among those who immigrated in the 1950s. The 1965–1974 cohort of immigrants had earnings ($31,100) comparable to the native-born. Immigrants who have lived in the United States a longer period of time are likely to be older than more recent immigrants. Yet, even when analyses that hold current age constant are performed, the pattern persists of earnings rising with

Table 14.14. Earnings of foreign-born men aged 25–64, by region of birth and period of immigration, 1990[a]

Period of immigration	Mean Earnings						Standard deviation Total
	Europe/ Canada[b]	Mexico	Other Latin America	Asia	Africa	Total[c]	
1985–90	$32,771	$11,082	$15,660	$22,369	$22,157	$19,966	$23,161
1975–84	39,148	14,494	19,878	29,363	30,610	24,086	24,877
1965–74	36,939	18,915	26,667	43,911	46,244	31,140	31,108
1960–64	39,242	21,620	38,818	42,946	42,615	35,945	33,171
1950–59	41,318	24,660	36,799	47,097	58,140	38,883	33,891
Before 1950	46,620	22,378	41,272	39,671	14,387	41,705	41,123
Total	$38,891	$16,139	$23,615	$32,028	$32,388	$27,647	$28,933
Standard deviation	$34,972	$13,902	$23,786	$32,562	$35,341	$28,933	

Source: 1990 Census of Population, Public Use Microdata Sample.
Note: Native-born earnings: mean $32,057; standard deviation $28,330.
[a] Excludes those with zero earnings.
[b] Includes Australia and New Zealand.
[c] Includes other areas not separately listed and country not specified.

duration in the United States, with the sharpest increase in the first few years, thereafter increasing at a slower rate. The increase in earnings with duration in the United States reflects the favorable effects on employment and pay rates of greater experience in the United States labor market, enhanced English-language fluency, and postmigration schooling, among other factors.

Earnings also varied systematically by country of origin. Overall, among the major regions, earnings are highest among the European/ Canadian immigrants (over $38,800), closely followed by the Asian immigrants ($32,000). The earnings of other Latin American ($23,600) and Mexican ($16,100) immigrants lag behind. Within each origin category, earnings increase with duration of residence, at least until the oldest cohort (pre-1950 immigrants). The steepness of this increase varies across country groups. It is flattest for the European/Canadian immigrants, since this group arrived with skills most readily transferable to the United States, including a high level of English-language fluency. The steepness of the profile is roughly similar for the other major source regions.

The pattern in earnings by region of origin reflects the impact of several factors. Differences in duration in the United States; for example, the longer duration of residence of the European/Canadian immigrants, account for some differences in earnings. Yet sharp differences exist even among immigrants who arrived in the same time period (Table 14.14). Immigrant earnings also increase with their level of education, although the effect of schooling on earnings is larger for the group (European/ Canadians) with the more highly transferable skills. Their higher-than-average level of schooling also gives the European/Canadian immigrants an earnings advantage. Geographic location in the United States, pre-immigration labor market experience, and marital status also influence earnings and vary across the birthplace groups.

Using European/Canadian immigrants as the benchmark, with other measured variables (age, education, time in the United States, marital status, region of residence, and urban/rural location) held constant, earnings are lower by about 15 percent for Asian immigrants, by about 26 percent for other Latin American immigrants, and by about 34 percent for Mexican immigrants. The differences in earnings by country of origin when other measured variables are the same reflect many unmeasured or unmeasurable factors, including the lower transferability of skills from countries whose economies and/or language differ from that of the United States, and differences in the quality of schooling in the origin, refugee status, English-language fluency, and training or licenses specific to the U.S. labor market. Discrimination may also account for part of these differences.

The earnings of immigrants can also be compared with the earnings of native-born men, when other variables are the same. When this is done it appears that recent immigrants have lower earnings than comparable native-born men, but that their earnings increase sharply with duration in the United States. As a result, other things the same, the earnings gap between immigrants and the native-born decreases with the duration of residence of the former. The earnings of male immigrants from non-refugee countries reach parity with native-born men at 10 to 20 years' duration in the United States, while those from countries where many of the migrants are refugees tend to have lower earnings and a later "catch-up," if it occurs at all. This finding of an earnings "catch-up" of economic migrants compared to native-born men, and the lower earnings of refugees, when other variables are the same, is not unique to the 1990 census. Similar patterns were found in analyses for the 1970 and 1980 censuses (Chiswick 1986). This suggests that although there may have been a decline in immigrant skills, as measured by years of schooling, and a shift in the source regions of immigrants, when schooling, country of origin, and other measured variables are the same, there does not appear to have been a decline over time in the unmeasurable dimensions of immigrant quality.

14.7.2. Public Assistance

Some observers fear that continued immigration will constitute a disproportionate drain on the welfare system. The 1990 census includes information on public assistance programs that provide cash benefits, such as Aid to Families with Dependent Children (AFDC), Supplemental Security Income (SSI), and other cash welfare programs. AFDC provides cash assistance to poor families with children, while SSI provides assistance to the poor who are aged or disabled. About 3.6 percent of the immigrants (2.6 percent for males, 4.7 percent for females) reported receiving any cash public assistance benefits in 1989, a proportion remarkably similar to the 3.9 percent (2.5 percent for males, 5.2 percent for females) among the native-born.[16]

There is no clear pattern in the receipt of cash public assistance benefits by duration of residence. Although incomes are lower during the early years in the United States, the major cash programs require either the presence of children in the family or a waiting period before benefits can be received. Among the major regions of origin, the proportion of immigrants receiving cash public assistance varies from 4.2 percent among Mexican immigrants to 1.6 percent for African immigrants. The variation by country of origin reflects differences in income and household structure. In general, these data seem consistent with a conclusion that immigrants use the welfare system at roughly the same rate as do the native-born.

14.7.3. Household Income

Household income is an important index of economic well-being. It is a complex measure because it combines the labor market earnings, property income, and money income from public and private transfers of all the household members. The fragmentation or consolidation of households can dramatically change the level and distribution of household income, even if the income of each household member does not change.

Overall, the income in 1989 of households in which the household head (householder) is foreign-born was only 1 percent larger than the native-born ($38,100, compared with $37,800 for the native-born). This difference does not arise from a larger proportion of aged, and hence lower-income households, among the native-born, because the proportion of the population aged 65 and older is about the same for the native-born and foreign-born (about 13 percent). There is, however, a different household structure among immigrants, with a larger number of workers per household.

Among both immigrant and native-born households, the lower the earning potential of the individual member, the larger the number of household members who work. If household members have low incomes, the household tends to have a larger number of adults living together and higher rates of labor force participation. Moreover, households with lower income from wages, salaries, and self-employment are more likely to be eligible for income transfer programs, including unemployment insurance, disability insurance, and welfare payments. As a result, the relative differences in household income are smaller across countries of origin and across immigrant cohorts than are the relative differences among the earnings of foreign-born men.[17]

The mean and standard deviation of household money income in 1989 are reported by region of origin and duration in the United States in Table 14.15. In general, household incomes increase with a longer duration of residence in the United States of the foreign-born head, but this generalization is tempered by declines among the longest duration immigrants,

Table **14.15.** Household income of the foreign-born, by region of birth and period of immigration, 1990[a]

Period of immigration	Mean income							Standard deviation total[c]
	Europe/ Canada[b]	Mexico	Other Latin America	Asia	Africa	Total[c]	
1985–90	$41,062	$23,227	$27,581	$31,859	$29,383	$30,981	$29,379
1975–84	49,685	25,714	30,823	43,333	43,594	36,701	33,077
1965–74	46,848	29,261	36,733	60,018	59,579	42,880	39,084
1960–64	47,868	33,545	46,307	56,959	51,046	46,050	40,164
1950–59	46,039	33,502	43,486	58,259	57,655	45,226	41,054
Before 1950	30,531	23,187	34,045	38,851	30,778	30,341	35,244
Total	$41,046	$27,328	$34,820	$45,617	$44,204	$38,104	$36,389
Standard deviation	$40,664	$22,328	$30,117	$41,032	$45,542	$36,389	

Source: 1990 Census of Population, Public Use Microdata Sample.
Note: Native-born: mean $37,838; standard deviation $33,785.
[a] Income of households in which the household head is foreign-born. Excludes those living in group quarters, those with no income, and vacant households.
[b] Includes Australia and New Zealand.
[c] Includes areas not separately identified and country not specified.

the cohorts with the largest proportion of aged. Differences exist by country of origin. Overall, Asian households have higher incomes than European/Canadian households, but the difference varies by duration of residence. More recent arrival cohorts of Asian immigrants have lower household incomes, but the cohorts that arrived in 1974 and earlier have substantially higher incomes than European/Canadian immigrants of the same duration in the United States. The larger number of workers per household and the steeper rise in labor market earnings with duration in the United States account for this pattern. The household income of the Mexican immigrants ($27,300) and other Latin American immigrants ($34,800) are far below the European/Canadian ($41,000) and Asian ($45,600) levels, and this pattern holds even when duration in the United States is the same.

14.7.4. Immigrants in Poverty

Although household money income is a useful measure of the household's capacity to purchase consumer goods and services in the marketplace, it is deficient because it does not take account of household structure, as measured by the number and age composition of household members. The 1990 census data provide an index of household money income relative to family size and structure. On the basis of the number of family members and their ages, the Census Bureau calculated the threshold poverty level income for that household. The household poverty index is the ratio of the household's reported money income divided by its calculated poverty threshold.

For the foreign-born population as a whole, 18.0 percent lived in households with money income below the poverty line, with little difference by gender (17.3 percent for males and 18.7 percent for females). This was substantially greater than the poverty rate for the native-born, which was 12.4 percent (10.8 percent for males and 13.9 percent for females). The higher poverty rate for females arises from the prevalence of single mothers, who have lower earnings and a larger number of children per household than do single fathers, and also from the prevalence of widows, who are more numerous and have lower incomes.

The poverty rate of the foreign-born reflects patterns seen above in the components of the poverty index, such as income and household structure. Overall, the poverty rate declines with duration in the United States until the oldest cohort of immigrants, those who arrived before 1950 (see Table 14.16). The pre-1950 immigrants are disproportionately elderly, many of whom are in retirement. For others, the poverty decline reflects

Table 14.16. Poverty rates of the foreign-born, by region of birth and period of immigration, 1990

Period of immigration	Europe/ Canada[a]	Mexico	Other Latin America	Asia	Africa	Total[b]
1985–90	22.7%	37.3%	28.1%	27.4%	24.6%	29.8%
1975–84	8.1	28.9	18.3	14.4	13.2	18.7
1965–74	6.4	23.6	12.0	6.6	6.4	12.5
1960–64	5.2	17.3	9.6	5.7	6.9	8.7
1950–59	5.8	17.8	10.9	5.5	9.6	7.9
Before 1950	9.0	20.5	11.2	10.6	3.1	10.6
Total	9.1%	29.0%	18.3%	16.5%	15.4%	18.0%

Source: 1990 Census of Population, Public Use Microdata Sample.
Note: Native-born (percent): 12.4.
[a] Includes Australia and New Zealand.
[b] Includes other areas not specified and country not reported.

both increased employment and increased wage rates that occur with duration of residence.

The variations in the poverty rate by country of origin are striking (Table 14.16). Among the foreign-born, the poverty rate varies from a low of 9 percent for European/Canadian immigrants, which is below the rate for the native-born (12 percent), to a high of 29 percent for Mexican immigrants, more than twice the rate for the native-born. These large differences in the incidence of poverty can be understood in terms of the differences in the underlying components of the index. For example, the higher level of education and greater English-language fluency of the European/Canadian immigrants compared with Mexican immigrants translate into higher earnings among those who work. The greater female labor supply and smaller family size of the European/Canadian immigrants compared with those of Mexican origin also results in greater household income and a smaller poverty threshold, and hence a lower poverty rate.

The highest poverty rate is experienced by females born in Mexico. Nearly one-third (32 percent) of Mexican-born females live in households with incomes below the poverty threshold. This extraordinarily high rate compared with other immigrant women is not limited to particular immigration cohorts, but rather appears to be a feature of all the cohorts. Such a high poverty rate stems, in part, from the lower skills, lower labor supply, and larger family size (higher fertility) of women born in Mexico.

14.8. The Consequences of Immigration: Summary, Conclusions, and Implications

This chapter has analyzed the demographic and economic characteristics of the foreign-born population of the United States as reported in the 1990 Census of Population. The strengths of census data include the large sample size and the rich array of questions asked in 1990. Its limitations include the inability to identify visa status, illegal aliens, and recipients of amnesty; the loss (after the 1970 census) of information on parental nativity; and the virtual absence of retrospective questions that address the dynamic nature of immigrant adjustment.

Three dominant themes emerge: immigration has increased absolutely and relatively; the diversity of immigrants has increased on nearly every measured characteristic; and immigrants converge impressively with the native-born in their demographic and economic characteristics. Over the past few decades immigration has been increasing, and in the most recent decade (1981–1990), 7.3 million individuals received permanent resident alien status, the equivalent of 3.2 percent of the population in 1980. By 1990 the foreign-born were 8.0 percent of the U.S. population (20 million people). This is the highest percentage of foreign-born in five decades. Even more dramatic has been the change in the source countries of immigrants. During the nineteenth and much of the twentieth centuries, immigrants came primarily from Europe and Canada. In recent decades immigration has been primarily from Asia, Mexico, and other parts of Latin America. In the 1980s, 85 percent of the immigrants were from Asia or Latin America, and by the 1990 census they were 67 percent of the foreign-born population.

The new immigration from Asia and Latin America shows more diversity in skills than the recent immigrants from the traditional (Europe/Canada) source countries. They occupy both high-skilled and low-skilled occupations. Many Asian immigrants in particular have high levels of education. More dramatic is the increased proportion of immigrants with very low levels of education, particularly among Mexican immigrants. The new immigrants are also less likely to arrive with English-language fluency.

As did the new immigrants from Southern and Eastern Europe at the turn of the century, the new immigrants of the late twentieth century tend to settle initially in a small number of metropolitan areas. With the passage of time, immigrants tend to spread out from their initial ports of entry. Their geographic concentration does, however, create a large disparity in the direct local area impact of immigrants.

The two basic conclusions from the analysis of the various demographic, skill, and economic characteristics of immigrants are diversity and convergence. In part because of the increased diversity in source countries, there is now greater heterogeneity among immigrants in nearly all demographic and economic characteristics, including fertility, education, English fluency, earnings, and household income. With a longer duration in the United States there tends to be a convergence in many of these characteristics among immigrants and with the native-born. With the passage of time immigrant fertility for those from high-fertility countries declines to the norm, all else the same, in the United States. Immigrant employment, English-language fluency, and earnings also increase with duration, and in the case of employment and earnings, even reach levels comparable to the native-born with similar measurable characteristics. The high unemployment and poverty rates of new immigrants decline with duration of residence.

The convergence of many characteristics of immigrants with the native-born is the optimistic side of the story. The pessimistic side exists as well. An increasing number and proportion of immigrants have been arriving with very low levels of skill, and even though there are improvements with a longer residence in the United States, these low levels of schooling, job training, and English-language fluency inhibit successful adjustment in the labor market. The results are very low earnings, often low employment, and hence very low household income and a high incidence of poverty. Moreover, these low-skilled immigrants are in direct competition for jobs, housing, and income transfer resources with the low-skilled population either born in or longterm residents of the United States. These problems are exacerbated by the geographic concentration of immigrants.

The American economy is undergoing a major restructuring in which higher skills and labor market flexibility are increasingly essential for employment at high wages. The opportunities are bleak for the successful employment at incomes significantly above the poverty level for the increasing number of lower-skilled immigrants. Nevertheless, the demand for immigrant visas is high and likely to increase because of even more limited job opportunities and high rates of population growth in many source regions. Moreover, the potential exists for large refugee flows from the former USSR, Eastern Europe, parts of Africa, and perhaps from China. Meanwhile, the strength and the stability of the United States will continue to attract economic migrants and refugees from all over the world.

The challenge to America in the past was the successful absorption of a large immigration of primarily unskilled workers into the economy. Although that challenge was successfully met at the end of the nineteenth century and earlier this century, the American economy and society have changed. The economy now offers far fewer opportunities for low-skilled workers. In addition, public policy has changed, and providing assistance to those in economic need has become an important role of government. Finally, the skills and other characteristics of potential immigrants are more heterogeneous than in the past. This situation necessitates continuous rethinking of all aspects of immigration policy—legal immigration, enforcement of immigration law, and refugee policy—to be sure that U.S. immigration policy and practice are consistent with the economic, humanitarian, and other goals of the United States. If this reevaluation is done, the United States will continue to meet the challenge and opportunities offered by immigration.

Notes

This chapter is a reprinting of the Chiswick–Sullivan essay that appeared in Reynolds (1995, volume two, chapter 5). The public use of Microdata files from the 2000 census of the U.S. was not available when this revision was completed.

We are indebted to the Russell Sage Foundation and the U.S. Bureau of the Census for invaluable support for this project. Additional funding came from the Venture 2000 project of the College of Business Administration, University of Illinois at Chicago and the Population Research Center of The University of Texas at Austin. Without the skillful research assistance of Michael Hurst and Grant Mallie, this project could not have been completed. Given the incompatibilities of our word processing programs, we are especially indebted for the assistance of Yvonne Marshall and Winona Schroeder. Additional technical support was provided by the Social Science Data Archive, University of Illinois at Chicago and the Office of Graduate Studies, The University of Texas at Austin. Finally, the essay has benefited substantially from the comments we received from our colleagues in this project and from the students in the sociology focus groups at The University of Texas at Austin. We are especially indebted to Reynolds Farley for his comments and assistance throughout this project. It should be noted, however, that the views expressed in this chapter and any errors of omission or commission are attributable solely to the authors.

1. Technically, "immigrants" refers to those who are awarded "legal permanent resident" status in the United States, which is a prelude to naturalization for the foreign-born. Immigrants may be economic migrants or refugees and enter the United States under kinship, skill, amnesty, or refugee provisions in U.S. immigration law. There are, however, other foreign-born individuals residing legally in the United States on tourist, student, temporary worker, and other temporary visas. In addition, there are illegal immigrants or illegal aliens, those in the United States without a lawful visa and those who have violated a condition of a lawful visa. Although the 1990 census provides information on whether a foreign-born person has become a US citizen, there are no data in the census on the visa status of aliens. Nor are there reliable data on the extent to which immigrants and illegal aliens were under-enumerated in the census. Throughout this study persons born abroad of American parents or born in Puerto Rico, the U.S. Virgin Islands, and other dependencies of the United States are treated as if they were neither foreign-born nor native-born.

2. Earlier census monographs on immigrants include Carpenter (1927); Hutchinson (1956); and Jasso and Rosenzweig (1990).

3. By way of contrast, the 1970 census included several important retrospective questions dropped from subsequent censuses, including questions on economic activity 5 years ago (employment status, occupation, and industry) and birthplace of parents.

4. The *Statistical Yearbook of the Immigration and Naturalization Service*, U.S. Department of Justice, is an invaluable source of administrative data on immigrants and illegal aliens. It is the primary source of data on annual flows of immigrants, apprehended illegal aliens, and beneficiaries of amnesty reported in this study.
5. Apprehensions of illegal aliens have increased since the late 1950s when they were fewer than 100,000 per year. There were about 161,000 per year in 1961–1970, 832,000 per year in 1971–1980, and 1.2 million per year in 1981–1992 (including 1.3 million in 1992). *Statistical Yearbook 1992:* Table 59.
6. There were 3.0 million applicants for legalization under the 1986 Act, of whom 74.7 percent were from Mexico, 5.5 percent from El Salvador, 2.3 percent from Guatemala, 2.0 percent from Haiti, and 1.1 percent from Colombia *Statistical Yearbook 1991*: Table 22). Nearly every country had at least some representation among the other 14.4 percent of applicants. For an analysis of the Immigration Reform and Control Act of 1986 and the characteristics of the applicants for amnesty, see Chiswick (1988) and *Statistical Yearbook 1991: 70–3.*
7. Passel and Woodrow (1984): 642–671; Passel and Woodrow (1987): 1304–23; Bean, King, and Passel (1983): 99–109; Bean, Browning, and Frisbie (1984): 672–91; U.S. General Accounting Office (1993).
8. For a detailed analysis of the educational attainment and school enrollment of the population, see Mare, in Reynolds (1995, Volume One).
9. There is little difference by gender. For an analysis of the school enrollment of immigrant children using the 1976 Survey of Income and Education, see Schultz (1984): 251–88.
10. For an analysis of labor force statistics in the 1990 census and trends over time for the population as a whole, see Wetzel, in Reynolds (1995, Volume One, chapter 2), and Kasarda, in Reynolds (1995, Volume one, chapter 5). For an analysis of the employment of immigrants using the 1976 Survey of Income and Education and the 1970 census, see Chiswick (1982).
11. For a detailed analysis of the employment and unemployment experiences of immigrants using census data, see Chiswick (1982).
12. For a similar analysis for 1980, see Frisbie et al. (1986): 74–99.
13. *Statistical Abstract of the United States: 1993*: Table 1376.
14. For a detailed analysis of income and poverty for the population as a whole using the 1990 Census, see Levy, in Reynolds (1995, Volume one, Chapter 1.)
15. *Statistical Abstract of the United States, 1993*: Table 682.
16. Analyzing data from the 1980 census, Jensen (1989) also reports a low incidence of receipt of cash public assistance.
17. Furthermore, the household income data include aged households. For the aged in a particular household, income may be a poor measure of their ability to consume since many are living in owner-occupied dwellings, receive large noncash transfers (e.g., Medicare), and are drawing down their savings.

References

Anderson, Margo (1988). *The American Census: A Social History*, New Haven, CT: Yale University Press.

Bartel, Ann P. (1989). "Where Do the New Immigrants Live?", *Journal of Labor Economics* 7: 371–91.

Bean, Frank D., Harley L. Browning, and W. Parker Frisbie (1984). "The Socio-demographic Characteristics of Mexican Immigrant Status Groups: Implications for Studying Undocumented Mexicans", *International Migration Review* 18: 672–91.

—, Allan G. King, and Jeffrey S. Passel (1983). "The Number of Illegal Migrants of Mexican Origin in the United States: Sex-Ratio Based Estimates for 1980", *Demography* 20: 99–109.

— and Gray Swicegood (1985). *Mexican American Fertility Patterns*, Austin: University of Texas Press.

—, Georges Vernez, and Charles B. Keely (1989). *Opening and Closing the Doors: Evaluating Immigration Reform and Control*, Santa Monica, CA and Washington, DC: RAND Corporation and Urban Institute.

Blau, Francine (1992). "The Fertility of Immigrant Woman: Evidence from High-Fertility Source Countries", in George J. Borjas and Richard B. Freeman (eds.) *Immigration and the Work Force: Economic Consequences for the United States: and Source Areas*, Chicago: University of Chicago Press, 93–133.

Bonacich, Edna (1984). "Some Basic Facts: Patterns of Asian Immigration and Exclusion", in Lucie Cheng and Edna Bonacich (eds.), Labor Immigration Under Capitalism: Asian Workers in the United States before World War II. Berkeley, CA: University of California Press, 60–78.

Briody, Elizabeth K. (1987). "Patterns of Household Immigration into South Texas", *International Migration Review* 21: 27–47.

Cafferty, Pastora San Juan, Barry R. Chiswick, Andrew M. Greeley, and Teresa A. Sullivan (1983). *The Dilemma of American Immigration: Beyond the Golden Door*, New Brunswick, NJ: Transaction Press.

Carpenter, Niles (1927). *Immigrants and Their Children*, 1920, Washington, DC: U.S. Government Printing Office.

Chiswick, Barry R. (1982). *The Employment of Immigrants in the United States*, Washington: American Enterprise Institute.

— (1986). "Is the New Immigration Less Skilled than the Old?", *Journal of Labor Economics* 4: 168–92.

— (1988). "Illegal Immigration and Immigration Control", *Journal of Economic Perspectives* 2: 101–115.

— and Paul W. Miller (1992). "Language in the Immigrant Labor Market", in Barry R. Chiswick (ed.), *Immigration, Language and Ethnicity: Canada and the United States*, Washington, DC: American Enterprise Institute, 229–96.

— and — (1994). "The Determinants of Post-Migration Investments in Schooling", *Economics of Education Review* 13.

Chiswick, Carmel U., Barry R. Chiswick, and George Karras (1992). "The Impact of Immigrants on the Macroeconomy", *Carnegie-Rochester Conference Series on Public Policy* 37: 279–316.

Clark, William A.V. and Peter A. Morrison (1993). "The Demographic Context of Minority Political Strength", Paper presented at the Annual Meetings of the Population Association of American, Cincinnati, Ohio.

De la Puente, Manuel (1993). "Why are People Missed or Erroneously Included by the Census: A Summary of Findings from Ethnographic Coverage Reports", Report prepared for the Advisory Committee for the Design of the Year 2000 Census. Mimeo.

Farley, Reynolds (ed.) (1995). *State of the Union: America in the 1990s*, Volumes I and II, New York: Russell Sage Foundation.

Filer, Randall K. (1992). "The Effect of Immigrant Arrivals on Migratory Patterns of Native Workers", in George J. Borjas and Richard B. Freeman (eds.), *Immigration and the Work Force: Economic Consequences for the United States and Source Areas*, Chicago: University of Chicago Press, 245–69.

Frey, William (1994). "The Changing Geographic Distribution of the U.S. Population", in *1990 Census Monograph*, Vol. I, Social and Economic Trends. New York: Russell Sage Foundation.

Frisbie, W. Parker, Frank D. Bean, Robert Kaufman and Jan E. Mutchler (1986). "Immigration and Household Structure Among the Mexican Origin Population of the United States, in Harley L. Browning and Rodolfo de la Garza (eds.), *Mexican Immigrants and Mexican Americans: An Evolving Relation*, Austin, TX: Center for Mexican American Studies, 74–99.

Glazer, Nathan (1954). "Ethnic Groups in America", in Morroe Berger, Theodore Abel, and Charles Page (eds.), Freedom and Control in Modern Society. New York: Van Nostrand, 158–73.

Greeley, Andrew M. (1971). *Why Can't They Be Like Us? America's White Ethnic Groups.* New York: E.P. Dutton.

Hagan, Jacqueline Maria and Nestor P. Rodriguez (1992). "Recent Economic Restructuring and Evolving Intergroup Relations in Houston", in Louise Lamphere (ed.), *Structuring Diversity: Ethnographic Perspectives on the New Immigration*, Chicago: University of Chicago Press, 145–72.

Hirschman, Charles O. (1978). "Prior U.S. Residence Among Mexican Immigrants", *Social Forces* 56:1179–202.

Hutchinson, Edward P. (1956). *Immigrants and Their Children. 1850–1950*, New York, John Wiley.

Jasso, Guillermina and Mark R. Rosenzweig (1990). *The New Chosen People: Immigrants in the United States*, New York: Russell Sage Foundation.

Jasso, Guillermina and Mark R. Rosenzweig (1986). "Family Reunification and the Immigration Multiplier: U.S. Immigration Law, Origin-Country Conditions, and the Reproduction of Immigrants", *Demography* 23: 291–311.

Jensen, Leif (1989). *The New Immigration: Implications for Poverty and Public Assistance Utilization*, New York: Greenwood Press.

Kasarda, Jack (1994). "Changes in Industrial Structure and Implications of the Changing Locations of Employment", in *1990 Census Monograph*, Vol. 1, Social and Economic Trends. New York: Russell Sage Foundation.

Keely, Charles B. (1971). "Effects of the Immigration Act of 1965 on Selected Population Characteristics of Immigrants to the United States", *Demography* 8: 157–69.

— (1975). "Effects of U.S. Immigration Law on Manpower Characteristics of Immigrants", *Demography* 12: 179–92.

Levy, Frank (1994). "Changes in the Distribution of Income and Trends in Poverty", in *1990 Census Monograph*, Vol. 1, Social and Economic Trends, New York: Russell Sage Foundation.

Lieberson, Stanley (1980). *A Piece of the Pie*, Berkley, CA. University of California Press.

— and Mary C. Waters (1990). *From Many Strands: Ethnic and Racial Groups in Contemporary America*, New York: Russel Sage Foundation.

Mare, Robert (1994). "Changes in Educational Attainment, School Enrollment and Skill Levels", in *1990 Census Monograph*, Vol. 1, Social and Economic Trends. New York: Russell Sage Foundation.

Massey, Douglas S., Rafael Alarcon, Jorge Durand and Humberto Gonzalez (1987). *Return to Aztlan: The Social Process of International Migration*, Berkley, CA: University of California Press.

Passel, Jeffrey S. and Karen A. Woodrow (1984). "Geographic Distribution of Undocumented Immigrants: Estimates of Undocumented Aliens Counted in the 1980 Census by State", *International Migration Review* 18: 642–71.

— and — (1987). "Change in the Undocumented Alien Population in the United States, 1979–1983", *International Migration Review* 21: 1304–23.

Pollard, Kelvin M. (1993). "Youth on the Cutting Edge of Diversity", *Population Today* 21: 3.

Portes, Alejandro and Robert L. Bach (1985). *Latin Journey: Cuban and Mexican Immigrants in the United States*, Berkley, CA: University of California Press.

— and Ruben Rumbaut (1990). *Immigrant America: A Portrait*, Berkley, CA: University of California Press.

Rindfuss, Ronald R. and James R. Sweet (1977). *Post-War Fertility Trends and Differentials in the United States*, New York: Academic Press.

Rodriguez, Nestor P. (1987). "Undocumented Central Americans in Houston: Diverse Populations", *International Migration Review* 21: 4–26.

Romero, Mary (1992). "Ethnographic Evaluation of Behavioral Causes of Census Undercount of Undocumented Immigrants and Salvadorans in the Mission

District of San Francisco, California", *Ethnographic Evaluation of the 1990 Decennial Census 18*, Washington, DC: U.S. Bureau of the Census.

Ryder, Norman B. (1955). "The Interpretation of Origin Statistics", *Canadian Journal of Economics and Political Science* 21: 466–79.

Schultz, T. Paul (1984). "The Schooling and Health of Children of U.S. Immigrants and Natives", *Research in Population Economics* 5: 251–88.

Sullivan, Teresa A. (1992). The Changing Demographic Characteristics and Impact of Immigrants in Canada, in Barry R. Chiswick (ed.), *Immigration, Language, and Ethnicity: Canada and the United States*, Washington, DC. American Enterprise Institute.

Tienda, Marta (1980). "Familism and Structural Assimilation of Mexican Immigrants in the U.S.", *International Migration Review* 14: 383–408.

Treas, Judith and Ramon Torrecilha (1994). "The Older Population: Demographic, Social and Economic Trends", in *1990 Census Monograph*, Vol. 1, Social and Economic Trends. New York: Russell Sage Foundation.

United States. United States Congress. General Accounting Office (1993). *Immigration Enforcement: Problems in Controlling the Flow of Illegal Aliens*, G AO/T-GGD-93-39.

United States. Department of Commerce. Bureau of the Census (1993). *Statistical Abstract of the United States, 1993*, 113th ed. Washington, DC: Government Printing Office.

— (1992). *Statistical Abstract of the United States, 1992*, 112th ed. Washington, DC: Government Printing Office.

— (1960). *Historical Statistics of the United States: Colonial Times to 1957*, Washington, DC: Government Printing Office.

United States. Department of Labor. Bureau of Labor Statistics (1991). *Employment and Earnings*, 38, 1.

United States. Department of Justice. Immigration and Naturalization Service (1993). *Advance Report: Immigration Statistics, Fiscal Year 1992*, Washington, DC: INS.

— (1992). *1991 Statistical Yearbook of the Immigration and Naturalization Service*, Washington, DC: INS.

Velasco, Alfredo (1992). "Ethnographic Evaluation of the Behavioral Causes of Undercount in the Community of Sherman Heights, California." *Ethnographic Evaluation of the 1990 Decennial Census 22*, Washington, DC: U.S. Bureau of the Census.

Wetzel, James (1994). "Trends in Labor Force Participation, Unemployment and Earnings", in *1990 Census Monograph*, Vol. 1, Social and Economic Trends. New York: Russell Sage Foundation.

15. Canadian Immigration Experience: Any Lessons for Europe?

Don J. DeVoretz and Samuel A. Laryea

15.1. Introduction

Canada embarked on an extensive eleven-year research programme in 1996 to investigate the economic, social, physical, and educational impact of immigrants on its three major cities. It is important to point out that this major research effort was only begun after Canada received several million immigrants in the postwar period. The economic motivation for and economic consequences of this substantial intake no doubt varies by historical epoch but what is most interesting to observe is that this substantial inflow took place with little substantive research or policy analysis. Until the 1990s only one book of substance was written by A. Green (1976) to analyse the postwar immigrant economic experience in Canada. It could be argued that the economic benefits from immigration were so obvious that at least until the mid-1970s the immigration policy was set with little critical economic analysis.

An inspection of Figure 15.1 allows some stylized facts to emerge from Canada's recent history. First, wide fluctuations occur in the gross immigrant inflow to Canada in terms of absolute admissions. The pre-modern period (i.e. 1947–67) was a product of postwar European resettlement coupled with family reunification. This flow was large by Canadian historical standards—often exceeding 1 per cent of Canada's base population.

The modern immigration period begins in 1967 when a new policy was introduced. Gross immigration flows in 1967 were high, over 220,000 or more than 1 per cent of the base population. However, throughout most of the modern period (1967–86) a secular decline occurred in Canadian immigration flows with important subpeaks in 1975/6 and 1980. Finally, by the early 1990s immigration levels rose to over 250,000 (1992) equally divided into economic and other (family reunification).

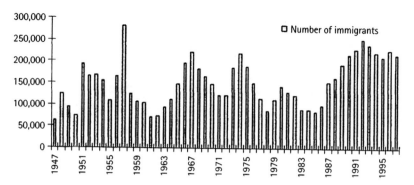

Figure 15.1. Canada's historical immigration flows
Source: Canada, C.I.C. Facts and Figures (annual)

15.2. Immigration Policy

This section focuses on Canada's recent immigration policies (1953–2000) in order to rationalize the immigration trends depicted in Figure 15.1. It emphasizes the relevant policy tools which in particular screened immigrants for their possible economic contributions. Our central aim is to argue that Canada's immigration policies, regardless of era or government in power, were largely designed to be highly selective with respect to the economic attributes of the *economically* assessed (independent, business, and assisted relatives) immigrants. Entry through other gates (family reunification, nominated relatives, or refugees) implied less stringent economic criteria.

15.2.1. Immigration Policy (1945–67)

Canada's postwar immigration policy was at first still under the regulations of the *1911 Immigration Act*. However, postwar policymakers realized the need to augment the limited entry principles of this dated act and by 1953 new legislation which still contained racist selection procedures was put into law. The 1953 *Immigration Act*, was initially permissive in terms of economic qualifications and total numbers admitted into Canada, but restrictive in terms of the admissible source countries. However, this early policy is important to understand for at least two reasons. First, the *1953 Immigration Act* remained essentially in place until 1978, albeit with substantial changes in its regulations. Moreover, the regulations derived from the 1953 *Immigration Act* were the central screening devices used to select the majority of the immigrant stock observed for most of the post-1971 period. In short, the econometric work of the 1980s and early 1990s reported extensively later in this essay is based on a foreign-born stock who largely entered under the 1953 *Immigration Act.*

In many ways the 1953 *Immigration Act* reaffirmed Canada's historical position of tailoring immigration policies to meet Canada's absorptive capacity. Specific countries and regions were identified as preferred areas under the then popular notation of 'absorptive capacity'. The United Kingdom, Western Europe, and the United States were cited as desirable source countries under the 1953 *Immigration Act* hence, the majority of these countries sent immigrants before 1960.

These absorption problems were not defined as economic ones, however. Rather, language, customs, and general social mores were the factors most often cited as absorptive criteria. Hawkins (1991: 38) states that the 1953 Act: 'gave the governor-in-council the all embracing power to refuse admission on the basis of... peculiar customs, habits or modes of life, [...][and] probable inability to become readily assimilated'. Throughout the 1950s, economic forces were present to remove this preoccupation with social absorption. Green (1976) argues that the postwar economic boom and the resulting demand for skilled workers required a more liberal immigration policy in terms of source countries.

Prior to 1968 the racist elements of the 1953 *Immigration Act* are self-evident in source country selection (Figure 15.2). The preferred areas by law—United Kingdom, Western Europe and the United States accounted for, on average 42 per cent of the movers in the 1950s. By contrast, under the act the nonpreferred regions (Africa, Asia, Australia, Other North and Central America, South America, and Oceania) were permitted to send (on

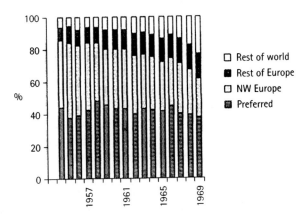

Figure 15.2. Distribution across source countries
Source: Statistics Canada (1994).

average) 7 per cent of the immigration flow between 1950 and 1968. Even with the changing economic forces (Green 1976) and growing political pressures (Hawkins 1991), Europeans as late as 1962 had a great advantage over non-Europeans since they could sponsor a wider range of kin. However, the source countries within Europe were changing. By the late 1950s Italians from the Mezzogiorno and unemployed or displaced Central Europeans entered the flow. Nonetheless, until 1967 Western Europe and the United States still provided over 50 per cent of Canada's immigrants while Southern Europe, Asia, Africa and South and Central America now accounted for 30 per cent of the 1962-7 immigrant flow.

15.2.2. Immigration Policy (1967–90)

In 1967, a point system was adopted to allow immigrants to Canada to be chosen on the basis of suitability to Canada and their ability to meet Canadian labour market needs while mitigating discrimination with respect to religion, race, or country of origin. In 1967, Canada's immigration policy became truly universalistic when the restriction on sponsorship of Asian relatives was dropped. Since then, regardless of country of origin, the method of assessment has been applied equally worldwide. This policy has been termed an open policy since the country of origin is not an entry criterion (Marr and Percy 1985: 62). The primary applicant in the independent or economic category now needed (circa 1967) fifty points or more earned from certain economic characteristics. These attributes included age, education, language, occupational demand, skill level, arranged employment, and province of final destination in Canada. In fact, as Coulson and DeVoretz (1993) note: 'During the 1967–74 period over 50 per cent of the required 50 points could be earned exclusively by the human capital measures of age, education, and language.' This policy shift did not take place in a vacuum. Other major immigrant receiving countries, especially the United States, admitted a large number of immigrants with human capital (Grubel and Scott 1965). Nonetheless, in contrast to the United States hemispheric quota system, Canada's point system was especially well designed to screen for the potential highly trained immigrant. Canada's point system was biased toward human capital criteria and accelerated the flow of highly trained movers from developing countries to Canada. This bias ultimately led to accusations that Canada was accelerating the brain drain from developing countries (DeVoretz and Maki 1980) under this modern period (1967–86) the total flow of human capital at 1995 replacement costs was over $30 billion from all source regions (Coulson and DeVoretz 1993).

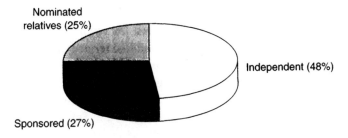

Figure 15.3. Immigration by class: summation, 1968–76
Source: Statistics Canada (1994).

As already noted, the open immigration policy since post-1967 with its point system resulted in a substantial change in the composition of immigrants, with a rise in the flow from less developed countries. But this changing source country composition also occurred in Australia and the United States. In later periods—post-1975 for the United States and post-1980 for Australia—Developing countries-sourced regions dominated these countries' immigrant inflows. These worldwide trends point to two underlying forces. First, as economic conditions improved in Europe, the supply of European immigrants declined not just to Canada, but to all destination regions. Next, Canadian policy, namely the point system, had a strong influence on their occupational or skill mix of the immigrant flow. For the 1968–76 period over 73 per cent of all immigrants were directly screened by the point system (covering independents and nominated relatives) with 25 per cent or more being judged as qualified professionals (Figure 15.3).

Notwithstanding the apparent early success of the post-1967 regulations, several criticisms were raised about the point system, resulting in the 1974 publication of a government 'white paper' on immigration (see Marr and Percy 1985). Its authors argued that the anticipated macroeconomic gains from immigration could not be documented. According to these critics, the presumed scale economies associated with a larger population were apparently not arising under expanding immigration. These critics further argued that if scale economies were sought they could be better achieved through free trade. In addition, some politicians noted that there was no precise immigrant control mechanism in the form of a yearly quota or target. Hence, a yearly immigrant target level and a greater policy emphasis on specific labour market criteria were proposed. As a result of these proposals the 1978 *Immigration Act* was passed. The new policy set three major goals for immigration: immigration targets should meet

Canadian demographic needs; foster family reunification, and be tied to Canadian labour market requirements. In comparison to the 1967 regulations, the 1978 *Immigration Act* could be termed a restrictive policy at least with respect to the independent or point-screened entry class. Other restrictions inherent in the 1978 act included specific yearly immigrant target levels to be tabled, in the preceding year, in the House of Commons and rationalized by testimony before a House Standing Committee. Immigrant entry under the *1978 Immigration Act* and in subsequent revisions circa 2002 could now occur via three main avenues: family reunification (family class); refugee class (convention refugees or designated class); or as a economic mover (assisted relative, entrepreneur, self-employed, investor, or independent).

Assessment in each entry class reflected varying degrees of scrutiny for possible labour market impacts. In particular, the 1978 policy linked entry into Canada under the *independent* class almost solely to labour market requirements. In addition, in periods of high unemployment economic immigrants in the independent group were reduced to nil by the imposition of an occupational bar. If occupational demand were deemed to be zero due to high unemployment in that particular occupation then the number of total points received under all other criteria by the perspective immigrant became irrelevant for admission. In short, adequate occupational demand became a necessary, but not a sufficient, criterion for entry under the independent class. For example, during the recession years 1982 through 1985, entrance to Canada under the independent worker category was prohibited, except in the case of arranged employment. Arranged employment required certification from a Canada Employment Centre which, in turn, required the employer to demonstrate that she/he had been *unable* to engage a Canadian citizen. The emphasis under the 1978 act and its subsequent regulations for *independent* immigrants moved from formal educational qualifications to explicit employment prospects. Coulson and DeVoretz (1993) noted that the 1978 *Immigration Act* revised the economic criteria from a human capital framework to a manpower planning one. Now for entry as an independent immigrant only 25 per cent of the (increased) seventy total points required for admission could be earned through the human capital attributes of age, education, and experience.

The 1978 policy clearly cannot be termed an open one. Rather, it reflected the view that scrutiny was required to ensure that immigration costs did not exceed benefits (Marr and Percy: 58). However, two contradictory forces appear in the 1978 policy which changed the labour market impacts of the post-1978 immigrant flow. First, the post-1978 emphasis on job certification potentially reduced the possibility of short-term unemployment for the independent class or points-assessed immigrants. On the other hand, expansion of the family reunification class after 1978 partially circumvented the job certification criterion for entry and opened the possibility of substantial negative economic impacts on wages and jobs. Moreover, the phenomenon of chain migration could arise under the 1978 Act with the total number of family reunified members being large over a long enough time horizon. An illustration will make this clear. In the first round, the original points assessed independent immigrant could sponsor his spouse and his parents. His parents could in turn sponsor the original immigrant's under nineteen-year-old brothers and sisters. These minor children, who are siblings of the original immigrant, could marry a foreign-born person prior to arrival and sponsor them and repeat the process ad infinitum. The family and siblings of the spouse of the original points assessed immigrant could also repeat the process. Thus, two possible infinite chains could arise.

In sum, the *1978 Immigration Act* substantially altered the gateways to enter Canada. As noted for the 1968–76 period (under the 1967 regulations of the 1953 *Immigration Act*) over 70 per cent of immigrants were screened in the independent class. This per cent dropped under the 1978 *Immigration Act* at first below 30 per cent (1975–82) and then to about 14 per cent of the total flow by the mid-1980s. To partially counteract this decline in the independent entry class, new entry classes were devised under the 1978 act. Self-employed or entrepreneurs and investor (after 1985) classes were now separately assessed on their ability to be self-financed or to create jobs. By the late 1980s these new categories in total represented 9 per cent of all movers.

15.2.3. 2002 Immigration Regulations

Dissatisfaction with the inability to control the size of particular entry gates—that is, family reunification and the resulting long processing queues and a host of other post entry legal problems—led to Bill C-26 being introduced in 2002. The proposed 2002 regulations unlike the 1978 *Immigration Act* had limited but far-reaching set of objectives. The primary objectives of the 2002 regulations were to control the skill composition across the entire immigrant flow and to reduce the outstanding backlog. To raise the skill composition and to end the long queues, the minimum point total has been raised from 70 to 80. In addition, under the 2002 act the independent selection criteria places a heavy emphasis on youth, official language skills, and previous job experience (relevant to Canada) which made the entry criteria even more select. The twin goals of this change are to shorten the queue and to improve the lagging economic performance of post-1986 immigrants.

In sum, these major policy changes from a closed (1953 to 1967) to open (post-1967) and then, increasingly restrictive immigration policy (after 1978) are strong *a priori* reasons to expect structural changes in the economic impact of Canadian immigrants over our study period. However, regardless of how many policy variations may appear over our study period the effectiveness of these changes must still be demonstrated. By taking successive economic snapshots during each immigrant policy regime we may detect if structural breaks actually occurred in each policy sub period. With the aid of census data, economic profiles for representative foreign-born and Canadian populations will be made for 1971, 1981, and 1996. The following Tables (15.1 to 15.3) report the important demographic and economic variables for each selected year's population by birth status. Next, each table reports (in columns 4 and 5) similar attributes but now for only the economically active (aged 25 to 65) groups who entered the labour force.

The first two columns in Table 15.1 report the *average* characteristics of the *entire* 1996 stock of Canadian and foreign-born populations

Table 15.1. Social and economic attributes by place of birth, 1996

All Canadian	All foreign	Variables	Econ. Canadian	Econ. foreign
2.93	3.45	Family size	2.99	3.46
41.9	44.4	Age	40.60	43.14
27.5	25.83	Hrs worked	40.68	40.92
43.2	42.53	Weeks worked	45.91	45.07
$28,099	$25,478	Total income	$34,323.76	$32,848.40
$21,919	$19,691	Wages & Salaries	$29,211.63	$27,572.80
$1,818	$1,738	Self-employment income	$2,262.38	$2,505.98
$840.35	$984.33	Investment Income	$755.09	$829.92
$46.20	$55.82	OAP	$2.72	$5.80
$398.33	$373.99	CPP	$98.26	$93.88
$735.75	$551.86	UIC	$628.77	$517.51
$854.55	$876.12	Other govt	$431.17	$429.84
$340.53	$383.71	Fam Allow	$374.88	$421.88
$2,383.14	$2,245.39	$Total Gov't	$1,535.80	$1,468.91

Source: 1996 Canadian Population Census, PUST microdata.

respectively unfiltered for labour force participation. Columns 4 and 5 present similar information for the 1996 economically active populations by birth status. To detect more accurately structural breaks in Canada's immigrant population over time, it is more meaningful to concentrate on active labour force participants as reported in the last two columns. The economically active foreign-born earned $1,475 less circa 1996 than their Canadian-born cohort. This shortfall in earnings is no doubt due to (among other factors) the fact that the immigrant stock worked one less week per year and were paid less salary. The last five rows in any column when summed indicate any population's draw on the federal treasury. For example, the economically active *foreign-born* group used $1,468 in federally financed pensions (OAP, CPP), unemployment insurance (UI), and family allowance (fam allow) and other programs. By contrast, the Canadian-born cohort used more ($1,535) of these services.

The data on the entire foreign-born and Canadian-born populations (columns 1 and 2) reveal two further trends circa 1996. Both the entire Canadian and foreign-born populations are older (41.9 and 44.4) and earn considerably less income ($28,099 and $25,478) than the economically active populations. These two factors cause both the Canadian-born and foreign-born to consume more public services ($2,383 and $2,245) than their economically active counterparts. It is clear that in 1996 Canada had two distinct subpopulations, an older and less affluent foreign-born group

Table 15.2. Social and economic attributes by place of birth, 1981

All Canadian	All foreign	Variables	Econ. Canadian	Econ. foreign
3.44	3.10	Family size	3.29	3.36
30.16	43.24	Age	40.81	43.1
21.7	22.5	Hours work	34.32	39.82
31.79	41.1	Weeks worked	46.90	47.2
$7962	$11,110	Total income	$22,647	$23,075
$6092	$8251	Wages & Salaries	$18,896	$19,400
$483	$719	Self-employment income	$2,110	$2,077
$516	$609	Investment Income	$821	$937
$303	$609	OAP	$8.22	$4.37
$74	$102	Family allowance	$308	$300
$135	$111	UIC	$226	$154
$153	$160	Other govt	$93.79	$59.90
$665	$982	$Total Gov't	$636	$518.27

Source: 1981 Canadian Population Census, PUST microdata.

and a younger and more affluent Canadian-born who intensively used more government social services.

Turning to the 1981 (Table 15.2) census we can observe the structural effects owing to immigration flows which predate the *1978 Immigration Act*. For an earlier period—1981—two changes appear in the respective stocks of economically active foreign-born and Canadian-born populations. The foreign-born worked more hours per week (5) in 1981 than the Canadian-born and this greater effort in the labour market yields a slightly larger income ($1,064) or wages and salaries ($504). In contrast to 1991, the greater 1981 earning power of the foreign-born stock resulted in the foreign-born using substantially fewer public services: ($518.27) than the Canadian-born-headed household ($636.01).

Turning to 1971, we would anticipate a major structural change in the pattern of reported variables given the limited economic scrutiny under the 1953 *Immigration Act*. This is borne out by the descriptive data in Table 15.3. Economic disadvantages for the economically active foreign-born again appear in 1971. Even though the average foreign-born head of household worked almost 5 more hours per week and 7 weeks more a year then their Canadian-born cohort, they earned $215 less in wages and salaries and $1396 less in total income than Canadians since they worked fewer weeks.

This review of the 1971–96 census data reveals two important points. First, in 1981 the economically active foreign-born earned more than the Canadian-born in the labour force. Moreover, by 1996 the foreign-born households consumed a greater number of public services than the Canadian-born average. In sum, the economic performance of Canada's immigrant population varies substantially across policy epochs.

Table 15.3. Social and economic attributes by place of birth, 1971

All Canadian	All foreign	Variables	Econ. Canadian	Econ. foreign
2.24	2.17	Family size	2.24	1.79
27.91	43.15	Age	42.15	48.89
21.7	22.5	Hours work	34.32	39.82
22.7	20.7	Weeks worked	43.5	39.50
$2,481	$3,945	Total income	$5,758	$4,362
$1,976	$3,010	Wages & Salaries	$4,577	$4,362
$181	$308	Self-employment income	$444	$466

Source: 1971 Canadian Population Census, PUST microdata.

15.3. Immigrant and Foreign-Born Substitution: A Theory and Some Facts

These stylized facts reported in Tables 15.1–15.3 arise from the employment opportunities and wage rates available to the foreign-born and the interaction between the Canadian-born and foreign-born workers in the labour market. The employment effects of immigration have been a rich source of policy debate since at least the turn of the century in Canada. Increased immigration, along with higher tariffs, and railroad investment helped form the cornerstone of Canada's early twentieth-century 'National Economic Policy'. The expressed goal of increasing immigration was to populate the prairies. The growing urbanization of immigrants and their changing skill mix (i.e. from farmers to urban artisans or semiskilled labour) led to fears of job displacement. The legacy of this historical research has not been lost since the modern policy debate has been sharply focused by this historical context.

For example, the earlier cited *Immigration Act of 1978* set in motion a 'Canada First' policy which was closely tied to unemployment and vacancy rates (Marr and Percy 1985). Several policy initiatives were set in place to limit the size and job displacement effect(s) presumably derived from this independent immigrant category. In sum, the period 1975–84 reflected an almost myopic concern with the issue of labour substitution. During the most recent period, 1985–2002, another shift in immigrant policy occurred reflecting a new view of the role of immigration and job creation. This led to the addition of new and explicit business and entrepreneurial immigrant entry classes. The *1985 Annual Report of Immigration Canada*, stated explicitly the then government's view on labour substitution: 'The federal government does not accept the popular misconception that immigrants take jobs away from Canadians. Immigrants contribute to economic growth and job creation by augmenting capital formation' (1985: 1).

Thus, in a twenty-six-year immigrant policy period (1976–2002) various governments have offered two conflicting hypotheses with respect to labour substitution; immigrants either create jobs, or they take jobs. The task now is to test this hypothesis formally. Modern immigrant labour market impacts in the Canadian labour force are complex. The vastly changing immigrant occupational mix, from semiskilled in the 1950s to highly human capital intensive in the 1970s, (Coulson and DeVoretz 1993), and then to business immigration in the 1980s (Globerman 1995) leads to several types of potential labour substitution or capital complementarity impacts. For example, will this heterogeneous immigrant flow differ in its degree of substitution by date of arrival? In other words, will pre-1978 immigrants substitute for skilled workers and post-1978 immigrants for unskilled? In addition, will the earlier or later arriving immigrant groups require or substitute for physical capital? Finally, is immigrant substitution industry specific? In other words, are tests of the displacement hypothesis sensitive to particular industry groupings? If so, what are these industries and their characteristics?

These are the main unanswered questions surrounding the nature of possible modern immigrant labour substitution in the Canadian economy. It is also important to note that the answer to each question leads to a particular corresponding policy implication for Canada's immigration selection criteria.

15.4. Displacement Model

To analyse the displacement (or wage compression) issue, elasticities of substitution between immigrant labour and Canadian-born labour must be computed from a production function which has been specified for all relevant Canadian industries. To clarify the estimating procedure a theoretical exposition of the displacement phenomenon follows.

Consider an immigrant receiving country that produces a single, non-exported output, by means of two inputs, capital, and homogeneous labour. The left panel of Figure 15.4 presents a situation in which the world

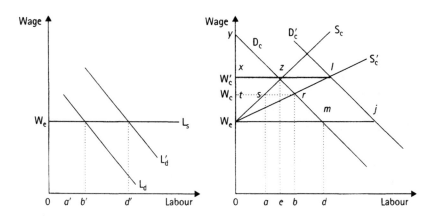

Figure 15.4. Labour market displacement model

supply of labour is perfectly elastic at wage rate (We).[1] The right panel shows the labour market in the immigrant receiving country, that is, Canada. If labour were to seek its maximum earnings, with negligible transportation and other costs, and with no institutional impediments, then, (od) workers would migrate to Canada. Thus, the Canadian labour supply would consist entirely of the foreign-born and its wage rate would fall to the world equilibrium level, or, (W_e). On the other hand, if Canada closed its borders, the wage rate in Canada would be (W_c). In addition, if independent events such as a rise in product price or increased complementary capital appeared in the economy, then these supply shifts induced by immigration could be offset by labour demand shifts. For example, with a partially open immigration policy (i.e. supply shifts to S'_c) the original equilibrium wage W_c would rise to W'_c with a shift in the demand curve equal to D'_c. Thus immigration under these special conditions would result in no domestic labour displacement and a rising wage rate.

Under a more realistic scenario for Canada immigrants arrive under a binding quota of (ab = a'b') workers, thus an increase in the labour supply from (S_c) to (S'_c) would result. In particular, this restraint on immigration appears appropriate for Canada after 1978 (Akbar and DeVoretz 1992). Now this limited increase in immigration, (ab), would have two important labour market consequences. First, the domestic wage rate would fall, and total employment would rise from (oe) to (ob). However, domestic employment declines from (oe) to (oa). Thus, immigrants displace domestic workers by the amount (ae). Second, when the wage rate falls from (W'_c) to (W_c), labour earnings change from (oxze) to (otrb), of which (otsa) accrues to Canadian-born workers and (asrb) to immigrants. The earnings of Canadian-born workers have fallen from (oxze) to (otsa). On the other hand, returns to nonlabour inputs or capital, have risen from (xyz) to (tyr). Hence, in this intermediate case Canadian capital owners benefit from immigration, while others, native-born labour, are injured. Finally, the existing wage differential of (W'_c-W_e), relative to the immigrant's opportunity cost is no doubt, substantial. Given such a substantial wage differential, a queue would form with immigrant applications exceeding yearly available slots.

The actual wage and employment changes resulting from any immigration flow depend upon the domestic elasticities of labour demand and supply, the magnitude of the quota, and other assumptions implicitly

[1] Perfect elasticity implies that within a relevant range all the labour demanded will be supplied at the prevailing wage We.

embedded in Figure 15.4. For example, the more inelastic the demand and supply relationships, the greater will be the reduction of domestic wages due to any given amount of immigration. Moreover, the displacement effect will be greater, the more elastic is the labour supply and the less elastic is labour demand.

Akbari and DeVoretz (1992) offer the following implicit production function to estimate labour substitution in Canada:

$$Yi = f(Ki, Ni, BIi, DIi) \tag{1}$$

where:
  Yi = Value added in industry i.
  Ki = Capital stock in industry i.
  Ni = Employed labour in industry i aged 15 years and over who were born in Canada.
  BIi = Employed labour in industry i aged 15 years and over who were born abroad and migrated to Canada prior to 1971.
  DIi = Employed labour in industry i aged 15 years and over who were born abroad and migrated to Canada after 1971.

The above production function was estimated by Akbari and DeVoretz in translog form for 125 Canadian manufacturing and nonmanufacturing industries using mid period or 1980 data to reflect the pre-1978 immigration policy. In terms of employment these, 125 industrial groupings represent approximately 93 per cent of the Canadian labour force circa 1980.

15.4.1. Initial Results: Canada-Wide 1981

Table 15.4 reports the estimated elasticities of complementarity. For convenience, pre-1971 immigrants are termed earlier immigrants, and those

Table 15.4. Elasticities of factor complementarities, 1980 (125 Canadian industries)

Elasticity between:	Value	Std error	t-value
Cdn-born and Earlier Immigrants (Cn,b)	−0.41	1.10	−0.37
Cdn-born and Recent Immigrants (Cn,d)	−0.41	2.46	−01.7
Cdn-born and Capital (Cn,k)	0.98	0.43	2.28[a]
Earlier and Recent Immigrants (Db,d)	1.45	9.39	0.15

Note: [a] A single asterisk indicates significance at the .05 level of significance.
Source: Akbari and DeVoretz (1992).

arriving later termed recent immigrants. This distinction between immigrant vintages is an attempt to explicitly recognize the hypothesis that the two immigrant pools are drawn from different populations. The corresponding policy issue which is being addressed is the effect of the 1967 immigration regulations. As noted above, only after 1967 did Canada truly employ a universalistic point system which did not discriminate by country of origin. We test to see if these policy regulations resulted in varying degrees of labour substitution vis a vis earlier or more recent immigrants.

It is observed from Table 15.4 that the elasticities of substitution between Canadian-born workers and earlier immigrants as well as between Canadian-born workers and recent immigrants are negative. This negative elasticity value implies that immigrant labour substitutes for Canadian-born labour. However, the corresponding t-values indicate that the elasticity coefficients are not statistically significant at the .05 level. Hence, the hypothesis that there is no displacement of Canadian-born workers by immigrants can be accepted for both the earlier and recent immigrant flows. Furthermore, it is also important to note that both the earlier and recent immigrants affect the employment of Canadian-born to the same extent (the elasticity values are identical). Hence, the hypotheses that the pre- and post-1971 immigrant pool have differential substitution effects with respect to the Canadian-born labour force must be rejected. Thus, circa 1980, there is no evidence to support the economy-wide displacement hypothesis or that immigrants were capital using. Critics often dismiss these economy-wide findings for Canada and cite examples of displacement in specific sectors. In other words, the critics argue that the above economy-wide findings may conceal substitution by subsectors. Thus, by disaggregating these tests it may be possible to reverse these economy-wide findings in certain subsectors.

15.4.2. Foreign-Born Intensive Industries

Critics are quick to pose the next obvious question: 'How robust are these findings?' The most obvious tactic to detect any significant substitution effect is to select those industries with a high concentration of foreign-born under the supposition that more foreign-born in the labour force would cause more substitution. A highly concentrated foreign-born industry is defined as any 3 digit *SIC* industry group with a greater than 23 per cent foreign-born labour force. A sampling of this subset of industries appears in Table 15.5.

Table 15.5. Ratio of foreign-born to total labour force from selected largest Canadian industries, 1980

Description	SIC #	Absolute #(000s) foreign-born	per cent of foreign-born
Meat and poultry	101	12.7	28
Bakery	107	12.3	30
Food (misc)	108	10.6	27
Plastics and fabricating	165	11.2	32
Men's clothing	243	19.0	45
Women's clothing	244	21.0	51
Household furniture	261	13.6	34
Universities & colleges	806	39.0	31
Hardware tool & cutlery	306	9.2	38
Metal stamping	304	10.0	29
Machine shops	308	7.5	32

Source: Akbari and DeVoretz (1992).

Several features of these selected industries are important to note. First, although many of the selected 59 industries are characterized by an unskilled labour force using labour intensive techniques (e.g. bakeries, clothing, and food processing) many groupings are highly skilled (e.g. universities, machine shops, metal stamping.) Thus, no generalization appears a priori for this subset of industries other than the preselected degree of concentration of foreign-born workers. Why a heavy concentration of foreign-born workers in this bizarre set of industries would cause displacement is open to speculation. One implicit hypothesis is that the job vacancy criteria under the *1978 Immigration Act* may have been inappropriately applied (DeVoretz 1995) or that members of the family reunification class entered some or all of these foreign-born labour intensive industries.

Table 15.6 reports the calculated elasticities of complementarity and associated test statistics for the foreign-born intensive industrial groupings. One result is obvious. Now, in these industries both recent and earlier immigrants are significant substitutes for Canadian-born labour. Also, capital is still not a significant complementary input to either recent or earlier immigrants. Finally, old and more recent immigrants are not substitutes for one another. These findings are in sharp contrast to the Canadian economy-wide results reported in Table 15.4.

Given the above results the actual degree of displacement between Canadian-born and foreign-born workers can be calculated for this subset

Table 15.6. Elasticities of factor complementary: above average in foreign-born intensive industries, 1980

Elasticity between:	value	Std error	t-value[a]
Canadian-born–Earlier Immigrants (Cn,b)	− .67	.33	− 9.3
Canadian-born–Recent Immigrants (Cn,d)	− .67	.25	− 2.68
Canadian-born–Capital (Cn,k)	1.08	1.35	.8
Recent Immigrants–Capital (Cd,k)	1.02	.65	1.57
Earlier Immigrants–Recent Immigrants (Cb,d)	.28	.21	1.33

Note: [a] A single asterisk indicates significance at the .05 level of significance.
Source: Akbari and DeVoretz (1992).

of 59 foreign-born intensive industries. For example, in the meat and poultry, clothing, and industry university groups the absolute marginal displacement of Canadian-born workers for each one-per cent rise in their immigrant labour force is respectively: 214; 582; 268 Canadian-born.

Clearly, the degree of displacement depends directly upon the labour intensive nature of the industry and the absolute number of Canadian-born workers in the industry. In general, across the preselected 59 industries a one per cent rise in foreign-born labour would have reduced Canadian-born employment circa 1980 by 2,543 workers.

15.4.3. Displacement in the 1990s

Major policy changes have occurred since 1981 which reflect the change in regulations under the 1978 *Immigration Act*. Most importantly, during the 1980s the pre-dominant entry gate became the family class group which was not assessed for its potential labour market impacts. Thus, the cross-elasticities of the more recent vintage of immigrants could have changed with respect to labour by 1991. Table 15.7 indicates that the 1991 results largely replicate the economy-wide findings for 1981.

Only the Canadian-born and recent immigrant elasticity value in the foreign intensive group (unreported) differs significantly between periods. This is, of course, an important exception. In 1981, in the foreign-born intensive industries Canadian-born labour and post-1971 immigrant arrivals were significant substitutes. By 1991 this pair had become insignificant complementary inputs. It should be noted that the significant substitution between Canadian-born labour and pre-1971 immigrants held in 1991, as it did in 1981.

This section posed one central question: 'Do immigrants displace Canadian-born workers?' and a host of subsidiary questions. We are now in a position

590   DON J. DEVORETZ AND SAMUEL A. LARYEA

Table 15.7. Elasticities of factor complementarities, 1991 (in 107 industries)

Elasticity between:	Value	Std error	t-value[a]
Canadian-born–Earlier immigrants (Cn,b)	− 0.97	.48	− 0.47
Native-born–Recent immigrants (Cn,d)	.96	1.05	1.01
Native-born–Capital (Cn,k)	0.91	1.02	1.93**
Recent Immigrants–Capital (Cd,k)	1.03	0.97	1.00
Earlier–Recent immigrants (Cb,d)	1.18	.39	0.47

Note: [a] A double asterisk indicates significance at the .10 level of significance.
Source: Author's calculations.

to answer these questions. First, economy-wide, there is no modern evidence circa 1981 or 1991 that the postwar stock of immigrants significantly displaced Canadian-born workers. In addition, this lack of substitution was invariant to date of arrival. Also, economy-wide, immigrants did not require a significant amount of physical capital upon entry while an expansion of the Canadian-born labour force did. This lack of economy-wide capital complementarity for immigrants, we believe, was a result of the on average high human capital content embedded in Canadian immigrants upon arrival circa 1967 to the 1990s (Coulson and DeVoretz 1993).

If one of Canada's continuing major immigrant policy goals is, in fact, the successful absorption of immigrants into the labour market then, the economy-wide findings indicate that this goal was met. The fact that these conclusions hold for two cross-sectional tests make these results more robust than they might first appear. First, these results reflect the long-term adjustment under several expansionist and restrictive policy regimes given that these economy-wide tests incorporate the stock of working immigrants who entered circa 1945 to 1990. Nonetheless, economy-wide, no labour displacement occurred. However, in the foreign labour intensive industries, significant labour substitution occurred between the foreign-born and Canadian born. A combination of factors, including a greater than average foreign labour content, and a large share of value added attributed to physical capital led to labour displacement in this sector. Equally important, under these conditions it is found that in this foreign intensive sub-sector, recent immigrants required a significant increase in physical capital. Moreover, the foreign intensive industrial subgroup does not conform to the stereotypical view of immigrant entry level industries. In fact, these industries include firms which use unskilled labour intensively, and other firms, which use highly skilled human capital intensively. These two types of immigrant streams reflect the two broad components of the overall immigrant flows which resulted from the post-1967 policy regimes. Immigrant policies after 1967 simultaneously selected immigrants with a greater level of human capital (1967–73) while later policies (post 1978) expanded the family reunification class reducing human capital (Coulson and DeVoretz 1993). This indicates the inherent policy dilemma of attempting to simultaneously achieve humanitarian and economic goals and avoid labour displacement.

15.5. Canadian–Born Wages and Immigration

Figure 15.2 indicates that in addition to labour displacement, immigration can lead to higher or lower wages for the resident labour force. For example, two mutually exclusive outcomes for wage and labour displacement appear in Figure 15.4. First, immigration under an expanding labour demand curve leads to greater native-born wages and employment due to the accompanying complementary human capital in the migration flow. In the opposite case both earnings degradation and labour displacement occur in the native-born labour force if immigrants have little complementary human capital. We now turn to the econometric results which sort through these wage outcomes.

15.5.1. Foreign-Born Wage Impacts: An Age-Cohort Approach

Most existing studies on the effects of immigration on wages, for example Grossman (1982), Lalonde and Topel (1991), Altonji and Card (1991), and Roy (1997), rely on variations in immigration levels across cities or Census Metropolitan Areas (CMAs) to identify the consequent change in relative wages of immigrants and the native-born. Friedberg and Hunt (1995) refer to this approach as cross-section differencing. A problem with cross-section differencing is that, in the presence of free trade within the recipient country and coupled with capital or labour mobility the result may be factor price equalization. Thus, an uneven distribution of immigrants across the country may not result (in the long run) in cross-section wage differences, since wages may be equalised by flows in goods or factors. Second, because immigrants are likely to be the most mobile workers as Newbold (1996) has established for Canada, they will probably move to those regions whose demand shocks have led to higher wages. Thus, an endogeneity problem ensues, prompting a naive econometrician possibly to conclude that greater immigrant densities will lead to higher wages.

To overcome these shortcomings, Laryea (1997) employs an age-cohort technique, developed by Suen (1994) to estimate the effects of immigration on wages. This approach estimates a two-stage constant elasticity of substitution (CES) model that aggregates immigrant groups by age cohorts and aggregate cohorts into effective labour, which is used to study the substitution relationships between age cohorts and between immigrant groups. One advantage of this immigrant cohort size approach is that immigrant age cohorts are not mobile at any one point in time.

A reoccurring policy question which motivates the age-cohort approach is: what should be the optimal age structure associated with Canada's immigration policy? The 1991 Canadian census reveals that 37 per cent of immigrants were aged 25–44 years at arrival, another 27 per cent between 15–24 years, while 28 per cent were younger than 15 years of age (see Statistics Canada, Catalogue No. 96–311E, 1994). Thus, the crucial issue which can also be explored using the age cohort methodology is whether the overall median age of Canada's immigrant population, that is, 23.6 years, has resulted in any wage effects on the resident population and other immigrant cohorts?

Laryea (1997) estimated the following reduced form equations from an aggregated two-staged CES production function. The equation estimated in the first stage is summarized as follows:

$$\log \ w_{ijk} = \alpha + X_{ijk}\gamma + (\rho_2 - 1)\log \ N_{jk} \tag{2}$$

In the second stage of the estimation procedure the following equation was estimated:

$$\log \ w_{ijk} = \alpha + X_{ijk}\gamma + (\rho_1 - \rho_2)\log \ M_j + (\rho_2 - 1)\log \ N_{jk} \tag{3}$$

where

w_{ijk} = wage rate of individual i in age cohort j and immigrant group k

X_{ijk} = an array of demographic characteristics (e.g. education, experience, marital status etc)

γ, ρ_1, ρ_2 = vector of parameters to be estimated

M_j = Labour supply from age cohort j

N_{jk} = Number of workers from immigrant group k in age cohort j.

The above equations were estimated by Laryea (1997) using data from the public use sample tape of individual records from the 1991 Canadian census. The sample was further classified in eight five-year cohorts ranging from the 25–29 year-old age group to the 60–64 year-old age

Table 15.8. The impact of a 20% increase in the stock of recent immigrants on wages

	25–29	30–34	35–39	40–44	45–49	50–54	55–59	60–64
Native-born	−.079%	−.047%	−.076%	−.102%	−.085%	−.070%	−.047%	−.037%
Early immig.	−.079%	−.047%	−.076%	−.102%	−.085%	−.070%	−.047%	−.037%
Recent Immig.	−.086%	−.069%	−.095%	−.120%	−.103%	−.088%	−.066%	−.056%

Source: Laryea (1997).

cohort. Individuals were also classified into four groups based on birth status. These are: (1) Canadian, (2) early immigrants (those who immigrated to Canada before 1970), middle vintage immigrants (those who immigrated between 1971 and 1980), and recent immigrants (those who immigrated to Canada after 1981). The raw count of the number of persons in these 8 × 4 subgroups gives the variable N_{jk} used in the wage model.

After the initial base runs, Laryea (1997) also conducted a simulation exercise involving a 20 per cent increase in the number of recent immigrants to ascertain the impact on wages. The results are summarized in Table 15.8.

The results show that the wage impacts of a 20 per cent increase in recent immigration levels on the native-born and other immigrant vintages are minimal. The wage decreases associated with this hypothetical inflow is no more than 1 per cent, ranging from −0.037 per cent for the native-born and early immigrants in the 60–64 year-old age cohort, to a high of −0.102 per cent for recent immigrants in the 40–44 year-old age cohort. Part of the reason why these wage impacts are so small can be attributed to the relatively small percentages of immigrants making up the total labour force. For example, recent immigrants constitute only 3.8 per cent of the effective labour supply of the 40–44 year-old age cohort, which in turn make up 18.9 per cent of the effective aggregate labour supply. Thus economy-wide it appears that the wage impacts of immigration flows are minimal and have no adverse impacts on Canadian labour markets.

15.5.2. Wage Impacts by Industries: A Panel Analysis

The absence of significant wage impacts of immigration flows economy-wide can mask the potential outcomes in the various industries in the economy. Estimating wage impacts across industries are also very important because certain industries serve as entry points for immigrants, and immigrants can potentially suppress wages of native-born workers in those industries (see Seward and Tremblay 1989). Laryea (1997) estimated the following random effects model to examine the impact of foreign-born labour on native-born wages by industry:

$$w_{it} = \alpha + \beta' X_{it} + u_i + \epsilon_{it} \tag{4}$$

where

w_{it} = hourly wage rate of native-born worker i in year t

X_{it} = Set of exogenous variables including the proportion of foreign-born workers in various industries between 1988 and 1990

ϵ_{it} = Traditional error term unique to each observation

u_i = error term representing the extent to which the intercept of the ith cross-sectional unit differs from the overall intercept.

β' = vector of estimated parameters

The above model was estimated using panel data from the 1988–90 Labour Market Activity Survey (LMAS). The model was estimated for the total sample and then by gender to address the outstanding literature, which suggests that females in particular may suffer a double negative effect as a result of their foreign birth status and gender (Beach and Worswick 1993). Laryea (1997) shows that looking at the total sample, and then the male and female subsamples separately, immigration had a positive impact on the wages of Canadians. The estimated wage elasticities suggest that a 1 per cent increase in the overall share of foreign-born labour results in a 1.1, 1.3 and 1.4 per cent increase in wages for all Canadians, Canadian males, and Canadian females respectively. However, when the data was disaggregated by industry, wage suppression was detected in the primary, transportation and storage, and retail and wholesale trade industries. This finding was detected in all 3 samples. The elasticities ranged from a low of 0.6 per cent in the primary industries for the female sample, to a high of 5.9 per cent in the transportation and storage industries for the male sample.

15.6. Immigrant Labour Market Experience

To this point this essay has concentrated on the rather benign effects of immigrants on the employment and earnings prospects of resident Canadians. It is clear, however, that the underlying theoretical paradigm of the preceding models—a neoclassical view of the labour market—may hide occupational or wage segmentation borne by the immigrants themselves. This section reviews the literature of Canadian immigrant occupational segmentation and subsequent wage discrimination. Hiebert (1997) implicitly asks if the relatively benign Canadian immigrant impacts in the dominant resident labour market is owing to occupational segmentation. In particular, Hiebert investigates the patterns of occupational distribution by ethnicity in Canada's three major cities: if immigrants are marginalized into urban ethnically concentrated occupations then this finding would be entirely consistent with limited wage effects or isolated occupational displacement reported on Canada's native-born population as reported above. Hiebert's study provides an index for measuring the degree of ethnic concentration by occupation. This index reports the ratio of the actual to the expected number of immigrants by ethnicity in occupations across Canada's three largest cities. We reproduce Hiebert's results for males and females in Vancouver in 1991.

Given the fact that the British are the dominant ethnic group in Vancouver it is obvious that an index of near unity should appear. Table 15.9 reports this trend for females of British descent in Vancouver. In the selected occupations reported the actual appearances in an occupation were close to the expected values for females of British ethnic origins with the exception of housecleaning (house). Jewish females were over represented in the human capital intensive occupations (law, teaching, university teachers) while South Asian, Filipino, and Vietnamese females are underrepresented in managerial law, teaching, and nursing occupations. On the

Table 15.9. Occupation by ethnic origin for females in Vancouver, 1991

Occupation	British	Jewish	South Asian	Filipino	Vietnamese
Manager	1.2	1.3	.5	.3	.6
Law	1.3	3.8	.3	.1	0
Teacher	1.3	2.6	.2	.2	.1
University	1.0	3.4	.8	0	1.3
Clerical	1.1	1.4	.7	.2	1.0
Sales	1.1	1.4	.7	.3	.6
House	.5	0	2.7	2.4	1.2
Labour	1.2	0	2.9	0	0
Taxis	.7	0	0	0	0
Nurses	1.2	.7	.5	.4	0

Source: Hiebert (1997), Table 5.

other hand, these latter ethnic groups of females were over represented in clerical, sales, and house cleaning occupations.

The male occupational patterns by ethnicity reported in Table 15.10 parallel that of the females in Vancouver. Again, British males are distributed near their expected numbers (i.e. ratio is near unity) while Jewish males are well above unity for the human capital intensive occupations. As with females, male ethnic groups from developing countries are under represented in these human capital intensive occupations.

Hiebert (1997) suggests that these patterns represent significant segmentation of immigrants upon arrival since the last three columns in each table represent the newest immigrant flows. Over time there is some evidence that male ethnic immigrants progressively move out of the secondary level jobs. However, for females there exists a double jeopardy in that female immigrants regardless of when they arrived are continuously employed as cleaners (Indo Canadian) and garment workers (Chinese). The daughters of these immigrants when born in Canada however break this pattern. Finally, Hiebert (1997) argues that there is no advantage for ethnic immigrants to migrate between Canada's three major cities since the occupational ethnic patterns are repeated for Toronto and Montreal.

Pendakur and Pendakur (1996) test for the degree of marginalization of immigrants in the Canadian labour market by decomposing the sources of earnings differences between ethnic groups. They test for double jeopardy in the Canadian labour market by first measuring whether immigrants earn less than the foreign-born in Canada when you control for the standard

Table 15.10. Occupation by ethnic origin for males in Vancouver, 1991

Occupation	British	Jewish	South Asian	Filipino	Vietnamese
Manager	1.2	1.7	.6	.4	.3
Law	1.3	3.4	.5	.2	.9
Teacher	1.3	2.1	.4	.2	.2
University	1.1	8.8	.5	.2	.2
Clerical	1.0	.8	1.0	1.7	.5
Sales	1.1	1.6	.9	.6	.4
MDs	1.1	8.8	.5	.2	0
Labour	1.2	0	1.3	0	0
Taxis	.7	0	6.1	.4	0
Farmers	1.0	.2	2.4	.6	2.7

Source: Hiebert (1997), Table 6.

human capital variables of age, education, etc. In addition, they test to see if simple ethnicity matters when you control for all of the obvious human capital characteristics as well as foreign birth status. The facts are straightforward. In an uncontrolled environment circa 1991 'there is a 21 per cent difference in mean lag earnings between visible minorities and whites'. Pendakur and Pendakur then estimate the age earnings functions for various combinations of ethnicity and foreign-birth status and perform Oaxaca type comparisons which are reported in Table 15.11.

Now with the aid of Table 15.11 it is possible to deduce the impact of ethnicity and foreign birth status by gender on earnings. The ideal situation in a controlled environment would be to explain all of the male (or female) observed earnings differences by human capital characteristics. However, Table 15.11 indicates that this is not possible in Canada using Pendakur and Pendakur's earnings equations. Turning to Table 15.11 and noting the first numerical entry is a value of 13 per cent allows the following interpretation. It suggests that if we gave Canadian-born white males the earnings characteristics (education, age, etc.) of the Canadian-born visible minorities the white males, earnings would fall only by 13 per cent of the required 21 per cent to eliminate the possibility of wage discrimination. In other words 8 per cent of the 21 per cent earnings difference between white and visible minority males is unaccounted for by human capital characteristics. This 8 per cent difference is owing to a difference in the earnings structure between ethnic and white earnings

Table 15.11. Oaxaca type comparisons by ethnicity in Canada, 1991

Sex	Birth	Ethnic	Canadian	by	Birth	Imm	by Birth
			White	Visible	Aborigine	White	Visible
Males	Canadian	White	compare	−2%	−9%	−3%	−21%
		Visible	−13%	−21%	NA	−14%	−30%
		Aborigine	−23%	NA	35%	NA	NA
	Immigrant	White	23%	14%	NA	10%	−12%
		Visible	10%	−2%	NA	−10%	−25
Females	Canadian	White	compare	2%	−5%	−1	−7
		Visible	1%	1%	NA	0	−7
		Aborigine	−13%	NA	−19%	NA	NA
	Immigrant	White	7%	6%	NA	−1	−2%
		Visible	9%	18%	NA	−8	−10

Source: Pendakur and Pendakur (1996), Table 4.

functions. What of the immigrants? If you apply immigrant characteristics to Canadian-born males' earnings functions and vice versa it is possible to deduce the affect of birth status on earnings. For example, exchanging white immigrant characteristics with white Canadian-born males leaves only a 3 per cent difference of earnings in favour of Canadian-born whites. However, if you gave the visibility minority immigrant males the characteristics of the white native-born males 21 per cent (i.e. −21 per cent) is still unaccounted by the earnings structure indicating the degree of discrimination. Moreover, if you observe in the last column in row 4 the value of −12 per cent indicates the degree of discrimination between white immigrants and visible minority immigrants if you equip the visible minority immigrants with the characteristics of white immigrants. In short, discrimination as measured in this sense drops but is still large on an ethnic basis alone. In fact, the only optimistic outcome for immigrants that can be derived from Table 15.10 in terms of the immigration process is the case when you equip visible minority immigrant males with visible minority Canadian-born characteristics. Now you would lower the earnings of the immigrant visible minority group!

In sum, Table 15.11 indicates that visible minority immigrants suffer large earnings penalties circa 1991 in Canada with the penalties greater for men than women. In addition, Pendakur and Pendakur (1996) argue that these penalties are the least in Vancouver and the greatest in Montreal owing to different labour market structures.

15.7. Summary

What lessons does the Canadian immigrant labour market experience yield for Europe? First, Canada's balanced immigrant programme of 50 per cent economic immigrants and 50 per cent other leads to minimal short-run displacement or wage compression in the Canadian-born segment of the labour market. Next, admitting immigrants with substantial amounts of human capital reinforces the above outcomes and reduces the need to equip new immigrant arrivals with additional (physical) capital. Paradoxically enough this relatively benign impact on the resident born is reinforced by initial occupational segmentation in Canada's labour market. Thus, Canada does have one overriding lesson to offer—economically screen at least one-half of an immigrant cohort for human capital characteristics and you minimize short-run labour market impacts.

References

Akbari, A. and DeVoretz, D. J. (1992). 'The substitutability of foreign-born labour in Canadian production: circa 1980', *Canadian Journal of Economics*, 25.

Altonji, J. G. and Card, D. (1991). 'The effects of immigration on the labour market outcomes of less-skilled natives', in J. Abowd and R. Freeman (eds.) *Immigration, Trade and the Labour Market* (Chicago: University of Chicago Press).

Beach, C. M. and Worswick, C. (1993). 'Is there a double negative effect on the earnings of immigrant women?', *Canadian Public Policy*, 19.

Coulson, R. G. and DeVoretz, D. J. (1993). 'Human capital content of Canadian immigration 1966–1987', *Canadian Public Policy*, 19.

De New, J. P. and Zimmermann, K. F. (1994). 'Native wage impacts of foreign-born labour: A random effects panel analysis', *Journal of Population Economics*, 7: 177–92.

DeVoretz, D. J. (1995). *Diminishing Returns: The Economics of Canada's Immigration Policy* (Toronto/Vancouver: C. D. Howe Institute/The Laurier Institution).

— and Maki, D. (1980). 'The size and distribution of human capital transfers from LDCs to Canada 1966–1973', *Economic Development and Cultural Change*, 28.

Friedberg, R. M. and Hunt, J. (1995). 'The impact of immigration on host country wages, employment and growth', *Journal of Economic Perspectives*, 9.

Globerman, S. (1995). 'Immigration and trade' in D. J. DeVoretz (ed.) *Diminishing Returns: The Economics of Canada's Immigration Policy* (Toronto/Vancouver: C. D. Howe Institute/The Laurier Institution).

Green, A. G. (1976). *Immigration and the Post-War Canadian Economy* (Toronto: Macmillan of Canada).

Grossman, J. B. (1982). 'The substitutability of natives and immigrants in production', *Review of Economics and Statistics*, 64.

Grubel, H. G. and Scott, A. D. (1965). 'The international flow of human capital,' *American Economic Review*, 56.

Hawkins, F. (1991). *Critical Years in Immigration: Canada and Australia Compared* (Montreal: McGill/Queens University Press).

Hiebert, D. (1997). 'The colour of work: labour market segmentation in Montreal, Toronto, and Vancouver, 1991', *RIIM Working Paper*, 97–02 (Vancouver: Centre of Excellence for Research on Immigration and Integration in the Metropolis).

Lalonde, R. J. and Topel, R. H. (1991). 'Labour market adjustment to increased immigration,' in J. Abowd and R. Freeman (eds.) *Immigration, Trade and the Labour Market* (Chicago: University of Chicago Press).

Laryea, S. A. (1997). 'The impact of foreign-born labour on wage rates in Canada', Department of Economics, Simon Fraser University, unpublished Ph.D. dissertation.

Marr, W. and Percy, M. (1985). 'Immigration policy and Canadian economic growth', in J. Whalley (ed.) *Domestic Policy and the International Environment* (Toronto: University of Toronto Press).

Newbold, K. B. (1996). 'Internal migration of the foreign-born in Canada', *International Migration Review*, 30.

Pendakur, K. and Pendakur, R. (1996). 'The colour of money: earnings differentials among ethnic groups in Canada', *RIIM Working Paper*, 96–03, Vancouver: Centre of Excellence for Research on Immigration and Integration in the Metropolis.

Roy, A. S. (1997). 'Job displacement effects of Canadian immigrants by country of origin and occupation', *International Migration Review*, 31.

Seward, S. B. and Tremblay, M. (1989). 'Immigrants in the Canadian labour force: their role in structural change', *IRPP Discussion Paper*, 89 B.2., Montreal: Institute for Research on Public Policy.

Statistics Canada (1994). *Canada's Changing Immigrant Population*, Catalogue No. 96–311E.

16. Europeans in the Antipodes: New Zealand's Mixed Migration Experience

Rainer Winkelmann

16.1. Introduction

The stagnation of real wages and rising unemployment rates for many types of workers since the late 1970s have led governments around the world to adopt policies to increase worker education. These policies were supported by arguments that emphasized the adverse role of an alleged relative decline in immigrants' education levels in generating those outcomes and rising income inequality more generally. Governments in many countries responded by changing their immigration policies in order to improve the skill levels of immigrants.

New Zealand is a prime example. As soon as the arguments about an increasing demand for 'skilled' workers began to emerge, this traditional immigration country swiftly changed the focus of its immigration policy away from a country-of-origin principle towards attracting more highly skilled migrants. Justifications for these changes often included a reference to desirable distributional effects of 'skilled' immigration and the idea that immigrants whose skills are in high demand adapt rapidly to conditions in the domestic labour market and are more likely to make a significant contribution to economic growth.

Substantial shifts in the composition of immigrants were the result. While the initial immigrants came predominantly from the United Kingdom, flows started to diversify after the Second World War. The 1960s and 1970s brought a wave of immigrants from the Pacific Islands, while the late 1980s and early 1990s saw a jump in the number of immigrants from Asia. The consequences of the resulting changes in the size and composition of immigration are controversial in academic and policy circles alike.

The objective of this paper is to shed some light on these policy changes and their effects on education, ethnic composition and relative labour market performance of immigrants in general. The paper describes New Zealand's current immigrant population against the background of its immigration history (Section 16.2), characterizes the country's current policies (Section 16.3), and analyses the labour market outcomes of New Zealand's immigrants (Section 16.4). Section 16.5 concludes by pointing out some potential lessons of New Zealand's experience for Europe.

16.2. The History of Immigration to New Zealand[1]

16.2.1. The First Century of European Immigration

New Zealand was first settled by the Maori, who arrived by canoe between 750 and 1350 AD from various Eastern Polynesian Islands. The first European contact was made in the late eighteenth century at a time when the Maori population was estimated around 100,000.[2] In 1840 when the Treaty of Waitangi established British sovereignty over the country, the number of European settlers did not exceed 2,000, whereas the Maori population had decreased to between 70,000 and 90,000. A systematic colonization by British migrants followed, and by the mid-1850s the European population was as large as the Maori one, and outgrew the Maori population fast thereafter. Between 1871 and 1892 alone, almost 114,000 people immigrated under an assisted immigration scheme resulting from the Immigration and Public Works Act of 1870, and the total population had reached 700,000 in 1892 (New Zealand Official Yearbook 1995: 40).

The large and steady inflow of migrants continued well into the 1900s. Immigrants had mostly British and Irish background, encouraged by a principle of free entry and assisted migration.[3] Since the late 1800s, New Zealand had actively restricted immigration from Asian (as well as Southern European) countries, and their numbers remained relatively low until the second half of the twentieth century. Assisted migration was terminated after the Great Depression (by the time of which the New Zealand population counted about 1.5 million) and was not reinstated for some time. As a consequence, immigration during the post-depression

[1] This section draws on Shroff (1988) and New Zealand Immigration Service (1997) where more details on New Zealand's immigration history can be found. Another source is Burke (1986). Summaries of empirical trends in gross and net migration data over the last few decades, together with some analysis, are given in Trlin and Spoonley (1986, 1992, 1997).

[2] New Zealand (or, in Maori, Aotearoa) was sighted by Dutch navigator Abel Tasman in 1642, but it was a further 127 years, in 1769, before British naval captain James Cook and his crew became the first Europeans to set foot on New Zealand soil.

[3] Formal independence from the United Kingdom was gained on 26 September, 1907.

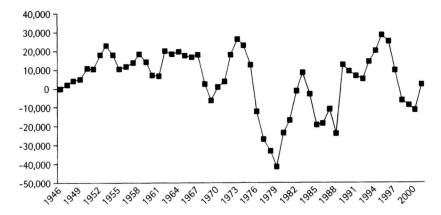

Figure 16.1. New Zealand net permanent and long-term migration, 1946–2001
Source: New Zealand Immigration Service. 1946–1969 are March years, 1970–2000 are calendar years, and 2001 is the October year.

years was limited, and a period of net-migration losses continued until after the end of the Second World War.[4]

16.2.2. The 1950s and 1960s

In 1947 the Government decided to reintroduce an assisted passage scheme, mostly for immigrants from the British Isles. In 1951, the Netherlands Migration Scheme was established as a bilateral assisted immigration scheme between the governments of the Netherlands and New Zealand. Both programmes targeted specific skills and occupations in high demand in New Zealand. Some provisions for family based migration were made.

The effects of these programmes can be clearly seen from Figure 16.1, where the annual permanent and long-term net-migration is plotted from 1946 to 2001. The figure shows the excess of arrivals of people intending to stay in New Zealand permanently or for twelve months or longer over the number of people departing permanently or for twelve months or longer (including New Zealanders).[5] It is apparent that net-migration

[4] New Zealand received only very small numbers of refugees from fascism or the Second World War.

[5] As New Zealand is an island nation, it has full control over its external borders and thus the statistics should be quite accurate. Nevertheless, net permanent and longterm migration is a less than ideal measure of immigration trends as it does not distinguish between returning citizens, foreign nationals on temporary visa (including, for instance, students) and genuine immigrants. Also, outmigration was always an important factor in New Zealand and fluctuated substantially over the period.

picked up gradually after 1947, eventually exceeding 20,000 in 1953. The net-migration gain remained relatively stable at between ten and twenty thousand per year throughout the 1950s and for most of the 1960s. Nevertheless, these annual flows constituted less than 1 per cent of the population at the time, and immigration had become a relatively small component of New Zealand's population growth compared with the early years of colonization.

The hallmark of the late 1950s and the early and mid-1960s was the emergence of truly diversified migration. For the first time, migrants of British and Irish origin no longer made up more than half of the permanent and longterm arrivals. This changing trend was also reflected in the country-of-origin composition of the New Zealand resident population as evident in Census data, although the changes were slow initially. In the three Census years 1945, 1956 and 1966, the share of the population born outside of New Zealand varied between 14 and 15 per cent. However, as shown in Table 16.1, the proportion of British and Australian-born residents among the overseas born declined by more than 10 percentage points, from 88.8 per cent in 1945 to 77.7 per cent in 1966. They were gradually replaced by immigrants from the Netherlands, the Pacific Islands, and, at this stage to a lesser extent, from Asia.

16.2.3. The 1970s and 1980s

The 1970s and 1980s were turbulent times for immigration. The ups and downs in net migration flows (see Figure 16.1) were the result of both cyclical policy decisions and lower transport costs that made outmigration

Table 16.1. New Zealand's changing population structure, 1945–66

Census Year	1945	1956	1966
Overseas born as % of total population	14.5	14.3	14.8
Country of Origin as % of overseas born population			
UK and Ireland	73.9	69.1	66.8
Australia	14.9	11.6	10.9
Netherlands	0.1	4.0	5.2
Pacific Islands	1.1	2.8	5.5
India	0.9	1.4	1.4
China (P.R.)	1.3	1.2	1.1

Source: NZ Official Yearbook, various issues.

rates more volatile and sensitive to economic conditions. A typical policy cycle would consist of a promotion of immigration during times of labour market shortages. The associated delays between recruitment and arrival of immigrants would mean that immigrants arrived during less favourable conditions, producing hostile attitudes in the population and a subsequent restriction of immigration.

The beginning of the 1970s saw the start of such a cycle, with intensive efforts to attract more immigrants via subsidized immigration schemes, a widening of the eligibility by source country (to most Western European states and the United States), and an intensive marketing campaign. At the time, agricultural prices were booming, New Zealand had virtually zero unemployment and ranked about tenth in the world in GDP per capita (New Zealand Official Yearbook 1995: 40). Permanent and longterm arrivals peaked at 70,000 in 1973/4, the year of the first oil-price shock. In addition to the adverse economic conditions, the sheer size of the inflow meant immense pressure on housing and schools and other services. Not surprisingly, brakes were put on soon. British ceased to be granted unrestricted access in April of 1974.[6] The general assisted schemes were abolished in 1975 and the Dutch scheme in 1976.

The other feature of the period was the continued trend towards more diversified immigration, a further shift towards immigrants from 'non-traditional' source countries, mostly the Pacific Islands. In 1976, occupational migration had been officially opened to a yet wider range of source countries although an explicit non-discriminatory immigration policy without regard for national or ethnic origin was adopted only a decade later. It was also in 1976 that a large number of Pacific Island *de facto* immigrants who had come to New Zealand with temporary work permits and overstayed gained residence status by way of general amnesty.

The effects of these changing migration flows on the composition of the New Zealand population are studied in the next table. The table is adopted from Winkelmann and Winkelmann (1998*b*). Data are from the Population Census and relate to the working age population (those aged 15–64). At the 1981 Census day, for instance, about 320 thousand working-age immigrants lived in New Zealand.[7] This amounted to 16.2 per cent of the total

---

[6] Coincidence or not, this was one year after Britain had joined the European Economic Community.

[7] The census is held at the end of February or beginning of March of the year. The definition of 'immigrant' in the census includes all people who were born overseas and resided in New Zealand on census day, independently of their official visa status (temporary or permanent residence, citizenship, etc.).

working age population. Among those immigrants, 12.1 per cent had arrived in the five-year period preceding the Census, i.e., between 1976 and 1980.

In 1981, 56 per cent of working-age immigrants were born in the UK or Ireland. This was a substantial reduction relative to the 67 per cent (in terms of the overall population) still observed in the 1966 Census. The main beneficiaries of the diversification were Europe and North America and the Pacific Islands, with a share of about 13 per cent each (among working-age immigrants). The Asian share remained at 6 per cent, although Asian immigration definitely started to pick up at the time, as Asians constituted 16 per cent of all recent immigrants who had arrived in the second half of the 1970s.

The trend towards increased diversity continued to be a strong force in the 1980s (and ever since). Among all persons who migrated to New Zealand between 1981 and 1985 and remained in the country until census day, only 28 per cent came from the British Isles, and the number of UK and Irish-born persons resident in New Zealand as a proportion of all working-age immigrants had decreased to just over half. By 1990, the percentage of migrants from the United Kingdom had fallen to 16 per cent (New Zealand Immigration Service, 1997). British migrants were increasingly replaced by Pacific Island and Asian nationals. In 1986, for instance, 22 per cent of recent immigrants originated from the Pacific Islands, and 18 per cent from Asia (see Table 16.2). By 1990, countries such as

Table 16.2. New Zealand's working age immigrant composition by region of origin, 1981 and 1986

| | 1981 census | | | | 1986 census | | | |
| | All immigrants | | 1976–80 cohort | | All immigrants | | 1981–85 cohort | |
	N	%	N	%	N	%	N	%
UK and Ireland	179,825	56.37	12,020	31.12	178,805	52.47	1,2325	27.52
Australia	27,487	8.62	5,527	14.31	29,189	8.56	4,717	10.53
Europe and North America	42,954	13.46	5,956	15.42	47,042	13.80	8,140	18.17
Pacific Islands	41,644	13.05	7,340	19.00	52,253	15.33	9,887	22.08
Asia	18,831	5.90	6,141	15.90	24,446	7.17	8,133	18.16
Other	8,295	2.60	1,638	4.24	9,072	2.66	1,585	3.54
Total	319,036	100.00	38,622	100.00	340,807	100.00	44,787	100.00

Source: Winkelmann and Winkelmann (1998b).

Hong Kong, Taiwan, and Malaysia had become major sources of immigration to New Zealand.

16.2.4. The 1990s

In terms of policy events, the changes of the 1990s were foreshadowed by the passing of the *Immigration Act 1987* (by the then Labour government) that heralded a substantial reorientation of policy. This Act was superseded by the *Immigration Amendment Act 1991* (under a national government) in which the current *point system* was established. Details of the policy changes are discussed in the next section. At this point, it suffices to say that the Acts promoted a further diversification of immigration flows by country-of-origin both directly and indirectly, and sought to establish and promote explicit channels for migration based on business and investment motives. Furthermore, the 1991 Act terminated the long-standing tradition of linking immigration to skill shortages and priority occupations, as the point system rewards professional experience and formal qualifications of any type. It also introduced an explicit annual target of initially 25,000 approvals.

The more open and flexible immigration policies had a substantial impact on the number of immigrants. This is most clearly seen in the number of annual residence approvals that are published by the New Zealand Immigration Service for more recent years (New Zealand Immigration Service, 1997).[8] Between 1982 and 1987, the number of annual approvals was around 10,000 per year. In 1988, approvals jumped to over 25,000 and remained there until 1994, when another increase to 43,000 occurred. In 1995 the approvals numbered 56,260, and in 1996 42,729 applications were approved. In combination with fewer than normal permanent and long-term departures, the net-migration gain in the mid 1990s was substantial (see Figure 16.1).[9]

As seen before in New Zealand's history, this large immigration wave, and the resulting pressure on urban centres, and a housing crisis in Auckland in particular, put migration back on the popular political agenda.[10] A 1995 policy review affected immigration in two ways. First,

---

[8] In New Zealand, citizenship can be obtained after three years of residence. Permanent residents have most citizen rights including vote.

[9] Note, though, that successful applicants do not necessarily enter New Zealand in the year they are granted residence, and there is some evidence that this effect may be of quantitative importance (Bedford 1996).

[10] In 1996, 31 percent of all people living in Auckland were foreign-born. See Winkelmann and Winkelmann (1998).

the selection criteria were changed (in particular with respect to English language proficiency), and secondly, the targeted number of new migrants that had in the meantime climbed up to 48,000 and 55,000, was lowered to 35,000 for the 1996/7 June year. Immigration flows proved to be responsive to the policy changes, and the number of approvals declined to 33,683 new immigrants in the year ended June 1997. This declining trend continued over the following years. At the same time, an increasing number of New Zealanders started to depart long-term, mostly to Australia. As a result, the external migration balance developed a deficit. The net-losses in permanent and long-term migration were 63,000 in 1998, 9,000 in 1999 and 11,300 in 2000, before a small surplus of 1700 was again reached for the year ending October 2001. It clearly is difficult for New Zealand to maintain a steady inflow of immigrants, such as the proclaimed goal of an average migration gain of 10,000 people per.

The 1994–6 immigration boom was controversial not only for its sheer magnitude, but also because of its composition. The top ten countries of approvals among the main categories in 1996 included Taiwan (12 per cent), China (12 per cent), India (8 per cent), South Korea (5 per cent), Hong Kong (4 per cent), and the Philippines (3 per cent). In the 1996 census, the proportion of Asians had increased to 21 per cent of all, and to 47 per cent of recently arrived (1991–5) foreign-born residents.

16.2.5. Summary and Implications for Current Policy

After the large inflows of the early colonization years, immigration, though still high by world standards, slowed down. In more recent decades, the composition of immigrants shifted away from 'traditional source' countries such as Great Britain towards neighbour countries (and trading partners) in the Pacific Islands and Asia. Today, New Zealand remains, with a land area similar to that of Colorado or the United Kingdom and a population of 3.8 million, a sparsely populated country.

Between 1946 and 1998, the overall population grew by 2.2 million. During this period, the population gain through permanent and long-term migration was only 258,911 persons, or 12.3 per cent of the total population growth. Nevertheless, it would be wrong to conclude that New Zealand had developed a hostile attitude towards immigration, or suffered from its remote location at the periphery of the world. While elements of xenophobia have been identified in the past (see, for instance, Shroff 1995), the policies of the last decade have been consistently pro-immigration. As a consequence, annual immigration flows have remained above 1 per cent of the population since 1988, reaching 1.6 per cent in 1995. This is well above the rates for other traditional immigration countries such as Australia (0.5 per cent), Canada (0.8 per cent) or the United States (0.3 per cent).[11]

New Zealand's problem was the very high rate of emigration. Therefore, the net-effect of external migration on New Zealand's population remained minor during the post Second World War period. The emigration rate was also very volatile. Therefore, the optimal immigration rate that would lead to a stable population growth without any undue pressures on infrastructure and social cohesion is very difficult (or impossible) to determine. The factors that make people emigrate have received little attention so far (one exception being Brosnan and Poot, 1987). In the case of previous immigrants returning to their country of origin, the lack of any settlement policy (provisions of post-arrival services intended to ease the integration of new immigrants) may be one such factor that is currently under review in policy circles.

16.3. Current Residence Policy

16.3.1. The Changing Policy Context

The two key immigration policy events during recent years were the passing of the *Immigration Act 1987* and the *Immigration Amendment Act* 1991. Pre-1987, immigration was subject both to an occupational priority list and to a preferred source country list.[12] A comprehensive review the New Zealand's immigration policy was conducted in 1986. Factors motivating this review included a desire to acknowledge New Zealand's location in the Asia-Pacific region (factors being that immigration from within this region might foster trade, attract investment, and increase cultural diversity), and a desire to tidy up some of the administrative and legal shortcomings of the old legislation (Burke 1986).

---

[11] In 1997, the Australian Prime Minister John Howard announced a reduction in the immigration intake to 68,000, compared to a targeted intake in New Zealand, a country one-fifth in population size, of 38,000.

[12] An occupational priority list (OPL) was in existence from the mid 1960s. In order to employ immigrants without OPL skills, the employer had to demonstrate that no suitable New Zealand resident was available. After 1976, the employment of immigrants from 'non-traditional' source countries with OPL skills became possible, provided their skills were not in demand in their home country and it was not possible to obtain migrants from preferred sources (New Zealand Immigration Service 1997).

Consequently, the *Immigration Act 1987* did away with the 'traditional source' preference for UK, Western European, and North American nationals. It rationalized the system of an occupational priority list in order to encourage the immigration of people with skills for which excess demand in New Zealand could be identified. Residence applications made on occupational grounds required a firm employment offer and were based on personal merit (with the exception of some bilateral preferential access arrangements with Australia, the Netherlands, and Western Samoa). Family reunification immigration continued.

The *Immigration Amendment Act 1991* went a significant step further by replacing the occupational priority list with a point system, attempting to increase New Zealand's stock of general human capital rather than using residency policy as a short-term labour market tool. The requirement of a job offer was abandoned, although a job offer increases an applicant's point score. A soft immigration target of 25,000 was introduced, but it was exceeded substantially after 1993, peaking at 56,000 residency approvals in 1995 (about 72 per cent of which were approved under the General Skills Category).

In October 1995, rules were tightened somewhat. For example, the minimum English language requirement was extended from just the principal applicant to all adult family members in both the General Skills and the Business Investor categories. In occupations where professional registration is required by law in New Zealand (such as for physicians, lawyers, and electricians), the registration must be obtained before points for these qualifications can be awarded. In addition, the tax treatment of investments by immigrants was changed.

As far as long-term migration is concerned, it appears that the introduction of the point system in 1991 was instrumental in encouraging diversified immigration, and Asian immigration in particular. Whether the policy was successful, in the sense of attracting individuals with high human capital who will succeed in the New Zealand labour market, is an issue that will be considered below.

16.3.2. The Point System

The 1991 *Immigration Amendment Act* established four main categories for obtaining permanent residence in New Zealand (in addition to refugee status). These were the *General* (in 1995 renamed to *General Skills*), *Business Investment* (in 1995 renamed to *Business Investor*), *Family*, and *Humanitarian* categories. In 1996, 61 per cent of all approvals came from the *General Skills* category, 25 per cent from the *Family* category, and 4 per cent from *Business Investments.* The exact proportions vary from year to year. But unlike for other countries, including Australia, Family reunification (for parent, siblings, dependent children, and partners) is not the major constituent part of current migration. The majority of immigrants come to New Zealand through the *General Skills* category and are thus directly subject to the selection criteria reflected in the point system.

Table 16.3 lists the elements of the points system after the October 1995 policy changes. The pass mark to gain residence stayed at 25 points over most of the period.

The relative 'prices' for immigrants' attributes have the following characteristics: first, there is an offsetting effect of age and experience. Some simple calculations help to illustrate the nature of the tradeoff. Assume that an applicant had an uninterrupted working career. In this case someone who started work at the age of eighteen obtains a maximum of 16 points for age and experience if aged 29–39 at the time of the application. For a starting age of twenty years, 16 points are reached for those aged thirty-nine on application. If the applicant started to work at the age of twenty-five, the maximum achievable number of points is 14 when aged forty-four. Despite the stepwise nature of the system, a general pattern emerges: In general, it is better to have started the working career at an early age. The prime-age range is between thirty and forty-five. And the optimal age is an increasing function of age at entry into the labour market.

Second, a minimum base qualification is not necessary to get over the pass mark if an offer of employment exists. In this case, 21 points can be obtained from the employability factors, and the difference between 25 and 21 can be filled by settlement points. However, if settlement factors do not apply, then both a qualification and, in most cases, an offer of employment will be necessary to gain entry into New Zealand. Finally, the 'returns' to a qualification beyond the base qualification are not very high (or even negative, if other factors are taken into account). In general, a PhD will be worse off than a Bachelor because the years spent as a student do not qualify as work experience.

In practice, potential migrants can compute their point score prior to application on their own. If the current pass mark is reached, an applicant can be certain to be granted residence, subject to common health and character requirements. At the time of this writing, the application fee was NZ$700 (approx. US$400), and a settlement fee of NZ$180 per person (NZ$720 maximum per family) was payable upon arrival in New Zealand.

Table 16.3. Summary of points scored in general skills category

Qualifications	
Base qualification	10
Advanced qualification	11
Master degree or higher	12
Employability	
Work experience	
2 years	1
4 years	2
6 years	3
8 years	4
10 years	5
12 years	6
14 years	7
16 years	8
18 years	9
20 years	10
Offer of employment	5
Age	
18–24 years	8
25–29 years	10
30–34 years	8
18–39 years	6
18–44 years	4
18–49 years	2
Maximum age: 55 years	
Settlement factors	
Settlement funds	
$100,000	1
$200,000	2
Partner's qualification	
Base qualification	1
Advanced qualification	2
New Zealand work experience	
1 year	1
2 years	2
Family sponsorship	3
Maximum settlement points	7

Source: Winkelmann and Winkelmann (1998*a*).

16.3.3. Other Entry Categories and Preferential Arrangements

Throughout the period, New Zealand had provisions for temporary entry as visitors (up to nine months), students (up to four years) or temporary workers (up to three years). As of 31 July 1996, there were 11,600 overseas students in New Zealand attending universities, polytechnics or schools. With several thousand each the two most numerous groups of temporary workers were fishing crew members and young people on working holidays undertaking casual work, such as fruit picking (New Zealand Immigration Service 1997).

Special entry provisions exist for Australian citizens who have practically unrestricted access. New Zealand citizenship is automatically granted for inhabitants of three islands in the Pacific, Niue, Tokelau, and the Cook Islands who have a combined population of little over 20,000. Citizens of Samoa can apply for residence under a special quota of 1,100 permits a year if they are aged between eighteen and forty-five and have an offer of full-time permanent employment. Finally, New Zealand has established an annual quota of up to 800 refugees that is managed in co-operation with the United Nations High Commissioner of Refugees.

16.4. The Labour Market Outcomes of Immigrants

16.4.1. New Zealand Research

General reviews of the research issues with special reference to New Zealand are given in Maani (1991), Chapple, Gorbey and Yeabsley (1994), and Chapple and Yeabsley (1996). A number of studies has analysed the determinants of migration flows (immigration or net-migration) to New Zealand using time-series techniques. Among them, Brosnan and Poot (1987) and Gorbey et al. (1997) deal with Trans-Tasman migration (i.e., net permanent and long-term migration between New Zealand and Australia), whereas Gani and Ward (1995) study the migration of highly skilled and professionally trained workers from Fiji to New Zealand. These studies generally find that migration is economically driven, as the real income differential has a significant impact on net-migration flows. Also, there is evidence for persistence, as current flows are significantly and positively related to previous flows.

Empirical research on the labour market outcomes of immigrants based on Census tabulations include Poot et al. (1988), Poot (1993), and Zodgekar (1997). The Poot et al. (1988) book analyses the labour force status of recent immigrants in the 1981 census, while Poot (1993) and Zodgekar (1997) study the relative incomes of immigrants in the 1986 and 1991 census, respectively.

Poot et al. (1988) show that in 1981 recent migrants from the UK, Australia, and North America had labour market activity patterns that were relatively similar to those of the New Zealand-born. By contrast, unemployment rates among recent immigrants from the Pacific Islands were several times higher than those of New Zealand-born workers and other immigrant groups. In order to explore the process of adjustment to the New Zealand labour market, the authors graphed age-standardized labour force participation and unemployment rates by length of residence for immigrants from the UK, Australia, and the Pacific Islands.

It was found that the rates of unemployment among male immigrants from the UK and Australia were initially higher than those of New Zealand-born males, but these rates declined to below New Zealand-born levels within three years of residence. Female unemployment rates for immigrants from Australia and the UK showed similar patterns of convergence to native rates within a few years. By contrast, immigrants born in the Pacific Islands appeared to take much longer to converge to the unemployment rates of the New Zealand-born (up to fifteen years).

Poot (1993) studied the median annual incomes of immigrants using data from the 1986 census. Using tabulated data, he controlled for the effects of age, occupation, country-of-origin and years since migration (using ten five year cohorts from 0 to 50 years). Overall, only Pacific Islanders behaved like typical migrants: they had a substantial income disadvantage upon entry, and a relatively steep years since migration-income profile. However, they did not reach parity with the income of New Zealand-born workers before thirty-five or forty years in New Zealand. UK-born immigrants typically outperformed New Zealand-born workers from the start (i.e. they did not have an initial entry disadvantage), while Australians were similar to New Zealand-born workers.

Zodgekar (1997) used 1991 Census data to analyse the socioeconomic characteristics and relative incomes of immigrants. He found that immigrant men's average income was 7.3 per cent above the average income of New Zealand-born men. Once he controlled for differences in the age and education distribution, this relative income advantage turned into a disadvantage of 3.9 per cent. He noted that immigrants from traditional source countries such as the UK had much higher average incomes than immigrants from the Pacific Islands and Asia, even after including the controls. He proposed one possible explanation for the relative disadvantaged position of Pacific Island migrants, namely that many of them came in the early 1970s in response to a labour shortage in manufacturing, a sector that had downsized substantially by 1991.

A common methodological feature of this previous research is the use of aggregate data or cross-tabulations. One reason was the previous policy of *Statistics New Zealand* not to grant access to unit-level data for reasons of confidentiality. This restriction was gradually lifted over recent years, and Winkelmann and Winkelmann (1998*a*, 1998*b*) represent the first studies of New Zealand's immigration experience based on unit-level census data, using the years 1981, 1986, and 1996 as observation points.[13] The following summary of immigrants' labour market outcomes over the previous thirty to forty years is based mainly on the original report (Winkelmann and Winkelmann 1998) where more details can be found.

16.4.2. A Socio-Economic Profile of New Zealand's Immigrants

16.4.2.1. The educational attainment of immigrants

In postwar New Zealand, immigration policies have targeted, in one way or another, immigrants with skills, either occupational skills, or, more recently, broadly defined 'general skills'. New Zealand being a country with a relatively high proportion of unskilled workers, importing skilled workers could be interpreted as a relatively inexpensive (since public subsidies to education, if any, are paid for by other countries) and immediate way to overcome a relative shortage in skilled labour. In theory, this change in relative supplies could benefit both unskilled New Zealand-born persons and, in particular, owners of New Zealand's capital stock. The argument for skilled immigration has been reinforced by another, namely that skilled immigrants make a greater contribution to economic activity, and hence the living standards of New Zealanders, than unskilled immigrants.

Table 16.4 lists the distribution of highest qualification for immigrants, recent immigrants, and New Zealand-born persons in 1981 and 1996. Judged by the evidence presented in this table, the policy was quite successful as immigrants had distinctively higher education levels than New Zealand-born persons.

The educational difference between immigrants and New Zealand-born persons was large: immigrants were about 30 per cent more likely to have

---

[13] The data comprised a 5 per cent random sample of New Zealand-born working-age residents, a 20 per cent random-sample of working-age persons born in the UK, and the full population of other immigrants. The 1991 Census was omitted as it contained no question on the year in which foreign-born residents first arrived in New Zealand.

Table 16.4. Educational attainment, New Zealanders, all immigrants and recent immigrants, 1981 and 1996 (%)

	None	School	Vocational	University
1981				
All immigrants	45.8	25.9	20.5	6.2
Recent immigrants	37.2	28.6	19.5	11.6
New Zealanders	49.5	26.7	16.9	3.6
1996				
All immigrants	23.3	31.9	27.8	15.5
Recent immigrants	13.5	35.3	22.9	24.7
New Zealanders	29.6	34.7	26.1	8.0

Note: Recent immigrants arrived between 1991 and 1995.
Source: Winkelmann and Winkelmann (1998*a*).

a post-school qualification than New Zealand-born persons in any of the census years, while recent immigrants were between 40 and 50 per cent more likely. In absolute terms, the gap in post-school qualifications between New Zealand-born persons and recent immigrants increased from 10 percentage points in 1981 to 14 percentage points in 1996. Moreover, relative to New Zealand-born persons with post-school qualifications, immigrants tended to have a higher proportion of university qualifications and a lower proportion of vocational qualifications. In 1981, for instance, about 37 per cent of recent immigrants with a post-school qualification had a university qualification, compared to only 18 per cent of New Zealand-born persons. By 1996, this proportion had increased to more than 50 per cent for recent immigrants, but remained unchanged for New Zealand-born persons.

16.4.2.2. Age

Table 16.5 shows the age distribution for the three working-age populations, all immigrants, recent immigrants, and New Zealand-born persons, for 1996. The average age of a New Zealander in the working-age population was thirty-six years whereas the average age of an immigrant was forty years. Of particular interest is the comparison of recent immigrants and New Zealand-born persons. It indicates how youthful immigrants are when they arrive, and hence how immigration affects the age distribution of New Zealand residents.[14]

---

[14] The age distribution of all immigrants, by contrast, reflects both the distribution of age-at-arrival as well as the size of immigrant flows over time, and the two components cannot be separated.

Table 16.5. 1996 Age distribution of working age of immigrants and
New Zealand-born persons

| Age | Immigrants | | |
	All	Recent	NZ-born
15–24	0.153	0.279	0.244
25–34	0.225	0.323	0.243
35–44	0.243	0.247	0.224
45–54	0.217	0.107	0.170
55–64	0.159	0.042	0.116
Average	39.5	32.3	36.1

Note: Recent immigrants arrived between 1991 and 1995.
Source: Winkelmann and Winkelmann (1998a).

Table 16.6. Parental and (de facto) marital status of immigrants and
New Zealand-born residents, 1996 (%)

| | Parent | | |
	Joint	Sole	Partner
All immigrants	40.9	4.7	71.1
Recent Immigrants	45.5	3.5	65.5
New Zealanders	33.9	6.8	60.0

Note: Recent immigrants arrived between 1991 and 1995.
Source: Winkelmann and Winkelmann (1998a).

Recent immigrants were on average about four years younger than New Zealand-born persons. This is consistent with the analysis in Poot et al. (1988) who used demographic projections of different immigration scenarios to show that an increase in net migration would tend to slow down the ageing of New Zealand's population.

16.4.2.3. Parental and marital status
Apart from age and education, parental status is one of the main determinants of labour market opportunities and outcomes, for women in particular.

Table 16.6 gives the proportion of parents with dependent children, either joint or sole, among all individuals living in a family situation for 1996.[15] Immigrants had a higher propensity to live with a partner than did

[15] A dependent child is here defined as any child under sixteen years.

Table 16.7. Proportion of immigrants speaking English proficiently, by region-of-origin, 1996

	Recent	All
Western Europe	0.982	0.984
Eastern Europe	0.871	0.914
North-East Asia	0.653	0.679
South-East Asia	0.837	0.878
South Asia	0.861	0.893
Pacific Islands	0.796	0.849
Other	0.968	0.991
Total	0.834	0.920

Source: Winkelmann and Winkelmann (1998a).

New Zealanders. 34 per cent of the New Zealand-born, and 41 per cent of all immigrants, were joint parents while the incidence of sole parenthood was 7 and 5 per cent, respectively. In other words, 17 per cent of all New Zealand parents were sole parents, compared to 10 per cent of all immigrant parents.

16.4.2.4. English language proficiency
The 1996 Census included a question on language proficiency.[16] Table 16.7 gives the proportion of working-age immigrants who listed English as one of the languages they were able to 'conduct an everyday conversation in', by region-of-origin: Western and Eastern Europe, North-East, South-East, and South Asia, Pacific Islands and other countries. 92 per cent of all immigrants from these regions living in New Zealand in 1996 'spoke English', based on the above definition.

Virtually all immigrants from Western Europe and all immigrants from other areas (including native English speakers such as US Americans and Canadians) spoke English. Recent immigrants from other regions had lower proficiency rates. 35 per cent of recent immigrants from Northeast Asia, and 20 per cent of recent immigrants from the Pacific Islands stated that they were not able to conduct an everyday conversation in English. The 'non-speaking rates' of recent immigrants from other Asian regions and Eastern Europe varied between 13 and 16 per cent.

---

[16] The exact question was: 'In which language could you have a conversation about a lot of everyday things?' with options English; Maori; Samoan; NZ sign language; and other (please specify).

16.4.3. The Labour Market Status of Immigrants

The main event in New Zealand's immigration history over the last decade was the shift in inflow composition away from the traditional source countries, the United Kingdom and Ireland, towards immigration from Asia and the Pacific Islands. How did this change in supply affect the relative labour market outcomes of immigrants?

Before trying to answer this question, it is worthwhile remembering that demand factors were subject to change as well. During the initial three decades of the postwar period, New Zealand had been a country with virtually no unemployment. Unemployment rates remained below 1 per cent of the labour force until 1978, when the unemployment rate increased to 2 per cent. Five years later, unemployment reached 6 per cent, and in the early 1990s, it was as high as 14 per cent if based on register statistics (Dalziel and Lattimore 1996). Also, a substantial restructuring of the economy took place as jobs in the service sector replaced those lost in manufacturing. Thus, immigrants arriving in New Zealand during the first half of the 1990s did face quite different labour market conditions upon entry compared to their peers who had arrived one or two decades earlier.

As Figure 16.2 shows, employment rates changed substantially between 1981 and 1996. The four panels plot employment rates (as a proportion of the working-age population) for New Zealand-born persons, immigrants and recent immigrants by age, for men and women and the two census years, respectively. For instance, the upper left panel is for men in 1981. The differences in employment rates between immigrants and New Zealand-born persons were not very large, except for young recent immigrants, which might be linked to their disproportionate participation in higher education. For all groups, mid-age employment rates were over 90 per cent.

By 1996, the situation had changed considerably. Male employment had fallen below 90 per cent for all groups and ages. However, the decline was much larger for recent immigrants, where employment rates did not reach 70 per cent even among those aged twenty-five to thirty-five, and declined rapidly for older persons.

The female employment rates in the lower part of Figure 16.2 exhibit the typical 'birth-dent' between the ages of twenty-five and thirty-five. Female employment tended to be lower than male employment in both in 1981 and 1996. However, convergence to the male levels took place for New Zealand-born women, as their employment rates increased between 1981 and 1996. The opposite was the case for immigrant women, and as

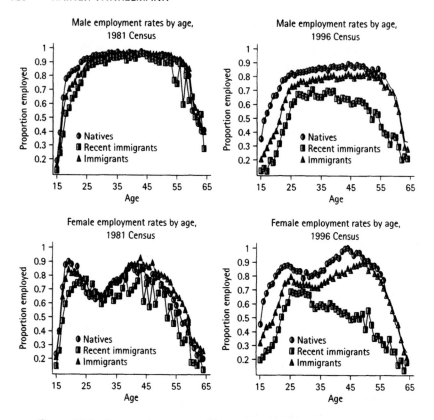

Figure 16.2. Age-employment profiles, men and women, 1981 and 1996
Source: Winkelmann and Winkelmann (1998*a*)

a consequence, the employment gap between immigrant and New Zeal-and–born women increased substantially. The declining relative perfor-mance of New Zealand's immigrants in the early 1990s was conspicuous. Possible explanations for this trend will be analysed below. First, however, it will be established that relative income followed a similar trend.

16.4.4. Income and Social Benefits

The forces that affected relative employment rates were likely at work for relative income as well. This is confirmed in Table 16.8. The first two columns give the unadjusted and adjusted relative incomes for employed residents in 1981 and 1996, respectively. The adjustment was based on a semi-logarithmic regression with log annual income as dependent variable and the independent variables hours of work (in the week prior to the census), a polynomial in age, three indicator variables for highest

Table 16.8. Relative income and welfare benefits, immigrants and New Zealanders, 1981 and 1996

	Relative income[a] (unadjusted/adjusted)		Welfare benefits[b]	
	1981	1996	1981	1996
All immigrants	1.05/0.94	0.99/0.89	0.347	0.227
Recent immigrants	0.83/0.81	0.84/0.75	0.245	0.181
New Zealanders			0.343	0.259

Notes: [a] Average nominal pre-tax total personal annual income from all sources. Grouped census data were converted continuous income measure using midpoints. Relative to New Zealand-born persons.
[b] Proportion of working age population receiving income from a social welfare benefit at some time during the last twelve months prior to the census.
Source: Winkelmann and Winkelmann (1998a).

qualification plus a dummy variable for immigrants. The reported adjusted relative income is obtained by taking the anti-log of the dummy coefficient. It provides a comparison of the incomes of immigrants and New Zealand-born workers who have otherwise similar characteristics. The adjustment is important as immigrants had relatively high levels of formal qualifications which renders a comparison with an 'average' New Zealand-born worker of questionable value.

This pattern is apparent in Table 16.8, where adjusted relative incomes of immigrants are always below the unadjusted ones. In 1981, for instance, an average immigrant's income was 5 per cent above the income of an average New Zealand-born worker. In comparison to 'similar' New Zealand-born workers, however, this advantage disappeared, and incomes were virtually identical on average. A similar adjustment effect was observed for recent immigrants in the two census years who always had incomes below those of established immigrants. As for employment, the relative position of recent immigrants was worse in 1996 than it was fifteen years earlier.

One issue associated with the income levels of (recent) immigrants is the extent to which immigrants use welfare benefits. A disproportionate use of the welfare system is one of the ways in which immigration could adversely affect the well being of New Zealand-born persons.[17] The available information only indicates whether or not a person has received at least one welfare benefit during the previous twelve months.[18] It does

[17] This is a highly simplified view. The real question is whether or not immigrants are net welfare recipients, i.e., whether they receive more welfare benefits than they contribute (through taxes or other payments) as a group over their lifetime.
[18] The benefit definition is very inclusive and includes many partial benefits, such as childcare subsidies, and some 'universal' benefits, such as the Family Benefit, which in 1981 was paid to all parents of children aged under sixteen years.

not give the benefit duration or the benefit level. Table 16.8 shows that immigrants had about the same probability as New Zealand-born persons of having received at least one benefit payment. In 1996, the proportion of New Zealand-born persons who had received a benefit dropped to 26 per cent, down from 38 per cent in 1986; and to 23 per cent, down from 37 per cent in 1986, for immigrants. This drop was likely caused by the abolition of the universal family benefit on 1 October 1986. Recent immigrants always were less likely than New Zealand-born persons to have received a benefit in all three census years.[19]

16.4.5. Region-of-Origin Differences

In sections 16.4.2–16.4.4 immigrants have been treated as a homogenous groups which they likely were not. In this section, the importance of region-of-origin differences will be highlighted. The following six regions are distinguished: UK and Ireland; Australia; Europe and North America; Pacific Islands; Asia; and other countries.[20] Although one could approach this issue in many ways, the particular focus here will be on trends in adjusted income differentials of employed recent immigrants. As shown in Winkelmann and Winkelmann (1998a) the substantive result would not be affected if one were to look at other aspects of labour market outcomes.

Two questions can be addressed with the information on adjusted income differentials by region-of-origin that is provided in Table 16.9.[21] First, how large were the differences between regions, and how did they change over time? From which sending countries came the more successful immigrants, and from which the less? And second, how much did the change in the composition of recent immigrants contribute to the declining fortunes of the 'average' recent immigrant in New Zealand?

In 1981, adjusted log-income differentials ranged from −0.074 for recent UK and Irish immigrants to −0.270 for recent Asian immigrants, a gap of about 20 log-points. The Pacific Islands, Asia, and Europe and North America were grouped closely together. By 1996, the gap had almost tripled to 57 log-points. The same regions were at the respective ends, and while the relative position of UK and Irish immigrants relative to the

---

[19] Immigrants are expected to have sufficient personal resources to maintain themselves and their dependants for at least the first twelve months of residence in New Zealand. During this period, they are not entitled to any income support benefits unless in severe financial hardship.

[20] Winkelmann (2000) provides an analysis based on subregions within the Europe and North America category.

[21] As in the previous section, the adjustment controls for hours of work, age, age squared, qualification, and gender.

Table 16.9. Adjusted income differentials and population shares of recent
immigrants by region-of-origin, 1981 and 1996

	Differential (diff$_{81}$)	Share (p$_{81}$)	Differential (diff$_{96}$)	Share (p$_{96}$)
UK and Ireland	−.074	36.85	.009	27.52
Australia	−.175	16.14	−.014	10.79
Europe and North America	−.262	15.07	−.186	17.04
Pacific Islands	−.233	14.62	−.444	6.01
Asia	−.270	13.10	−.566	27.16
Other countries	−.089	4.23	−.216	11.48
		100.00		100.00

Note: Differentials and shares are for employed recent immigrants.
Source: Winkelmann and Winkelmann (1998a).

New Zealand-born had improved, the opposite was the case for Asian immigrants.

Concurrently, the share of Asian immigrants had increased from 13 per cent of all recent employed immigrants in 1981 to 27 per cent of all recent employed immigrants in 1996.[22] Both factors contributed to a decline in the estimated relative income of an average immigrant. However, the changes within-regions was quantitatively not as important as the changes in composition towards immigrants from Asia, as is shown by the following decomposition exercise: let p denote the proportion of employed immigrants from a specific region among all recent employed immigrants. The overall log-income differential between recent immigrants and New Zealand-born residents in a given year is simply the weighted average of the region specific log-income differentials, where the weights are provided by the proportions

$$diff_t^{Total} = \sum_{i=1}^{6} diff_{it} p_{it}$$

or, in vector notation, $diff_t' p_t$, $t = 81,96$. Moreover, the overall change can be computed as:[23]

$$diff_{96}' \, p_{96} - diff_{81}' \, p_{81} = -0.236 - (-0.168) = -0.068$$

[22] The 1996 proportion of Asian recent immigrants among employed recent immigrants was much smaller than their overall share among all recent immigrants of 47 percent, as the Asian employment rate was very low.
[23] Note that the overall differential differs from Table 16.8, as no frequency weights were used in the context of the Table 16.8.

How much of this change is due to changes in composition, and how much to changes in region-specific differentials? Using the regression results, the change in the overall recent immigrant-New Zealand-born resident income differential can be decomposed as follows

$$diff_{96}' \; p_{96} - diff_{81}' \; p_{81} = diff_{96}' \; (p_{96} - p_{81}) + p_{81}' \; (diff_{96} - diff_{81})$$

The first term on the right side gives the overall change caused by a change in composition, evaluated at the 1996 differentials. From Table 16.9, $diff_{96}' \; p_{81} = -0.181$. Hence, the aggregate 1996 log-income differential would have amounted to -0.181 had the composition not changed between 1981 and 1996. The actual value was -0.236, and the difference between the two, 0.055 percentage points, is the increase in the (recent) log income differential that is due to compositional changes. This constitutes about 80 per cent of the total increase in the log-income differential. Alternatively, one could evaluate the change in composition using the 1981 differentials. The result is approximately the same.

The other 20 per cent of the increase was associated with increases in the entry income differentials for recent immigrants from specific regions. We cannot tell from the data whether these changes were caused by changes in unobserved characteristics (either quantity or returns) within countries, or by the changes in the receiving conditions in the New Zealand labour market that were mentioned at the beginning of Section 4.4.

16.4.6. Evidence on Assimilation

As suggested by the previous section, *cohort effects*, i.e. changing (adjusted) New Zealand-born immigrants' labour market differentials for successive immigrant cohorts at the time of arrival, were paramount. At the risk of being accused of oversimplification, the set of regions can be split into two categories: predominantly English speaking regions ('ESB': UK and Ireland, Australia, and Europe and North America) whose entry position (measured by the annual income for those in employment) improved over the last two decades,[24] and predominantly non-English speaking regions ('NESB': Asia and the Pacific Islands) whose entry position worsened. While the recent intake of immigrants from Asian and Pacific Island countries faced considerable initial problems, this issue is of less concern to policy makers and society if assimilation can be expected to be fast.

---

[24] To the point where certain immigrant groups actually 'outperformed' similar New Zealand-born in terms of labour market outcomes independently of duration of residence.

Using past data to predict the future assimilation of current arrivals obviously requires certain homogeneity assumptions. Winkelmann and Winkelmann (1998a) follow the common approach in the literature by assuming that the entry position may differ between cohorts, but that their convergence path towards the position of New Zealand-born workers is stable over cohorts (see, for instance, Borjas, 1994). In particular, they estimated the parameters of the following model using pooled data from the three Census years 1981, 1986, and 1996:

$$\log(y) = \alpha + X\beta + \sum_{k=1}^{8} \eta_k C_k + \delta YSM + \phi YSM^2$$
$$+ \gamma YEAR86 + \lambda YEAR93 + \varepsilon$$

where YSM stands for 'years since migration' and C_k, $k = $ pre60, 61–65, 66–70, 71–75, 76–80, 81–85, 86–90, 91–95 denote succesive cohorts. η_k measure the percentage difference in income between immigrants of cohort k and otherwise similar New Zealand-born residents *in the first year after arrival* (for YSM = 0), whereas δ and ϕ determine the rate of convergence. A typical income adjustment path for cohort k would feature an initial income disadvantage upon entry $(\eta_k < 0)$, combined with subsequently faster income growth for foreign-born workers $(\delta > 0)$. δ literally measures the relative income growth attributable to the first year of residence. If, as expected, ϕ is negative, then relative income growth slows by -2ϕ percentage points in each subsequent year, and income convergence occurs, if at all, after $\left(-\delta + \sqrt{\delta^2 - 4\phi\eta_k} \right)/2\phi$ years.[25] Moreover, the model can be generalized somewhat by interacting the qualification variables with both an immigrant dummy and the YSM polynomial. In this way, entry differentials between immigrants and New Zealand-born residents and convergence rates are allowed to vary by qualification levels.

Figure 16.3 summarizes the predicted income position of hypothetical immigrants and New Zealand-born residents over the life cycle, based on the estimated regression coefficients. The figure displays separate profiles by English-speaking background, sex, and education (school versus university). In all panels, the age at which the hypothetical immigrant entered New Zealand is set to twenty-five. Both the immigrant and the

---

[25] Selective outmigration may distort this inference. If, on average, the less successful migrants leave, then the estimated convergence rates will overstate the true economic progress of those who stay (see, for instance, Borjas 1994).

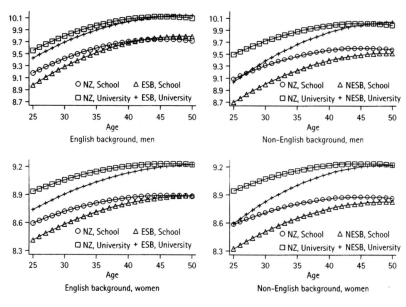

Figure 16.3. Age-log income profiles of immigrants and New Zealand-born residents, by English background and sex
Source: Winkelmann and Winkelmann (1998*a*)

New Zealand-born worker are followed from the age of twenty-five through to the age of fifty. Finally, both are assumed to work full-time (forty hours per week) and immigrants' entry differentials are assumed to equal the (arithmetic) cohort average for the group. In this context, the *y*-axis gives the predicted log-income for a worker with the specified characteristics. Differentials over the lifecycle (moving along a profile) or differentials over groups (moving across profiles) can be interpreted as approximate measures of relative (percentage) income differentials.

For example, the upper left graph of Figure 16.3 shows the age-income profiles of male English background migrants. The vertical distance between the two qualification curves gives the percentage difference in income between school graduates and university graduates of a given age. Both New Zealand-born residents and immigrants had substantial returns to a university qualification, about 38 per cent and (initially) about 46 per cent, respectively. The vertical distance between the immigrant and New Zealand-born resident curves, for a given qualification level, gives the approximate percentage difference in income between immigrants and New Zealand-born residents. This vertical difference tended to decline with age and eventually disappeared, after about eighteen years for school graduates and after about twenty years for university graduates. Hence, convergence was predicted to take place.

By allowing convergence profiles to differ by education level this analysis can shed light on the 'skill transferability hypothesis'. According to this hypothesis, immigrants face an initial disadvantage in the host labour market, relative to New Zealand-born residents with the same qualifications, because it takes time to generate credible information about the true value of the qualification, or, in the case of some professions, to obtain the required licence. As a consequence, more highly qualified immigrants are likely to face a larger initial disadvantage than others, and also have faster subsequent convergence rates as the true value of their qualifications is revealed.

Figure 16.3 shows that this hypothesis appears not to be supported by the experience of English background male immigrants. To the contrary, less qualified ESB immigrants had a larger initial income disadvantage and faster subsequent adjustment rates. However, the transferability hypothesis is supported by the experience of non-English background immigrant men, depicted in the upper right panel of Figure 16.3, as more qualified non-English background migrants had a substantially larger entry disadvantage but also faster subsequent income growth. The difficulty of NESB immigrants in making productive use of their qualifications upon arrival is illustrated by the low initial returns to a university qualification (relative to a school degree) of only 33 per cent (compared to 46 per cent for ESB migrants).

As expected, the overall income differentials relative to New Zealand-born residents were much larger for NESB migrants than for ESB migrants. NESB migrants with university qualification are predicted to reach parity with similar New Zealand-born residents, although it will take about twenty years. NESB migrants with school qualification only are unlikely to reach New Zealand-born resident income levels within the time horizon of this analysis.

Are women different? The two lower panels of Figure 16.3 repeat the previous type of analysis for female immigrants. Female profiles tended to be flatter than male ones. There were two contributing factors. First, female returns to experience were smaller (as were the returns to qualifications). Incomes of female New Zealand-born residents increased by 35 per cent over the 25-year period, compared to an increase by 54 per cent for males. Second, female immigrants had slower rates of convergence. The differences between ESB and NESB migrants were less pronounced than those for men, and convergence was achieved after about 25 years for ESB immigrants and NESB immigrants with university qualification.

To summarize, the results indicate that a typical immigrant entered with an income shortfall of about 20–30 per cent relative to a similar New Zealand-born resident. This shortfall tended to disappear after 20–30 years of residence. Immigrants with English speaking background clearly 'out-performed' non-English-speaking background migrants.

16.4.7. Effects on New Zealanders

The limited research on the effects of immigration on New Zealand-born workers that has been undertaken so far has concentrated on macro-economic variables, in addition to some studies involving the housing market. For instance, Poot (1986) reports estimates from a dynamic model whereby the aggregate unemployment rate in t is explained by its own lags and by a current and past values of an immigration variable, defined as net permanent and longterm migration as a proportion of the population size. Poot also takes into account that the causality may run the other way around. The general conclusion is that immigration has no strong shortrun influence on macroeconomic variables but is itself highly endogenous and Granger-caused by macroeconomic conditions.

A lot of additional research, preferably based on micro-level data, will be required before a firmer picture on the wage and employment effects of immigration on skilled and unskilled New Zealand-born workers will emerge.

16.5. Lessons for Europe

Each country's main objective is to design its policies so as to improve its national welfare. One of the most contentious issues concerning immigration policy is: how likely immigrants are to succeed in the domestic labour market; how much difficulty do they have in finding employment at all, and employment commensurate with their qualifications in particular? Are their tax contributions higher than those of the natives? Is their need for social assistance lower relative to that of the natives? The benefits of immigration to the host country are likely to be higher if immigrants fully realize their productive potential and perform well in the labour market. What, if any, is then the lesson of New Zealand's experience for future revisions of immigration policy in Europe? Despite being located as far away from Europe as possible in terms of geography, New Zealand is a country that in many ways has preserved more similarity with its European (here: British) heritage than did Australia, Canada, or the United States. From this point of view, its experience should be relevant.

This survey has shown that as many of the enthusiastic expectations associated with the general economic reforms of the 1980s were disappointed by subsequent economic development, the experiences with the point system were mixed as well. While some features of the system worked quite well (e.g., it is a transparent, rational system with reduced bureaucratic overhead and, to some extent, it gives better control over immigrant numbers), it has failed to bring into the country the promised steady stream of economically successful migrants who contribute to New Zealand's economic growth. While the levels of formal qualifications of the first cohort of immigrants admitted under the point system were very high indeed, compared to the New Zealand born population or to previous cohorts of immigrants, their unemployment rates were exceptionally high as well, and their income levels quite low. The New Zealand experience suggests that a controlled immigration policy with an emphasis on highly-skilled immigrants does not by itself guarantee a successful integration of immigrants.

References

Bedford, R. (1996). 'International migration, 1995: some reflections on an exceptional year', *New Zealand Journal of Geography*, April, 21–33.

Borjas, G. (1994). 'The economics of immigration', *Journal of Economic Literature*, 32(4): 1667–1717.

Brosnan, P. and Poot, J. (1987). 'Modelling the determinants of Trans-Tasman migration after the Second World War', *The Economic Record* 63: 313–29.

Burke, K. (1986). 'Review of immigration policy', *Appendix to the Journals of the House of Representatives*, 1986–7.

Chapple, S. and Yeabsley, J. (1996). 'A framework for the assessment of the economic and social effects of immigration', NZIER report to the Department of Labour.

—, Gorbey, S. and Yeabsley, J. in collaboration with Poot, J. (1994). 'Literature review on the economic impact of immigration', NZIER Working Paper No. 95/5, NZIER report to the Department of Labour.

Cook, L. (1997). 'New Zealand's current and future population dynamics', Paper presented at the Population Conference held in Wellington on 12–14 November 1997.

Dalziel, P. and Lattimore, R. (1996). *The New Zealand Macroeconomy. A Briefing on the Reforms* (Auckland: Oxford University Press).

Gani, A. and Ward, B. D. (1995). 'Migration of professionals from Fiji to New Zealand: A reduced form supply-demand model', *World Development* 23, 9: 1633-7.

Gorbey, S., James, D. and Poot, J. (1997). 'Population forecasting with endogenous international migration: the case of New Zealand', *International Regional Science Review.*

Maani, S. (1991). 'Consequences of current immigration in New Zealand: an economic overview', University of Auckland, Department of Economics Discussion Paper No. 87.

New Zealand Immigration Service (1995). *A Review of New Zealand's Residence Policies: the "Targeted" Immigration Streams* (Wellington).

— (1997). *New Zealand Immigration Policy and Trends*, document prepared for the population conference, Wellington, 13-14 November 1997.

Poot, J. (1986). *Immigration and the Economy: A Review of Recent Australian Findings on the Economic Consequences of Immigration and the Relevance of these Findings for New Zealand* (Wellington: Institute of Policy Studies).

— (1988a). 'International migration and the New Zealand economy: a trans-Tasman Comparison', Baker, L. and Miller, P. (eds.) *The Economics of Immigration: Proceedings of a Conference*, 22-3 April 1987 (Canberra, Australian Government Printing Service).

— (1988b). 'The New Zealand labour force: a demographic outlook', Crothers, C. and Bedford, R. (eds.) *The Business of Population* (Wellington, New Zealand Demographic Society).

— (1993). 'Adaptation of migrants in the New Zealand labour market', *International Migration Review*, 27(1): 121-39.

— (1998). 'The impact of immigration on labour markets and urban infrastructure in Australia and New Zealand', in C. Gorter, P. Nijkamp and J. Poot (eds.) *Crossing Borders: Regional and Urban Perspectives on International Migration* (Avebury, Aldershot (in press)).

Poot, J., Nana, G. and Philpott, B. (1988). *International Migration and the New Zealand Economy: A Long-Run Perspective* (Wellington: Victoria University Press for the Institute of Policy Studies).

Shroff, G. (1988). 'New Zealand's immigration policy', *New Zealand Official Yearbook* 1988-89: 193-207.

Statistics New Zealand (1995). *New Zealand Official Yearbook* (Wellington).

Trlin, A. and Spoonley, P. (eds.) (1986). *New Zealand and International Migration. A Digest and Bibliography, Number 1* (Department of Sociology, Massey University).

— (eds.) (1992). *New Zealand and International Migration. A Digest and Bibliography, Number 2* (Department of Sociology, Massey University).

— (eds.) (1997). *New Zealand and International Migration. A Digest and Bibliography, Number 3* (Department of Sociology, Massey University).

Wearing, B. (1993). 'New Zealand's immigration policies and Immigration Act (1987): comparisons with the United States of America', in Ivan Light and Parminder Bhachu, *Immigration and Entrepreneurship: Culture, Capital, and Ethnic Networks* (Transaction: New Brunswick and London), 307–27.

Winkelmann, L. and Winkelmann, R. (1997). 'Determining the relative labour force status of Maori and non-Maori using a multinominal logit model', *Labour Market Bulletin*, 1997(1): 24–62.

— (1998a). *Immigrants in the New Zealand Labour Market: A Study of their Labour Market Outcomes* (Wellington: New Zealand Department of Labour).

— (1998b). 'Immigrants in the New Zealand labour market: a cohort analysis using 1981, 1986 and 1996 census data', *Labour Market Bulletin* 1998:1 and 2, 34–70.

Winkelmann, R. (2000). 'The labour market performance of European immigrants in New Zealand in the 1980s and 1990s', *International Migration Review*, 34(1): 33–5.

Zodgekar, A. V. (1997). 'Immigrants in New Zealand Society', Occasional Papers in Sociology and Social Policy, No 10, 1997, Victoria University of Wellington.

Index

Achiram, E. 470, 475
Adebahr, H. 222
affirmative action 189, 276
Afghanistan, migrants 215, 217
Afonso, S. I. C. 432
Africa, migrants 434
  from Italy 306
  to Denmark 61, 62, 64, 71, 72
  to France 268, 269, 273, 275, 283, 287
  to Germany 215, 217
  to Israel 468, 469, 470, 475
  to Italy 317, 318, 319, 328
  to Portugal 416, 436, 438, 439, 443-4
  to Spain 411
  to Sweden 38, 51
  to United Kingdom 118, 123, 125, 132,
    134, 135, 141, 145, 149
  unemployment 139, 140, 145, 146-7,
    148
  to United States 511-14, 539, 544-6
  educational level 531, 532
  income and poverty 557, 560-2
  labour force participation 539, 544-6
  occupational status 544-6
ageing population 223, 241, 242
agricultural sector 392
  Greece 343, 369, 370, 371, 373, 374,
    376, 377
  Israeli settlements 465-7, 469, 496
  Spain 389, 393, 394
  U.S. 516, 543, 544, 545, 546, 547
Akbari, A. 586, 588, 589
Alba, R. 283
Albanian migrants 10
  to Greece 338, 342, 346, 357, 362
  to Italy 316-18, 320, 321-2,
    328, 329
Algerian migrants in France 4, 268, 269,
    271, 274, 273, 281, 283, 284
  assimilation 282-4
  impact of 291-2
  return migration 288, 289
  socioeconomic position 288, 297-8
  statistics 268-9, 271, 272, 275
Almeida, J. C. F. de 432
Almeida, C. 426, 428

Altonji, J. 412, 591
Alves, M. 441, 442
Amaro, R. R. 441-2
Amir, S. 482, 484
amnesties 276, 292, 293, 605
  aggravating illegality 358-9
  United States 509, 516, 517, 525, 563
Andersen, L. M. 83
Anderson, M. 529
Angrist, J. 291, 299
Antillean migrants in the Netherlands 173,
    181-6, 189, 190, 191
  earnings 183, 184
  education 181-3
  unemployment 185, 186
Antolin, P. 223, 390, 396, 400, 401
Antunes, M. L. M. 420, 422, 426, 432
Anwar, M. 129
Arellano, M. 390, 408
Argentina
  Italian migrants to 306, 310, 312
  Jewish population 461
  Spanish migrants to 392, 393
Armenians in U.S. 521
Arroteia, J. C. 420, 431, 433
Ashton-Vouyoucalos, S. 365
Asia, migrants 436
  asylum seekers in Germany 215
  to Canada 595, 596
  to Denmark 60-4, 71, 72
  to France 269, 271, 275, 276, 281, 286
  to Greece 338
  to Israel 468-70, 475, 481
  to Italy 316-19
  to New Zealand 601, 602, 604, 606, 608,
    609, 618, 622, 623
  to Spain 411
  to Sweden 38, 51
  to United Kingdom 132, 134, 135
  unemployment 138-40, 145, 147, 148, 153
  to United States 511-12, 513, 514,
    519, 528
  educational level 531-3, 536, 564
  income and poverty 561, 562
  labour force participation 539, 544-6
  occupational status 544-6

assimilation 2, 3, 423
  and country similarities 5
  defined 278
  and endogamy 423
  ethnic diversity 497
  France 264-5, 278-90
  Germany 226-42
  homogeneity 496, 497
  Israel 11, 472-3, 480-91, 495, 497
  as policy, UK 127, 130
  right to refuse 278
asylum seekers 5
  Denmark 69
  France 274-5, 276
  from Bosnia 26
  Germany 201-3, 214-18
    welfare benefits 238, 239, 240, 241
  Netherlands 173, 178-9, 191
  Portugal 440
  psychological disease 36, 37
  Sweden 25-6
  United Kingdom 117, 121-2, 126
  United States 515, 516, 519
Atchison, J. 352
Aussiedler see under Germany,
    ethnic Germans
Australian migration
  assisted passages 352
  earnings gap 228
  from Denmark 61
  from Greece 337, 352, 368
  from Italy 306
  from United Kingdom 114, 118, 119
  immigration policy 354-5
  language fluency 133, 134
  to Israel 470
  to New Zealand 604, 606, 608, 609, 610
    614, 622
Austria 4, 8, 18, 489
  migrants from Italy 306
Àvila, P. 441

Bacchetta, P. 307, 315
Bach, R. L. 517
Baganha, M. 415-57
Baillet, D. 288
Baillet, P. 281
Baines, D. E. 160, 161, 163, 164
Baldacci, E. 327
Baldwin-Edwards, M. 356
Bangladeshi migrants
  in Portugal 438

  in United Kingdom 132-5, 149, 154
    employment 139, 140, 143, 145,
      147-9, 159
    numbers 118, 119
Bar-Chaim, Y. 476, 477, 482
Barabas, G. 249
Barosa, J. P. 426, 427
Barreto, A. 426, 428
Barrett, A. 89-112
Barry, F. 99
Bartel, A. P. 521
Bauer, T. 2, 5, 6, 197-261, 295
Beach, C. M. 594
Bean, F. D. 515, 553
Becker, G. S. 359
Beenstock, M. 482, 492-4, 500
Behrman, J. R. 154
Bein, A. 465, 467, 468
Belgium, migrants 4
  from Italy 306, 310
  to France 273
Bell, B. D. 152, 154, 164, 165
Ben-Porath, Y. 488, 498-9
Bender, S. 234
Bengtsson, T. 15-58
Bentolila, S. 223, 390, 398, 399
Benz, W. 204
Bernard, H. R. 365
Bernardt, Y. 192
Berthoud, R. 134-5, 137
Betz, F. H. 205
Bevelander, P. 28-9
Birindelli, A. M. 305, 308, 314
Black, R. 355
Blackaby, D. H. 138-9, 140,
    152-5, 159
Blanchard, O. 390, 398
Blau, F. 553
Blejer, M. I. 493
Boeri, T. 2
Bohning, W. R. 372
Bonacich, E. 513
Bonjour, D. 326
Borjas, G. 6, 139, 153, 154, 160, 243,
    351, 352, 625
  assimilation 154, 226, 227, 481
  earnings 154
  on human capital 228
  on impact on natives 243, 480, 485, 486
  on Irish immigrants 104
  on policy 447
Borrel, C. 269-70, 283

Börsch-Supan, A. 242
Bosnia 22, 26, 37
Botsas, E. L. 363, 364
Bovenkerk, F. 187
Bover, O. 223, 389–414
Boyer, G. R. 105
Bradley, J. 99, 107
brain drain 164–5, 351
  Canadian immigration 576
  Ireland 95, 102, 105
Branquinho, I. 426
Brazil, migrants
  from Italy 306, 309, 312
  from Portugal 418, 421
  to Italy 318
  to Portugal 10, 436, 437, 438, 442
  to Spain 392
Breen, R. 101
Brettell, C. 421, 426–7
Briody, E. K. 548
British Nationality Act (1948) UK 126
Brooks, D. 163
Brosnan, P. 609, 613
Brücker, H. 2, 198, 243, 291
Brun, F. 293
Bruto da Costa, A. 442
Büchel, F. 238, 239–40
Buhr, P. 239
Bulgarian migrants to Greece 338, 346, 357, 363
Burda, M. C. 223
Burke, K. 609
business cycle effects 162, 279, 298
  Germany 209, 210
  Sweden 22, 30
Butaud, J.-P. 279–80

Cafferty, P. S. J. 514
Cagiano de Azevedo, R. 307, 315
Caille, J.-P. 286
Callan, T. 101
Camp David Accord 490
Canada 10–12, 573–99
  2002 immigration regulations 578–82
  absorptive capacity 575
  Bill C-26, 579
  Canada First policy 583
  decrease in skill levels 480
  earnings 228, 581, 594, 597
  economic criteria 578
  family reunification 573, 574, 578
  goals for immigration 576–7
  history of immigration 602

human capital 576, 597–8
immigrants
  from Britain 114, 118, 119
  from Greece 355
  from Italy 306
  from Portugal 421
  health of 36, 37
  labour market experience 594–8
  social and economic attributes 580, 581, 582
  wage discrimination 595, 597
immigration policy 9–13, 351, 352, 574–82
  (1945–67) 574–6
  (1967–90) 576–9
  restrictive 576, 580
  Jewish population 461, 595–6
  labour market impacts 578–9
  labour market participation 581–2
  labour substitution 583–4
    displacement model 584–91
    foreign-born industries 587–9
  legislation 577, 580, 582, 586, 587
  migrants to Israel 470
  migrants to U.S. 511–12, 513, 514, 518,
    531, 533, 535, 536
    income and poverty 561, 562, 563
    labour force participation 539, 542,
      543, 544–6
    occupational status 544–6
  occupation by ethnic origin 597–8
  occupation by ethnic origin 597–8
  point system 578–80
    and settlement location 522
  preferred regions
  refugee class 578
  sender countries 575
  skill criteria 576–7, 579
  wage discrimination 595
  wage impacts 579, 591–3
    by industry 593–4
  welfare consumption 581–2
Card, D. 250, 412, 486, 591
Caribbean migrants 4
  in United Kingdom 132–5,
    140, 141
    numbers 118, 119, 123, 149
    unemployment 143, 147, 148
  in United States 511, 514
Carlos, L. P. 443
Carpenter, N. 513
Castro, P. 442, 443
catch-up 33–4
  see also human capital
Cebula, R. J. 359

Cerase, F. 315
chain migration
  Canada 579
  Netherlands 178–91
  United Kingdom 119, 163
  United States 515, 517
Chaney, E. 427
Chapple, S. 613
Chile, migrants 21, 22
China, migrants
  to France 276, 286
  to New Zealand 604, 608
  to Portugal 438, 442
  to United Kingdom 132, 134, 135
  to United States 513, 516, 518
Chiswick, B. R. 139, 140, 152, 153, 155,
    296, 481, 483
  employment model 141, 144, 147,
    148, 154
  on human capital 139, 226, 500
  and language skills 482, 500
  on U.S. immigration 507–74
Chiswick, C. U. 508
Christoffersen, H. 83
circular migration 1
citizenship 125, 126, 264, 266–7
Clark, K. 138, 152, 155
Clark, W. A. V. 529
Coleman, D. A. 119, 120, 121, 126
Collaros, T. A. 376
Colombian migrants to U.S. 518
Comitas, L. 365
Common Nordic Labour Market 23,
    26–7, 45
Commonwealth Immigrants Acts (UK) 123,
    124, 125
Constant, A. 2, 228–31,
    234, 263–302
Corcoran, M. P. 102
Cordeiro, A. 427, 441
Cortesão, L. 443
Coulson, R. G. 574, 578, 583, 590, 591
Cramer, U. 234
Craveiro, J. 443
creuset français 278, 297
crime and immigrants 328
Crowley, J. 278–9, 285
Cuba
  migrants to U.S. 518, 519
  Spanish migrants to 392
Curtis, J. 105–6
Czechoslovakian migrants in Sweden 20, 34

Da Vanzo, J. 400
Dagevos, J. M. 185, 187, 189
Dale, A. 103–4
Dalziel, P. 619
Daveri, F. 313
Davis, K. 435
Dayan, J.-L. 282–3, 287
De la Puente, M. 519, 549
de Melo, J. 198
decolonization 4, 8, 9, 123, 173, 273
  Netherlands 177, 178, 179, 191
  Portugal 439, 444–6
Decressin, J. W. 224
Del Boca, D. 303–35
Delis, D. I. 369
Della Pergola, S. 461
Dell' Aringa, C. 325
Deneuve, C. 277
DeNew, J. P. 244–6
Denmark 4, 5, 6, 7, 44, 59–85
  emigrants 66–8
    to Sweden 21, 23, 27
  employment and migration 66–7
  and EU 59–60
  family reunification 61, 63, 65, 69
  guest workers 59, 60, 62, 64, 68, 69
    stop 69, 84
  immigrants
    employment 72, 73, 75, 77, 80–4
    geographical mobility 83–4, 73
    integration of 7, 79, 80–1
    proportion of 15, 83
    Swedish 15
  immigration policy 69–70
  income transfers 79, 81–3, 85
  internal mobility 60
  labour force participation 74–7
  labour market integration 60, 69–80
    participation by country of origin 71–2
  migration flows 84–60, 61–9
  net migration period 59
  Nordic migration flows 62, 63, 64–6, 67–8
  recruitment policy 4
  refugees 74–5, 70–80
  return migration 66, 68
  unemployment 69, 70–81, 84
  welfare issues 80–85
  worker flows 65–9
determinants of migration 2, 120–1
  Ireland 96–102
DeVoretz, D. J. 573–600
Dex, S. 152

Dietz, B. 197–261
Dikaiou, M. 354, 355, 365, 373
Dinkel, R. 242
discrimination 75–8, 84
  Denmark 69
  earnings and wages 33, 53, 559
  France 263, 276, 284–6, 298
  gender 78
  Israel 484
  Netherlands 187–8, 193
  Portugal 446
  second generation immigrants 17, 28, 39–41
  skin colour 45, 128, 129
  United Kingdom 128–30, 158
    immigration policy as 126
Dobson, J. 117, 122
Dogas, D. 341
Dolado, J. J. 390, 391, 398, 411
Dominican Republic, migrants to U.S. 518
Drinkwater, S. 136, 139, 155
Duce, R. 411
Dunn, T. A. 229, 233
Dustmann, C. 159, 214, 228, 229, 230, 231

earnings and wages 5, 7, 6, 11, 47–9, 481
  Canada 581, 585, 597, 598
  Denmark 77–9, 84
  discrimination 33, 77–8
  France 271, 279–81, 296, 297
  Germany 228–33, 242–50
    and years of residence 233
  and Irish emigration 105–7
  Israel 481, 487–4
  Italy 322–3, 326–7
  and marital status 156, 158
  Netherlands 183–4
  returns to education UK 155–8
  second generation immigrants 40–1
  Sweden 32–5, 41
  United Kingdom 149–160, 159
    geographical location 156, 158
  United States 481, 555–9, 565
Easterlin, R. A. 474, 487–8
Eastern Europe
  agreements with Germany 218–19
  ethnic Germans 204–5
  Jewish population 461
  migrants 2, 5, 191
    illegal 320
    to Sweden 15, 20, 37, 38
    to Denmark 76, 77
    to Germany 214–15, 235, 253

  to Greece 338, 342
  to Israel 465, 469
  to Italy 316–19, 321, 328, 329
  to New Zealand 618
  to United Kingdom 123–4
  to United States 520–1
Eban, A. 468, 471
Eckstein, Z. 477, 483
economic growth 45, 46, 373–6, 377
  Germany 205, 206, 209, 212, 224–5
  and immigration 45–6, 192, 498–9
  and internal migration 224–5
  Ireland 105–8
  Israel 460–1, 486–91, 498
education levels 31–2, 76, 77
  decline in 479–80
  Denmark 67
  Greece 348, 372–3
  Irish emigrants 94–5, 101, 103, 110
  Italy 319
  Netherlands 180–3
  and parental capital 78–85
  returns to 155–8, 481
    New Zealand 626, 627
  Sweden 41–2
  United Kingdom 133–7, 155–8, 165–6
Eisenstadt, S. N. 466
Ekberg, J. 34, 46, 47
El Salvador, migrants to U.S. 518, 519, 520
Eliav, M. 474
Elizur, D. 492, 494–5
Emke-Poulopoulou, I. 349
Empire Windrush 119
employment 28–32, 41, 44, 47–9,
    177, 184, 485
  and education 31–2
  Germany 233–6
  Israel 486
  as motive for migration 177
Entzinger, H. B. 444
Esteves, M. de C 436 439–40, 441, 445
Ethiopian migrants
  to Greece 355
  to Israel 471, 472, 473, 478–9, 484
  to Italy 318
ethnic enclaves 32, 35
  and language fluency 134–5
ethnic origin (ancestry) 520–1
ethnic minorities and migrants 113
  see also United Kingdom
ethnicity 442, 444, 446
ethnocentrism 187, 188

Europe
  asylum seekers in Germany 215
  Danish migration flows 61, 62, 64, 65, 66-7
  Greek migrants to 337
  immigration 1980s and 1990s 433-6
  labour migration (1950-74) 418-20
  legal foreign residents 436
  migrants to Canada 575-8
  migrants to Israel 468, 470
  migrants to New Zealand 606, 622
  migrants to U.S. 511, 512-13, 531, 533,
    535, 536, 539
    income and poverty 561, 562, 563
    labour force participation 539, 542,
    543-6
    occupational status 544, 545, 546
  migration policies 419-20
  phases of postwar migration 4
  recruitment 419
  see also Eastern Europe; European Union
European Union
  and Common Nordic Labour Market 26-7
  and Denmark 60-1
  and Greece 339
  measuring immigration 3
  migrants to Italy 316, 318
  migration policies 435, 447, 446, 448
  and Portugal 430-1
  and skilled migration 2
European Voluntary Workers
    programme 123-4

Fabbri, F. 159
Faini, R. 2, 198, 223, 310-13, 368
Fakiolas, R. 354, 355, 356, 358, 372, 373, 377
family reunification 5, 352, 420
  and assimilation 41
  Canada 573, 578, 579, 582, 588, 591
  Denmark 59, 60, 61, 63, 65, 69, 84
  France 264-5, 269, 274, 275, 296, 297
  Germany 202, 203, 210, 211, 212, 214,
    216, 217, 254, 352, 355, 354
  Greece 355-7, 361, 365
  Italy 318, 328
  Netherlands 173, 178, 191
  New Zealand 610
  Portugal 421
  and refugees 26
  Sweden 19, 20-1, 22, 25, 26
  United Kingdom 120, 121, 125-6, 132
  United States 514-15, 517, 527, 547-8,
    549, 552

Felderer, B. 242
female immigrants
  assimilation 482
  Canada 598
  Denmark 73, 75, 78
  early retirement 37, 38, 39
  education, Netherlands 181, 182
  France 282, 283, 287-8, 279, 280, 293
  Germany 229, 230, 235-6
  integration, labour market 28, 29, 30-4
  Irish emigrants 92-3
  Italian emigrants 313-14
  labour force participation 73, 75, 78,
    235-6, 594, 595
    France 269, 278
    Netherlands 184, 185
  Portugal 443, 437
  United States 531, 538-9, 547
    poverty 562, 563
  wages 33, 229, 230, 326-7
Ferrão, J. 431, 434, 442, 446
Ferreira, E. S. 426, 428, 432, 443
Fetzer, J. S. 295
Filer, R. K. 522
Filias, V. 370
financial responsibility for
    immigrantsm, 83, 85
Finland, migrants 15, 16, 18-19
  health of 36
  to Sweden 19, 21, 22, 24, 27, 37, 46, 47, 65, 66
Fischer, P. A. 47, 65-7
Fitzgerald, J. D. 105-6
Fournier, I. 284
France 8, 263-300
  assimilation model 264, 448
  asylum seekers 274-5, 276
  business cycle effects 296
  citizenship 266-7, 271
  colonies 4, 7, 9, 263
  demand for skills 277
  discrimination 263, 276-7, 284
  education system 285-6
    as discriminatory 286
  family reunification 274, 275
  Front National 295
  housing problems 273, 274
  illegal immigrants 263, 274, 276
    amnesties 276
  immigrant population 267-9
    age distribution 269
    by nationality 268-9
    earnings 271, 279-81, 297

education 270-2
effect of policy 296
fertility 271-2
geographical distribution 270
impact on wages and employment 290-4
integration 278-9, 298, 297, 299
limited occupations 277
political rights 271
real estate behaviour 272
residential location 285
self-employment 286-8, 290
sex composition 269
socioeconomic characteristics 270
welfare rights 271
immigration legislation 272-7
immigration policy 9, 264, 272, 294, 297, 299
insertion 278
Jewish migrants 281
jus soli principle 3, 266, 275
labour market assimilation 276-7, 278-90
les sans-papiers 263
Mahgrebians 283, 284, 285
Italian immigrants 306, 310, 312, 313
migrants to US 512
motives for immigration 296
naturalization rate 271
number of immigrants 263
Portuguese immigrants 418, 421,
    422-5, 426, 430, 432-3
public opinion 294-5
scientific visas 277
second generation migrants 264, 265, 266
sender countries 268-9
Spanish immigrants 390, 394-5, 396
unemployment 270-1
    impact of immigrants 290-4
wages 248-9, 485
see also Algerian migrants
Freidberg, R. M. 481
Freire, J. 442
Freitas, M. J. 442
Frey, M. 214
Fricke, J. 238
Friedberg, R. 242, 290, 591
Friedrich, K. 222
Fuborg, G. 164, 165

Gabaay, Y. 498
Gabanyi, A. 214
Galli, G. 258, 332, 333
Gallo, G. 326
Gang, I. 228, 245, 248-9, 253

Gani, A. 613
Garvey, D. 117
Gavosto, A. 323
Gazioglu, S. 140, 152, 154
Geary, P. T. 98
Genari, P. 258
Germany 3, 4, 8, 197-255
assimilation and integration 226-42
    earnings 228-33
    and human capital 226-30, 233,
        236, 249
asylum seekers 200, 201-2, 203, 214,
    215-16, 217-18, 238
    treaties 218
citizenship criteria 199
effect of business cycle 209
emigration 18, 215
    to France 273
    to Israel 466
    to US 512, 518, 519
employment 233-6
ethnic Germans 5, 8-9, 199, 200, 202,
    203, 204-5, 214-15, 206
    assimilation 9, 255
    earnings gap 229, 232-3, 228
    economic position 205
    labour market integration 234, 235-8
    quota system 220-1
    source countries 210, 220, 221
family reunification 352
foreign population and labour force
    (1955-73) 207
    (1974-88) 212
Greek immigrants 337-8, 340-1, 352-3
    integration policy 353
    remittances 354, 360, 366, 368, 369
growth rate 489
guest workers 208
    earnings gap 228, 229-30, 231-2
    regulation of 219, 253, 254
history of immigration 199-21, 199, 203
    aftermath of socialism 199, 202, 203,
        215-21
    consolidation 199, 201, 202-3, 211-15
    manpower recruitment 199, 200-3, 206-11
    war adjustment 199, 200, 201, 204-6
immigration
    from GDR 199, 225, 227, 232-3, 234-8
    motives for 203
    and native employment 247, 250-4, 253
    numbers (1954-2000) 204
    wage effects 592, 595

Germany (*cont.*)
  internal migration 221-5
    constraining factors 223-4
    destination areas 222
    and unemployment 223-5
  Italian immigrants 306, 310, 312, 313
  job mobility 237-8
  jus sanguinis principle 3, 199
  labour market 197-8, 242-3
    mis-match 197
  language proficiency 354
  migration agreements 218-19, 352, 354
  migration policy 4-5, 197, 363
  pensions 241
  Portuguese immigrants 418, 421,
    430, 431
  recruitment 4, 206-11
  return migration 213-14, 216, 217
  seasonal workers 218-220
  self-employment 234-5, 255
  Spanish immigrants 390, 394-5, 396
  Swedish immigrants 15
  unemployment 197, 208-9, 211-12,
    217, 233-6
    by nationality 213
    regional 252
  wages 242-50, 485
  welfare contributions 238-42
    asylum seekers 238, 239, 240
    ethnic Germans 238, 239, 240
    GDR migrants 237
    guest workers 238, 241
    positive impact 240-1
ghettos, formation of 83, 85
Gieseck, A. 240
Gil, L. 401
Giusti, F. 308
Glaude, M. 269-70, 283
Glazer, N. 521
globalization 1, 13, 263, 435, 446-7, 448
Globerman, S. 583, 586
Glytsos, N. P. 337-88
Godinho, V. M. 417, 426
Góis, P. 415-57
Goldberg, I. 493
Golini, A. 305, 308, 314
Gonçalves, A. 422
Gordon, M. 423
Gorjão-Henriques, M. 443
Gould, J. D. 312
Goux, D. 277
Graham, D. H. 309

Granier, R. 280
Graversen, B. K. 83
Great Britain *see* United Kingdom
Greece 10, 337-83
  agreement with Germany 206, 355, 357
  agricultural sector 369, 370, 371, 373-4
  education 348, 372-3
  emigration 18, 231, 337-42
    age and sex 346-7
    causal factors 359-66
    destinations 337, 363
    determinants of 363, 364
    effects of 352-3
    and employment 364
    and labour market adjustment 369-73
    occupation and skills 348
    policies 353-6
    and policies of host country 351-3
    regional contributions 342-5
    and repatriation 339-42
    to Germany 213, 337-8, 340-2, 346-8, 363
    to Sweden 22, 24, 34, 37, 46
    to United States 513
  ethnic Greeks 341, 355, 356, 359
  factor substitution 373-5
  family reunification 346, 351-3, 356,
    358, 361, 365
  growth rate 489
  history of migration 337-48
  illegal immigrants 338, 342, 343, 344, 346
    356-7, 363, 372
    and agriculture 371
    legalization 358-9
    policy 379
  immigration 338, 342, 434
    age and sex 346
    determinants 364, 365
    integration 355
    policies 338-9, 355-9, 379
    positive trade effects 371, 377, 378
    role of municipalities 358-9
    settlement areas 344-6
  income effects 373-6
  legalization policies 356-9
  legislation 338, 355-6
  political refugees 342
  remittances 348-50, 354, 374-6
    determinants of 366-8
  repatriation 337, 338, 382
  return migration 337, 338, 340-2, 343,
    353, 365-6, 371
    and integration 355-6

reasons for 365-6
regional basis 345
skill acquisition 347-8, 374, 376, 377
urban regions 370-1
self employment 373
total net migration (1960-99) 340
unemployment 371, 373
urbanization and migration 370-1, 376
vocational skills 372
Greeley, A. M. 514, 521
Green, A. G. 576, 573, 575
Green Cards, Greece 356-9
Green, D. A. 480
Greenwood, M. J. 160, 221, 228, 242, 400, 403
Grillo, F. 326
Groenendijk, K. 191
Gross, D. M. 292
Grossman, J. B. 243, 591
Grubel, H. G. 576
Guatemalan migrants to US 518, 519
guest workers 4, 5, 351, 352
    Denmark 59, 60, 62, 63, 64, 68, 69, 72, 84
    Germany 202, 206, 208, 211, 219
        earnings gap 228-9, 232
Guibentif, P. 443
Guinea-Bissau 438, 441

Hagan, J. M. 519
Haisken-DeNew, J. P. 244, 245, 246
Haiti, migrants to U.S. 516
Halevi, N. 474
Halpin, B. 104
Hampsink, R. 191
Hannan 99-100
Hargreaves, A. G. 298
Harmsen, H. 200
Hartog, J. 179, 184
Hatton, T. 105, 113-166, 308, 311-12,
    392, 393
Hatzius, J. 245, 247, 251
Haus, L. 276
Hawkins, F. 575, 576
health of immigrants 34-8, 49, 53, 475
heart disease among immigrants 36
Heijke, J. A. M. 177-8, 179
Héran, F. 271-2, 286, 290
Hercowitz, Z. 485, 486
Hiebert, D. 595, 596
Hippmann, H. 222
Hirschman, C. O. 517
Hjarnø, J. 77
Hollifield, J. F. 296

Hong Kong, migrants to
    New Zealand 607, 608
Honohan, P. 106
Hornsby-Smith, M. P. 103-4
housing 24, 83-85, 273, 274
    Israel 470, 471, 485, 492, 493
Howard, C. 126
Hughes, G. 400
Hughes, J. G. 103
Hükum, P. 287
human capital
    Canada 576, 578, 583, 590, 591, 595, 596,
        597, 598
    country-specific 35, 39, 227, 228, 229
    and discrimination 41-5, 53
        Sweden 39, 41-5, 54
    and earnings in Germany 228-30, 233
    effect on integration 12
    and European Union 1, 2
    Irish 1990s inflow 109
    Israel 466, 473, 476, 478, 480, 484, 496
    Netherlands 184, 193
    and point system 610
    Portuguese returnees 421-2, 428
    returns to 483
    theory 188, 226, 279, 310, 359-60
    transferability 5
    United Kingdom 139, 148, 158, 159, 160
    and wage effects 249
humanitarian immigration 5, 26
Hummelgaard, H. 73, 75, 76, 77, 83
Hunt, J. 242, 250, 253-4, 290, 291, 591
Hurst, M. E. 140, 144, 148
Husted, L. 77-8

illegal immigration 1, 2, 9, 434-5, 447
    France 274, 276, 293, 297
    from Portugal 426, 432
    Germany 203, 218
    Greece 338, 342, 343, 346, 356, 358, 371, 372
        legalization 358-9
    Irish to U.S. 101, 102
    Israel 501
    Italy 319-21, 328, 329
    and legalization 358-9
    Portugal 440, 442
    Spain 410
    United States 514, 515-17, 566, 567
immigration 2-6
    balancing ageing 192
    as beneficial 3
    and business cycle 162

immigration (*cont.*)
  effect on growth 45-6
  effects on earnings and wages 47-9
  and employment 47-9, 180
  employment as motive 177
  and geographical distance 177-8
  immigrant defined 266, 391, 566
  impact on consumption 292
  impact of 330
  see also earnings and wages; female
    immigrants *and individual countries*
Immigration Act 1990 (US) 516
Immigration Acts (UK) 125, 126
Immigration and Asylum Act 1996 (UK) 126
Immigration and Nationality Acts (U.S.) 514
Immigration Reform and Control Act 1986
India, migrants 4
  to Greece 357
  to New Zealand 604, 608
  to Portugal 438, 441
  to UK 123, 133, 139, 140, 149
    educational level 134, 135, 136
    employment 137, 138, 143, 147, 148
    numbers 118, 119, 121, 132
    wages 157
  to United States 518, 520
Indonesian migrants to Netherlands 4, 173,
    177, 178
Iran, migrants
  asylum seekers 217
  to Denmark 60, 61, 63
  to Greece 355
  to Sweden 31-2
Iraqi migrants 60, 61, 63, 355
Ireland 6-8
  1990s inflow 108-9, 110
    educational level 108, 110
    and GNP 107, 109
    labour market effects 108-9, 110
  age of migrants 93-4, 95
  components of population change 90-1
  determinants of migration 96-102, 109
    education 100, 101, 102
    labour markets 96-8, 101
    socioeconomic status 101
    unemployment 97, 98-9
  education of migrants 94-5
  effects of emigration 105-7
    growth 105-7
    wages 105-6, 107, 110
  emigration
    assimilation of 103-4

  by age 93
  by sex 92-3, 95
  destinations 91-2, 95
  motives for 101, 102
  to New Zealand 603, 604, 606
  to U.S. 512
  wage effects 161
  history of migration 89, 90-5, 110
  migrants in UK 6-7, 135, 158
    education 149
    occupational distribution 152
    unemployment 137, 140, 145
  migration flows 114-15, 117
  occupation of migrants 94-5
  return migration 7, 93, 101
  unemployment and migration 97, 98-9
Israel 10-11, 459-501
  absorption policies 495-8
  agricultural settlements 465, 466, 467, 469,
    474, 496
    Arab population 465, 472
  assimilation 11, 480-91
    model 497
  direct absorption 472-3, 495
  economic growth 460-1, 486-91, 498
  employment impacts 486
  growth rate 489
  housing 470, 471, 485, 492, 493
  human capital 471, 473, 476, 478, 484
  immigration
    (1882-1948) 465-7
    (1948-51) 467-9
    (1952-66) 469-70
    (1967-88) 470-2
    (1989-98) 472-3
    age 473
    educational level 473-80
    financial aid 468
    ideological 459
    living conditions 475-6
    numbers 459
    occupational distribution 476-7
    sender countries 465-6, 468, 470
    settlement areas 473
    settlement process 468-9
    Soviet 459
    statistics 462-5, 468, 469-70
  Jewish-Arab conflict 461, 467-8
  labour market impacts 481-6
  Law of Return 460
  occupational convergence 482-4
  Operation Moses 471, 478

Operation Solomon 459, 472
out migration 470, 471
policies 460, 472-3
population composition 461
population growth 460, 463-5, 469-70,
    471-2, 490
return migration 470, 491-5
    motives 491-2
unemployment 486, 496, 497
wage convergence 481, 483-4
and World Jewry 461-8
Italy 9, 303-31
emigration 18, 304-16
    characteristics of migrants 307
    destinations 305
    economic effect 315
    motivation 310-13
    rate (1876-1985) 304
    regional contribution 305
    remittances 314-15
    restrictions 309-10
    return migration 305, 307, 315
    social and demographic effects 313-16
    to Canada 576
    to France 271, 272, 274, 281
        return migration 289-90
    to Germany 211, 213, 231
    to United States 518, 520
    wage factors 310-13
employment effects 323-8
family reunification 318, 328
history of migration 303
illegal immigrants 319-21, 328, 329
immigration 316-30, 434
    age and households 318
    determinants of 321-2
    education 319
    effect on economy 322-8
    gender composition 318
    occupational characteristics 319
    sender countries 303, 316-17
    territorial distribution 316, 318
integration evidence 326-8
internal migration 303
labour market effects 322-8
legislation 321
policy 308-10, 328-30
self-employment 318, 319
trade unions 309, 323
treaty with Germany 206, 207, 208
unemployment 303, 322, 324-6, 327-8
and wages 322-3, 326-7

welfare payments 327
Izquierdo, A. 410

Jamaican migrants 119, 123, 124, 518
Japan
    growth rate 488-9, 490
    migrants to US 513, 518
Jasso, G. 492, 515
Jayet, H. 270, 293-4
Jensen, L. 525
Jensen, T. 75, 77
Jewish
    Agency 467, 468
    Arab conflict 461, 467-8
    migrants in Canada 461, 595, 596
    population worldwide 461
Jimeno, J. 401, 411
Jones, C. 129, 485
Jones, T. 132, 137, 153
jus sanguinis principle 3, 199, 445
jus soli principle 3, 266, 275, 445
Justino, D. 443

Kanetakis, 343, 344
Karr, W. 234
Karras, G. 508
Kassimati, K. 356
Katseli, L. T. 337-88
Katz, Y. 474
Kay, D. 127
Kee, P. 184
Keely, C. B. 514, 515
Keenan, J. G. 97, 99
Kenyan migrants 125, 128, 141, 142,
    145, 146, 148
King, R. 355, 356
Klinov-Malul, R. 474
Koller, B. 235, 236
Korean migrants to U.S. 518
Kousis, M. 373
Krämer, K. 222
Kugler, A. 291, 299
Kurdistan, migrants 5, 122, 217, 320, 322
Kuznets, S. 488-9, 498

labour force participation
    Canada 581-4
    Denmark 71-2, 74-80
    and discrimination 75-7
    and language skills 76
    United Kingdom 138-48
    United States 538-41

labour market 3, 5–6, 7–13
  Canadian immigrants' experience 598
  effects 8, 9–10, 16
    and economic screening of
      immigrants 574
    integration 13, 28–45, 52, 54, 70–80
    mis match 52, 187, 197
    performance 619–620
      determinants of 226–7
      and human capital 41–5
      and second generation immigrants 44
labour migration period 4
labour substitution model 583–584
LaLonde, R. 481, 591
Lamdani, R. 494
language proficiency 76, 84, 499–500, 534
  Canada 580
  France 277, 282
  Germany 219, 220–1, 231, 236
  Israel 478, 482, 483, 493, 494, 500
  and labour market performance 43, 44,
    53, 133–5, 139
  Netherlands 188, 189, 189–90, 191, 193
  New Zealand 611, 621
  and return migration 493, 494
  Sweden 43
  teaching 25, 69, 70, 354, 526–7,
  United Kingdom 133–6, 154, 158, 159
  United States 530, 533–537
Laryea, S. A. 573–600
Latin America 62, 317, 318
  Italian immigrants 306
  migrants to Sweden 20, 38, 51
  migrants to United States 511–12, 513,
    514, 531, 535, 539
    labour force participation 539, 542–3,
      544–6
      occupational status 544, 545, 546
  Spanish immigrants 410–11
Lattimore, R. 619
Layton-Henry, Z. 126, 127, 128, 129
Le Grand, C. 34, 45
Le Pen, Jean-Marie 275
Le Saout, D. 287
Leandro, M. E. 427, 432
Lebanese migrants 60, 61, 63, 355
Lebok, U. 242
Lee, E. S. 495
Leeds, E. 427, 428
legislation 354, 355
  Canada 577, 580, 582, 586, 587
  France 264, 272–7

Germany 205, 218
Greece 338, 355–6
Italy 308–310, 321, 328–30
  on labour market integration 70
New Zealand 609, 611–13
Portugal 445
Spain 393
United Kingdom 122–6, 128–30
  race relations 128–30
United States 514, 515–16, 528, 529
Leite, C. 422
Leslie, D. 136–39, 152–55, 159
Lianos, T. P. 364, 365
  illegal immigrants 338, 342, 357,
    363–4, 371, 374
Licht, G. 229, 230, 231
Lieberson, S. 513, 521
Lifschitz, C. 479
Linardos-Rylmon, P. 371
Lifshitz, G. 467, 471, 473, 479
Lucas, R. E. B. 362
Lundborg, P. 66
Lundh, C. 15–58
Luvumba, F. M. 443
Lynch, J. P. 294

Ma Mung, E. 287
Maani, S. 613
McCormick, B. 152, 223, 400
McDowell, J. M. 160, 228, 242
Machado, F. L. 441, 442, 443–4, 446
Mackensen, R. M. 222
McLean, E. 373
McMaster, I. 162
McNabb, R. 152
Maki, D. 576
Malheiros, J. 431, 434, 441, 442, 443
Manfrass, K. 353
Marciano, J. P. 280
Markova, E. 358, 363, 365, 377
Maroulis, D. 375
Marques, J. C. L. 430, 433
Marques, M. M. 443
Marr, W. 578, 576, 577, 583
Massey, D. S. 120, 231, 517
Mathiessen, P. C. 79
Maurin, E. 277
Melas, G. K. 369
Melchior, M. 75–6
Menezes, M. 441, 443
Merens, J. G. F. 188
Merrick, T. W. 309

Metcalf, H. 137
Metzer, J. 487
Mexican migrants to U.S. 511–12, 513, 514,
    517–19, 536
  educational level 531–3, 537, 564
  fertility 554–5, 556, 563
  household structure 548, 549
  income 560, 561, 562, 563
  labour force participation 539–41
  language fluency 533, 535
  occupational status 544, 545, 546
migration
  determinants of 2, 364
  and development 375–6
  and ethnic minorities 113
  measurements of 3
  motives 5, 396
  phases of postwar 4
  typology of systems 119
  virtual 1
  see also illegal immigration; immigration;
    unskilled migrants
migratory nets 429, 431, 432, 433, 446
Miles, R. 127
Miller, P. W. 296, 482, 532
miscegenation 127
Modood, T. 134–5, 137
Mogensen, G. V. 79
Moldavian migrants 10, 357
Moluccans 173, 177
Moreno, J. L. 315
Morocco
  migrants in France 269, 271, 274, 281, 283
    return migration 289
  migrants to Italy 317, 318, 320, 321,
    326–7, 329
  migrants to Netherlands 173, 177–8, 189,
    190, 191
    earnings 183–4
    education 181–3
    labour market participation 184, 185, 186
  migrants to Portugal 438
  treaty with Germany 206
Morrison, P. A. 529
mortality of immigrants 36
motives for migration 22, 613
  four factors 362
  France 296
  Greece 359–66
Moussourou, L. M. 376
Mühleisen, M. 234, 237, 251, 252
Münz, R. 203, 217, 221, 444

Murphy, P. D. 139, 154
Murteira, M. 426

Natale, M. 328
National Congress of Emigration and
    Immigration 309
National Front parties 128, 129, 295
Nationality Act 1948 (UK) 123, 126, 129
Nationality Act 1981 (UK) 126, 129
neighbourhood characteristics 78–9, 85
Neri, F. 325
Netherlands 5, 8, 9, 173–96
  admission criteria 191
  agreement with New Zealand 603, 610
  asylum seekers 191
  decolonization 4, 8, 177, 178, 179, 183
  economic effects of immigration 192
  education 180–3
  emigrants to New Zealand 604, 606, 610
  family reunification 173, 178, 191
  geographical mobility 189
  integration policy 192–3
  internal migration 176
  job mobility 189–90
  labour market 179–90
    participation 184–9, 192, 194
    policy 174, 180, 186, 188, 194
    position of immigrants 173–4, 177
  number of immigrants 173
  occupational positions 174
  periods of immigration 173
  policy 190–3
  population growth 174–6
  recruitment (1964–75) 177, 179
  recruitment policy 4
  second generation immigrants 182
  unemployment 174, 179–80, 184–9, 194
    demand factors 186–7
    explanations 186–9
    supply factors 186, 188
  wage effects 248
networks 345, 361, 362, 363, 373, 377, 378,
    429, 446
  Portugal 431, 432, 433–4
Neuman, S. 459–506
New Commonwealth immigration see
    United Kingdom
New Zealand 600–9
  agreement with Netherlands 603
  assisted passages 602, 603, 605
  British immigrants 114, 118
  Business Investments criterion 607, 610, 611

New Zealand (*Cont.*)
  Danish immigrants 61
  determinants of migration 613
  emigration 609
  Family category 611
  General Skills category 611
  history of immigration 601-9
  immigrants
    age 617
    assimilation evidence 624-8
    education levels 616, 627
    effect on natives 628
    employment 619-20
    income 620-2, 623-8
    labour market outcomes 613-28
    labour market status 619-20
    language proficiency 618
    parental and marital status 617
    region of origin differences 622-4
    socioeconomic characteristics 614
    welfare benefits 621
  immigration
    (1950s and 1960s) 603-4
    (1970s and 1980s) 604-7
    (1990s) 607-8
    annual target 607, 610
    occupational 609
  legislation 610, 612-13
  point system 610, 611-13
    criteria 612-13
    and human capital 611
  policy 12, 13
    current residence 612-16, 609-13
    impact of current 608-9, 611-12
  population composition 606-7
  preferential arrangements 610
  refugees 613
  restrictions on immigration 605
  skill criterion 607
  unemployment 614, 619, 622, 628
Newbold, K. B. 591
Nickell, S. J. 164, 180
Nielsen, H. S. 77-80, 81, 83
Niesing, W. 187, 188, 189
Noam, G. 479
North Africa, Spanish migrants to 392
North America 436
  Danish migrants 61, 71, 72
  migrants in Sweden 38, 52
  migrants to New Zealand 606, 614, 622
  see also Canada; United States
Norway 15, 27

  employment integration 79, 81
  migrants to Denmark 71, 72
  migrants to Sweden 21, 23, 27, 66
Nunes, A. S. 426

Oaxaca, R. 139, 153
O'Connell, P. J. 109
Ofer, G. 476, 477, 482
O'Gráda, C. 90, 94, 95, 97-100
Ohliger, R. 203
Ohlsson, R. 17, 28, 43, 47
oil price shock effects 4, 419
  Denmark 59, 63, 64, 84
  Germany 206, 211, 214, 222, 224
  Greece 349, 361
  New Zealand 605
  Portugal 419, 422
Olano, A. 405
Operation Moses 471, 478
Operation Solomon 459, 472
O'Rourke, K. 89, 105, 106, 161
Orrje, H. 82
Ottosen, M. H. 75, 76

Pacelli, L. 326
Pacheco, N. 443
Pacific Islands, migrants to New Zealand 604, 605, 608, 618, 619
  income 622
  incomes 613-15
  percentage 606
Paes, I. S. 443
Pakistani migrants 10
  to Denmark 61, 63, 65, 68, 71, 72, 78
  to Greece 338, 351
  to Portugal 438
  to United Kingdom 123, 134, 135, 137, 140, 141, 149
    numbers 118, 119, 132
    unemployment 136, 138, 139, 143, 145, 147, 148
    wages 157, 158, 159
Palestine, Jewish immigration 459
Papademetriou, D. G. 346, 372, 375, 377
Papanikos, G. 352
parental capital 78, 85
Pasqua, Charles 275
Patiniotis, N. 353
Pedersen, P. J. 59-87
Peixoto, J. 430, 442
Pelagidis, T. 378
Pendakur, K. 596, 597, 598, 600
Pendakur, R. 596, 597, 598, 600

Percy, M. 576, 577, 578, 583
Pereira, A. M. 415–57
Pereira, M. M. 443
Pereira, P. T. 231, 415–57
Perista, H. 443
Peru, migrants to Italy 318, 329
Petrinioti, X. 356
Petropoulos, N. 341, 343, 345, 348, 363, 373
Phillipines, migrants
   to Canada 595, 596
   to Greece 338, 363
   to Italy 316–18, 320, 321, 329
   to New Zealand 608
   to United States 513, 518, 519
Pimenta, M. 442
Pintado, X. 426
Pinto da Cunha, C. 441
Piore, M. J. 419
Pires, R. P. 434, 439
Pischke, J.-S. 229, 231, 245, 246, 247, 251–2
Pissarides, C. 162, 400
Poinard, M. 421, 423
point system 610–15
   Canada 522, 576–7
   New Zealand 610–15
Poland, migration
   to Denmark 60, 62
   to France 271
   to Germany 210, 214, 218, 219, 220
   to Greece 357
   to Israel 465
   to Italy 318, 320, 326
   to Sweden 20, 34
   to United States 513, 518, 520
policy, migration 2, 3, 12, 350–1, 447–8
   Denmark 69–70
   Europe 418–20
   focus on economic channels 3
   France 264
   future requirements 330, 331, 379–80, 565
   Germany 197, 363
   Greece 338–9, 353–60, 379
   Italy 308–10, 328–30
   Netherlands 190–3
   Sweden 16–18, 20, 22, 23–6, 35
   United Kingdom 119–30, 166
Polish Resettlement Act 1947 123
political parties, anti-immigration 128, 129, 295
political tensions 484, 525
   Denmark 7, 70, 85
   France 264, 299
Pollard, K. M. 526

Poot, J. 609, 613, 614, 617, 628
Portes, A. 517, 521
Portugal 9, 10, 415–48
   data limitations 416, 430, 439–41
   decolonization 439, 444, 445
   discrimination 446
   emigration 417–34
      (1950–74) 418–25
      (1980s and 1990s) 429–31
      composition of migrants 420–1, 422
      construction workers 430
      destinations 418, 421
      illegal 426, 432
      impact on economy 427
      motives 426
      numbers 420, 421
      social framework 417
      to France 268, 269, 271, 273, 274, 280, 281, 282
      return migration 289
      to Germany 213, 231–2
   ethnicity 444
   and European Union 430–1
   family reunification 421
   illegal immigrants 440, 442
   immigration 423–4, 434
      (1980s and 1990s) 436–43
      assimilation 423
      endogamy 423
      high visibility of 416
      numbers 436–7
      occupations 424–5
      socioeconomic profiles 436–8
      jus sanguinis 445
   Luso-Africans 443–4, 446
   migration statistics 415
   PALOPs 416, 438, 440, 444–39, 446
   remittances 415–25
   return migration 416, 421–2, 439
      human capital 32, 421–2
   second generation immigrants 443
   self employment 447
   treaty with Germany 206
   unemployment 426
Potsdam conference 204
poverty in United States 561–5
Powell, Enoch 128
Psacharopoulos, G. 152
public sector revenues and welfare 60, 79–82, 85
Pudney, S. 155
Puerto Rico 489, 492
Puig, J.-P. 291

Rabi, C. 470, 475, 476
race relations policy in UK 127-30
racial discrimination 127-30, 187, 298, 513
Raffelhüschen, B. 223
Ramos,F. A. 492
refugees 121-2, 276, 612
    in Denmark 60, 63, 64, 65, 69-78, 81-4
    in Greece 341, 355
    in Sweden 15, 16, 20, 21-3, 25, 26, 35, 37,
        41, 51, 53
    in United States 515, 516, 519
Reichling, G. 205
Reilly, B. 101, 102, 104
remittances 375
    determinants of 366-9
    global 374
    Greece 348-50, 354, 366-8
        and trade balance 349-51
    Italy 314-15
    leakage to imports 376
    motives for
    Portugal 415-16
    Spain 395
restrained migration period 4-5
return migration 1, 66, 90, 101, 360
    Denmark 68
    discouraging 494-5
    France 274, 288, 289
    Germany 202, 216, 230, 231
    Greece 338, 340-2, 343, 353, 365-6, 371
        skill acquisition 347-8
    Ireland 7, 89-91, 94-96, 99, 101-10
    Israel 491-5
    Italy 307, 315
    Netherlands 177, 179, 192
    Portugal 416, 421-2, 438
    Spain 392, 393, 395
    Sweden 17, 20-2, 34
    United Kingdom 159
Ribeiro, F. G. Cassola 428
Ribeiro, M. 432
Richard, J.-L. 285
Rindfuss, R. R. 553
Ringe, M. J. 164
Riphahn, R. 228, 240
Rivera-Batiz, F. L. 245, 248-9, 253
Rocha, E. 427
Rocha, Nuno 425
Rocha-Trindade, M. B. 426, 427, 428, 431
Rodenas, C. 395, 397, 407
Rodriguez, N. P. 519
Røed, M. 65, 67

Romanian migrants 10
    to Germany 210, 214
    to Greece 357, 358
    to Italy 316, 318, 320, 321, 329
    to Portugal 438
Ronge, V. 220
Rosenzweig, M. R. 492, 515
Rosholm, M. 77, 79
Rossi, F. 258, 332
Rossi, S. 334
Rouault, D. 289
Roy, A. S. 591
Rumbaut, R. 521
Russell, S. S. 361
Ryder, N. B. 521

Saint-Maurice, A. 434, 441, 444
Salt, J. 121, 126, 447
Sanchez Alonso, B. 391, 392, 393
Santillana, I. 396
Sapir, A. 363, 364
Sarris, A. 363, 365, 372
Sava, N. 352, 353
Scandinavian migrants to U.S. 512
Schiff, M. 361
Schmähl, W. 239, 241
Schmidt, C. M. 199, 200, 205, 226, 227, 234
    earnings 228-9, 230, 231, 232-3
    labour market effects 242, 243, 249
    occupations 237
Schröder, L. 67
Schulz, E. 235-6
Schultz, T. W. 352
Schultz-Nielsen, M. L. 79, 80, 81
scientific visas 277
Scott, A. D. 576
Scott, K. 15-58
second generation immigrants 44, 75, 76,
        121, 131, 182
    Denmark 78, 84, 85
    France 264, 265, 266
    Irish in Britain 103-4, 110
    Sweden 39-41
Segal, E. 479
Seifert, W. 229, 233, 236
Seiring, K. 235-6
self-employment
    France 286-8, 290
    Germany 234-5, 255
    Greece 373
    Italy 318, 319
    Portugal 447

Sweden 16, 32, 49, 54
  United Kingdom 136, 137
  United States 537, 542, 544, 545,
    556, 560
Senegal, migrants 10, 329
Serrão, J. 417, 426
settlement patterns 133
Seward, S. B. 594
Sexton, J. J. 90
Shachmurove, Y. 234
Shields, M. A. 135, 140, 141, 149, 153,
  154, 155, 159
Shroff, G. 608
sickness benefits 35, 37, 38-9
Sicron, M. 466
Silberman, R. 283, 284
Silva, M. 423, 428, 432
Simon, J. l. 485-6
Simon, R. J. 294
Six Day War 470, 471
Sjaastad, L. A. 359
Skellington, R. 122
skilled labour migration 1, 6, 13, 372, 613
  Denmark 68
Smith, A. D. 485
Smith, N. 70
Soares, F. 427
socialism, dissolution of 4
Somalian migrants 60, 64, 355
Sori, E. 307, 313-14
South Africa 114, 118, 148, 470
South America 436
  Spanish migrants to 389, 392-4
South Korean migrants 608
Soviet Union, migration
  Jewish 492
  to Israel 471-3, 476-9, 482-3, 485
  to U.S. 483, 513, 516, 518, 519, 521
Spain 9, 10, 389-414
  agriculture 389, 393, 394
  Civil War 389, 394
  data sources 391-2
  emigration
    causal factors 392-3, 396
    destinations 392, 394-6
    regional differences 393-4, 395
    to France 271, 273, 274, 281, 289
    to Germany 213, 231
    to Portugal 436
    to South America 389, 392-4
    and wage gap 393
  growth rate 489

  history of migration 389-96
  illegal immigrants 410
  immigration 390-1, 410-12, 434
    countries of origin 411
    labour market effects 411-12
    policy 10, 411
    Portuguese 433
  internal migration 390
    (1960-82) 396-9
    (1983-99) 399-410
    causal factors 396-8
    characteristics of migrants 400-3
    and education 401-3
    and employment 390
    house prices 401, 402, 403, 405, 406,
      407, 409
    rural to urban 404
    and service sector 407, 408
    wages and employment 396-9,
      402-3, 407
  legislation 393
  remittances and trade balance 395
  return migration 289, 392, 393, 395
  treaty with Germany 206
  unemployment 390, 398-9, 400-1, 402-4
Spencer, I. R. G. 123, 125, 127, 128
Sri Lanka
  asylum seekers 122
  migrants to Denmark 60
  migrants to Germany 215
  migrants to Italy 329
  migrants to UK 118, 143, 147, 148
Stahl, C. W. 375
Stahl, H.-M. 421, 426, 432
Stark, O. 360, 362
Stein, J. 447
Steiner, V. 229, 230, 231
Straubhaar, T. 47, 65-7, 313
Strozza, S. 320, 326, 328
Sudan, migrants 355
suicide rates of immigrants 37
Sullivan, T. A. 507-67
Surinam, migrants to Netherlands 173, 178,
    179, 189, 190, 191, 192
  earnings 183, 184
  education 181, 182, 183
  labour market participation 184, 185, 186
Sutherland, H. 101
Swamy, G. 368
Sweden 4-7, 15-54
  composition of immigrants 16
  country-specific human capital 35, 39, 41-5

Sweden (cont.)
  Danish migration to 63, 64, 65, 68
  early retirement 25, 37–8, 52
  earnings and wages 32–5, 41, 47–9
  economic growth 45–6
  educational level of immigrants 40,
    42, 52
  effect of business cycle 22, 30
  effects on labour market 16
  emigration 15, 63, 64
  employment 47–9, 51, 52
  family reunification 19, 20–1, 22,
    25, 26
  health of immigrants 36–7
  history of immigration 15–16, 51
  housing market 24
  immigrant population 15, 17
  immigration policy 35, 51
    restrictive 16, 24–6, 51
  integration of migrants 7, 25, 79
  labour immigration 16, 18–19, 23–5,
    29, 46, 49, 50
  labour market integration 28–45, 52
    employment rates 28–9, 30–3
    performance 20, 41, 43, 44
    unemployment 29–32, 41
  migration exchange 17, 19
  migration history 17–22
  migration policy 16, 18, 20, 23–6
    liberalization 23–4
    restrictive 24–6
  motives for immigration 22
  multicultural model 448
  occupational mobility 34
  phases of immigration 18, 19–20
  recruitment 4, 23
  refugees to 19–20, 25
  return migration 19–22, 34
  second generation immigrants 39–41
    earnings 40–1
    education 40
    employment rates 40
  self-employment 32, 49
  sender countries 18, 22, 23
  social mobility 34
  social welfare 31
  trade unions 24, 25, 48, 54
  unemployment 15, 16, 19, 28–32, 41,
    47–9, 52, 54
  work permits 23–4
Sweet, J. R. 553
Swicegood, G. 553

Switzerland 4, 5, 8, 306, 433
  Spanish immigrants 390, 394–5
Szulkin, R. 34

Taiwan 518, 607, 608
Tapinos, G. 273
Tavares, L. 423
Thatcher, Margaret 129
Thave, S. 289
Thierry, X. 289
Thurow, L. C. 187
Tienda, M. 548
Tinguy, A, de 342
Topel, R. 481, 591
Torrecilha, R. 527
Tournakis, I. 349
Trace, F. 108
trade unions
  France 275–6
  Italy 309, 323
  Netherlands 180
  Sweden 16, 24, 25, 48, 54
translation services 527
Treas, J. 527
Tremblay, M. 594
Tribalat, M. 281–2, 423, 424
Trigal, L. 433
Tsamourgelis, Y. 371
tuberculosis among immigrants 36
Tunali, I. 154, 492
Tunisia 274, 283, 329
  treaty with Germany 206
Turkey, emigration 5, 18
  asylum seekers 122, 217
  to Denmark 59, 61, 62, 64, 65, 68, 71,
    72, 76, 77, 84
  to France 268, 269, 270, 271, 273, 286
  to Germany 213, 214, 231
  to Greece 355
  to Netherlands 173, 177–8, 189,
    190, 191
    earnings 183, 184
    education 181, 182, 183
    labour market participation 184–6
  to Sweden 22, 37
  to United Kingdom 140, 154
  treaty with Germany 206

Übersiedler see under Germany, from GDR
Ugandan Asian refugees 122, 125
Ukrainian migrants to Greece 357
Ulrich, R. 217, 221, 239, 241

unemployment 1, 6
  Denmark 69, 71–80, 84
  and educational level 76, 77
  female 75, 78
  France 270–1
    impact of immigrants 291–4
  Germany 197, 208–9, 211–12, 213, 217,
    233–6, 247, 250–4
  and internal migration 223–5
  Greece 371, 373, 376
  and Irish migration 97, 98–9, 105–7, 110
  Israel 486, 497
  Italy 303, 322, 324–6, 327–8
  Netherlands 179–80, 184–9
  New Zealand 614, 619
  second generation immigrants 70, 74, 75, 84
  Spain 390, 398–9, 400–1, 402–4
  Sweden 15, 16, 47–9
  and time of residence 74, 165
  United Kingdom 136, 139–40, 141–8, 165
    and human capital 139
  United States 540–1
  welfare incentives 79–80
Unger, K. 343, 365, 371–3
United Kingdom
  assimilation 8
  asylum seekers 121–2, 126
  Black British 132
  business cycle effects 162
  census data 130–3
  citizens and patrials 125
  colonial immigration 4, 8, 123
  data sources 115–16
  determinants of immigration 120–1
  discrimination 158
  earnings and wages 152–8, 159
  economic incentives and policy 119–22
  education 133–7, 155–8, 166
  emigration
    destinations 114, 117–18
    to Canada 595, 596
    to Denmark 71, 72
    to New Zealand 602–8, 623
    to United States 512, 518
  employee characteristics 149, 150–2
  ethnic minorities 130, 131–3
    education 150
    employment rates 142–3
    labour market status 136, 137–8
    language fluency 139
    unemployment 136, 139–40, 141–8
  and EU 121

family reunification 120, 121, 125–6,
    132
  growth rate 490
  health of immigrants 36–7
  historical pattern 114–15
  immigration policy 8, 119, 120, 122–30,
    166, 351
    as discrimination 126
    evolution of 122–7
    restrictive 5, 124–5
  Irish immigrants 6–7, 92, 95
    assimilation 102–4
    second generation 103–4
    socioeconomic level 103, 104
  Jewish population 461
  language fluency 133–6, 154, 158, 159
  migration flows 1964–98 116
  net migration 116–17, 160–1, 162
    by country 118
  New Commonwealth immigrants 4, 118–19,
    120, 122, 123, 163
    restriction of 124–5
  numbers and distribution of
    immigrants 130–3, 141
  occupational distribution 150–1, 152,
    159, 164
  postwar migration 115–19
  race-relations 8, 127–30
  regional demand for labour 162–3
  second generation immigrants 131
  settlement patterns 133, 163
  skill levels 133–6
  source regions 141
  unemployment 165
    by region 145–6
  unskilled immigrants 163–4, 165
  voucher system 124, 125
  wages 149–58, 248, 249
United States 10, 11, 12, 507–67
  census data 507–9, 563–4
    limitations of 508
  children and education 526–7
  convergence 11
  diversity of immigrants 11, 563
  earnings 228, 296, 481
  education system 515
  employer responsibilities 515
  family reunification 514–15, 517
  future policy requirements 565
  future refugees 565
  growth rate 490
  health of immigrants 36–7

United States (*cont.*)
  historical trends 509-12
    illegal immigrants 508-9, 514,
      515-17, 566, 567
    amnesty 509
    numbers 517, 519
  immigrants 203
    age 518, 525-6
    British 114, 115, 117, 118, 119
    by state 523, 524, 525
    consequences of 563-5
    demographic characteristics 516,
      563, 564
    earnings 556-9
    educational attainment 530-3
    employment status 537-41
    fertility 551-6, 564
    geographical location 521-3, 524, 564
    Greek 337, 351, 352, 365
    household income 560-1, 564
    household structure 547-2, 560
    Irish 91-2, 95, 96, 101, 102, 104
    Italian 306, 312
    and labour market 537-47
    local impact 523-6
    marital status 552-3
    numbers 508, 517-18
    occupational attainment 542-7
    political power 527-30
    Portuguese 421
    poverty 561-3, 564, 565
    public assistance 559-60
    school enrollment 536-7
    senior 527
    skills 530, 564
    Soviet Jewish 483
  immigration policy 350-2
    regional impact 522, 525
    restrictive 513-14
  investors 514, 515
  Jewish population 461
  language proficiency 134, 533-6, 564, 565
  legislation 514, 515-16, 528, 529
  measuring immigration 3
  Mexico border entry 514, 515
  migration to Israel 470
  naturalization 527-30
    politics 527-30
  preference system 514
  prohibition of illiterate 309
  quota system 309-10, 329, 351
  racial prejudice 513
    redistricting 529
    refugees 516
    sender countries 511-21, 564
    voting rights 528-9
    wages 243, 485, 515
    U.S. and Mexico 517
    unskilled migrants 1, 11
  Denmark
  Ireland 94-5
    and labour market 163-4, 165, 565
Uruguay, Spanish migrants to 392

Valagão, M. M. 427
Vallet, L.-A. 286
Van Dugteren, F. 190
Van Ours, J. C. 173-96
Vanberg, M. 222
Veenman, J. 173-96
Velasco, A. 548
Velilla, P. 389-414
Velling, J. 199, 245, 246-7, 251-3
Venturini, A. 303-35, 324-6, 342
Vernez, G. 515
Vietnamese migrants
  to Canada 595, 596
  to Denmark 61, 63
  to United States 518, 519
Villosio, C. 324, 325, 326
Vinokur, A. 476, 477, 482
Virdee, S. 130, 137
virtual migration 1
Vitali, L. 327
Vitali, O. 305
vocational training 75, 76, 78
Voges, W. 238
Vogler, M. 231
Vriend, N. 179, 184

Wadensjö, E. 82
Wadsworth, J. 400
wages *see* earnings and wages
Wagner, G. 239
Walsh, B. M. 90, 94, 95, 96-7, 98,
  99, 103, 106, 107
Ward, B. D. 613
Waters, M. C. 521
Weber, A. 239
Weil, P. 278-9, 285
Weiss, Y. 477, 483
welfare 85
  Canada 581-582
  Denmark 68, 70, 79-81, 85

as disincentive 79–80
Israel 485–6
Italy 327
Netherlands 180, 183, 193
New Zealand 624–5
Sweden 31, 49–50
  sickness benefits 35, 37,
    38–9, 52
United States 525, 526, 559–60
Wendt, H. 223
Wheatley Price, S. 113–72
Wihtol De Wenden, C. 274
Williamson, J. 308, 311–12,
    392, 393
Winkelmann, L. 615, 622, 623–5
Winkelmann, R. 237, 250–1, 601–31
Winter-Ebmer, R. 245, 253
Wolfe, B. L. 154
women see female
work permits
  Germany 206, 209, 219–20
  Sweden 19, 23–4, 48
  United Kingdom 121, 164
Worswick, C. 594

Yeabsley, J. 613
Yugoslavian migrants
  asylum seekers 217
  to Denmark 59, 60, 61, 62, 64, 65, 68, 71, 72, 84
  to France 280, 281
  to Germany 213, 231
  to Italy 316, 317, 318, 322, 326, 329
  to Netherlands 173, 191
  to Sweden 18, 19, 20, 24, 34, 37, 38, 46
    early retirement 37, 38
  to United States 520
  treaty with Germany 206

Zaire 10
Zamagni, V. 314
Zilberfarb, B.-Z. 499
Zimmermann, K. F. 1–14, 197–261, 296, 300,
    353, 485, 486
Zionist Movement 459, 461, 462, 465, 467
Zodgekar, A. V. 613, 614
Zografakis, S. 372
Zolberg, A. R. 431, 444
Zolotas, X. 351, 354, 369
Zwintz, E. 197–261